FIELD GUIDE TO THE
PALMS OF THE AMERICAS

FIELD GUIDE TO THE

Palms of the Americas

ANDREW HENDERSON,
GLORIA GALEANO, AND
RODRIGO BERNAL

PRINCETON UNIVERSITY PRESS, PRINCETON, NEW JERSEY

Copyright © 1995 by Princeton University Press
Published by Princeton University Press, 41 William Street,
Princeton, New Jersey 08540
In the United Kingdom: Princeton University Press, Chichester,
West Sussex

Library of Congress Cataloging-in-Publication Data

Henderson, Andrew, 1950–
Field guide to the palms of the Americas / Andrew Henderson,
  Gloria Galeano, and Rodrigo Bernal.
      p.   cm.
Includes bibliographical references (p.   ) and index.
ISBN 0-691-08537-4 (cl)
      1. Palms—America—Identification.   I. Galeano, Gloria.
  II. Bernal, Rodrigo.   III. Title.
  QK495.P17H44   1995
  584'.5'097—dc20   94-30080

This book has been composed in Baskerville
Designed by Jan Lilly

Printed in the United States of America

10 9 8 7 6 5 4 3 2 1

CONTENTS

FOREWORD

AMAZING. I thought it would be another twenty years before something as useful as this came out. Everyone who picks up this book is probably aware of how important palms are. They get a lot of media attention compared with other groups of tropical plants. They look so different from the surrounding vegetation that we spot them immediately. But what most people do not realize is how poorly palms are understood. Little by little we have seen the emergence of a few checklists of American palms for different regions, guides to palm species in some small areas, detailed technical monographs of a few genera, and some attempts at keys to the palm genera. With this patchwork of information there has been enormous confusion of names and distribution, and this situation was expected to continue for some time. The palm specialists may have understood what was going on, but for the rest of us working in the field it was a confusing mess.

This book is a shot in the arm for the study of palms. It is a guide to 550 species in the field, not a taxonomic revision. But the authors, experts who are well qualified to do it, have made a bold move to bring good sense, order, and simplicity to the taxonomy of American palm species. It brings the taxonomic dirty laundry out into the sun where we can all examine it and challenge it. It's going to shock some people who consider every genetic variant as a different species to see so many names lumped under one species. It will shock others to be giving up so many of the names they have been using for so long, and to see the geographic ranges increase by leaps and bounds. But it is done with the support and assistance of most of the authors' botanical and ecological colleagues who know from work in the field that this is long overdue.

As a field guide it is going to delight everyone who has ever done ecological inventories, ethnobotanical surveys, or otherwise had to identify palms in the American tropics. We now have a standard of species names to use from one country to the next and with which to communicate. And we have a means of getting to those names in places where no adequate local floras exist, that is, in most of the American tropics. If we encounter a new species or distribution record, we will now quickly be aware of it. And we can distinguish those that are candidates for more conservation attention, either because they can help sustain humans and other animals in an ecosystem context, or because they may soon go extinct, or both.

With the numerous illustrations, range maps, highlighted distinguishing characters, local names, checklists by country, and list of synonyms, the authors have gone out of their way to make it easier to get palms identified. Make no mistake, palms are a difficult group, and it will never be effortless to identify them, especially if they are immature or without reproductive structures. But with this book the prospect of correctly identifying palms has gone from being almost hopeless to being a rewarding challenge. If we can spend less effort tearing our hair out identifying them we should be able to focus more effort on the ethnobiology, conservation, management, population ecology, genetic variation, and evolution of this most elegant and valuable group of plants.

Robin B. Foster
Smithsonian Tropical Research Institute, Panama; Field Museum of Natural History, Chicago; Conservation International, Washington, D.C.; and Selby Botanical Garden, Sarasota, Florida

ACKNOWLEDGMENTS

WE GRATEFULLY acknowledge the National Geographic Society for their support in the completion of the manuscript of this book. The following persons reviewed parts of the manuscript or helped in various ways: Henrik Balslev, Finn Borchsenius, John Brown, Greg de Nevers, Carol Gracie, Michael Grayum, William Hahn, Donald Hodel, Dennis Johnson, John Mitchell, Onaney Muñiz, Larry Noblick, Renata Pardini, Roger Sanders, Helen Sanderson, Tom Zanoni, and Scott Zona. Flor Chávez helped with the preparation of the maps, and Alba Arbeláez illustrated the generic key. Plate 3 (*Schippia concolor*) was provided by Dr. Andrew Kahl, and Plate 13 (*Juania australis*) by the Bailey Hortorium of Cornell University. All other photographs were taken in the field by the authors. This book is the outcome of our taxonomic research over the last twelve years, and we are grateful to our respective institutions for their support during this time.

FIELD GUIDE TO THE
PALMS OF THE AMERICAS

INTRODUCTION

Hay palmas de seis o de ocho maneras, que es admiración verlas,
por la diformidad fermosa dellas
[There are palms of six or eight kinds, which are a wonder to look at,
because of their beautiful diversity]

Christopher Columbus, February 1493

PREAMBLE

Palms are the quintessential tropical plants. In the popular imagination they symbolize the tropical landscape. There are good reasons for this. Palms are confined almost exclusively to the tropics, where they have diversified into dozens of genera and hundreds of species and have occupied almost every habitat. Indeed, palms are among the world's largest plant families, both in terms of number of species and in abundance. But it is also their distinctive appearance and apparently simple architecture that makes them instantly recognizable and memorable, so that the concept of the palm tree is universal.

Beyond the symbolic association, the careful observer will soon realize that palms play a major role in tropical ecosystems. Palms abound in tropical rain forests, where they are major components of the canopy and conspicuous elements of the understory; they grow near mangrove swamps, where they often make up large, homogeneous stands; they comprise the dominant vegetation of some permanently inundated areas and line the margins of tropical rivers for hundreds of kilometers; they form huge stands of many millions of individuals and grow in dense groves in the mixed rain forests. Palms grow also in the high mountains, where they are sometimes conspicuous elements of the montane forest landscape; some of them thrive in arid areas, although only where the water table is high. Palms are often the only trees surviving in cleared areas; they are planted in gardens and yards, along city avenues, and even as indoor plants. Palms are the food source for such diverse animals as bears, peccaries, coyotes, monkeys, toucans, parrots, weevils, and hundreds of other mammals, birds, fish, and insects. For many of these animals, palms are major components of their diet.

But it is humans who have exploited palms to the highest degree. Palms rank with grasses and legumes as one of the most useful plant groups worldwide. In particular, for aboriginal cultures in the Americas, palms are by far the most important plants. A traditional Indian family, for example in the Amazon region, lives in a house where the floors and walls are made from split palm stems; the roof is thatched with leaves of another palm, and still another one is used to make the stairs; the family sleeps in hammocks made with strong fibers obtained from palm leaves; they keep their foods in baskets woven with palm stems or palm leaves, stir the fire with fans woven from palm leaflets, cook palm fruits gathered from their garden plot, drink beverages fermented from wild palm fruits, and extract oil from others; they enrich their diet with protein from insect larvae that live in palm stems and even extract salt from the burned stems and leaves of other species. With their weapons made from palm stems and palm leaves, they hunt wild animals, which themselves feed heavily on palm fruits. Palms provide them with materials for making toys, body ornaments, ceremonial clothes, and many other items. In some places, even coffins are made from the hollowed-out stem of a palm. Amerindian cultures could be accurately termed palm cultures. For not only do palms provide for almost every material necessity, but also they are a vital part of their spiritual lives and are intimately associated with myth, religion, and theories on the origin of the world.

Botany has seen in the last decade, especially in the Americas, a boom in the scientific study of palms. Many monographic and floristic works have been undertaken, as have studies on palm ecology, reproductive biology, and exploitation of promising species. Science is thus beginning to recognize what aboriginal societies have known since ancient times: the vital role played by palms in the tropical ecosystem.

Some History and Species Concepts

This book is intended as a field guide to the identification of naturally occurring palms in the Americas. Although it is written by taxonomists, it is intended for nonspecialists. As such, some aspects of taxonomic methodology and history need explanation.

Taxonomy is the science of discovering, describing, naming, and classifying species or groups of species. Much botanical taxonomic research is carried out in herbaria. An herbarium is essentially a museum, or library, of plant specimens preserved by pressing and drying. The specimens, which usually consist of a short, leafy stem with flowers and/or fruits, are mounted on stiff paper sheets, together with a label, and stored in cabinets. An herbarium specimen will last indefinitely as long as it is kept dry and free from insects. Most herbaria are associated with either university botany departments, natural history museums, or botanical gardens. The largest herbarium in the Americas is at The New York Botanical Garden, with over five million specimens; this institution also holds the largest collection of American palms, but there are significant collections at many other institutions. Taxonomic research, or herbarium taxonomy, has been traditionally based on the study of the morphology of plants, as seen from herbarium specimens. This is often supplemented by anatomical or biochemical data. Results of botanical taxonomic research are published as either a flora, which is an account of all the plants of a defined area, or a monograph, which is an account of a defined group of plants, usually a genus or family. Herbarium specimens are thus very important, and are the basis of our knowledge of the taxonomy of plants.

Herbarium collections are built up slowly over many years and rely on the work of field collectors, who are often the taxonomists themselves. Palms are actually more difficult to collect than most other plants, because they are large and often spiny. For this reason they have traditionally been poorly represented in herbaria and consequently poorly understood taxonomically. Until relatively recently, palm floras and monographs have seldom been of much practical value in identifying the palms of a region or of a genus.

Some of the earliest herbarium specimens of American palms were collected by Nikolaus Jacquin in the Caribbean in the years 1755 to 1759. On his return to Europe, Jacquin described them using the binomial system of nomenclature that had been recently established by Linnaeus. In this system species are known by two names, a genus name and a species name, followed by the author's name (often abbreviated). So, for example, a palm collected by Jacquin from the Caribbean coast of Colombia is known as *Bactris major* Jacq. Written knowledge of American palms proceeded sporadically for the next fifty years, until the appearance of Carl von Martius, the greatest of all palm botanists. Martius, a German, traveled in Brazil during the years 1817 to 1821. He collected almost every palm he saw, particularly from the Amazon region and, on his return to Germany, described and illustrated them in a magnificent book. This monograph, a three-volume, large-folio work called *Historia Naturalis Palmarum* (Martius, 1831–53; 1823–37; 1837–53), not only contained descriptions of Martius's South American collections, but all the knowledge of palms known at the time. It has never been surpassed, and is still the foundation of our knowledge.

Martius was followed by various other palm botanists in the American tropics during the latter part of the nineteenth century, notably Anders Oersted, Hermann Wendland, Alfred Russel Wallace, Richard Spruce, João Barbosa Rodrigues, James Trail, and Hermann Karsten. Each of these made substantial contributions. Barbosa Rodrigues was the most prolific of them, and he produced another classic of palm taxonomy, *Sertum Palmarum Brasiliensium* (Barbosa Rodrigues, 1903). At the end of the century, two important works on the genera of palms appeared in *Die Natürlichen Pflanzenfamilien* (Drude, 1887) and *Genera Plantarum* (Bentham and Hooker, 1883). These summarized the work of earlier botanists, and generic boundaries were thus relatively well understood at the end of the nineteenth century.

The most important figures in palm taxonomy during the first half of the twentieth century were a German, Max Burret, and an American, Liberty Hyde Bailey. Burret was essentially a herbarium botanist working in Berlin, and he had little field experience. He had an extremely narrow species concept, and described almost every herbarium specimen he received as a new species. Burret was matched in this narrow concept of species by Bailey, working at Cornell University. Despite Bailey's extensive field experience, he also described many specimens as new species based on the slightest differences. For example, a small, spiny palm from the Amazon region was first described by Martius in 1826 as *Bactris simplicifrons*. This is a rather variable species, and was redescribed six times by Bailey (and nine times by Burret and six times by

Barbosa Rodrigues). This overdescription of palm species was based on an herbarium species concept. In this approach, if a specimen looks different from others in the herbarium, it is automatically described as a new species. This led to such a profusion of names that identification of specimens became almost impossible. Bailey had a visionary outlook, however, and in 1951, at the age of ninety-three, he was planning "to make a classification of all the genera, and to describe every genus. It would be a 'Genera Palmarum'" (Uhl and Dransfield, 1987). Bailey brought Harold Moore to Cornell in 1948 to carry out the work. Moore's premature death in 1980 left his generic monograph of palms unfinished, and it was not until 1987 that Bailey's dream was fulfilled with *Genera Palmarum; a classification of palms based on the work of Harold E. Moore, Jr.* (Uhl and Dransfield, 1987).

While Moore concentrated his attention on generic limits and relationships on a world scale, taxonomy of American palms at the species level was neglected. It had been left by Barbosa Rodrigues, Burret, Bailey, and others in a chaotic state with literally hundreds of names and no way to apply them to real species in nature. One of the first investigators to try to resolve this problem was the Dutch botanist Jan Wessels Boer, working in Suriname and Venezuela in the 1960s. He collected palms extensively in the field, and appreciated the great natural variation within species. He realized that many so-called species were in fact synonyms of older species (many of them first described by Martius), and he consigned these names to synonymy. For example, he recognized the natural variation in *Bactris simplicifrons*, and he placed the names of almost all the minor variants that had been described by Barbosa Rodrigues, Burret, and Bailey into synonymy. His palm flora of Suriname (Wessels Boer, 1965) and monograph of the geonomoid palms (Wessels Boer, 1968) were the first useful treatments of American palms at the species level to be published. The reason for this was that the species concept used by Wessels Boer was more realistic and took into account the extensive morphological variation of palms. Over the last decade a new generation of botanists, many of them natives of tropical countries, has become interested in palms, and our knowledge of the taxonomy of American palms is now based on extensive field work, well-collected specimens, appreciation of variation in nature, and realistic species concepts. Our Guide is based on the work of these botanists.

OUR species concept in this field guide is necessarily a broad one. There are several reasons for this. First, this Guide is not a taxonomic treatment but a field guide for nonspecialists. For this reason we have tended to combine closely related and doubtfully distinct species and also groups of species that we consider to be part of species complexes. There are, however, other reasons why we have adopted a broad species concept. Taxonomists must fit every herbarium specimen into a hierarchy of taxa, either species, subspecies, or variety; a specimen cannot be excluded, it must go somewhere. And yet palms in nature do not always occur in discrete, easily defined species. Just the opposite. The reality is that many species are divided throughout their ranges into a patchwork of local forms, whose individual ranges expand and contract with environmental change and which may form hybrid zones where they meet. Furthermore, we estimate that at least 10 percent of the species of American palms are what we call "species complexes." We define these as widespread and variable species that usually contain several more or less distinct forms, joined to each other by intermediates. Often, in a restricted area, two or more forms occur together and appear, and indeed behave, as distinct species. Over their entire range, however, these forms merge into one another. In some cases, where this variation has been studied in detail, we recognize the forms taxonomically as subspecies or varieties, in other cases not.

Our species concept is as follows. We view species as series of distinct populations, which may or may not interbreed at any one time, and which may be quite distinct from one another vegetatively and quantitatively, according to their adaptation to local environments. These populations may be very dynamic over time and their ranges may contract and expand, and then they may interbreed. What unites them as species is their similar reproductive structures (inflorescences, flowers, and fruits). Many species are thus quite "messy" and not easy to understand. Herbarium taxonomy does not have the methodology (and certainly not the number of specimens) to fully understand this kind of variation. We therefore present species as broadly defined entities, and at the same time point out subspecific variation as understood from the specimens available. The understanding of subspecific variation falls more within other fields, such as experimental taxonomy, pollination biology, population biology, cytology, genetics, and molecular systematics. Tropical woody plants, such as palms, have seldom been studied using these methodologies. The many problems remaining in palm taxonomy should be addressed at this level.

FROM the above discussion it can be seen that species concepts have changed over the years. Our particular concept means that in several instances we have not accepted the species of previous botanists. We do not imply that we are "right" and the others are "wrong," but stress that we have a different concept. We have tried to strike an even balance throughout the Guide, and often the differences in opinions are merely a question of ranking.

A consequence of changing species concepts is that names of species change. In fact, one of the main criticisms of taxonomic research made by nontaxonomists, such as horticulturalists, is that taxonomists continually change names. There are several reasons for this. Because there are so many superfluous names—those of Barbosa Rodrigues, Burret, and Bailey, for example—it is quite common for a palm to become known by a later name while an earlier name is overlooked. For example, a common species of *Bactris* in the Amazon region was referred to by Wessels Boer as *Bactris monticola*, a name introduced by Barbosa Rodrigues in 1875, and it has become widely known by this name. But unfortunately this species had already been described by Martius in 1826 as *Bactris maraja*, and this is the correct name. Because of the laws of botanical nomenclature, one of which is the priority of earlier published names, taxonomists often have no choice but to change a name. As taxonomic research proceeds, the number of name changes becomes fewer and fewer. There are also genuine scientific disagreements among taxonomists. Some botanists with a broad outlook will "lump" species together because they consider the characters used to separate them as trivial. In the case of two closely related genera, the lumping of the two genera will cause generic names to change. For example, we believe that the palm formerly known as *Jessenia bataua* is better placed in the genus *Oenocarpus*, and so we refer to it as *Oenocarpus bataua*, although this name will be unfamiliar to many people. We made this change because we believe that the characters that had been used to separate the two genera were either inconsistent or insufficient.

This, the analysis of characters, is at the heart of most taxonomic problems. Some characters that were previously thought to be important in separating species, or even genera, can now be seen to be trivial. For example, *Attalea funifera* has tall and aerial stems throughout most of its range, and short and subterranean stems at the northern end. These short-stemmed populations were separated as a distinct species, *A. acaulis*, by Burret. The reproductive structures of both are identical, however, and we recognize the two populations as the same species. There are many other such examples of variation, especially in leaf division, degree of spinyness, and size of stems and leaves. Fruit size and color, in particular, can vary greatly within a species, depending on local factors. In the case of species complexes, variation has usually led to many names. One of the most important reasons for this variation is the environment; in other words, palms are variable morphologically because they live in variable environments.

There are perhaps other reasons for the overdescription of American palms. Some taxonomists have looked for "new species" as if this were the only goal of taxonomy. Of course, those who look for differences between "species" will surely find them. This, coupled with a natural propensity to want more rather than less, has resulted in the hundreds of "species" that we have today. It is very easy to describe a new species, and very difficult to understand variation within an "old" one.

PALMS AND PALM REGIONS

There are approximately 200 genera and 1500 species of palms in the world. The family has a pantropical distribution, with a few species reaching northern subtropical areas in the United States, Mediterranean Europe, the Middle East, and northern India through China and Korea to southern Japan; in the Southern Hemisphere they extend into northern Argentina and central Chile, southeast Africa, southeast Australia, and New Zealand. Extreme limits of palm distribution are 44°N for *Chamaerops humilis* in Europe, and 44°18'S for *Rhopalostylis sapida* in New Zealand. Nevertheless, the highest concentration of palms occurs near the equator (Moore, 1973).

In general terms, palm genera are endemic to major continental areas, none of them being pantropical. Notable exceptions are the coconut, *Cocos nucifera*, widespread in the tropics but probably of western Pacific origin (Harries, 1978); the genera *Raphia* and *Elaeis*, shared by Africa and America; *Chamaerops*, which grows in Europe and northern Africa; and five genera, *Livistona, Phoenix, Borassus, Hyphaene*, and *Calamus*, shared by Africa and Asia (Moore, 1973).

Sixty-seven genera and 550 species occur naturally in the Americas. The largest genera are *Chamaedorea, Bactris*, and *Geonoma*, which together make up about one third of all palm species. Most, but not all, American palms occur within the tropics, the area between the Tropic of Cancer (23° 27'N) and the Tropic of Capricorn (23° 27'S) (fig. 1). Several species occur outside these latitudes, for example *Sabal palmetto* in the southeastern USA, which grows at 34°N, and *Jubaea chilensis* in Chile, which grows at 36°S. For this reason we prefer to call them American palms rather than Neotropical.

Except for a few widespread genera, notably *Bactris, Geonoma, Chamaedorea, Acrocomia, Euterpe, Prestoea*, and *Desmoncus*, all American palm genera are mostly confined to, or at least most diversified in, one of seven major regions:

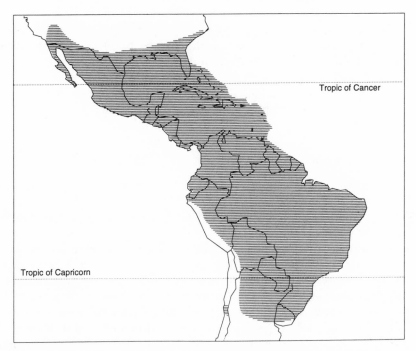

Tropic of Cancer

Tropic of Capricorn

FIGURE 1. DISTRIBUTION OF AMERICAN PALMS.

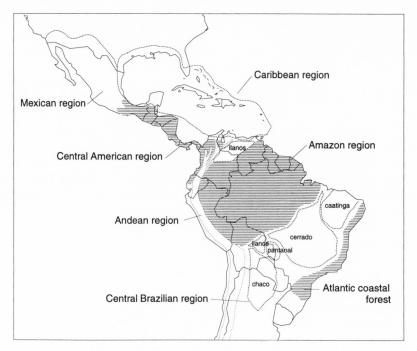

Figure 2. Regions.

the Mexican region; the Central American region; the Caribbean region; the Amazon region; the Andean region; the Central Brazilian region; and the Atlantic Coastal Forest (fig. 2). Each of these regions contains various vegetation types and are recognized here more for convenience; they are not intended as natural regions. For each we discuss, in very general terms, its extent, geology and topography, climate, vegetation, and characteristic palms. Here we also define the terms we shall use later in the habitat descriptions.

The Mexican Region

The Mexican region comprises the drier, inland deserts and mountains of Mexico and adjacent parts of the United States (Texas, New Mexico, Arizona, California). Although a very large and diverse area, it contains few palms, since most of the region is arid and outside the tropics. The region consists of mountain ranges, dry lowlands, and deserts. The northwestern part contains the Sonoran Desert, including the adjacent Mojave Desert and Baja California. This area receives between 50 and 400 mm of rain per year and has a vegetation dominated by plants adapted to very dry areas, such as cacti. To the east rises the great Sierra Madre Occidental, separating the Sonoran Desert from the Chihuahua Desert of central Mexico. This inland desert is separated from the Caribbean by another great mountain range, the Sierra Madre Oriental.

Few palms occur in the Chihuahua Desert, or in the Sierras. *Brahea moorei* and *Sabal urseana* grow in thorn or oak forest in the foothills. The Sonoran Desert, however, contains two genera, *Brahea* and *Washingtonia*, with about five species between them, and the latter genus is endemic. They almost always occur where groundwater is present, for example on hillside seeps or canyon washes, and they are often found on limestone soils.

The Central American Region

The Central American region extends from southern Mexico to Panama, and from there down the Pacific lowlands of western Colombia and northwestern Ecuador. We also include here the inter-Andean valleys of the Ríos Magdalena and Cauca in Colombia, and the forests of the Catatumbo region in northwestern Venezuela. It is a diverse area, geologically and climatically, and in vegetation types. The section from the Mexico-Guatemala frontier to western Panama has a mountainous backbone of volcanoes (eastern Panama has lower mountains that are not part of this volcanic formation). Some of these volcanoes reach 4000 m elevation, and many of them are still active. On either side of this mountainous backbone are narrow coastal plains. The eastern side of the mountains is referred to as the Atlantic slope, and the western side as the Pacific slope. The Pacific lowlands continue into Colombia and Ecuador. The climate of the region is dominated by the interaction of the northeastern trade winds and the mountain range. Rainfall along the Atlantic slope is generally higher, from 2500 to 6000 mm per year. The Pacific slope is somewhat drier, and has a longer dry season. Annual average rainfall ranges from 1000 to 1500 mm. Some areas in the central highlands, in rain shadow areas, receive a lot less rain. This situation is reversed along the Pacific slope of Colombia and Ecuador. These are regions of very high rainfall, mostly over 3000 mm but to 12,000 mm per year in some places.

Vegetation of the region is influenced by these geological and climatic factors. Along the drier, more seasonal Pacific coast of Central America deciduous forests are widespread. Higher up the mountain slopes, premontane and montane rain forest occurs. In areas of lower rainfall, especially in the northern part of Central America and southern Mexico, pine-oak forests are common. Along the Atlantic coast, lowland rain forest is widespread, and there are also restricted areas of lowland rain forest on the Pacific side, notably in Chiapas, Mexico, and on the Osa Peninsula in Costa Rica. Here and for the other regions, we define lowland rain forest as that occurring below 500 m elevation; premontane rain forest between 500 and 1000 m elevation; and montane rain forest from 1000 to about 2500 m elevation. Few palms, or any other plants, follow exactly these elevational boundaries, but rather lowland rain forest species gradually drop out between 500 and 1000 m elevation, and premontane species gradually drop out over 1000 m elevation. Conversely, montane species are sometimes found below 1000 m.

The Central American region is rich in palms and contains approximately twenty-five genera and 150 species. Most of these are from the genus *Chamaedorea*, which is extraordinarily diverse in the region. The genus has two centers of diversity: Mexico and Guatemala, and Costa Rica and Panama. Endemic genera in the Central American region include *Cryosophila*, *Schippia*, *Synechanthus*, *Neonicholsonia*, and *Calyptrogyne*. Other genera are most diversified in this area but extend into other regions. *Pholidostachys* has four species but one of them reaches the Amazon region east of the Andes; *Reinhardtia* has five species in Central America and one in Hispaniola. Both *Bactris* and *Geonoma* are diverse along the Atlantic lowlands, while *Attalea* and a couple of other species of *Bactris* are common along the Pacific side. The Pacific lowlands of Colombia are very rich in species. Here, because of high rainfall, several Andean species occur at low elevations, for example *Chamaedorea linearis*, *Euterpe precatoria* var. *longevaginata*, and *Prestoea ensiformis*, showing that perhaps rainfall is more important than elevation in influencing palm distributions.

Deforestation and habitat destruction in the Central American region except for the Pacific Coast of Colombia, are more severe than perhaps in any other region in the world, and the rate of destruction is extremely rapid. Most of the deciduous forests of the Pacific coast in Central America are now turned over to agriculture, as are the accessible mountain slopes. Some large blocks of lowland forest remain on the Atlantic coast—in Belize, Honduras, Nicaragua, and Panama—but in general these lowland forests are much fragmented. The valley of the Río Magdalena in Colombia, an area of high endemism for palms, is being severely deforested.

The Caribbean Region

The Caribbean region includes the Greater and Lesser Antilles, and the coastal plain of the United States (Florida, Texas), Mexico (especially the Yucatán peninsula), and Belize. It also includes the northern coastal plain of Colombia and Venezuela. The Greater Antilles comprise the four largest islands of the Caribbean: Cuba, Hispaniola (Haiti and the Dominican Republic), Jamaica, and Puerto Rico. The Lesser Antilles comprise an arc of small, relatively young volcanic islands from Anguilla in the northwest to Grenada in the southeast, a distance of some 800 km. There are also a few other islands such as the Caymans, the San Andrés Islands, Aruba, Curaçao, and Bonaire.

It is hardly possible to generalize on the climate of this large region. The dominant weather pattern comes from the east, and east-facing mountain regions can receive from 1000 to 2000 mm average rainfall per year. On the other hand, rain shadow areas can receive as little as 600–700 mm per year. The vegetation of the region thus ranges from premontane and montane rain forest in mountainous areas to thorn scrub or desert in rain shadow areas. There are two Greater Antillean habitats which support an interesting vegetation. One consists of limestone outcrops, called *mogotes* in Cuba, which are extremely well-drained outcrops of almost pure limestone with very little soil;

and the second one is the open savannas formed on serpentine soils, which are particularly well developed in central and eastern Cuba.

The Caribbean region contains approximately twenty-one genera and eighty species. It is particularly rich in coryphoid genera, for example *Thrinax, Coccothrinax, Zombia, Acoelorrhaphe, Serenoa, Rhapidophyllum,* and *Colpothrinax.* Other endemic genera are *Pseudophoenix, Gaussia, Gastrococos,* and *Calyptronoma. Copernicia* and *Roystonea* are diverse, but these also reach South America, the former reaching southeastern Brazil and Paraguay. Certain Caribbean habitats have a characteristic palm flora. *Thrinax, Coccothrinax,* and *Pseudophoenix* are common in coastal areas on alkaline soils; *Coccothrinax* and *Copernicia* in savannas; *Gaussia* and *Thrinax* on *mogotes* in Cuba and Puerto Rico; and *Prestoea* and *Calyptronoma* in Antillean rain forests. In the Lesser Antilles a group of mainland genera, *Euterpe, Syagrus,* and *Aiphanes,* have representative species, and *Desmoncus* also just reaches the area.

Deforestation and habitat destruction are particularly severe in some of the Greater Antillean islands. In Haiti, for example, only 2 percent of the original forest remains. Endemic species such as *Attalea crassispatha* have been driven to the point of extinction. Many of the spectacular endemics of lowland areas in Cuba, for example some *Copernicia* and *Coccothrinax* species, are also greatly threatened.

The Andean Region

The Andean region extends from Venezuela to Colombia, Ecuador, Peru, Bolivia, Chile, and Argentina. This narrow, volcanic mountain chain, over 8000 km long, consists of multiple ranges. Starting in the north, we include the Cordillera de la Costa in Venezuela, and its continuation to the east, including the Península de Paria. The Venezuelan Andes, in the northwestern part of the country, are usually referred to as the Cordillera de Mérida. In Colombia there are actually three ranges and one outlier: the Cordillera Occidental, which is separated from the Cordillera Central by the valley of the Río Cauca, and the Cordillera Oriental, including the Sierra de Perijá, separated by the Río Magdalena valley. The outlier is the Sierra Nevada de Santa Marta. The southern Andes of Ecuador, Peru, Bolivia, and Chile contain various cordilleras but these are not separated by large river valleys.

Rainfall is very unevenly distributed in the Andes. In tropical areas, where palms occur, there are two rainy seasons per year. Highest rainfall is at intermediate elevations (500–1500 m) and decreases with increasing elevation. Western and eastern slopes receive about 1500 to 2000 mm per year, and the Cordillera Central in Colombia receives more rain than the two other cordilleras. The interandean valleys are mostly dry at low elevations, but their slopes are wet. In southern Ecuador and continuing through Peru into Chile, the western slopes receive very little rain and there are deserts at sea level. Eastern slopes are very wet. Because of its very varied topography and climate there are dozens of habitats in the Andes, ranging from desert to rain forest.

As far as palms are concerned, we only need to consider here premontane and montane rain forest.

The Andean region contains a very interesting palm flora (Moraes et al., in press). Twenty-one genera and eighty-six species are found in the main cordilleras, and a few more occur in the northern Venezuelan mountains, the Cordillera de la Costa and the Peninsula de Paria. Two genera, *Ceroxylon* and *Parajubaea*, are endemic, and several other genera are highly diversified, but each with a few species reaching other areas. *Aiphanes* and *Wettinia*, for example, contain forty-three species between them, most of them along the Andes, but a few species also grow in adjacent regions. Other genera that are highly diversified, or at least very abundant, in the Andes are *Dictyocaryum* and *Prestoea*. From a vegetation point of view, the Andes are often divided into a northern and southern part, with a low pass, the Huancabamba Depression, in Peru near the frontier with Ecuador, as the boundary. Some genera are more diverse in the northern Andes—*Aiphanes* and *Wettinia*, for example. For several palms the Depression marks the "crossover" point, where species from the wet western slopes of the Cordillera Occidental in Colombia cross to the wet eastern slopes of the Andes in Peru. Examples are *Chamaedorea linearis* and *Prestoea ensiformis*. *Bactris macana*, *Aiphanes aculeata*, and *Syagrus sancona* also cross here, but their distribution may be anthropogenic.

The Amazon Region

The Amazon region is by far the largest of our seven regions, and is over 6.5 million square kilometers in extent. It includes all of the immense lowland rain forests of the Amazon and Orinoco basins, as well as those of the Guianas (Guyana, Suriname, French Guiana). We also include Trinidad here, since from the point of view of its vegetation it is really an extension of the mainland. Not all of the area is at low elevations. In the northern part, in an area known as the Guayana Highland, spectacular flat-topped mountains, or *tepuis*, occur. In this area, mostly in southern Venezuela but also reaching adjacent Colombia, Brazil, and Guyana, mountains can reach 3000 m elevation, but most are nearer 2000 m or less. The best known of these are Neblina, Roraima, Duida, and Chimantá. These mountains support quite a different type of vegetation, as we shall see below. The climate of the Amazon region, in concert with its geology, is highly variable. Rainfall is high, typically over 1500 mm annually, and reaching 6000 mm in some western parts. Rainfall is not evenly distributed throughout the year, and there are marked dry seasons in most places. The vegetation of the Amazon region is also surprisingly variable. There are large areas of open savannas, and in the south the rain forest gives way to deciduous forest or *cerrado*. There are also smaller areas of specialized vegetation, such as the *campinas* of the upper Rio Negro, which are low, open forests that form on nutrient poor, white sand soils. In the Guayana Highland region there are mountainous areas of premontane or montane rain forest. Most of the Amazon region, however, is covered by lowland rain forest. Because there are so many rivers in the region it is common to divide this forest into either inundated forest (i.e., forests along river flood plains which flood annually, called *várzea* in Brazil) or noninundated forest (i.e., forests that occur on land which is never inundated, called *terra firme* in Brazil). The plants of each forest type are distinct, and the *várzea* has a distinct palm flora.

The Amazon region is still mostly covered with its natural vegetation. The most recent estimate gave the figure of 12 percent deforestation. Considering its large size and favorable climate, the Amazon region actually has relatively few palms. Henderson (1994) estimated that thirty-four genera and 189 species and varieties occur in the region. Of these, eight (24 percent) genera and 140 (75 percent) species and varieties were endemic. These palms are not evenly distributed throughout the region. The most diverse area is the western part, especially in Colombia, Ecuador, and Peru. Approximately seventy-five species and varieties occur in this area, and the Iquitos region of Peru is perhaps the richest in palm species in all of the Americas. The northeastern part of the Amazon region is also diverse, with about forty taxa. Rather surprisingly, the high-elevation regions of the Guayana Highland contain few palms, and only one species, *Prestoea tenuiramosa*, can really be considered endemic. A handful of other palms also occur there but are also found either in the lowlands or in the Andes. There are fewer palms south of the Amazon, in the southeastern part of the region, and only about thirty-five taxa are found there. The most speciose genera in the Amazon region are *Bactris*, *Geonoma* and *Astrocaryum*. Among them they comprise ninety-five species and varieties. Usually the understory of the forest is full of these palms. Other palms are important for their abundance, and, for example, *Mauritia flexuosa* is extremely common and abundant throughout the Amazon region. In fact, it is the sheer abundance of individuals, not diversity of species, that makes palms so important in Amazon ecosystems.

The Central Brazilian Region

The Central Brazilian region includes the drier regions of central and northeastern Brazil and adjacent Bolivia, Paraguay, Uruguay, and Argentina. This region contains a mixture of various vegetation types, including the *caatinga* of northeastern Brazil, the *cerrado* of central Brazil, the *pantanal* of southwestern Brazil, the *chaco* of Paraguay and adjacent areas, the *llanos* of Bolivia, and the open grasslands and savannas of Argentina and Uruguay. All these regions have rather low, strongly seasonal rainfall that does not permit the development of evergreen forest.

The *caatinga* occurs in northeastern Brazil, mostly in the states of Ceará, Piauí, and central Bahia. It develops in areas that receive less than 800 mm of rainfall per year, and even this is unevenly distributed in a short wet season. In some years no rain at all falls. Soils are sandy or rocky and are generally poor in nutrients, except for some limestone areas. The vegetation is characterized by short, deciduous, many-branched shrubs with twisted stems, and cacti are also common. In the southwest, the *caatinga* merges into the *cerrado*. This is a large area of over 1.5 million square kilometers in central Brazil found mostly in the states of Bahia, Goiás, Mato Grosso, Mato Grosso do Sul, Minas Gerais, and São Paulo. It is centered on an upland area of east-central Brazil called the *planalto*, and lies between 400 and 1100 m elevation. Rainfall is between 700 and 1750 mm per year, and there is a distinct dry season of about six months. Typical vegetation consists of open woodland or savanna, and the trees are often stunted and twisted with thick bark and leaves. A more specialized vegetation type, *campo rupestre*, is really an extension of the *cerrado*. It occurs over 600 m elevation in the Brazilian states of Bahia, Goiás, and Minas Gerais. It differs in its rocky soils and generally has a different flora.

In the center of South America, where Brazil, Bolivia, and Paraguay meet, is a large, low-lying area of over 100,000 square kilometers, known as the *pantanal* ("swampland"). It is formed in the basin of the Río Paraguay and is relatively new and unstable from a geological point of view. Annual average rainfall is about 1200 mm, and most of it falls in the wet season, from December to March. Then the whole area, except for low islands, becomes flooded. The vegetation is a blend of Amazon elements along with plants from both the *chaco* to the south and *cerrado* to the east. The *chaco* can be considered intermediate between desert and savanna. It is found in Paraguay and adjacent Bolivia and Argentina. It is a large region, about 1300 km from north to south and 350–400 km from west to east. The region is low-lying and seldom exceeds 500 m elevation. Rainfall is low, and varies between 550 and 760 mm per year. The *llanos* of Bolivia are tropical savannas. The climate is strongly seasonal, and rainfall is generally less than 1500 mm per year, concentrated in a short wet season. Vegetation ranges from open grassland to more or less closed woodlands. Open grasslands, known as *pampas*, occur to the south, in southern Brazil, Argentina, and Uruguay.

The Central Brazilian region and adjacent areas contain about eleven genera and forty-four species of palms. *Trithrinax* is endemic to the region, and both *Syagrus* and *Butia* are very diverse there. Species of *Attalea, Allagoptera,* and *Acrocomia* are also common. Few palms can exist in the dry *caatinga*, but some species of *Syagrus* and *Attalea* are found there, and *Copernicia prunifera* is abundant in places. There are several palms in the *cerrado*, almost all of them with short and subterranean stems. They are in the genera *Acrocomia, Allagoptera, Astrocaryum, Attalea, Butia,* and *Syagrus*. The palm flora of a small area of *cerrado* near São Paulo has been well described by Medeiros-Costa and Panizza (1983). Palms are fewer in *campo rupestre*, but some species of *Syagrus* are endemic to these regions. *Copernicia alba* and *Attalea phalerata* are two of the few palms occurring in the *pantanal*. Two genera, *Copernicia* and *Trithrinax*, are found in the *chaco*. In particular, *Copernicia alba* forms massive stands of millions of trees in some areas, called "palmares" (Markley, 1955). One species of *Trithrinax* occurs in the *chaco*, but other species occur farther south in the grasslands of Uruguay and northern Argentina.

The Atlantic Coastal Forest

Our last region, the Atlantic Coastal Forest of Brazil, stretches from the state of Rio Grande do Norte in the north to Rio Grande do Sul in the south, a distance of more than 4000 km. It is separated from the *caatinga* and *cerrado* by a zone of deciduous forest. Although very long, the coastal forest is rather narrow, and in most places is scarcely 150 km wide. It does, however, broaden in the southern part and just reaches Argentina. Here it merges with *Araucaria* forests. There are mountains along the southern part of this coastal region, principally the Serra do Mar and the Serra do Mantiqueira. The forest owes its existence to the very high rainfall in this part of coastal Brazil. Ocean winds, coming from the east, are forced to rise by the coastal mountains, and thus lose their moisture. Annual rainfall ranges from 1800 mm per year in the northern part to over 4000 mm in certain parts of the south. Unlike the Amazon region, the dry season here is almost negligible. The forest composition is rather homogeneous compared with the Amazon, but various habitats exist. Near the coast is a narrow zone, from 2 to 20 km wide, of *restinga* vegetation. This consists of low, shrubby vegetation on nutrient-poor, sandy soils. Part of the *restinga* is made up of old sand dunes, formed by sea level changes in the past, now covered by forest. Moving inland, steep, forested hills rise up from the coast. At higher elevations, between 700 and 1600 m elevation, the forest gives way to the more open vegetation, called *campo rupestre* in Brazil. This is discussed in more detail in the preceding section. Still farther inland the Atlantic Coastal Forest gives way to either *cerrado* or deciduous forest, or, in the south, to *Araucaria* forests.

The Atlantic Coastal Forest contains ten genera and approximately forty species of palms. Only one genus, *Polyandrococos*, is endemic, but endemism at the species level is high. Typical palms of the *restinga* are *Polyandrococos caudescens*, *Syagrus schizophylla*, and *Allagoptera arenaria*. On old dunes *Attalea funifera* is very common and in places completely dominates the landscape. On the steep, forested hills rising from the coast, *Euterpe edulis* and various species of *Bactris* and *Geonoma* are common, as well as *Attalea*. A few species from the Amazon region also occur here, for example *Bactris hirta* and *B. acanthocarpa*, emphasizing the probable links that may have existed in the past between the two forests.

The Atlantic Coastal Forest has suffered more from deforestation than most areas; it is estimated that over 95 percent of the original forest cover has been destroyed since the Europeans first arrived.

OUTLINE OF THE BOOK

This Guide includes all naturally occurring palms in the Americas. The only cultivated palm included is the coconut. We make no further reference to other cultivated palms since there are already several books on the subject (e.g., Blombery and Rodd, 1982; Boyer, 1992; Gibbons, 1993). The following three sections present the classification, the morphology, and a key to genera of American palms. In the first section we give an outline of the latest classification of palms, and the one we use for the order of genera. This system is taken from Uhl and Dransfield (1987). In the second section we discuss the morphology of palms. The technical terms used in the generic and species descriptions and keys are defined. The defining characters of the palm family as a whole are also given, as well as those characters that distinguish it from similar families, or false palms (e.g., Cyclanthaceae). In the third section we give a key to the identification of American palms, with some technical terms illustrated.

The main part of the book, containing the species accounts, is organized in the following way. For each genus, a short description is provided to give an idea of the general morphology of the genus as seen in the field. Much more detail on palm genera, in particular on flower and fruit structure, can be found in Uhl and Dransfield (1987). Derivation of generic names is taken from a variety of sources, but many come from a long series of short articles by Harold Moore that appeared in *Principes* ("What's in a Name"). Generic descriptions are followed by short discussions on the number of species and their distribution and also a reference to the most recent or useful monographs. Most genera with more than ten species have keys, but in some genera, such as *Ceroxylon*, where identification does not represent a problem, no key is given.

Species within each genus are in alphabetical order. We give the currently accepted Latin name of each. Some familiar species will be found under unfamiliar names; lists of synonyms are given in Appendix II.

Common names follow the species name. We have chosen the most widely used common names, giving a maximum of two from each country. Occasionally we include an Indian name when this may be useful. Users should, however, be aware that common names are very variable, and the same species will often be given different names by local people. On the other hand, many different species can be given the same common name. For example, in the Brazilian Amazon all *Geonoma* are "ubim." The more useful the species, the more consistent the name. The country abbreviations after common names are as follows:

Ang = Anguilla	DR = Dominican Republic
Arg = Argentina	Ecu = Ecuador
Bah = Bahamas	ElS = El Salvador
Bar = Barbados	FrG = French Guiana
Bel = Belize	Gre = Grenada
Ber = Bermuda	Gua = Guatemala
Bol = Bolivia	Gud = Guadeloupe
Bra = Brazil	Guy = Guyana
Cay = Cayman Islands	Hai = Haiti
Chi = Chile	Hon = Honduras
Col = Colombia	Jam = Jamaica
CR = Costa Rica	Luc = St. Lucia
Cub = Cuba	Mar = Martinique
Dom = Dominica	Mon = Montserrat

Nic = Nicaragua	Tob = Tobago
Pan = Panama	Tri = Trinidad
Par = Paraguay	Uru = Uruguay
Per = Peru	USA = United States of America
PR = Puerto Rico	Ven = Venezuela
SAI = San Andrés Islands, Colombia	Vin = St. Vincent
Sur = Suriname	VIs = Virgin Islands

Field characters are those that can be easily seen in the field, usually without the aid of a hand lens. Characters in italics in the species descriptions are diagnostic characters that in combination distinguish that species from others in the genus.

Ranges are given by political units (countries, and states or departments), and these can be supplemented by the distribution maps. Identification in this Guide is much easier if country and state or department locality are known (as well as elevation). Following the country we give state or department (except in the case of a few widespread species) from where the species has either been collected or recorded; however, species no doubt occur in states or departments not given by us. Note that in both Cuba and Ecuador we use the older departmental boundaries. In habitat descriptions we use the terms that have already been discussed above in the section on palm regions.

Uses follow range and habitat. Almost all palms have at one time or another been used for some purpose, especially the leaves for thatching and the fruits for eating. We have tried to give the most important and common uses. A great deal more information on the uses of palms has been given in a bibliography by Balick and Beck (1990).

In the notes sections we discuss subspecific division, where appropriate, and give other information on the species and its variation. We also take note of similar species and how to distinguish them, and of conservation status if that species is threatened in any way. Here we also provide references to other works on the natural history and ecology of the species. This kind of information is often scattered in the scientific literature, and we have tried to bring it together here.

The color plates are chosen to show typical features of each genus, as observed in the field. Each genus is illustrated, and the number of illustrations for each is proportional to the number of species in that genus. For *Chamaedorea*, however, we provide fewer plates because the genus has already been well illustrated by Hodel (1992a).

The distribution maps are designed to give an idea of the total range of the species. These are taken from recent monographs and floras, herbarium specimens, and our own observations. Almost all palms, however, have patchy distributions, and any given species will not occur throughout its range. When a species has a very small range, or a small outlying population, it is arrowed. Most maps have the Andean region outlined with a dotted line.

The checklist of species by country (Appendix I) is designed as an additional aid in identification, especially in narrowing down the range of possibilities. Do not forget that many new country records are to be expected.

TABLE 1. RELATIONSHIPS OF GENERA OF AMERICAN PALMS.

Subfamily (-oideae)	Tribe (-eae)	Subtribe (-inae)	Genus
Coryphoideae	Corypheae	Thrinacinae	*Trithrinax*
			Chelyocarpus
			Cryosophila
			Itaya
			Schippia
			Thrinax
			Coccothrinax
			Zombia
			Rhapidophyllum
		Livistoninae	*Colpothrinax*
			Acoelorraphe
			Serenoa
			Brahea
			Copernicia
			Washingtonia
		Sabalinae	*Sabal*
Calamoideae	Calameae	Raphiinae	*Raphia*
	Lepido-caryeae		*Mauritia*
			Mauritiella
			Lepidocaryum
Ceroxyloideae	Cyclospatheae		*Pseudophoenix*
	Ceroxyleae		*Ceroxylon*
			Juania
	Hyophorbeae		*Gaussia*
			Synechanthus
			Chamaedorea
			Wendlandiella
Arecoideae	Iriarteeae	Iriarteinae	*Dictyocaryum*
			Iriartella
			Iriartea
			Socratea
		Wettiniiane	*Wettinia*
	Areceae	Manicariinae	*Manicaria*
		Leopoldiniinae	*Leopoldinia*
		Malortieinae	*Reinhardtia*
		Euterpeinae	*Euterpe*
			Prestoea
			Neonicholsonia
			Oenocarpus
			Hyospathe
		Roystoneinae	*Roystonea*
	Cocoeae	Butiinae	*Butia*
			Jubaea
			Cocos
			Syagrus

TABLE 1. (*Continued*)

Subfamily (-oideae)	Tribe (-eae)	Subtribe (-inae)	*Genus*
			Lytocaryum
			Parajubaea
			Allagoptera
			Polyandrococos
		Attaleinae	*Attalea*
		Elaeidinae	*Barcella*
			Elaeis
		Bactridinae	*Acrocomia*
			Gastrococos
			Aiphanes
			Bactris
			Desmoncus
			Astrocaryum
	Geonomeae		*Pholidostachys*
			Welfia
			Calyptronoma
			Calyptrogyne
			Asterogyne
			Geonoma
Phytelephantoideae			*Phytelephas*
			Ammandra
			Aphandra

The list of accepted names and synonyms (Appendix II) includes all names, followed by their authors, that have been applied to American palms. Also included here are hybrids and uncertain names. We have taken these from recent monographs, as well as from Glassman (1972) and Index Kewensis (1993).

CLASSIFICATION OF AMERICAN PALMS

Table 1 shows relationships of the genera of American palms (Palmae or Arecaceae). It is the most recent and widely used classification, taken from Uhl and Dransfield (1987). Our list here does not exactly agree with that of Uhl and Dransfield; we include *Jessenia* in *Oenocarpus; Catoblastus* in *Wettinia;* and *Maximiliana, Orbignya,* and *Scheelea* in *Attalea.*

MORPHOLOGY OF AMERICAN PALMS

Palm stems are always woody and never herbaceous. They are typically tall and solitary, but can have many modifications. They can be erect, leaning, or creeping along the ground. Occasionally tall, aerial stems can be swollen at the base (*Gaussia, Jubaea*) or at the middle (*Colpothrinax, Iriartea*). Short and subterranean stems are also common. In one genus, *Desmoncus*, stems are elongate and climbing. Often stems are covered with dead, persistent leaf remains, while others are clean and have the leaf scars clearly visible. A few genera have root spines on the stems (*Cryosophila*, *Mauritiella*), and members of the tribe Bactridinae commonly have spiny stems. Also very common are shoots or rhizomes that develop at the base of stems, resulting in plants with clustered stems. Some clusters that form from basal shoots are very large and dense, others, which form from rhizomes, are rather small or open.

Leaves of palms can be instantly divided into two kinds, either *palmate* (i.e., fan shaped) or *pinnate* (i.e., feather shaped). All members of the subfamily Coryphoideae have palmate leaves, as do a few genera in the Calamoideae. All other palms have pinnate leaves, although often leaves are simple but still pinnately veined. Many palm leaves are covered in various short hairs, scales, or woolly scales; this condition is referred to as *tomentose*. Whether palmate or pinnate, leaves of palms are divided for convenience into four parts. At the base is a *sheath* that encircles the apical part of the stem. In a few genera (for example, *Euterpe*, *Roystonea*, *Socratea*) the sheath is closed and tubular and forms a crownshaft, but in most palms it is open. Some sheaths are very fibrous on the margins, and a few others consist entirely of reticulate fibers. The sheath is almost continuous into the *petiole*, but at the top of the sheath in most species there is a small continuation above the point of insertion of the petiole. In most palms this sheath continuation is small and inconspicuous, but in some it is well developed (e.g., *Oenocarpus*) while in *Desmoncus* it is elongate. Petioles are short to elongate, and rounded or more commonly channeled on the upper surface. The part of the leaf that actually bears the leaflets is called the *rachis*. In palmate leaves the rachis may be rather short (*Sabal*, *Mauritia*) or absent. In the former case, where the blade has a rachis, the leaf is referred to as *costapalmate*. In some Coryphoideae a small, flaplike structure is developed at the junction of the petiole and blade; in some species of *Copernicia* this is very well developed. Leaflets are always folded, and in palmate leaves and simple pinnate leaves this gives the familiar folded or plicate look to the leaves. The shape of leaflets varies tremendously, but most have a central midvein. In most palmate-leafed palms leaflets are linear and commonly fused at the base with one another, giving the characteristic fan-shaped leaf. Pinnate-leafed palms also often have linear leaflets, but various other shapes, such as lanceolate or sigmoid, are common. The apex of most leaflets tapers to a point, but in all species of the tribe Iriarteeae (and in *Aiphanes* and one species of *Bactris*) the leaflets have jagged margins or tips. Most species of Calamoideae have spines on the leaves, and all species in the Bactridinae have spiny leaves. In one genus, *Desmoncus*, the few apical leaflets of the leaves are often modified into reflexed hooks, called *acanthophylls*, an adaptation to the climbing habit of this genus.

Palms are either bisexual, bearing both male and female (or bisexual) flowers on the same plant; or less commonly unisexual, bearing only male or female flowers. Flowers are borne on compound structures known as *inflorescences*. At first sight the inflorescence appears rather complex, but actually consists of variations on a rather simple theme. Inflorescences always occur in the axils of leaves. Usually only one inflorescence is found in each axil, but several occur together on occasion (some species of *Aiphanes, Chamaedorea, Wettinia*). The position of the inflorescence at flowering time can be a good character for identification; it can be borne either among the leaves or below the leaves. In palms with crownshafts (most Iriarteeae and Euterpeinae) inflorescences are borne below the leaves. Inflorescences are spicate (i.e., they have a single flowering branch) or branched to one or more orders. The basal, nonbranched axis of the inflorescence is called the *peduncle*. It is often covered by bracts. The first bract on the peduncle is called the *prophyll* (although this is often difficult to see because it is hidden by the leaf sheath). In Coryphoideae, Calamoideae, and Ceroxyloideae there are several other bracts on the peduncle, called *peduncular bracts*, but in the Arecoideae there is only one peduncular bract, and this is usually conspicuous, and can be large and woody and deeply grooved (*Attalea, Syagrus*). The *rachis* is the axis of the inflorescence which actually bears the flowering branches, and again in Coryphoideae and Calamoideae it may be covered in bracts. In fact, one of the characters that defines the Calamoideae are the numerous, overlapping bracts that cover the peduncle, rachis, and flowering branches. In Arecoideae these bracts are present but are so reduced as to be hardly visible. The flowering branches themselves are either smooth or covered in hairs (*Euterpe*). In all genera of the Geonomeae the flowering branches are pitted, and the flowers are borne in these pits.

Flowers of palms are usually small and many hundreds can occur on an inflorescence. As already mentioned, they can be bisexual, with both stamens and carpels, or unisexual, with either stamens or carpels. A typical bisexual palm flower has three sepals, three petals, six stamens, and three carpels. From this simple pattern very many different types have evolved, and common changes involve the fusion of various parts, and increase or decrease in stamen number. In the Coryphoideae, the least specialized subfamily, flowers are usually borne singly and have a simple pattern, although carpels range from free to incompletely or completely joined. In the Calamoideae, the unisexual flowers bear reduced remnants of either stamens or carpels; male flowers have reduced carpels, called the *pistillode*, and female flowers have reduced stamens, called *staminodes*. In the Ceroxyloideae, flowers are also mostly unisexual, and there is considerable fusion of either sepals or petals, or both. In some genera of the Ceroxyloideae, such as *Wendlandiella* and *Synechanthus*, flowers can be arranged in short rows. In the largest subfamily, the Arecoideae, flowers are arranged in groups of three, consisting of one central female flower with two lateral male flowers. Often, however, at the ends of the flowering branches, the male flowers occur in pairs without the central female flower. In the most specialized subfamily, the Phytelephantoideae, flowers are very unusual, with male flowers consisting of a mass of stamens, and females having very long, fleshy sepals and petals and elongate stigmas and styles. These flower types define the subfamily.

Palm fruits are very variable in shape and size, ranging from small, globose, pea-sized fruits less than 0.5 cm in diameter to large, obovoid fruits more than 10 cm in diameter. Fruits contain three outer layers surrounding a seed. The outermost layer, the *epicarp*, is usually thin and often colored. In the Calamoideae (*Raphia, Mauritia, Mauritiella, Lepidocaryum*) it is covered with overlapping scales , and this is one of the defining characters of the subfamily. In some other genera (e.g., *Phytelephas, Manicaria*) it is warty and uneven, and in the Bactridinae it is occasionally spiny. The middle layer of the palm fruit is called the *mesocarp*. It is fleshy, fibrous, or dry and in many palms it is rich in oil. The inner layer of the fruit, covering the seed, is called the *endocarp*. In most palms it is relatively thin and inconspicuous, but in the Cocoeae, especially in the Attaleinae, it is very thick and bony, and sometimes difficult to break open. Palm fruits are usually one-seeded, but occasionally two or more seeds occur together. The seed consists of a large amount of endosperm and a small embryo, which is either apical, lateral, or basal. The endosperm is either homogeneous (i.e., plain) or ruminate (i.e., with indentations of the seed coat). Germination of palm seeds is quite variable, and can be either adjacent-ligular, in which the new shoot develops next to the seed and is enclosed by a tubular structure; remote-ligular, in which the shoot develops away from the seed on a short stalk, but is still enclosed by a tubular structure; or remote-tubular, similar to the former but lacking the tubular structure. The first seedling leaf is either simple, bifid, pinnate with a short rachis, or pinnate with a long rachis.

Many of the characters listed above occur in other plants, and occasionally other families can be confused with palms. The most important characters of the palm family are the woody stem; the folded, or plicate, leaf; and the compound inflorescence covered by bracts. The family Cyclanthaceae is common in the understory of American tropical rain forests and is often confused with palms. Most cyclanths are epiphytic plants that climb by roots, something palms never do. Terrestrial cyclanths have herbaceous stems, and are never woody like the palms. Their leaves are often bifid, and these can be confused with simple, pinnate-leafed palms, but in cyclanths the veins typically run up to the leaf apex, whereas veins in palms end along the margins. When cyclanths have palmate leaves, they can be confused with palmate-leafed palms, but cyclanths have three thick principal veins, and very long cylindrical petioles. The inflorescence of cyclanths is also very distinct, in being thick, spicate, and covered with four-sided female flowers. Two other groups of nonflowering plants are occasionally confused with palms: cycads and tree ferns. The former can usually be distinguished by their thick, fleshy, nonplicate leaves and cones, and the latter by their thin, nonplicate leaves, with spores on the lower surface of the leaflets.

KEY TO THE GENERA OF AMERICAN PALMS

This key is intended to provide a complement to the visual identification of the Guide. It is completely artificial, aimed for quick identification of a palm in the field, using vegetative characters as much as possible. Therefore, the key does not show the relationships between the genera, and related genera can appear far apart.

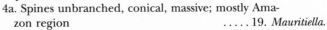

1a. Leaves fan shaped, palmate, or costa-palmate, i.e., leaf-
    lets radiating from the apex of the petiole or from a cen-
    tral costa, the blade appearing circular or almost so.
  2a. Palms with spines on the stems, leaf sheath, petiole,
    or leaflet margins.
    3a. Spines on the stems.
      4a. Spines unbranched, conical, massive; mostly Ama-
        zon region   . . . . . 19. *Mauritiella.*
      4b. Spines branched, slender; Central American re-
        gion   . . . . . 3. *Cryosophila.*
    3b. Spines on the leaf sheath, on the petiole, or on the
    leaflet margins.
      5a. Spines as hardened fibers of the leaf sheath.
        6a. Stems to 1 m tall, often creeping; southeastern
          United States   . . . . . 9. *Rhapidophyllum.*
        6b. Stems taller than 1 m, not creeping.
          7a. Southeastern South America (Bolivia to
            Uruguay)   . . . . . 1. *Trithrinax.*
          7b. Hispaniola (Dominican Republic, Haiti)
                                   . . . . . 8. *Zombia.*

      5b. Spines along the petiole margins or along the
      leaflet margins.
        8a. Spines along the leaflet margins; Amazon re-
         gion   . . . . . 20. *Lepidocaryum.*
        8b. Spines along the petiole margins.
          9a. Stems clustered.
            10a. Stems short and subterranean or creep-
              ing along the ground   . . . . . 12. *Serenoa.*
            10b. Stems tall and aerial   . . . . . 11. *Acoelorraphe.*
          9b. Stems solitary.
            11a. Cuba and Hispaniola, northern and east-
              ern South America   . . . . . 14. *Copernicia.*
            11b. Southwestern United States, Mexico, Bel-
              ize, Guatemala, El Salvador, Honduras.
             12a. Fruits less than 1 cm long; inflores-
               cence rachis bracts split lengthwise, hang-
               ing down   . . . . . 15. *Washingtonia.*
             12b. Fruits more than 1.5 cm long; inflores-
               cence rachis bracts neither split nor hang-
               ing down   . . . . . 13. *Brahea.*

2b. Palms lacking spines (but in some species of *Brahea* the petiole with short, blunt teeth).
13a. South America.
14a. Leaf sheath and petiole base split lengthwise.

15a. Leaf with a prominent costa along which the leaflets are inserted (i.e., costapalmate); northern South America north of the Amazon region
..... 16. *Sabal.*

15b. Leaf without a costa, the leaflets inserted directly at the petiole apex; western Amazon region
..... 4. *Itaya.*

14b. Leaf sheath and petiole base not split lengthwise.
16a. Large palms; stems 30 cm or more in diameter; fruits covered with overlapping scales like a snake's skin
..... 18. *Mauritia.*
16b. Small to medium-sized palms; stems less than 15 cm diameter; fruits not covered with scales
..... 2. *Chelyocarpus.*
13b. Central America and the Greater Antilles.
17a. Ripe fruits white.
18a. Leaf sheath and petiole not split lengthwise; blade divided in two large lobes
..... 5. *Schippia.*
18b. Leaf sheath and petiole split lengthwise; blade not divided in two lobes
..... 6. *Thrinax.*
17b. Ripe fruits black, brown, purplish red, or purple-black.

19a. Seed with a net of deep grooves, somewhat resembling a brain
..... 7. *Coccothrinax.*
19b. Seed smooth.
20a. Leaflets stiff; petioles often with short, blunt teeth
..... 13. *Brahea.*
20b. Leaflets with pendulous tips.
21a. Leaves with a short central costa; tall palms, sometimes with a swollen stem
..... 10. *Colpothrinax.*
21b. Leaves with a long costa that extends almost along the whole blade, or if costa is short, then small palms with subterranean stems
..... 16. *Sabal.*
1b. Leaves pinnate, i.e., leaflets arranged along a central rachis, or pinnately veined if simple.

22a. Fruits covered with large scales, somewhat resembling a snake's skin; leaves 8 m long or more .....17. *Raphia.*
22b. Fruits not resembling a snake's skin; leaves usually shorter than 8 m.
  23a. Stems and/or leaves spiny (the smallest species of *Bactris* sometimes spiny only along the margins of the leaflets).

    24a. Climbing palms; leaf rachis modified into a whip provided with hooks (but *Desmoncus stans* of Costa Rica not climbing, and with no whip)
          .....55. *Desmoncus.*
    24b. Nonclimbing palms; stems tall and aerial or short and subterranean; leaf rachis not modified.
      25a. Spines short and stout, confined to petiole and sheath margin.

        26a. Stems creeping; ripe fruits red; Central America and northern South America .....52. *Elaeis*
        26b. Stems erect, or short and subterranean; ripe fruits yellowish; southern South America (Brazil, Paraguay, Argentina, Uruguay) ....42. *Butia.*
      25b. Spines slender, needle-like or flattened, present on the stems, leaves, and usually also on the inflorescences.
        27a. Leaflets jagged at the tip, wedge-shaped to linear (see also *Bactris caryotifolia* of southeast Brazil) .....55. *Aiphanes.*

        27b. Leaflets not jagged at the tip.
          28a. Female flowers (and fruits) scattered along the flowering branches; leaflets usually green on lower surface (but note *Bactris bidentula, B. hatschbachii, B. vulgaris* with leaflets white below) .....56. *Bactris.*
          28b. Female flowers (and fruits) on basal parts of flowering branches; leaflets usually white or glaucous on the lower surface
            29a. Spines strongly flattened; usually in rain forest .....58. *Astrocaryum.*
            29b. Spines needle-like; rather dry, seasonal areas.
              30a. Stems markedly swollen; fruits yellow to orange; Cuba .....54. *Gastrococos.*
              30b. Stems occasionally swollen; fruits yellowish green to yellowish brown; widespread .....53. *Acrocomia.*
  23b. Stems and leaves without spines (rarely, stilt roots spiny).

31a. Leaflets with the margins and tips jagged, with
numerous veins radiating from the leaflet base,
and ending at different lengths along the margin,
often each leaflet divided lengthwise to the base in
several leaflets arranged in different planes.

 32a. Stilt roots tall, loosely arranged (and possible
  to see through), covered with sharp conical
  spines   . . . . . 31. *Socratea.*

 32b. Stilt roots poorly developed, or, if well developed, then dense (and impossible to see
  through the cone).

  33a. Small understory palms less than 10 m tall.

   34a. Fruits smooth, less than 2 cm long; Ama-
    zon region   . . . . . 29. *Iriartella.*

   34.b Fruits hairy, or, if glabrous, longer than 2
    cm; Andean region and adjacent lowlands

           . . . . . 32. *Wettinia.*

  33b. Larger canopy or subcanopy palms, more
   than 10 m tall.

   35a. Leaflets whitish on lower surface, each
    leaflet divided lengthwise into equally wide
    leaflets   . . . . . 28. *Dictyocaryum.*

   35b. Leaflets green on lower surface, un-
    divided, or divided lengthwise into leaflets
    of different widths.

    36a. Inflorescence buds horn-shaped and
     pendulous, only one at each node; stems
     often swollen in middle . . . . . 30. *Iriartea.*

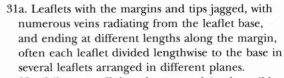

    36b. Inflorescence buds shaped like a short
     club, erect, often multiple per node;
     stems always cylindrical . . . . . 32. *Wettinia.*

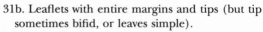

31b. Leaflets with entire margins and tips (but tip
sometimes bifid, or leaves simple).

 37a. Fruit with a woody, often very thick, stonelike
  endocarp, marked with three germinating pores
  (like the "eyes" of a coconut).

  38a. Fruit more than 20 cm diameter; cultivated
   palms, often along sandy shores ("coconuts")

          . . . . . 44. *Cocos.*

38b. Fruit less than 15 cm diameter; naturally
occurring palms.
 39a. Andean highlands, above 1500 m elevation . . . . . 47. *Parajubaea.*
 39b. Palms of lower elevations.
  40a. Inflorescences spicate, usually more
than 50 cm long.
   41a. Stems usually short and subterranean; stamens 6–18. . . . . . 48. *Allagoptera.*
   41b. Stems usually tall and aerial; stamens
60–120 . . . . . 49. *Polyandrococos.*

  40b. Inflorescences branched, or, if spicate,
then less than 50 cm long.

   42a. Fruits splitting at maturity along
three lines, exposing the relatively thin
endocarp; Brazil (Espírito Santo, Rio
de Janeiro, Sâo Paulo) . . . . . 46. *Lytocaryum.*
   42b. Fruits usually not splitting at maturity.

    43a. Leaflets pointed at tips; male
flowers sunken in pits in the flowering branches . . . . . 51. *Barcella.*
    43b. Leaflets unequal and/or bifid at
tips; male flowers not sunken in pits.
     44a. Fruits usually more than 4.5 cm
long, often with more than one
seed; inflorescences of two kinds,
with all male flowers, and with
both male and female flowers, and
both kinds on the same plants
        . . . . . 50. *Attalea.*
     44b. Fruits usually less than 4.5 cm
long; usually one-seeded; inflorescences with both male and female
flowers.
      45a. Peduncular bract usually
grooved, not tomentose; pores
near base of endocarp; petiole
without spinelike projections
(but note *Syagrus coronata* and *S.
schizophylla*).
       46a. Stems less than 50 cm
diameter; east of the Andes
        . . . . 45. *Syagrus.*
       46b. Stems to 1 m diameter; west
of the Andes in Chile . . . . . 43. *Jubaea.*

45b. Peduncular bract usually not
grooved, often tomentose; pores
near or just below middle of endocarp; petiole usually with spinelike projections (but note *Butia
archeri, B. campicola, B. micro-
spadix*, and *B. purpurascens* . . . . 42. *Butia.*
37b. Fruits without a woody endocarp, or if this is
present, then without three germinating pores.

47a. Rather small and delicate understory palms
with subterranean or slender and canelike
stems that are markedly ringed.
48a. Stems green.
49a. Leaf sheaths green.

50a. Inflorescences with two or more
bracts besides the prophyll.

51a. Palms with flowers of both sexes;
flowers arranged in lines of 8–13
along the flowering branches; ripe
fruits red, seeds grooved and brain-
like   . . . . . 25. *Synechanthus.*
51b. Plants with either male or female
flowers; flowers solitary or in groups
of 2–3, not in lines; ripe fruits black
or red, seeds not grooved like a brain
                          . . . . . 26. *Chamaedorea.*
50b. Inflorescences with one bract besides
the prophyll.
52a. Plants with both male and female
flowers; widespread in northern
South America and Panama
                          . . . . . 40. *Hyospathe.*
52b. Plants with either male or female
flowers; western Amazon region in
Peru and adjacent Brazil and Bolivia
                          . . . . . 27. *Wendlandiella.*
49b. Leaf sheaths brownish.
53a. Flowering branches with deep pits
that cover the flowers before flowering
                          . . . . . 64. *Geonoma.*

53b. Flowering branches without pits, the
flowers superficial   . . . . . 37. *Prestoea.*

48b. Stems brownish or grayish.
   54a. Flowering branches with deep pits that
   cover the flowers before flowering.
     55a. Peduncular bract inserted at top of
     peduncle apex, usually falling off at
     flowering and leaving a distinct scar
                    . . . . . 62. *Calyptrogyne.*

     55b. Peduncular bract inserted at or near
     base of peduncle.
       56a. Leaves simple or unequally pin-
       nate, or if the leaflets are equal, then
       rather narrow; peduncular bract not
       strongly fibrous.
         57a. Bracts that cover the pits im-
         mersed in the flowering branch;
         leaves simple   . . . . . 63. *Asterogyne.*
         57b. Bracts that cover the pits not
         immersed in flowering branch;
         leaves pinnate or simple . . . . . 64. *Geonoma.*
       56b. Leaflets almost of equal width;
       peduncular bract strongly fibrous or
       woody   . . . . . 59. *Pholidostachys.*
   54b. Flowering branches without pits, the
   flowers superficial.
     58a. Leaflets with a strongly unequal
     apex, sometimes several leaflets united
     along their margins into a broad seg-
     ment that is dentate at apex . . . . 35. *Reinhardtia.*

     58b. Leaflets pointed, not unequal at
     apex.
       59a. Inflorescences horsetail shaped.
                       . . . . . 39. *Oenocarpus.*

       59b. Inflorescences not horsetail
       shaped.

         60a. Fruits globose   . . . . . 37. *Prestoea.*

         60b. Fruits ellipsoid.

           61a. Inflorescences spicate; fruits
           pointed at apex; Nicaragua to
           Panama   . . . . . 38. *Neonicholsonia.*

61b. Inflorescences branched;
fruits rounded at apex; Panama
and northern South America
..... 40. *Hyospathe.*

47b. Larger and stouter palms of the forest canopy or subcanopy, or sometimes massive
palms of the understory, with subterranean or
rather short and thick stems.

62a. Leaves with groups of leaflets joined
along their margins, forming large leaflets
that are toothed at apex, the large leaves
sometimes appearing almost undivided
..... 33. *Manicaria.*

62b. Leaflets free, not joined along their margins.
63a. Fruits large and woody, grouped in
spherical heads, the epicarp with woody,
conical, or sharply pointed projections.

64a. Petiole to 2 m long, cylindrical
..... 66. *Ammandra.*
64b. Petiole less than 1 m long, flattened
above.
65a. Leaf sheath with abundant long fibers   ..... 67. *Aphandra.*
65b. Leaf sheath not fibrous, or the fibers not abundant   ..... 65. *Phytelephas.*
63b. Fruits rather small and not in heads,
the epicarp smooth.
66a. Leaf sheath long and closed, forming a prominent cylindrical crown
shaft.

67a. Massive palms with stout stems
more than 30 cm diameter; inflorescences branched to three orders
..... 41. *Roystonea.*
67b. Slender palms with stems 15–25
cm in diameter; inflorescences
branched to one order   ..... 36. *Euterpe.*

66b. Leaf sheath short and/or open, or if long, then not forming a cylindrical crown shaft.

68a. Inflorescences branched to 3–5 orders.

69a. Lowlands of the Caribbean region.

70a. Stems more or less swollen with closely spaced leaf scars .... 21. *Pseudophoenix.*

70b. Stems almost cylindrical, tapering toward the apex .... 24. *Gaussia.*

69b. South America and the Juan Fernández Islands.

71a. Sandy soils along blackwater rivers in the Amazon region .... 34. *Leopoldinia.*

71b. The Andes and Juan Fernández Islands.

72a. Highlands of the Andes above 1000 m .... 22. *Ceroxylon.*

72b. Juan Fernández Islands .... 23. *Juania.*

68b. Inflorescences branched to 1–2 orders.

73a. Flowers borne in deep pits in the flowering branches.

74a. Flowering branches more than 2 cm diameter; Central American and Andean regions .... 60. *Welfia.*

74b. Flowering branches less than 1 cm diameter; the Greater Antilles .... 61. *Calyptronoma.*

73b. Flowers borne superficially on the flowering branches.

75a. Inflorescences horsetail shaped; fruits pointed at apex .... 39. *Oenocarpus.*

75b. Inflorescences with spreading branches; fruits rounded at apex .... 36. *Euterpe.*

THE PALMS OF THE AMERICAS

1. TRITHRINAX

This small genus from subtropical southern South America contains some of the most cold and drought-resistant American palms. Stems are short to tall, clustered or solitary, and are covered, at least near the top, with persistent, fibrous, spiny leaf sheaths. Older stems often lose this covering. Leaves are palmate, 5–35 in number, and form a rather dense crown. The leaf sheaths consist of reticulate fibers, and at the top these form outward and downward pointing spines. Petioles are long and have smooth margins. The origin of the name of the genus comes from the leaf shape; *Thrinax* comes from the Greek word meaning a trident or three-pronged fork and so *Trithrinax* refers to three tridents. The leaflets are either stiff or somewhat flexible, slightly to deeply bifid and sharply pointed at the tips. Inflorescences are borne among the leaves and are branched to two or three orders. They are covered with numerous, inflated bracts. Flowers are bisexual with six stamens and three free carpels. There is considerable variation in the relative lengths of sepals, petals, and styles, and this has been used to separate the species. Fruits are one-seeded, globose to ellipsoid, and initially white or yellowish white but eventually black. Seeds have ruminate endosperm and the seedling leaf is simple.

Trithrinax contains three species, distributed in subtropical southern South America in Brazil, Bolivia, Paraguay, Argentina, and Uruguay. They grow in seasonally dry regions, open areas, or deciduous forest at low elevations. Only three species are accepted here although Pingitore (1978) recognized five. This small and poorly known genus is in need of a modern revision. It is considered one of the least specialized genera of palms. It belongs to the Coryphoid subfamily, itself considered unspecialized. The flowers of *Trithrinax*, with three sepals, three petals, six stamens, and three free carpels and having simple floral anatomy (Magnano, 1973), are considered to represent the basic type of flower from which all other palm flowers are evolved.

It is also of biogeographic interest because it is the first link in a chain of closely related genera. *Trithrinax* occurs in southern South America, followed by the South and Central American *Chelyocarpus*, *Itaya*, *Cryosophila*, and *Schippia* and finally the Caribbean *Coccothrinax*, *Thrinax*, and *Zombia*. This kind of chain of related genera is quite common in American palms, and often one of the terminal genera will contain the most species, in this case *Coccothrinax*. This distribution pattern indicates a Southern Hemisphere origin for this group of palms.

Trithrinax is a distinctive genus that is not likely to be confused with any other in the field except for the occasionally co-occurring *Copernicia alba*, from which it most obviously differs by its clustered stems, spiny leaf sheaths, and smooth petiole margins.

Trithrinax brasiliensis
(Map 1, Plate 1)
"Carandaí," "burití" (Bra)
Field characters. Stems solitary or clustered, 2–15 m tall and 7–35 cm diameter, covered with persistent, fibrous, spiny leaf sheaths. Leaves 5–35; *leaflets somewhat flexible, briefly bifid and pointed at the tips.* Fruits globose to ellipsoid, 0.8–1.5 cm diameter, yellowish.
Range and habitat. Southern Brazil (Paraná, Rio Grande do Sul, Santa Catarina); open, dry, inland areas, or rarely in *Araucaria* forests near streams (Gubert, 1987).
Uses. In southern Brazil and elsewhere it is

sometimes cultivated as an ornamental; the leaflets are used locally to weave hats.
Notes. Reitz (1974) reported that this species flowered in October and fruits ripened from May to July. In Paraná it flowers in August and fruits are ripe in February; however, local people report that the palm produces fruits only every seven years.

Trithrinax campestris
(Map 2)
"Saro" (Arg), "caranday" (Uru)
Field characters. Stems clustered or solitary, to 6 m tall and 20–25 cm diameter, covered with

persistent, fibrous, spiny leaf sheaths. Leaves 12–35, the old ones persistent; *leaflets very stiff and leathery, briefly bifid, the tips very sharply pointed and spinelike.* Fruits globose to ellipsoid, 0.8–1.5 cm diameter, yellowish.

Range and habitat. Argentina (Córdoba, Entre Ríos, Salta, San Luis, Santa Fé, Tucumán) and western Uruguay; open, dry areas, especially along dry stream margins, at low elevations.

Uses. The leaves are used for thatching.

Trithrinax schizophylla
(Map 3, Plate 1)
"Carandillo," "saro" (Arg, Bol), "burití" (Bra), "caranday-i" (Par)
Field characters. Stems clustered or solitary, 2–6 m tall and 12–20 cm diameter, covered at the top with persistent, fibrous, spiny leaf sheaths. Leaves 10–25, glaucous; *leaflets somewhat flexible, deeply bifid for one- to two-thirds their length,* the tips sharply pointed. Fruits globose or subglobose, 0.8–1.5 cm diameter, yellowish white.

Range and habitat. Southwestern Brazil (Mato Grosso do Sul), south and central Bolivia (Santa Cruz), western Paraguay (Alto Paraguay, Concepción, Presidente Hayes), and northern Argentina (Chaco, Formosa, Jujuy, Salta); near watercourses in dry, deciduous thorn forests of the *chaco* region and adjacent areas, below 400 m elevation.

Uses. The stems are occasionally used in construction; the leaves are used for thatching and making hats and baskets.

2. CHELYOCARPUS

This small genus from northwestern South America occurs both west and east of the Andes. Stems are small to moderate, solitary or clustered, and erect or leaning. Leaves are palmate, 10–20 in number, and form a rather open crown. The densely woolly sheath is not split, thus distinguishing the genus from the closely related *Itaya*, in which the sheath is split. Petioles are long and have smooth margins. The leaf blade is circular in outline, usually whitish on the lower surface and is split into two halves; each half is again split into groups of wedge-shaped leaflets. The arching inflorescences, borne among the leaves, are branched to one or two orders and have 1–4 inflated, peduncular bracts. Flowering branches are numerous and bear small, solitary, bisexual flowers. The fruits are one- to two-seeded, globose, greenish yellow or brown when ripe. In one species the surface is corky and cracked; in fact, the name *Chelyocarpus* comes from the Greek words meaning "turtle carapace-fruited," an allusion to the appearance of the cracked surface of the fruits of this species. The seeds have homogeneous endosperm and the seedling leaf is bifid.

Chelyocarpus contains four species, three of them distributed in the western Amazon region and the fourth in the Pacific lowlands of Colombia (Moore, 1972; Kahn and Mejía, 1988).

Chelyocarpus chuco
(Map 4)
"Hoja redonda" (Bol), "caranaí," "carnaubinha" (Bra)
Field characters. Stems solitary or clustered, 5–12 m tall and 8–12 cm diameter. Leaves 14–17; blade 1.5–2 m diameter, *green on the lower surface, split into 22–42 wedge-shaped leaflets.* Inflorescences branched to 2 orders, with 2 peduncular bracts; flowering branches numerous, 1–8 cm long; fruits globose, 1.5–2 cm diameter, one-seeded, yellowish green, becoming dark brown when ripe, *smooth.*

Range and habitat. Brazil (Acre, Rondônia) and Bolivia (Beni, Pando); along the Río Madeira and its tributaries near the Brazil-Bolivia frontier; common in swampy areas in inundated forest near rivers, or in adjacent forest on non-inundated soils, below 200 m elevation.

Uses. The leaves used for thatching and to weave hats.

Chelyocarpus dianeurus
(Map 5, Plate 1)
"Nolí" (Col)
Field characters. Stems solitary, erect or slightly leaning, 3–15 m tall and 6–9 cm diameter. Leaves 13–15; blade 1–2 m diameter, *whitish on the lower surface, deeply split into 7–14 leaflets,* these bifid at the tips. Inflorescences branched

to one order, with 2 peduncular bracts; flowering branches about 50, to 16 cm long; fruits globose, 1.7–2 cm diameter, one-seeded, greenish, yellowish, or whitish, *smooth.*

Range and habitat. Pacific lowlands of Colombia (Chocó, Valle); understory of lowland rain forest on well-drained soils, most common on slopes, near sea level.

Uses. The woolly covering of the sheaths has been used to stuff pillows.

Chelyocarpus repens
(Map 6)

Field characters. Stems solitary, *leaning or creeping, to 1 m tall and 9 cm diameter.* Leaves 10–20; blade 1.2–1.5 m diameter, *whitish on lower surface, split into 4–7 leaflets.* Inflorescences branched to one order, with only one peduncular bract; flowering branches 25–35, very short; fruits globose, to 2.5 cm diameter, 1–2-seeded, greenish, *smooth.*

Range and habitat. Known from two small areas near Iquitos in the Peruvian Amazon (Loreto); lowland rain forest, more abundant on non-inundated soils, but also in inundated areas, below 200 m elevation.

Chelyocarpus ulei
(Map 7, Plate 1)
"Xila" (Bra), "sacha aguajillo" (Per)

Field characters. Stems solitary, erect, 1–8 m tall and 4–7 cm diameter. Leaves 10–15; blade 1–1.5 m diameter, *whitish on the lower surface, deeply split into 5–12 leaflets.* Inflorescences branched to one or rarely two orders, with 2 peduncular bracts; flowering branches numerous, 7–20 cm long; fruits globose, 2–2.5 cm diameter, one-seeded, brown, *markedly cracked and corky.*

Range and habitat. Western Amazon region in Colombia (Amazonas), Ecuador (Morona-Santiago), Peru (Loreto, Pasco, San Martín, Ucayali), and Brazil (Acre); lowland rain forest in inundated or noninundated areas, below 500 m, rarely to 900 m elevation.

Uses. Vegetable salt is extracted from the burned stems by the Miraña Indians in Colombia.

3. CRYOSOPHILA

This small genus of medium-sized palms is immediately recognizable by the spines that cover the stems. These spines are slender, sharply pointed, and branched and are derived from roots that grow directly from the stems. They are more numerous nearer the base of the stems and often become fewer and less branched higher up. Stems are solitary or rarely clustered and are erect or occasionally arched. Leaves are palmate, 5–35 in number and are borne on elongate petioles. Sheaths are tomentose and the sheath and petiole base are split lengthwise in all but one species. The blade is circular in outline, split to the middle into equal halves, and each half is again divided into numerous groups of leaflets. In most species each leaflet is again partially split, giving a 2–3-lobed apex. The blades are often whitish gray on the lower surface. Inflorescences are borne among the leaves and are branched from 1–3 orders. They are exserted through the split leaf sheath and are pendulous or rarely erect at flowering time. They are rather short and compact and not longer than the petioles. Both rachis and peduncle are covered with several inflated, densely white-tomentose bracts, each partially enclosing the next, and these are usually deciduous at flowering time. Flowers are bisexual, small, and whitish and are densely crowded on the flowering branches. There are six stamens and three free carpels. Fruits are one-seeded, globose, ellipsoid, obovoid, or pear shaped, white and smooth. The endosperm is homogeneous and the seedling leaf is simple and narrowly lanceolate.

Cryosophila contains nine species (Evans, 1992a), distributed from western Mexico to northwestern Colombia, from sea level to 1700 m elevation. The origin of the name is unknown, but can be translated from the Greek words meaning "cold-loving," perhaps in reference to the northern habitat of one species in Mexico. Most species grow in lowland rain forest, but *C. nana* grows in dry, deciduous forests. Many species are usually found on alkaline soils. Several are narrow endemics and Evans (1992a) reported that four of the nine species were endangered.

The genus is rather uniform. Species have been separated mainly on the basis of size and shape of fruit and on other minor characters. Evans (1992b) recognized the difficulty of finding characters that differentiated the species. A further problem in the genus is that the Central American rain forests are much fragmented, making it usually impossible to tell if local variants are really distinct from one another, or if intermediates once occurred in the intervening areas. For these reasons, we suspect that the actual number of species in the genus is lower than that given by Evans (1992a).

Cryosophila cookii
(Map 8)
"Escobón," "súrtuba" (CR)
Field characters. Stems solitary, 7–14 m tall and 11–20 cm diameter, densely covered with a tangled mass of root spines. Leaves 10–35; blade split into 66–80 leaflets, whitish gray on the lower surface. *Inflorescences branched to one order,* pendulous, *the flowering branches closely arranged in groups that extend spirally along the rachis,* with about 15 rachis bracts, these deciduous at flowering time; fruits ellipsoid, to 2 cm long and 1.3 cm diameter, white.
Range and habitat. Atlantic lowlands of Costa Rica (Limón); lowland rain forest, about 100 m elevation.
Notes. Evans (1992a) estimated that the total population of this species was not more than 100 adult plants, a few of them in the Tortuguero National Park.

Cryosophila grayumii
(Map 9)
"Bijagua," "palma real" (CR)
Field characters. Stems solitary, rarely clustered, 0.7–5 m tall and 5–9 cm diameter, often arched, densely covered with root spines. Leaves 9–32; blade split into 36–50 leaflets, these grayish white on the lower surface. Inflorescences branched to 2 orders, pendulous, with 12–22 rachis bracts, these deciduous at flowering time; fruits globose to ellipsoid, 1.2–2 cm long and 1–1.6 cm diameter, white.
Range and habitat. Pacific slope in Costa Rica (Puntarenas); lowland rain forest, on limestone soils, at 100–600 m elevation.
Notes. Known from 2 small areas in a very restricted habitat. Evans (1992a) recognized 2 subspecies, but these seem scarcely different from one another.

Cryosophila guagara
(Map 10, Plate 2)
"Guágara" (CR)
Field characters. Stems solitary, 6–10 m tall and 7–13 cm diameter, covered throughout with root spines. Leaves 18–28; blade divided into

44–66 leaflets, these white on the lower surface. Inflorescences usually branched to 2 orders, pendulous, *with 23–36 rachis bracts, these semipersistent after flowering time;* fruits ovoid to almost globose, 1.3–2 cm diameter, white.
Range and habitat. Pacific lowlands of Costa Rica (Puntarenas, San José) and adjacent Panama (Chiriquí); lowland rain forest, to 500 m elevation.
Uses. The leaves are commonly used for thatching.
Notes. Large populations still exist in the Corcovado National Park in Costa Rica. In other places, where the species was formerly abundant, it is now becoming rare due to habitat destruction.

Cryosophila kalbreyeri
(Map 11)
"Barbasco," "palma de escoba" (Col), "guágara chica," "nupa" (Pan)
Field characters. Stems solitary or rarely clustered, 1–5 m tall and 4–11 cm diameter, erect or arched, covered with root spines. Leaves 10–32; blade split into 36–56 leaflets, these whitish gray on the lower surface. Inflorescences branched to two orders, pendulous, with 14–26 rachis bracts, *these deciduous but some persistent after flowering time;* fruits ± globose, 1.2–1.9 cm long and 1.1–1.7 cm diameter, white.
Range and habitat. Eastern Panama (Darién, Panamá) and Colombia (Antioquia, Bolívar, Córdoba, Sucre); rain forest, at 300–1200 m elevation.
Notes. Evans (1992a) divided this species into 3 subspecies, but these are scarcely distinct from one another.

Cryosophila macrocarpa
(Map 12)
"Nolí" (Col)
Field characters. Stems solitary, to 5 m tall and 12 cm diameter, erect or arched, covered with root spines. Leaves to 30; blade split into 58–64 leaflets, whitish gray on the lower surface. Inflorescences branched 2–3 orders, pen-

dulous, with 10 rachis bracts, these ± deciduous at flowering time; *fruits ellipsoid, 3.1– 3.6 cm long and 2.6–2.9 cm diameter*, white.
Range and habitat. Colombia (Chocó); lowland rain forest, at 20 m elevation.
Notes. Distinguished by its larger fruits. Several other palms from the very wet forests of the Chocó region also have large fruits, for example *Attalea cuatrecasana* and *Bactris maraja*.

Cryosophila nana
(Map 13)
"Escoba," "zoyamiche" (Mex)
Field characters. Stems solitary, 0.6–5 m tall and 5–10 cm diameter, densely covered with root spines. Leaves 6–13; *leaf sheath and petiole base not split lengthwise; blade divided into 26– 48 leaflets, these green on the lower surface.* Inflorescences usually branched to 2 orders, pendulous, with 9–22 rachis bracts, these deciduous at flowering time; fruits almost globose, 1.2–1.9 cm diameter, white.
Range and habitat. Pacific coastal Mexico (Colima, Chiapas, Guerrero, Jalisco, Michoacán, Nayarit, Sinaloa); dry, deciduous forest, often in pine-oak woodlands, at 200–1000(–1700) m elevation.

Cryosophila stauracantha
(Map 14)
"Give-and-take" (Bel), "escoba" (Gua, Mex)
Field characters. Stems solitary, 1–10 m tall and 5–12 cm diameter, densely covered with root spines. Leaves 18–24; blade divided into 32–50 leaflets, these whitish gray on the lower surface. Inflorescences branched to 2 orders, pendulous, with 16–32 rachis bracts, these deciduous at flowering time; *the apical ones joined at the tips and falling together*; fruits ± globose, 1.1–1.4 cm diameter, white.
Range and habitat. Mexico (Campeche, Chiapas, Quintana Roo, Tabasco), northern Guatemala (Alta Verapaz, Izabal, Petén), and Belize; lowland rain forest, at sea level to 600 m elevation.

Cryosophila warscewiczii
(Map 15)
"Guáguara," "palma de escoba" (CR)
Field characters. Stems solitary, 1–12 m tall and 4–15 cm diameter, erect or rarely arched, densely covered with root spines. Leaves 9–27; blade divided into 38–68 leaflets, these whitish gray on the lower surface. Inflorescences branched to 2 orders, pendulous, with 16–40 rachis bracts, these deciduous at flowering time; *fruits globose or ovoid, 2–2.6 cm long and 1.8–2.3 cm long*, white.
Range and habitat. Southern Nicaragua (Río San Juan, Zelaya), Costa Rica (Alajuela, Cartago, Heredia, Limón), and Panama (Bocas del Toro, Coclé, Colón, San Blas); lowland rain forest, at sea level to 1200 m elevation.
Notes. Henderson (1984a) studied pollination (as *C. albida*) in Costa Rica. He found that two genera of small beetles, *Derelominus* and *Mystrops*, were the probable pollinators.

Cryosophila williamsii
(Map 16)
"Mojarillo," "palmiche" (Hon)
Field characters. Stems solitary, 3–7 m tall and 7–10 cm diameter, erect or arched, covered with root spines. Leaves 17–25; blade divided into 44–56 leaflets, these whitish gray on the lower surface. *Inflorescences erect*, branched to two orders, with 14–19 rachis bracts, these deciduous at flowering time; fruits globose to ellipsoid, 1.3–1.8 cm long and 1.3–1.5 cm diameter, white.
Range and habitat. Honduras (Santa Bárbara, west side of Lago Yojoa); lowland rain forest on steep slopes with limestone soils, at 600– 700 m elevation.
Notes. Evans (1992a) reported that only a few thousand individuals remained in a few square kilometers of forest.

4. ITAYA

This genus was discovered recently, in 1972, along the Río Itaya in Peru, from which it gets its name. Stems are solitary and of medium size. Leaves are palmate, 11–25 in number, and the sheath is very woolly and split basally lengthwise, thus distinguishing the genus from the closely related *Chelyocarpus*. The petiole is elongate and has smooth margins. The blade is silvery gray or white on the lower surface, circular in outline, and split into a few groups of wedge-shaped leaflets. The tips of the leaflets are serrate, giving the outline of the leaf a very attractive appearance. The arching inflorescences are branched to two orders and are borne among the leaves. They do not project beyond the leaves. There are several peduncular bracts and these are woolly tomentose.

.

The flowering branches are numerous with solitary, creamy white, small, bisexual flowers, which have 15–19 stamens. These flowers are somewhat unusual in being open while still within the bracts. Fruits are one-seeded, almost globose, with some variation to ovoid or obovoid and yellowish green. The seed has homogeneous endosperm and the seedling leaf is simple, elliptic, and whitish on the lower surface.

Itaya contains one species in the western Amazon region (Moore, 1972; Henderson, 1994). It can be separated from the most closely related genera *Chelyocarpus* and *Cryosophila* by its split sheath and petiole base. Uhl and Dransfield (1987) considered *Itaya* a more specialized genus than *Cryosophila* and *Chelyocarpus* because of anatomical and floral characteristics.

Itaya amicorum
(Map 17, Plate 2)
"Xila" (Bra), "marimiipa" (Col: Miraña)
Field characters. Stems solitary, to 4 m tall and 9–10 cm diameter. Leaves forming a wide crown, with long petioles; blade circular in outline, about 2 m diameter, split to the base into 10–16 equally broad leaflets (the leaf looking like a cartwheel), silvery gray or whitish on lower surface. Inflorescences with numerous flowering branches up to 10 cm long, whitish in flower; fruits almost globose, with some variation to obovoid or ovoid, 2–2.5 cm long and 1.5–2 cm diameter, yellowish green.

Range and habitat. Western Amazon region in Colombia (Amazonas), Peru (Loreto), and Brazil (Amazonas); an uncommon understory palm growing both in noninundated areas and in wet areas along rivers, in lowland rain forest, below 300 m elevation.

Uses. The leaves are used to thatch temporary shelters. Salt is extracted from the burned trunks by Miraña Indians in Colombia.

Notes. At one time it was considered to have a narrow range and to be endangered (Moore, 1977). It is now known to have a more widespread, although somewhat patchy, distribution (Henderson, 1994).

5. SCHIPPIA

This genus contains one little-known species discovered in Belize in 1932 by the Australian-born botanist William A. Schipp. Stems are solitary and of medium size and they are typically obscured by persistent, dead leaves which hang from the crown. In areas where burning is frequent, stems are covered with corky bark. Leaves are palmate and about 6–15 in number. The woolly tomentose sheath is split at the base lengthwise and the elongate petiole has smooth margins. The blade is circular in outline, green on the lower surface, and is divided into about thirty narrow, pointed leaflets. Inflorescences are branched to two orders, are borne among the leaves, and are covered with three, woolly-tomentose peduncular bracts. Flowers are small and white and are borne on short stalks. Both bisexual and male flowers occur on the same inflorescence, with the bisexual flowers occurring near the base of the flowering branches. There are six stamens and a single carpel. Fruits are one-seeded, globose, rather large, and white. The epicarp splits irregularly when the fruits are ripe to expose the white mesocarp. The endosperm is homogeneous and the seedling leaf is simple and lanceolate.

Schippia is a genus of one species occurring in Belize and possibly adjacent Guatemala.

Schippia concolor
(Map 18, Plate 3)
"Silver pimento," "mountain pimento" (Bel)
Field characters. Stems solitary, 5–10 m tall and 5–10 cm diameter. Leaves 6–15; petiole to 2 m long; blade circular in outline, about 1 m diameter, green on the lower surface, divided into about 30 leaflets. Inflorescences branched to 2 orders, with 3 woolly-tomentose peduncular bracts; fruits globose, to 2.5 cm diameter, white.

Range and habitat. Belize and probably northern

Guatemala (Petén); patchily distributed in lowland rain forest, or often in pine forest, to 500 m elevation.

Notes. Often found with *Thrinax radiata*, which differs in its nonlobed leaf, and *Cryosophila*

stauracantha which has a spiny trunk. Frequent fires affect regeneration in some populations. The conservation status of this species has been assessed by Balick and Johnson (in press).

6. THRINAX

This small Caribbean genus is closely related to the following two genera, *Coccothrinax* and *Zombia*. Its name is derived from the Greek word meaning trident, in reference to the leaves. Stems are short to moderate, almost always solitary, and usually swollen at the base. They are often covered, at least near the top, with persistent, fibrous leaf bases. Leaves are palmate, 6–17 in number, and form a rather dense crown. Sheaths are fibrous, densely white-tomentose, and are split lengthwise (thus distinguishing the genus from *Coccothrinax* and *Zombia*, in which the leaf sheath is not split). The petiole is either elongate or short and smooth along the margins. The leaf blade is divided to about halfway or more into numerous leaflets. These are linear-lanceolate, green or gray-waxy on the lower surface, and often curled over at the tips. Inflorescences are branched to two orders and are borne among the leaves, either greatly or scarcely exceeding them. The elongate peduncle and rachis are covered with sheathing bracts, but the primary branches, which hang down from the rachis, are free from bracts. The small bisexual flowers are borne on short stalks, although these are almost absent in some species. The sepals and petals are greatly reduced to a single cupule with six teeth, and there are 5–15 stamens and a single carpel. Fruits are one-seeded, globose, small, and white or yellowish white at maturity (as opposed to purple-black or purple-red in *Coccothrinax*). Seeds have homogeneous endosperm and lack the grooves of *Coccothrinax* and *Zombia*. The seedling leaf is simple, narrow, and lanceolate.

Thrinax contains seven species, distributed throughout the northwestern Caribbean, usually in coastal regions. Read (1975) recognized four species and three more were added by Borhidi and Muñiz (1985) when they included *Hemithrinax* in *Thrinax*. Borhidi and Muñiz recognized two subgenera, which are best separated from each other by the smaller inflorescences with few primary branches near the top of the rachis in subgenus *Hemithrinax*; and the larger inflorescences with primary branches all along the rachis in subgenus *Thrinax*. The situation is perhaps more complex and the whole group, including the related genera *Coccothrinax* and *Zombia*, needs a modern systematic revision.

The simple flowers with their much reduced perianth and exserted anthers and stigmas have been considered adaptations to wind pollination (Read, 1975). Insects, however, are also probably involved in pollen transfer (Uhl and Moore, 1977).

Thrinax compacta
(Map 19)
"Yarey," "yuraguancillo" (Cub)
Field characters. Stems 2.5–15 m tall and to 30 cm diameter. Leaf sheaths with a few, thin fibers; petiole elongate, to 1.5 m long; blade with 60–70 leaflets, the middle ones to 1.4 m long, lighter green on the lower surface. *Inflorescences short, not or shortly exceeding the leaves, with a few primary branches crowded near the top*; flowers and fruits borne on short stalks less

than 1 mm long; fruits globose, to 9 mm diameter, white.
Range and habitat. Cuba (Oriente, Sierra de Nipe); limestone cliffs on rocky outcrops (*mogotes*).
Notes. Distingiushed by its compact inflorescences.

Thrinax ekmaniana
(Map 20, Plate 3)
"Palmita de jumagua" (Cub)

Field characters. Stems 2–4 m tall and 3–5 cm diameter, the upper part covered with persistent, dead leaves. Leaf sheaths with a few coarse fibers; *petiole short (to 10 cm long), giving the leaves a clustered appearance;* blade with 30–36 leaflets, the middle ones 40–50 cm long, stiff, gray on the lower surface. *Inflorescences slender, erect, with 3 primary branches at the top, exceeding the leaves;* flowers and fruits not borne on stalks; fruits globose, to 9 mm diameter, white.

Range and habitat. Cuba (Las Villas); known only from a small, isolated, limestone hill *mogote* where it grows on steep, rocky cliffs. A very rare palm in Cuba with a small range and few individuals.

Thrinax excelsa
(Map 21)
"Broad thatch" (Jam)
Field characters. Stems 3–11 m tall and 12.5–20 cm diameter. Leaf sheaths with fine fibers; petiole elongate, 1.2–2.2 m long; blade with 52–65 leaflets, the middle ones 1.1–1.7 m long, *gray-waxy on the lower surface.* Inflorescences arching, not exceeding the leaves, with 10–17 primary branches all along the rachis; *flowers and fruits borne on stalks more than 1 mm long;* fruits globose, 0.8–1.1 cm diameter, white.

Range and habitat. Jamaica, John Crow Mountains; open, exposed areas in honeycomb limestone rocks, at 300–800 m elevation.

Thrinax morrisii
(Map 22)
"Broom palm" (Ang), "buffalo-top" (Bah), "miraguano" (Cub), "palma de escoba" (PR), "brittle-thatch" (USA)
Field characters. Stems 1–11 m tall and 5–35 cm diameter. Leaf sheaths with fine fibers; petioles elongate, 27–84 cm long; blade with 43–58 leaflets, the middle ones 55–75 cm long, *gray-waxy on the lower surface.* Inflorescences arching, exceeding the leaves, with 9–21 primary branches; *flowers and fruits borne on very short stalks less than 1 mm long;* fruits globose, 3.5–4.5(–8) mm diameter, white.

Range and habitat. United States (Florida Keys), Bahamas, Cuba, Navassa Island, Puerto Rico, and western Lesser Antilles (Anguilla, Barbuda); dry, deciduous woodlands or open, coastal regions, often on limestone soil, usually at low elevations.

Uses. The stems are used as poles, and the leaves are very commonly used for thatching and for weaving various items.

Thrinax parviflora
(Map 23)
"Broom palm," "thatch pole" (Jam)

Field characters. Stems 1–13 m tall and 5–15 cm diameter. Leaf sheaths with fine fibers; petiole elongate, 0.3–1.6 m long; blade with 35–60 leaflets, the middle ones 38–96 cm long, *green on the lower surface.* Inflorescences arching, not greatly exceeding the leaves, with 7–22 primary branches, *these granular-hairy at flowering time;* flowers and fruits borne on stalks more than 1 mm long; fruits globose, 6.5–7.5 mm diameter, white.

Range and habitat. Jamaica; exposed and eroded limestone hills with deciduous, open woodland, usually below 900 m elevation.

Notes. Two subspecies were recognized by Read (1975): subsp. *parviflora*, with the leaf segment tips conspicuously twisted and the inflorescences shorter than the petioles; and subsp. *puberula*, with the leaf segment tips not twisted and the inflorescences equal to or longer than the petioles.

Thrinax radiata
(Map 24, Plates 3 & 4)
"Guano de costa" (Cub), "guanillo" (DR), "latanier-la-mer" (Hai), "thatch" (Jam), "chit" (Mex), "thatch palm" (USA)
Field characters. Stems 1.5–12 m tall and 6–13 cm diameter. Leaf sheaths with fine fibers; petiole elongate, 36–94 cm long; blade with 51–63 leaflets, the middle ones 0.7–1.1 m long, *lighter green on the lower surface.* Inflorescences arching, not exceeding the leaves, with 13–21 primary branches, *these smooth at flowering time;* flowers and fruits borne on stalks more than 1 mm long; fruits globose, 7–8 mm diameter, white.

Range and habitat. Northwestern Caribbean in Mexico (Quintana Roo, Yucatán), Cayman Islands, Belize, Honduras (Atlántida, Islas de la Bahía), United States (Florida), Bahamas, Jamaica, Cuba, and Hispaniola; coastal regions on limestone or sandy soil close to the sea, often in sand-dune scrub.

Uses. The leaves are commonly used to weave hats and other items; and the stems are occasionally used as poles.

Notes. Some specimens may have clustered stems with shoots coming from short rhizomes. Orellana and Ayora (1993) described the population structure of this species in the Yucatán peninsula in Mexico; and Ayora and Orellana (1993) described soil factors influencing its distribution.

Thrinax rivularis
(Map 25)
Field characters. Stems (1–)6–8 m tall and to 8 cm diameter, swollen at the base. Leaf sheaths with a few coarse fibers; *petiole short, to 33 cm long, giving the leaves a crowded appearance;* blade

with 40–50 leaflets, the middle ones 58–68 cm long, lighter green on the lower surface. Inflorescences exceeding the leaves, *with 3 primary branches near the top*, flowers and fruits not on stalks; fruits globose, 1.3–1.5 cm diameter, yellowish white.

Range and habitat. Cuba (Oriente, Sierra de Moa); wet savannas or wooded areas near streams on savanna margins, on serpentine soils near the sea.

Notes. Borhidi and Muñiz (1985) recognized 2 varieties: var. *rivularis*, with stems 6–8 m tall; and var. *savanarum*, with stems 1–4 m tall.

7. COCCOTHRINAX

This moderately large and very variable genus is confined to the islands of the Caribbean, especially Cuba, and adjacent Mexico and Florida. It gets its name from a combination of the Latin word for a berry, "coccus," and *Thrinax*. Stems are small to medium sized and often covered with fibrous leaf sheaths. In some species the leaf sheath fibers are very long, fine, and pendulous, in others they are short, thick, and rigid and can be spinelike at the tip. Leaves are palmate, 8–22 in number, with an elongate, nonspiny petiole which is not split at the base lengthwise. This distinguishes *Coccothrinax* from the similar genus *Thrinax*, in which the petioles are split at the base. The leaf blade is often circular in outline and is divided to about the middle into numerous, long or short, narrow leaflets. The veins of the leaflets are joined by transverse veinlets in a few species and this can be a useful character in identification. In some species the leaflets are abruptly narrowed and we refer to this as a "shoulder." Leaflets are often silvery gray on the lower surface. Inflorescences are branched to two orders and are borne among the leaves. The elongate peduncle and rachis are covered with sheathing bracts, but the primary branches, which hang down from the rachis, are free from bracts. Flowers are borne on short stalks. They are bisexual with 6–13 stamens and one carpel; the sepals and petals are greatly reduced to a cupular perianth. Fruits are one-seeded, globose, or subglobose, small, and purple-red, purple-black, or brown at maturity (as opposed to white in *Thrinax*); occasionally they are warty. Although the endosperm is homogeneous, the seeds are penetrated by deep grooves and resemble a brain. The seedling leaf is simple and narrow.

Coccothrinax contains fourteen species distributed throughout the Greater Antilles (especially Cuba) and Lesser Antilles and other Caribbean Islands, including Trinidad and Tobago. They are also found in adjacent Florida and the Yucatán Peninsula of Mexico. They usually grow in open areas, coastal regions, woodlands, or scrub woodlands on limestone, sandy, or serpentine soils, usually at low elevations.

This genus is very poorly known botanically and is much in need of a modern revision. Most work has been done on Cuban species (León, 1939; Muñiz and Borhidi, 1981), but the genus has never been studied in its entirety. Although about forty-nine species are recognized, with thirty-six of them in Cuba, here we accept only fourteen. We believe that many of the other species described in the genus should be recognized as either subspecies or varieties (see also Nauman and Sanders, 1991a). After a modern revision, however, especially of Cuban and Hispaniolan plants, more species may be recognized. There appear to be local endemics confined to certain soils, and hybridization is probably common in the genus. Recently, Kowalska et al. (1991) have begun to use chemical data for taxonomy of the genus.

These handsome palms are sometimes cultivated, but are too slow-growing to make popular ornamentals. Many also have specialized soil requirements. Nauman and Sanders (1991b) have provided a key to cultivated plants, but have pointed out that some of them may be of hybrid origin.

KEY TO THE SPECIES OF COCCOTHRINAX

1a. Bahamas.
  2a. Leaf blade green on both surfaces; leaf sheath extended for 10–30 cm
    above petiole insertion   ..... *C. inaguensis.*
  2b. Leaf blade silvery or gray on lower surface; leaf sheath not extended
                                                 ..... *C. argentata.*
1b. Caribbean region, excluding Bahamas.
  3a. Western Caribbean (Mexico, Honduras, Cayman Islands, San Andrés,
    United States, Jamaica)   ..... *C. argentata.*
  3b. Eastern Caribbean (Cuba, Hispaniola, Puerto Rico, Virgin Islands, the
    Lesser Antilles, Margarita Island, Trinidad and Tobago).
    4a. Southeastern Caribbean (Lesser Antilles, Puerto Rico, Trinidad, To-
      bago, Virgin Islands, Margarita Island)   ..... *C. barbadensis.*
    4b. Cuba and Hispaniola.
      5a. Hispaniola.
        6a. Leaves one-third to one-half circular in outline; fruits brown-
          ish, fibrous, covered with small, pointed warts   ..... *C. ekmanii.*
        6b. Leaves three-quarters to fully circular in outline; fruits purple,
          fleshy, smooth.
          7a. Stems stout, usually swollen, 20–30 cm or more in diame-
            ter   ..... *C. spissa.*
          7b. Stems slender, not swollen, 4–12 cm diameter.
            8a. Leaf sheath 2-layered, with closely woven fibers less than
              0.5 mm thick (burlaplike)   ..... *C. argentea.*
            8b. Leaf sheath 2–3-layered, with coarsely woven fibers 0.5–
              2 mm thick.
              9a. Stems tall and slender, sometimes twisted or con-
                torted, often swaying in the wind   ..... *C. gracilis.*
              9b. Stems shorter and stouter, not twisted or contorted,
                not swaying in the wind   ..... *C. miraguama.*
      5b. Cuba.
        10a. Leaf sheath 2-layered, with closely woven fibers less than 0.5
          mm thick.
          11a. Leaf sheath fibers greatly elongate and pendulous.
            12a. Petiole very short, giving a compact crown; north coast
              of Matanzas, near the sea   ..... *C. borhidiana.*
            12b. Petiole elongate, giving an open crown; inland in west-
              ern Cuba (Las Villas, Matanzas, Pinar del Río, Santa
              Clara)   ..... *C. crinita.*
          11b. Leaf sheath fibers not elongate and pendulous.
            13a. Transverse veinlets absent   ..... *C. argentata.*
            13b. Transverse veinlets present   ..... *C. hiorami.*
        10b. Leaf sheath 2–3–layered, with looser, coarser fibers 1–9 mm
          thick.
          14a. Fruits brownish, fibrous, covered with small, pointed
            warts; leaves one-third to one-half circular in outline
                                                 ..... *C. ekmanii.*
          14b. Fruits purple, fleshy, smooth; leaves one-half to fully circu-
            lar in outline.

15a. Tip of leaf sheath not spiny   ..... *C. miraguama.*
15b. Tip of leaf sheath spiny.
    16a. Leaves half to three-quarters circular in outline; inflorescences short, curved down below the leaves
                                                ..... *C. salvatoris.*
    16b. Leaves three-quarters to fully circular in outline; inflorescences elongate, erect above the leaves.
        17a. Leaflets somewhat flexuous at the tips, 0.6–1 m long, green on the lower surface   ..... *C. gundlachii.*
        17b. Leaflets rigid at the tips, 23–52 cm long, silvery gray or occasionally green on the lower surface
                                              ..... *C. pauciramosa.*

Coccothrinax argentata

(Map 26)
"Silvertop" (Bah), "thatch palm" (Cay), "yuraguana de costa" (Cub), "silver thatch palm" (Jam, USA), "knacás" (Mex), "palmicha" (SAI)

Field characters. Stems solitary, sometimes with basal shoots, 1–10 m tall and 3–20 cm diameter. *Leaf sheaths 2-layered, the fibers fine (0.5 mm thick, rarely to 1 mm thick) and closely woven, not forming spines at the tip;* blade half to fully circular in outline, silvery gray, golden brown or metallic green (rarely patchy gray) on lower surface, transverse veinlets absent; leaflets 39–54, somewhat flexuous at the tip, the middle ones 30–100 cm long with a nonsplit, basal part 4–40 cm long. Inflorescences short and curved down below the leaves, with 2–9 primary branches; fruits globose, 0.5–1.3 cm diameter, purple-black.

Range and habitat. Western Caribbean in Mexico (Quintana Roo, Yucatán), Honduras (Islas de la Bahía), the Bahamas (Caicos, Great Inagua, San Salvador), Cayman Islands, Colombia (San Andrés Islands), Cuba (at least Matanzas, Oriente), United States (Florida), and Jamaica; usually near the sea in open areas or partially closed woods, often on dunes, on sandy soils overlying limestone, at low elevations or rarely to 500 m.

Uses. The trunks are used in construction and the leaves are commonly used for thatching. It is often retained or planted as an ornamental. At one time the leaves were important for twisting into ropes in the Cayman Islands (Read, 1988).

Notes. This is a widespread and variable species. Although it has been divided into various local species, here we treat these as one. There appear to be, however, 2 forms, one northern and one southern. The northern one corresponds to typical *Coccothrinax argentata*, with 2–6 primary branches and 1–3(–5) mm long flower stalks, while the southern one corresponds to *C. fragrans* and has (4–)6–9 primary

branches and (3–)4–7 mm long flower stalks. Each of these forms is again divided into local, geographic varieties. Thus viewed the species have an almost circular distribution in the northwestern Caribbean, as follows (named species are given in parentheses, but note we treat these as synonyms): Florida and the northwestern Bahamas (*C. argentata*), northern coast of Cuba (*C. litoralis*), eastern Cuba (*C. fragrans*), Jamaica (*C. jamaicensis*), Cayman Islands (*C. proctori*), and Mexico (*C. readii*).

Orellana and Ayora (1993) described population structure in the Yucatán peninsula in Mexico; and Ayora and Orellana (1993) described soil factors influencing its distribution. Nauman (1990) reported intergeneric hybrids occurring in Florida between *Coccothrinax argentata* and *Thrinax morrisii.*

Coccothrinax argentea

(Map 27)
"Guano" (DR), "latanye maron," "latanye savann" (Hai)

Field characters. Stems solitary or occasionally clustered, to 10 m tall and 5–10 cm diameter. Leaf sheaths 2-layered, the fibers fine (less than 0.5 mm thick) and closely woven and burlaplike, not forming spines at the tip; blade fully circular, silvery gray on lower surface, *transverse veinlets present;* leaflets to 30, somewhat flexuous at the tip, the middle ones 35–60 cm long, with a nonsplit, basal part 3–12 cm long. Inflorescences short and curved down below the leaves, with 2–10 primary branches; fruits globose, 0.6–1.2 cm diameter, purple-black.

Range and habitat. Hispaniola (Dominican Republic, Haiti); on limestone hills in open areas or pine woods, to 500 m elevation.

Uses. The leaves are used to thatch houses and make brooms (Read, 1988).

Notes. A very common palm which seems to persist and reproduce in disturbed areas. Plants from the north coast of the Dominican Republic are larger than usual and sometimes have swollen stems. They may represent a distinct taxon (Thomas Zanoni, pers. comm.). On the east coast of the Dominican Republic plants approach morphologically their Puerto Rican neighbor, *C. barbadensis*.

Coccothrinax barbadensis
(Map 28)
"Latanier balai" (Gud, Mar), "palma de abanico" (PR), "latanier" (Luc, Dom, Tri), "silver palm" (VIs)
Field characters. Stems solitary, 2.5–15 m tall and 5–18 cm diameter. Leaf sheaths 2-layered, the fibers fine (less than 0.5 mm thick) and closely woven, burlaplike, not forming spines at the tip; blade silvery gray on lower surface, *transverse veinlets present*; leaflets 36–60, somewhat flexuous at the tip, the middle ones 65–80 cm long, the nonsplit basal part less than 25(–35) cm long. Inflorescences short and curved down below the leaves, with 3–10 primary branches; fruits globose, purple-black, 0.6–1.2 cm diameter; seeds with 6 or more narrow, branched grooves.
Range and habitat. Lesser Antilles (Leeward and Windward islands: Antigua, Barbados, Barbuda, Dominica, Guadeloupe, Marie Galante, Martinique, St. Lucia), Puerto Rico, Trinidad, Tobago, the Virgin Islands, and Venezuela (Margarita Island); coastal or scrub woodland on limestone soils, from sea level to 300(–600) m elevation.
Uses. The leaves are used to thatch houses.
Notes. It probably occurred formerly on all Leeward and Windward islands but is now exterminated on many of them (Read, 1979). Although closely related to *Coccothrinax argentea*, it can be distinguished by its larger, nonsplit base of the leaf.

Coccothrinax borhidiana
(Map 29, Plate 4)
"Guano" (Cub)
Field characters. Stems solitary, 1–7 m tall and 8–20 cm diameter. Leaves closely spaced on short petioles and the *crown appearing very dense*; leaf sheath 2-layered, the fibers fine (less than 0.5 mm thick) and loosely woven, *elongate and pendulous at the tips*; blade three-quarters circular in outline, green on lower surface; leaflets 32–36, rigid, the middle ones 60–65 cm long with a nonsplit basal part 22–25 cm long. Inflorescences erect above the leaves, becoming pendulous; primary branches 4–5; fruits globose, 7–9 mm diameter, violet-purple.
Range and habitat. Cuba (Matanzas); in dwarf vegetation on raised limestone beaches near the sea.

Uses. The leaves are occasionally used for thatching.
Notes. This beautiful palm is confined to a small, coastal area and is in danger of extinction (Borhidi and Muñiz, 1983).

Coccothrinax crinita
(Map 30, Plate 4)
"Guano barbudo," "guano petate" (Cub)
Field characters. Stems solitary, 2–10 m tall and 8–20 cm diameter. *Leaf sheaths 2-layered, the fibers fine (less than 1 mm thick) and closely woven, with the tips greatly elongate and pendulous and covering the stem*; blade almost circular in outline, silvery gray or almost green on lower surface, cross veinlets absent; leaflets 32–56, somewhat flexuous at the tip, the middle ones 40–100 cm long, with a nonsplit, basal part 22–25 cm long. *Inflorescences erect to arching above the leaves*, with 4–5 primary branches; fruits globose to subglobose, 0.7–2 cm diameter, black.
Range and habitat. Cuba (Las Villas, Matanzas, Pinar del Río, Santa Clara); low-lying, seasonally flooded savannas or sometimes hilly areas, on serpentine soils, from sea level to 300 m elevation.
Uses. It is often planted as an ornamental; the leaves are used for thatching.
Notes. This is a very rare palm in Cuba, which now persists only in cleared fields and pastures, where it does not reproduce. Borhidi and Muñiz (1983) regard it as being in danger of extinction. It is, however, commonly cultivated and is a popular ornamental. Muñiz and Borhidi (1981) recognized 2 subspecies: subsp. *crinita*, with longer and denser leaf sheath fibers, from western Cuba; and subsp. *brevicrinis*, with shorter leaf sheath fibers, from central Cuba.

Coccothrinax ekmanii
(Map 31)
"Gwenn" (Hai)
Field characters. Stems solitary, 3–15 m tall and 5–8(–20) cm diameter, usually covered with persistent leaf bases. *Leaf sheaths 2-layered, the fibers thick (more than 2 mm diameter), coarsely woven, the tips forming spines*; blade one-third to one-half circular in outline, silvery gray on lower surface, transverse veinlets absent; leaflets 16–25, rigid, the middle ones 20–40 cm long, with a nonsplit, basal part 8–9 cm long. Inflorescences short curved down below the leaves, with 3–5 primary branches; fruits subglobose, 5–6 mm diameter, *brownish, fibrous, covered with small, pointed warts*.
Range and habitat. Cuba (Oriente) and Hispaniola (Dominican Republic, Haiti); rocky hills

or dry areas in scrub forest on limestone soils near the sea.

Notes. First described in its own genus, *Haitiella*.

Coccothrinax gracilis
(Map 32)
"Latanier" (Hai)

Field characters. *Stems tall and slender, sometimes twisted or contorted, often swaying in the wind,* to 10 m tall and 15 cm diameter. *Leaf sheaths 2–3-layered, the fibers thicker (0.5–2 mm thick), coarsely woven, rounded at the tip and not forming spines;* blade fully circular in outline, silvery gray on lower surface, transverse veinlets absent; leaflets to 40, the middle ones to 65 cm long with a nonsplit basal part to 20 cm long. Inflorescences small and curved down below the leaves, primary branches 5–6; fruits 6–8 mm diameter.

Range and habitat. Hispaniola (Dominican Republic, Haiti); open places near the sea, on limestone soil, at low elevations.

Notes. Closely related to *Coccothrinax miraguama* and only kept separate here because of its tall, often twisted stems. In some places it grows near the sea and is tolerant of salt water and salt spray.

Coccothrinax gundlachii
(Map 33)
"Yuraguana" (Cub)

Field characters. Stems solitary, 4–10 m tall and 7–20 cm diameter. Leaf sheaths 2-layered, the fibers coarse (1–4 mm thick), *forming spines at the tip;* blade three-quarters to fully circular in outline, green on lower surface, transverse veinlets absent; leaflets 30–45, somewhat flexuous at the tip, the middle ones 0.6–1 m long, with a basal, nonsplit part 18–33 cm long. *Inflorescences elongate, erect above the leaves,* with 4–10 primary branches; fruits globose, 1–1.3 cm diameter, purple-black.

Range and habitat. Central and eastern Cuba (Camagüey, Santa Clara, Oriente); low, open areas or open woods near the sea.

Notes. Distinguished by the large size of its stem and leaves, but is related to the smaller *Coccothrinax pauciramosa.*

Coccothrinax hiorami
(Map 34)

Field characters. Stems solitary, 6–12 m tall and 7–15 cm diameter. *Leaf sheaths 2-layered, closely woven, the fibers fine (0.1–0.5 mm thick), not forming spines at the tip;* blades three-quarters to fully circular in outline, silvery gray on the lower surface, *transverse veinlets present;* leaflets 40–64, the middle ones 50–80 cm long, with a nonsplit basal part 15–18 cm long. Inflores-

cences long, with 4–8 primary branches; fruits globose, 0.9–1.1 cm diameter, black.

Range and habitat. Cuba (Oriente); open, sandy areas near the sea.

Notes. It occurs in extreme eastern Cuba, nearest to *Coccothrinax argentea* in Hispaniola and can be considered the Cuban version, or even a variety of the latter. It differs only in its longer leaflets and more numerous primary inflorescence branches. The cross veins of this species are not easy to see and require a hand lens with back light.

Coccothrinax inaguensis
(Map 35)
"Thatch palm" (Bah)

Field characters. Stems solitary, 2–5 m tall and 6–8 cm diameter. *Leaf sheaths 2-layered, closely woven with fine strands (less than 1 mm thick), forming an entire, apical extension 10–30 cm long above the petiole;* leaf blade dull green on lower surface, cross veins absent; leaflets 39–47, 36–49 cm long, somewhat flexuous at the tips, with a 20 cm or less nonsplit basal part, bifid at the tip for 5–11 cm. Inflorescences small, curved down below the leaves; fruits globose, 1.2–1.3 cm diameter, purple.

Range and habitat. Bahamas (Caicos, Great Inagua, San Salvador) and possibly Cuba; thickets on limestone or sandy soil near the sea.

Notes. Closely related to *Coccothrinax argentata,* but can be recognized by its "inverted umbrella-shaped" leaf blades. It occurs in the southern Bahamas and may have been introduced into the northern island of San Salvador. Here it hybridizes with *C. argentata* (Roger Sanders, pers. comm.). It is also probable that *C. victorini,* a poorly known Cuban species, is conspecific, in which case the latter name would have priority.

Coccothrinax miraguama
(Map 36, Plate 5)
"Miraguano," "yuraguana" (Cub)

Field characters. Stems solitary, 1–15 m tall and 4–12 cm diameter. *Leaf sheaths 2–3-layered, the fibers thicker (0.5–2 mm thick), coarsely woven, rounded at the tip and not forming spines;* blade one-third to fully circular in outline, silvery gray or green on lower surface, transverse veinlets absent; leaflets 18–50, *rigid,* the middle ones 22–65 cm long with a nonsplit basal part 4–24 cm long. Inflorescences small and curved down below the leaves, primary branches 1–4; fruits 5–12 mm diameter, purple-black or rose-purple.

Range and habitat. Widespread in Cuba and Hispaniola; low, open, coastal areas, open woods, rocky places, savannas, or *mogotes*, on limestone, serpentine, or sandy soils.

Uses. The leaves are widely used for making a variety of woven items and for thatching.

Notes. Variation in this widespread species is still very poorly understood, and in Cuba it has been split into numerous species, subspecies, or varieties. Here we recognize 3 informal forms: the first, based on *Coccothrinax miraguama*, with a 2-layered, closely woven leaf sheath and 18–50 leaflets, from Cuba; the second, based on *C. yuraguana*, with a 3-layered, closely woven leaf sheath and 18–36 leaflets, from Cuba and possibly Hispaniola; and the third, based on *C. scoparia*, with a 2-layered, loosely woven leaf sheath and 30–40 leaflets, from Hispaniola.

Coccothrinax pauciramosa
(Map 37)
"Yuraguana," "yuraguana vestida" (Cub)

Field characters. Stems solitary, (0–)2–5(–15) m tall and 4–8(–20) cm diameter. Leaf sheaths 2–3-layered, *the fibers coarse (2–5 mm thick), loosely woven, with the tips forming spines*; blade three-quarters to fully circular in outline, silvery gray or occasionally green on lower surface, transverse veinlets absent; leaflets 16–32, *stiff and rigid with a pronounced "shoulder,"* the middle ones 23–52 cm long, with a nonsplit, basal part 3–14 cm long. *Inflorescences elongate, erect above the leaves*, with 1–10 primary branches; fruits purple-black, 0.7–1.2 cm diameter.

Range and habitat. Eastern Cuba (Camagüey, Holguín, Oriente); limestone hills or serpentine savannas, at low elevations.

Coccothrinax salvatoris
(Map 38)
"Yuraguana" (Cub)

Field characters. Stems solitary, 4–8 m tall and 8–10 cm diameter. *Leaf sheaths 2-layered, the fibers coarse (3–6 mm thick), woody, forming spines at the tip*; blade one-half to three-quarters circular in outline, gray on lower surface, transverse veinlets absent; leaflets 38–42, rigid, the middle ones 26–56 cm long, with a nonsplit basal part 10–20 cm long. *Inflorescences short, curved down below the leaves*, with 2–4 primary branches; fruits subglobose, 5–8 mm diameter, purple-black.

Range and habitat. Eastern Cuba (Camagüey, Oriente); open places on limestone soils, to 500 m elevation.

Coccothrinax spissa
(Map 39)
"Guano" (DR)

Field characters. Stems solitary, *usually swollen but always stout*, 3–8 m tall and 20–30 cm diameter. Leaf sheaths 2-layered, the fibers fine (0.5 mm thick) and closely woven, burlaplike, not forming spines at the tip; blade silvery gray on the lower surface, *transverse veinlets present*; leaflets to 45, the middle ones to 75 cm long, the nonsplit basal part more than 20 cm long. Inflorescences short to medium, curved down below the leaves, with 3–4 primary branches; fruits globose, 1.1–1.2 cm diameter, dark purple.

Range and habitat. Hispaniola (Dominican Republic, Haiti); dry, open areas or woodland margins, below 400 m elevation.

Notes. This species is closer to *Coccothrinax barbadensis*, although it grows with *C. argentea* in one area. The swollen stem that characterizes this species does not occur in all populations; sometimes stems are stout but not swollen.

8. ZOMBIA

This genus is closely related to both *Thrinax* and *Coccothrinax*, but differs in a few details. The generic name is taken from the local name of the palm in Haiti, "zombi," from where it was first described. Stems are short, clustered, and covered with persistent leaf sheaths. Leaves are palmate and 9–12 in number. The leaf sheaths consist of stout, reticulate fibers which are spiny and outward and downward pointing at the top of sheath. These spiny fibers readily distinguish the genus from its relatives. Petioles have smooth margins and are not split at the base. The blade is split into numerous, lanceolate leaflets, and these are slightly bifid at the tips. Leaflets are gray-white on the lower surface. Inflorescences are branched to two orders and are borne among the leaves. Flowers are borne singly along the flowering branches. They are bisexual, with 9–12 stamens and one carpel. Sepals and petals are greatly reduced to a cupular perianth.

Fruits are one-seeded, globose, or slightly oblong and white. The seeds are deeply lobed with homogeneous endosperm. The shape of the seedling leaf is not known.

Zombia contains one species, distributed in the Greater Antillean island of Hispaniola and occurring in both Haiti and the Dominican Republic. It grows in dry, hilly regions at low elevations and, at least in the Dominican Republic, always on serpentine soils. This palm is becoming very rare in Haiti due to habitat destruction (Henderson et al., 1990).

It is similar to both *Thrinax* and *Coccothrinax*, from which it can be easily distinguished by its clustered stems with fibrous, spiny leaf sheaths. In cultivation it forms hybrids with *Coccothrinax*.

Zombia antillarum
(Map 40, Plate 5)
"Latanye pikan," "latanye zombi" (Hai),
"guanito" (DR)
Field characters. Stems clustered, to 3 m tall and 5 cm diameter, forming small, dense clumps, covered with stout, reticulate fibers, these spiny and outward and downward pointing at tip of sheath. Leaves gray-white on lower surface. Inflorescences shorter than the leaves; fruits globose to oblong or pear-shaped, 1.5–2 cm diameter, white.
Range and habitat. Hispaniola (Dominican Republic, Haiti); dry, hilly, inland or occasionally coastal regions, at low elevations, in areas of 1000–1500 mm annual rainfall.
Uses. The leaves are used in weaving hats and making brooms in Haiti. It is a popular ornamental.

9. RHAPIDOPHYLLUM

This unusual genus contains one species and occurs only in North America. Stems are very short, clustered, often partly creeping, and are covered with persistent, spiny leaf sheaths. Leaves are palmate and about fifteen in number. The leaf sheaths consist of numerous soft fibers and fewer, upward pointing, stout, needle-like spines. The generic name refers to these spines, derived from the Greek words "rhapidos," a rod, and "phyllon," a leaf. Petioles are smooth on the margins and the blade is split into numerous leaflets. These are slightly silvery white on the lower surface. Inflorescences are branched to one order and are borne among the leaves. They are very short and compact and are scarcely exserted from the leaf sheaths and so are almost hidden from view. They are covered with 4–6 short peduncular bracts. Flowers are unisexual, and usually individual plants bear either male or female flowers, rarely both kinds. They are densely crowded along the rather short flowering branches. Male flowers have six stamens and female flowers have three free carpels. Fruits are one-seeded, globose or ovoid, brownish, and are covered with easily removed hairs. The endosperm is homogeneous and the seedling leaf is simple.

Rhapidophyllum contains one species, which occurs in the southeastern United States. It grows in wet places in woods at low elevations. This genus is very distinct, but in the field may be confused with *Sabal minor* or *Serenoa repens*. It differs from both of these in its upward-pointing, stout, needle-like leaf sheath spines.

Rhapidophyllum hystrix
(Map 41, Plate 5)
"Needle palm" (USA)
Field characters. Stems clustered, very short, to 1 m tall and 8–10 cm diameter, often creeping along the ground and then rooting, producing suckers, covered at the top with numerous soft fibers and fewer, upward-pointing, stout, needle-like leaf sheath spines. Leaves about 15. Inflorescences hidden among the leaf sheaths; fruits globose or obovoid, 1 cm diameter, brownish, with easily removed hairs.
Range and habitat. Southeastern United States (Florida, Georgia, Mississippi, North Caro-

lina); sporadically occurring on the coastal plain in wet areas in deciduous woods, swamp forests, or hammocks, usually on calcareous soils.

Uses. It is occasionally planted as an ornamental. It may be one of the most cold-tolerant palms, withstanding temperatures of − 20°C (Clancy and Sullivan, 1990).

Notes. This is a rare species and is considered endangered (Clancy and Sullivan, 1990). Pollination has been studied by Shuey and Wunderlin (1977), who found the main pollinator to be a curculionid beetle; and demography has been studied by Clancy and Sullivan (1990).

10. COLPOTHRINAX

Stems in this small genus are tall, stout, solitary, columnar, or markedly swollen. In fact, the genus gets its name from the Greek word meaning swollen and translates as the swollen-stemmed *Thrinax.* Leaves are palmate, 12–30 in number, and form a rather dense crown. Leaf sheaths are fibrous and the old leaves and fibers commonly persist on the top of the stem, giving the palms an "untidy" appearance. The elongate petioles have smooth margins and there is a small "flap" on the upper surface where the petiole joins the blade. The rachis is very short, giving a costapalmate leaf. The blade is split to about halfway into many, stiff, leathery, green leaflets and each of these is again briefly bifid at the tip. Inflorescences are borne among the leaves and are branched to four orders. They are large and project well beyond the leaves and are covered with numerous, sheathing, brown-tomentose bracts. Flowers are arranged in spirals along the flowering branches. They are small, bright orange-red at anthesis and bisexual, with six stamens and three carpels. Fruits are one-seeded, globose, and brown or black. Seeds have homogeneous endosperm and the seedling leaf is simple.

Colpothrinax contains two species, one confined to Cuba and the other to Central America. This distribution represents a common pattern in American palms with related species in both the Greater Antilles and Central America and is repeated, for example, in *Gaussia, Reinhardtia,* and *Calyptronoma-Calyptrogyne.* In many cases the Greater Antillean representative is larger and grows in more open areas than the Central American one.

This genus is similar to and may be confused in the field with both *Sabal* and *Copernicia.* It differs from *Sabal* in its very fibrous sheaths and short rachis in the leaf blade, and from *Copernicia* (in Cuba) in its markedly swollen trunk and nonthorny petiole margins.

Colpothrinax cookii
(Map 42)
"Shan" (Gua)
Field characters. Stems columnar, 7–8 m or more tall and 20–35 cm diameter, occasionally covered with dead, persistent old leaf bases and long fibers. Leaves 12–30, circular in outline; blade divided into about fifty equal leaflets, these abruptly pendulous at the tip. Inflorescences shorter than the petioles; fruits globose, 1.5–2 cm diameter, brown or black.
Range and habitat. Patchily distributed on the Atlantic slope of Guatemala (Alta Verapaz), Costa Rica (Cordillera de Talamanca), and Panama (Panamá), also possibly in Belize; premontane or montane rain forest in moun-

tainous regions, especially on ridges, at 800–1200 m elevation.
Notes. Guatemalan populations are somewhat different from Panamanian ones, and it is possible there are two distinct species here.

Colpothrinax wrightii
(Map 43, Plate 6)
"Palma barrigona" (Cub)
Field characters. Stems greatly swollen near or below the middle, solitary, 5–10 m tall and 30–40 cm diameter (twice as much or more at swelling). Leaves about 12. Inflorescences shorter than the leaves; fruits globose, 1–1.5 cm diameter, brown or black.
Range and habitat. Western Cuba (Pinar del Río,

Isla de Pinos); in savannas on quartzite soils, at low elevations.

Uses. The leaves are commonly used for thatching and it is rare to see a palm from which the leaves have not been harvested. The swollen stems are used for various purposes, for example as canoes, water barrels, or water troughs; the fruits are fed to domestic animals.

11. ACOELORRAPHE

This genus of one species occurs in the western Caribbean region, especially near the sea. Stems are moderate in size, clustered, and form small to large clumps. They are almost always covered with the remains of persistent, spiny leaf bases. On older plants, however, these leaf bases fall away, leaving a clean stem. Petioles are covered along their margins with stout, sharp thorns; and there is a conspicuous "flap" on the upper surface at the junction of petiole and blade. Leaves are palmate and 9–15 in number. The blade is bright green on the upper surface and somewhat silvery on the lower surface. It is split to below the middle into numerous, stiff leaflets and these are again bifid at the tips. These rigid leaflets stick straight up and give the leaves a very distinctive appearance. Inflorescences are covered with numerous sheathing, peduncular bracts. They are branched to four orders, slender, and greatly exceed the leaves, sticking up well above the crown. It is a combination of these elongate inflorescences and stiff leaflets that gives the plants their characteristic appearance. Flowers are small, bisexual, and are borne in small groups along the flowering branches. Fruits are one-seeded, globose, small, and black. The seed lacks the impressed raphe (a depression or seam on the seed) of related palms, hence the generic name, from the Greek words "a" (without), "coelos" (hollow), and "raphe" (seam). The endosperm is homogeneous and the seedling leaf is linear and simple.

A genus of one species (Bailey, 1940), widely distributed in the Caribbean in the southern United States, Cuba, and on the Atlantic coast of Mexico, Belize, Guatemala, Honduras, Nicaragua, and Costa Rica.

Acoelorraphe wrightii
(Map 44, Plate 6)
"Hairy Tom palmetto" (Bel), "guano preto" (Cub), "tasiste" (Gua, Mex), "tique" (Hon), "everglades palm," "paurotis palm" (USA)
Field characters. Stems clustered, in groups of 2–15 or more, 1–4 m tall and 5–15 cm diameter, covered with persistent sheaths and petioles. Leaves 9–15; petiole with thorns along the margins; leaflets numerous, stiff. Inflorescences borne among the leaves, greatly exceeding them, brown at flowering time; fruits globose, 5–9 mm diameter, orange-brown, becoming black.

Range and habitat. Throughout the western Caribbean in the United States (southern Florida), the Bahamas (Eleuthera, New Providence, Andros), Cuba (Habana, Pinar del Río, Santa Clara), Colombia (San Andrés, Providencia), Mexico (Campeche, Chiapas, Quintana Roo, Tabasco, Veracruz, Yucatán), Belize, Guatemala (Petén), Honduras (Atlántida, Colón, Gracias a Dios), Nicaragua (Zelaya), and Costa Rica (Alajuela); low-lying areas inundated by fresh or brackish water, thickets in savannas, or occasionally in pine woods, often near the sea, at low elevations.

12. SERENOA

This is the second coryphoid genus, after *Rhapidophyllum*, which is endemic to the southeastern United States. It was named for Sereno Watson (1826–1892), an eminent North American botanist. Stems are short, often subterranean or creeping along the ground, or rarely upright. They are clustered, with the clusters arising from suckers that are produced on the stem. Stems on older plants often have a distinctive covering of old leaf bases which form a regular pattern. Leaves are palmate, with the sheaths disintegrating into a mass of fine fibers. The margins of the petioles have small, recurved thorns. The blade is split to below the middle into rather few, broad, green, or rarely glaucous leaflets, and these are bifid at the tips. Inflorescences are borne among the leaves and are branched to three or four orders. They are covered with rather few bracts and scarcely exceed the leaves. Flowers are bisexual, with six stamens and three carpels. They are arranged in spirals along the densely tomentose flowering branches. Fruits are one-seeded, ellipsoid to subglobose and blue-black at maturity. The seeds have homogeneous endosperm and the seedling leaf is simple.

Serenoa contains one species, which occurs in the southeastern United States.

Serenoa repens
(Map 45, Plate 6)
"Saw palmetto" (USA)

Field characters. Stems clustered, usually subterranean, horizontal and creeping, or occasionally upright, forming dense colonies, covered with persistent leaf bases. Leaves palmate, numerous; petiole with small thorns; leaflets stiff, either green or rarely blue-gray. Inflorescences shorter than the leaves; fruits subglobose to ellipsoid, 1.6–2.5 cm long and 1.2–1.9 cm diameter, dark blue to black.

Range and habitat. Southeastern United States (Alabama, Florida, Georgia, Mississippi, the Carolinas, Virginia); often very abundant in the understory of pine woods and also in open areas and on sand dunes. It is most common on the lower coastal plain in southern Georgia and Florida.

Uses. The form with blue-gray leaves is sought after as an ornamental. The seeds are used in traditional medicine to treat enlarged prostates. Currently the seeds are being investigated in Europe for antiestrogen receptor effects (Di Silverio et al., 1992).

Notes. It may be confused in the field with low-growing species of *Sabal*, e.g., *S. miamiensis* and *S. etonia*, from which it can be distinguished by its thorny petioles and noncostapalmate leaf.

Fire is frequent in the habitat of *Serenoa repens* and the palm is adapted to withstand frequent burning (Bristo, 1969). The subterranean and horizontal stem is insulated by the leaf base remains. Fire stimulates shoots from stems and these are the primary method of reproduction. Flowering takes place from April to June and fruits are mature in September and October. It is regarded as a weed in areas where pine is a commercial crop. Branch and inflorescence production has been described by Fisher and Tomlinson (1973).

13. BRAHEA

This genus includes some popular palms of subtropical gardens, cultivated for their attractive foliage and prominent inflorescences. It was named after the Danish astronomer Tycho Brahe (1546–1601). Stems are short and subterranean or aerial, medium sized or large, solitary or clustered, with very close rings, and are often partially covered by persistent leaf bases. Leaves are palmate or costapalmate and 5–30 in number. The sheaths are fibrous and the petioles are long and smooth or sparsely to densely covered along the margins with small to large thorns. A short to long, thin "flap" is present on the upper surface at the junction of petiole and blade. The leaf blade is circular in outline and is divided to the middle or more into regular, usually stiff leaflets. These are usually shortly bifid at the tips. Inflorescences are branched to four orders and are borne among the leaves, which they often greatly exceed. The flowering branches are sometimes crowded and are often tomentose. Flowers are small, whitish, and bisexual, with six stamens and three carpels. The sepals, petals, and carpels are often tomentose. Fruits are one-seeded, globose to ovoid, greenish yellow, yellowish brown to brown, purplish dark blue or black, and are usually smooth but can be slightly hairy. The endosperm is homogeneous and the seedling leaf is simple and narrowly lanceolate.

As treated here, *Brahea* includes nine species, all distributed in Mexico, including one on the island of Guadalupe off the coast of Baja California. Two species also extend into Guatemala and one reaches Belize, El Salvador, Honduras, and Nicaragua. They grow in rather dry or semidesert areas, mostly in open sites on rocky, limestone soils, associated with low scrub or thorn vegetation. Some species thrive under the shade of oak or pine forest. The genus ranges from sea level to 2000 m elevation, but most species occur above 1000 m.

Brahea is one of the most poorly understood genera among American palms, and variation of most species is not yet well defined. Most characters previously used for separating species (leaf color, petiole spines, inflorescence length, fruit shape and size) seem to have been overemphasized, leading to such a proliferation of names that the identification of a particular specimen was extremely difficult (Bailey, 1937, 1943; Moore, 1951; Quero, 1989). Our treatment of *Brahea* must be considered tentative, and it is intended to allow at least for the identification of the most common or characteristic species. Most of the poorly known species will probably turn out to be synonyms of the widespread *B. dulcis*, and they have been treated as such here.

Brahea is very closely related to *Acoelorraphe*, *Copernicia*, and *Serenoa*, and reasons for keeping these genera separate seem more traditional than biological.

Brahea aculeata
(Map 46)
"Palmilla" (Mex)
Field characters. Stems solitary, 3–4 m tall and to 20 cm diameter. Leaves 8–10, forming a very loose crown, *yellowish green*; petiole with sharp, distantly spaced thorns; blade divided to two-thirds its length into 30–40 rigid leaflets. Inflorescences shorter than the leaves, branched to two orders, with 3–4 primary branches; *fruits almost globose, 2–2.5 cm diameter*, black.
Range and habitat. Western Mexico (Sonora, Sinaloa, Durango) in southern part of Sonora Desert; very dry areas, on rocky soils, to 600 m elevation.
Uses. The leaves are used for thatching and for weaving into hats and saddle blankets.

Brahea armata
(Map 47)
Field characters. Stems solitary, massive, to 15 m tall and 45 cm diameter. Leaves 25–30, forming a rather dense, rounded crown, *bluish green*; petiole 1–1.5 m long, with curved, sometimes bifid thorns along margins; blade divided to about the middle in 40–60 rigid leaflets. *Inflorescences numerous, arching 1 m or more beyond the leaves*; fruits almost globose to ovoid, to 2 cm diameter, brownish black.
Range and habitat. Northwestern Mexico (Baja California, Sonora); desert canyons and cliffs on rocky soils, at low to medium elevations.
Notes. Easily mistaken for *Washingtonia*, which differs in its green foliage and in its usually pendulous leaflet tips. *Brahea brandegeei* is also very similar but differs in its leaves, which are green on the upper surface, and inflores-

cences, which are shorter than its leaves. Both species of *Washingtonia* and *B. armata* occur together at one site in Baja California, near Cataviña Arroyo (Cornett, 1987a).

Brahea brandegeei
(Map 48)
"Palma negra," "palma de tlaco" (Mex)
Field characters. Stems solitary, 10–12 m tall and to 30 cm diameter. Leaves green on the upper surface, *glaucous on the lower surface*; petiole *strongly thorny*; blade divided to about half its length into many stiff leaflets. *Inflorescences slightly shorter than leaves*, much branched; fruits almost globose, 1.5–2 cm diameter, shiny brown or lighter with brown stripes.
Range and habitat. Northwestern Mexico (southern Baja California, Sonora); arid canyons and mountains, to 350 m elevation.
Notes. It differs from the similar *Brahea armata* in its leaves, which are green rather than bluish on the upper surface. It is easily mistaken for *Washingtonia robusta*, which has leaf bases persisting longer on the stem, leaflets with pendulous tips and smaller fruits. Plants described from Sonora as *Erythea elegans* are included here.

Brahea decumbens
(Map 49)
Field characters. Stems clustered, to 2.5 m tall and 15–20 cm long, creeping along the ground, old plants forming thickets. Leaves 6–8, *shiny glaucous; petiole with very fine thorns only near base*; blade rather small and circular, divided to three-quarters its length into several stiff leaf-

lets. Inflorescences slightly shorter than leaves; fruits not known.

Range and habitat. Northeastern Mexico (San Luis Potosí, Tamaulipas); very dry, open areas, on rocky limestone hills of the Sierra Madre Oriental, at 1000–2000 m elevation.

Brahea dulcis
(Map 50, Plate 6)
"Palma de sombrero" (ElS), "suyate" (Hon), "capulín," "soyate" (Mex)
Field characters. Stems solitary or clustered, 2–7 m tall and 12–20 cm diameter, erect or often leaning. Leaves 10–15, dull green to somewhat glaucous; petiole with marginal thorns 2–4 mm long; blade split to half its length into 30–50 rigid leaflets. *Inflorescences exceeding the leaves*, arching; *flowering branches rather thick, densely tomentose, the tomentum obscuring the solitary flower buds*; fruits ovoid to obovoid, 0.9–1.6 cm long, brownish or greenish, tomentose.
Range and habitat. Widespread in eastern and southern Mexico and extending north along the Pacific coast (Coahuila, Colima, Durango, Guerrero, Jalisco, Michoacán, Nuevo León, Oaxaca, Puebla, Sinaloa, Sonora, Tamaulipas, Zacatecas) and south to Guatemala, Belize, El Salvador, Honduras (Comayagua, Francisco Morazán), and Nicaragua (Madriz); hillsides in dry, open, or wooded areas, often in oak forests, on rocky, calcareous soils, at 300–1700 m elevation.
Uses. The stems are used in construction; the leaves for thatching; and the leaf fibers are woven into ropes. The fruits are edible (Guzmán-Rivas, 1984).
Notes. Most of the poorly known entities described in *Brahea* will probably prove synonyms of this variable and widespread species. These segregates are difficult to separate in the field (Bailey, 1943; Erikson, 1992) and in the herbarium, and they probably represent only local morphological variation. McVaugh (1993) separated *B. pimo* from *B. dulcis* and we follow this here.

Brahea edulis
(Map 51)
Field characters. Stems solitary, 10–12 m tall and to 40 cm diameter. Leaves about 20, green; *petiole smooth or with short thorns*; blade divided to half its length into many stiff leaflets. *Inflorescences shorter than leaves*; fruits globose, 2.5–3.5 cm diameter, black.
Range and habitat. Mexico, island of Guadalupe, 250 km west off the coast of Baja California; rocky slopes and cliffs in desertlike vegetation, to 1000 m elevation.

Notes. Goats introduced to Guadaloupe in 1830 have stripped the natural vegetation and made it impossible for any seedlings of this species to develop. It was reported long ago to be rare (Bailey, 1937) and it is now believed that it will eventually become extinct in the wild (Gunther and Mahalick, 1988).

Brahea moorei
(Map 52)
Field characters. Stems solitary, *short and subterranean* or to 30 cm tall. Leaves 5–6; *petiole smooth, without thorns*; blade circular, about 70 cm diameter, *markedly chalky white on lower surface*, with 35–45 stiff leaflets. Inflorescences erect, projected beyond leaves; fruits ellipsoid to almost globose, 6–7 mm diameter, purplish, slightly hairy at first.
Range and habitat. Northeastern Mexico (Hidalgo, Querétaro, San Luis Potosí, Tamaulipas); shade of oak woods on limestone outcrops of the Sierra Madre Oriental, at 1600–1900 m elevation.

Brahea nitida
(Map 53)
Field characters. Stems solitary, 8–10 m tall and to 30 cm diameter. Leaves 15–20, markedly white on lower surface; *petiole without thorns*; blade divided into 50–70 stiff leaflets. Inflorescences projected far beyond leaves; fruits ellipsoid, to 1.5 cm long and 1 cm diameter, light dull yellow to greenish yellow.
Range and habitat. Mexico (Colima, Guerrero, Jalisco, Michoacán, Nayarit, Oaxaca, Sinaloa, and possibly Chiapas) and Guatemala (Alta Verapaz); dry areas on limestone hills, often among pines and oaks, at 900–1500 m elevation.
Notes. We are following Quero (1989) in considering *Brahea prominens* as conspecific with *B. nitida.*

Brahea pimo
(Map 54)
Field characters. Stems solitary, 2–5 m tall and to 20 cm diameter. Leaves 10–15, dull green or glaucous; petiole with irregularly spaced marginal thorns 1–3 mm long; blade split to about three-quarters its length into numerous leaflets. Inflorescences exceeding the leaves; *flowering branches tomentose, but the tomentum not obscuring the clustered flower buds*; fruits ovoid to obovoid, 1–1.5 cm diameter, yellow.
Range and habitat. Western Mexico (Guerrero, Jalisco, Michoacán, Nayarit); hillsides and near streams in pine-oak forest, at 1100–1600 m elevation.

14. COPERNICIA

This moderately large genus was named for the Polish astronomer Nicolaus Copernicus (1473–1543). Stems are small to large and are solitary or rarely clustered. Leaves are palmate, 30–40 in number, and often persist on the plant even after they have died. This "skirt" of dead leaves gives some species a very striking appearance. The petiole can be either very short or elongate and the margins are covered with recurved thorns. In certain species these thorny petioles persist on the stem after the leaf blade has fallen. Some species bear a very prominent "flap" at the junction of the petiole and blade. The shape of the blade in outline varies from circular to wedge shaped. Leaflets are numerous, often waxy on the lower surface and occasionally spiny on the margins. Inflorescences are borne among the leaves and often exceed them and are branched to six orders. Flowering branches bear either tubular or bristle-like bracts at their bases and vary considerably in length and diameter. This variation of the flowering branches is used to separate closely related species. Flowers are bisexual, with six stamens and three united carpels. Fruits are one-seeded, globose or ovoid, and black at maturity. The seeds have ruminate endosperm and the seedling leaf is simple.

Copernicia contains thirteen species, most of which occur in Cuba except for two in Hispaniola and three in South America. Species are very variable, especially the wide-ranging *C. hospita*, and are not easy to distinguish from one another. The most recent revision is that of Dahlgren and Glassman (1961, 1963), who recognized twenty-five species. The South American and Hispaniolan species are closely related and are the least specialized of the genus. The Cuban species are the most specialized and many are endemic to serpentine soils. Some of them are among the most spectacular of American palms. They are also the most endangered (Moya et al., 1989). All species grow in drier, open regions or open woodlands at low elevations.

The taxonomy of the genus is further complicated by the amount of hybridization that takes place. Table 2 shows the hybrids that have been recorded.

The genus is very similar to other coryphoid genera, especially *Brahea* and *Acoelorraphe* (which perhaps should be included in it). In the wild, in Cuba and Hispaniola, *Copernicia* is likely to be confused only with *Acoelorraphe*, *Coccothrinax*, or *Sabal*. It differs from *Acoelorraphe* in its usually solitary, stout stems (versus slender, clustered stems); from *Coccothrinax* in its recurved thorns on the petiole margins (versus petioles with smooth margins); and from *Sabal* in its palmate (versus costapalmate) leaf. In southern South America the only species of *Copernicia* present can be distinguished from the co-occurring *Trithrinax* by its nonspiny leaf-sheath fibers.

TABLE 2. HYBRIDS IN *COPERNICIA*.

Parent 1	Hybrid	Parent 2
C. hospita	*C.* x *burretiana*	*C. macroglossa*
C. hospita	*C.* x *occidentalis*	*C. brittonorum*
C. hospita	*C.* x *shaferi*	*C. cowellii*
C. hospita	*C. sueroana*	*C. rigida*
C. hospita	*C.* x *textilis*	*C. baileyana*
C. gigas	*C.* x *vespertilionum*	*C. rigida*

Key to the Species of Copernicia

1a. South America.
  2a. Argentina, Bolivia, Brazil (Mato Grosso, Mato Grosso do Sul) and Paraguay ..... *C. alba.*
  2b. Northern South America.
    3a. Northeastern Brazil ..... *C. prunifera.*
    3b. Colombia and Venezuela ..... *C. tectorum.*
1b. The Caribbean.
  4a. Hispaniola.
    5a. Blade bluish, waxy on lower surface; petiole thorny on the margins; north coast of Haiti ..... *C. ekmanii.*
    5b. Blade green, not waxy on lower surface; petiole with few thorns on the margins; Haiti and Dominican Republic ..... *C. berteroana.*
  4b. Cuba.
    6a. Leaf blade wedge shaped in outline.
      7a. Flowering branches with small, bristle-like bracts ..... *C. gigas.*
      7b. Flowering branches with tubular bracts.
        8a. Flowering branches 1–2.6 cm long and 0.3–1 cm diameter; stems 1.5–7 m tall and 12–20 cm diameter ..... *C. macroglossa.*
        8b. Flowering branches 4.5–9 cm long and 1–3 mm diameter; stems 10–15 m tall and 25–36 cm diameter ..... *C. rigida.*
    6b. Leaf blade circular in outline.
      9a. Stems 4–20 m tall.
        10a. Flowering branches smooth ..... *C. glabrescens.*
        10b. Flowering branches hairy.
          11a. Stems massive, often swollen, to 40(–60) cm diameter ..... *C. baileyana.*
          11b. Stems smaller, not swollen, 12–30 cm diameter.
            12a. Flowering branches 0.5–3.5 cm long ..... *C. hospita.*
            12b. Flowering branches 5 cm long ..... *C. brittonorum.*
      9b. Stems 1.2–2.5 m tall ..... *C. cowellii.*

Copernicia alba
(Map 55, Plate 7)
"Caranday" (Arg, Bol, Par), "carandá" (Bra), "palma blanca" (Arg, Bol, Par), "palma negra" (Arg, Bol, Par)
Field characters. Stems 8–30 m tall and 17–22 cm diameter, columnar, at least the younger ones covered with persistent leaf bases. Leaves spreading, glaucous when young; petiole elongate; blade circular in outline, gray-waxy on the lower surface, nonthorny on the margins. Inflorescences exceeding the leaves; flowering branches 3–7 cm long and 1–1.5 mm diameter, hairy, *with tubular bracts*; fruits ovoid, 1–2 cm long and 0.9–1.7 cm diameter, black.
Range and habitat. Subtropical southern South America in Brazil (Mato Grosso, Mato Grosso do Sul), Bolivia (Beni, Santa Cruz), Paraguay (Alto Paraguay, Central, Concepción, Cordillera, Neembucú, Paraguarí, Presidente Hayes), and Argentina (Chaco, Formosa, Santa Fé); low-lying, seasonally inundated savannas, in areas where flooding is followed by complete drying out. Its distribution is centered on the *chaco* region of Paraguay and adjacent countries.
Uses. The stems are cut and commonly used in various kinds of construction; and the leaves are woven into a variety of items.
Notes. Markley (1955) described the habitat of this species in Paraguay based on aerial surveys. The palms occurred over several thousand square kilometers of the *chaco*, generally in "palmares," or grassy plains with palms. Markley estimated that the largest palmar contained possibly half a billion individual palms. Moraes (1991) described the reproductive biology of this species in Bolivia. Flowering took place in August to October, at the end of the dry season, and fruiting from October to May.

Seeds were dispersed by the large ostrichlike rhea, *Rhea americana.*

Copernicia baileyana
(Map 56)
"Yarey" (Cub)
Field characters. Stems *10–20 m tall and 40(–60 cm diameter at the swelling),* columnar or swollen, smooth (at least in older trees). Leaves spreading; petiole elongate, with a short or well-developed "flap" at the junction with the blade; blade circular in outline, gray-waxy on lower surface, nonthorny on the margins, *the leaflets stiff and erect at the tips.* Inflorescences greatly exceeding the leaves; flowering branches to 8 cm long and 3–4 mm diameter, hairy, *with tubular bracts;* fruits globose or obovoid, 1.8–2.3 cm long and 1.8–2 cm diameter, black.
Range and habitat. Central and eastern Cuba (Camagüey, Las Villas, Oriente); savannas and woodlands, at low elevations.
Uses. The leaves are used to weave hats, baskets, and other items and also for thatching.
Notes. The larger number and greater length of the leaflets, together with their stiffly erect tips, give the leaves of this palm a very distinctive appearance, which it shares only with *Copernicia gigas.*

Copernicia berteroana
(Map 57, Plate 7)
"Dyaré" (Hai), "yarey" (DR)
Field characters. Stems 4–5 m tall and to 20 cm diameter, columnar, smooth. Leaves spreading; petioles elongate; blade circular in outline, green on lower surface, nonthorny on the margins. Inflorescences just exceeding the leaves; flowering branches to 13 cm long and 1–2 mm diameter, hairy, *with very small, bristle-like bracts;* fruits ovoid, 2 cm long and 1.8 cm diameter, black.
Range and habitat. Hispaniola (Dominican Republic, Haiti); low-lying, flat regions in areas of low rainfall. It also occurs on Curaçao, near the coast of Venezuela, but is probably planted there.
Uses. The leaves are used for thatching.
Notes. Becoming increasingly rare in Haiti due to continued habitat destruction (Henderson et al., 1990).

Copernicia brittonorum
(Map 58)
"Jata de costa" (Cub)
Field characters. Stems to 12 m tall and 12–18 cm diameter, columnar, smooth. Leaves spreading; petiole elongate; blade circular in outline, green or lightly waxy on lower surface,

nonthorny on margins. *Inflorescences greatly exceeding the leaves;* flowering branches to 5 cm long and 0.5–1.5 mm diameter, hairy, *with tubular bracts;* fruits globose, 1.2–1.5 cm diameter, black.
Range and habitat. Western Cuba (Las Villas, Pinar del Río); open places and woodlands, at low elevations.
Uses. The leaves are used for weaving various items, including hats and straps.
Notes. Very closely related to *Copernicia hospita* and is only kept separate here because of its longer flowering branches.

Copernicia cowellii
(Map 59)
"Jata enana" (Cub)
Field characters. Stems *1.2–2.5 m tall* and to 17 cm diameter, columnar, covered with persistent, dead leaves. Leaves stiffly erect; *petiole very short;* blades circular in outline, gray-waxy on lower surface, nonthorny on the margins, the leaflet tips blunt. *Inflorescences greatly exceeding the leaves;* flowering branches 3–4 cm long and 1–1.5 mm diameter, hairy, *with tubular bracts;* fruits globose, 1.3–1.7 cm diameter, black.
Range and habitat. Eastern Cuba (Camagüey); savannas on serpentine soils.
Uses. The leaves are used for weaving various items.
Notes. Closely related to *Copernicia hospita* and possibly conspecific; it is only distinguished by its smaller size, which is probably related to its serpentine habitat.

Copernicia ekmanii
(Map 60)
"Om de pay," "jamm de pay" (Hai)
Field characters. Stems 3–4 m tall and 15–20 cm diameter, columnar, smooth. Leaves spreading; petiole elongate, thorny on the margins; blade circular in outline, *bluish, gray-waxy on lower surface, thorny on the margins.* Inflorescences scarcely exceeding the leaves; flowering branches to 5 cm long and 1 mm diameter, *with very small, bristle-like bracts;* fruits ovoid, to 2 cm long and 1.7 cm diameter, black.
Range and habitat. North coast of Haiti (Nord Ouest); rocky shores near the sea. It is very rare in the wild (Henderson et al., 1990).
Uses. The leaves make a very durable and sought-after thatching material.

Copernicia gigas
(Map 61)
"Barrigón" (Cub)
Field characters. Stems 15–20 m tall and to 50 cm diameter, columnar, *smooth in older trees but with persistent leaves on younger ones.* Leaves

spreading; petiole elongate, with a well-developed "flap" at junction with blade; *blade wedge shaped in outline*, gray-waxy on the lower surface, *usually thorny on the margins, the leaflets stiff and erect at the tips*. Inflorescences exceeding the leaves; flowering branches to 11 cm long and 2–3 mm diameter, hairy, *with very small, bristle-like bracts*; fruits globose, 2–2.2 cm diameter, black.

Range and habitat. Eastern Cuba (Camagüey, Las Villas, Oriente); woodlands and open areas.

Uses. The leaves are used for thatching.

Notes. The long leaflets with their stiffly erect tips give this species a distinctive appearance, like that of *Copernicia baileyana*. Dahlgren and Glassman (1963) considered that a palm described as *C. vespertilionum* was a hybrid between *C. gigas* and *C. rigida*. This palm got its name from the Latin word for a bat, "vespertilio," in reference to the bat's habit of roosting among the leaves; and its common name, "jata de murciélagos," from the same source ("bat copernicia"). Taboada (1979) described the association between two species of bats, *Mormopterus minutus* and *Tadarida laticaudata*, and the palm. The bats use the "skirt" of dead, persistent leaves as their natural roosting site and the concave petioles as nesting sites. They deposit guano at the base of the palm, which in turn fertilizes the tree.

Copernicia glabrescens
(Map 62)
"Guano," "guano blanco" (Cub)

Field characters. Stems 4–6 m tall and 12–15 cm diameter, columnar, *covered with persistent leaf bases*. Leaves spreading; petiole elongate; blade circular in outline, gray-waxy on lower surface, nonthorny on margins. *Inflorescences greatly exceeding the leaves*; flowering branches 0.5–1.5 cm long and 0.5–1.5 mm diameter, smooth, *with tubular bracts*; fruits globose, 1.7–2 cm diameter, black.

Range and habitat. Western Cuba (Habana, Matanzas, Pinar del Río); savannas and open areas, at low elevations.

Notes. Very closely related to *Copernicia hospita* and perhaps conspecific. The only difference between the two is the smooth, nonhairy flowering branches of *C. glabrescens*.

Copernicia hospita
(Map 63, Plate 7)
"Guano cano," "yarey" (Cub)

Field characters. Stems 4–8 m tall and 12–30 cm diameter, columnar or rarely somewhat swollen, solitary or rarely with basal shoots,

smooth (at least on older trees). Leaves spreading; petiole elongate; blade circular in outline, gray-waxy on lower surface, nonthorny on the margins. Inflorescences exceeding the leaves; flowering branches 0.5–3.5 cm long and 1–2.5 mm diameter, *hairy, with tubular bracts*; fruits globose, 1.7–2 cm diameter, black.

Range and habitat. Throughout Cuba (Camagüey, Habana, Las Villas, Matanzas, Oriente, Pinar del Río); open savannas, woodlands, and occasionally coastal regions adjacent to mangrove swamps, at low elevations.

Uses. The hard and durable stems are extensively used for fence posts; and the leaves are woven into hats, panniers, and baskets.

Notes. A widespread and variable species that has previously been divided into several, poorly characterized taxa. Here we prefer to recognize one species, although further study may reveal local varieties or subspecies.

Copernicia macroglossa
(Map 64, Plate 7)
"Jata de Guanabacoa" (Cub)

Field characters. Stems 1.5–7 m tall and 12–20 cm diameter, columnar, *usually with a "skirt" of persistent, dead leaves at top*. Leaves *stiffly erect and densely crowded; petiole very short or absent*, with a well-developed "flap" at junction with blade; *blade wedge shaped in outline*, green or gray-waxy on lower surface, often thorny on margins. Inflorescences exceeding the leaves; flowering branches 1–2.6 cm long and 0.3–1 cm diameter, *hairy, with tubular bracts*; fruits globose, 1.5–2 cm diameter, black.

Range and habitat. Western and central Cuba (Camagüey, Habana, Las Villas, Matanzas); savannas and other open places.

Uses. The stems are used as fence posts.

Copernicia prunifera
(Map 65, Plate 8)
"Carnaúba" (Bra)

Field characters. Stems 10–15 m tall and 15–25 cm diameter, columnar, the younger ones covered with persistent leaf bases spirally arranged around the stem. Leaves spreading; petiole elongate; blade circular in outline, gray-waxy on lower surface, nonthorny on the margins. Inflorescences longer than the leaves; flowering branches to 12 cm long and 1.5–2.5 mm diameter, *hairy, with very small, bristle-like bracts*; fruits ovoid, to 2.7 cm long and 2.2 cm diameter.

Range and habitat. Northeastern Brazil (Alagoas, Bahia, Ceará, Maranhão, Paraíba, Pernambuco, Piauí, Rio Grande do Norte, Sergipe,

Tocantins, and just reaching eastern Mato Grosso); *caatinga*, low-lying areas, especially along river or lake margins that are liable to seasonal flooding followed by seasonal or prolonged drought.

Uses. This is an important palm as a source of wax, which is taken from the lower surfaces of the leaves. It was formerly much exploited (Johnson, 1972), and there are still factories in the northeast of Brazil that refine the wax and sell it for domestic or international use. It is currently used, for example, in the manufacture of coatings for medicine capsules.

Copernicia rigida
(Map 66)
"Jata," "jata guatacuda" (Cub)
Field characters. Stems 10–15 m tall and 25–36 cm diameter, columnar, usually with a "skirt" of persistent dead leaves at top. Leaves stiffly erect; petiole short or absent, with a well-developed "flap" at junction with blade; *blade wedge shaped in outline*, gray-waxy on lower surface, *with thorns along the margins*. Inflorescences exceeding the leaves; flowering branches 4.5–9 cm long and 1–3 mm diameter, *with tubular bracts*; fruits globose, 1.7–1.9 cm diameter, black.

Range and habitat. Central and eastern Cuba (Camagüey, Las Villas, Oriente); woodlands, savannas, and open areas, at low elevations.

Uses. The stems are cut and used as fence posts; the leaves are used for thatching.

Copernicia tectorum
(Map 67, Plate 8)
"Sará" (Col), "cobija," "palma llanera" (Ven)
Field characters. Stems 8–10 m tall and 25–30 cm diameter, columnar, at least the younger ones covered with persistent leaf bases. Leaves spreading; petiole elongate; blade circular in outline, green on the lower surface, nonthorny on the margins. Inflorescences just exceeding the leaves; flowering branches to 17 cm long and 1–2 mm diameter, *with very small, bristle-like bracts*; fruits ovoid, 2.5–3 cm long and 1.5–2 cm diameter, brown.

Range and habitat. Northern Colombia (Atlántico, Cesar Guajira, Magdalena) and northern Venezuela (Bolívar, Cojedes, Guárico, Portuguesa, Zulia); low-lying, seasonally inundated savanna areas. Like other South American species, this palm can withstand both long droughts and long floods in its highly seasonal habitat.

Uses. The leaves are used for various purposes, such as weaving baskets and thatching houses, and the durable stems are used as house posts.

Notes. It often has persistent leaf bases covering the stem. The adaptive significance of this is not known, but Putz and Holbrook (1989) reported that the litter that accumulated in the leaf bases was richer in organic matter and nutrients than the surrounding soil. Strangler figs (*Ficus* spp.) commonly germinated and grew in the leaf bases, eventually rooting in the ground and displacing the host palm.

15. WASHINGTONIA

This genus contains some of the most familiar and widely planted ornamental palms in subtropical areas of the world. It was named in honor of George Washington. Stems are robust, solitary, and stout and erect. Leaves are palmate, about thirty in number, large and heavy and naturally hang after death for several years. If they are not removed they form a complete "skirt" reaching from the top of the stem to the ground. Older and taller plants, however, tend to shed their old leaves completely. The petiole is covered along the margins with curved thorns. The blade is costapalmate, circular in outline, and is split into numerous stiff or pendulous leaflets, each bearing long threads hanging from the lower surface. Inflorescences are branched to three or four orders and are borne among the leaves, but project out from the crown. The rachis bracts are conspicuous and are split lengthwise and hang down. Flowering branches are numerous, short, and slender and bear small, solitary, bisexual flowers. These have six stamens and three carpels. Fruits are one-seeded, oblong to globose, smooth and black. Seeds have homogeneous endosperm and the seedling leaf is simple.

Washingtonia contains two species of desert palms, from southern California and western Arizona to northwestern Mexico. Both species can be seen together in Baja California near Cataviña (Cornett, 1987a). The genus needs a modern taxonomic revision. The last attempt to understand the species was by Bailey (1936a). He recognized two very closely related species, which differed only in very subtle characters. The specific status of these deserves reconsideration in the light of current understanding of morphological variation in palms.

Washingtonia filifera
(Map 68, Plate 8)
"California fan palm," "desert palm" (USA)
Field characters. Stems to 15 m tall or more and about 1 m diameter. *Leaves forming a loose and open crown; petiole of young palms green and not markedly thorny; blade lacking a tawny patch on the base of the lower surface; leaflets markedly pendulous and with abundant threads;* fruits globose to oblong, about 1 cm diameter, black.
Range and habitat. United States (southern California, western Arizona) and Mexico (Baja California); desert and arid regions, along streams in canyons and in open areas where groundwater is present.
Uses. Planted as an ornamental in streets and parks in many tropical and subtropical cities. It is resistant to freezing and easy to grow.
Notes. A wealth of information on this species has been given by Cornett (1989), including some spectacular photographs of the palm in its native habitat. It can withstand not only extreme heat, with summer temperatures sometimes reaching 56°C (127°F), but also extreme cold. Cornett (1987b) found that these palms could survive temperatures of -28°C (-11°F). They can also grow in areas of extreme alkaline soil with a pH of 9.2. Fires occur frequently in these oases, and it has been suggested that natural fires not only increase fruit production of the palms, but also encourage seedling growth by removing competing vegetation. The recent report of unexpectedly

low genetic differentiation between isolated populations of *W. filifera* (McClenaghan and Beauchamp, 1986) has led to a debate on the origins of the desert fan palm. For a long time the palm was thought to be a relic of a former widespread distribution, broken up into its present fragmented range by climatic change. However, the new genetic findings suggest that seeds are frequently dispersed between oases by coyotes or birds, both of which eat the fruit. Hicks (1989) suggested that the palm owed its present distribution almost entirely to Cahuilla Indians, who planted the palms in oases.

Washingtonia robusta
(Map 69)
"Mexican fan palm" (USA)
Field characters. Stems more slender and taller, to 22 m tall. *Leaves forming a compact crown; petiole of young palms brown and markedly thorny; blade with a tawny bright patch on the base of the lower surface* (specially marked on young leaves); *leaflets usually stiff and with abundant threads in young leaves, drooping and with few threads with age;* fruits globose to oblong, about 1 cm diameter, black.
Range and habitat. Northwestern Mexico (Baja California, Sonora); canyons and along watercourses and in wet places, also near the sea.
Uses. Faster growing than *Washingtonia filifera* and more commonly planted as an ornamental.

16. SABAL

This is one of the most common genera of palms in the Caribbean region and adjacent areas. It was named by the French botanist Adanson, but the derivation of the name is unknown. Stems are usually smooth and gray, solitary, short and subterranean or large and erect. The split leaf bases may persist for some time, giving the stem a characteristic reticulate appearance. Leaves are costapalmate, 10–30 in number, with a long, smooth petiole. The costa is arched downwards, giving the blade a three-dimensional shape. A short to long "flap" is present on the upper surface at the junction of the petiole and costa. Leaflets are few to numerous and are joined at the base. In two species the leaflets are unequally joined; pairs of leaflets are separated almost to the base of the leaf, but within each pair the leaflets are joined by their inner margins to varying distances. Often the leaflets have threads along the margins which hang down from the leaf. Inflorescences are borne among the leaves and are branched to four orders. They are often as long or longer than the leaves, erect to pendulous, and sheathed by numerous bracts. Flowering branches are rather short and slender. Flowers are creamy white, small and bisexual, with six stamens. Fruits are one-seeded (rarely two- or three-seeded), globose, pear shaped or broader than long, small and black, with a sweet, fleshy mesocarp. The endosperm is homogeneous and the seedling leaf is simple and linear-lanceolate.

Sabal contains sixteen species (Zona, 1990; Quero, 1991), distributed in and around the Caribbean region in Bermuda, the Greater Antilles, southeastern United States, Mexico, Central America, and through northern Colombia and Venezuela to Trinidad. Most species grow in rather dry areas, ranging from dry forest and thorn forest to moist forest. They are well adapted to open environments and only a few are forest plants. Each species has its own soil preferences, from beachside dunes to rich alluvial soils. The genus ranges in elevation from sea level to 1500 m, but most species are found below 500 m.

The flowers of many species are visited by different species of bees and members of the families Megachilidae and Halictidae are considered the principal pollinators (Zona, 1990).

The fleshy mesocarps of *Sabal* fruits attract a wide variety of birds (robins, mockingbirds, ravens, larks, pigeons, jays) and mammals (bears, raccoons, bats), which act as seed disperses. Long distance dispersal by birds has been suggested as an explanation for the distribution of *Sabal* throughout the islands of the Caribbean and for the patchy distribution of *Sabal mauritiiformis* (Zona, 1990; see also below). The most widely distributed species of *Sabal* are those with small fruits. Water dispersal has been suggested as a mode of dispersal for some species, e.g., *S. palmetto* and *S. minor*.

The treatment of *Sabal* in this Guide closely follows the recent monograph of Zona (1990). This work is of interest in that it touches on a current biogeographical controversy, the origin of the Greater Antillean fauna and flora. Some scientists believe that long-distance dispersal to the islands accounts for the current distributions of animals and plants, while others believe that the islands have had a mobile geological history and their current biota is derived from former contact with the mainland. Zona supports the former idea, believing that species of *Sabal* reached the islands by long-distance dispersal over water.

Species of *Sabal* can be separated from other palmate-leafed palms in the Caribbean region by the smooth, nonthorny petiole and long, arching costa that gives the leaf a three-dimensional shape.

KEY TO THE SPECIES OF SABAL

1a. Stems short and subterranean or to 2 m tall.
    2a. Inflorescences shorter than the yellow-green leaves   ..... *S. etonia.*
    2b. Inflorescences as long or longer than the green leaves.
        3a. Inflorescences branched to 2 orders; fruits 0.6–1 cm long   ..... *S. minor.*
        3b. Inflorescences branched to 3 orders; fruits 1.4–1.7 cm
           long   ..... *S. miamiensis.*
1b. Stems erect, 4–20 m tall.
     4a. Southeastern United States (North Carolina to Florida) and the Caribbean.
        5a. Stems more than 35 cm diameter.
           6a. Inflorescences erect or ascending (especially early in development)   ..... *S. maritima.*

6b. Inflorescences arched or pendulous.
  7a. Fruits globose, 0.7–1.1 cm diameter   ..... *S. causiarum.*
  7b. Fruits pear shaped, 1.1–1.4 cm diameter   ..... *S. domingensis.*
5b. Stems 15–35 cm diameter.
  8a. Bermuda   ..... *S. bermudana.*
  8b. Cuba, the Bahamas, and southeastern United States.
    9a. Inflorescences erect or ascending (especially early in develop-
      ment)   ..... *S. maritima.*
    9b. Inflorescences arched or pendulous.
      10a. Leaves strongly arched; all leaflets joined for more or less
        the same distance, not in pairs   ..... *S. palmetto.*
      10b. Leaves not strongly arched, only moderately so; leaflets
        joined in pairs (or threes) for about half their length, the
        pairs only shortly joined   ..... *S. yapa.*
4b. Southern United States (Texas) through Central America and northern South America.
11a. All leaflets joined for more or less the same distance, not in pairs,
the leaf appearing rather regular.
  12a. Western and southern Mexico (Sonora to Guerrero and the Distrito Federal).
    13a. Inflorescences more or less pendulous, shorter than the
    leaves; Río Balsas basin   ..... *S. pumos.*
    13b. Inflorescences arching, as long or longer than the leaves.
      14a. Leaves evenly green; flowering branches often thin and
      curled; Sinaloa to Jalisco   ..... *S. rosei.*
      14b. Leaves glaucous; flowering branches stiff; Sonora to Chi-
      huahua   ..... *S. uresana.*
  12b. Northeastern and eastern Mexico (including the Yucatán Peninsula), south to coastal Guerrero and Oaxaca.
    15a. Fruits globose to slightly pear shaped, 1.5–2 cm diameter.
      16a. Broadest leaflet 6–7 cm wide   ..... *S. gretheriae.*
      16b. Broadest leaflet 3.2–5.3 cm wide   ..... *S. mexicana.*
    15b. Fruits conspicuously pear shaped, 1.1–1.4 cm
    diameter   ..... *S. guatemalensis.*
11b. Leaflets joined in pairs for half their length, the pairs joined for
one-third their length, the leaf appearing untidy.
  17a. Leaflets joined in groups of 2–3 for almost their entire length,
  the groups joined for about one-third their length   ..... *S. mauritiiformis.*
  17b. Leaflets joined in groups for about half their length, the groups
  joined for about one-sixth their length   ..... *S. yapa.*

Sabal bermudana
(Map 70)
"Bermuda palm," "Bermuda palmetto" (Ber)
Field characters. Stems solitary, to 7 m tall and 20–35 cm diameter. Leaves 15–25, with a very long costa; leaflets 85–95, *rigid, joined at the base for about half their length.* Inflorescences branched to 3 orders, arching, not exceeding the petioles; fruits slightly pear shaped to almost globose and slightly narrowed at base, 1.3–1.9 cm diameter, black.

Range and habitat. Bermuda; open areas both in dry and marshy habitats.
Notes. Very similar to *Sabal palmetto* but differs in its larger, slightly pear-shaped fruits.

Sabal causiarum
(Map 71, Plate 8)
"Palma cana" (DR); "palma de sombrero," "yarey" (PR)
Field characters. Stems solitary, *very stout*, to 10 m tall and 35–70 cm diameter. Leaves 20–30,

with a prominent costa; leaflets 60–120, rigid, arranged in many planes, with many threads along the margins. Inflorescences branched to 3 orders, arching or pendulous, *projected beyond the leaves*; fruits globose, 0.7–1.1 cm diameter, black.

Range and habitat. Southern Hispaniola in southwestern Haiti and eastern Dominican Republic, Puerto Rico, and the island of Anegada (British Virgin Islands); often forming dense and extensive colonies on sandy soils of coastal plains, from sea level to 100 m elevation.

Uses. The leaves are used for making hats, baskets, and mats. The practice of making hats in Puerto Rico has decreased in recent years (Henderson, 1984b).

Notes. *Sabal causiarum, S. domingensis,* and *S. maritima* form a complex of closely related species that may better be regarded as conspecific.

Sabal domingensis
(Map 72)
"Palma cana" (DR), "latanier-chapeau" (Hai)
Field characters. Stems solitary, very stout, to 10 m tall and 60 cm diameter. Leaves 20–30, with a prominent costa; leaflets about 90, arranged in different planes, with threads along the margins. Inflorescences branched to three orders, arching, as long as the leaves or longer; *fruits pear shaped, 1.1–1.4 cm diameter,* black.

Range and habitat. Hispaniola, from northwestern Haiti to central Dominican Republic, and also recently discovered in Cuba (Oriente) (Zona, 1992); secondary vegetation, at 100–1000 m elevation.

Uses. The leaves are extensively used for thatching and for weaving hats, baskets, mats, and other items.

Notes. A poorly known species, separated from *Sabal causiarum* by its larger, pear-shaped fruits.

Sabal etonia
(Map 73)
"Scrub palmetto" (USA)
Field characters. Stems solitary, *short and subterranean*, but sometimes erect and then to 2 m tall. *Leaves 4–7, yellow-green*, with a prominent costa; leaflets 25–50, rigid, *joined for a short distance at base*, with threads along the margins. Inflorescences typically branched to two orders, with a bushy appearance, ascending, shorter than the leaves; fruits almost globose but slightly broader than long, 0.9–1.5 cm long and 0.8–1.3 cm diameter, brownish black.

Range and habitat. United States (central and southeastern Florida); sandy soils in the understory of pine-oak woodlands along the central Florida ridge. Zona and Judd (1986) have

discussed the distribution and ecology of this species.

Notes. Large populations are protected in the Ocala National Forest and Archbold Biological Station in Florida.

Sabal gretheriae
(Map 74)
Field characters. Stems solitary, to 8 m tall and 20–30 cm diameter, covered apically with persistent leaf bases. Leaves about 30; leaflets 100–120, rigid. Inflorescences branched to 3 orders, arching, as long as the leaves; fruits globose or obovoid, 1.6–2 cm diameter, black.

Range and habitat. Mexico (Quintana Roo); open, disturbed areas on sandy soils, at low elevations.

Notes. Quero (1991) has discussed the differences between this newly described species and the co-occurring *Sabal yapa*. This new species, however, may better be treated as a local form of the widespread and variable *S. mexicana*, although its chromosomes are different (Palomino and Quero, 1992).

Sabal guatemalensis
(Map 75)
Field characters. Stems solitary, to 15 m tall and 35 cm diameter. Leaves 20–25, with a prominent, strongly arched costa; *leaflets 80–100, rigid, pointing upwards*. Inflorescences branched to 3 orders, arching, as long as leaves; fruits pear shaped, often wider than long, 1–1.4 cm long and 1.1–1.4 cm diameter, black.

Range and habitat. Southern and eastern Mexico (Chiapas, Oaxaca, Yucatán) to Guatemala (Flores, El Progreso, Zapaca); dry areas, often in disturbed habitats associated with human activity.

Notes. Closely related to *Sabal mexicana*, which differs only in its somewhat larger, globose fruits and the calyx shape. Mexican populations have been considered as *S. mexicana* by Quero (1989); both species are perhaps better regarded as conspecific.

Sabal maritima
(Map 76)
"Guana cana," "palma cana" (Cub), "bull thatch" (Jam)
Field characters. Stems solitary, stout, to 15 m tall (but usually smaller) and 25–40 cm diameter. Leaves about 25, *forming a rather open crown, the blades gently undulate, with a prominent, strongly arching costa*; leaflets 70–110, rigid, horizontally spreading, with threads between leaflets. Inflorescences branched to 3 orders, erect (but may become arching in fruit), as long as the leaves; fruits pear shaped

to almost globose, but slightly broader than long, 0.8–1.4 cm diameter, black.

Range and habitat. Cuba and Jamaica; scrubby or disturbed vegetation, on sandy and limestone-derived soils, often locally common and persisting in pastures, from sea level to 600 m elevation.

Uses. The leaves are used for thatching.

Notes. It occurs with *Sabal palmetto* in Cuba, but is distinguished from that species by its erect inflorescences and more spreading, almost horizontally arranged leaflets. Positive identification of some individuals may need study of vein pattern in leaflets (see differences in Zona, 1990).

Sabal mauritiiformis
(Map 77, Plate 9)
"Botán" (Bel, Gua), "palma amarga" (Col), "palma de guagara" (Pan), "carat" (Tri), "carata," "palma redonda" (Ven)

Field characters. Stems solitary, *slender*, 10–20 m tall and 15–20 cm diameter, *markedly swollen at base*. Leaves 10–25, with a prominent costa; leaflets 90–150, *whitish on lower surface*, joined in groups of 2–3, *soft and with pendulous tips, the leaf appearing quite open*, without threads along the margins. Inflorescences branched to 4 orders, erect to arching, *projected beyond leaves*; fruits globose to slightly pear shaped, 0.8–1.1 cm diameter, black.

Range and habitat. A remarkably patchy range in central Mexico (Chiapas, Oaxaca, Tabasco, Veracruz), northern Guatemala (Petén), Honduras (Gracias a Dios), Belize, eastern Costa Rica (Limón), eastern Panama (Darién, Panamá), the upper Río Cauca Valley (Valle) in Colombia, the Caribbean lowlands of Colombia (Atlántico, Bolívar, Córdoba, Guajira, Sucre), upper Rio Magdalena Valley (Cundinamarca, Tolima), and Venezuela (Barinas, Bolívar, Cojedes, Falcón, Lara, Zulia), and Trinidad, but not El Salvador, or Nicaragua; locally very abundant in dry to wet areas, from sea level to 1000 m elevation, but most abundant below 500 m. Common in disturbed areas and left in pastures.

Uses. The leaves are a prized thatching material.

Sabal mexicana
(Map 78)
"Palma de sombrero" (ElS), "palma de micharo," "soyate" (Mex)

Field characters. Stems solitary, to 15 m tall and 20–35 cm diameter, with leaf bases persisting at least near the top, *often flowering when the stem is still very short*. Leaves 10–25, with a prominent and strongly arching costa; leaflets 80–115, rigid and ascending, with threads along the margins. Inflorescences branched to

3 orders, arching, as long as the leaves; fruits globose to slightly broader than long, 1.5–1.9 cm long and 1.4–1.7 cm diameter, black.

Range and habitat. Southern United States (southern Texas), through the Atlantic and Pacific coasts of Mexico (Guerrero, Oaxaca, San Luis Potosí, Tamaulipas, Veracruz, Yucatán) and extending into Honduras (Cortés), El Salvador (San Vicente), and Nicaragua (Boaco, Chinandega, León, Madriz, Matagalpa); dry lowlands, often in disturbed habitats. One of the most widespread and common palms in Mexico.

Uses. The leaves are used for thatching and for making hats; the stems are used as fence posts. The palm hearts and fruits are eaten (Quero, 1989).

Notes. Closely related to *Sabal guatemalensis* (see differences under the latter). Co-occurrence of both species is probably secondary and anthropogenic (Zona, 1990). Lockett (1991) considered that palms in the lower Rio Grande in Texas were hybrids between *S. minor* and *S. mexicana*.

Sabal miamiensis
(Map 79)
"Miami palmetto" (USA)

Field characters. Stems solitary, *short and subterranean*. Leaves 3–6, with a prominent costa; leaflets 35–70, rigid, *joined for a short distance at base*. Inflorescences branched to 3 orders, arching, as long or longer than the leaves; fruits broader than long, 1.4–1.7 cm long and 1.6–1.9 cm diameter, black.

Range and habitat. United States (southern Florida in the vicinity of Miami); outcrops of oolitic limestone near sea level. Probably already extinct, as most of its habitat has been urbanized (Zona, 1990).

Notes. It grows with the very similar *Sabal etonia*, but differs in its large, arching inflorescences branched to 3 orders and larger fruits.

Sabal minor
(Map 80)
"Dwarf palmetto," "latanier" (USA)

Field characters. Stems solitary, *short and subterranean*, but sometimes erect and then to 2 m tall and 10–20 cm diameter. *Leaves 4–10, dark green*, with a weakly developed costa; *leaflets 15–65, rigid, joined for a short distance at base*, the leaf appearing rather circular. *Inflorescences typically branched to 2 orders, erect, projecting beyond leaves*; fruits globose or slightly broader than long, 0.6–1 cm long and 6–8 mm diameter, brown to black.

Range and habitat. United States (Alabama, Arkansas, Florida, Louisiana, Mississippi, North Carolina, southern Oklahoma, South Carolina,

Texas); common on rich alluvial soils in the understory of broad-leaf deciduous forest.

Notes. Flowering takes place from April to August. In central and northern Florida it occurs with the similar *Sabal etonia*, which differs in its yellow-green leaves, bushy inflorescences shorter than leaves, and larger fruits.

Sabal palmetto
(Map 81, Plate 9)
"Guana cana," "palma cana" (Cub), "cabbage palm," "palmetto" (USA)
Field characters. Stems solitary, 6–20 m tall and 20–35 cm diameter. Leaves 15–30, with a prominent, strongly arching costa; leaflets 50–95, rigid, erect, joined for one-third their length, with threads along the margins. Inflorescences branched to 3 orders, arching, as long as leaves or longer; fruits globose or slightly broader than long and pear shaped, 0.8–1.4 cm long and 0.8–1.4 cm diameter, black.
Range and habitat. Widespread in Bahamas, western Cuba, and southeastern United States (Georgia, Florida, North Carolina, South Carolina); from coastal dunes and tidal flats to river banks and seasonally inundated savannas, often in disturbed vegetation, near sea level.
Uses. The leaves are used for thatching.
Notes. In Cuba it occurs with *Sabal maritima*; the differences are discussed under that species. Floral biology (Brown, 1976a) and dispersal and predation (Brown 1976b) have been studied. In Florida, the palmetto weevil, *Rhynchophorus cruentatus*, completes its life cycle in *Sabal palmetto* (Weissling et al., 1993). Currently some coastal populations of this palm in Florida are dying out, possibly as a result of increased salinity of the water.

Sabal pumos
(Map 82)
"Palma real," "pumos" (Mex)
Field characters. Stems solitary, 4–15 m tall and 15–35 cm diameter. Leaves 15–25, with a prominent costa; leaflets 60–80, joined for one-third their length, with threads along the margins. Inflorescences branched to 3 orders, arching to pendulous, *much shorter than leaves*; fruits slightly broader than long, almost globose, *1.4–2.3 cm long and 1.2–1.9 cm diameter, greenish brown-black.*
Range and habitat. Mexico in the Río Balsas basin (Guerrero, Guanajuato, Jalisco, México, Michoacán, Zacatecas, and possibly Morelos); locally abundant on sandy soils in the transition zone between tropical deciduous forest and oak forest, at 600–1300 m elevation. Much of its range is now transformed into pastures, where the species seems to thrive.

Uses. The mesocarp of the fruit is edible; the leaves are used for thatching.

Sabal rosei
(Map 83)
"Palma de llano" (Mex)
Field characters. Stems solitary, 6–15 m tall and 15–30 cm diameter. Leaves 15–30, *with a long and prominent, strongly arching costa*; leaflets 60–80, rigid, ascending, *those of each side of the costa arranged in one plane.* Inflorescences as long as leaves, arching, branched to 3 orders; fruits slightly broader than long, almost globose, 1.5–2.2 cm long and 1.3–2.0 cm diameter, greenish brown-black.
Range and habitat. Mexico (Nayarit, Jalisco, Sinaloa); savannas, deciduous to semideciduous forest, and now abundant in disturbed areas, to 1000 m elevation.

Sabal uresana
(Map 84)
"Palma blanca" (Mex)
Field characters. Stems solitary and stout, to 20 m tall and 30–40 cm diameter. Leaves 15–35, *markedly glaucous to bluish*, with a prominent arching costa; leaflets 60–75, rigid, ascending, with or without threads along the margins. Inflorescences branched to 3 orders, arching, as long as the leaves; fruits broader than long, almost globose or slightly pear-shaped, to 1.6 cm long and 1.3 cm diameter, brown or black.
Range and habitat. Mexico in the foothills of the Sierra Madre Occidental (Chihuahua, Sonora); uncommon in thorn forest and oak forest along watercourses and valleys, from sea level to 1500 m elevation, but most populations growing above 650 m.
Uses. The leaves are used for thatching.
Notes. Related to *Sabal rosei*, but differs in its glaucous-bluish leaves and the somewhat smaller fruits.

Sabal yapa
(Map 85)
"Thatch palm" (Bel), "botán" (Bel, Gua), "palma guano" (Cub), "cana" (Mex)
Field characters. Stems solitary, *slender, to 20 m tall and 15–26 cm diameter.* Leaves 15–20, green, *the costa not prominent*; leaflets 90–115, *joined in groups of 2–3 for about half their length, the groups only shortly joined.* Inflorescences branched to 3 orders, erect; fruits globose to pear shaped, 1–1.3 cm long and 4–6 mm diameter, black.
Range and habitat. Mexico (Yucatán peninsula in Campeche, Quintana Roo, Yucatán), Belize, and western Cuba (La Habana, Pinar del Río); low-lying areas on well-drained, limestone soils, originally in deciduous woodlands but now persisting in open areas.

17. RAPHIA

This genus is one of only two American palm genera that also occurs in Africa, and it is the only American scaly-fruited palm with pinnate leaves. Stems are solitary or clustered, upright or short and subterranean. Leaves are pinnate, 5–15 or more in number, erect, and spiny. The numerous leaflets are either regularly arranged and spread in the same plane or are clustered and spread in different planes. The leaves of *Raphia* are the longest of any flowering plant and those of *Raphia regalis* from central Africa can reach 25 m long. A fiber is extracted from the leaves, called raffia, hence the name of the genus. Raffia was for a long time used by gardeners to tie up plants. Inflorescences are borne at the top of the stem, are branched to two orders, and are pendulous, large, and heavy. Like other calamoid palms, they are covered with numerous overlapping bracts. Each stem bears several inflorescences, but these develop over a relatively short period, and after flowering and fruiting the stem dies. Another stem in the same clump then grows to flowering size. The numerous, woody flowering branches bear solitary, unisexual flowers, but male and female flowers occur on the same inflorescence. Female flowers are borne at the base and males toward the top of each branch. Fruits are one-seeded, ellipsoid, reddish brown, and covered with overlapping scales. Seeds have ruminate endosperm and the seedling leaf is pinnate or bifid.

Raphia contains about twenty-eight species (Otedoh, 1982), distributed throughout wet areas of Africa and Madagascar, except for the American *Raphia taedigera*. One other African species, *Raphia farinifera*, is naturalized in the Lesser Antillean islands of Martinique and Guadeloupe (Read, 1979).

Some authors have considered that the presence of *Raphia taedigera* in the Americas is due to the introduction of seeds brought from Africa by slaves. Otedoh (1977) emphasized the similarities between the African *R. vinifera* and the American *R. taedigera* and considered the latter introduced. Evidence from ecological studies is conflicting; Anderson and Mori (1967) believed some Central American populations were pioneer communities, possibly as a result of recent introduction. On the other hand, Devall and Kiester (1987) considered the same populations as representing climax communities. It is interesting to note that both *Raphia* and *Elaeis*, the only two genera shared by both America and Africa, have a disjunct distribution in Central America and northwestern Colombia, on one side of the continent, and the lower Amazon on the other side. Their general pattern of distribution is surprisingly similar.

Raphia taedigera
(Map 86, Plates 9 & 10)
"Jupatí" (Bra), "pángana" (Col), "yolillo" (CR), "matomba" (Pan)
Field characters. Stems clustered with 5–6 or more stems, 1–6 m tall and 20–40 cm diameter, erect, covered with persistent, dead leaf bases. Leaves 5–15, to 10 m long, ascending and curved toward the top, with a plumose appearance; leaflets 136–205 each side, irregularly arranged, and spreading in different planes, with short spines along the margins and veins. Inflorescences pendulous, more than 2 m long; fruits ellipsoid to oblong, 5–7 cm long and 3–4 cm diameter, covered with large, reddish brown, overlapping scales.

Range and habitat. Atlantic and Pacific coasts of Central America in Nicaragua (Zelaya), Costa Rica, and Panama, estuary of Río Atrato in northwestern Colombia (Antioquia, Chocó), and the estuary of the Amazon in Brazil (Pará); forming large stands in lowland tropical rain forest in permanently swampy areas, usually near the sea.

Uses. Although species in Africa are extensively used, the American species has relatively few uses. In Colombia the long petioles are used as poles, and in Brazil thin strips from the surfaces of the petioles are used to make shrimp traps, bird cages, and related items.

18. MAURITIA

This small genus was named for Count Johan Mauritz van Nassau-Siegen (1604–1679), a Dutch field marshall and governor of a company in Suriname. Stems are very large, solitary, or very rarely clustered, gray, and columnar or rarely swollen. Leaves are costapalmate, 6–20 in number, large and heavy, and are borne on elongate, rounded petioles. The blade is circular in outline and deeply split in half, and each half is again split into numerous leaflets. Leaflets have small spines along the margins. The tips of the leaflets tend to spread in different planes, giving the leaf a three-dimensional appearance. Individual plants bear either male or female flowers, but not both. Inflorescences are very large; they are borne among the leaves and are branched to two orders. They are pendulous and are covered with numerous overlapping bracts. The woody flowering branches are arranged in two rows and are densely covered with small flowers. Male flowers are borne in pairs and females are solitary. Fruits are one-seeded, globose, oblong or ellipsoid, large, and are covered with small, overlapping, reddish brown to reddish orange scales. Seeds have homogeneous endosperm and the seedling leaf is palmate.

Mauritia contains two species (Henderson, 1994), one of which is widely distributed throughout wet areas in northern South America east of the Andes and just reaching Trinidad, and the other is more narrowly distributed in the Amazon region.

Mauritia carana
(Map 87)
"Caraná" (Bra, Col, Ven), "canangucha de sabana" (Col), "aguaje" (Per)
Field characters. Stems 10–15 m tall and to 30 cm diameter, with a few persistent dead leaves hanging from the top. Leaves 6–12; *sheath with many fine fibers, these forming a mass that obscures the leaf sheaths*; blade about 2 m long and 3.5 m wide, split into about 150 leaflets. Inflorescences 3–4 m long, with 16–36 flowering branches; *fruits nearly globose*, 4.5–7 cm diameter, dark reddish brown, *the scales 3–4 mm wide.*
Range and habitat. Amazon region of Colombia (Amazonas, Guainía, Guaviare), Venezuela (Amazonas), Peru (Loreto), and Brazil (Amazonas); forest or open forest on poorly drained, white sand soils, usually in areas of blackwater rivers, at low elevations.
Uses. Not used as much as *Mauritia flexuosa*, but the fibers of the sheaths are occasionally used to make brooms and the leaves are commonly used for thatching.

Mauritia flexuosa
(Map 88, Plate 10)
"Caranday-guazú," "palma real" (Bol), "burití," (Bol, Bra), "mirití" (Bra), "aguaje" (Col, Per), "canangucho" (Col, Ecu), "moriche" (Col, Ven), "morete" (Ecu), "ite palm" (Guy)
Field characters. Stems 3–25 m tall and 30–60 cm diameter, smooth, rarely swollen, with a few dead leaves hanging from the crown. Leaves 8–20; *sheath clearly visible, covered with a few coarse fibers*; blade about 2.5 m long and 4.5 m wide, split into about 200 stiff or pendulous leaflets. Inflorescences pendulous in fruit, more than 2 m long, with 25–40 flowering branches; *fruits very variable, oblong, globose, or ellipsoid*, to 7 cm long and 5 cm diameter, orange-reddish to brown-reddish, *the scales to 6 mm wide*; mesocarp bright yellow and oily.
Range and habitat. Widely distributed throughout northern South America east of the Andes, especially in the Amazon region, in Colombia, Venezuela, the Guianas, Trinidad, Ecuador, Peru, Brazil, and Bolivia; usually in permanently swampy areas where it forms extensive, high-density stands, also in gallery forest along rivers in savannas, usually below 500 m elevation but sometimes reaching 900 m on eastern Andean slopes.
Uses. One of the most extensively used palms in the Amazon region. The soft pulp of the fruits is eaten directly, dried and made into flour, or fermented; it is a nutritious and important part of the diet of many indigenous groups in the Amazon (Borgtoft Pedersen and Balslev, 1990; Galeano, 1991). In Iquitos, Peru, the trade in fruits is important economically (Padoch, 1988). Ice cream and preserves are made from the mesocarp and sold in many parts of the city. In Brazil, oil is extracted from the fruits at a domestic level. String is obtained from the leaf fibers of young leaves and

is used to make ropes, hammocks, baskets, and similar items. The spongy part of the petiole is used to make mats and can be used for paper production (De los Heros and Bueno Zárate, 1980–81). Inside the fallen stems, larvae of the beetle *Rhynchophorus palmarum* develop, and these are eaten and highly appreciated by indigenous people. Wine and starch are obtained from the sap of the stem (Borgtoft Pedersen and Balslev, 1990). These authors gave many other minor uses and considered that this species was promising for extractivism and agroforestry.

Notes. Pollination of plants in Ecuador has been described by Ervik (1993). Fruits, usually borne in the dry season, play an important role in the diet of some animals such as collared peccaries (*Tajassu tajacu*), white-lipped peccaries (*Tajassu pecari*), agouties (*Dasyprocta fuliginosa*), pacas (*Agouti paca*), and various birds, turtles, and fish. Some of these animals also disperse the fruits (Urrego, 1987; Goulding, 1989). Individuals with leaves spreading in one plane are sometimes encountered (Kahn, 1988).

19. MAURITIELLA

This genus is essentially a smaller version of *Mauritia*, hence its generic name, and it has sometimes been included there. It is immediately distinguished from *Mauritia* by its smaller, clustered stems, which are covered, at least near the base, with short, stout, conical root spines. Near the very base of the stem these root spines form a mound of roots. Leaves are costapalmate, 4–10 in number, almost circular in outline and white-waxy on the sheath, petiole, and lower surface of the leaflets. The sheaths are partially closed and usually somewhat swollen. Petioles are elongate and rounded in cross section. The blade is split almost to the base into numerous, linear-lanceolate leaflets and, although not obvious, the leaflets are usually spiny on the margins. Inflorescences are covered with overlapping bracts. They are branched to two orders, and the flowering branches are short and arranged in one plane. The small flowers are crowded on the branches, with plants bearing either male or female flowers, but not both. Male flowers are borne singly while female flowers are clustered, and this arrangement also distinguishes the genus from *Mauritia*. Fruits are one-seeded, ellipsoid or ellipsoid-oblong, moderate sized, and covered in reddish brown, overlapping scales. Endosperm is homogeneous and the seedling leaf is bifid (unlike the palmate seedling of *Mauritia*).

Mauritiella contains three species (Henderson, 1994), one of which is widespread in northern South America and the other two have more restricted ranges. They are typical palms of savanna regions, blackwater river margins, or other wet, periodically inundated areas. This small genus has at one time or another been included in *Mauritia*, but the differences between the two seem to justify recognition of two separate genera. Apart from the obvious differences in the clustered stems with root spines of *Mauritiella*, there are other differences in the arrangement of the flower clusters. They are, however, clearly closely related to one another and also to the following genus, *Lepidocaryum*.

Mauritiella aculeata
(Map 89, Plate 10)
"Buritirana," "caranaí" (Bra), "morichito" (Ven)
Field characters. Stems 3–8 m tall and 7–10 cm diameter, forming large colonies and often leaning over the margins of streams or rivers. Leaves 5–9; blade split into 68–80 pendulous leaflets, these 1–2 cm wide. Fruits oblong-ellipsoid, 4–5 cm long and 3–4.5 cm diameter, reddish brown.
Range and habitat. Upper Rio Negro region of

Colombia (Guainía, Vaupés), Venezuela (Amazonas, Apure), and Brazil (Amazonas); along inundated margins of blackwater streams and rivers, at low elevations. A very characteristic species of the Rio Negro and its tributaries, appearing from just above Manaus all the way to Colombia and Venezuela.

Mauritiella armata
(Map 90, Plate 11)
"Buriticillo" (Bol), "buritirana," "caranaí"

(Bra), "cananguchillo" (Col), "moretillo" (Ecu), "aguajillo" (Per), "morichito" (Ven)
Field characters. Stems clustered or less often solitary, 2–20 m tall and 7.5–14(–30) cm diameter, forming small clumps. Leaves 4–10; blade split into 80–120, stiff or arching leaflets, these 1.5–3.5 cm wide. Fruits globose, ovoid, or ellipsoid-oblong, 2.5–3.5 cm long and 2–3 cm diameter, reddish brown.
Range and habitat. Very widespread in the Amazon region and adjacent areas in Colombia (Amazonas, Caquetá, Guaviare, Guainía, Meta, Putumayo, Vaupés, Vichada), Venezuela (Amazonas, Bolívar), Guyana, Surinam, Ecuador (Napo), Peru (Loreto, San Martín), Brazil (Acre, Amazonas, Bahia, Goiás, Mato Grosso, Minas Gerais, Pará, Pernambuco, Piauí, Rondônia, Roraima, Tocantins), and Bolivia (La Paz, Pando, Santa Cruz); common in a variety of habitats, including savannas, river margins, lowland rain forest, or gallery forest, usually at low elevations but occasionally reaching 1400 m on mountain slopes in the Guayana Highland.

Notes. Small palms with stems 1–2 m tall, leaves with about 25 leaflets each, and small fruits to 3 cm long are found in white sand savannas of the upper Rio Negro region of Brazil and Colombia, and possibly Venezuela. These populations seem to be a distinct species, apparently the one described as *Mauritiella pumila* by Wallace (1853).

Mauritiella macroclada
(Map 91)
"Quitasol" (Col)
Field characters. Stems solitary or clustered, to 10 m tall and 15 cm diameter. Leaves 6–12; blade split into about 60 leaflets, these to 4.5 cm wide. Fruits ellipsoid-oblong, 2–2.5 cm long and 1.8–2 cm diameter, reddish brown.
Range and habitat. Pacific coast of Colombia (Antioquia, Chocó, Nariño, Valle) and Ecuador (Esmeraldas); seasonally or permanently inundated areas, at low elevations but occasionally reaching 1000 m elevation on western Andean slopes (although probably planted there).

20. LEPIDOCARYUM

A genus of small-sized, understory palms, closely related to the two preceding genera. Stems are slender, clustered, conspicuously ringed, and sometimes form large colonies by rhizomes. Leaves are palmate, 8–20 in number, and are borne on distinctive, rounded, long petioles. The blade is deeply divided into two halves, and each half is again divided into 2–11 leaflets. These are weakly spiny along the margins and veins. Plants bear either male or female inflorescences, but not both. Inflorescences are branched to two orders and are borne among the leaves. They are erect in flower but become pendulous in fruit. The peduncle is much longer than the rachis, and both are covered with several tubular and sheathing peduncular bracts. The short rachis bears a few primary branches arranged in one plane, and these bear the shorter flowering branches. Fruits are one-seeded, ellipsoid to globose, beaked at the apex, and covered with overlapping reddish brown, red, or orange-red scales. The name *Lepidocaryum* means fruits covered with scales, which is a distinctive characteristic of this genus as well as of the very closely related *Mauritia* and *Mauritiella*. The endosperm is homogeneous and the seedling leaf is bifid.

This is a genus of one species with three varieties, widely distributed in the Amazon region (Henderson, 1994).

Lepidocaryum tenue
(Map 92, Plate 11)
"Caraná" (Bra, Col), "burityzinho" (Bra), "pui" (Col), "caraña," "irapai" (Per), "morichito" (Ven)
Field characters. Stems clustered, 1–4 m tall and 1.5–3 cm diameter, sometimes forming large colonies by rhizomes. Leaves 8–20, with an elongate petiole; blade deeply divided into 4–

22 leaflets, these 48–75 cm long and 1–8 cm wide, rarely wider. Inflorescences with 2–16 primary branches and numerous, short flowering branches; fruits ellipsoid to globose, beaked at the apex, 1.5–3 cm long and 1–2 cm diameter, covered with reddish brown, red or orange-red scales.
Range and habitat. Widely distributed throughout the western Amazon region in Colombia,

Venezuela, Peru, and Brazil and possibly Guyana; on well-drained or inundated soils, or sometimes on inundated, white-sand soils, at low elevations. Vegetative reproduction through the growth of underground stems (rhizomes) allows the formation of large colonies. Where conditions are suitable, it becomes an important and conspicuous understory species (Kahn and Mejía, 1987).

Uses. The leaves are an important thatching material, especially in Amazonian Peru.

Notes. This is a rather variable, complex, and poorly understood species. The division of the leaf, the number of inflorescence branches, as well as the fruit shape are very variable. Henderson (1994) has recognized 3 varieties, although intermediate forms can be found in some areas: var. *tenue*, with the leaves divided into 4(–8) broad leaflets and inflorescences with 4–14 primary branches, from Colombia (Amazonas, Vaupés), Peru (Loreto, San Martín), and Brazil (Acre, Amazonas, Pará); var. *gracile*, with the leaves divided into 4–19 unequal leaflets and inflorescences with 5–14 primary branches, from Brazil (eastern Amazonas, western Pará, northern Mato Grosso) and possibly Guyana; and var. *casiquiarense*, with the leaves divided into 16–22 narrow leaflets and inflorescences with 2–6 primary branches, from the upper Rio Negro region of Colombia (Amazonas, Guainía), Venezuela (Amazonas, Bolívar), and Brazil (Amazonas).

21. PSEUDOPHOENIX

This small genus is confined to the Caribbean and named because of its supposed resemblance to the date palm, *Phoenix*. The two genera are, however, not closely related. Stems are solitary, moderate or tall, often swollen and are smooth, gray, or white-waxy. Leaves are pinnate, 10–20 in number, and form a rather open crown. Sheaths are gray-green and somewhat waxy and form a short, open, and somewhat swollen crown shaft. The linear leaflets are glaucous and are irregularly arranged and spread in different planes, thus giving the leaf a plumose appearance. The large inflorescences are borne among the leaves and are branched to five orders. The flowers are bisexual on the basal parts of the flowering branches, but male flowers only are found on the upper parts. Flowers and fruits are borne on short stalks and this is one of the distinguishing features of the genus. Fruits are one- to three-seeded, globose or lobed, red, and almost always have the persistent sepals and petals present at the base. The endosperm is homogeneous and the seedling leaf is simple and narrowly linear.

Pseudophoenix contains four species (Read, 1968, 1969) distributed in the Caribbean islands and adjacent to Mexico and United States. They often grow near the sea on sandy or calcareous soils but can also grow inland on dry hillsides.

This very distinctive genus is only likely to be confused in the wild with *Roystonea* and *Gaussia*. It differs from the former by its smaller size, less well-developed, gray-green, waxy crown shaft, much-branched inflorescences, and stalked flowers and fruits with persistent sepals and petals; and from the latter by its stalked flowers and fruits.

Pseudophoenix ekmanii
(Map 93)
"Cacheo" (DR)
Field characters. Stems solitary, swollen, 4–6 m tall and 20(–80) cm diameter. Leaflets with brown scales on the lower surface. Inflorescences pendulous; *flower and fruit stalks slender, more than 5 mm long;* fruits globose (or 2–3-lobed), 1.8–2.2 cm diameter, reddish.
Range and habitat. Barahona Peninsula of the Dominican Republic; dry, open hillsides on calcareous soils.

Uses. It was formerly much used as a source of palm wine. The stems were cut down and the pith removed, especially from the swollen part and the sap squeezed out and fermented.

Pseudophoenix lediniana
(Map 94, Plate 11)
"Pal," "ti palmis maron" (Hai)
Field characters. Stems solitary, 10–20 m tall and to 30 cm diameter, columnar or slightly swollen at the base, *white waxy with prominent rings.* Leaflets lacking brown scales on lower

surface. Inflorescences pendulous; *flowers and fruits on stalks less than 4 mm long*; fruits globose or lobed, about 1.8 cm diameter, reddish.

Range and habitat. Southwestern peninsula of Haiti (L'Ouest); known only from the steep sides of one river valley in a dry region. It is rare in the wild (Henderson et al., 1990).

Uses. The fruits are collected and fed to domestic animals.

Pseudophoenix sargentii
(Map 95)
"Palma de guinea" (Cub), "cacheo" (DR), "kuká" (Mex), "cherry palm" (USA)

Field characters. Stems solitary, columnar, or slightly swollen, 4–8 m tall and to 30 cm diameter, *gray. Leaflets with brown scales on lower surface.* Inflorescences either erect or arching; fruits globose or 2–3-lobed, 1.2–1.7 cm diameter, red.

Range and habitat. United States (Florida), Bahamas, Belize, Cuba, Hispaniola (Dominican Republic, Haiti), Mexico (Quintana Roo), and Dominica (Read, 1969); near the sea on well-drained, sandy, or limestone soils. It is one of the few salt-tolerant palms (Quero, 1981).

Uses. It is occasionally planted as an ornamental.

Notes. Read (1968) recognized two subspecies and three varieties: subsp. *sargentii*, with inflo-rescences 0.7–1.2 m long, from Florida, Mexico, and Belize; and subsp. *saonae*, with inflorescences 0.9–1.7 m long, from the Bahamas, Hispaniola, and Cuba. This latter subspecies was further divided into two varieties: var. *saonae*, with the leaves gray-green on lower surface and fruits less than 1.5 cm diameter, from the Bahamas, Hispaniola, and Cuba; and var. *navassana*, with the leaves white or silvery on lower surface and fruits more than 1.5 cm diameter, from Navassa Island (off the western peninsula of Haiti).

Durán and Franco (1992) studied demography of subsp. *sargentii* in Mexico.

Pseudophoenix vinifera
(Map 96, Plate 12)
"Cacheo" (DR), "katié" (Hai)

Field characters. Stems solitary, large and *markedly swollen*, 7–25 m tall and 30–40 cm diameter (more at swelling), gray. *Leaflets with brown scales on lower surface.* Inflorescences pendulous; fruits globose or 2–3-lobed, 2–2.5 cm diameter, reddish.

Range and habitat. Hispaniola (Dominican Republic, Haiti); dry, open hillsides.

Uses. The leaves are used for thatching and the fruits fed to domestic animals. This was formerly a source of palm wine which was extracted in the same way as from *Pseudophoenix ekmanii.*

22. CEROXYLON

This Andean genus contains some of the most spectacular American palms, and a mountain slope covered with *Ceroxylon* is an unforgettable sight. The genus also contains some of the tallest palms in the world and those growing at the highest elevations. Stems are solitary, slender or stout, and those of *Ceroxylon quindiuense* can reach 60 m tall. They are usually marked with oblique rings, leaf scars, and covered with a more or less thick layer of wax that often gives the trunk a white appearance. The name *Ceroxylon* refers to this covering of wax and comes from the Greek words "keros," meaning wax, and "xylon," meaning wood. Leaves are pinnate, 5–30 in number, and often form an almost circular crown. Leaflets vary from regularly arranged and spreading in the same plane to irregularly arranged in clusters and spreading in different planes. Leaflets are linear, leathery, sometimes plicate, and variously tomentose on the lower surface. Plants are unisexual and bear inflorescences with either male or female flowers, but not both. The large, curved inflorescences are branched to several orders and are borne among the leaves. They are often conspicuous because they project well below the leaves, and several are usually present at the same time. Peduncular bracts are several and are covered in woolly tomentum, like the peduncle. Flowering branches commonly have a zigzag appearance and bear small, solitary, unisexual flowers. Male and female flowers are similar; males have 6–18 stamens. Fruits are one-seeded, globose, small, red to orange-red, and either smooth, warty, or tuberculate. Seeds have homogeneous endosperm and the seedling leaf is simple and whitish on the lower surface.

Ceroxylon contains eleven species, distributed throughout the Andes, from Venezuela and Colombia to Ecuador, Peru, and Bolivia. They grow in areas of high rainfall, in montane rain forest, usually above 2000 m elevation, less commonly in premontane forest between 800 and 2000 m elevation. Some species form large stands in relatively restricted areas, others have scattered populations in a wide range.

Ceroxylon is a very interesting genus, both phylogenetically and geographically. It is restricted to the Andes and is the terminal and most speciose genus in a chain of genera stretching from Madagascar (*Ravenea*), Australia (*Oraniopsis*), and the Juan Fernández Islands (*Juania*) to the Andes. An understanding of the relations among these genera and other trans-Pacific patterns would help solve one of the enigmas in the biogeography of palms.

Ceroxylon alpinum
(Map 97)
"Palma de cera" (Col), "palma de ramo," "palma real" (Ecu)
Field characters. Stems 8–20(–30) m tall and about 20 cm diameter, gray-brownish to whitish, covered with a thin layer of wax. Leaves 14–25, horizontally spreading, forming an almost circular crown; leaflets 94–130 per side, *regularly arranged and horizontally spreading in the same plane, the apical ones sometimes joined,* the lower surface with a thick yellowish to whitish tomentum. Fruits globose, 1.6–2 cm diameter, orange-red, *conspicuously pebbled.*
Range and habitat. Patchily distributed on the northwestern slopes of the Cordillera de la Costa in Venezuela (Distrito Federal) and Cordillera de Mérida (Táchira), western and eastern slopes of the Cordillera Occidental and Central in Colombia (Antioquia, Caldas, Quindío, Valle), and western slopes of the Cordillera Oriental (Cundinamarca) in Colombia and the northwestern slopes of the Central Cordillera in Ecuador (Pichincha); montane rain forest, at 1400–1800(–2000) m elevation.
Uses. The young leaves are cut for use on Palm Sunday; the trunks are used for fences or house walls; and fruits are used to feed pigs.
Notes. Two subspecies are recognized (Galeano, in press): subsp. *alpinum* in Colombia and Venezuela and subsp. *ecuadorense* in Ecuador. They are separated on the basis of differences in male flowers. The habitat of this species has been extensively deforested and transformed into agricultural land, mainly coffee plantations. Because of this the survival of the species is severely threatened. Fruiting season in Colombia seems to be in March and April of every other year.

Ceroxylon amazonicum
(Map 98)
"Ramo" (Ecu)

Field characters. Stems 8–12 m tall and 20–25 cm diameter, rarely taller, grayish to whitish, with a thin layer of wax. Leaves 14–22, forming an almost circular crown; leaflets 99–106 per side, *regularly arranged and horizontally spreading in the same plane,* but the apical ones appearing in a vertical position because of bending of the leaf rachis, the lower surface with a rather thin whitish or yellowish tomentum. Fruits globose, 1.7–2 cm diameter, orange-red, smooth.
Range and habitat. Southeastern Ecuador (Morona-Santiago, Zamora-Chinchipe), on the eastern slopes of the Andes; premontane or lower montane rain forest, at 820–1200 m elevation. It occurs at the lowest elevation of any *Ceroxylon* and grows with other low to mid-elevation palms such as *Iriartea deltoidea, Wettinia maynensis,* and *Oenocarpus bataua.*

Ceroxylon ceriferum
(Map 99)
"Palma de cera" (Col), "ramo bendito" (Ven)
Field characters. Stems 10–25 m tall and 25–30 cm diameter, grayish brown to whitish, covered with a rather thin layer of wax. Leaves 8–20, horizontal or ascending and curved; leaflets 100–116 per side, *regularly arranged and spreading in the same plane,* horizontal at base, in a vertical position toward the top due to the bending of the leaf rachis, rigid, on the lower surface with a rather thick yellowish to brownish tomentum. Fruits globose, 1.5–1.8 cm diameter, orange-red, *minutely but densely granulose or pebbled.*
Range and habitat. South-facing slopes of the Cordillera de la Costa and Cordillera de Mérida in Venezuela (Aragua, Distrito Federal, Táchira), Serranía de Perijá along the Colombian-Venezuelan frontier, and the Sierra Nevada de Santa Marta in Colombia (Guajira, Magdalena); montane rain forest, at 2000–2800 m elevation.

Uses. The young leaves are cut for Palm Sunday.
Notes. Sometimes forming large stands of hundreds of palms. Ripe fruits are eaten by the military macaw (*Ara militaris*) and other species of macaws (Burret, 1929a). Braun (1976) discussed flowering and fruiting, germination, and leaf development of this species in Venezuela.

Ceroxylon echinulatum
(Map 100)
"Palma real," "pumbo" (Ecu)
Field characters. Stems 12–20 m tall and 25–30 cm diameter, greenish to whitish, with a thin layer of wax. Leaves 8–17, forming an almost circular crown; leaflets 91–102 per side, *regularly arranged and spreading in the same plane, completely pendulous*, sometimes the apical ones joined at the tips, the lower surface with a very thick whitish or yellowish tomentum. Fruits globose, about 2 cm diameter, orange-red, *conspicuously and densely covered with short blunt spines*.
Range and habitat. Eastern or rarely western slopes of the Andes in Ecuador (El Oro, Napo, Zamora-Chinchipe); montane rain forest, at 1800–1920 m elevation.
Uses. The stems are used as fences or in house construction; young leaves are cut for use on Palm Sunday; and the fruits are used to feed pigs. The basal portion of the peduncle is boiled and used in salads.
Notes. Large and dense stands with thousands of palms are still common in forest, or conserved in pastures.

Ceroxylon parvifrons
(Map 101, Plate 12)
"Palma ramo," "palma real," "ramo" (Col, Ecu)
Field characters. Stems 4–15 m tall and 8–21 cm diameter, grayish to grayish brown, sometimes green toward the top, with a very thin layer of wax. Leaves 5–17, *ascending and conspicuously arched*; leaflets 40–84 per side, *regularly arranged, ascending, and very rigid and plicate*, the lower surface with a yellowish to brownish tomentum. Fruits globose, 1.5–2.5 cm diameter, orange-red to bright red, smooth.
Range and habitat. Widespread throughout the Andes of Colombia (Antioquia, Cauca, Huila, Nariño, Norte de Santander, Putumayo, Quindío, Tolima, Valle), Venezuela (Mérida), Ecuador (Azuay, Loja, Pichincha, Zamora-Chinchipe), Peru (Amazonas), and Bolivia (La Paz); montane rain forest, at 2000–3150 m elevation but most common above 2600 m.
Uses. The young leaves are cut for Palm Sunday.
Notes. Often found with *Geonoma weberbaueri*; both grow at the highest elevation of any palm

in the world. Probably occurring throughout Peru but not yet collected.

Ceroxylon parvum
(Map 102)
"Palma amarilla," "vicuña palmito" (Bol)
Field characters. Stems 2.5–10 m tall and 9–17 cm diameter, greenish to grayish, with a very thin layer of wax. Leaves 11–20, *horizontal and arched, forming a circular crown*; leaflets 96–120 per side, *irregularly arranged and spreading in different planes, pendulous at the tips*, usually less than 3 cm wide (the narrowest in the genus), with a very thin, whitish tomentum on the lower surface. Fruits globose, 1.2–1.8 cm diameter, orange-red, smooth.
Range and habitat. Andean slopes in Ecuador (Loja), Peru (Cuzco), and Bolivia (La Paz, Santa Cruz); montane rain forest, but now mostly in forest remnants or open pastures, at 1400–1780 m elevation.
Uses. The stems are used for house construction; and the leaves are used for thatching and as forage for cattle.
Notes. This is the smallest species in the genus.

Ceroxylon quindiuense
(Map 103, Plate 12)
"Palma de cera" (Col)
Field characters. Stems 15–50 m tall (rarely to 60 m) and 20–40 cm diameter, silvery white with a thick layer of wax, at least in adults. Leaves 18–30, horizontally spreading, forming an almost circular crown (in young trees the leaves ascending); leaflets 70–110 per side, *regularly arranged and spreading in the same plane*, pendulous, the lower surface with a whitish or yellowish, thick and woolly tomentum. Fruits globose, 1.7–1.9 cm diameter, orange-red to bright red, smooth.
Range and habitat. Colombia, eastern and western slopes of the Cordillera Central (Antioquia, Quindío, Risaralda, Tolima), western slopes of the Cordillera Occidental (Valle), and eastern slopes of Cordillera Oriental (Cundinamarca, Norte de Santander, Putumayo); montane rain forest, at 2000–3000 m elevation.
Uses. The young leaves are cut for Palm Sunday; and stems are used for fences and for house walls. It is also cultivated in parks in Bogotá. The extraction of the wax that covers the stem was an important economic activity in the Quindío region in the nineteenth century. The wax was used to make candles that were sold in town markets. In order to scrape the wax the palms were climbed, or more frequently the taller palms were cut down, which destroyed hundreds of palms.
Notes. This is the most famous species in the

genus and is the national tree of Colombia. Large populations of massive palms, some of them reaching 60 m tall, became a legend to European explorers in the Andes of Colombia in the nineteenth century. The large remaining stands are still one of the wonders of the world. Ripe fruits are eaten by jays (*Cyanocorax yncas*), thrushes (*Turdus fuscater*) and toucanets (*Aulacorhynchus prasinus*) and by the rare and endangered yellow-eared parrot (*Ognorhynchus icterotis*). The fleshy palm heart is eaten by the spectacled bear (*Tremarctos ornatus*), which can climb the smaller trunks.

Ceroxylon sasaimae
(Map 104)
"Palma de ramo," "palma real" (Col)
Field characters. Stems 8–15(–20) m tall and 20–30 cm diameter, brownish to grayish, with a very thin layer of wax. Leaves about 15, horizontally spreading in a *dense crown*; leaflets 93–110 per side, *rigid, irregularly arranged in clusters and spreading in different planes,* with a rather dense tomentum on lower surface. Fruits globose, 1.5–1.8 cm diameter, orange-red, smooth.
Range and habitat. Western slope of the Cordillera Oriental in Colombia (Cundinamarca); montane rain forest, at 1400–1800 m elevation.
Uses. The young leaves are cut for Palm Sunday.
Notes. A poorly known species, from a very small area, where the only known population survives in coffee plantations.

Ceroxylon ventricosum
(Map 105, Plate 13)
"Palma de cera" (Col), "palma real," "palma de tambán" (Ecu)
Field characters. Stems stout and massive, to 30 m tall and 35–42 cm diameter, completely silvery white with a thick layer of wax. Leaves 12–20, *horizontally spreading;* leaflets 120–160 per side, *more or less pendulous, the middle ones irregularly arranged and spreading in slightly different planes, the basal and apical ones regularly arranged and spreading in the same plane,* the lower surface with a rather thin, whitish tomentum. Fruits globose, 1.5–1.8 cm diameter, orange-red, smooth.
Range and habitat. Western slopes of the Cordillera Central and Oriental in southwestern Colombia (Cauca, Nariño, Putumayo) to southern Ecuador (Bolívar, Carchi, Cotopaxi, Zamora-Chinchipe); montane rain forest or in forest remnants or pastures, on slopes at 2000–3000 m elevation but most common above 2500 m.
Uses. The stems are used for house construction

and for fences. In Ecuador the fruits are used to feed pigs and in the fruiting season pigs are let free to feed in the forest. The palms are thus somewhat protected. It is cultivated in parks in Quito.
Notes. Sometimes forming large stands of thousands of individuals. At first sight it may easily be mistaken for *Ceroxylon quindiuense,* but the leaves of *C. ventricosum* have a somewhat plumose appearance because of the clustered middle leaflets; and the ranges of the 2 species apparently do not overlap.

Ceroxylon vogelianum
(Map 106)
"Palma de ramo," "palma negra" (Col)
Field characters. Stems 3–13 m tall and 10–20 cm diameter, sometimes bending at the top, green, yellowish green to brownish, clean or usually covered with a very thin layer of wax. Leaves 6–15, *markedly plumose and curved,* forming an almost circular crown with a ragged appearance; leaflets 70–110 per side, *irregularly arranged in clusters and spreading in different planes, with pendulous tips,* the lower surface with a very thin, whitish to yellowish, rarely brownish, tomentum. Fruits globose, 1.5–1.8 cm diameter, red to orange-red, *with reticulate grooves.*
Range and habitat. Throughout the Andes in Colombia (Antioquia, Boyacá, Caquetá, Chocó, Huila, Norte de Santander, Putumayo, Risaralda, Santander), Venezuela (Lara, Táchira), Ecuador (Loja, Napo, Zamora-Chinchipe), Peru (Huánuco, Junín, Pasco), and Bolivia (Santa Cruz); montane rain forest, at 1900–3000 m elevation but most common above 2500 m.
Uses. The young leaves are cut for Palm Sunday; and the stems are used for house construction.
Notes. Although this is one of the most common palms throughout the high elevations of the Andes, large populations are rarely found; usually the palms are scattered on mountain ridges.

Ceroxylon weberbaueri
(Map 107)
Field characters. Stems 5–10 m tall, grayish, with a thin layer of wax. *Leaflets numerous, irregularly arranged in clusters but appearing almost regularly arranged,* the lower surface with whitish, thick tomentum. Fruits globose, about 1.5 cm diameter, red, *pebbled.*
Range and habitat. Eastern Andean slopes in Peru (Cuzco, Pasco); montane rain forest, at 1800–2000 m elevation.
Notes. This is a very poorly known species.

23. JUANIA

A genus of one species, named after its island home, the Juan Fernández Islands. Stems are solitary, of moderate height, and are greenish white with obvious leaf scars. Leaves are pinnate, 18–20 in number, stiffly arching, and covered in small scales. The leaf sheaths form an open, short crown shaft and the petiole is rather short. Leaflets are numerous, linear, and are regularly arranged and spread in the same plane. Inflorescences are branched to two orders and are borne among the leaves but arch out below them, especially when in fruit. There are several, somewhat woody, peduncular bracts. Individual plants are unisexual and bear either male or female flowers. Male flowers have six stamens and female flowers have three fused carpels. Fruits are one-seeded, globose, orange-red, and smooth. The endosperm is homogeneous and the seedling leaf is simple and linear.

This is a genus of one species (Moore, 1969a), confined to Masatierra in the Juan Fernández Islands. It is of great interest in being a member of a group of related genera which have a southern Pacific distribution track; see notes under *Ceroxylon*.

Juania australis
(Map 108, Plate 13)
"Chonta" (Chi)
Field characters. Stems solitary, to 15 m tall and 26 cm diameter, markedly ringed. Leaves arching; leaflets to 80 per side, regularly arranged and spreading in the same plane. Inflorescences borne among the leaves, with sev-

eral, woody bracts; fruits globose, 1.5–1.8 cm diameter, orange-red.
Range and habitat. Chile (Masatierra, Juan Fernández Islands); steep slopes and ridges in lowland rain forest, at 200–800 m elevation.
Notes. Even though it has a narrow distribution, it is apparently not threatened with extinction (Moore, 1969a; Stuessy et al., 1983).

24. GAUSSIA

A small Caribbean genus, named in honor of the German astronomer and mathematician Carl Friedrich Gauss (1777–1855). Stems are always solitary, grayish white, of medium height, usually leaning, and often swollen at the base and tapered toward the top. This swollen base is developed even in seedlings. An unusual feature of the genus is that the stout roots are often visible and form a small cone at the base of the stem. Leaves are pinnate, 3–10 in number, and form an open crown; in some species they are arranged almost in one plane. The leaf sheaths form a short, open crownshaft. The leaflets are usually regularly arranged in two rows along each side of the rachis but usually spread in different planes, giving the leaves a plumose appearance. The leaflets are slightly swollen at the point of insertion with the rachis. Inflorescences are branched to two or three orders, are borne among the leaves and often arch beyond them, and, like other ceroxyloid palms, have numerous peduncular bracts. Male and female flowers are present on the same inflorescence, but are arranged in an unusual manner. There are short rows of flowers, of which the lowest one is female and the rest male. Fruits are 1–3-seeded, globose or lobed, usually red, and have basal stigmatic remains. The endosperm is homogeneous but the shape of the seedling leaf is not recorded.

This is a genus of five species distributed in the western Caribbean region (Quero and Read, 1986; Moya et al., 1991).

Gaussia attenuata
(Map 109, Plate 13)
"Palma de sierra" (PR)

Field characters. Stems gray, swollen at the base, and gradually tapering toward the top, to 15 m tall and 15–25 cm diameter. Leaves 5–7, spirally arranged; leaflets linear, 2.5–4 cm wide, very closely spaced and spreading almost in the same plane or in somewhat different planes. Inflorescences branched to two orders, exserted well beyond the leaves; fruits globose or lobed, 1(–3)-seeded, 1.4–1.6 cm long and about 1.2 cm diameter, orange-red.

Range and habitat. Puerto Rico; on steep-sided, extremely well-drained limestone hills (*mogotes*) in areas of strongly seasonal rainfall.

Notes. Henderson (1984b) has described the habitat of this palm in Puerto Rico.

Gaussia gomez-pompae
(Map 110)

Field characters. Stems almost columnar, 10–14 m tall and to 30 cm diameter. Leaves to 10, spirally arranged; leaflets linear-lanceolate, 4–4.6 cm wide, regularly arranged and spreading in different planes. Inflorescences branched to two orders; fruits globose, 1.5–1.6 cm diameter, orange-red.

Range and habitat. Mexico (Oaxaca, Tabasco, Veracruz); forest in steep, rocky places on limestone soils.

Gaussia maya
(Map 111)
"Palmasito" (Bel), "cambo," "palma cimarrona" (Mex)

Field characters. Stems almost columnar, often leaning, 5–20 m tall and 10–15(–30) cm diameter, gray. Leaves 6–8, spirally arranged; leaflets linear-lanceolate, 3–4 cm wide, regularly arranged in 4 ranks along the rachis, but spreading in different planes. Inflorescences branched 1–2 orders; fruits globose or bilobed, 1–1.5 cm diameter, bright red.

Range and habitat. Mexico (Quintana Roo), Guatemala (Petén), and Belize; forest in rocky places on limestone soils, at low elevations.

Uses. The long-lasting stems are used for construction.

Gaussia princeps
(Map 112, Plate 14)
"Palma de sierra" (Cub)

Field characters. Stems whitish, *markedly swollen at the base, gradually tapering toward the top*, to 8 m or more tall and 30 cm diameter at the swelling. Leaves 3–6, arranged almost in one plane; leaflets linear-lanceolate, less than 4 cm wide, regularly arranged but spreading in different planes. Inflorescences branched to 2 orders, erect, and exserted well beyond the leaves; fruits obovoid, 1(–3)-seeded, to 1 cm long and 7 mm diameter, orange-red.

Range and habitat. Cuba (Pinar del Río); on steep-sided, extremely well-drained limestone hills (*mogotes*) in areas of strongly seasonal rainfall.

Notes. This species, growing with the palmate-leaved *Thrinax morrisi*, occurs in a remarkable habitat for a palm, where it can hardly be mistaken for any other species.

Gaussia spirituana
(Map 113)

Field characters. Stems whitish, *markedly swollen at the base, gradually tapering toward the top*, to 7 m tall and 30–35 cm diameter at the swelling. Leaves 5–6; leaflets linear-lanceolate, more than 4 cm wide, regularly arranged but spreading in different planes. Inflorescences branched to 2 orders, erect, and exserted well above the leaves; fruits globose, to 1 cm diameter, orange-red.

Range and habitat. Central Cuba (Sancti Spiritus, Sierra de Jatibonico); on steep-sided, extremely well-drained limestone hills (*mogotes*), at 200 m elevation, in areas of strongly seasonal rainfall.

Notes. Similar to the other Cuban species, *Gaussia princeps*, but differing in its broader leaflets and smaller fruits.

25. SYNECHANTHUS

This genus contains two species of small understory palms. Stems are solitary or clustered, smooth, green, and markedly ringed. Leaves are pinnate, or sometimes simple, to twelve in number and completely smooth. The leaf sheaths are open but form a short green crownshaft. Leaflets are few to numerous and are regularly or irregularly arranged and often of unequal width. Inflorescences are borne among or below the leaves, are branched to one or two orders, and are enclosed in bud by 5–6 papery peduncular bracts. The peduncle is long and bears numerous, very slender, yellowish flowering branches, with the proximal ones branched again. The shape of the inflorescence, with elongate peduncle and erect flowering branches, is very distinctive and reminiscent of a broom. The flowers are small and arranged in rows of 6–14, the basal one of each row female, the others male. These rows of flowers alternate on opposite sides of the flowering branches. The origin of the generic name comes from this arrangement, from the Greek words "synechos," meaning together, and "anthos," meaning a flower. Male flowers have either three or six stamens. Fruits are one-seeded, ellipsoid to globose, small, bright red at maturity, and have a fleshy mesocarp. The seed separates easily from the mesocarp, is brown, ellipsoid to globose, and grooved like a brain. The endosperm is homogeneous to deeply ruminate and the seedling leaf is bifid.

Synechanthus contains two species (Moore, 1971), distributed throughout the Central American region from southern Mexico to western Ecuador, in wet forest from sea level to 1200 m elevation. The ranges of both species, one in the north and the other in the south, scarcely overlap in eastern Costa Rica and southeastern Nicaragua. This genus can be mistaken for the more common and closely related *Chamaedorea*, which differs in its flower arrangements. Furthermore, species of *Chamaedorea* often have a yellowish line along the undersurface of the petiole, do not have the extremely fleshy fruit with easily separating seed, and also lack the grooved, brainlike seed of *Synechanthus*.

Synechanthus fibrosus
(Map 114)
"Monkey-tail palm" (Bel), "corocilla" (Hon)
Field characters. Stems solitary, to 6 m tall and 2–3 cm diameter, aerial or sometimes short and subterranean. Leaves to 12, pinnate, to 1.5 m long; *leaflets 10–23 per side, arranged in groups of 2–6,* spreading in slightly different planes, all leaflets (except apical ones) with one principal vein. Inflorescences borne among the leaves, to 1 m long, with a very long peduncle and numerous flowering branches, *the basal ones branched*; fruits globose to ellipsoid, 1.4–2.1 cm long; *seed with homogeneous or slightly ruminate endosperm.*
Range and habitat. Atlantic slope of southern Mexico (Chiapas, Oaxaca, Veracruz), Belize, Guatemala (Alta Verapaz, Izabal), Honduras (Atlántida, Olancho, Yoro), Nicaragua, and eastern Costa Rica (Cartago, Limón); lowland to montane rain forest, from sea level to 1200 m elevation.
Notes. It has become increasingly popular as an ornamental in the last decades.

Synechanthus warscewiczianus
(Map 115, Plate 14)
"Palmilla" (Col, Pan)
Field characters. Stems clustered, to 6 m tall and 5 cm diameter, or sometimes a single stem and several basal shoots. Leaves to 10, to 2 m long, *simple or regularly or irregularly divided into 2–31, one-veined or several-veined leaflets, broad several-veined leaflets often intermixed with narrow, one-veined ones.* Inflorescences to 1 m long, with a long peduncle and numerous, *unbranched* flowering branches; fruits almost globose to ellipsoid, 1.5–3.2 cm long; *seeds with deeply ruminate endosperm.*
Range and habitat. Nicaragua (Zelaya), Costa Rica (Cartago, Heredia, Limón, Puntarenas), Panama (Canal Area, Darién, Panamá, San Blas, Veraguas), and the Pacific lowlands of Colombia (Antioquia, Cauca, Chocó, Valle), and western Ecuador (Esmeraldas); lowland to montane rain forest, from sea level to 1200 m elevation.

26. CHAMAEDOREA

This large, predominantly Central American genus contains some of the most commonly cultivated ornamental palms. Stems are green, with prominent nodes, usually solitary or less often clustered, and seldom exceed 3 m in height. Indeed, the derivation of the name comes from a combination of Greek words meaning "gift from the ground," presumably a reference to the small size of most species. Leaves are very variable and can be either simple or pinnate. Simple leaves are bifid and often have toothed margins. Unlike perhaps almost all other New World palms, leaves of *Chamaedorea* are usually smooth and not tomentose or scaly. Inflorescences are very variable; they can be spicate or branched to one or two orders, and although usually solitary they can be multiple with up to eight inflorescences at each node. Several papery peduncular bracts are present and this, together with the smooth leaves, distinguishes *Chamaedorea* from other understory palms (e.g., *Geonoma, Hyospathe*). Plants bear either male or female flowers, but not both. Flower arrangement is variable, either solitary, in short lines, or very close and sometimes joined one to another. Male flower structure is also variable, and in one group of species the petals are joined at tips and there joined to the top of the pistillode and the flowers open by lateral slits. Fruits are one-seeded, globose, or variously ovoid or ellipsoid, small, black, or red, and in some species are densely crowded on the flowering branches. In one group of species the thickened petals are persistent on the fruits. The endosperm is homogeneous and seedling leaf is usually bifid or, in a few species pinnate.

Chamaedorea is the largest genus of palms in the Americas. As treated here it contains seventy-seven species, most of them in rain forest in mountainous regions of Central America. Hodel (1992a), who recognized ninety-six species, has provided an excellent illustrated treatment of the genus. Subsequently Hodel (1992b) recognized four more species. Our treatment is based on Hodel's work and differs only in details of ranking. The taxonomy of *Chamaedorea* has been greatly influenced by the work of horticulturalists and we tend to recognize fewer species. Hybrids are commonly formed in cultivation and presumably exist in the wild.

Chamaedorea is the terminal and most speciose genus in a chain of related genera. This starts in the Mascarene Islands, in the Indian Ocean, with *Hyophorbe* and continues with *Wendlandiella* in South America, *Synechanthus* in South and Central America, and *Chamaedorea* in Central America.

An interesting phenomenon occurs in the petals of the male flowers. In one group of species these are joined at the tips and also joined to the top of the pistillode. These flowers open by lateral slits between the petals. Because of this character, these species have been grouped in subgenus *Chamaedorea*. Most species in this subgenus have a counterpart in subgenus *Chamaedoreopsis*, characterized by the male flowers with free petals that open normally. In most cases the species of each pair occur together, and some of them are so strikingly similar to each other that it is hard to believe that they are truly distinct species and do not just represent a variation in the degree of spreading of the petals. Examples of these species pairs include the following: *C. amabilis–C. sullivaniorum, C. palmeriana–C. pumila, C. parvifolia–C. pittieri, C. pinnatifrons–C. oblongata, C. glaucifolia–C. plumosa, C. geonomiformis–C. rigida, C. graminifolia–C. seifrizii, C. liebmannii-C. whitelockiana*, and *C. rojasiana–C. dammeriana*. Only a few species with joined petals do not have a counterpart with free petals; this group includes *C. warscewiczii* and two of the most distinctive species in the genus, *C. elatior* with climbing stems and *C. klotzschiana* with clustered leaflets.

Another remarkable feature of the genus is that so many species are solitary stemmed. In the other large, understory genera of American palms, for example *Geonoma* and *Bactris*, almost all species have clustered stems.

Some species are becoming rare in the wild because collectors dig up plants of the more desirable species. A further danger to wild populations is the collection of leaves for the cut-flower business.

Positive identification of *Chamaedorea* species often requires information on inflorescence and flower structure. This is not always available because plants bear either male of female flowers. Thus we have tried to make the key as independent from these characters as possible, but floral information is still required at some places in the key. Nevertheless, if floral information is unavailable, it is still possible to proceed by trying both entries in the key. In most cases there will be fewer than ten species to choose from, and even some of these can be discarded using additional information provided in the key. Finally there will be only a few species to be compared in the text and in the maps. Measurements of leaflets are from those on the middle or lower part of the rachis. Note also that many species appear twice or more times in the key, either because they are variable and/or because they occur in more than one region.

KEY TO THE SPECIES OF CHAMAEDOREA

1a. Central America.
  2a. Mexico, Guatemala, Belize, El Salvador.
    3a. Stems solitary.
      4a. Leaves simple, the blades bifid.
        5a. Blade only very briefly bifid, 12–22 cm long   . . . . . *C. tuerckheimii.*
        5b. Blade bifid to one-third their length or more, more than 22 cm long.
          6a. Blade leathery, rigid.
            7a. Leaves with metallic-blue sheen   . . . . . *C. metallica.*
            7b. Leaves without metallic-blue sheen.
              8a. Leaves with a velvety aspect, blue-gray-green in color; female inflorescences spicate   . . . . . *C. adscendens.*
              8b. Leaves not velvety, green; female inflorescences with 3–5 flowering branches   . . . . . *C. rigida.*
          6b. Blade rather thin.
            9a. Blade obscurely nerved, usually oblong   . . . . . *C. geonomiformis.*
            9b. Blade obviously nerved, usually obovate.
              10a. Blade with 11–18 primary veins per side.
                11a. Blade with 11–13 primary veins per side; male inflorescences spicate; flowers whitish   . . . . . *C. castillo-montii.*
                11b. Blade with 12–18 primary veins per side; male inflorescences branched; flowers yellow to orange.
                  12a. Female inflorescences spicate (rarely with 2–4 branches)   . . . . . *C. ernesti-augustii.*
                  12b. Female inflorescences with 2–4 flowering branches   . . . . . *C. stricta.*
              10b. Blade with 6–10 primary veins per side.
                13a. Male flowers with petals joined at tips and there joined to the pistillode, the flowers opening by lateral slits.
                  14a. Female inflorescences spicate   . . . . . *C. simplex.*
                  14b. Female inflorescences with 2–15 flowering branches (rarely spicate).
                    15a. Blade with 7 primary veins per side . . . . *C. rojasiana.*
                    15b. Blade with 10 primary veins per side   . . . . . *C. pinnatifrons.*
              13b. Male flowers with petals free at tips.
                16a. Male flowering branches erect or spreading; female inflorescences spicate or bifurcate; fruiting perianth bright orange; Mexico   . . . . . *C. queroana.*

16b. Male flowering branches pendulous; female
inflorescences with 1–5 flowering branches;
fruiting perianth brownish; Guatemala

..... *C. volcanensis.*

4b. Leaves pinnate.

17a. Climbing palms; apical leaflets progressively reduced and
pointing backwards ..... *C. elatior.*

17b. Nonclimbing palms; apical leaflets not reduced.

18a. Leaflets 2–10 per side.

19a. Leaf rachis 50 cm or more long.

20a. Leaflets less than 2.5 cm wide ..... *C. radicalis.*

20b. Leaflets more than 2.5 cm wide.

21a. Female inflorescences spicate or bifurcate.

22a. Male inflorescences multiple at each node,
spicate ..... *C. nationsiana.*

22b. Male inflorescences solitary at each node,
with 2–13 flowering branches.

23a. Male flowers densely crowded, touching
one another ..... *C. arenbergiana.*

23b. Male flowers very dense but not touching
one another ..... *C. volcanensis.*

21b. Female inflorescences with 3–20 flowering
branches.

24a. Male flowers ± densely arranged on the flowering branches.

25a. Leaflets 8–12 per side ..... *C. volcanensis.*

25b. Leaflets usually 12–25 per side (rarely as
few as 6) ..... *C. tepejilote.*

24b. Male flowers loosely arranged on the flowering branches.

26a. Leaf sheath apex white; leaflets thin

..... *C. pinnatifrons.*

26b. Leaf sheath apex green; leaflets rather
thick. ..... *C. oblongata.*

19b. Leaf rachis less than 50 cm long.

27a. Leaves with metallic-blue sheen ..... *C. metallica.*

27b. Leaves without metallic-blue sheen.

28a. Leaf rachis to 20 cm long.

29a. Leaflets backwards pointing, the apical pair
with toothed margins ..... *C. tenerrima.*

29b. Leaflets not backwards pointing, the apical
pair not toothed.

30a. Female inflorescences with 1–5 flowering
branches.

31a. Leaflets with a velvety aspect, leathery,
blue-gray-green ..... *C. adscendens.*

31b. Leaflets rather thin, not leathery or velvety, green.

32a. Apical leaflets very wide, at least
twice as broad as the others combined.
   33a. Male flowers with petals free at
      the tips; growing at 600–1000 m el-
      evation   ..... *C. castillomontii.*
   33b. Male flowers with petals joined at
      the tips and there joined to the pis-
      tillode, flowers opening by lateral
      slits; growing at 1200–2600 m eleva-
      tion   ..... *C. rojasiana.*
32b. Apical leaflets not considerably wider
than the others.
   34a. Stems very short, appearing al-
      most stemless.
      35a. Leaflets to 2 cm wide, rather
         obscurely nerved, often attached
         at right angles to the rachis
             ..... *C. pachecoana.*
      35b. Leaflets 3 cm wide or more,
         conspicuously nerved, normally
         attached   ..... *C. queroana.*
   34b. Stems well developed, upright.
      36a. Leaf sheath tubular; leaves ar-
         ranged in several planes.
         37a. Fruiting peduncle and flow-
            ering branches very thin and
            pendulous   ..... *C. fractiflexa.*
         37b. Fruiting peduncle and flow-
            ering branches not very thin
            ..... *C. whitelockiana.*
      36b. Leaf sheath almost completely
         open; leaves arranged in 3 planes
            ..... *C. lehmannii.*
30b. Female inflorescences with 6–20 flowering
branches.
   38a. Leaflets somewhat thick and leathery;
      top of leaf sheath green; male flowers
      with petals free at the tips   ..... *C. oblongata.*
   38b. Leaflets rather thin; top of leaf sheath
      white; male flowers with petals joined at
      the tips, and there joined to the pis-
      tillode, the flowers opening by lateral slits
         ..... *C. pinnatifrons.*
28b. Leaf rachis 20–50 cm long.
   39a. Leaves with metallic-blue sheen   ..... *C. metallica.*
   39b. Leaves without metallic-blue sheen.
      40a. Female inflorescences with 6 or more flow-
         ering branches.

41a. Petals of male flowers joined at the tips
and there joined to the pistillode, the
flowers opening by lateral slits ..... *C. pinnatifrons.*
41b. Petals of male flowers free.
  42a. Female flowers with bright orange
  petals   ..... *C. sartorii.*
  42b. Female flowers with green or greenish yellow petals.
    43a. Fruits reddish   ..... *C. radicalis.*
    43b. Fruits black.
      44a. Leaflets somewhat thick and
      leathery   ..... *C. oblongata.*
      44b. Leaflets thin, not leathery.
        45a. Male flowering branches
        pendulous; female flowering
        branches thick, with blunt
        tips   ..... *C. parvisecta.*
        45b. Male flowering branches
        erect; female flowering
        branches slender, spinose
        tipped   ..... *C. whitelockiana.*
40b. Female inflorescences with 1–5 flowering
branches.
  46a. Leaflets to 2.5 cm wide.
    47a. Fruits reddish   ..... *C. radicalis.*
    47b. Fruits black.
      48a. Leaflets leathery, dark gray-green
                     ..... *C. pittieri.*
      48b. Leaflets rather thin; leaves ar-
      ranged in three planes   ..... *C. lehmannii.*
  46b. Leaflets more than 2.5 cm wide.
    49a. Petals of female flowers orange ..... *C. sartorii.*
    49b. Petals of female flowers green or
    greenish.
      50a. Petals of male flowers joined at
      the tips and there joined to the pis-
      tillode, the flowers opening by lat-
      eral slits   ..... *C. pinnatifrons.*
      50b. Petals of male flowers free at the
      tips.
        51a. Leaf sheath tubular   ..... *C. parvisecta.*
        51b. Leaf sheath almost completely
        open.
          52a. Leaflets leathery, dark gray-
          green   ..... *C. pittieri.*
          52b. Leaflets rather thin.
            53a. Petiole minutely white
            spotted; male flowering
            branches erect or spread-

ing; female inflorescences
spicate or bifurcate;
fruiting perianth bright or-
ange; Mexico   . . . . . *C. queroana.*
   53b. Petiole not white spotted; male flowering
   branches pendulous; female inflorescences with
   1–5 flowering branches;
   fruiting perianth brownish;
   Guatemala   . . . . . *C. volcanensis.*
18b. Leaflets 10–100 per side.
  54a. Leaflets 10–20 per side.
    55a. Leaflets irregularly arranged in clusters   . . . . . *C. klotzschiana.*
    55b. Leaflets regularly arranged.
      56a. Leaf sheath, petiole, and rachis densely and min-
      utely white spotted or pitted   . . . . . *C. vulgata.*
      56b. Leaf sheath, petiole, and rachis not white spot-
      ted.
        57a. Leaflets to 2.5 cm wide.
          58a. Male and female inflorescences spicate
            . . . . . *C. oreophila.*
          58b. Male inflorescences with 2–35 flowering
          branches; female with 1–35 branches.
            59a. Female flowers green; males in linear
            groups of 2–5 near the base of the flow-
            ering branches; fruits reddish   . . . . . *C. radicalis.*
            59b. Female flowers yellow or greenish yel-
            low; males solitary; fruits black.
              60a. Female inflorescences spicate or bi-
              furcate; flowers of both sexes greenish
              yellow, with free petals   . . . . . *C. pachecoana.*
              60b. Female inflorescences with 5–35
              flowering branches; flowers of both
              sexes yellow, with joined petals.
                61a. Male flowers with petals joined al-
                most to the tips, the flowers open-
                ing by a terminal pore; growing
                mostly below 1400 m elevation . . . . . *C. elegans.*
                61b. Male flowers with petals joined at
                the tips, and there joined to the
                pistillode, the flowers opening by
                lateral slits; mostly growing above
                1200 m elevation   . . . . . *C. liebmannii.*
        57b. Leaflets more than 2.5 cm wide.
          62a. Petioles of young leaves covered with black
          tomentum   . . . . . *C. carchensis.*
          62b. Petioles of young leaves lacking black to-
          mentum.

63a. Male and female inflorescences spicate.
    64a. Guatemala   . . . . . *C. nationsiana.*
    64b. Mexico   . . . . . *C. oreophila.*
63b. Male and female inflorescences with 2–
    50 flowering branches.
    65a. Leaflets lanceolate to sigmoid, 2.5–
        12 cm wide.
        66a. Male flowers rather loosely ar-
           ranged, the petals joined at the
           tips, opening by lateral slits.
           67a. Leaflets 10–14 per side; Mex-
              ico (Oaxaca, Puebla, Veracruz)
                       . . . . . *C. schiedeana.*
           67b. Leaflets 2–8 per side; wide-
              spread   . . . . . *C. pinnatifrons.*
        66b. Male flowers densely crowded, the
           petals free at the tips   . . . . . *C. tepejilote.*
    65b. Leaflets linear or linear-lanceolate,
        1–3 cm wide.
        68a. Stems lacking or to 30 cm tall
                     . . . . . *C. ibarrae.*
        68b. Stems to 2.5 m tall.
           69a. Leaflets contracted at the base
                     . . . . . *C. elegans.*
           69b. Leaflets not contracted at the
              base   . . . . . *C. keeleriorum.*
54b. Leaflets more than 20 per side.
    70a. Leaflets to 36 per side, rather wide and regularly ar-
    ranged along the rachis, spreading in one plane.
        71a. Inflorescences of both sexes spicate   . . . . . *C. oreophila.*
        71b. Inflorescences with 5–100 flowering branches.
           72a. Small palms, taller individuals to 2 m tall, but
              usually smaller   . . . . . *C. elegans.*
           72b. Medium-sized palms, 2–5 m tall.
              73a. Leaflets sigmoid   . . . . . *C. tepejilote.*
              73b. Leaflets linear-lanceolate   . . . . . *C. woodsoniana.*
    70b. Leaflets 50–100 per side, very narrow and irregu-
    larly arranged in clusters, spreading in several planes,
    the leaves markedly plumose.
        74a. Leaflets 50–70 per side; petiole and rachis usu-
        ally glaucous   . . . . . *C. glaucifolia.*
        74b. Leaflets to 85 per side; petiole and rachis green
                     . . . . . *C. plumosa.*
3b. Stems clustered.
    75a. Climbing palms; apical leaflets progressively reduced and point-
    ing backwards   . . . . . *C. elatior.*
    75b. Nonclimbing palms; apical leaflets not reduced.
        76a. Leaves simple.

77a. Stems extending on or under the ground (stolons or rhizomes).

    78a. Stems creeping on the ground (stolons); blades bifid
    to two-thirds their length; flowers orange; fruits globose
    . . . . . *C. stolonifera.*

    78b. Stems underground (rhizomes); blades bifid to one-
    half their length; flowers yellowish green; fruits ellipsoid
    . . . . . *C. brachypoda.*

77b. Stems erect   . . . . . *C. nubium.*

76b. Leaves pinnate.

    79a. Leaflets 5–20 per side.

        80a. Leaflets to 3 cm wide.

        81a. Stems forked, creeping and appearing stemless; usu-
        ally growing near fast-running waters   . . . . . *C. cataractarum.*

        81b. Stems not forked, erect; habitat diverse, but usually
        not by fast-running waters.

            82a. Male inflorescences with 15–30 flowering
            branches   . . . . . *C. costaricana.*

            82b. Male inflorescences with up to 15 flowering
            branches.

                83a. Mountain regions at 1500–2500 m elevation
                . . . . . *C. nubium.*

                83b. Lowlands, to 500 m elevation   . . . . . *C. seifrizii.*

        80b. Leaflets more than 3 cm wide.

        84a. Stems to 1 cm diameter; leaflets 6–11 per side.

            85a. Stems rhizomatose, forming loose colonies; leaf-
            lets 6–8 per side   . . . . . *C. rhizomatosa.*

            85b. Stems erect, forming dense colonies; leaflets 9–
            11 per side; fruits orange-red or red   . . . . . *C. microspadix.*

        84b. Stems 2–10 cm diameter; leaflets usually 12–26.

            86a. Leaflets with 5–10 primary veins; male flowers
            densely crowded; fruits ellipsoid to ovoid   . . . . . *C. tepejilote.*

            86b. Leaflets with one primary vein and 2 secondary
            veins on either side; male flowers not densely
            crowded; fruits globose to ellipsoid   . . . . . *C. costaricana.*

    79b. Leaflets 20–42 per side.

        87a. Stems forked, creeping and appearing stemless; usually
        growing near fast-running waters   . . . . . *C. cataractarum.*

        87b. Stems not forked, erect; habitat diverse, but usually not
        by fast-running waters.

            88a. Leaf sheaths with a prominent flap on either side at
            the top   . . . . . *C. costaricana.*

            88b. Leaf sheaths without a flap at the top.

                89a. Leaflets 1.5–3 cm wide, with a primary vein and
                1–2 secondary veins on either side of it.

                    90a. New shoots emerging from tops of basal, per-
                    sistent leaf sheaths   . . . . . *C. hooperiana.*

                    90b. New shoots not emerging from leaf sheaths.

91a. Leaflets with one secondary vein on either
side of primary vein; male flowers with petals
joined at the tips and there joined to the
pistillode, the flowers opening by lateral slits
. . . . . *C. graminifolia.*
91b. Leaflets with 2 submarginal secondary
veins on either side of the primary vein;
male flowers with petals not joined at the
tips   . . . . . *C. pochutlensis.*
89b. Leaflets 3.5–10 cm wide, with 5–10 primary veins
. . . . . *C. tepejilote.*
2b. Honduras, Nicaragua, Costa Rica, and Panama.
92a. Stems clustered.
93a. Stems 0.4–1 cm diameter.
94a. Stems with rhizomes; flowers green   . . . . . *C. brachypoda.*
94b. Stems without rhizomes; flowers yellow   . . . . . *C. nubium.*
93b. Stems 1–10 cm diameter.
95a. Male flowers densely crowded; fruits ellipsoid to ovoid . . . . *C. tepejilote.*
95b. Male flowers not densely crowded; fruits globose.
96a. Leaf sheaths with a prominent flap on either side at top
. . . . . *C. costaricana.*
92b. Leaf sheaths without a flap at the top   . . . . . *C. seifrizii.*
92b. Stems solitary.
97a. Leaves simple, or with up to 2 basal leaflets.
98a. Primary veins 8–17 per side.
99a. Blades to 25 cm long.
100a. Blades bifid to one-third or one-half their length.
101a. Petiole 2–15 cm long   . . . . . *C. geonomiformis.*
101b. Petiole 25–60 cm long   . . . . . *C. stricta.*
100b. Blades bifid from one-half to three-quarters their
length.
102a. Blades 7–10 cm wide   . . . . . *C. verecunda.*
102b. Blades 13–30 cm wide.
103a. Blades thick, stiff, or somewhat leathery.
104a. Leaf sheaths tubular   . . . . . *C. correae.*
104b. Leaf sheaths open   . . . . . *C. pumila.*
103b. Blades thin, papery   . . . . . *C. palmeriana.*
99b. Blades more than 25 cm long.
105a. Male flowers with petals joined at the tips and there
joined to the pistillode, the flowers opening by lateral
slits.
106a. Female inflorescences with 1–3 flowering branches
. . . . . *C. geonomiformis.*
106b. Female inflorescences usually with 5–15 flowering
branches.
107a. Leaflets 2–4 per side, the apical one much
wider than the others; Panama (Darién)   . . . . . *C. murriensis.*
107b. Leaflets 2–8 per side, the apical one not much
wider than the others; widespread   . . . . . *C. pinnatifrons.*

105b. Male flowers with petals not joined at the tips.
   108a. Primary veins prominent above, blades appearing corrugated.
      109a. Blades leathery.
         110a. Blades bifid to half their length or more . . . . . *C. pumila.*
         110b. Blades bifid to one-third their length . . . . . *C. sullivaniorum.*
      109b. Blades not leathery . . . . . *C. robertii.*
   108b. Primary veins not prominently elevated above, blades flat, not corrugated.
      111a. Petiole to 7 cm long . . . . . *C. rigida.*
      111b. Petiole 25–60 cm long . . . . . *C. stricta.*
98b. Primary veins 20–50 per side.
   112a. Blades bifid to one-fifth to one-quarter their length.
      113a. Leaf margins conspicuously toothed; female inflorescences spicate or bifurcate . . . . . *C. amabilis.*
      113b. Leaf margins toothed but not conspicuously so; female inflorescences with 3–6 flowering branches . . . . . *C. deneversiana.*
   112b. Blades bifid to more than one-quarter their length.
      114a. Male inflorescences multiple, 4–10 at each node; male flowers green; fruits obovoid-globose, 1–1.5 cm long . . . . . *C. deckeriana.*
      114b. Male inflorescences solitary at each node; male flowers yellow; fruits globose, 0.7–1.3 cm long . . . . . *C. allenii.*
97b. Leaves pinnate, with more than 5 leaflets per side.
   115a. Leaflets 8–12 cm wide, glossy, shiny on the lower surface, with prominent veins; Panama (Coclé) . . . . . *C. lucidifrons.*
   115b. Leaflets usually narrower, not glossy nor shiny with prominent veins; widespread.
      116a. Flowers bright orange to yellow-orange.
         117a. Leaflets 5–10 per side; female inflorescences with 4–8 flowering branches . . . . . *C. sartorii.*
         117b. Leaflets to 36 per side; female inflorescences with about 50 flowering branches . . . . . *C. woodsoniana.*
      116b. Flowers green to yellow or whitish.
         118a. Male flowers with petals joined at the tips and there joined to the pistillode, the flowers opening by lateral slits.
            119a. Leaf rachis to 35 cm long . . . . . *C. parvifolia.*
            119b. Leaf rachis usually longer than 35 cm.
               120a. Fruits maturing from green to orange-yellow to black . . . . . *C. pinnatifrons.*
               120b. Fruits maturing from green to black.
                  121a. Apical leaflet much wider than the others . . . . . *C. warscewiczii.*
                  121b. Apical leaflet not much wider than the others . . . . . *C. macrospadix.*

118b. Male flowers with petals not joined at the tips.
  122a. Male flowers densely crowded.
    123a. Female inflorescences spicate or with up to 3
    flowering branches; female flowers densely
    crowded, touching one another.
      124a. Male inflorescences with 8–10 flowering
      branches   . . . . . *C. arenbergiana.*
      124b. Male inflorescences spicate or with a few
      flowering branches   . . . . . *C. allenii.*
    123b. Female inflorescences with 5–20 flowering
    branches; female flowers not touching one anoth-
    er   . . . . . *C. tepejilote.*
  122b. Male flowers not densely crowded, separated.
    125a. Leaf sheaths open; stems short or lacking.
      126a. Leaflets running into and continuous with
      the rachis.
        127a. Leaflets not decreasing markedly in
        length toward top of rachis.   . . . . . *C. pygmaea.*
        127b. Leaflets decreasing markedly in length to-
        ward top of rachis.
          128a. Leaflets 20–30 per side; female inflo-
          rescences with 60–100 short, stiff, very
          thin flowering branches   . . . . . *C. brachyclada.*
          128b. Leaflets 12–20 per side; female inflo-
          rescences with 2–15 thick flowering
          branches.
            129a. Leaflets with nonwavy margins . . . . *C. scheryi.*
            129b. Leaflets with wavy margins
                   . . . . . *C. undulatifolia.*
      126b. Leaflets not running into the rachis   . . . . . *C. pittieri.*
    125b. Leaf sheaths tubular; stems usually elongate,
    erect, or creeping.
      130a. Petioles gray-green and/or densely white
      spotted.
        131a. Leaflets 2–4 per side, the apical pair
        much wider than the others combined.
          132a. Apical pair of leaflets bifid to about
          three-quarters their length.
            133a. Leaflets with prominent veins   . . . . *C. correae.*
            133b. Leaflets obscurely veined   . . . . *C. guntheriana.*
          132b. Apical pair of leaflets bifid from one-
          fifth to one-quarter their length
                  . . . . . *C. deneversiana.*
        131b. Leaflets 7–9 per side, the apical pair
        much shorter than the others   . . . . . *C. microphylla.*
      130b. Petioles green, not densely white spotted.
        134a. Leaflets thin-papery   . . . . . *C. selvae.*
        134b. Leaflets thick or medium textured.
          135a. Leaflets thick, rather leathery; inflores-
          cences borne below the leaves   . . . . . *C. oblongata.*

135b. Leaflets medium textured; inflorescences borne among the leaves
..... *C. dammeriana.*

1b. South America.
136a. Leaves simple or with an additional pair of leaflets at the base.
137a. Blades bifid from one-fifth to one-quarter their length.
138a. Leaf margins conspicuously toothed; female inflorescences
spicate or bifurcate ..... *C. amabilis.*
138b. Leaf margins toothed but not conspicuously so; female inflorescences with 3–6 flowering branches ..... *C. deneversiana.*
137b. Blades bifid from one-third to three-quarters their length.
139a. Blades bifid to three-quarters their length; flowers bright orange; Peru ..... *C. fragrans.*
139b. Blades bifid from one- to two-thirds their length; flowers green
to yellow.
140a. Female inflorescences with 3–10 flowering branches
..... *C. pinnatifrons.*
140b. Female inflorescences spicate or bifurcate.
141a. Blades 0.4–1 m long.
142a. Leaflets with 8–10 almost equally prominent veins;
male inflorescences solitary at each node; northwestern
Colombia ..... *C. allenii.*
142b. Leaflets with a prominent primary vein and 1–2 secondary veins on either side of it; male inflorescences
multiple at each node; Amazon region ..... *C. pauciflora.*
141b. Blades to 30 cm long; northwestern Colombia ..... *C. pumila.*
136b. Leaves pinnate, with 3 or more leaflets per side.
143a. Stems less than 50 cm long, creeping, the palm appearing stemless ..... *C. pygmaea.*
143b. Stems erect, usually longer than 50 cm.
144a. Leaflets with 6–10 equally prominent veins, a midrib not easily
recognizable.
145a. Inflorescences spicate or with up to 3 flowering branches;
northwestern Colombia ..... *C. allenii.*
145b. Inflorescences with 5–53 flowering branches.
146a. Fruits black; staminate flowers densely crowded, touching one another ..... *C. tepejilote.*
146b. Fruits red; staminate flowers separated, not crowded
..... *C. linearis.*
144b. Leaflets with a midrib and 1–2 secondary veins on either side.
147a. Leaflets 30–39 per side ..... *C. angustisecta.*
147b. Leaflets 3–14 per side.
148a. Inflorescences spicate; male inflorescences several at
each node; ..... *C. pauciflora.*
148b. Inflorescences with 3–14 flowering branches; male and
female inflorescences solitary at each node.
149a. Leaflets 3 per side, the apical one much wider than
the others; Colombia (Antioquia). ..... *C. murriensis.*
149b. Leaflets 2–8 per side, the apical one not much wider
than the others; widespread ..... *C. pinnatifrons.*

Chamaedorea adscendens
(Map 116)

Field characters. Stems solitary, to 2.5 m tall and 1 cm diameter, erect. Leaves 5–7, pinnate or rarely simple and bifid; leaflets (1–)2–6 per side, obovate-lanceolate, to 16 cm long and 2.5–3.5 cm wide, *leathery, blue-gray-green, with a velvety aspect.* Inflorescences dissimilar; males with 2–10 pendulous flowering branches; females spicate, erect; fruits globose or ovoid, to 8 mm diameter, black, with thickened, persistent petals.

Range and habitat. Atlantic slope in Belize (Toledo) and Guatemala (Alta Verapaz, Petén); forest, often on limestone soils, to 700 m elevation.

Notes. Unusual in the texture of its leaflets.

Chamaedorea allenii
(Map 117, Plate 14)

Field characters. Stems solitary, 1–2 m tall and 1.5–2 cm diameter, erect or creeping. Leaves 3–6, pinnate, or occasionally simple and bifid; leaflets (1–)7–11 per side, lanceolate, 25–35 cm long and 3–6.5 cm wide. Inflorescences dissimilar; males solitary at each node, spicate or occasionally with few flowering branches, *pendulous, with rows of closely arranged flowers; females spicate, erect, with densely crowded flowers touching one another on a thickened flowering branch;* fruits globose, angled by mutual pressure, 0.7–1.3 cm diameter, orange when immature, ripening black, with thickened, persistent petals.

Range and habitat. Costa Rica (Alajuela, Cartago, Guanacaste, Heredia, Limón, Puntarenas, San José), Panama (Chiriquí, Coclé, Darién, San Blas), and northwestern Colombia (Antioquia, Chocó, Risaralda); premontane rain forest, at 100–1250 m elevation.

Notes. Our treatment of this species differs somewhat from that of Hodel (1992a), who separated two other species, *Chamaedorea crucensis* and *C. zamorae*, based on minor details. The following species are also very similar to *C. allenii* and all are closely related to one another: *C. arenbergiana*, *C. deckeriana*, and *C. nationsiana.* Positive identification may prove difficult if flowering plants of both sexes are not present.

Chamaedorea amabilis
(Map 118)

Field characters. Stems solitary, 1–2 m tall and 0.7–1 cm diameter, erect or somewhat leaning. Leaves 4–5, simple; *blades broadly obovate,* shallowly to deeply bifid, 30–50 cm long and 15–25 cm wide, *strongly plicate and toothed on the margins.* Inflorescences erect; males with 3–7 flowering branches; females spicate or occa-

sionally bifurcate; fruits globose to oblong, to 1.2 cm long and 9 mm diameter, black, with persistent, thickened petals.

Range and habitat. Atlantic slope in Costa Rica (Alajuela, Cartago, Heredia, San José) and Panama (Coclé, Colón); premontane rain forest, at 450–1000 m elevation.

Uses. It is much prized as an ornamental and has been stripped from the forest for sale, thus much reducing wild populations (Hodel, 1988).

Notes. Similar to *Chamaedorea palmeriana,* which differs mainly in its more deeply bifid leaves and higher-elevation habitat.

Chamaedorea angustisecta
(Map 119)

"Siyeyi" (Bol), "sangapilla" (Per)

Field characters. Stems solitary, 1.5–4 m tall and 2–3 cm diameter. Leaves 5–8, pinnate; *petioles and rachis distinctively mottled white;* leaflets 30–39 per side, linear-lanceolate, 33–48 cm long and 1.5–3.5 cm wide. Inflorescences dissimilar; *males multiple, up to 7 at each node,* with 9–16 pendulous flowering branches; females solitary at each node, with 9–16 erect flowering branches; fruits ellipsoid, 1.3–1.6 cm long and 0.5–0.8 cm diameter, black, with thickened, persistent petals.

Range and habitat. Andean foothills of Peru (Ayacucho, Cuzco, Junín, Madre de Dios, Ucayali), Brazil (Acre), and Bolivia (Beni, La Paz); lowland rain forest on noninundated soils, below 700 m elevation.

Chamaedorea arenbergiana
(Map 120)

"Chim" (Gua), "pacaya" (Hon)

Field characters. Stems solitary, to 4 m tall and 2–3 cm diameter, erect or rarely creeping. Leaves 4–6, pinnate; leaflets 8–10 per side, oblong-lanceolate, *to 60 cm long and 15 cm wide.* Inflorescences dissimilar; *males solitary at each node, with 8–10 pendulous flowering branches, with densely arranged flowers; females spicate or bifurcate, with densely crowded flowers touching one another on a thick flowering branch;* fruits globose to oblong, *angled from mutual pressure,* to 1.9 cm long and 1.2 cm diameter, black, with thickened, persistent petals.

Range and habitat. Mexico (Chiapas, Oaxaca, Veracruz), Guatemala (Alta Verapaz, Baja Verapaz, Huehuetenango, San Marcos), Honduras (Atlántida), and possibly El Salvador, Nicaragua, Costa Rica, Panama, and northwestern Colombia; rain forest on slopes, at 100–1800 m elevation.

Notes. The range of this species from El Salvador southwards is not confirmed; see notes under *Chamaedorea allenii.*

Chamaedorea brachyclada
(Map 121)

Field characters. Stems solitary, often short and subterranean, 2–3 cm diameter, erect or creeping. Leaves 3–5, pinnate; leaflets 20–30 per side, linear-lanceolate, to 30 cm long and 2–3 cm wide, decreasing markedly in length toward top of rachis, *the lower margins continuous with and running into the rachis.* Inflorescences dissimilar, often arising from near ground level, borne on a long peduncle; males with 40–50 flowering branches; females bottle-brush-like, with 60–100 branches; fruits globose, 3–5 mm diameter, black, with persistent, thickened petals.

Range and habitat. Pacific coast of Costa Rica (Puntarenas, San José) and Panama (Chiriquí); montane forest on steep slopes, at 1000–1400 m elevation.

Notes. Together with *C. pygmaea, C. scheryi,* and *C. undulatifolia,* forms a group of similar species.

Chamaedorea brachypoda
(Map 122)
"Pacaya" (Gua)

Field characters. Stems clustered, *forming large clumps by rhizomes,* 1–2 m tall and 5–7 mm diameter. Leaves 5–8, simple; blades broadly oblanceolate, bifid to one-half their length, to 30 cm long and 22 cm wide, slightly toothed at the margins. Inflorescences erect; males and females with 4–8 short flowering branches; fruits ellipsoid, 0.5–1 cm long, black, with thickened, persistent petals.

Range and habitat. Atlantic slope in Guatemala (Izabal) and Honduras; lowland rain forest, at 150 m elevation.

Uses. Commonly cultivated as an ornamental.

Notes. To the north and/or at higher elevations, this species is replaced by the similar *Chamaedorea nubium.*

Chamaedorea carchensis
(Map 123)

Field characters. Stems solitary, to 1(–5) m or more tall and 2.5–5 cm diameter, erect or sometimes creeping. Leaves 3–6, pinnate, *to 3 m long, the petioles of young leaves often covered with black tomentum;* leaflets 15–22 per side, lanceolate, to 60 cm long and 3.5–5.5 cm wide. Inflorescences dissimilar, erect or arching, often appearing from ground level, borne on a long peduncle; males with 20–75 flowering branches; females with 18–50 branches; fruits globose, 0.9–1 cm long, black, with persistent, thickened petals.

Range and habitat. Atlantic slope in Mexico (Chiapas) and Guatemala (Alta Verapaz,

Huehuetenango); montane forest on rocky slopes, at 900–1600 m elevation.

Notes. Closely related to *Chamaedorea woodsoniana,* but differs in its less numerous leaflets and black tomentum on the young leaves.

Chamaedorea castillo-montii
(Map 124)

Field characters. Stems solitary, to 50 cm tall and 1.5–2.5 cm diameter, erect or creeping. Leaves 12–15, simple or pinnate; simple leaves with obovate, deeply bifid blades, scarcely toothed on the margins, markedly plicate, with 11–13 primary veins per side, pinnate leaves with a few (2–5) linear-lanceolate leaflets to 20 cm long, the apical one always wider. *Inflorescences spicate,* the males pendulous, the females arching, *both with closely arranged, whitish flowers;* fruits oblong, to 1.3 cm long and 7 mm diameter, black, with persistent, thickened petals.

Range and habitat. Atlantic slope in Guatemala (Alta Verapaz, Izabal); premontane or montane rain forest on limestone soils, at 600–1000 m elevation.

Notes. Closely related to and perhaps not distinct from *Chamaedorea robertii* from Costa Rica and Panama.

Chamaedorea cataractarum
(Map 125)
"Guayita de los arroyos" (Mex)

Field characters. Stems to 2 m long and 2–4 cm diameter, *forked at the base, clustered and forming large clumps,* but creeping and appearing stemless. Leaves 4–5, pinnate; leaflets 13–20 per side, linear-lanceolate, to 30 cm long and 2.5 cm wide. Inflorescences solitary, with 6–15 pendulous flowering branches, *thickened with closely spaced flowers;* fruits ovoid-oblong, to 1 cm long and 6–8 mm diameter, black, with thickened, persistent petals.

Range and habitat. Atlantic slope in Mexico (Chiapas, Oaxaca, Tabasco); rain forest along streams and rivers, by rapids or waterfalls, usually on limestone soils, at 300–1000 m elevation.

Notes. Unusual in its forked stems (Fisher 1974) and streamside habitat, where it is frequently inundated.

Chamaedorea correae
(Map 126)

Field characters. Stems solitary, to 1 m tall and 5–10 mm diameter, creeping and rooting. Leaves 4–5, simple or with 2 leaflets per side; petiole gray-green; *leaf sheaths tubular; blades deeply bifid,* 15–25 cm long and 20–30 cm wide, *with leathery, gray-green, lanceolate to sigmoid lobes,* with prominent veins. Inflorescences erect, borne well below the leaves; males with 2–3 flowering branches; females spicate or rarely with 2 branches; fruits globose to ellipsoid, black, 5–8 mm long.

Range and habitat. Atlantic slope in Panama (Coclé, Colón, Panamá, Veraguas); premontane rain forest or wind-swept, dwarf forest on slopes of the continental divide, at 800–1000 m elevation.

Notes. Similar to *Chamaedorea guntheriana,* but differs in its larger leaves with wider lobes.

Chamaedorea costaricana
(Map 127)
"Pacaya" (CR, ElS), "tenera" (Gua), "pacayita" (Nic)

Field characters. Stems clustered, forming colonies by rhizomes, 3–8 m tall and 1–6 cm diameter, erect or leaning on other vegetation. Leaves 3–6, pinnate, *usually the sheaths with a prominent flap on either side at the top;* leaflets 15–30 per side, linear-lanceolate to lanceolate, 25–40 cm long and 2.5–5 cm wide, with one primary vein and 2 secondary veins on either side. Inflorescences erect or pendulous, with 6–30 flowering branches, usually the females with fewer; fruits globose to ellipsoid, 1.2–1.3 cm long and 0.7–1 cm diameter, black, with persistent, thickened petals.

Range and habitat. Throughout Central America in eastern Mexico (Chiapas), Guatemala (El Quiche, San Marcos), El Salvador, Honduras (Comayagua, Distrito Central, Francisco Morazán, Yoro), Nicaragua (Madriz), Costa Rica (Heredia), and Panama (Coclé) (not recorded in Belize); rain forest, at 50–2300 m elevation.

Notes. This is a widespread and variable species that is commonly cultivated in Central America. It is very similar to *Chamaedorea woodsoniana* and some forms may be difficult to tell apart from this species. Hodel (1992a) separated *C. quezalteca* as a distinct species, but we include it here.

Chamaedorea dammeriana
(Map 128)
"Sirik" (CR)

Field characters. Stems solitary, to 1 m tall and 7–8 mm diameter, erect or creeping. Leaves 4–15, pinnate, occasionally simple and deeply bifid; *leaflets 2–7 per side, oblong-lanceolate, to 20 cm long and 4–5 cm wide, the apical one much wider.* Inflorescences borne among the leaves; males with 2–10 flowering branches; females spicate or with 2–5 erect branches; fruits globose to ovoid, 0.8–1.5 cm long, 0.5–0.8 cm diameter, black, with persistent, thickened petals.

Range and habitat. Atlantic and Pacific slope in Costa Rica (Alajuela, Guanacaste, Heredia,

Limón) and Panama (Bocas del Toro, Colón, Panamá); rain forest, at 200–1100 m elevation.

Notes. Hodel (1992a) separated *Chamaedorea chazdoniae* as a distinct species, but we include it here.

Chamaedorea deckeriana
(Map 129)

Field characters. Stems solitary, 0.3–2 m tall and 2–3 cm diameter, erect or rarely creeping. Leaves 4–5, *simple;* blades obovate, bifid to half their length, 50–70 cm long and 25–35 cm wide, with toothed margins. *Inflorescences spicate, erect, the males multiple, 4–10 at each node, with densely crowded flowers on a pendulous flowering branch, the females one at each node, with densely crowded flowers on a thick flowering branch;* fruits obovoid-globose but angled by mutual pressure, 1–1.5 cm long and 0.5–1 cm diameter, red-orange when immature, ripening black, with persistent, thickened petals.

Range and habitat. Atlantic slope in Costa Rica (Alajuela, Cartago, Guanacaste, Heredia, Limón, Puntarenas) and Panama (Bocas del Toro, Colón, San Blas); rain forest, to 900 m elevation.

Notes. See notes under *Chamaedorea allenii.*

Chamaedorea deneversiana
(Map 130)

Field characters. Stems solitary, to 2 m tall and 1.3–1.6 cm diameter, erect or creeping. Leaves 3–4, simple, rarely pinnate with a few basal leaflets; petiole gray-green; *blades oblong, 50–80 cm long and 12–25 cm wide, bifid to one quarter their length, with toothed margins.* Inflorescences with 3–10, pendulous flowering branches; fruits ellipsoid, 7–8 mm long and 5–6 mm diameter, black.

Range and habitat. Panama (San Blas, Veraguas) and Ecuador (Carchi, Cotopaxi, Pichincha); lowland to premontane rain forest, to 850 m elevation.

Notes. Very similar to, and probably conspecific with, *Chamaedorea warscewiczii.*

Chamaedorea elatior
(Map 131)
"Tepejilote," "junco de bejuco" (Gua, Mex)

Field characters. Stems solitary or rarely clustered, *sprawling or climbing,* 1–20 m tall and 0.8–2 cm diameter. Leaves 5–15, pinnate, rarely bifid; leaflets 10–55 per side, linear to linear-lanceolate, 18–45 cm long and 1.5–5 cm wide, *those near the apex of the leaf modified into climbing hooks.* Inflorescences erect, branched, with up to 35 flowering branches; fruits globose, 0.8–1.1 cm diameter, black, with persistent, thickened petals.

Range and habitat. Atlantic slope and occa-

sionally on the Pacific slope in Mexico (Chiapas, Oaxaca, Puebla, Veracruz), Guatemala (Huehuetenango, Sacatepéquez), and Honduras; rain forest, at 100–1500 m elevation.
Uses. The stems are occasionally used to weave baskets.
Notes. A remarkable species, being the only climbing *Chamaedorea.* The modification of the apical leaflets into climbing hooks exactly mimics those of *Desmoncus.* In Veracruz, Mexico, flowering takes place between February and June (Aguilar, 1986).

Chamaedorea elegans
(Map 132)
"Chaté," "pacaya" (Gua), "palmilla" (Mex)
Field characters. Stems solitary, 0.3–2 m tall and 0.8–1.5 cm diameter, erect or often leaning. Leaves 5–8, pinnate; *leaflets 11–21 per side, linear or linear-lanceolate, contracted at the base.* Inflorescences erect, branched with 5–35 erect flowering branches; fruits globose, 4–7 mm diameter, black, with thin petals, these mostly nonpersistent.
Range and habitat. Atlantic (and rarely Pacific) slope in Mexico (Chiapas, Hidalgo, Oaxaca, Puebla, San Luis Potosí, Tabasco, Veracruz), Guatemala (Alta Verpaz, Huehuetenango, Petén), and Belize; rain forest, often on limestone soils, to 1400 m elevation.
Uses. Very widely cultivated as an ornamental and in the nursery trade often referred to as the parlor palm or "neanthe bella." Hodel (1992a) reported that each year millions of seeds, mostly from wild plants, are collected in Mexico and exported.
Notes. Placed in its own subgenus because of its unusual flowers. The petals of both male and female flowers are joined and open only by a small, 3-angled pore at the tips. It would be very interesting to know how this species is pollinated. In Veracruz, Mexico, it flowers from May to October (Aguilar, 1986).

Chamaedorea ernesti-augustii
(Map 133)
"Guaya," "guayita" (Mex)
Field characters. Stems solitary, 0.8–2 m tall and 1–1.5 cm diameter, erect. Leaves 5–8, simple; *blades broadly wedge shaped-obovate, bifid to about half their length, 25–60 cm long and 20–30 cm wide,* with 12–18 primary veins per side. Inflorescences erect, males with 13–25 pendulous flowering branches, densely covered with flowers; females spicate (rarely with 2–4 branches), *with bright orange flowers;* fruits subglobose to ellipsoid, 1–1.5 cm long and 0.8–1 cm diameter, black, with thin petals, these mostly nonpersistent.
Range and habitat. Atlantic slope in Mexico

(Chiapas, Oaxaca, Tabasco, Veracruz), Guatemala (Alta Verapaz, Huehuetenango, Izabal, Petén), Belize, and Honduras (Atlántida, Comayagua, Yoro); rain forest, often on limestone soils, at 100–1000 m elevation.
Uses. It is a commonly planted ornamental.
Notes. Flowering takes place from March to May in Veracruz, Mexico (Aguilar, 1986). Biomass and nutrient allocation have been studied by Bullock (1984).

Chamaedorea fractiflexa
(Map 134)
Field characters. Stems solitary, to 1 m tall and 5–8 mm diameter, erect or creeping. Leaves 3–8, pinnate; leaf sheaths tubular; leaflets 5–8 per side, lanceolate to sigmoid, to 13 cm long and 3.5 cm wide. Inflorescences borne among the leaves; males with 5 flowering branches; *females with up to 3 very thin and pendulous branches;* fruits globose, 7–8 mm diameter, black, with persistent, flattened petals.
Range and habitat. Pacific slope in Mexico (Chiapas) and Guatemala (Quezaltenango, San Marcos); montane rain forest, at 2000–2900 m elevation.
Notes. Similar to *Chamaedorea parvisecta.*

Chamaedorea fragrans
(Map 135)
"Sangapilla" (Per)
Field characters. Stems clustered, 2–4 m tall and 0.5–1 cm diameter, erect. Leaves to 4, simple; *blades deeply bifid, 30–50 cm long, the lobes 6–9 cm wide, toothed along the margins.* Inflorescences erect; males and females with 1–8 flowering branches; flowers bright orange, very fragrant; fruits ellipsoid, to 1.2 cm long and 0.6 cm diameter, black.
Range and habitat. Eastern Andean slopes of Peru (Cuzco, Huánuco, San Martín); lowland or premontane rain forest on steep slopes, at 400–800 m elevation.

Chamaedorea geonomiformis
(Map 136)
"Capuca-capocha" (Gua), "pacaya" (Hon)
Field characters. Stems solitary, 1.5–2 m tall and 0.5–1 cm diameter, erect or leaning. Leaves 5–10, *simple;* blades oblanceolate to oblong-elliptical, 15–30 cm long and 10–15 cm wide, *obscurely nerved.* Inflorescences erect or pendulous; males with 1–6 pendulous flowering branches, females with 1–3 erect flowering branches; fruits globose, 0.8–1.2 cm diameter, black, with persistent, thickened petals present.
Range and habitat. Atlantic slope in southern Mexico (Chiapas, Oaxaca, Veracruz), Guatemala (Alta Verapaz, Izabal, Petén), Belize,

Honduras (Atlántida), and Pacific slope in Costa Rica (Puntarenas); rain forest, usually on limestone soils, at 100–1000 m elevation.
Uses. Commonly cultivated as an ornamental.
Notes. Plants on the northern and southern edge of the range of this species commonly have somewhat smaller leaves, and these forms have been described as a separate species. Hodel (1992a) separated *Chamaedorea tenella*, from Costa Rica, as distinct but we include it here. See comments on species pairs following genus description.

Chamaedorea glaucifolia
(Map 137)
"Kiba" (Mex)
Field characters. Stems solitary, to 4 m tall and 2–3.5 cm diameter, erect. Leaves 3–5, pinnate; *petiole and rachis usually glaucous; leaflets 50–70 per side, narrowly linear to linear-lanceolate, irregularly arranged in clusters and spreading in different planes*, 30–35 cm long and 0.5–1.2 cm wide. Inflorescences similar, with 12–30 flowering branches; fruits globose, 0.7–1 cm diameter, black, with thickened petals.
Range and habitat. Atlantic slope in Mexico (Chiapas); slopes in rain forest, often on exposed limestone, at 500–1000 m elevation.
Notes. Very similar to *Chamaedorea plumosa*, but differs in its glaucous petiole and male flowers.

Chamaedorea graminifolia
(Map 138)
"Chapai" (Bel)
Field characters. Stems clustered, to 3 m tall and 2–3 cm diameter, *often glaucous*. Leaves 4–6, pinnate; *sheath, petiole, and rachis usually glaucous; leaflets 22–42 per side, linear to linear-lanceolate*, regularly arranged and spreading in the same plane or the basal few clustered and spreading in different planes, to 40 cm long and 1.5–2.5 cm wide, with one secondary vein on either side of primary vein. Inflorescences erect, males and females similar with 10–35 flowering branches; fruits globose, 0.6–1 cm diameter, black, with thickened, persistent petals.
Range and habitat. Atlantic slope in Mexico (Chiapas), Guatemala (Alta Verapaz), Belize, and northern Costa Rica (Alajuela); rain forest, often on limestone soils, at 700–1500 elevation.

Chamaedorea guntheriana
(Map 139)
Field characters. Stems solitary, to 3 m tall and 5–7 mm diameter, creeping. Leaves 4–5, pinnate; petiole gray-green; leaflets 2–4 per side, the apical pair widest, the middle ones to 15 cm long and 3 cm wide, lanceolate, *leathery*,

gray-green. Inflorescences erect; *males and females spicate or bifurcate*; fruits globose, to 6 mm diameter, black, with persistent, thickened petals.
Range and habitat. Panama (Panamá); windswept, dwarf, premontane forest on continental divide, at 900–1000 m elevation.
Notes. Similar to both *Chamaedorea correae* and *C. verecunda* and all three form a species complex.

Chamaedorea hooperiana
(Map 140)
Field characters. Stems clustered, the new shoots emerging from tops of basal, persistent leaf sheaths, to 4 m tall and 2–2.5 cm diameter. Leaves 5–7, pinnate; leaflets 20–26 per side, lanceolate, to 40 cm long and 1.8 cm wide, with one primary vein and two secondary veins on either side. Inflorescences erect, *males and females similar with 40–50 flowering branches*; fruits globose, 7–8 mm diameter, black, with thickened, persistent petals.
Range and habitat. Atlantic slope in Mexico (Veracruz); montane rain forest, at 1000–1500 m elevation.

Chamaedorea ibarrae
(Map 141)
"Cib" (Mex)
Field characters. Stems solitary, very short, eventually to 30 cm tall. Leaves pinnate; leaflets up to 17 or more per side, to 24 cm long and 2.5–3 cm wide, linear-lanceolate, regularly or occasionally irregularly arranged. Inflorescences erect, similar, appearing to arise directly from the ground, with 3–6 flowering branches; fruits obovoid, 0.8–1 cm long and 5–7 mm diameter, black, with persistent, thickened petals.
Range and habitat. Atlantic slope, or rarely Pacific slope in Mexico (Chiapas) and Guatemala (Huehuetenango); montane rain forest or pine-oak forest, usually on limestone soils, at 1600–2600 m elevation.
Notes. Similar to the southern *Chamaedorea brachyclada*.

Chamaedorea keeleriorum
(Map 142)
Field characters. Stems solitary, to 4 m tall and 1.5–2.5 cm diameter, erect. Leaves 3–4, pinnate; leaflets 12–17 per side, linear-lanceolate, to 30 cm long and 4 cm wide. Inflorescences with 8–40 flowering branches; fruits globose to ovoid, 0.8–1 cm long and 6–8 mm diameter, black, with thickened, persistent petals.
Range and habitat. Pacific slope in Mexico (Chiapas) and Guatemala (Quezaltenango, Saca-

tepéquez, Sololá); montane rain forest, at 1500–2500 m elevation.

Notes. Very similar to and possibly conspecific with *Chamaedorea whitelockiana.*

Chamaedorea klotzschiana
(Map 143)
"Tepejilote" (Mex)

Field characters. Stems solitary, 1–4 m tall and 1.5–3 cm diameter, erect. Leaves 4–6, pinnate; leaflets 12–20 per side, lanceolate to sigmoid, *irregularly arranged in clusters and spreading in different planes,* 20–40 cm long and 3.5–6 cm wide. Inflorescences erect, males and females with 12–20 flowering branches; fruits globose to ovoid, 0.9–1.2 cm long and 0.7–0.9 cm diameter, black, with persistent, thickened petals.

Range and habitat. Atlantic slope in Mexico (Veracruz); rain forest, at 500–1250 m elevation.

Notes. Very distinctive because of its clustered leaflets which spread in different planes. Flowering takes place between October and June (Aguilar, 1986).

Chamaedorea lehmannii
(Map 144)
"Chiquilote" (Gua)

Field characters. Stems solitary, to 2 m tall and 1–2 cm diameter, erect. Leaves 5–7, pinnate, *arranged in 3 planes;* leaflets to 8 per side, lanceolate, to 20 cm long and to 2 cm wide. Inflorescences erect, with 2–6 flowering branches; fruits globose, 6–7 mm diameter, black, with persistent, thickened petals.

Range and habitat. Atlantic slope in Guatemala (Alta Verapaz, Baja Verapaz, El Progreso, Zacapa); montane rain forest, at 1400–2600 m elevation.

Chamaedorea liebmannii
(Map 145)

Field characters. Stems solitary, to 4 m tall and 2 cm diameter, erect, sometimes the palm flowering when still stemless. Leaves 4–9, pinnate; leaflets 13–18 per side, linear to narrowly lanceolate, 16–30 cm long and 1.5–3 cm wide. Inflorescences with 18–26 flowering branches, *the lower ones often branched;* fruits globose, to 1 cm diameter, black.

Range and habitat. Atlantic slope in Mexico (Chiapas, Oaxaca, Puebla, Veracruz) and Guatemala (Huehuetenango); rain forest, at 1200–1800 m elevation.

Chamaedorea linearis
(Map 146, Plate 15)
"Caña de San Pablo" (Col), "shúcshu" (Per)

Field characters. Stems solitary, 2–10 m tall and 2–8 cm diameter, erect or occasionally creep-

ing. Leaves 3–8, pinnate; leaflets 11–62 per side, lanceolate to almost sigmoid, 16–85 cm long and 2.5–12 cm wide. Inflorescences erect, *the males multiple, 3–18 at each node,* the female solitary at each node, both male and female with 5–53 flowering branches, the males with flowers clustered; *fruits globose to ellipsoid, 0.8–2.5 cm diameter, red.*

Range and habitat. Throughout the Andes of Venezuela, Colombia, Ecuador, Peru, and Bolivia, between 500 and 2800 m, but descending to 50 m in the Pacific lowlands of Colombia and Ecuador; rain forest on mountain slopes or lowland areas.

Notes. It has a very broad ecological tolerance and is widespread and variable. We have included *Chamaedorea latisecta* and *C. smithii* here, two species kept separate by Hodel (1992a).

Chamaedorea lucidifrons
(Map 147)

Field characters. Stems solitary, to 2 m tall and 2–3 cm diameter, erect. Leaves 3–5, pinnate; leaflets to 7 per side, sigmoid, 30–35 cm long and *8–12 cm wide, glossy, shiny on the lower surface, with prominent veins.* Inflorescences borne on elongate peduncles, females with 7–11 flowering branches; fruits globose, 5–6 mm long, orange, with persistent thickened petals.

Range and habitat. Panama (Coclé); rain forest, at 600 m elevation.

Notes. Very similar to and possibly only a local leaf form of *Chamaedorea pinnatifrons.*

Chamaedorea macrospadix
(Map 148)

Field characters. Stems solitary, to 3 m tall and 1.5–2.5 cm diameter, erect or creeping. Leaves 3–7, pinnate; leaflets 7–13 per side, lanceolate, to 37 cm long and 5 cm wide, *glossy on the lower surface.* Inflorescences erect, *borne on an elongate peduncle;* males with 10–25 flowering branches, females with 8–15 branches; fruits oblong, 0.7–1 cm long and 6–8 mm diameter, black, with thickened, persistent petals.

Range and habitat. Atlantic and Pacific slopes in Costa Rica (Alajuela, Cartago, Limón, Puntarenas, San José); lowland to montane rain forest, often on limestone soil, at 100–1300 m elevation.

Notes. We include here *Chamaedorea pedunculata,* a species kept separate by Hodel (1992a).

Chamaedorea metallica
(Map 149)
"Metálica" (Mex)

Field characters. Stems solitary, 0.3–3 m tall and 0.5–1.5 cm diameter, erect. Leaves 4–16, simple or pinnate, *with a metallic-blue sheen;* simple

leaves with blades wedge shaped-obovate, 20–30 cm long and 12–15 cm wide, pinnate leaves with 3–8 sigmoid leaflets per side, to 7 cm long and 2.5–6.5 cm wide. Inflorescences erect, males with 5–12, pendulous flowering branches, *densely covered with flowers*, females spicate or with 2–4 branches, *with bright orange flowers*; fruits globose-ellipsoid, black, 1–1.2 cm long and 8–9 mm diameter, with thin petals, these mostly nonpersistent.
Range and habitat. Atlantic slope in Mexico (Oaxaca, Veracruz); lowland rain forest, often on limestone soils, to 600 m elevation.
Notes. Commonly planted as an ornamental and admired for the distinctive metallic-blue sheen of its leaves. In Veracruz, flowering takes place from March to August (Aguilar, 1986).

Chamaedorea microphylla
(Map 150)
Field characters. Stems solitary, to 1 m tall and 1.5 cm diameter, erect, *white spotted.* Leaves 3–5, pinnate; *petiole minutely white spotted*; leaflets 7–9 per side, lanceolate to oblong, 10–17 cm long and 3–4 cm wide, the top pair much shorter than the others. Inflorescences erect, with 7–12 flowering branches, the females usually fewer than the males; fruits oblong, to 6 mm long and 4 mm diameter, black, with persistent, thickened petals.
Range and habitat. Panama (Chiriquí); rain forest on wet, windswept ridges, at 1000 m elevation.

Chamaedorea microspadix
(Map 151)
"Palmilla" (Mex)
Field characters. Stems clustered, to 3 m tall and 1 cm diameter, erect or leaning, *forming dense colonies.* Leaves pinnate; leaflets 9–11 per side, lanceolate, to 25 cm long and 4–5 cm wide. Inflorescences erect or pendulous, with 3–6 flowering branches; *male flowers in pairs or short rows*; fruits globose, to 1 cm diameter, *orange-red or red, with persistent, thickened perianth.*
Range and habitat. Mexico (Hidalgo, Querétaro, San Luis Potosí, Veracruz); forest, usually on limestone soils, at 800–1500 m elevation.

Chamaedorea murriensis
(Map 152)
Field characters. Stems solitary or clustered, 2–3.5 m tall and 2–3 cm diameter, erect. Leaves 7–10, pinnate; leaflets 2–4 per side, sigmoid, 25–32 cm long and 5–7 cm wide, *the apical one much wider than the others.* Inflorescences similar; flowering branches 11–15; fruits globose to oblong, to 1.2 cm long and 9–10 mm diameter, black, with persistent, thickened petals.

Range and habitat. Panama (Darién) and Colombia (Antioquia); montane rain forest, at 700–1500 m elevation.
Notes. Very similar to, and perhaps conspecific with, *Chamaedorea warscewiczii.*

Chamaedorea nationsiana
(Map 153)
Field characters. Stems solitary, to 2.5 m tall and 2–3 cm diameter, erect. Leaves 5–6, pinnate; leaflets to 11 per side, lanceolate, to 53 cm long and 9 cm wide. *Inflorescences spicate, the males pendulous, multiple, to 8 at each node, with densely crowded flowers; females solitary, erect, with densely crowded flowers on a thickened flowering branch*; fruits globose but angled from mutual pressure, 1–1.5 cm diameter, black, with thickened, persistent petals.
Range and habitat. Atlantic slope in Guatemala (Izabal); rain forest on limestone soils, to 900 m elevation.
Notes. See comments under *Chamaedorea allenii.*

Chamaedorea nubium
(Map 154)
Field characters. Stems clustered, forming small colonies, 1–3 m tall and 0.8–1 cm diameter, erect or creeping. Leaves 4–7, simple or pinnate; blades widely oblanceolate, deeply bifid, to 45 cm long and 30–35 cm wide, the margins only slightly toothed, pinnate leaves with 6–13 linear-lanceolate leaflets per side. Inflorescences erect or arching, dissimilar; males with up to 15 flowering branches; females with up to 10 branches (rarely spicate); flowers yellow; fruits globose to ovoid, 1–1.4 cm long, black, with persistent, thickened petals.
Range and habitat. Mexico (Chiapas, Guerrero, Oaxaca), Guatemala (Alta Verapaz, Baja Verapaz, El Progreso, Huehuetenango, Quezaltenango, San Marcos, Zacapa), El Salvador (Chalatenango, Santa Ana), and Honduras (Lempira); premontane or montane rain forest on mountain slopes, at 1500–2500 m elevation.
Notes. Similar to the southern *Chamaedorea brachyclada.* We include here *C. skutchii*, a species kept separate by Hodel (1992a).

Chamaedorea oblongata
(Map 155)
"Xaté macho" (Gua), "tepejilote" (Mex), "pacayita" (Nic)
Field characters. Stems solitary, 1–3 m tall and 1–2.5 cm diameter, erect or creeping. Leaves 3–8, pinnate; leaflets 3–9 per side, *somewhat thick and leathery,* lanceolate to oblong, 17–40 cm long and 3.5–10 cm wide. Inflorescences erect, with 6–25 flowering branches; fruits ovoid-ellipsoid, 0.8–1.4 cm long and 6–8 mm

diameter, black, with persistent, thickened petals.

Range and habitat. Atlantic slope in Mexico (Campeche, Chiapas, Oaxaca, Puebla, Quintana Roo, Tabasco, Veracruz), Guatemala (Alta Verapaz, Izabal, Petén), Belize, Honduras (Atlántida), and Nicaragua (Jinotega, Matagalpa); lowland forest, below 350 m elevation.

Uses. Widely cultivated as an ornamental.

Notes. Very similar to *Chamaedorea pinnatifrons*, but differs in the structure of its male flowers (see comments on species pairs following genus description). Here we include *C. paradoxa*, a species kept separate by Hodel (1992a).

Chamaedorea oreophila
(Map 156)
"Tepejilote" (Mex)
Field characters. Stems solitary, 0.4–3 m tall and 0.6–2 cm diameter, erect. Leaves 5–13, pinnate; leaflets 14–25 per side, lanceolate, 16–35 cm long and 1.4–4 cm wide. *Inflorescences spicate, erect, the males pendulous, 4–8 at each node, with densely crowded flowers, the females erect, one at each node, with densely crowded flowers on a thickened flowering branch*; fruits ovoid-ellipsoid, 0.6–1.3 cm long and 4–8 mm diameter, *red, crowded on the flowering branch*, with persistent, thickened petals.
Range and habitat. Atlantic slope in Mexico (Oaxaca, Veracruz); rain forest, often on limestone soils, at 1000–1500 m elevation.
Notes. In Veracruz, flowering takes place between April and August, but also at other times of year (Aguilar, 1986).

Chamaedorea pachecoana
(Map 157)
"Pacaya" (Gua)
Field characters. Very small plants. Stems solitary, to 0.3 m tall and 7–10 mm diameter, erect or creeping. Leaves 6–12, pinnate; leaflets 7–11 per side, oblong-lanceolate to sigmoid, 4.5–12 cm long and 1.5–2 cm wide, *often attached at right angles to rachis*. Inflorescences erect; males with 2–6 flowering branches; females spicate or bifurcate; fruits globose to ovoid, 6–8 mm diameter, black, with thickened, persistent petals.
Range and habitat. Pacific slope in Guatemala (Quezaltenango, San Marcos, Sololá); montane rain forest, at 1200–1500 m elevation.
Notes. In its leaflets attached at right angles it resembles *Chamaedorea tenerrima*.

Chamaedorea palmeriana
(Map 158)
Field characters. Stems solitary, to 1 m tall and 0.7–1 cm diameter, erect or somewhat lean-

ing. Leaves to 7 or more, simple; *blades broadly oblanceolate, deeply bifid*, 22–25 cm long and to 20 cm wide, strongly plicate and toothed on the margins. Inflorescences erect; males with 2–7 flowering branches; females spicate or rarely with 2–3 branches; fruits globose to ovoid, to 1.2 cm long and 0.8–1 cm diameter, black, with persistent, thickened petals.
Range and habitat. Atlantic slope in Costa Rica (Alajuela, Cartago, Heredia, Limón, San José) and Panama (Chiriquí, Veraguas); rain forest, at 450–1800 m elevation.
Notes. See comments under *Chamaedorea amabilis* (of which this is possibly a local leaf form).

Chamaedorea parvifolia
(Map 159)
Field characters. Stems solitary, to 2 m tall and 1.5 cm diameter, but usually flowering when stemless. Leaves 5–8, *pinnate, to 35 cm long; leaflets 4–5 per side*, lanceolate, to 16 cm long and 2.5–2.8 cm wide. Inflorescences erect, with 3–5 erect flowering branches; fruits small, globose.
Range and habitat. Pacific slope in Costa Rica (Alajuela, Cartago, Puntarenas, San José); montane forest, at 1500–2700 m elevation.
Notes. Very similar to *Chamaedorea lehmannii* and *C. pittieri*, which differ mostly in their male flowers with free petals.

Chamaedorea parvisecta
(Map 160)
"Pacaya" (Gua)
Field characters. Stems solitary, to 2 m tall and 5–7 mm diameter, erect. Leaves 3–5, pinnate; *leaf sheaths tubular*; leaflets to 10 per side, lanceolate, to 20 cm long and 4.5 cm wide. Inflorescences erect to horizontal; males with 4–18 pendulous flowering branches; females with 3–10 thick, blunt-tipped branches; fruits globose to ovoid, to 1 cm long and 9 mm diameter, black, with persistent, thickened petals.
Range and habitat. Atlantic slope in Mexico (Chiapas) and Guatemala (Alta Verapaz, Baja Verapaz, El Progreso, Huehuetenango, Zacapa); montane rain forest, at 1400–2500 m elevation.

Chamaedorea pauciflora
(Map 161, Plate 15)
"Suma-yuca" (Ecu), "sangapilla" (Per)
Field characters. Stems solitary, 0.3–2 m tall and 1–2 cm diameter, erect. Leaves 4–9, simple or rarely pinnate; simple leaves bifid, to 75 cm long and 25–40 cm wide, pinnate leaves with 4–7, linear to sigmoid leaflets per side. Inflorescences dissimilar; *males spicate, multiple, to 7 at each node; females spicate, solitary at the nodes*

(rarely 2 at each node); fruits ellipsoid, 1.2–1.5 cm long and 5–8 mm diameter, black, with persistent, thickened petals.

Range and habitat. Western Amazon region in Colombia (Amazonas, Putumayo), Ecuador (Napo, Morona-Santiago, Pastaza, Zamora-Chinchipe), Peru (Huánuco, Loreto, Madre de Dios, San Martín, Ucayali), Brazil (Acre, Amazonas, Mato Grosso, Rondônia), and Bolivia (Pando); rain forest in inundated or noninundated areas, below 1000 m elevation.

Chamaedorea pinnatifrons
(Map 162, Plates 15 & 16)
"Jatatilla" (Bol), "ubim" (Bra), "molinillo," "San Pablo" (Col), "chontilla" (Ecu), "pacaya" (Gua), "tepejilotillo" (Mex), "cashipana" (Per), "molinillo" (Ven)

Field characters. Stems solitary, 0.5–4.5 m tall and 0.5–3 cm diameter, erect or sometimes sprawling and then rooting at the nodes. Leaves 3–10, pinnate or rarely simple; *leaflets (2–)4–8 per side, sigmoid* or rarely almost lanceolate, 11–40 cm long and 2–15 cm wide, simple leaves with up to 10 primary veins per side. Inflorescences erect to horizontal, male and female similar, with 2–45 flowering branches, most commonly with 5–20, males pendulous, females ± stiff; fruits globose to ellipsoid, rarely sickle shaped, 0.5–1.5 cm long and 0.4–0.5 cm diameter, passing (always?) from green to orange or red and finally ripening black.

Range and habitat. Southern Mexico through Central America in Belize, Guatemala, Honduras, Nicaragua, Costa Rica, Panama and into Venezuela, Colombia, Ecuador, Peru, Brazil, and Bolivia; lowland to montane forest, at 40–2700 m elevation.

Uses. A kitchen instrument is made from the lower part of the stem and roots and used to stir chocolate, whence the common name "molinillo."

Notes. One of the most widespread and variable palms in the Americas, both latitudinally and elevationally. Hodel (1992a) recognized several segregates based mostly on leaf characters; we have included these here (*Chamaedorea falcifera, C. neurochlamys, C. serpens, C. verapazensis*). Pollination has been studied in Peru (Listabarth, 1993a).

Chamaedorea pittieri
(Map 163)
Field characters. Stems solitary, 0–2 m tall and 1–2 cm diameter, erect (but often appearing stemless). Leaves 5–9, pinnate; leaflets 5–8 per side, lanceolate, 10–20 cm long and 2–3 cm wide, *dark gray-green, leathery.* Inflorescences erect, with 2–6 flowering branches; fruits

globose to oblong, to 1 cm long and 6–7 mm diameter, black, with thickened, persistent petals.

Range and habitat. Pacific slope in Costa Rica (Puntarenas) and Panama (Chiriquí, Panamá); montane rain forest, at 1100–1800 m elevation.

Notes. Closely related to, but geographically separated from *Chamaedorea lehmanii*. It is also very similar to *C. parvifolia*, which differs in the male flowers with petals joined at the tips (see comments on species pairs following the genus description).

Chamaedorea plumosa
(Map 164)
Field characters. Stems solitary, to 4 m tall and 4–6.5 cm diameter, erect. Leaves 7–9, pinnate; *leaflets to 85 per side, linear, irregularly arranged in clusters and spreading in different planes and giving the leaf a plumose appearance.* Inflorescences dissimilar, males with up to 100 flowering branches, females with 30–45 branches; fruits globose, to 1.1 cm diameter, black.

Range and habitat. Mexico (Chiapas); deciduous forest, often on limestone, at 600–1200 m elevation.

Notes. Very similar to *Chamaedorea glaucifolia*, but this differs in its glaucous petiole and rachis and male flowers with the petals joined at the tips (see comments on species pairs following the genus description).

Chamaedorea pochutlensis
(Map 165)
"Canelilla" (Mex)
Field characters. Stems clustered, 2–5 m tall and 1.5–3 cm diameter, erect or leaning, *forming dense clumps.* Leaves 2–5, pinnate; leaflets 11–33 per side, lanceolate, 12–40 cm long and 1–3 cm wide, *swollen at point of attachment,* with 2 submarginal secondary veins on either side of primary vein. Inflorescences erect with 6–28 flowering branches (males with more, females with fewer); fruits globose-ellipsoid, 1.2–1.5 cm long and 0.8–1 cm diameter, black, with thickened, persistent petals.

Range and habitat. Pacific slope in western Mexico (Colima, Durango, Guerrero, Jalisco, Michoacán, Nayarit, Oaxaca, Sinaloa); rain forest or oak forest, on steep slopes and often in canyons, at 50–2000 m elevation.

Notes. It is the northern counterpart of and very similar to *Chamaedorea costaricana*. This differs only in the flaps at the top of its leaf sheaths.

Chamaedorea pumila
(Map 166)
Field characters. Stems solitary, 25–50 cm tall and 0.8–2 cm diameter, erect or creeping, *the*

plant usually appearing stemless. Leaves 5–15, *simple*, blades obovate to elliptic, bifid for half their length or more, 15–40 cm long and to 17 cm wide, toothed on the margins, *thick and leathery and sometimes mottled gray-green.* Inflorescences erect, dissimilar; males with 4–10 flowering branches; females spicate or rarely bifurcate; fruits globose, 0.6–1 cm diameter, black, with persistent, thickened petals.
Range and habitat. Atlantic and Pacific slope in Costa Rica (Alajuela, Cartago, Guanacaste, Heredia, Limón, Puntarenas, San José); lowland to montane rain forest on steep slopes, at 400–1500 m elevation.
Uses. It is widely cultivated as an ornamental. In several localities whole populations of this species have been dug up by collectors, threatening the species with extinction.
Notes. Hodel (1992a) separated *Chamaedorea minima*, but we include it here.

Chamaedorea pygmaea
(Map 167)
Field characters. Stems solitary, 0–75 cm tall and 1–2 cm diameter, erect or creeping, *plants often appearing stemless.* Leaves 3–8, simple or pinnate; simple blades 20–30 cm long, 6–15 cm wide, bifid for one-third their length, pinnate leaf with 9–20 leaflets per side, lanceolate, 12–18 cm long and 1–15 cm wide, *the lower margins running into and continuous with the rachis.* Inflorescences dissimilar; males with 10–25 flowering branches; females spicate or bifurcate; fruits oblong, 0.6–0.8 cm diameter, black, with thickened, persistent petals.
Range and habitat. Atlantic and Pacific slope in Guatemala (Izabal), Costa Rica (Alajuela, Heredia, Puntarenas), Panama (Chiriquí, Darién, Veraguas), and northwestern Colombia (Antioquia); rain forest, at 200–2000 m elevation.
Notes. Together with *Chamaedorea brachyclada, C. scheryi*, and *C. undulatifolia*, this forms a group of similar species. Hodel (1992a) separated *Chamaedorea stenocarpa*, but we include it here.

Chamaedorea queroana
(Map 168)
Field characters. Stems solitary, 0–1 m tall and 2–3 cm diameter, erect or creeping, *plants appearing stemless.* Leaves 4–5, simple or pinnate; *petiole minutely white spotted;* blades to 25 cm long and 18 cm wide, bifid to more than one-half their length, margins slightly toothed at the tips, with 8–10 primary veins per side, pinnate leaves with 3–10, lanceolate leaflets per side, to 16 cm long and 3–4 cm wide. Inflorescences erect, dissimilar, males with 6–13 flowering branches, females spicate or bifurcate; fruits ovoid, to 1.4 cm long and 7–8 mm diameter, black, with thickened, persistent petals.

Range and habitat. Atlantic slope in Mexico (Oaxaca); rain forest, at 1300 m elevation.

Chamaedorea radicalis
(Map 169)
Field characters. Stems solitary, (0–)3–4 m tall and 2.5–3 cm diameter, erect. Leaves 4–8, pinnate; leaflets 10–18 per side, linear-lanceolate, to 40 cm long and 1–2.5 cm wide. Inflorescences erect, dissimilar; male with 8–20 flowering branches; females with 1–20 branches; *male flowers in linear groups of 2–5 at base of flowering branch;* fruits ellipsoid, to 1.2 cm long and 9 mm diameter, *reddish*, with thickened, persistent petals.
Range and habitat. Mexico (Hidalgo, Nuevo León, San Luis Potosí, Tamaulipas); oak forest, often on limestone soils, to 1000 m elevation.

Chamaedorea rhizomatosa
(Map 170)
Field characters. Stems clustered, to 2.5 m tall and 7–9 mm diameter, erect or creeping, *forming loose colonies by rhizomes.* Leaves 3–6, pinnate; leaflets 6–8 per side, lanceolate, to 25 cm long and 5 cm wide. Inflorescences with 12 flowering branches; fruits unknown.
Range and habitat. Mexico (Oaxaca); pine-oak forest in rocky places, at 1400 m elevation.

Chamaedorea rigida
(Map 171)
"Kum" (Gua)
Field characters. Stems solitary, 1.5–2 m or less tall and 1–1.5 cm diameter, erect or creeping, flowering when still appearing stemless. Leaves 10–15, simple, *with very short petioles;* blades obovate, deeply bifid to half their length, 35–45 cm long and 14 cm wide, *glossy green, leathery and rigid,* scarcely toothed on the margins. Inflorescences with 3–5 erect flowering branches; fruits globose, 7–8 mm diameter, black, with persistent, thickened petals.
Range and habitat. Atlantic slope in Mexico (Oaxaca); rain forest on steep slopes, at 1700–1900 m elevation.

Chamaedorea robertii
(Map 172)
Field characters. Stems solitary, to 50 cm tall and 2–5 cm diameter, erect or creeping, the plant appearing stemless. Leaves 5–7, simple; blades elongate-obovate, *deeply bifid, markedly plicate,* 40–50 cm long and 20 cm wide, *the margins toothed.* Inflorescences spicate, the males pendulous, the females arching, both with densely arranged flowers; fruits globose, 7 mm diameter, black, with persistent, thickened petals.
Range and habitat. Atlantic slope in Costa Rica

(Alajuela, Guanacaste, Heredia, San José) and Panama (Bocas del Toro, Chiriquí, Coclé, Veraguas); premontane and montane rain forest, at 650–1500 m elevation.
Notes. Closely related to and perhaps not distinct from the Guatemalan *Chamaedorea castillomontii*.

Chamaedorea rojasiana
(Map 173)
"Molinillo," "pacaya" (Gua)
Field characters. Stems solitary, to 1 m tall and 0.6–1 cm diameter, erect. Leaves 3–6, pinnate or occasionally simple; blades with up to 7 primary veins per side, pinnate leaves with 2–5 sigmoid leaflets per side, 13–22 cm long and 2.5–9 cm wide. Inflorescences dissimilar; males spicate or with 2–10 pendulous flowering branches; females spicate or with 2–5 arching branches; fruits globose to ellipsoid, 0.7–1.1 cm diameter, purple-black.
Range and habitat. Mexico (Chiapas) and Guatemala (Alta Verapaz, Baja Verapaz, El Progreso, Huehuetenango, Quezaltenango, San Marcos, Sololá, Zacapa); montane rain forest, at 1200–2600 m elevation.
Notes. Strikingly similar to *Chamaedorea dammeriana*, which differs mainly in its male flowers with spreading petals (see comments on species pairs following genus description). It is also similar to *C. pinnatifrons*.

Chamaedorea sartorii
(Map 174)
"Tepejilote" (Mex)
Field characters. Stems solitary, 0.6–4 m tall and 0.8–1.6 cm diameter, erect. Leaves 3–6, pinnate; leaflets 5–10 per side, sigmoid, 20–40 cm long and 4–7 cm wide. Inflorescences erect, branched, *males with up to 30 pendulous flowering branches, densely covered with flowers*, females with 4–8 branches, *with bright orange petals*; fruits ellipsoid-ovoid, 0.9–1.2 cm long and 7–8 mm diameter, black, with thin petals, *these mostly nonpersistent*.
Range and habitat. Atlantic slope in Mexico (Oaxaca, Puebla, Veracruz) and Honduras (Atlántida, Olancho); rain forest, often on limestone soils, at 100–1300 m elevation.
Uses. It is occasionally planted as an ornamental.
Notes. Very similar to *Chamaedorea pinnatifrons* and *C. oblongata*, but differs in its male flowers with orange petals. Flowering takes place between September and March in Veracruz, Mexico (Aguilar, 1986).

Chamaedorea scheryi
(Map 175)
Field characters. Stems solitary, often short and

subterranean, to 15 cm tall and 1–3 cm diameter, erect or creeping. Leaves 4–6, pinnate; leaflets 16–20 per side, linear-lanceolate to almost sigmoid, 20–35 cm long and 2.5–4 cm wide, decreasing markedly in length toward top of rachis, *the lower margin running into and continuous with the rachis*. Inflorescences erect, dissimilar, often arising from near ground level, borne on an elongate peduncle; males with 15–30 flowering branches; females with 4–9 branches; fruits globose, 5–7 mm diameter, black, with persistent, thickened petals.
Range and habitat. Atlantic slope in Costa Rica (Alajuela, Cartago, Heredia, San José) and Panama (Chiriquí, Coclé); rain forest, at 800–2000 m elevation.
Notes. Together with *Chamaedorea brachyclada*, *C. pygmaea*, and *C. undulatifolia*, this forms a group of similar species.

Chamaedorea schiedeana
(Map 176)
"Pacaya" (Mex)
Field characters. Stems solitary, to 3 m tall and 2.5–3 cm diameter, erect. Leaves 3–5, pinnate; *leaflets 10–14 per side, lanceolate to sigmoid, to 30 cm long and 3–4 cm wide*. Inflorescences dissimilar, borne on an elongate peduncle; males with 20–45 flowering branches, females with 15–20 branches; fruits globose, 6–9 mm diameter, black, with thickened, persistent petals.
Range and habitat. Atlantic slope in Mexico (Oaxaca, Puebla, Veracruz); montane rain forest, often on limestone soils, at 900–1600 m elevation.
Notes. Closely related to *Chamaedorea pinnatifrons*, but differs in its more numerous leaflets.

Chamaedorea seifrizii
(Map 177)
"Xaté" (Bel, Gua)
Field characters. Stems clustered, forming clumps, to 3 m tall and 1–2 cm diameter, erect or leaning. Leaves 4–5, pinnate; leaflets 5–18 per side, very variable in shape, from linear to lanceolate, or almost sigmoid, 20–35 cm long and 0.8–3 cm wide. Inflorescences erect with 4–12 flowering branches; fruits globose, to 8 mm diameter, black, with persistent, thickened petals.
Range and habitat. Mexico (Campeche, Quintana Roo, Tabasco, Yucatán), Belize, Guatemala (Petén), and Honduras (Islas de la Bahía); open woods or forest, often on limestone soils in areas liable to seasonal inundation, to 500 m elevation.
Notes. Unusual in preferring low-lying, seasonally inundated areas, especially in the Yucatán Peninsula of Mexico. Once cultivated by the Maya, this is one of the most widespread spe-

cies of *Chamaedorea* in cultivation, where it is possibly more common than in the wild (Hodel, 1992a). Hodel (pers. comm.) suggests that *Chamaedorea donnell-smithii* may be the correct name for this species.

Chamaedorea selvae
(Map 178)
Field characters. Stems solitary, to 2 m tall and 2 cm diameter, erect. Leaves 4–5, pinnate; leaflets 3–8 per side, lanceolate to sigmoid, to 45 cm long and 9 cm wide, *the apical pair sometimes very large.* Inflorescences dissimilar; males with up to 17 flowering branches; females with up to 11 branches; fruits oblong, to 7 mm long and 5 mm diameter, black, with persistent, thickened petals.
Range and habitat. Atlantic slope in Nicaragua (Río San Juan) and Costa Rica (Alajuela, Heredia, Limón, San José); lowland rain forest, below 200(–700) m elevation.
Notes. This species is probably conspecific with *Chamaedorea lucidifrons* (M. Grayum, pers. comm.).

Chamaedorea simplex
(Map 179)
"Pacaya" (Gua)
Field characters. Stems solitary, to 1 m tall and 0.5–1.2 cm diameter, erect or creeping. Leaves 3–6, *simple; blades broadly obovate, bifid to three-quarters their length or more,* the lobes to 20 cm long and 5 cm wide, scarcely toothed on the margins, with 6–7 primary veins per side. *Inflorescences spicate,* the males pendulous, the females arching; fruits ellipsoid to oblong, 0.9–1.2 cm diameter, black, with persistent, thickened petals.
Range and habitat. Atlantic slope in Mexico (Chiapas) and Guatemala (Alta Verapaz, Baja Verapaz, Huehuetenango); montane rain forest, at 1100–1500 m elevation.

Chamaedorea stolonifera
(Map 180)
Field characters. Stems creeping along the ground (stoloniferous) and forming colonies, 1–2 m tall and 0.5–0.8 cm diameter. Leaves 5–8, simple; blades oblong-lanceolate, bifid to two-thirds their length, to 30 cm long and 25 cm wide. Inflorescences erect, with 2–7 flowering branches, the males pendulous and densely covered with flowers, *the female flowers bright orange;* fruits globose, 7–9 mm diameter, black, *with thin petals, these mostly nonpersistent.*
Range and habitat. Atlantic slope in Mexico (Chiapas); rain forest, usually on limestone soils, at 600–800 m elevation.
Uses. It is commonly cultivated as an ornamental.

Chamaedorea stricta
(Map 181)
Field characters. Stems solitary, to 1.5 m tall and 2.5–3 cm diameter, but usually appearing stemless. Leaves 3–7, erect, simple, with a 25–60 cm long petiole; *blades almost rectangular, 20–75 cm long and 13–28 cm wide, bifid for about one-third their length,* with 12–17 primary veins per side. Inflorescences erect, males with 7 flowering branches, females with 2–4; fruits almost globose, 8 mm diameter.
Range and habitat. Pacific slope in Mexico (Chiapas), Guatemala (San Marcos), Costa Rica (San José), and Panamá (Veraguas); rain forest, at 850–1900 m elevation.
Notes. Very similar to *Chamaedorea rigida,* but differs in its longer petioles and poorly developed stems.

Chamaedorea sullivaniorum
(Map 182)
Field characters. Stems solitary, creeping to erect, to 25 cm tall and 1–1.5 cm diameter. Leaves 10–15, *simple;* blades oblong, 25–40 cm long and 10–17 cm wide, bifid to one third their length, *leathery, the margins conspicuously toothed.* Inflorescences erect, dissimilar; males with 4–8 flowering branches, females spicate or bifurcate; fruits globose, 6–8 mm diameter, black.
Range and habitat. Pacific and Atlantic slope in Costa Rica (Limón, Puntarenas, San José) and Atlantic slope in Panama (Bocas del Toro to Colón) and an unconfirmed record in eastern Panama (San Blas) and two records from western Colombia (Antioquia, Chocó), one of them from the late nineteenth century; rain forest, at 600–1500 m elevation on the Atlantic slope but below 400 m in the Pacific lowlands of Costa Rica.
Notes. Similar to *Chamaedorea pumila,* but differs in its shortly bifid leaves.

Chamaedorea tenerrima
(Map 183)
Field characters. Stems solitary, to 1.5 m tall and 7 mm diameter, erect or creeping. Leaves 4–5, pinnate; leaflets 2–7 per side, *sigmoid, backwards-pointing, with toothed margins, the lower margin continuing over the rachis,* to 11 cm long and 2.5 cm wide, the apical pair much wider than the others. Inflorescences erect, dissimilar; males with up to 10 flowering branches; females with 2–3 branches; fruits globose, 6–7 mm diameter, black.
Range and habitat. Atlantic slope in Guatemala (Alta Verapaz, Baja Verapaz); rain forest, at 900–1600 m elevation.
Notes. Very unusual in its backward-pointing leaflets.

Chamaedorea tepejilote
(Map 184, Plate 16)
"Palmito dulce" (CR), "pacaya," "tepejilote" (ElS, Gua, Mex), "caña verde" (Pan)
Field characters. Stems solitary or sometimes clustered, 2–7 m tall and 2–10 cm diameter, erect or rarely creeping. Leaves 3–7, pinnate; leaflets 6–25 per side, sigmoid, 16–70 cm long and 3.5–10 cm wide, with 5–10 primary veins. Inflorescences dissimilar; *males solitary or rarely multiple and 2–5 at each node, with 7–50 pendulous flowering branches, with densely crowded flowers; females solitary or rarely multiple with 2–4 at each node, with 5–20 erect, thickened flowering branches with densely crowded flowers;* fruits ellipsoid to ovoid, 1–1.5(–2) cm long and 7–8 mm diameter, black, with persistent, thickened petals.
Range and habitat. Southern Mexico (Chiapas, Oaxaca, Veracruz) and Central America in Guatemala, Belize, El Salvador, Honduras, Nicaragua, Costa Rica, and Panama and reaching western Colombia (Chocó, Valle); forest, often on limestone soils, to 1600 m elevation.
Uses. Very commonly cultivated in parts of Central America, particularly Guatemala, for its edible male inflorescences. The unopened inflorescences, which resemble ears of corn and are locally known as "pacaya," are collected and sold in markets and eaten as a vegetable (Cook and Doyle, 1939; Hodel, 1992a; Castillo Mont et al., 1994).
Notes. Hodel (1992a) separated *Chamaedorea alternans* as distinct, although it appears to be only a local form and we include it here. Various ecological aspects of this species have been studied in Mexico: biomass allocation (Oyama and Dirzo, 1988); growth and reproduction (Oyama, 1990); defoliation (Oyama and Mendoza, 1990); seed predation (Oyama, 1991), herbivory (Oyama and Dirzo, 1991), population structure (Oyama et al., 1992), and age and height (Oyama, 1993).

Chamaedorea tuerckheimii
(Map 185)
"Guonay" (Mex)
Field characters. Very small palms. Stems solitary, 0.3–1 m tall and 3–7 mm diameter, creeping. Leaves 7–12, simple; blades wedge shaped-obovate, *very briefly bifid,* 12–22 cm long and 3.5–7.5 cm wide, *strongly plicate and with toothed margins.* Inflorescences dissimilar, erect; males with 7–16 flowering branches, females spicate or bifurcate; fruits ovoid to ellipsoid, 0.8–1.2 cm long and 6–9 mm diameter, black, with persistent, thickened petals present.
Range and habitat. Mexico (Oaxaca, Veracruz)

and Guatemala (Alta Verapaz); rain forest, at 900–1500 m elevation.
Notes. This is one of the smallest American palms and an attractive ornamental. It has been practically exterminated in the wild by collectors.

Chamaedorea undulatifolia
(Map 186)
Field characters. Stems solitary, to 1 m tall and 1–1.5 cm diameter, creeping. Leaves 3–5, pinnate; leaflets 12–18 per side, lanceolate to sigmoid, 12.5–19 cm long and 1.5–2.5 cm wide, decreasing markedly in length toward top of rachis, *with wavy margins, these running into the rachis at the point of insertion.* Inflorescences dissimilar, erect, *borne on an elongate peduncle;* males with up to 30 flowering branches; females with 2–6 branches; fruits globose to ellipsoid, to 8 mm long and 6 mm diameter, black, with persistent, thickened petals.
Range and habitat. Costa Rica (Alajuela, Cartago, Heredia, Puntarenas, San José); premontane or montane rain forest along the continental divide, at 800–1700 m elevation.
Notes. Closely related to *Chamaedorea brachyclada, C. scheryi,* and *C. pygmaea* and the four form a natural group.

Chamaedorea verecunda
(Map 187)
Field characters. Stems solitary, to 75 cm long and 3.5–5 mm diameter, creeping or erect. Leaves 8–11, *simple;* blades obovate, *9–16 cm long and 7–10 cm wide,* bifid to half their length, gray-green. Inflorescences erect, *males and females spicate,* very short; fruits ellipsoid, to 1 cm long, black, with thickened, persistent petals.
Range and habitat. Panama (Chiriquí); rain forest on the continental divide, at 1200–1400 m elevation.
Notes. This distinctive, dwarf species is closely related to both *Chamaedorea correae* and *C. guntheriana.*

Chamaedorea volcanensis
(Map 188)
Field characters. Stems solitary, to 1 m tall and 2–3 cm diameter, erect. Leaves 4–5, pinnate, rarely simple and bifid; *leaflets 8–12 per side, 25–35 cm long, and 4–7.5 cm wide,* lanceolate to sigmoid, simple leaves with 7–9 primary veins per side. Inflorescences dissimilar; males with 2–13 pendulous flowering branches; females with 1–5 spreading branches; fruits oblong to ovoid, to 1.2 cm long and 8 mm diameter, black, with persistent, thickened petals.
Range and habitat. Pacific slope in Guatemala

(Quezaltenango, San Marcos, Suchitepéquez); montane rain forest, at 1200–2000 m elevation.

Chamaedorea vulgata
(Map 189)
Field characters. Stems solitary, to 2 m tall and 1–2 cm diameter, erect, densely and minutely white spotted. Leaves 3–5, pinnate; *sheath, petiole, and rachis densely and minutely pitted or white spotted*; leaflets 10–16 per side, lanceolate or linear-lanceolate, 35–50 cm long and 4–9 cm wide. Inflorescences erect on elongate peduncles; males and females with 3–12 flowering branches; fruits globose to obovoid, 8–9 mm long, black, with persistent, thickened petals.
Range and habitat. Mexico (Oaxaca, Chiapas) and Guatemala (Quezaltenango, San Marcos); pine-oak or montane rain forest on slopes, at 1300–2350 m elevation.
Notes. Hodel (1992a) separated *Chamaedorea foveata* as distinct, but we include it here.

Chamaedorea warscewiczii
(Map 190)
Field characters. Stems solitary, to 4 m tall, 1.5–3.5 cm diameter, erect or creeping. Leaves 4–8, pinnate; leaflets 4–7 per side, *sigmoid, 25–37 cm long, 2–13 cm wide, the apical pair of leaflets wider than the others.* Inflorescences erect, dissimilar; males with 15–25 pendulous flowering branches, females with 7–15 spreading branches; fruits ovoid or globose, to 1.3 cm long and 7 mm diameter, black.
Range and habitat. Atlantic slope in Costa Rica (Alajuela, Cartago, Guanacaste, Heredia, Limón, Puntarenas, San José) and Panama (Coclé, Colón, Darién, Herrera, Panamá, San Blas, Veraguas); rain forest on slopes, to 750 m elevation.

Notes. Similar to *Chamaedorea pinnatifrons.* Hodel (1992a) separated *C. matae*, but we include it here.

Chamaedorea whitelockiana
(Map 191)
Field characters. Stems solitary, to 2 m tall and 1–1.3 cm diameter, erect. Leaves 5–7, pinnate; leaf sheaths tubular; leaflets 7–13 per side, lanceolate, to 15 cm long and 3 cm wide. Inflorescences erect; males with 12–15 erect flowering branches; females with 6–8 branches, these *spinose-tipped*; fruits globose, 7–8 mm diameter, black, with thickened petals.
Range and habitat. Pacific slope in Mexico (Chiapas, Oaxaca); pine-oak forest, at 1400–1900 m elevation.
Notes. Close to *Chamaedorea parvisecta* but differs in its pendulous male flowering branches and other details. It is also strikingly similar to *C. liebmanii*, which differs in the joined petals of the male flowers (see comments on species pairs following genus description).

Chamaedorea woodsoniana
(Map 192)
"Tepejilote" (Mex)
Field characters. Stems solitary, *5–12 m tall and 5–10 cm diameter.* Leaves 4–6, pinnate; *leaflets to 36 per side, linear-lanceolate, 30–65 cm long and 3.5–5 cm wide.* Inflorescences dissimilar, erect; *males with up to 100 flowering branches, females with up to 50*; fruits globose to oblong, 1–2 cm long and to 1 cm diameter, black, with persistent, thickened petals.
Range and habitat. Mexico, Belize, Guatemala, Honduras, Nicaragua, Costa Rica, Panama, and probably adjacent Colombia (Chocó); montane forest, at 800–2000 m elevation.
Notes. This is one of the largest species in the genus.

27. WENDLANDIELLA

This genus has traditionally been considered to be closely related to *Chamaedorea*, but may in fact be closer to *Synechanthus*. It was named in honor of Hermann Wendland (1825–1903), a German botanist and horticulturalist in Hannover who studied and grew palms, particularly those from Central America. The palms of this genus are small and easily overlooked in the forest and thus poorly collected and studied. Stems are green, small, and slender and often form clumps. Leaves are usually pinnate, 4–11 in number and are smooth and not tomentose. Sheaths are partially closed but do not form a crownshaft. The few leaflets are irregularly arranged in loose clusters, but sometimes the leaf is simple. The small inflorescences are borne below the leaves and can be spicate or branched to one or two orders. There are only two bracts on the peduncle, apart from the prophyll, and this character distinguishes the genus from *Chamaedorea*, which has more than two peduncular bracts. Individual plants bear either all male or all female flowers, but not both. Male flowers, with six stamens, are arranged in short, vertical rows along the flowering branches, while the female flowers are borne singly or in pairs. Fruits are one-seeded, ellipsoid, and black at maturity. The endosperm is homogeneous and the seedling leaf is bifid.

Wendlandiella contains one species (Henderson, 1994), distributed in the western Amazon region. It is in need of more collection and study to determine its relationship with other genera. Pollination has been studied by Listabarth (1993a), who concluded that flowers were wind pollinated.

Wendlandiella gracilis
(Map 193, Plate 16)
"Chontilla," "ponilla" (Per)
Field characters. Stems clustered or solitary, green, 0.3–1.5 m tall and 0.4–1 cm diameter. Leaves 4–11, simple or with 2–6 leaflets per side; leaflets irregularly arranged. Inflorescences usually borne below the leaves; fruits ellipsoid, 0.8–1 cm long and about 0.5 cm diameter, orange or orange-red.
Range and habitat. Western Amazon region in

Peru, Brazil, and Bolivia; low-lying, wet areas or occasionally well-drained places in rain forest, usually below 500 m elevation.
Notes. Three varieties are recognized (Henderson, 1994): var. *gracilis*, with 4–6 leaflets per side, from Peru (Huánuco, Loreto) and Brazil (Acre); var. *polyclada*, with 2 leaflets per side, from Peru (Loreto); and var. *simplicifrons*, with simple leaves, from Peru (Madre de Dios, Pasco) and Bolivia (La Paz, Pando).

28. DICTYOCARYUM

This genus, the first of the stilt-root palms, contains a few species that are confined mostly to mountain regions. Stems are tall, stout, erect, columnar or swollen, white or gray, and are solitary or rarely clustered. They are supported by a cone of numerous, closely spaced stilt roots, and these are covered with rather blunt spines. Leaves are pinnate, 3–6 in number and spread horizontally in a rather open crown. The leaf sheaths are closed and form a distinct crownshaft and the petiole is very short. Leaflets are split lengthwise into numerous, equally wide segments, and these spread in different planes, giving the leaf a plumose appearance. The segments are jagged on the apical margins and are white-gray waxy on the lower surface. Inflorescences are branched to one or two orders and are borne below the crown shaft. In bud they are either erect and straight or pendulous and horn shaped and are covered with numerous deciduous bracts. The scars of these bracts are clearly visible on the peduncle after they have fallen, and their number helps in identification of species. Inflorescences are usually very large and at flowering time are conspicuous, with the numerous, yellowish flowering branches spreading in various directions. Flowers are unisexual, yellowish white, and are borne in threes of a central female and two lateral males all along the flowering branches. Fruits are one-seeded, usually globose, and greenish yellow. The epicarp splits irregularly when mature to reveal the white mesocarp. The genus is named from the Greek words "dikyton," a net, and "karyon," a seed, in reference to the reticulate veins covering the seed. The endosperm is homogeneous and the seedling leaf is bifid.

Dictyocaryum contains three species (Henderson, 1990) distributed in Venezuela, Colombia, Ecuador, Peru, and Bolivia and also just reaching Panama, Guyana, and Brazil. They grow in mountainous areas on steep, forested slopes, usually between 1000 and 2000 m elevation, in areas of high rainfall. They rarely occur in lowland rain forest. This genus is very similar to *Iriartea*, from which it differs by its more or less equally wide leaf segments, which are white-gray waxy on the lower surface. *Dictyocaryum* also occurs at higher elevations than *Iriartea.*

Dictyocaryum fuscum
(Map 194)
"Palma araque" (Ven)
Field characters. Stems solitary, stout and erect, to 22 m tall and 20 cm diameter, *not swollen,* supported by a dense cone of stilt roots. Leaves 4–6, with a plumose appearance. Inflorescences very large, *the buds horn shaped and curved downward, with 9–11 bracts (or bract scars);* fruits globose, 2–3 cm diameter, greenish yellow.
Range and habitat. Cordillera de la Costa in Venezuela (Aragua, Carabobo, Distrito Federal, Miranda, Yaracuy); montane forest, at 1000–1800 m elevation.
Uses. The wood has been used in cabinet making.

Dictyocaryum lamarckianum
(Map 195, Plate 17)
"Barrigona" (Col), "palma real" (Ecu), "palma barrigona" (Pan), "basanco" (Per)
Field characters. Stems solitary, stout and erect, to 25 m tall and 40 cm diameter, *often swollen near the middle,* supported by a dense cone of stilt roots. Leaves 3–6, with a plumose appearance. Inflorescences very large, *the buds erect, with 8–9 bracts (or bract scars);* fruits globose, 2.5–3 cm diameter, greenish yellow.
Range and habitat. Patchily distributed from eastern Panama (Darién) through the Andes of Colombia (Antioquia, Caquetá, Huila, Magdalena), Venezuela (Táchira), Ecuador (Cotopaxi, Morona-Santiago, Napo), Peru (Pasco,

San Martín), and Bolivia (La Paz); montane rain forest on steep slopes, at 1000–2000 m elevation. It often forms very large and magnificent stands on forested Andean slopes, usually in areas of high rainfall (3500–6000 mm per year). Below 1000 m elevation it is replaced as the dominant palm by *Iriartea deltoidea.*
Uses. The hard, durable stems are often used in construction; in Colombia they are used as coffins by Emberá Indians.

Dictyocaryum ptarianum
(Map 196)
"Bombona paso" (Col), "pona colorada" (Per)
Field characters. Stems solitary, *rarely clustered,* stout and erect, to 20 m tall and 20 cm diameter, *not swollen,* supported by a cone of stilt roots. Leaves 4–5, with a plumose appearance. Inflorescences very large, *the buds horn shaped and curved downwards, with 8–10 bracts (or bract scars);* fruits globose, 2–3.5 cm diameter, greenish yellow.
Range and habitat. Mountains of the Guayana Highland of Venezuela (Amazonas, Bolívar) and Guyana; montane rain forest on steep slopes, at 800–1700 m elevation. Small, rare, lowland populations occurring below 300 m are known in the western Amazon region in Colombia (Amazonas), Peru (Loreto), and Brazil (Acre).
Uses. The stems are used in construction; the leaves are occasionally used for thatching.

29. IRIARTELLA

Palms of this genus resemble a smaller version of *Iriartea,* hence the generic name. The two genera may not be as closely related as previously thought, however. Stems are slender, erect, clustered (rarely solitary), and form loose, open colonies by elongate basal shoots or by rhizomes. Sometimes these basal shoots arise directly from the stem at some distance above the ground. There is a short cone of stilt roots but it is usually obscured by leaf litter. Leaves are pinnate, 3–8 in number, and form an open crown. The leaf sheaths are closed and form a poorly developed crownshaft, covered with irritant hairs. These leaf sheath hairs distinguish the genus from all others. Leaflets are simple, broadly lanceolate to almost rhombic, spread in the same plane and have jagged apical margins. Inflorescences are branched to one order and are borne among the leaves at flowering time but are below the leaves in fruit. There are 3–5 papery peduncular bracts and these sheath the peduncle. Flowers are unisexual and are borne in threes of a central female and two lateral males. Both flowers and the few flowering branches are green, and inflorescences are hard to see in the forest. Fruits are one-seeded, usually ellipsoid, scarlet, orange, or brownish, and the epicarp splits irregularly when mature to reveal the white mesocarp. The endosperm is homogeneous, and the seedling leaf is simple with jagged apical margins.

Iriartella contains two species (Henderson, 1990), distributed in the central and western Amazon region of Colombia, Venezuela, Guyana, Peru, and Brazil. They grow in lowland rain forest at elevations below 1000 m. The two species are very common understory palms in the Amazon region. They can easily be distinguished from all other palms by their moderate, clustered stems, leaf sheaths with irritant hairs, and simple leaflets with jagged margins. *Wettinia drudei* is superficially similar, but lacks irritant hairs and has hairy fruits. The two species of *Iriartella* differ from one another in small floral details (although *I. setigera* is generally larger than *I. stenocarpa*) and their ranges generally do not overlap, except in southeastern Colombia.

Iriartella setigera
(Map 197, Plate 17)
"Paxiubinha" (Bra), "macanilla" (Ven)
Field characters. Stems 2–12 m tall and 2–4 cm diameter, forming loose clusters, supported by a small cone of black stilt roots. Leaves 6–8; leaflets spreading in the same plane. Inflorescences borne among the leaves; fruits ellipsoid, rarely almost globose, 1.4–1.7 cm long and 0.7–1 cm diameter, scarlet, orange, or brown.
Range and habitat. Southeastern Colombia (Amazonas, Caquetá, Guainía, Vaupés, Vichada), southern Venezuela (Amazonas, Bolívar), Guyana, and Brazil (Amazonas, Pará, Roraima); lowland rain forest on noninundated soils, occasionally in inundated areas, usually below 500 m but rarely reaching 1000 m elevation.

Uses. The slender, straight stems were at one time used to make blowguns.

Iriartella stenocarpa
(Map 198)
"Paxiubinha de macaco" (Bra), "casha ponita" (Per)
Field characters. Stems 1–3 m tall 1–2 cm diameter, forming loose clusters, supported by a small cone of black stilt roots. Leaves 3–5; leaflets spreading in the same plane, or rarely the leaf simple. Inflorescences borne among the leaves; fruits ellipsoid, 0.9–1.5 cm long and 5–7 mm diameter, orange.
Range and habitat. Western Amazon region in Colombia (Amazonas), Peru (Junín, Loreto, Madre de Dios, Pasco, Ucayali), and Brazil (Acre); lowland rain forest on noninundated soils, below 500 m elevation.

30. IRIARTEA

This genus was named for Bernado de Iriarte (1735–1814), a Spanish politician and patron of the sciences. Stems are large, stout, erect, gray, solitary, and columnar or often swollen. They are supported by a dense cone of closely spaced, black, spiny stilt roots. Leaves are pinnate, 4–7 in number and horizontally spreading in a rather open crown. The leaf sheaths form a distinct, grayish green crownshaft. The leaflets have jagged apical margins and are split lengthwise into unequal segments; these spread in different planes, thus giving the leaf a plumose appearance. The basal segment of each leaflet is much wider than the others; it is pendulous, which gives the leaf a very characteristic, almost three-dimensional appearance. Inflorescences are branched to one or two orders and are covered by up to sixteen woody, deciduous bracts. These bracts, some of them very large, fall in a pile under the tree as the inflorescence develops. The scars of the bracts are easy to see on the peduncle after they have fallen. Inflorescences and inflorescence buds are clearly visible on the stem below the crown shaft. Buds develop below the leaves, becoming large, pendulous, and horn shaped before opening. At flowering time inflorescences are very large, with the white, pendulous flowering branches hanging almost candelabra-like. Flowers are unisexual and borne in threes of a central female and two lateral males along the flowering branches. Male flowers have 10–17 stamens. Fruits are one-seeded, globose, greenish yellow, and the epicarp splits irregularly at maturity to reveal the white mesocarp. The endosperm is homogeneous and the seedling leaf is simple and elliptical, with jagged margins.

Iriartea is a genus of one species (Henderson, 1990), occurring from Nicaragua south to Bolivia and extending into the western Amazon region of Colombia, Venezuela, and Brazil. It grows in lowland and montane rain forest between 150 and 1300 m elevation. It can be distinguished from all other genera of large stilt root palms (*Dictyocaryum*, *Socratea*, *Wettinia*) by its often swollen stems, green lower surface of the leaflets and large, pendulous, horn-shaped inflorescence buds. It is very commonly confused with *Socratea*, with which it often occurs, but can be distinguished by its dense cone of black stilt roots and horn-shaped buds.

Iriartea deltoidea
(Map 199, Plate 17)
"Copa" (Bol), "paxiúba barriguda" (Bra), "barrigona" (Col), "maquenque" (CR), "bomba" (Ecu), "huacrapona" (Per), "barriguda" (Ven)
Field characters. Stems solitary, large, swollen or columnar, to 25 m tall and 30(–70 at swelling) cm diameter, supported by a dense cone of black, closely spaced, spiny stilt roots. Leaves 4–7; leaflets divided and spreading in different planes, giving the leaf a plumose appearance. Inflorescences borne below the leaves, the buds large (to 2 m long), pendulous, and horn shaped; bracts (or bract scars) to 16, woody; fruits globose, 2–2.8 cm diameter, greenish yellow.
Range and habitat. Central America in Nicaragua, Costa Rica, and Panama and south through the Pacific lowlands of Colombia and Ecuador, the Andes of Colombia, Ecuador, Peru, and Bolivia and extending into the western Amazon region in Colombia, Venezuela, and Brazil; in a variety of habitats, from premontane forest on steep Andean slopes to lowland rain forest along stream margins, at 0–1300 m elevation.
Uses. The stems are split and the outer durable

part is commonly used in house construction. Pinard (1993) has studied the effect of stem harvesting on populations in Acre, Brazil. Specimens with swollen stems, growing near streams or rivers in the lowland Amazon region, are cut and used as temporary canoes. In the Chocó region of Colombia the swollen parts of the stems are used as coffins.
Notes. Extremely abundant on eastern Andean slopes below 1000 m elevation. Individuals in the Andes, near the upper elevational limit of the species, often have columnar, nonswollen stems (intermixed with a few swollen-stemmed individuals). Individuals in populations below 300 m elevation, which occur along stream and river margins in the western Amazon region, often have greatly swollen stems. The reason for this elevational variation in stem swelling is not known, but occurs in other palms. Flowers of *Iriartea* are pollinated by bees (Henderson, 1985); Roubik (1989) described the succession of different social bees visiting the inflorescences and collecting pollen of *Iriartea* in Panama. Fruits are copiously produced and from the tree are eaten by toucans and monkeys; fruits that fall on the ground are eaten by peccaries, rodents, and red and gray brocket deer.

31. SOCRATEA

This genus was named for the philosopher Socrates. Stems are gray, tall, and solitary or rarely clustered and are supported by an open cone of spiny, brown stilt roots. The genus is immediately recognizable by these roots. Leaves are pinnate, 4–7 in number, and the leaf sheaths form a distinct crownshaft. Individual leaflets are jagged at the tips and are split lengthwise (except *Socratea salazarii*) into numerous segments; these spread into various planes, giving the leaf a plumose appearance. The tips of the segments are often pendulous and this is characteristic for some species. Inflorescences are branched to one order and are erect in bud and hidden within the leaf sheath, but become visible and pendulous below the leaves at flowering time. They are covered with 3–5 thin, deciduous peduncular bracts. Flowering branches are rather few and short, but are generally quite thick. The white, unisexual flowers are borne in threes of a central female and two lateral males, and they are densely crowded along the flowering branches. Male flowers have 17–145 stamens but are very short lived and fall from the inflorescences within a day or so of opening. Fruits are one-seeded, ellipsoid or ovoid, yellowish or brownish, and the epicarp splits irregularly at maturity to reveal the white mesocarp. The endosperm is homogeneous and the seedling leaf is bifid with jagged apical margins.

Socratea contains five species (Henderson, 1990). One, *S. exorrhiza*, is widely distributed from Nicaragua south to Bolivia and all across northern South America, occurring in lowland forest below 1000 m elevation; the other four species have narrower ranges, occurring in Andean and adjacent regions in lowland or montane forest to 1800 m elevation.

This genus is similar to the other genera of stilt root palms (*Dictyocaryum, Iriartea, Iriartella, Wettinia*), but can be distinguished by its open cone of brown, spiny stilt roots. It is usually possible to see right through the cone, whereas in the other genera the stilt roots are very close together and the cone is not transparent.

Socratea exorrhiza
(Map 200, Plate 18)
"Pachuba" (Bol), "paxiúba" (Bra), "zancona" (Col), "bombón" (Ecu), "awara-monbin" (FrG), "jira" (Pan), "cashapona" (Per), "macanilla" (Ven)
Field characters. Stems solitary, 8–20 m tall and 12–18 cm diameter, supported by an open cone of about 25 spiny stilt roots. Leaves about 7, with a plumose appearance; *leaflets divided into segments, these pendulous at the tips.* Inflorescences with 4–6 bracts; *flowering branches to 17, 30–40 cm long and 2–3 mm diameter;* fruits ovoid or ellipsoid, *not beaked at the top,* 2.5–3.5 cm long and 1.5–2 cm diameter; yellowish.
Range and habitat. Widely distributed from Nicaragua south through Central and South America to Bolivia and east through Venezuela, the Guianas, and Brazil; lowland to premontane rain forest, from sea level to 1000 m elevation.
Uses. The most useful part of this palm is the hard and durable outer part of the lower stem. The stem is cut, split into sections, and the inner soft pith is discarded. The sections are used in house construction, especially for the walls and floors. The reason that the outer part of the stem is so hard and durable is because the vascular bundles, which are themselves highly sclerified, are concentrated in the outer region of the stem; the central pith consists of soft cells. There are many other minor uses of this palm; for example, sections of the spiny stilt roots are often used as manioc graters.
Notes. The flowers of *Socratea exorrhiza* are pollinated by small curculionid and nitidulid beetles (Henderson, 1985). A great variety of arboreal mammals, bats, and birds feed on its fruits, including monkeys, squirrels, currassows, oil birds, and toucans. The fruits that fall to the ground are eaten by peccaries, agoutis, and other small rodents (Henderson, 1990).

Socratea hecatonandra
(Map 201)
"Zancona" (Col), "crespa" (Ecu)
Field characters. Stems solitary, to 20 m tall and 30 cm diameter, supported by an open cone of about 30 stilt roots. Leaves about 7, with a plumose appearance; *leaflets divided and the segments stiff and not pendulous, appearing in 4 planes from a distance, golden-brown on lower surface.* Inflorescences with 4 bracts; *flowering branches 7–12, to 80 cm long and 7–8 mm diameter;* fruits ellipsoid, *beaked at the top,* 4–5 cm long and 2–2.5 cm diameter, yellowish green.
Range and habitat. Pacific coastal region of western Colombia (Chocó, Valle, and one possible record from the Cordillera Central in Antioquia) and Ecuador (Los Ríos, Pichincha); lowland rain forest, from sea level to 750 m elevation.

Socratea montana
(Map 202)
"Gualte" (Ecu)
Field characters. Stems solitary, to 23 m tall and 17 cm diameter, supported by an open cone of about 30 stilt roots. Leaves 5–8, with a plumose appearance; *leaflets divided and the segments arching at the tips.* Inflorescences with 4 bracts; *flowering branches 7–9, to 82 cm long and 11–13 mm diameter;* fruits ellipsoid, *beaked at the top,* about 3.5 cm long and 2.5 cm diameter, yellowish green.

Range and habitat. Pacific slope of the Cordillera Occidental in Colombia (Antioquia, Chocó, Nariño) and northern Ecuador (Esmeraldas, Pichincha); montane rain forest on steep slopes, at 900–1800 m elevation.

Uses. The outer sections of the split stem are used in construction.

Notes. This species and the following are very similar and may eventually be treated as local forms of a single, widespread species. *Socratea rostrata* would then be the correct name.

Socratea rostrata
(Map 203)
"Crespa" (Ecu)

Field characters. Stems solitary, to 25 m tall and 13 cm diameter, supported by an open cone of 15–26 stilt roots. Leaves 4–7, with a plumose appearance; *leaflets divided and the segments abruptly pendulous at the tip.* Inflorescences with 4 bracts; *flowering branches 8–11, to 60 cm long and 5 mm diameter;* fruits ellipsoid, *beaked at the top,* about 3.5 cm long and 2.5 cm diameter, yellowish brown.

Range and habitat. Eastern Andean slopes in southern Colombia (Caquetá) and Ecuador (Morona-Santiago, Pastaza); montane forest, at 1000–1400 m elevation.

Uses. The palm hearts and immature seeds are occasionally eaten.

Socratea salazarii
(Map 204, Plate 18)
"Cashapona de altura" (Per)

Field characters. Stems solitary or rarely clustered, 7–16 m tall and 6–12 cm diameter, supported by an open cone of stilt roots. Leaves 6–7; *leaflets not divided into segments.* Inflorescences with 3–4 bracts; *flowering branches 3–8, 20–35 cm long and to 1 cm diameter;* fruits ellipsoid-ovoid, *not beaked at the top,* 2.5–3.5 cm long and 2–2.5 cm diameter, yellowish.

Range and habitat. Eastern Andean foothills and adjacent Amazon lowlands in Peru (Amazonas, Loreto, Madre de Dios, Pasco, San Martín, Ucayali), western Brazil (Acre) and northern Bolivia (La Paz); lowland rain forest, at 300–700 m elevation.

32. WETTINIA

This moderately large genus, the last of the stilt-root palms, was named after King Frederick August of Saxony, of the house of Wettin. Stems are medium sized to tall, very hard, and solitary or occasionally clustered. They are supported by a low, dense cone of warty to spiny stilt roots. Leaves are pinnate, 4–8 in number, hairy, with a conspicuous, often grayish green to purplish green cylindrical crownshaft. Leaflets are numerous, regularly arranged, and of two kinds. Most lowland and middle elevation species have undivided, narrowly elliptical to almost fan-shaped leaflets that are arranged in the same plane, whereas most highland species have the leaflets split lengthwise into many narrow segments; these are arranged in different planes, giving the leaf a plumose appearance. Leaflets of both types have several prominent veins, and the margins are jagged toward the apex. Apical leaflets typically form a triangular fan. Inflorescences are spicate or branched to one order and usually bear either male or female flowers. They develop under the crown shaft and in most species are arranged in rings of 3–15 at each node, the central bud larger, the lateral ones progressively smaller, with sometimes only the central one developing to flowering. The central bud is either male or female, and the lateral buds are usually all male and only rarely one or two of them develop to flowering. Inflorescence buds are covered with 5–8 bracts. Male inflorescences are very similar in all species; the flowers have 6–20 stamens, not totally covered by the petals. The one-seeded fruits are either loosely arranged and then globose to ellipsoid, or tightly packed along the flowering branch(es) with the infructescence appearing sausage shaped and the fruits prismatic to pyramidal because of mutual pressure. Fruits are usually one-seeded, ellipsoid, globose, prismatic, or pyramidal and are often misshapen by mutual pressure. They are usually more or less hairy and in several species are densely covered with short hairs. The endosperm is either homogeneous or ruminate, and the seedling leaf is simple, elliptical, with jagged margins toward the apex.

Wettinia is a rather homogeneous group of twenty-one species distributed from central Panama and northern Venezuela south to Bolivia; but it is most diverse in the wettest areas of Pacific Colombia, where ten species occur. Here they are among the most conspicuous and characteristic palms of lowland and montane forests. Otherwise, species of the genus are rather uncommon, except for a few locally abundant ones. They are distributed from sea level to 2600 m elevation, but most species grow between 500 and 2000 m, some of them being characteristic of the Andean montane forests. The genus is poorly represented in the lowlands east of the Andes, with only three species reaching the lowlands of the western Amazon region. All species are typical of the primary or disturbed forests, where they seem to regenerate readily in clearings or forest edges, but none is known to regenerate in deforested areas.

The sexual expression of the species in this genus is very interesting and deserves more attention. The central bud of two or more consecutive nodes develops into a female inflorescence, and then the central bud of one or more nodes produces a male inflorescence. Thus the palm periodically changes its functional sex, alternately acting as a female or a male. The presence of multiple inflorescences at the same node is an uncommon trait that has evolved independently in several unrelated genera (Fisher and Moore, 1977). Its biological significance remains unknown. In *Wettinia*, when young palms begin to flower, they produce only one bud per node, and the number of buds increases as the palm gets older. In some of the species with undivided leaflets and branched, compact infructescences, buds are solitary throughout the life of the plant, with one or two lateral buds occasionally occurring besides the central one.

Until very recently species of *Wettinia* were treated as two genera, *Catoblastus* and *Wettinia*. The former included all species with fruits loosely arranged along the flowering branches, whereas palms with tightly packed fruits were referred to *Wettinia*. Close packing appears to have evolved more than once and thus the group is better treated as a single genus (Bernal, in press).

Wettinia is closely related to *Socratea*, from which it differs by its multiple buds, unisexual inflorescences, hood-shaped peduncular bracts, and structure of the male and female flowers. In the field, *Wettinia* is readily separated from *Socratea* by its dense cone of stilt roots covered with blunter spines.

KEY TO THE SPECIES OF *WETTINIA*

1a. Leaflets undivided, narrowly elliptical to broadly triangular, the leaf appearing flat.
    2a. Fruits densely arranged in compact infructescences, their sides angled through mutual pressure.
        3a. Infructescences consisting of 1–7 cylindrical, sausagelike flowering branches (after the fruits fall, the branches are visible).
            4a. Panama and west of the Andes and the inter-Andean valleys in Colombia.
                5a. Panama   *W. panamensis.*
                5b. Colombia and Ecuador.
                    6a. Infructescences with 3–7 flowering branches; Pacific lowlands of Colombia and Ecuador   *W. quinaria.*
                    6b. Infructescences spicate; basins of the Ríos Magdalena and Sinú in Colombia   *W. hirsuta.*
            4b. East of the Andes.

7a. Stems solitary; infructescences branched or spicate.
  8a. Infructescences with 4–6 thick and short branches; stems
      to 12 m tall; Colombia, Ecuador, and Peru   . . . . . *W. maynensis.*
  8b. Infructescences spicate; stems to 6 m tall; Peru (Pasco)
                                                   . . . . . *W. longipetala.*
7b. Stems clustered; infructescences mostly spicate   . . . . . *W. augusta.*
3b. Infructescences consisting of a narrowly to broadly ellipsoid mass of
    fruits (after the fruits fall, the many rather short flowering branches
    are visible.)
  9a. Surface of the infructescences rather flat, the fruits prismatic,
      with flat or slightly rounded tops.
    10a. Fruits dark brown, with hard spines   . . . . . *W. castanea.*
    10b. Fruits green to pale brown, spineless, with small warts
                                                   . . . . . *W. verruculosa.*
  9b. Surface of the infructescences very irregular, the fruits elliptical,
      with blunt tops   . . . . . *W. oxycarpa.*
2b. Fruits loosely arranged along the branches, or at least not so close as
    to change each other's shape.
  11a. Panama and the Pacific lowlands of Colombia and Ecuador.
    12a. Leaflets narrowly elliptical; dead leaves persistent on the palm
         for some time, hiding the crownshaft; fruits broadly ellipsoid
                                                   . . . . . *W. aequalis.*
    12b. Leaflets broadly triangular; dead leaves cleanly falling from the
         palm, the crownshaft clearly visible; fruits narrowly ellipsoid to al-
         most cylindrical   . . . . . *W. radiata.*
  11b. Cordillera de la Costa in Venezuela, the eastern slopes of the
       Andes and western Amazon region.
    13a. Stems clustered.
      14a. Stems 3–6 m tall; leaflets 10–15 per side; to 400 m elevation
                                                   . . . . . *W. drudei.*
      14b. Stems 6–20 m tall; leaflets 20–30 per side; 400–2000 m ele-
           vation   . . . . . *W. praemorsa.*
    13b. Stems solitary.
      15a. Stems to 10 m tall, 15 cm diameter; leaflets 8–9 cm wide
                                                   . . . . . *W. anomala.*
      15b. Stems to 7.5 m tall, 4–7 cm diameter; leaflets 3.5–7 cm wide.
        16a. Leaflets 10–15 per side, 26–54 cm long, 4–7 cm wide; to
             500 m elevation   . . . . . *W. drudei.*
        16b. Leaflets 26–29 per side, 58–67 cm long, 3.5–4.5 cm wide;
             1300–2000 m elevation.   . . . . . *W. aequatorialis.*
1b. Leaflets divided lengthwise to the base into 3–12 segments, these ar-
    ranged in different planes, the leaf appearing plumose.
  17a. Fruits densely arranged in compact infructescences, their sides angled
       through mutual pressure   . . . . . *W. fascicularis.*
  17b. Fruits loosely arranged along the branches, or at least not so close as
       to change each other's shape.
    18a. Leaves arranged in one plane.
      19a. Small palms to 6 m tall; southeastern Ecuador   . . . . . *W. minima.*
      19b. Tall palms, 12–20 m tall; Colombia.

20a. Western slopes of the Cordillera Occidental; seeds with homogeneous endosperm.
21a. Leaf sheaths purplish to greenish, almost glabrous; 1700–
2100 m elevation.   ..... W. disticha.
21b. Leaf sheath dark brown to black, densely tomentose, like
an animal's fur; 2400–2600 m elevation   ..... W. lanata.
20b. Eastern slopes of the Cordillera Oriental; seeds with ruminate endosperm   ..... W. microcarpa.
18b. Leaves spirally arranged.
22a. Stems 3–8 m tall; infructescences with 2–7 branches; fruits narrowly ellipsoid to almost cylindrical   ..... W. radiata.
22b. Stems 10–20 m tall; infructescences with 20 or more branches;
fruits broadly ellipsoid to globose   ..... W. kalbreyeri.

Wettinia aequalis
(Map 205)
"Ratonera", "sapa" (Col), "gualte" (Ecu)
Field characters. Stems solitary, 6–8 m tall and
10–12 cm diameter, with stilt roots to 50 cm
long. Leaves 5–6, *the dead ones persistent and
hanging, obscuring the prominently warty crownshaft*; leaflets 19–34 per side, horizontally
spreading in the same plane, undivided, narrowly elliptical. Inflorescences 5–8 at each
node; *infructescences with (1–)2–8 long, pendulous flowering branches*; fruits loosely arranged, ellipsoid, brownish yellow at maturity
and then cracking open and exposing the
seed; endosperm homogeneous.
Range and habitat. Atlantic slope of Panama
(San Blas, Veraguas) through the Pacific lowlands of Colombia (Cauca, Chocó, Nariño
Valle) to western Ecuador (Los Rios, Pichincha); lowland or premontane rain forests,
between sea level and 500 m elevation.
Uses. Like all species in the genus, the hard
stems are used in construction, especially for
walls of houses. The Emberá Indians of Colombia use the stems for making blowguns.
Notes. There is a gap in the range of this species
in northwestern Colombia. The co-occurring
Wettinia radiata has fewer, wider, almost triangular leaflets that are sometimes split into several segments, and it has narrower, almost cylindrical fruits.

Wettinia aequatorialis
(Map 206)
Field characters. Stems solitary, 5–7.5 m tall and
4–7 cm diameter, with stilt roots to 70 cm
long. Leaves 4–6, with a prominent green
crownshaft; *leaflets 22–29 per side, undivided,
very long and narrow.* Inflorescences 1–3 at
each node; infructescences with 18–20 flowering branches; fruits ellipsoid, 1.8–2 cm long,
green with rusty-red, velvety hairs; endosperm
homogeneous.

Range and habitat. Eastern Andean slopes of
southern Ecuador (Morona-Santiago, Zamora-
Chinchipe); premontane or montane rain forest, at 1300–2000 m elevation.

Wettinia anomala
(Map 207)
"Corunta" (Col), "quilli ruya" (Ecu)
Field characters. Stems solitary, to 15 m tall and
15 cm diameter, with stilt roots to 30 cm long.
Leaves 4–7, with prominent gray to green
crownshaft; leaflets 22–43 per side, undivided,
regularly arranged, pendulous, *brownish below.*
Inflorescences 5–17 at each node; infructescence with 31–50 pendulous flowering
branches; *fruits loosely arranged*, ellipsoid, 1.7–
1.8 cm long, brownish; endosperm homogeneous.
Range and habitat. Eastern slopes of the Andes
from southern Colombia (Caquetá, Putumayo) to northern Ecuador (Napo); rain forest, at 1100–1500 m elevation.

Wettinia augusta
(Map 208)
"Pachiuba de macaco" (Bra), "ponilla" (Per)
Field characters. Stems clustered, 3–12 m tall and
3–12 cm diameter. Leaves 4–8; leaflets 16–29
per side, undivided. Inflorescences 5–8 at
each node; infructescences spicate, sausagelike, or sometimes with 2–4 branches; *fruits
densely packed and prismatic to pyramidal, white-
hairy*; endosperm homogeneous.
Range and habitat. Western Amazon region in
southern Colombia (Amazonas), Peru (Amazonas, Cuzco, Huánuco, Loreto, Madre de
Dios, San Martín), western Brazil (Acre), and
northern Bolivia (La Paz), but not recorded in
Ecuador; lowland or premontane rain forest,
usually on slopes but occasionally in inundated areas, to 800 m elevation.

Notes. Wettinia maynensis differs in its larger size and infructescences with 4–6 short, thick branches.

Wettinia castanea
(Map 209, Plate 18)
"Gualte" (Col, Ecu), "macana" (Col)
Field characters. Stems solitary, to 7 m tall and 20 cm diameter, with stilt roots to 1.1 m long. Leaves 4–5; *crownshaft with prickly hairs*; leaflets 33–35 per side, undivided, regularly arranged, pendulous. Inflorescences 1–3 at each node; *infructescences a compact, ellipsoid dark brown cone* to 40 cm long and 20 cm wide; fruits densely arranged, pyramidal, to 4 cm long and 2.5 cm diameter, *with hard, thick, dense, chestnutlike spines*; endosperm homogeneous.
Range and habitat. Pacific slopes of the Andes in northern Colombia (Antioquia, Chocó); locally abundant in montane rain forest, at 1300–1800 m elevation.
Notes. Wettinia castanea, W. oxycarpa, and W. verruculosa form a group of closely related and vegetatively similar species that are easily separated by the fruits but harder to recognize in the field when sterile or in male flower. In this group, W. castanea is the only species in which old leaves fall cleanly and do not remain decaying on the palm.

Wettinia disticha
(Map 210, Plate 19)
"Macana" (Col)
Field characters. Stems solitary, 10–17 m tall and to 17 cm diameter, with stilt roots to 1.8 m long. Leaves 4–6, *conspicuously arranged in one plane*; crownshaft purplish; leaflets 27–33 per side, each divided to the base into 2–7 narrow, arching segments, these spreading in different planes, in total 90–130 segments per side. Inflorescences 7–11 at each node; infructescences with 15–24 pendulous flowering branches; fruits loosely arranged, globose to ellipsoid, to 2.5 cm diameter, green with scattered, short, tawny hairs; endosperm homogeneous.
Range and habitat. Pacific slope of the Andes in Colombia (Antioquia, Cauca, Valle); montane forest, at 1700–2100 m elevation. Locally very abundant and often conserved in open lands, where it is unable to regenerate.
Notes. Four species of *Wettinia* have leaves arranged in one plane, a character otherwise very uncommon among palms. *Wettinia lanata* grows at higher elevations and differs in the dark brown, thickly woolly crownshaft, the woolly hairs on the leaves, and the larger fruits.

Wettinia drudei
(Map 211)
"Pachiubinha" (Bra), "pachuba" (Col), "pona" (Col)
Field characters. Stems small, 3–6 m tall and 2–3.5 cm diameter, clustered and forming open colonies. Leaves about 5; leaflets to 14 per side, short and undivided. Inflorescences 1–3 at each node; infructescences with 5–9 branches, *with loosely arranged fruits*; fruits ellipsoid, 2–3 cm long and 0.5–1 cm diameter, warty, brown-to-mentose; endosperm homogeneous.
Range and habitat. Western Amazon region in Colombia (Amazonas, Caquetá, Putumayo), Ecuador (Pastaza), Peru (Amazonas, Loreto), and western Brazil (Amazonas); lowland rain forest in inundated or noninundated areas, below 500 m elevation.

Wettinia fascicularis
(Map 212, Plate 19)
"Macana" (Col)
Field characters. Stems solitary, 5–18 m tall and 5–18 cm diameter, with stilt roots to 1.1 m tall. Leaves 4–5; leaflets 17–29 per side, *each lengthwise divided to the base into 3–13 narrow segments*, the total number of segments 120–125, spreading in all directions, *the apical half of each segment abruptly pendulous*, the leaf markedly plumose. Inflorescences usually 3 at each node; *infructescences an ellipsoid cone 20–40 cm long and 8–24 cm wide*, passing from green to brown, with numerous flowering branches; fruits densely arranged, pyramidal or irregularly shaped, warty; endosperm homogeneous.
Range and habitat. Northern end of the Cordillera Central in Colombia (Antioquia), the Pacific slopes of the Cordillera Occidental (Antioquia, Cauca, Valle), and eastern Andean slopes from southern Colombia (Caquetá, Putumayo) to northern Ecuador (Napo); montane rain forest, at 1200–2000 m elevation. Abundant on western Andean slopes but only occasional on eastern slopes.
Notes. Populations at the northern end of the range are considerably smaller and have been regarded as a different species.

Wettinia hirsuta
(Map 213, Plate 19)
"Palma mazorca," "zancaraño" (Col)
Field characters. Stems solitary, 4–12 m tall and 8–11 cm diameter, with stilt roots to 35 cm long. Leaves 5–7; crownshaft grayish green, *with purplish, prickly hairs*; leaflets 25–41 per side, undivided. Inflorescences 5–12 at each node, males and females always spicate; infructescences very dense, sausagelike; fruits densely arranged, narrow, densely hairy, dark brown; endosperm homogeneous.

Range and habitat. Colombia, in the middle valley of the Río Magdalena (Antioquia, Santander) and the upper Río Sinú (Córdoba); lowland to montane rain forest, at 400–1300 m elevation.

Notes. Threatened by extensive deforestation and is rare in most areas.

Wettinia kalbreyeri
(Map 214, Plate 20)
"Gualte" (Col, Ecu), "macana" (Col)

Field characters. Stems solitary, rarely clustered, 10–20 m tall and 10–20 cm diameter, with stilt roots to 1 m long. Leaves 4–5, *with a prominent, green crownshaft*; leaflets 19–26 per side, each divided to base into 2–4 narrow, *arching segments*, in total about 68–123 segments per side, spreading in different planes. Inflorescences to 15 at each node; infructescences with 7–20 pendulous flowering branches; fruits loosely arranged, globose to shortly ellipsoid, 2.4–3.5 cm long, *shortly-hairy, green*, sometimes with minute warts; endosperm homogeneous.

Range and habitat. Western slopes of the Andes from northern Colombia (Antioquia) to southern Ecuador (El Oro) and the northern end of the Cordillera Central in Colombia (Antioquia to Risaralda) and occasionally on eastern slopes of the Cordillera Oriental in Colombia (Caquetá); premontane and montane rain forests, at 600–2100 m elevation but more common at 1200–1600 m.

Uses. The hard stems have been widely used in construction and for fences, which partly accounts for its current scarcity in the central Andes.

Notes. Variable in the shape of the fruits and the amount of hairs on the leaves.

Wettinia lanata
(Map 215)

Field characters. Stems solitary, 5–9 m tall and 10–13 cm diameter, with stilt roots to 70 cm long. *Leaves 4, arranged in one plane, crownshaft prominent, dark brown, thickly woolly*; leaflets 24–25 per side, each divided to base into 4–8 rigid segments, the total number of segments about 75 per side, spreading in different planes. Inflorescences 3 at each node, with 9–11 pendulous flowering branches; fruits loosely arranged, globose, about 4 cm diameter, hairy; endosperm homogeneous.

Range and habitat. Colombia, restricted to a small area on the western slope of the Cordillera Occidental (Cauca, Chocó, Valle); abundant in cloud forest, at 2100–2600 m elevation.

Notes. Replaced by *Wettinia disticha* below 2100 m elevation.

Wettinia longipetala
(Map 216)

Field characters. Stems solitary, to 6 m tall. Leaves 5–6; leaflets about 30 per side, undivided. Inflorescences spicate; infructescences sausagelike; fruits densely packed, to 2.5 cm long, prismatic to pyramidal, *surpassed by the persistent petals*; endosperm homogeneous.

Range and habitat. Peru, eastern Andean slopes (Pasco); premontane and montane rain forests, at 700–1200 m elevation.

Notes. Known from a very small area that is threatened by deforestation.

Wettinia maynensis
(Map 217)
"Corunta" (Col), "gualte" (Ecu), "camonilla," "pullo coroto" (Per)

Field characters. Stems solitary, 6–14 m tall and 8–15 cm diameter. Leaves 5–10, *the old leaves hanging for some time and decaying on the palm*; leaflets 31–43 per side, undivided, pendulous. Inflorescences 3–9 at each node; infructescences with 5–7 spreading, short, and stout flowering branches, each crowded with densely packed fruits and appearing sausagelike; fruits densely crowded, prismatic to pyramidal, rounded at apex, 1.8–2.5 cm long and 1.5–2 cm diameter, covered with white hairs; endosperm homogeneous.

Range and habitat. Eastern slopes of the Andes and adjacent Amazon lowlands, from southern Colombia (Caquetá, Putumayo), Ecuador (Morona-Santiago, Napo, Pastaza, Zamora-Chinchipe), and Peru (Amazonas, Huánuco, Junín, Loreto, Pasco, San Martín); lowland, premontane, and montane rain forest, at 200–1600 m elevation.

Uses. The stems used as posts in construction.

Notes. The similar *Wettinia quinaria* has a different range, cleanly falling leaves, and longer and thinner infructescence branches.

Wettinia microcarpa
(Map 218)
"Mapora" (Col)

Field characters. Stems solitary, 7–12 m tall and to 12 cm diameter, with stilt roots to 70 cm long. *Leaves 4–5, arranged in one plane*; crownshaft grayish green; leaflets 23–32 per side, divided to base in 3–6 segments, *the outer segment of each leaflet very broad and to 40 cm wide*, in total 63–85 segments per side, spreading in different planes. Inflorescences to 11 at each node; infructescences with 26–27 flowering branches; fruits loosely arranged, almost globose, 2.5 cm long; *endosperm ruminate.*

Range and habitat. Eastern Andes of Colombia (Norte de Santander and most probably oc-

curring also in adjacent Venezuela); montane rain forest, at 2200–2400 m elevation. It is uncommon, but locally abundant in the Tamá National Park.
Uses. The stems used as posts in construction.

Wettinia minima
(Map 219)
Field characters. Stems to 6 m tall and 2.5–3 cm diameter. *Leaves arranged in one plane,* with a short but prominent crownshaft; leaflets short, divided to the base into 4–7 segments, these spreading in different planes. Inflorescences with 4–7 flowering branches; fruits ellipsoid to almost globose, 1.5–1.6 cm diameter, *smooth; endosperm slightly ruminate.*
Range and habitat. Known only from the Cordillera de Cutucú in Ecuador (Morona-Santiago); montane rain forest, at 1500–1700 m elevation.

Wettinia oxycarpa
(Map 220)
"Gualte" (Col, Ecu)
Field characters. Stems solitary, to 15 m tall and 15 cm diameter, with stilt roots to 90 cm long. Leaves about 6, *the dead ones persistent for some time, hanging and decaying over the infructescences;* crownshaft prominent; leaflets 25–27 per side, undivided, *horizontally spreading in the same plane.* Inflorescences 1–3 at each node; *infructescences with numerous flowering branches,* the fruits tightly packed into a compact, ellipsoid cone to 40 cm long and 20 cm wide; *fruits ellipsoid and acute at apex,* to 3.5 cm long, light brown, velvety; endosperm homogeneous.
Range and habitat. Pacific slopes of the Andes from northern Colombia (Chocó) to northern Ecuador (Carchi, Esmeraldas); rather uncommon in premontane and montane rain forest, at 400–1200 m elevation.

Wettinia panamensis
(Map 221)
"Chonta" (Pan)
Field characters. Stems solitary, 3–16 m tall and 5–10 cm diameter, with stilt roots to 60 cm long. Leaves 4–8; leaflets 20–31 per side, undivided, pendulous. Inflorescences 3–6 at each node; male inflorescence spicate or with 2–3 flowering branches; *infructescences spicate,* rarely with 2–4 branches, the fruits very densely packed, dark brown; endosperm homogeneous.
Range and habitat. Panama (Coclé, Colón, San Blas), mostly along the continental divide and the Atlantic slope; rain forest, between sea level and 1200 m elevation.
Notes. Palms in San Blas, Panama, near the Colombian border, have infructescences with up

to 4 branches and might be mistaken for *Wettinia quinaria,* although the smaller number of leaflets are diagnostic. It has also long been confused with *Wettinia hirsuta* of Colombia, which has prickly hairs on the crownshaft, a larger number of leaflets, and petals longer than the fruits.

Wettinia praemorsa
(Map 222)
"Mapora," "maquenco" (Col), "prapa" (Ven)
Field characters. Stems clustered, occasionally solitary, to 10 per plant, to 15 m tall and 15 cm diameter, often with small developing shoots. Leaves 4–6; crownshaft prominent, grayish green; leaflets undivided, 20–30 per side, spreading in the same plane, pendulous, or occasionally divided into 2–8 segments, these spreading in different planes and then the leaf plumose. Inflorescences 4–12 at each node; infructescences with 16–26 pendulous flowering branches; fruits loosely arranged, ellipsoid, 2.2–2.9 cm long, green to finally yellowish brown, cracking open at maturity; *endosperm ruminate*
Range and habitat. Venezuela, on the Atlantic slopes of the Cordillera de la Costa and Cordillera de Mérida (Cojedes, Miranda, Táchira), eastern and western slopes of the Sierra de Perijá, and eastern slopes of the Andes in Colombia (Norte de Santander to Caquetá), also in the Sierra de la Macarena; premontane and montane rain forest, at 400–2400 m elevation but most common between 1000 and 1500 m.
Uses. The resistant stems are used for fences.
Notes. The only Andean *Wettinia* with clustered stems. Isolated populations in Colombia have solitary stems and divided leaflets and have been described as a separate species.

Wettinia quinaria
(Map 223, Plate 20)
"Memé" (Col), "gualte" (Col, Ecu)
Field characters. Stems solitary, 7–15 m tall and 15–20 cm diameter, with stilt roots to 1 m long. Leaves 4–6, *the crown often appearing like an x when seen from a distance;* crownshaft grayish green; leaflets 34–58 per side, undivided, pendulous. Inflorescences 5–7 at each node; infructescences with 4–7 thick, flowering branches, densely crowded with whitish to brownish fruits, appearing sausagelike; fruits prismatic to narrowly pyramidal, with rounded apex, 2–3.5 cm long and 1.5–2.5 cm diameter, dark brown, often with long, loose, white hairs; endosperm homogeneous.
Range and habitat. Colombia, west of the Andes (Antioquia, Cauca, Chocó, Nariño, Valle) to northern Ecuador (Esmeraldas); very abun-

dant in lowland to premontane rain forest, from sea level to 1000 m elevation. It is one of the most common palm trees of the Pacific coast of Colombia.

Uses. The split stems are one of the most widely used materials for walls, preferred to other species in the genus. They are also used for making blowguns.

Notes. Unlike any other palm in the area because of its infructescences. *Wettinia panamensis* has spicate or few-branched infructescences, 20–31 leaflets per side and a different range. *Wettinia maynensis* has shorter and thicker fruiting branches, and dead leaves persist for some time. Also has a different range.

Wettinia radiata
(Map 224)
"Palma sapa," "vaqueta" (Col)
Field characters. Stems solitary, 4–9 m tall and 7–10 cm diameter, with stilt roots to 70 cm long. Leaves 5–6; leaflets 11–17 per side, undivided, *these very broad and almost triangular,* sometimes divided into 2–7 narrow segments, these spreading in different planes. Inflorescences 3–5 at each node; infructescences with 3–5 long, pendulous flowering branches; fruits narrowly ellipsoid to almost cylindrical, loosely arranged, to 4 cm long and 2 cm diameter,

yellow, sometimes slightly hairy, cracking open when ripe; endosperm homogeneous.

Range and habitat. Eastern Panama (Darién) through the Pacific lowlands of Colombia (Antioquia, Cauca, Chocó, Valle); lowland or premontane rain forest, between sea level and 1000 m elevation. Very common and sometimes abundant in inundated areas, such as the forests of *Prioria copaifera* (Leguminosae) in northwestern Colombia.

Wettinia verruculosa
(Map 225)
Field characters. Stems 8–10 m tall and 15–18 cm diameter, with stilt roots to 80 cm long. Leaves 5–6, *the dead ones persistent and decaying on the palm;* crownshaft prominent; leaflets 36–40 per side, undivided regularly arranged and spreading in the same plane. Inflorescences solitary at each node; infructescences a compact, ellipsoid cone to 40 cm long and 25 cm wide; fruits densely arranged, pyramidal, green to brown, the surface with small, dense warts; endosperm homogeneous.

Range and habitat. Restricted to a small area on the western slopes of the Andes in southern Colombia (Nariño) and northern Ecuador (Carchi); montane rain forest, at 1200–1400 m elevation.

33. MANICARIA

This small and very unusual genus is widespread but patchily distributed in Central and northern South America. Stems are moderate to large, but are almost always covered with old, persistent leaves and leaf bases and accumulated litter. Dry, dead leaves hang down from the top of the stem and make a distinctive rustling sound in the wind. Although usually solitary the stems sometimes appear to be forked. Leaves are usually very large, pinnate or simple, 5–25 in number and strongly plicate. Most often the leaves are at least partially pinnate with several broad, nonsplit leaflets. These nonsplit leaflets are briefly split at the tips, giving the leaves a characteristic serrated margin. Inflorescences are branched to one or rarely two orders and are borne among the leaves; they are often hidden by leaf bases or other debris. They are enclosed by an unusual, fibrous, seamless, brown peduncular bract that persists over the inflorescence until it is split by the developing fruits. The relatively large, unisexual flowers are crowded along the flowering branches, with the females near the base and the males along the upper part. Male flowers have 26–34 stamens. The most unusual feature of the genus is the fruits. These are one- to three-seeded, globose or lobed, dusty brown, and are covered with short, pyramidal, woody projections. The endosperm is homogeneous and the seedling leaf is bifid with a toothed apical margin.

A genus of one species (Henderson, 1994) distributed from Guatemala southwards all through Central America and northern South America. It is rather patchily distributed, but is generally more common in coastal areas. The genus is unusual morphologically and has no obvious relatives.

Manicaria saccifera

(Map 226, Plate 20)

"Bussú" (Bra), "jíquera," "ubí" (Col), "palmier toulouri" (FrG), "yolillo" (Gua), "troolie" (Guy), "escomfra" (Nic), "guágara" (Pan), "truli" (Sur), "temiche" (Ven)

Field characters. Stems solitary or less often forked, 0.5–10 m tall and 15–20 cm diameter, covered with old leaves and debris. Leaves 5–25, stiff and erect, very large, 2–8 m long; leaf margins serrate. Inflorescences covered by a fibrous, nonopening peduncular bract; fruits globose or 2–3-lobed, 4–6 cm diameter, brown, covered with short, pyramidal projections.

Range and habitat. Patchily distributed throughout the Atlantic coast of Central America in Guatemala, Belize, Honduras, Nicaragua, Costa Rica, and Panama and northern South America in Colombia (Amazonas, Antioquia, Chocó, Valle, Vaupés, Vichada), Venezuela (Amazonas, Delta Amacuro, Monagas, Sucre), Trinidad, the Guianas, Ecuador (Esmeraldas), Peru (Loreto), and Brazil (Amazonas, Pará); usually near the sea in low-lying, inundated areas but also inland in inundated areas in lowland forest, usually at low elevations, very rarely to 1200 m elevation (Cerro Marahuaca, Venezuela).

Uses. The leaves are very commonly used for thatching and it is the preferred species where it occurs in quantity. The peduncular bract is used as a hat and is made into various handicrafts for tourists. Previously this was a very important species to the Warao Indians of Delta Amacuro in Venezuela (Wilbert, 1976). Sago, or palm starch, was harvested from the stems; weevil grubs were collected from fallen stems; the leaves were used for thatching and as sails for small canoes; the peduncular bract was made into hats; the liquid endosperm of the fruits was drunk; and several parts of the palm were used medicinally.

34. LEOPOLDINIA

This genus was named by Martius in honor of his patron, the Archduchess Leopoldina of Austria. It is a small and very unusual genus confined to the central Amazon region. Stems are solitary or clustered, of medium size, and covered with the persistent remains of the leaf sheaths. These sheath fibers are of two very different types, either short and reticulate or long and fibrous. Leaves are pinnate and 10–25 in number. Leaflets are numerous, linear, regularly arranged, and spread in the same plane. Inflorescences are borne among the leaves and are branched to three orders. The numerous flowering branches are densely brown-tomentose. Flowers are unisexual and extremely small and are arranged in threes of a central female and two lateral males. Often, however, inflorescences appear to bear either mostly male or mostly female flowers. Fruits are one-seeded, rounded or kidney shaped in profile but more or less flattened (and thus unique among palms). The mesocarp is fleshy and edible, with reticulate coarse fibers and air spaces. The endosperm is homogeneous and the seedling leaf is bifid.

Leopoldinia contains three species confined to the central Amazon region, particularly the white-sand, blackwater regions of the upper Rio Negro (Henderson, 1994). They commonly occur along beaches or river margins where they are seasonally inundated and in some areas endure months of inundation. The unusual, flattened fruits appear adapted to dispersal by water, and the mesocarp contains large intercellular air spaces, probably an adaptation for floating (Kubitzki, 1991). The genus has no obvious relatives and appears isolated both phylogenetically and geographically.

Leopoldinia major

(Map 227)

"Jará," "yará" (Bra), "chiquichiqui," "morichita" (Ven)

Field characters. Stems 3–8 m tall and 5–10 cm diameter, *clustered and forming large colonies,* covered, at least apically, with *reticulate, stiff, reddish brown, 1–2 mm thick fibers.* Leaves about

11; leaflets somewhat pendulous. Fruits flattened, irregularly rounded, almost kidney shaped, 3–4 cm long and 3–4 cm diameter, dull orange-red.
Range and habitat. Rio Negro region of Colombia (Vaupés), Venezuela (Amazonas), and Brazil (Amazonas); margins of blackwater streams and rivers.

Leopoldinia piassaba
(Map 228, Plate 21)
"Piassaba" (Bra), "chiquichiqui" (Col, Ven), "fibra" (Col)
Field characters. Stems solitary, 4–5(–10) m tall and to 15 cm diameter, appearing much wider because of the *persistent, dense covering of long, loose, pendulous brown fibers.* Leaves 14–16, with spreading leaflets. Fruits irregularly globose, *scarcely flattened, 3–5.5 cm diameter,* orange-brown to purplish-brown.
Range and habitat. Upper Rio Negro region of Colombia (Guianía), Venezuela (Amazonas), and Brazil (Amazonas); sandy soils near blackwater streams and rivers, rarely on white-water rivers.
Uses. The fibers ("piassaba") from the stems are gathered and traded locally. They were more

important previously and were at one time exported to Europe, where they were manufactured into brooms (Wallace, 1853; Spruce, 1860). They are still an important item of trade locally (Putz, 1979; Bernal, 1992; Lescure et al., 1992). A drink is made from the fruits.

Leopoldinia pulchra
(Map 229, Plate 21)
"Jará" (Bra), "yará" (Col), "cucurito" (Ven)
Field characters. Stems *solitary* or rarely clustered, 1.5–7 m tall and 4–10 cm diameter, covered, at least apically, with *reticulate, stiff, reddish brown, 3 mm thick fibers.* Leaves 10–25, the leaflets stiffly spreading to slightly arching. Fruits rounded or kidney shaped, flattened, *2–2.3 cm diameter,* reddish brown or purple.
Range and habitat. Colombia (Guianía, Vaupés) and Venezuela (Amazonas, Apure), and from there down the Rio Negro to Manaus in Brazil (Amazonas) and rarely south or east of Manaus in Amazonas and Pará; sandy beaches of blackwater streams and rivers, occasionally by white-water rivers.

35. REINHARDTIA

The name of this small genus honors the Reinhardt family, some of whom were prominent nineteenth century Danish biologists. Stems are slender, very small to rather large, and are solitary or more commonly clustered. Leaves are pinnate or simple and 6–20 in number. The leaf sheaths are closed but do not form crownshafts, rather they disintegrate into an interwoven, fibrous covering. Leaves are of three kinds; in some species there are numerous linear leaflets, in others there are only 2–3 broad, compound leaflets made up of several nonsplit leaflets; in one species the leaves are small, simple and elliptical. The leaflets are very characteristic in their strongly unequal tips, with one half markedly longer than the other half. These unequal tips make the apex of the compound leaflets and the margins of the simple leaves appear toothed. In some species there are small windows between the folds of the compound leaflets, close to the rachis. Inflorescences are borne among the leaves and are spicate or branched to one order, or to two orders when the lower branches are bifurcate. Only one peduncular bract is present and the peduncle is usually elongate. Flowers are small and creamy white and arranged in threes of a central female and two lateral males; males have 8–40 stamens. The flowering branches turn red in ripe fruit. Fruits are one-seeded, ellipsoid, ovoid or obovoid, small, and purplish black at maturity. The seed has homogeneous or ruminate endosperm and the seedling leaf is simple or bifid.

Reinhardtia contains six species (Moore, 1956, 1957; Read et al., 1987) distributed from southwestern Mexico throughout Central America to Panama. Two species reach northwestern Colombia and one is endemic to the Dominican Republic. All species inhabit the understory of lowland rain forest, usually at low elevations but occasionally reaching 1600 m. None of the species is able to regenerate in disturbed areas.

Morphological variation within the genus follows an almost linear sequence, ranging from the tall *Reinhardtia elegans* of southern Mexico, with large, pinnate leaves and inflorescences branched to one or two orders, progressing through the smaller species of Central America, with fewer, compound leaflets and inflorescences with fewer flowering branches, and ending with the dwarf *R. koschnyana* in Panama and Colombia, with minute, simple leaves and spicate inflorescences. This variation in size along a latitudinal gradient parallels variation found in other genera of palms along elevational gradients in the Andes (e.g., *Wettinia*). It is noteworthy that two of the species that reach the northernmost latitudes in Mexico also reach the highest elevations.

None of the species is particularly abundant in the wild, and there are few records of local names and uses. Species of *Reinhardtia* have been in cultivation by enthusiasts since the nineteenth century, but none has become very common.

Reinhardtia elegans
(Map 230)
"Palmito" (Hon)
Field characters. Stems solitary, 2.5–6 m tall and to 4 cm diameter. Leaves 10–12; *leaflets 38–40 per side, linear*, regularly arranged, and spreading in the same plane. Inflorescences with a 1 m long peduncle; flowering branches 4–9, the lower ones sometimes bifurcate; fruits ellipsoid, 1.6–1.8 cm long and 0.9–1.2 cm diameter, purple-black; *seeds with deeply ruminate endosperm.*
Range and habitat. Atlantic slope in southern Mexico (Oaxaca, Chiapas) and Honduras (Olancho); evergreen forest, at 1000–1600 m elevation.
Notes. Easily mistaken for a species of *Chamaedorea*, but differs in its fibrous leaf sheath, bifid leaflets with unequal tips, and single peduncular bract.

Reinhardtia gracilis
(Map 231)
"Coquito," "coyolito" (Mex)
Field characters. Stems solitary or clustered, to 2.5 m tall and 1.5 cm diameter, brown, the upper part covered with persistent leaf sheaths. Leaves 6–20; petiole almost as long as the 12–45 cm long blade; leaflets typically 2 (rarely 3–4) per side, *the apical ones considerably wider than the others, incompletely split and with small "windows" at the base.* Inflorescences as long as the leaves or slightly longer, with a long peduncle; flowering branches 3–11, the basal ones sometimes bifurcate; fruits obovoid, 1.2–1.6 cm long, purple-black; *endosperm homogeneous.*
Range and habitat. Atlantic slope of southern Mexico, Belize, Guatemala, Honduras, Nicaragua, and eastern Costa Rica; rain forest, to 1300 m elevation.
Notes. Variable in terms of leaf size and inflorescence branching, as well as number of stamens. Moore (1957) separated four varieties: var. *gracilis*, with larger leaves and larger male

flowers, from Belize, Guatemala (Izabal, Petén), Honduras (Atlántida, Gracias a Dios), and Nicaragua (Zelaya); var. *tenuissima*, with small leaves and large male flowers, from Mexico (Oaxaca); var. *gracilior*, with small leaves and small male flowers, from southern Mexico (Chiapas, Oaxaca, Veracruz), Belize, and Honduras (Atlántida, Gracias a Dios); and var. *rostrata*, with larger leaves and small male flowers, from Nicaragua (Chontales, Zelaya) and Costa Rica (Alajuela, Cartago, Limón, San José). Mendoza and Franco (1992) studied clonal integration of var. *gracilior* in Mexico.

Reinhardtia koschnyana
(Map 232, Plate 21)
Field characters. Stems clustered, forming small clumps by rhizomes, 40–70 cm tall, 4–8 mm diameter. Leaves 6–14, *simple*, blade 15–23 cm long and 6–7.5 cm wide, with toothed margins. *Inflorescences spicate*, longer than the leaves; fruits obovoid, 1.1–1.3 cm long and 6–8 mm diameter, purple-black; seed with homogeneous endosperm.
Range and habitat. Honduras (Gracias a Dios), Nicaragua (Zelaya), Costa Rica (Alajuela), Panama (Darién), and northwestern Colombia (Antioquia, Chocó); lowland rain forest, at low elevations.
Notes. One of the smallest American palms, and endangered throughout its range.

Reinhardtia latisecta
(Map 233, Plate 21)
Field characters. Stems clustered, in clumps of 8–9, to 8 m tall and 6–7 cm diameter. Leaves about 10; petiole to 45 cm long; blade 1–1.5 m long, *with 2–3 broad compound leaflets*, the apical one much broader than the others, *all with small windows between the folds on either side of the rachis.* Inflorescences longer than leaves, with a long peduncle; flowering branches 15–19; fruits ellipsoid or ovoid, 1.7 cm long, purple-black; *seed with deeply ruminate endosperm.*

Range and habitat. Belize, Honduras (Gracias a Dios), Nicaragua (Zelaya), and western Costa Rica (Guanacaste, Puntarenas); lowland rain forest, from sea level to 100 m elevation. Not recorded with certainty from Guatemala.

Notes. *Reinhardtia gracilis* is a similar species but differs in its smaller habit and leaves and homogeneous or scarcely ruminate endosperm.

Reinhardtia paiewonskiana
(Map 234)
"Coquito," "manacla" (DR)

Field characters. Stems solitary, 6–12 m tall and to 14 cm diameter. Leaves about 12; *leaflets 55–57 per side, linear-lanceolate,* regularly arranged and spreading in the same plane. Inflorescences projecting beyond the leaves; flowering branches 4–10; fruits ovoid to subglobose, 2–2.2 cm diameter, purple-black; *seed with ruminate endosperm.*

Range and habitat. Dominican Republic; premontane rain forest on slopes, at 800–1200 m elevation.

Notes. This is an isolated species, but not unexpected since many Central American genera have outliers in the Greater Antilles. It is probably most closely related to *Reinhardtia elegans.*

It grows with *Prestoea acuminata* and *Calyptronoma plumeriana.*

Reinhardtia simplex
(Map 235)
"Upuká" (Hon)

Field characters. Stems clustered, to 1.2 m tall and 8 mm diameter, brown. Leaves 8–20; *blade simple, elliptical, to 20 cm long, shortly bifid at the apex, or with an elliptical apical lobe and an additional leaflet on either side of the rachis.* Inflorescences projecting beyond the leaves, with a long peduncle; *flowering branches 3–7, short;* fruits obovoid, to 1.5 cm long, purple-black; seeds with homogeneous endosperm.

Range and habitat. Honduras (Atlántida, Colón, Gracias a Dios), Nicaragua (Chontales, Jinotega, Río San Juan, Zelaya), Costa Rica (Alajuela, Cartago, Guanacaste, Heredia, Limón, Puntarenas), Panama (Bocas del Toro, Colón, Darién, Panamá), and northwestern Colombia (Chocó, near the Panamanian frontier); rain forest, from sea level to 1000 m elevation.

Notes. Differs from *Reinhardtia gracilis* in its elliptical, shortly bifid leaf without windows; and from *R. koschnyana* in its taller stems and branched inflorescences.

36. EUTERPE

This genus is considered by many people to contain the most beautiful American palms. Its name is derived from the Greek goddess of song and poetry, Euterpe, one of the nine Muses of Greek mythology. Stems are medium to large, gray, slender and solitary or clustered. Leaves are pinnate, 5–18 in number, and dead leaves fall immediately from the stem, giving the plant a "clean" appearance. The leaf sheaths form a prominent crownshaft, ranging in color from green to bright orange, and this is one of the most distinctive features of the genus. Leaf sheaths, petioles, and the rachis are often covered with large, black scales. Leaflets are numerous, linear, long, narrow, and usually pendulous, giving the leaves a very elegant appearance. Inflorescences are branched to one order and are borne below the crownshaft. The numerous flowering branches are usually densely hairy, distinguishing *Euterpe* from the very similar *Prestoea.* Flowers are unisexual and are borne in threes of a central female and two lateral males. Fruits are one-seeded, globose or rarely ellipsoid, and purple-black. The endosperm is homogeneous or less often ruminate, and the seedling leaf is bifid, palmate, or pinnate.

Euterpe contains seven species (Henderson and Galeano, in press), distributed from Central America all through northern South America and just reaching the Lesser Antilles. These very graceful palms are easily recognizable by their slender, gray stems, prominent crownshaft, and narrow, pendulous leaflets. The genus differs from the closely related *Prestoea* in a number of technical characters, but in general *Euterpe* can be recognized by its well-developed crownshaft and narrow, and usually pendulous leaflets.

Euterpe broadwayi
(Map 236)
"Manicol" (Dom), "manac" (Tri)

Field characters. Stems usually clustered or occasionally solitary, 8–20 m tall and 20–25 cm diameter, gray, often with a prominent and visible cone of roots at the base. Leaves 10–16; crownshaft green or tinged reddish brown; *leaflets more or less pendulous. Flowering branches 0.7–1 cm diameter, densely covered with whitish brown hairs;* fruits globose, purple-black, 1–1.4 cm diameter; *endosperm homogeneous; seedling leaf pinnate.*

Range and habitat. Northern Trinidad, Tobago, and Lesser Antilles (Dominica, Grenada, St. Vincent); premontane forest on mountain ridges, at 600–1000 m elevation.

Uses. The palm heart is occasionally eaten.

Euterpe catinga
(Map 237, Plate 22)
"Açaí da catinga" (Bra), "asaí de sabana" (Col), "manaca" (Col, Ven)

Field characters. Stems clustered or solitary, 4–16 m tall and 3.5–15 cm diameter, gray, with a visible cone of roots at the base. Leaves 6–11; *crownshaft usually orange, often with a mass of flimsy, black fibers at the top; petiole and rachis with black scales; leaflets more or less horizontally spreading.* Flowering branches 2.5–4 mm diameter, densely covered with short, whitish brown hairs; fruits globose, purple-black, 0.8–1.3 cm diameter; *endosperm homogeneous; seedling leaf bifid.*

Range and habitat. Western Amazon region of Colombia, Venezuela, Peru, and Brazil, in open forest on poorly drained, acidic, white-sand soils below 350 m elevation and mountain regions of the Guayana Highland of Venezuela, Guyana, and Brazil and also just reaching the Andes in Ecuador and Peru, in wet places in forest patches at 1100–1800 m elevation.

Uses. The stems are used in construction; the leaves for thatching; and the fruits to make a drink.

Notes. Two varieties are recognized (Henderson, 1994): var. *catinga*, with moderately scaly petiole and rachis and nonleathery leaflets with fewer scales and dots on lower surface, from low elevations in the western Amazon region to high elevations in the western Guayana Highland, in Colombia (Amazonas, Caquetá, Guainía, Guaviare, Vaupés), Venezuela (Amazonas, Bolívar), Peru (Loreto), and Brazil (Amazonas); and var. *roraimae*, with densely scaly petiole and rachis and leathery leaflets with scales and dots on lower surface, from high elevations in the Guayana Highland of Venezuela (Amazonas, Bolívar), Guyana, and Brazil (Amazonas), and also just reaching the Andes in Ecuador (Pastaza) and Peru (Huánuco).

Euterpe edulis
(Map 238)
"Yayih" (Arg), "juçara," "palmito" (Bra)
Field characters. Stems solitary or very rarely clus-tered, 5–12 m tall and 10–15 cm diameter, gray, with a visible cone of roots at the base. Leaves 8–15; crownshaft green, sometimes tinged orange or red; *leaflets horizontally spreading or occasionally pendulous. Flowering branches 2 mm thick, densely covered with very short hairs;* fruits globose, purple-black, 1–1.4 cm diameter; *endosperm homogeneous; seedling leaf palmate.*

Range and habitat. Atlantic coast of Brazil (Alagoas, Bahia, Espírito Santo, Minas Gerais, Paraíba, Paraná, Pernambuco, Rio de Janeiro, Rio Grande do Norte, Rio Grande do Sul, Santa Catarina, Sao Paulo, Sergipe) and reaching inland at least to Brasília, and just reaching Argentina (Misiones) and Paraguay (Alto Paraná); coastal forest on steep slopes and forest patches farther inland, from sea level to 1000 m elevation.

Uses. The palm heart, or palmito, of this species is considered one of the best tasting, and for a long time it was the principal source of wild-gathered palmito. The palm has been locally exterminated in many areas because the growing point of the solitary stem is cut when the palmito is harvested. There are now efforts in various parts of Brazil to grow the palm in plantations and to produce hybrids that have clustered stems (EMBRAPA, 1987).

Euterpe longebracteata
(Map 239)
"Açaí chumbo," "açaí da mata" (Bra)
Field characters. Stems solitary or occasionally clustered, 5–15(–20) m tall and 5–8 cm diameter. Leaves 8–9; *crownshaft green; leaflets pendulous.* Flowering branches 1.5–2 mm diameter, densely covered with stiff, whitish, branched hairs; fruits globose, 1–1.2 cm diameter, purple-black; *endosperm homogeneous;* seedling leaf not known.

Range and habitat. Venezuela (Amazonas, Bolívar, Delta Amacuro), Guyana and Brazil (Amazonas, Mato Grosso, Pará); lowland rain forest on noninundated or inundated soils, at low elevations.

Euterpe luminosa
(Map 240)
"Guayaquil," "palma palanca" (Per)
Field characters. Stems clustered, but usually only one of a cluster well developed, 5–11 m tall and 5–7 cm diameter. Leaves 9–12; crownshaft green; *leaflets more or less pendulous, very narrow. Flowering branches 2 mm diameter, loosely to densely covered with reddish brown hairs; fruits ellipsoid, 2 cm long and 1 cm diameter; endosperm homogeneous; seedling leaf pinnate.*

Range and habitat. Known from a small area of Andean Peru (Pasco); very wet montane rain forest on steep slopes, at 2000–2500 m elevation.

Uses. The straight, slender stems are cut and used as poles.

Euterpe oleracea
(Map 241, Plates 22 & 23)
"Açaí" (Bra), "murrapo," "naidí" (Col), "pinot" (FrG), "manaka" (Sur), "manac" (Tri)
Field characters. Stems clustered with several stems per clump, gray, 3–20 m tall and 7–18 cm diameter, with a cone of visible roots at the base. Leaves 8–14; crownshaft green or tinged dark brown, yellow-green, dull red, or purple; leaflets pendulous. Flowering branches 3–4 mm diameter, densely covered with whitish brown hairs; fruits globose, purple-black, 1–2 cm diameter; endosperm ruminate; seedling leaf bifid.
Range and habitat. Pacific coast of Colombia (Antioquia, Chocó, Nariño, Valle, and the middle Magdalena valley in Antioquia and Santander) and Ecuador (Esmeraldas, Pichincha), and coastal regions of Venezuela (Bolívar, Delta Amacuro, Sucre), Trinidad, the Guianas, and Brazil (Amapá, Maranhão, Pará, Tocantins); low-lying, wet areas, often near the sea in tidal areas but also further inland along river margins.
Uses. This is an important palm throughout its range. The palm heart is eaten or canned and exported, and the fruits are made into a drink. This, known as açaí in Brazil, is a very important part of the diet in Belém and surrounding areas of the Amazon estuary (Strudwick and Sobel, 1988). Because of its abundance and clustered stems, there has been much research on the economic possibilities of this species in the Amazon estuary (e.g., Calzavara, 1972; Urdaneta, 1981), and currently it is the focus of studies on management and sustainable harvesting (Anderson, 1988).
Notes. Swamps in French Guiana dominated by Euterpe oleracea have been described by Oldeman (1969). The palm develops upright roots, or pneumatophores, in these areas.

Euterpe precatoria
(Map 242, Plate 23)
"Mountain cabbage" (Bel), "açaí" (Bra), "asaí," "palmiche" (Col), "wassaï" (FrG), "huasi" (Per), "manaca" (Ven)

Field characters. Stems solitary or rarely clustered, 3–20 m tall and 4–23 cm diameter, gray, usually with a mound of visible roots at the base. Leaves 5–10(–20); crownshaft green or tinged lighter green or yellow; leaflets pendulous. Flowering branches 3–5 mm diameter, densely covered with whitish hairs; fruits globose, purple-black, 0.9–1.3 cm diameter; endosperm homogeneous; seedling leaf pinnate.
Range and habitat. Central America in Belize, Guatemala, Honduras, Nicaragua, Costa Rica, and Panama and northern South America in Colombia, Venezuela, Trinidad, the Guianas, Ecuador, Peru, Brazil, and Bolivia. It grows in a variety of habitats; in the Amazon region it is common along margins of rivers in seasonally inundated forest at low elevations; in mountain areas it grows in wet forest, to 2000 m elevation.
Uses. The stems are widely used in construction; the fruits are used in making a drink; and the roots are used medicinally.
Notes. Two varieties are recognized (Henderson, 1994): var. longevaginata, with shorter, solitary, or clustered stems, wider, ± horizontally spreading leaflets and smaller inflorescences, from low to high elevations in Central America in Belize, Guatemala, Honduras, Nicaragua, Costa Rica (including Cocos Island), Panama, and from low to high elevations in the Andes and adjacent areas in Colombia (Antioquia, Boyaca, Chocó, Guajira, Santander, Valle), Venezuela (Barinas, Carabobo, Cojedes, Falcón, Lara, Miranda, Monagas, Tachira, Yaracuy), Ecuador (El Oro, Esmeraldas, Zamora-Chinchipe), Peru (Amazonas, Madre de Dios, San Martín), Brazil (Acre), and Bolivia (La Paz); and var. precatoria, with tall, solitary stems, narrow, strongly pendulous leaflets and larger inflorescences, from low elevations in the Amazon region and adjacent areas in Colombia (Amazonas, Meta, Norte de Santander, Vaupés, Vichada), Venezuela (Amazonas, Anzoátegui, Apure, Bolívar, Monagas, Zulia), Trinidad, the Guianas, Ecuador (Morona-Santiago, Napo), Peru (Amazonas, Cusco, Loreto, Madre de Dios, Pasco, San Martín), Brazil (Acre, Amazonas, Pará, Rondônia), and Bolivia (Beni, Pando, Santa Cruz).

37. PRESTOEA

This medium-sized, predominantly Andean genus is closely related to Euterpe and has often been confused with it. It differs, however, in several important characters. The genus was named for Henry Prestoe, government botanist and superintendent of the Botanic Gardens in Trinidad from 1864 to 1886. Stems are short to medium sized and usually clustered, or at least have shoots at the base. Stems are often covered with old, persistent leaf bases. Leaves are pinnate, less commonly simple, 4–12 in number, and are usually horizontally spreading. The leaf sheaths are not closed and do not form a crownshaft (in contrast to *Euterpe*), except for a partial crownshaft in *Prestoea acuminata*. Leaflets are almost always broad, linear-lanceolate, and spread horizontally (not narrow, linear, and pendulous as in *Euterpe*). Inflorescences are branched to one order and are borne among the leaves and are often erect or arching. The peduncle is usually elongate and rounded in cross section. Unlike *Euterpe*, the flowering branches are not densely covered with hairs. A very distinctive characteristic of the flowering branches is that they change color, from white at flowering time to reddish at fruiting time. Flowers are unisexual and are borne in threes of one central female and two lateral males. Fruits are one-seeded, globose (or very rarely ellipsoid), and purple-black. The seed almost always has ruminate endosperm, and the seedling leaf is either bifid or pinnate, but is unknown in several species.

Prestoea contains eleven species (Henderson and Galeano, in press), most of them understory or midcanopy palms of mountainous areas of Central America and the Andes.

KEY TO THE SPECIES OF *PRESTOEA*

1a. Stems large, to 15 m tall and 20 cm diameter; leaflets numerous, 33–58 per side, or leaf simple; inflorescences stout, rachis 26–82 cm long with 10–101 flowering branches.
    2a. Leaflets with prominent, brown scales on the lower surface, especially on the midvein.
        3a. Sheaths partially closed and forming a crownshaft, cleanly falling; widespread in the Antilles, Central America, and the Andes
                . . . . . *P. acuminata.*
        3b. Sheaths open and not forming a crownshaft, often persistent on the stem; Guayana Highland region of Venezuela and adjacent Brazil and Guyana   . . . . . *P. tenuiramosa.*
    2b. Leaflets without prominent, brown scales on the lower surface.
        4a. Leaf simple; Colombia (Antioquia)   . . . . . *P. simplicifolia.*
        4b. Leaf regularly pinnate, rarely simple, or with a few separate leaflets.
            5a. Leaflets abruptly narrowed at the tips; inflorescences short with peduncle 8–30 cm long   . . . . . *P. decurrens.*
            5b. Leaflets tapering gradually at the tips; inflorescences elongate with peduncle 27–93 cm long   . . . . . *P. ensiformis.*
1b. Stems slender, to 5 m tall and 2–5 cm diameter, usually less; leaflets usually few, 5–38 per side, or occasionally leaf simple; inflorescences slender, rachis 0–46 cm long with usually less than 50 flowering branches.
    6a. Leaves simple, or more often with a few narrow basal leaflets and a very broad apical leaflet; petiole with woolly, reddish brown tomentum; Venezuela (Sucre) and Trinidad   . . . . . *P. pubigera.*
    6b. Leaves regularly pinnate or simple; petiole with flattened, brown tomentum; Central America, Andean region, and western Amazon region.
        7a. Flowering branches usually numerous, 27–59 (–101), rarely less angular, almost rectangular in cross section; Andean region in Colombia, Venezuela, Ecuador, and Peru   . . . . . *P. carderi.*
        7b. Flowering branches few, 1–20, rounded; Central America, Pacific

lowlands in Colombia, or western Amazon region and adjacent Andes.

8a. Leaflets elliptical or almost sigmoid; inflorescences spicate or with 2–11 flowering branches; eastern Panama and Pacific coast of Colombia   . . . . . *P. pubens.*

8b. Leaflets linear-lanceolate; inflorescences branched with 2–20 flowering branches.

9a. Leaflets abruptly narrowed to a fine tip, (21–)33–38 per side; western Amazon region and adjacent Andes in Colombia, Ecuador, and Peru   . . . . . *P. schultzeana.*

9b. Leaflets gradually tapering, 17–33 per side; Central America (Nicaragua to western Panama).

10a. Apical leaflet wider than the others; flowering branches (2–)3–8(–20); peduncle densely brown-tomentose; Nicaragua to western Panama   . . . . . *P. longepetiolata.*

10b. Apical leaflet not wider than the others; flowering branches 9–16; peduncle smooth; Panama   . . . . . *P. roseospadix.*

Prestoea acuminata
(Map 243, Plate 23)
"Palma ramosilla" (Bol), "palmicho" (Col, Ven), "palmito dulce" (CR), "palma justa" (Cub), "manaca" (DR), "maquenque" (Pan), "palma de sierra" (PR)
Field characters. Stems solitary or clustered, (3–)6–15 m tall and 4–20 cm diameter. Leaves 4–10; *sheath partially closed and forming a purple to purple-green, open crownshaft;* rachis (0.6–)1.1–2.6 m long with 30–52(–82), linear-lanceolate leaflets per side. Inflorescences horizontal; peduncle 3–20 cm long; flowering branches 23–117; fruits globose or rarely almost ellipsoid, 1–1.2(–1.8) cm diameter, purple-black; endosperm ruminate; seedling leaf bifid.
Range and habitat. Greater Antilles in eastern Cuba, Hispaniola, and Puerto Rico, Lesser Antilles, Tobago (absent from Trinidad), Central America in Nicaragua, Costa Rica, and Panama, and Colombia (Antioquia, Boyacá, Caldas, Chocó, Cundinamarca, Huila, Magdalena, Meta, Nariño, Norte de Santander, Putumayo, Risaralda, Santander, Tolima, Valle), Venezuela (Aragua, Falcón, Mérida, Monagas, Táchira, Trujillo, Yaracuy), Ecuador (Azuay, Carchi, Cotopaxi, Loja, Morona-Santiago, Napo, Pastaza, Pichincha, Zamora-Chinchipe), Peru (Cajamarca, Huánuco, Junín, Pasco, San Martín), and Bolivia (La Paz); mountainous areas, especially the Andes, in premontane and montane areas on steep slopes, at 1000–2000 m elevation in the Andes but usually much lower in the Antilles.
Uses. The leaves are commonly used for thatching, especially in the Antilles. In Ecuador the palm hearts are harvested and canned for local and international consumption (Balslev and Henderson, 1987a).

Notes. It may be confused with *Euterpe,* but the purple-green crownshaft is not completely closed and the flowering branches are not densely covered with hairs. It is very widespread and consequently very variable and has been given numerous names. In the Andes it is widespread although never very abundant, but in the Antilles it can form large stands, for example the famous "palm brakes" of Puerto Rico. Here the fruits are the preferred food source of the endangered Puerto Rican parrot, *Amazona vittata.* Some ecological aspects of this palm have been studied in Puerto Rico: demography (Van Valen, 1975), long-term growth rates, leaf production, and age (Lugo and Batlle, 1987), root systems (Frangi and Ponce, 1985); ecosystem dynamics (Frangi and Lugo, 1985); hurricane damage (Frangi and Lugo, 1991); soil-plant relationships (Johnston, 1992); seed size, seedling, and stem density and wood (Weaver, 1992); and fruit fall (Lugo and Frangi, 1993).

Prestoea carderi
(Map 244, Plate 24)
"Palmita" (Ecu), "chucshomasha" (Per)
Field characters. Stems clustered, 0.5–4 m tall and 3–4(–10) cm diameter. Leaves 3–6(–10); sheath open and not forming a crownshaft; rachis 1–2.4 m long with 13–36(–54), linear-lanceolate leaflets per side, or rarely leaves simple. *Inflorescences erect; peduncle (0.4–)0.8–1.4 m long; flowering branches (7–)21–59(–101);* fruits globose, 0.7–1 cm diameter, purple-black; endosperm ruminate; seedling leaf bifid.
Range and habitat. Cordillera Central and Oriental in Colombia (Antioquia, Caquetá, Putumayo, Tolima), Cordillera de la Costa and

Cordillera de Mérida in Venezuela (Táchira, Yaracuy), and eastern Andean slopes in Ecuador (Morona-Santiago, Pastaza, Santiago-Zamora) and Peru (Amazonas, Huánuco); montane rain forest on steep slopes, at 1000–1950 m elevation.

Notes. Known from isolated populations throughout its range. The most common form has regularly pinnate leaves, but local populations of plants with simple leaves are known from Colombia and Peru.

Prestoea decurrens
(Map 245, Plate 24)
"Chapil" (Col), "caña lucia" (CR)

Field characters. *Stems green,* clustered with several stems in a clump, rarely solitary, 1.4–7 (–10) m tall and 3–12 cm diameter. Leaves 4–10; sheath semi-open and forming a partial crownshaft, but this obscured by persistent leaf bases; *rachis 1.2–3.1 m long with 35–58 linear-lanceolate leaflets per side.* Inflorescences erect; *peduncle 8–30 cm long;* flowering branches (10–) 30–70; fruits globose, 0.7–1.1 cm diameter, purple-black; endosperm ruminate; seedling leaf pinnate.

Range and habitat. Nicaragua, Costa Rica, Panama, western Colombia (Antioquia, Cauca, Chocó, Nariño, Valle), and western Ecuador (Carchi, Cotopaxi, Esmeraldas, Pichincha); lowland or premontane rain forest, especially common along streams and rivers, from sea level to 800(–1500) m elevation.

Prestoea ensiformis
(Map 246)
"Rabihorcao" (Col), "chontilla" (Ecu), "cuyol," "palmita" (Per)

Field characters. Stems clustered or solitary, 2.5–9 m tall and 3–13 cm diameter. Leaves 5–12; sheath open and not forming a crownshaft; rachis 0.4–2.3 m long with 36–49 linear-lanceolate leaflets per side, occasionally these incompletely split to give a simple or almost simple leaf. *Inflorescences erect; peduncle 27–93 cm long;* flowering branches (13–)18–60; fruits globose, 0.7–1 cm diameter, purple-black; endosperm deeply ruminate; seedling leaf bifid.

Range and habitat. Costa Rica, Panama, western Andean slopes of Colombia (Chocó, Nariño, Risaralda, Valle), and Ecuador (El Oro, Esmeraldas, Los Ríos) and eastern Andean slopes of Ecuador (Morona-Santiago, Pastaza, Zamora-Chinchipe) and Peru (Cusco, Huánuco); premontane or montane rain forest on mountain slopes, at 350–1800 m elevation.

Prestoea longepetiolata
(Map 247)
"Surtua" (CR)

Field characters. Stems solitary or clustered, 0.5–

3(–6) m tall and 2–5 cm diameter. Leaves 4–6; sheath open and not forming a crownshaft; rachis 1.1–2 m long with 17–33 linear-lanceolate leaflets per side. Inflorescences erect, becoming arched in fruit; *peduncle 0.1–1 m long; flowering branches (2–)3–8(–20)* fruits globose, 0.8–1 cm diameter, purple-black; endosperm ruminate; seedling leaf bifid.

Range and habitat. Nicaragua (Jinotega, Matagalpa), Costa Rica (Alajuela, Cartago, Puntarenas, San José), and western Panama (Chiriquí, Bocas del Toro); montane rain forest on steep slopes, at (600–)1000–1500(–2100) m elevation.

Prestoea pubens
(Map 248)
"Siler burwi" (Pan)

Field characters. Stems clustered, 1.4–3.5 m tall and 2–5 cm diameter. Leaves 4–10; sheath open and not forming a crownshaft; rachis 0.5–1.8 m long, with 8–20 *elliptical or almost sigmoid leaflets per side.* Inflorescences arching; peduncle 6–50 cm long; *flowering branches 1–11;* fruits globose, 0.8–1 cm diameter, purple-black; endosperm ruminate; seedling leaf not recorded.

Range and habitat. Panama and Colombia; lowland and premontane rain forest on steep slopes, between sea level and 900 m elevation.

Notes. Two varieties are recognized (Henderson and Galeano, in press); var. *semispicata*, with 1(–4) flowering branches and fruits with scarcely ruminate endosperm, from Panama (Coclé, San Blas); and var. *pubens*, with 3–10 flowering branches and fruits with deeply ruminate endosperm, from Colombia (Cauca, Valle).

Prestoea pubigera
(Map 249, Plate 24)
"Amari" (Tri), "palmillo" (Ven)

Field characters. *Stems solitary,* 3–4(–8) m tall and 3–3.5 cm diameter. Leaves 8–9, *with reddish brown, woolly tomentum;* sheath open but forming a semi-crownshaft; rachis 45–80 cm long with 5–7, linear, *irregularly wide leaflets, the apical one much wider than the others or occasionally the leaf simple.* Inflorescences horizontal; peduncle 8–10(–22) cm long; flowering branches 17–60; fruits globose, 0.8–1.2 cm diameter, purple-black; endosperm ruminate; seedling leaf bifid.

Range and habitat. Trinidad (Northern Range) and northwestern Venezuela (Peninsula de Paria, Sucre); premontane and montane forest on ridges and steep slopes, at 700–1300 m elevation.

Uses. In Trinidad the leaves are occasionally used for thatching.

Notes. An unusual species, not only in its small,

Euterpe-like inflorescences, but also in its restricted and somewhat isolated range.

Prestoea roseospadix
(Map 250)
"Manaca" (Pan)
Field characters. Stems solitary, 0.3–3 m tall and 8–10 cm diameter. Leaves 4–6; sheath open and not forming a crownshaft; rachis 1.1–2 m long with 21–27 linear-lanceolate leaflets per side. *Inflorescences erect*; peduncle 16–38 cm long; flowering branches 9–16; fruits globose, 7–8 mm diameter, purple-black; endosperm deeply ruminate; seedling leaf unknown.
Range and habitat. Western Panama (Bocas del Toro, Chiriquí); montane rain forest on steep slopes, at 1200–2100 m elevation.

Prestoea schultzeana
(Map 251)
"Chincha," "palma de pantano" (Ecu)
Field characters. Stems clustered, rarely solitary, 0.2–5 m tall and 3–5.5 cm diameter. Leaves 4–10; sheath open and not forming a crownshaft; rachis 1.2–2.2 m long with (21–)33–38 linear-lanceolate leaflets per side. *Inflorescences arching*; peduncle 45–80 cm long; *flowering branches 5–13*; fruits globose, 0.7–1 cm diameter, purple-black; *endosperm slightly ruminate; seedling leaf pinnate.*
Range and habitat. Eastern Andean foothills and adjacent Amazon regions of Colombia (Amazonas, Putumayo), Ecuador (Morona-Santiago, Napo, Pastaza), and Peru (Amazonas, Loreto, Pasco); lowland rain forest in flat areas liable to inundation, usually near streams, below 400 m or occasionally reaching 900 m elevation.

Prestoea simplicifolia
(Map 252, Plate 24)
"Lindona" (Col)
Field characters. Stems solitary or clustered, 2–8 m tall and 5–7 cm diameter. Leaves 4–12; sheath open and not forming a crownshaft; rachis 1.4–1.8 m long; *blade simple, bifid at the apex, strongly plicate. Inflorescences curved down*; peduncle 48–86 cm long; flowering branches 32–48; fruits globose, 0.9–1.4 cm diameter, purple-black; seedling leaf bifid.
Range and habitat. Colombia (Antioquia), known only from a small area in the Cordillera Occidental; montane forest on steep slopes, at 950–1600 m elevation.
Notes. One of the most distinctive and rare members of the genus, immediately recognizable by its large, simple leaves. It is only likely to be confused with simple-leafed plants of *Prestoea ensiformis*, from which it differs by its larger fruits and different range.

Prestoea tenuiramosa
(Map 253)
"Manicole palm" (Guy), "manacachilla" (Ven)
Field characters. Stems solitary or clustered, 4–10 m tall and 8–20 cm diameter. Leaves 7–15; sheath open and not forming a crownshaft; rachis to 1.8 m long with 38–45, linear-lanceolate leaflets per side. *Inflorescences erect, elongate*; *peduncle 26–30 cm long; flowering branches about 40*; fruits globose, 1–1.2 cm diameter, purple-black; endosperm deeply ruminate; seedling leaf not recorded.
Range and habitat. Venezuela (Amazonas, Bolívar) and Guyana and just reaching Brazil (Amazonas); montane forest or dwarf forest on the slopes of table-top mountains of the Guayana Highland, at 1200–2000 m elevation.

38. NEONICHOLSONIA

This small, Central American genus is closely related to both *Euterpe* and *Prestoea* and is only distinguished by detailed flower and fruit characters. It was named for George Nicholson (1847–1908), an English botanist, nurseryman, and horticulturalist. Stems are solitary, short, and generally subterranean. Leaves are pinnate and 4–9 in number. Although the leaf sheaths are partially subterranean, they are closed but do not form a crownshaft. The linear-lanceolate leaflets are regularly arranged and spread in the same plane. Inflorescences are spicate and are borne on an elongate peduncle. They are erect and project well above the leaves. Flowers are arranged in threes of one central female and two lateral males, and are closely spaced along the flowering branch. Fruits are one-seeded, ellipsoid-oblong, and purple-black. The apical stigmatic remains on the fruit distinguishes the genus from *Euterpe* and *Prestoea*, which have subapical or lateral remains. The endosperm is deeply ruminate and the seedling leaf is bifid.

Neonicholsonia contains one species (Henderson and Galeano, in press), distributed in Central America. It grows in the understory of lowland rain forest.

Neonicholsonia watsonii
(Map 254, Plate 25)
"Coladegallo" (CR)
Field characters. Stems solitary, short, and subterranean. Leaves 4–9; leaflets linear-lanceolate, glossy green, regularly arranged and spreading in the same plane. Inflorescences spicate, held erect above the leaves; fruits ellipsoid-oblong, 0.9–1 cm long and 0.5–0.6 cm diameter, black.
Range and habitat. Honduras (Gracias a Dios),

Nicaragua (Río San Juan, Zelaya), Costa Rica (Alajuela, Guanacaste, Puntarenas), and Panama (Chiriquí); lowland rain forest on slopes or ridges, at low elevations, occasionally reaching 600 m.
Notes. It can be mistaken for a *Chamaedorea*, but differs in its elongate, spicate inflorescence with both male and female flowers and fruits with an apical stigmatic residue (basal in *Chamaedorea*).

39. OENOCARPUS

This genus of medium-sized to large palms is especially diverse in the northwestern Amazon region. Stems are slender to stout, solitary or clustered, conspicuously ringed, and brown to gray. Leaves are pinnate (simple in *O. simplex*), 5–16 in number and in one species they are arranged in one plane. Leaf sheaths are open but in most species form a partial crownshaft. They are green to purple and the margins have strong, wiry fibers. In one species, *O. circumtextus*, the sheaths consist of a net of interwoven fibers, which completely cover the stem. Leaflets are numerous and are either regularly arranged along the rachis and spread in the same plane, or clustered and spread in different planes. They are narrowly to broadly linear and are usually grayish to whitish on the lower surface. Inflorescences are borne below the leaves and are branched to one order (spicate or bifurcate in *O. simplex*). The long, pendulous flowering branches are closely spaced on the lower surface of the short rachis, and the inflorescence thus resembles a horse's tail. This immediately distinguishes the genus from all others. Flowers are borne in threes of one central female and two lateral males; and male flowers have six stamens (7–20 in *O. bataua*). Fruits are one-seeded, ellipsoid to globose, and purple-black. The mesocarp is usually very oily and the seed is covered by flattened, longitudinal fibers. The endosperm is homogeneous or rarely ruminate and the seedling leaf is slightly to deeply bifid or palmate. The embryo is very large.

Oenocarpus contains nine species (Balick, 1986; Henderson, 1994), distributed in northern South America, reaching south to Brazil and Bolivia and extending north into Central America. All species grow within the Amazon region and only three of them extend beyond. They are usually lowland palms, reaching 1000 m elevation on Andean slopes and at least to 700 m in the Guayana Highland. The highest concentration of species occurs in the northwestern Amazon region of Colombia.

Species in this genus are typical of rain forest or gallery forest and some of them are extremely abundant. *Oenocarpus bataua* is one of the most familiar palms of South American lowland forests. Some of the smaller species are typical elements of the understory, whereas others are tall canopy palms.

The species of *Oenocarpus*, especially the taller ones, are widely appreciated by people throughout northern South America for their nutritious fruits, from which a delicious drink is obtained (the name *Oenocarpus* literally means wine-fruit), as well as an oil very similar to olive oil in its taste and chemical composition (Balick, 1986). The protein of the mesocarp is comparable in quality to good animal protein (Balick, 1986). The Spanish name "milpesos" (one thousand pesos) by which *O. bataua* is widely known in Colombia may well refer to the usefulness of this species. Domestication of this and other species in the genus has been recommended (National Academy of Sciences, 1975).

The fruits of species of *Oenocarpus*, especially those of the canopy species, are a major component in the diet of the oil bird (*Steatornis caripensis*) (Snow, 1962; Snow and Snow, 1978). This nocturnal cave-dwelling bird apparently locates palm fruits by sight, picks them in flight, and swallows them whole, later regurgitating the seeds. The oil bird is known to fly long distances every night (Hilty and Brown, 1986), and it probably plays a major role in the dispersal of *Oenocarpus*.

Oenocarpus is closely related to *Prestoea*, but is readily separated by its horsetail-shaped inflorescence and the whitish lower surface of the leaflets. The genus *Jessenia*, separated on the basis of the larger number of stamens and the ruminate endosperm, is better included under *Oenocarpus* (Bernal et al., 1991).

Hybrids are common in the genus and those in table 3 have been recorded.

TABLE 3. HYBRIDS IN *OENOCARPUS*.

Parent 1	Hybrid	Parent 2
O. bacaba	*O.* x *andersonii*	*O. minor*
O. bataua	Unnamed hybrid	*O. mapora*
O. bataua	Unnamed hybrid	*O. bacaba*

Oenocarpus bacaba
(Map 255)
"Bacaba" (Bra), "manoco," "milpesillo" (Col), "comou" (FrG), "lu" (Guy), "unguraui" (Per), "koemboe" (Sur), "seje pequeño" (Ven)
Field characters. Stems solitary, 8–20 m tall and 15–25 cm diameter. Leaves 10–15, spreading, to 6 m long; leaflets 75–115 per side, irregularly arranged in clusters of 2–7 and spreading in different planes, *the leaf slightly but noticeably plumose.* Inflorescences long and slender, very similar to a horse's tail, reddish in fruit; fruits almost globose, to 2 cm diameter, dark purple-black; seedling leaf palmate.
Range and habitat. Northern South America east of the Andes and north of the Rio Amazonas, in Colombia (Amazonas, Guainía, Vaupés, Vichada), Venezuela (Amazonas, Bolívar, Delta Amacuro), the Guianas, and Brazil (Amapá Amazonas, Pará Roraima); widespread throughout lowland areas on noninundated soils, reaching 1000 m elevation in the Guayana Highland.
Uses. The fruits are used for making a beverage.
Notes. Superficially similar to *Oenocarpus bataua*, with which it often occurs, but this latter has leaflets regularly arranged and spreading in the same plane, a broader and shorter inflorescence and ellipsoid fruits with ruminate endosperm.

Oenocarpus balickii
(Map 256, Plate 25)
"Sinamillo" (Per)
Field characters. Stems solitary, 7–14(–20) m tall and 6–12 cm diameter. Leaves 7–11; leaflets 80–179 per side, narrow, *irregularly arranged in tight clusters of 2–6 and spreading in many planes.*

Inflorescences borne below the leaves, with 46–103 flowering branches; fruits globose-ellipsoid, 1.5–1.8 cm long, 1–1.5 cm diameter, purple-black; seedling leaf palmate.
Range and habitat. Western Amazon region in Colombia (Amazonas), Venezuela (Amazonas), Peru (Loreto, Madre de Dios, San Martín), and Brazil (Acre, western Amazonas, Rondônia), and Bolivia; lowland rain forest on noninundated soils, at 150–350 m elevation.
Uses. A beverage is occasionally prepared from the fruits.
Notes. Unmistakable in its solitary stem and narrow leaflets spreading in many planes. It is reminiscent of *Syagrus*, but it is easily distinguished from that genus by the whitish lower surface of leaflets, pendulous flowering branches and purple-black fruits.

Oenocarpus bataua
(Map 257, Plate 25)
"Batauá," "patauá" (Bra), "milpesos," "seje" (Col), "trupa" (Col, Pan), "chapil" (Ecu), "patawa" (FrG), "turu" (Guy), "unguraui" (Per), "komboe" (Sur), "yagua" (Tri), "aricaguá" (Ven)
Field characters. Stems solitary, 4–26 m tall and 15–45 cm diameter. Leaves (5–)9–20, *rather erect and very long (to 8 m); leaf sheaths with numerous soft fibers interspersed with long, rigid, black fibers;* leaflets numerous, 65–100 per side, broad, regularly arranged and spreading in the same plane, conspicuously whitish on lower surface. Inflorescences massive and broad, typically several developing simultaneously; flowering branches yellowish in flower, turning reddish brown in fruit; fruits ellipsoid, 2.5–4.5 cm long and 2.2–2.5 cm diameter,

dark purple-black; *endosperm ruminate*; seedling leaf bifid.

Range and habitat. Widespread throughout northern South America, on both sides of the Andes, reaching south to central Brazil and northern Bolivia and extending into Trinidad and eastern Panama. One of the most common palms of lowland rain forest and in gallery forests of the *llanos* in Colombia and Venezuela. Grows both in noninundated and in inundated soils, in the latter often forming very large stands. Usually at low elevations but reaching 1000 m on eastern Andean slopes.

Uses. A much-appreciated beverage is prepared from the fruits. This can be further boiled to obtain a clear oil very similar to olive oil. Because of the quality of the oil and its high content in the fruit, this species has been repeatedly recommended as an oil crop with a large underexploited potential (National Academy of Sciences, 1975; Balick, 1979). The trunks are used in construction; the leaves are woven into improvised carrying baskets for game; and leaf sheath fibers are used for blowgun darts. There are many other minor uses.

Notes. A very characteristic canopy palm, easily spotted from the air. In western Colombia and Ecuador it can be mistaken for the common "amargo" (*Welfia regia*), which has less erect and more arching leaves that are green on the lower surface, inflorescences with fewer, thicker flowering branches, and fruits laterally compressed with two keels. East of the Andes, it can be mistaken for *Oenocarpus bacaba*, which has slightly but noticeably plumose leaves and a long and slender inflorescence.

Two varieties are recognized (Henderson, 1994): var. *bataua*, with the male part of the flowering branches flexuous with loosely spaced flowers (or flower scars), widespread in the Amazon region and beyond; and var. *oligocarpa*, with the male part of the flowering branches straight with closely spaced flowers, from the northeastern Amazon region in Venezuela (Bolívar), Trinidad, and the Guianas. Sist and Puig (1987) studied regeneration, population dynamics, and dispersal of this variety in French Guiana.

Oenocarpus circumtextus
(Map 258, Plate 26)
Field characters. Stems solitary, 3–6 m tall and to 8 cm diameter, *completely covered by a dense net of interwoven leaf sheath fibers.* Leaves 7–8; *leaflets 16–19 per side, narrowly elliptical,* regularly arranged and spreading in the same plane, pendulous. Inflorescences borne among the leaves, *with a long peduncle hidden among the leaf sheaths* and numerous pendulous flowering branches, these reddish in fruit; *peduncular*

bract persistent; fruits ellipsoid, to 1.7 cm long and 1 cm diameter; seedling leaf narrowly wedge shaped, shallowly bifid at apex.

Range and habitat. Colombia (Amazonas, in a small area near La Pedrera on the Río Caquetá, near the Brazilian frontier, but said to occur also further north in Vaupés); common among the low and shrubby vegetation of white-sand areas and on the granitic or quartzitic rocky outcrops, where it is often the dominant plant and forms dense stands.

Oenocarpus distichus
(Map 259, Plate 26)
"Bacaba" (Bra)
Field characters. Stems solitary, 5–10(–20) m tall and 8–18(–25) cm diameter. Leaves 9–12, *arranged in one plane*; leaflets 40–130 per side, the basal and middle leaflets irregularly arranged in clusters of 2–7 and spreading in different planes, *giving the leaf a markedly plumose appearance.* Inflorescences long and slender, with 51–161 pendulous flowering branches, these reddish in fruit; *fruits globose to ellipsoid,* 1.8–2 cm long and 1.5–1.7 cm diameter, purple-black; seedling leaf palmate.

Range and habitat. Southern margins of the Amazon region, south of the Rio Amazonas, in Brazil (Maranhão, Mato Grosso, Pará, Rondônia, Tocantins) and Bolivia (Beni, Santa Cruz); lowland rain forest, savanna margins, rocky areas, on noninundated soils, to 350 m elevation.

Uses. The fruits are used for making a beverage and for oil extraction.

Notes. Unmistakable because of its leaves, which are arranged in one plane. Plants in Brazil (Mato Grosso) and Bolivia (Beni, Santa Cruz) have been treated as separate species (*Oenocarpus discolor* and *O. tarampabo*; Balick, 1986), but all are better treated as one.

Oenocarpus makeru
(Map 260)
"Makeru" (Col: Yukuna)
Field characters. Stems solitary, 5–8 m tall and 7–8 cm diameter, longitudinally cracked. Leaves about 12; leaflets about 65 per side, regularly arranged and spreading in the same plane, *green on the lower surface.* Inflorescences borne below the leaves; flowering branches 107–125, pendulous; fruits ovoid, 2.2–2.6 cm long and 1.4–1.7 cm diameter, purple-black; *seeds with ruminate endosperm*; seedling leaf palmate.

Range and habitat. Colombia (Amazonas, known from a small area around La Pedrera, on the Río Caquetá, near the Brazilian frontier); lowland rain forest bordering an area of white sand, at 200 m elevation.

Notes. Possibly a hybrid between *Oenocarpus*

bataua and *O. mapora*. It differs from *O. bataua* in its shorter leaves with the leaflets green on the lower surface and smaller fruits.

Oenocarpus mapora
(Map 261, Plate 26)
"Bacaba" (Bol), "bacabai," "bacabinha" (Bra), "pusuy," "don Pedrito" (Col), "maquenque" (Pan), "ciamba," "sinamillo" (Per), "mapora" (Ven)
Field characters. Stems 2–12, clustered, 5–15 m tall and 4–17 cm diameter. Leaves 6–8, with long and prominent dark green sheath; leaflets 40–90 per side, narrow, *basal and middle leaflets irregularly arranged in clusters of 2–4 and spreading in different planes, apical ones regularly arranged and spreading in the same plane.* Inflorescences borne below leaves, with 60–100 flowering branches, these reddish in fruit; fruits ellipsoid to ovoid, 2–3 cm long and 1.5–2.5 cm diameter; seedling leaf palmate.
Range and habitat. Widespread throughout northwestern South America on both sides of the Andes, from Colombia and western Venezuela to Ecuador, eastern Peru (Loreto, San Martín), western Brazil (Amazonas to Acre), and northern Bolivia (Pando), and extending into Central America in Panama and western Costa Rica (Puntarenas); common in lowland rain forest, on noninundated soils, occasionally reaching 1000 m but usually at lower elevations.
Uses. A beverage is occasionally prepared from the fruits; leaflet midveins are used for basketry; and the leaf is used by the Emberá shamans of Colombia in healing rituals.
Notes. The only clustered-stemmed *Oenocarpus* west of the Andes. It is very similar to (and perhaps better regarded as conspecific with) *O. minor*, which differs in its smaller size and mostly regularly arranged leaflets. Populations on the Pacific coast of Colombia have been treated as a different subspecies (*O. mapora* subsp. *dryanderae*), but this seems unnecessary. Demography has been studied in Panama (de Steven, 1986).

Oenocarpus minor
(Map 262)
"Bacaba-miri," "bacabinha" (Bra), "milpesillo" (Col)
Field characters. Stems solitary or clustered, 2–8 m tall and 4–7 cm diameter. Leaves 4–13; leaflets 50–70 per side, narrow, regularly arranged and spreading in the same plane, or occasionally with clusters of 2–3 leaflets. Inflorescences borne below the leaves, with 29–72 flowering branches, these reddish in fruit and resembling a short horse's tail; fruits globose-ellipsoid, 1.5–2 cm long and 1.3–1.5 cm diameter, purple-black; seedling leaf palmate.
Range and habitat. Central and western Amazon region in Colombia (Amazonas) and Brazil (Amazonas, Pará, Rondônia); lowland rain forest on noninundated soils, at low elevations.
Notes. Balick (1986) recognized two subspecies, but this has not been accepted by other authors (Bernal et al., 1991).

Oenocarpus simplex
(Map 263, Plate 27)
Field characters. Stems 2–3 in a cluster, canelike, 3–4 m tall and 1.5–1.8 cm diameter. Leaves 5–8, reddish when young, erect, *simple, narrowly wedge shaped, shallowly bifid at apex,* 75–90 cm long and 15–20 cm wide. Inflorescences borne among the leaves, *spicate or bifurcate,* with persistent peduncular bract, reddish in fruit; fruits oblong-ellipsoid, 2.2–2.7 cm long and 1.3–1.4 cm diameter, purple-black; seedling leaf simple, bifid.
Range and habitat. Colombia (Amazonas, known from a small area near La Pedrera on the Río Caquetá, near the Brazilian border); understory of lowland rain forest on noninundated soils, at 200 m elevation.
Notes. This remarkable species, with simple leaves and spicate or bifurcate inflorescences, discovered as recently as 1990, is the smallest in the genus and suggests the close affinity of *Oenocarpus* and *Prestoea*.

40. HYOSPATHE

This genus contains one of the most widespread and common understory palms in the American tropics and perhaps also one of the most variable. The name is a Greek translation of the Brazilian Indian name for the palm, "tajassu ubi," which in English means pig leaf. Stems are solitary or clustered, small and slender, and erect or creeping. They are green or brownish, smooth, and have prominent internodes. Leaves are small, simple to pinnate, and 3–10 in number. The leaf sheaths are green and tubular and form a rather elongate crownshaft in one species. The leaf blade varies greatly, from small and simple to irregularly divided into unequal leaflets or regularly divided into equal leaflets. The small inflorescences develop below the leaves and are branched to one order. In bud they are enclosed by a prophyll and one peduncular bract and have few to numerous slender, flowering branches. The flowers are arranged in threes of one central female and two lateral males and are cream colored to pinkish or purplish. Male flowers are rather unusual in being borne on short stalks, and in one species both male and female flowers are borne on stalks. The inflorescence rachis becomes a showy bright red color in fruit. Fruits are one-seeded, ovoid to globose, or almost cylindrical and purple-black. Endosperm is homogeneous and the seedling leaf is bifid.

Hyospathe contains two species (Skov and Balslev, 1989). One is widespread throughout northern South America and reaches Panama and Costa Rica and the other is a narrow endemic on eastern Andean slopes in Ecuador. The genus is typical of the understory of rain forest, from sea level to 2000 m, but is more frequently found in the lowlands below 1000 m elevation. The ability of plants to survive in a low-light environment has been suggested as an explanation of its wide elevational range (Skov and Balslev, 1989), a hypothesis in conflict with the fact that many other understory palms are more restricted in elevation.

The large variation in plant size, leaf division, and inflorescence size in the most common species, *Hyospathe elegans*, led earlier botanists to the recognition of a number of separate species in the genus; these were not accepted by Skov and Balslev (1989).

Hyospathe elegans

(Map 264, Plate 27)

"Ubim-rana" (Bra), "palmita" (Col), "mandi" (Ecu), "waï" (FrG), "nibbi-brit" (Guy), "palmicho" (Per), "mapora" (Ven)

Field characters. Stems solitary or clustered with up to 8 stems, 1–8 m tall and 1–3 cm diameter, green. Leaves 5–11; leaf blade very variable among and within populations, either very small and simple and 20–50 cm long, or irregularly divided into 2–few, unequal, sickle-shaped leaflets, with broad and narrow leaflets often intermixed, or sometimes the leaf with to 26 equal, narrow, one-veined, sickle-shaped leaflets. *Inflorescences developing several nodes below the leaves*; flowering branches 3–31(–55); fruits ellipsoid to ovoid, 1–1.3 cm long and 0.5–1.2 cm diameter, black.

Range and habitat. Costa Rica (Limón, Puntarenas), Panama (Coclé, Darién, San Blas) throughout northern South America in Colombia, Venezuela, the Guianas, Ecuador, Peru, Brazil, and Bolivia; lowland to montane rain forest, from sea level to 2000 m but most common below 1000 m elevation.

Uses. Several Indian tribes in the Amazon region chew the palm hearts to prevent dental cavities; and the Mirañas of Colombia use them mixed with the roots of *Euterpe precatoria* as a cure for flu (Galeano, 1991). In Ecuador and Peru the stems are sharpened and used as spears (Skov and Balslev, 1989).

Notes. Variation in leaf division is correlated with plant size; small, simple leaves being more common in small palms, whereas larger, divided leaves are more frequent in larger palms. The seeds are dispersed by birds and mammals (Zona and Henderson, 1989). *Hyospathe elegans* can be mistaken for understory species of *Chamaedorea*, *Geonoma* and *Prestoea*. Species of *Chamaedorea* usually do not have unequally segmented leaves and differ in the unisexual inflorescences enclosed in several bracts; the fruits lack mesocarp fibers. Species of *Geonoma* have coarser leaves, brownish stems, and the flowers sunken in conspicuous pits on the flowering branches. The understory species of *Prestoea* can be separated by their elongate inflorescences and globose fruits.

Hyospathe macrorhachis

(Map 265)

Field characters. Stems solitary, creeping, to 2 m long and 2.5 cm diameter, reddish brown, the upper 10–20 cm covered with old, persistent leaf sheaths. Leaves 3–10, to 1 m long; leaf blade either simple, to 50 cm long, bifid to one-half of its length, or divided into 3–4 broad, sickle-shaped leaflets per side. *Inflorescences borne among the leaves, erect, to 60 cm long, with a long rachis (to 35 cm), the peduncular bract persistent;* fruits ellipsoid to ovoid, to 1.2 cm long and 9 mm diameter, black.

Range and habitat. Eastern Andean slopes of Ecuador (Morona-Santiago, Pastaza); understory of montane forest, at 1000–1850 m elevation.

41. ROYSTONEA

This small genus is confined to the Caribbean and adjacent countries and contains some of the commonest palms in the region. Together with *Sabal* it typifies the Caribbean landscape. It was named for Roy Stone, a general in the United States Army who served in Puerto Rico. Stems are tall, solitary, whitish gray, gray-brown, or mauve-brown and are often swollen. Leaves are pinnate, 12–18 in number and the leaf bases form a distinctive, green crownshaft. Leaflets are numerous, linear to linear-lanceolate, and are arranged in two rows along the rachis and spread in different planes, giving the leaf a somewhat plumose appearance. Inflorescences are borne below the leaves at the base of the crownshaft and in bud are either as long as or shorter than the crownshaft. They are branched to three orders and contain numerous flowering branches. One unusual feature of the genus, perhaps unique in palms, is that the interior of the inflorescence bud before it opens is full of "packing" in the form of millions of very small fluffy, branched hairs. After the bract opens these fall and blanket the ground below the palm. Flowers are either male or female and are arranged in threes of one central female and two lateral males. Flowers are variously colored, and this is a useful character for identifying species. Fruits are one-seeded, globose to ellipsoid or obovoid, small and purple-black or variously red or brown. The stigmatic remains are basal on the fruit and in one species they are star shaped. Endosperm is homogeneous and the seedling leaf is simple.

Roystonea contains ten species, distributed throughout the Caribbean and adjacent regions (Zona, in press). They are all rather similar and are distinguished by details of flowers and fruits. However, usually only one species occurs in a locality or habitat (except in eastern Cuba), and so they are not difficult to identify. They often occur naturally in low-lying, inundated areas but can colonize disturbed areas in a variety of habitats and are very commonly planted. One apparent adaptation to their Caribbean habitat is that plants lose their leaves early in hurricanes and are thus able to withstand strong winds without being blown down.

Roystonea altissima
(Map 266)
"Mountain cabbage" (Jam)
Field characters. Stems *gray-brown, columnar,* to 20 m tall and 25–35 cm diameter. Leaves about 15; lowest leaves hanging below the horizontal. Peduncular bract about 1 m long, shorter than the crownshaft; *male flowers violet;* fruits obovoid, 1.1–1.5 cm long and 0.6–1 cm diameter, purple-black.
Range and habitat. Jamaica; hills and mountains in inland areas, on limestone soils, to 800 m elevation.

Roystonea borinquena
(Map 267)
"Palma caruta," "palma real" (DR), "palmis," "palmiste" (Hai), "palma real" (PR)
Field characters. Stems *gray-brown, swollen,* to 15 m tall and 25–50 cm diameter. Leaves 15 or fewer; lowest leaves hanging below the horizontal. Peduncular bract 0.9–1.6 m long, as long as the crownshaft; *male flowers yellow;* fruits

subglobose to ellipsoid, 1.1–1.5 cm long and 0.9–1.3 cm diameter, brown to black.
Range and habitat. Puerto Rico, Hispaniola (Dominican Republic, Haiti), and Virgin Islands; widespread and very common in a variety of habitats, especially disturbed areas or fields, to 1000 m elevation.
Uses. The fruits are an important source of food for pigs and other farm animals, and the flowers are a pollen source for honey bees. There are also several minor uses (Zanoni, 1991).

Roystonea dunlapiana
(Map 268)
"Caviche" (Hon), "yagua" (Hon, Nic)
Field characters. Stems *whitish gray, columnar,* to 20 m tall and 40 cm diameter. Leaves 12–15; lowest leaves hanging below the horizontal. Peduncular bract about 2 m long, as long as the crownshaft; *male flowers white;* fruits obovoid, 1.2–1.4 cm long and 0.8–1 cm diameter, purple-black.

Range and habitat. Caribbean coast of Mexico (Quintana Roo), Honduras (Atlántida), and Nicaragua (Zelaya); low-lying, inundated areas, tidal estuaries or mangrove swamps.

Roystonea lenis
(Map 269)
"Palma conga," "palma de seda" (Cub)
Field characters. Stems whitish gray, often swollen, to 20 m tall and 35–47 cm diameter. Leaves about 15; lowest leaves hanging below the horizontal. Peduncular bract about 1.8 m long, shorter than the crownshaft; *male flowers white;* fruits ellipsoid, 1.1–1.4 cm long and 0.8–1.1 cm diameter, purple-black.
Range and habitat. Eastern Cuba (Oriente); open areas, at 350–450 m elevation.

Roystonea maisiana
(Map 270)
"Palma negra" (Cub)
Field characters. Stems whitish gray, to 20 m tall and 25–50 cm diameter. Leaves about 15; lowest leaves hanging below the horizontal. Peduncular bract shorter than the crownshaft; *male flowers white;* fruits ellipsoid, 1–1.4 cm long and 7–9 mm diameter, purple-black.
Range and habitat. Eastern Cuba (Oriente); open places, at 350–450 m elevation.

Roystonea oleracea
(Map 271, Plate 27)
"Cabbage palm" (Dom, Bar), "mapora" (Col, Ven), "royal palm" (Lesser Antilles)
Field characters. Stems whitish gray, very large, columnar or slightly swollen, 18–40 m tall and 46–66 cm diameter. Leaves 16–22; lowest leaves held ± horizontally. Peduncular bract about 1.5 m long, shorter than the crownshaft; *male flowers white;* fruits ellipsoid, 1.3–1.7 cm long and 0.8–1 cm diameter, purple-black.
Range and habitat. Lesser Antilles (Guadaloupe, Dominica, Martinique, Barbados), Trinidad, Tobago, northern Venezuela (Barinas, Bolívar, Carabobo, Cojedes, Falcón, Monagas, Yaracuy), and northeastern Colombia (Arauca, Casanare, Meta); low-lying, wet areas near the sea in the Caribbean, or in gallery forest in savannas liable to inundation in Colombia and Venezuela, to 1600 m elevation.
Uses. This is the tallest and most majestic of the royal palms and is commonly planted as an ornamental. It is naturalized in the Guianas.

Roystonea princeps
(Map 272)
"Marsh cabbage" (Jam)
Field characters. Stems whitish gray, columnar or slightly swollen, to 20 m tall and 25–40 cm di-ameter. Leaves about 15; lowest leaves hanging below the horizontal. Peduncular bract about 1.8 m long, as long as the crownshaft; *male flowers white;* fruits globose to ellipsoid, 1.2–1.8 cm long and 0.8–1 cm diameter, purple-black.
Range and habitat. Southwestern Jamaica; low-lying, wet areas.

Roystonea regia
(Map 273, Plate 28)
"Yagua" (Hon, Mex), "palma criolla" (Cub), "palma real" (Cub, Hon, Mex), "royal palm" (USA)
Field characters. Stems whitish gray, columnar or regularly or irregularly swollen, 7–30 m tall and 40–57 cm diameter, swelling to 60–75 cm. Leaves 15–18; lowest leaves hanging below the horizontal. Peduncular bract 0.8–1.6 m long, shorter than the crownshaft; *male flowers white;* fruits ellipsoid to obovoid, 0.9–1.5 cm long and 0.7–1.1 cm diameter, reddish brown or purple-black.
Range and habitat. United States (Florida), Bahamas, Mexico (Campeche, Tabasco, Veracruz, Yucatán), Belize, Honduras (Atlántida, Cortes), Cayman Islands, and Cuba; in hammocks (Florida), woods, or open savannas, usually in wet places but now very common in disturbed areas. It is still extremely abundant in Cuba and locally common and reproducing well in its restricted habitat in southwest Florida (Scott Zona, pers. comm.).
Uses. Very commonly planted as an ornamental throughout the American tropics and elsewhere. In Cuba this species has a host of uses (Zona, 1991). The stems are cut into planks for house construction; the fruits are fed to animals and are a source of oil; the leaves are used for thatching; the leaf sheaths ("yagua") are used to cover tobacco bales; and the stems are occasionally made into furniture.
Notes. In Florida it flowers from January to July and fruits from April to October (Jones, 1983). Other ecological aspects of this species are provided by Jones. *Roystonea elata,* described from Florida and here regarded as a synonym, is actually the oldest name for this species, if indeed the Florida populations are the same species as those from Cuba. However, we have refrained from changing the name until the matter is studied in more detail.

Roystonea stellata
(Map 274)
"Palma blanca" (Cub)
Field characters. Stems whitish gray, to 15 m tall. Peduncular bract about 1.2 m long, shorter than the crownshaft; *male flowers white;* fruits

ellipsoid, 0.9–1.1 cm long and 8–9 mm diameter, purple-black, *with a star-shaped stigmatic scar.*

Range and habitat. Eastern Cuba (Oriente, Maisí region); open areas, at low elevations.

Notes. Either very rare or extinct in the wild (Zona, in press).

Roystonea violacea
(Map 275)
"Palma morada," "palma roja" (Cub)

Field characters. Stems mauve-brown to mauve-gray, to 15 m tall and 34 cm diameter. Leaves about 15; lowest leaves hanging below the horizontal. Peduncular bract about 1.2 m long, shorter than the crownshaft; *male flowers violet;* fruits globose to ellipsoid, 1.2–1.4 cm long and 7–9 mm diameter, purple-black.

Range and habitat. Eastern Cuba (Oriente, Maisí region); open places, at 350–450 m elevation.

42. BUTIA

This small genus is very closely related to *Syagrus,* and at one time or another some of its species have been included there. Stems are rough and often covered with persistent leaf bases. They are either moderately tall and stout or short and subterranean. Leaves are pinnate, 3–32 in number, and are strongly arched. The petioles are usually covered with coarse spines (unlike the smooth petioles of most species of *Syagrus*), although several species have nonspiny, fibrous petioles. The genus gets its name from these spines and is a Portuguese corruption of an Indian word meaning toothed or spiny. Leaflets are numerous, linear, and usually spread stiffly, forming a V shape. They are often glaucous and have large brown scales on the lower surface. Inflorescences are branched to one order, or rarely spicate, and are borne among the leaves. The peduncular bract is usually smooth or scarcely grooved on the outer surface (unlike the grooved bract of *Syagrus*), and in some species it is densely tomentose. Flowering branches range from few to numerous, and in the larger species the basal ones are sometimes bifurcate. Flowers are unisexual and are borne in threes of one central female and two lateral males. Male flowers have six stamens; the filaments are often inflexed at the tips, thus further distinguishing the genus from *Syagrus.* Fruits are one- to three-seeded, globose or ovoid, and often yellowish or brownish purple. The thick, bony endocarp has three pores near or just below the middle (compared to the basal pores of *Syagrus*). Seeds have homogeneous endosperm and the seedling leaf is simple.

Butia contains eight species (Glassman, 1979). Our treatment differs from Glassman's in that we transfer *Butia campicola* from *Syagrus* and place *B. arenicola* in synonymy under *B. paraguayensis.* Some species, particularly the ones with short and subterranean stems, are extremely variable, and this variation is still not well understood. *Butia* is a genus of subtropical southern South America, growing in open areas in southern Brazil, eastern Paraguay, northeastern Argentina, and northern Uruguay. Many species are becoming rare because their habitat—open grasslands and *cerrado*—is being turned into farmland.

The larger species, such as *Butia capitata,* are commonly cultivated in subtropical parks and gardens (Bailey, 1936b). *Butia capitata* has been crossed in cultivation with *Syagrus romanzoffiana* to produce x *Butiarecastrum nabonnandii* (Moore, 1982).

Butia archeri
(Map 276)
"Coqueirinho do campo" (Bra)
Field characters. Stems solitary, *short and subterranean* or sometimes to 1 m tall. Leaves arching; *petiole without spines on the margins,* fibrous; leaflets 28–44 per side, regularly arranged and

stiffly spreading, forming a V shape. Peduncular bract smooth or slightly grooved; *flowering branches 15–31;* fruits ellipsoid, 1.8–2 cm long, brown.

Range and habitat. Southern Brazil (Distrito Federal, Goiás, Minas Gerais, São Paulo); *cerrado* vegetation in open grasslands.

Notes. Silberbauer-Gottsberger (1973) studied floral biology and insect visitors of this species (as *Butia leiospatha*) in Brazil. She found that a variety of insects, including wasps, bees, flies, and beetles, were pollinators, attracted to the nectar produced by male and female flowers. Scarab beetles removed and buried fruits that had fallen to the ground and used them as oviposition sites.

Butia campicola
(Map 277)

Field characters. Stems solitary or clustered, *short and subterranean.* Leaves 3–9, arching; *petiole without spines on the margins,* fibrous; leaflets 14–16 per side, grayish, stiffly spreading, forming a V shape. *Inflorescences spicate; peduncular bract brown-tomentose, slightly grooved;* fruits ovoid, 1.5–2 cm long and 1 cm diameter, brown.

Range and habitat. Paraguay (Candeniyú, Cordillera); open grassy areas on sandy soils.

Notes. Treated by Glassman (1987) as a species of *Syagrus.*

Butia capitata
(Map 278)
"Butiá-da-praia," "cabeçudo" (Bra), "butiá" (Uru)

Field characters. Stems solitary, *1–6 m tall* and 25–50 cm diameter, rough. Leaves 18–32, arching; *petiole with coarse spines along the margins;* leaflets 44–80 per side, glaucous, more or less regularly arranged and stiffly spreading, forming a V shape. *Peduncular bract almost smooth or with shallow grooves on outer surface,* glaucous; *flowering branches 50–99;* fruits ovoid, 1.8–3.5 cm long and 1.2–2.2 cm diameter, yellowish or orange-brown.

Range and habitat. Southern Brazil (Bahia, Goiás, Minas Gerais, Paraná, Santa Catarina, Rio Grande do Sul) and Uruguay (Montevideo); open areas or *cerrado* on sandy soils, at low elevations.

Notes. The non-*cerrado* populations from the southern part of the range, in Brazil (Paraná, Santa Catarina, Rio Grande do Sul) and Uruguay (Montevideo), are somewhat different and grow in *restinga* vegetation. They should perhaps be recognized as a separate species, in which case *Butia odorata* would be the correct name (Larry Noblick, pers. comm.).

Butia eriospatha
(Map 279, Plate 28)
"Butiá," "butiá-da-serra" (Bra)

Field characters. Stems solitary, *3–6 m tall and to 50 cm diameter, rough.* Leaves 25–30, arching; *petiole with coarse spines along the margins;* leaflets 50–95 per side, glaucous, regularly arranged and stiffly spreading, forming a V shape. *Peduncular bract covered on outer surface with dense, brown tomentum;* flowering branches numerous, to 125; fruits globose, 1.7–1.9 cm diameter, yellowish.

Range and habitat. Southern Brazil (Paraná, Rio Grande do Sul, Santa Catarina); open areas and *Araucaria* forests.

Uses. The fruits are soaked in alcohol to produce a popular drink.

Butia microspadix
(Map 280)

Field characters. Stems solitary, *short and subterranean.* Leaves 4–7, arching; *petiole without spines, fibrous;* leaflets 19–29 per side, regularly arranged and stiffly spreading, forming a V shape. Peduncular bract smooth or scarcely grooved, *covered with dense, brown tomentum;* flowering branches 11–16; fruits ovoid, to 2 cm long and 1 cm diameter, brownish.

Range and habitat. Southern Brazil (Paraná, São Paulo); open grasslands, to 1000 m elevation.

Butia paraguayensis
(Map 281, Plate 29)
"Yatay enano" (Arg), "butiá" (Bra), "yatay" (Par)

Field characters. Stems short and subterranean, occasionally reaching 4 m tall and 8–20 cm diameter, covered with persistent leaf bases. Leaves 5–7, strongly arching; *petiole with coarse spines along the margins;* leaflets 32–53 per side, glaucous, regularly arranged and stiffly spreading, forming a V shape. *Peduncular bract smooth or sparsely tomentose, without grooves; flowering branches 18–43;* fruits ovoid, 2–3.9 cm long and 1–2.5 cm diameter, yellowish, 1–2-seeded.

Range and habitat. Southern Brazil (Mato Grosso do Sul, Paraná, Rio Grande do Sul, São Paulo), Paraguay (Amambay, Caaguazú, Canendiyú, Concepción, Cordillera, Misiones, Neembucú, San Pedro), Argentina (Corrientes, Misiones), and northern Uruguay; open *cerrado* vegetation on sandy soils, at low elevations.

Notes. Closely related to and perhaps not distinct from *Butia yatay.*

Butia purpurascens
(Map 282)
"Butiá" (Bra)

Field characters. Stems solitary, *1–4 m tall* and 15–16 cm diameter, covered with persistent leaf bases. Leaves 12–22, arching; *petiole without spines on the margins, fibrous;* leaflets 38–58 per side, regularly arranged and stiffly spreading, forming a V shape. *Peduncular bract smooth or slightly grooved; flowering branches 50–79;*

fruits ovoid, 2.3–2.9 cm long and 1–1.3 cm diameter, purple or brownish.
Range and habitat. Brazil (Goiás); *cerrado* vegetation, to 750 m elevation.

Butia yatay
(Map 283)
"Yatay" (Arg), "palma yatay" (Uru)
Field characters. Stems solitary, *8–10 m tall and to 40 cm diameter*, rough. Leaves 30 or more; *petiole covered with coarse spines*; leaflets 68–72 per side, regularly arranged and stiffly spreading,

forming a V shape. *Peduncular bract usually with shallow grooves; flowering branches to 100 or more;* fruits ovoid, 3–4.2 cm long and 2.5–2.8 cm diameter.
Range and habitat. Southern Brazil (Rio Grande do Sul), Argentina (Corrientes, Entre Ríos, Santa Fé), and Uruguay; forming large stands in open, flat areas on sandy soils.
Notes. Crovetto and Piccinini (1951) have described the habitat and associated plants of this species in Argentina.

43. JUBAEA

This Chilean genus gets its name from a king of Numidia, Juba II (about 50 B.C. to A.D. 24), who was interested in botany. Stems are massive, solitary, dark gray, and are markedly and sometimes irregularly swollen at or near the base and generally taper toward the apex. Leaves are pinnate, 40–50 in number, and form a dense crown. They are borne in a few tight spirals and cleanly fall when dead and do not persist on the stem. Sheaths are open and are rather fibrous. Petioles are also fibrous, but are short and not really distinct from the sheaths. The numerous linear, stiff leaflets are more or less irregularly arranged along the rachis, but spread in the same plane. They are somewhat glaucous and are covered with brownish scales on the lower surface. Inflorescences are large and pendulous and are branched to one order. The single peduncular bract is woody and is densely covered on the outer surface with brown, feltlike tomentum. Flowers are unisexual and are borne in threes of one central female and two lateral males along the flowering branches. The staminate flowers are slightly unusual among related genera in being borne on a short stalk and in having up to eighteen stamens. Fruits are one-seeded, irregularly globose, brown, and have a thick endocarp with three pores below the middle. The endosperm is homogeneous and the seedling leaf is narrow and simple.

This genus of one species (Glassman, 1987) is of great botanical interest, not only for its isolated and rather dry habitat but also because of its relationships. *Jubaea* is a relict of a Southern Hemisphere distribution track of several related genera (the subtribe Butiinae; see Moraes and Henderson, 1990), starting from the west in Africa (*Jubaeopsis*) and continuing east to Madagascar (*Voanioala*), Melanesia (*Cocos*), Chile (*Jubaea*), Bolivia (*Parajubaea*), and ending in southern Brazil (*Syagrus, Butia, Lytocaryum, Allagoptera, Polyandrococos*). A recently extinct genus, *Paschalococos*, from Easter Island (Dransfield et al., 1984; Dransfield, 1991) also fits into this track. This southern Pacific distribution pattern is evident in other groups of palms.

Jubaea chilensis
(Map 284, Plate 29)
"Palma chilena," "palma de coquitos" (Chi)
Field characters. Stems solitary, massive, 8–15 m tall and to 1 m or more diameter, irregularly swollen, usually widest at the base and tapering toward the apex, dark gray. Leaves forming a dense crown; leaflets stiffly spreading, green or blue-gray, appearing regularly arranged. Inflorescences borne among the

leaves; fruits almost globose, one-seeded, 3.5–4 cm long and 3–4 cm diameter, brownish.
Range and habitat. Chile (Aconcagua, O'Higgins, Valparaiso); Andean foothills in dry river valleys or open hillsides in seasonally dry regions with a Mediterranean climate, at low elevations. Formerly more common in Chile between 32° and 35°S (Río Limarí to Curicó), but now confined to a few small areas, principally La Campana National Park and near Co-

calán (Zizka, 1989). It is one of the most southerly occurring genera of palms.

Uses. It was formerly the source of palm wine, which was made from the sap of the cut trunks, and this led to the demise of many *J. chilensis* populations. Currently the "nuts" (i.e., endocarps and seeds) are sold locally and internationally as a snack food, and honey ("miel de palma") is extracted (by tapping) from the stems. The palm is also a popular ornamental in Chile, as far south as Valdivia and other warm temperate regions. There is currently an active research program in Chile aimed at the sustainable harvest of honey and fruits from this palm.

Notes. Darwin (1845) wrote: "These palms are, for their family, ugly trees." However, the magnificent stands of *Jubaea chilensis* at La Campana are one of the wonders of the palm world, rivaling *Ceroxylon* and *Dictyocaryum* of the Colombian Andes in their beauty. Flowering is from November to December and fruits are ripe from January onwards.

44. COCOS

The best-known palm in the Americas, the coconut, is the only species of this genus. Stems are large and solitary, gray and often leaning, and are conspicuously swollen at base. Leaves are pinnate, 25–30 in number, and form a graceful crown. The leaf sheath is open and very fibrous. Leaflets are linear, numerous, and regularly arranged along the rachis and spread in the same plane. Inflorescences are borne among the leaves and are branched to one order. The peduncular bract is somewhat woody. Flowers are unisexual and are borne in threes of one central female and two lateral males at the base of the flowering branches, where the large female flowers are easily visible. The one-seeded fruits are very distinctive, mostly because of their large size. The origin of the name is from the Portuguese or Spanish word "coco," meaning a nut or a seed. The outer layer is green, orange, or yellow, depending on variety. Inside is a fibrous layer, and this gives coconuts their ability to float. A thick, bony endocarp protects the inner layer of endosperm. The inside of the seed is hollow and contains liquid endosperm. The seedling leaf is simple.

This is a genus of one species, which is widely cultivated throughout tropical areas of the world, especially along sandy coasts. The origin of the coconut palm is unknown. Harries (1978) believed it may have originated in the western Pacific. Buckley and Harries (1984) and Gruezo and Harries (1984) found what they considered to be self-sown, wild-type coconuts in Australia and the Philippines, respectively.

Cocos nucifera
(Map 285, Plate 29)
"Coco"

Field characters. Stems solitary, often leaning, to 20 m tall and 20–30 cm or more diameter. Leaves 25–30; leaflets 75–100 per side, regularly arranged and stiffly spreading in the same plane. Inflorescences borne among the leaves; fruits ovoid, 20–30 cm long and 12–20 cm diameter, green to reddish brown.

Range and habitat. Commonly planted throughout tropical areas in the Americas, usually at low elevations but occasionally seen up to 1000 m elevation.

Uses. The coconut is very useful at the domestic level, and is an important commercial crop, producing coconut oil, coir, and toddy. Coconut oil is obtained from the dried endosperm (known as copra) and has been used in the manufacture of soap and margarine. Coir is obtained from the fibrous mesocarp and is used to weave mats and rugs. Toddy is sugar-containing sap which is tapped from unopened inflorescences and often fermented into an alcoholic drink. The most important commercial plantations have always been in the Old World, particularly in the Philippines and Indonesia. In the Americas, only Trinidad, Tobago, Jamaica, Mexico (Guzmán-Rivas, 1984), and some of the Lesser Antilles have had coconut industries, but they have suffered from hurricanes and a disease known as lethal yellowing (McCoy, 1983). Coconut palms are still important in the Caribbean and other regions, as landscape plants in tourist areas. Apart from these major uses, the coconut has a host of minor uses.

45. SYAGRUS

This large genus is widespread in South America and is especially diverse in dry areas of central and eastern Brazil. The name is derived from a Latin word meaning a kind of palm tree. Stems are small to large, solitary or less often clustered, and aerial or short and subterranean. Leaves are pinnate (simple in some populations of *Syagrus smithii*) and 6–30 in number. They are sometimes arranged in distinctive rows. The sheath is often fibrous on the margins and the petiole is occasionally covered with spinelike fibers. Leaflets are few to numerous, narrow, linear, often glaucous, stiff or flexuous, often briefly and asymmetrically bifid at the tips and have brown scales on the lower surface. They are either regularly arranged and spreading in the same plane, or more often clustered and spreading in different planes. Inflorescences are borne among the leaves, branched to one order or sometimes spicate, with few to numerous flowering branches. The peduncular bract is typically persistent, woody, or sometimes papery and is usually grooved on the outer surface. Flowers are unisexual and are borne in threes of one central female and two lateral males; male flowers have six stamens. Fruits are one- to two-seeded, ovoid, ellipsoid, or globose, small to medium sized, yellow, orange, green, brown, or red, and often have a prominent beak. The mesocarp is fibrous and the endocarp thick and woody or bony, with three basal pores. The shape of the endocarp cavity in cross section varies from round to triangular and is a good character for identification in some species. The endosperm is homogeneous, or ruminate in a few species, and the seedling leaf is simple and narrowly elliptical.

As treated here, *Syagrus* contains thirty species distributed in South America, from Colombia east to French Guiana and south to Uruguay and northern Argentina, with one species endemic to the Lesser Antilles. The genus is particularly diverse in the central Brazilian region. Most species are typical of dry areas, in *caatinga, cerrado,* or savanna, often on sandy or rocky soils, or sometimes growing directly on granitic outcrops. Only a few species grow in rain forest in the Amazon region and Atlantic coastal forest, and only two species reach the Andes.

Several species of *Syagrus* are often found in the same area and hybridization seems to be common (Glassman, 1968, 1970, 1987; Noblick, 1991). At least six natural hybrids have been recognized; see notes under *S. coronata.*

Some species of *Syagrus* are very variable, and herbarium taxonomy has resulted in a proliferation of specific names for local forms that we think should be recognized as part of widespread, variable species. This seems to be particularly true for the small, short-stemmed species, which grow in extreme conditions, often within rock crevices. Thus, although for the purpose of this guide the classification of species largely follows Glassman (1987), we have departed somewhat from it, especially in the recognition of fewer species in the *Syagrus petraea* complex. Noblick's (1991) treatment of *Syagrus* for Bahia, Brazil, has been a major source of information for the species of that area.

Syagrus is the closest relative of the coconut and most species in the genus have been included at one time in the genus *Cocos.* There is now a consensus in keeping both genera separate, although more for traditional rather than biological reasons. The seeds of most species of *Syagrus* are edible and they taste like coconut. Mesocarp of some species is also edible.

KEY TO THE SPECIES OF *SYAGRUS*

1a. Lesser Antilles; stems 15–20 m tall, markedly swollen at base . . . . . *S. amara.*
1b. South America; stems usually shorter and not swollen at the base.
  2a. The Andes and Amazon regions (sometimes reaching adjacent parts of the central Brazil region).
    3a. Fruits globose to ovoid or pear shaped.
      4a. Fruits globose, longitudinally grooved; Suriname and French Guiana . . . . . *S. stratincola.*
      4b. Fruits ovoid to pear shaped, not grooved; Guyana and Brazil (Amazonas, Maranhão, Mato Grosso, Pará, Piauí, Tocantins) . . . . *S. cocoides.*
    3b. Fruits ellipsoid.
      5a. Fruits 6–8 cm long; western Amazon region in Colombia (Amazonas), Peru (Amazonas, Loreto, Ucayali), and Brazil (Acre, western Amazonas) . . . . . *S. smithii.*
      5b. Fruits 3–4 cm long; Amazon or Andean region.
        6a. Large palms with stems 7–30 m tall and 20–30 cm diameter; leaves with 122–180 leaflets per side; inflorescences with 78–200 flowering branches; Andes and southwestern Amazon region . . . . . *S. sancona.*
        6b. Smaller palms with stems 1–15 m tall and 4–15 cm diameter; leaves with 51–110 leaflets per side; inflorescences with 6–37 flowering branches; Amazon region.
          7a. Endocarp cavity triangular in cross section; northeastern Amazon region in the Guianas and northern Brazil . . . . . *S. inajai.*
          7b. Endocarp cavity rounded in cross section; northwestern Amazon region and northern Venezuela . . . . . *S. orinocensis.*
  2b. Central Brazilian region and Atlantic coastal forest, occasionally reaching Amazon region, especially in open areas and savannas.
    8a. Stems upright, more than 0.5 m tall.
      9a. Leaves conspicuously arranged in 5 vertical rows, the leaf bases persistent along the stem in 5 rows.
        10a. Petiole-like extension of the leaf sheath with spinelike, woody, flattened fibers; leaflets green; stems 3–12 m tall . . . . . *S. coronata.*
        10b. Petiole-like extension of the sheath lacking woody fibers; leaflets glaucous; stems 0.5–5 m tall . . . . . *S. glaucescens.*
      9b. Leaves spirally arranged, not in conspicuous rows.
        11a. Leaf sheath with fibrous, spiny, serrate margins . . . . . *S. schizophylla.*
        11b. Leaf sheath margins not spiny nor serrate.
          12a. Stems solitary.
            13a. Leaflets regularly arranged and spreading in the same plane, erect, the leaf looking like a V . . . . . *S. botryophora.*
            13b. Leaflets irregularly arranged in clusters and spreading in different planes.
              14a. Small to medium-sized palms, stems 1–8 m tall and 6–20 cm diameter.
                15a. Atlantic coastal rain forest of Brazil; fruits cinnamon to orange-brown . . . . . *S. picrophylla.*

15b. *Cerrado*, woodland, or seasonal forest.
  16a. Fruits large, 6.5–7 cm long and 3–3.2 cm di-
    ameter; Brazil (Espírito Santo, Minas Gerais)
    . . . . . *S. macrocarpa.*
  16b. Fruits medium sized, 2.5–3.5 cm long and
    1.5–1.8 cm diameter; widespread.
    17a. Leaflets 2–3 cm wide, with obvious cross
      veins; flowers white to cream; fruits light
      green   . . . . . *S. comosa.*
    17b. Leaflets 0.5–2 cm wide, without obvious
      cross-veins; flowers yellow; fruits yellowish
      . . . . . *S. flexuosa.*
14b. Large palms, stems 5–20 m tall and 25–50 cm diameter.
  18a. Leaflets with the tips abruptly bent downwards
    and pendulous; endocarp cavity very irregular in
    cross section   . . . . . *S. romanzoffiana.*
  18b. Leaflets stiff; endocarp cavity circular or almost
    so in cross section.
    19a. Fruits 6–8 cm long, yellow, with a prominent
      brown beak; seed with ruminate endosperm
      . . . . . *S. pseudococos.*
    19b. Fruits 4–5.5 cm long, light greenish to yellow
      green; seed with homogeneous endosperm
      . . . . . *S. oleracea.*
12b. Stems clustered.
  20a. Leaflets regularly arranged and spreading in the same
    plane; fruits broadly ellipsoid, bright orange   . . . . . *S. ruschiana.*
  20b. Leaflets arranged in clusters of 2–5 and spreading in
    different planes; fruits ellipsoid to narrowly ellipsoid,
    light green to yellow.
    21a. Leaflet tips very rigid and spinelike; leaves white-
      tomentose throughout   . . . . . *S. campylospatha.*
    21b. Leaflets tips not spinelike; leaves green   . . . . . *S. flexuosa.*
8b. Stems short and subterranean, or upright and to 0.5 m tall (rarely
  more).
  22a. Leaflets regularly arranged and spreading in the same plane.
    23a. Lower portion of the leaf sheath with stiff, flattened fibers,
      which form narrow, toothlike projections   . . . . . *S. vagans.*
    23b. Lower portion of the leaf sheath without stiff fibers.
      24a. Leaflets glaucous on upper surface; inflorescences covered
        with a fine, dense, grayish white tomentum   . . . . . *S. werdermannii.*
      24b. Leaflets green on upper surface; inflorescences glabrous.
        25a. Inflorescences with 5–31 flowering branches; fruits
          dark orangish brown; Brazil (central Bahia); in rock
          crevices   . . . . . *S. harleyi.*
        25b. Inflorescences spicate or sometimes with up to 9 flow-
          ering branches; fruits green with brown tomentum; wide-
          spread; open areas.

26a. Peduncular bract papery; Brazil (Mato Grosso)
.... *S. leptospatha.*
26b. Peduncular bract woody; widespread in central and
eastern Brazil and Paraguay.
27a. Eastern Brazil (southern Goiás, Mato Grosso do
Sul) and eastern Paraguay ...... *S. graminifolia.*
27b. Brazil (Bahia, Mato Grosso do Sul, Minas Gerais,
Pará, Piauí, Rondônia, São Paulo), eastern Bolivia
(Santa Cruz), and eastern Paraguay (Amambay,
Caaguazú) ...... *S. petraea.*
22b. Leaflets in clusters of 2–5 on the rachis.
28a. Leaflet tips very rigid and spinelike; leaves white-tomentose
throughout ...... *S. campylospatha.*
28b. Leaflets tips not spinelike; leaves green or the leaflets white
on lower surface, but not white-tomentose throughout.
29a. Leaflets bluish green or glaucous.
30a. Leaflets 44–64 per side; Brazil (Minas Gerais) ...... *S. duartei.*
30b. Leaflets 18–36 per side; Brazil (Bahia) ...... *S. microphylla.*
29b. Leaflets green.
31a. Flowering branches short and gnarled; Brazil (Minas
Gerais, São Paulo) ...... *S. pleioclada.*
31b. Flowering branches not gnarled; widespread.
32a. Western Bolivia; flowering branches 4–13 on an
elongate rachis ...... *S. cardenasii.*
32b. Widespread; flowering branches less than 9 on a
short rachis.
33a. Leaflets 9–50 per side; flowers yellowish to
orangish ...... *S. petraea.*
33b. Leaflets 57–82 per side; flowers white to cream
...... *S. comosa.*

Syagrus amara
(Map 286)
"Yattahou," "coco nain" (Dom), "petit coco
de bois" (Gud), "petit coco" (Mar), "mocho"
(Mon)
Field characters. Stems solitary, 15–20 m tall and
10–20 cm diameter, *markedly swollen at the base.*
Leaves 12–15, to 3 m long; leaflets 102–106
per side, rigid, irregularly arranged in clusters
of 2–3 and spreading in different planes, *but
the leaf not markedly plumose.* Inflorescences with
about 50 flowering branches; fruits ellipsoid,
5–7 cm long and 3.5 cm diameter, *orange; endosperm ruminate, with a central cavity.*
Range and habitat. Lesser Antilles in Montserrat,
Guadeloupe, Dominica, Martinique, and St.
Lucia; dry to wet coastal areas, below 300 m
elevation.
Notes. One of the largest species of *Syagrus*,
which was formerly treated as a genus of its
own, *Rhyticocos.* The only comparable palm in
the area is the coconut, which is easily sepa-

rated by its leaning stem, lighter foliage with
leaflets spreading in the same plane and
larger fruits.

Syagrus botryophora
(Map 287)
"Pati," "patioba" (Bra)
Field characters. Stems solitary, 6–18 m tall, 15–
25 cm diameter. Leaves 10–15, about 3 m
long, with an arching rachis; leaflets 100–150
per side, *rigid, ascending, forming a V-shape, regularly arranged and spreading in the same plane.* Inflorescences with a woody, very thick, deeply grooved
peduncular bract; flowering branches 30–50;
fruits ellipsoid, 3.5–4.5 cm long and 2.2–2.5
cm diameter, whitish to yellowish green.
Range and habitat. Atlantic coast of Brazil
(southern Sergipe, Bahia, northern Espírito
Santo); lowland rain forest on lateritic clayey
soils, below 400 m elevation. A record from
Bolivia (Glassman, 1987; Balslev and Moraes,

1989) is apparently based on a misidentification.

Uses. The stems are used in construction and the seeds are rich in edible oil.

Syagrus campylospatha
(Map 288)
"Yatay-mi" (Par)

Field characters. Stems clustered, *short and subterranean* or to 1.5 m tall. Leaves to 1.5 m long, whitish tomentose throughout; *leaflets 30–50 per side, rigid,* irregularly arranged in clusters of two but spreading in the same plane, *the tips rigid and spinelike.* Inflorescences erect, with a woody peduncular bract; *flowering branches 18–35;* fruits ellipsoid, beaked, to 2 cm long and 1 cm diameter, yellowish.

Range and habitat. Paraguay, east of the Río Paraguay (Concepción, Cordillera, Paraguarí); open *cerrado* or scrub on sandy soil, at low elevations.

Syagrus cardenasii
(Map 289, Plate 30)
"Corocito," "saro" (Bol)

Field characters. Stems clustered or solitary, short and subterranean, rarely to 0.5(–2) m tall. Leaves 8–12, 1–3 m long; rachis 0.6–1.6 m long; leaflets 32–74 per side, irregularly arranged in clusters and spreading in different planes, grayish. Inflorescences erect, with 4–13 flowering branches; fruits ovoid, 2.2–3 cm long and 1.6–2 cm diameter, brownish.

Range and habitat. Bolivia (Chuquisaca, Santa Cruz); seasonal forest on dry banks, at 400–1800 m elevation.

Uses. The mesocarp, which tastes like pineapple, is eaten.

Syagrus cocoides
(Map 290, Plate 30)
"Jatá," "piririma" (Bra)

Field characters. Stems solitary, 1.3–9 m tall and 6–10 cm diameter. Leaves 14–22, to 4 m long; rachis 1–3 m long; leaflets 55–100 per side, *flaccid,* arranged in clusters of 2–4 and spreading in different planes, *the leaf only slightly plumose.* Inflorescences with 4–15 flowering branches; *fruits ovoid to pearshaped,* 3.5–5 cm long and 2–2.5 cm diameter, yellowish brown.

Range and habitat. Guyana and Brazil (Amazonas, Maranhão, Mato Grosso, Pará, Piauí, Tocantins); open rocky areas as well as lowland rain forest, at low elevations.

Notes. Easily mistaken for *Syagrus inajai,* which differs in its ellipsoid (i.e., not pear shaped) fruits and wider leaflets with prominent cross veins on the upper surface.

Syagrus comosa
(Map 291)
"Babão," "catolé" (Bra)

Field characters. Stems solitary, (0–)1–7 m tall and 6–12 cm diameter, often covered with persistent petiole bases, *sometimes flowering when still stemless.* Leaves 6–12, about 1.5 m long; leaflets 38–82 per side, *very closely arranged* in clusters of 2–4 and spreading in different planes. Inflorescences with a long peduncle; peduncular bract woody, deeply grooved; flowering branches (1–)2–19; fruits ellipsoid, 2.5–3 cm long and 1.5–1.8 cm diameter, *light green.*

Range and habitat. Central and eastern Brazil (Bahia, Goiás, Mato Grosso, Mato Grosso do Sul, Maranhão, Minas Gerais, Pará, Piauí, Tocantins); open areas of *cerrado* vegetation, especially on rocky slopes, to 1200 m elevation.

Uses. The fruits are edible.

Notes. Stemless palms were treated by Glassman (1987) as *Syagrus acaulis,* but we include them here.

Syagrus coronata
(Map 292)
"Licuri," "ouricuri" (Bra)

Field characters. Stems solitary, 3–12 m tall and 20–25 cm diameter, *covered along the upper half or more with persistent petiole remains arranged in 5 slightly twisted vertical rows.* Leaves 15–30, *arranged in 5 slightly twisted vertical rows, margins of the sheath and its petiole-like extension armed with woody flattened fibers;* rachis to 2.8 m long; leaflets 80–130 per side, rigid, arranged in clusters of 2–5 and spreading in different planes, *whitish on the lower surface.* Inflorescences with a woody, deeply grooved peduncular bract; flowering branches 34–78; fruits ellipsoid, 2.5–3 cm long and 1.7–2 cm diameter, yellow green to orange, with brown tomentum and appearing brownish at first sight.

Range and habitat. Eastern Brazil, east of the Rio São Francisco (Alagoas, Bahia, northern Minas Gerais, southern Pernambuco, Sergipe); very abundant in *caatinga* and seasonal semideciduous forests, extending also into the *restinga* and into transitional vegetation between the *caatinga* and other vegetation types. It is a very common species; the number of trees in the state of Bahia alone was once estimated as approximately one-half billion (Bondar, 1942).

Uses. This is an extremely useful palm. The palm heart, sweet-tasting mesocarp, and seeds are edible; ground-up leaves are fed to cattle; ground-up seeds are fed to fowl; oil from the seeds is used for making soaps; and wax from the undersurface of leaflets is used for making torches and was formerly an item of trade.

Notes. Easily mistaken for *Syagrus oleracea,* which

TABLE 4. HYBRIDS IN *SYAGRUS*.

Parent 1	Hybrid	Parent 2
S. coronata	Unnamed hybrid	*S. microphylla*
S. coronata	*S.* x *camposportoana*	*S. romanzoffiana*
S. coronata	*S.* x *costae*	*S. oleracea*
S. coronata	*S.* x *matafome*	*S. vagans*
S. coronata	*S.* x *tostana*	*S. schizophylla*

differs in its spirally arranged leaves (not in 5 rows), fibrous petiole margins, and larger fruits. *Syagrus coronata* hybridizes with several co-occurring species (Glassman, 1987; Noblick, 1991). At least five hybrids have been recognized (Table 4), most represented by a few trees in any particular area. *Syagrus* x *costae*, which grows in *cerrado* in Pernambuco, is apparently the only one forming large stands. It differs from *S. coronata* in its leaves, which usually are not arranged in rows (although individuals with leaves in five rows are sometimes found), in the softer petiole fibers, and in the short internodes. The only hybrid *Syagrus* with leaves always in five rows is *S.* x *camposportoana*, which differs in its more robust size and in its fruit cavity being irregular instead of smooth.

Syagrus duartei
(Map 293)
"Coco de lapa," "coqueirinho" (Bra)
Field characters. Stems solitary, *short, and subterranean.* Leaves 6–12, to 1.2 m long; rachis 51–90 cm long; leaflets 44–64 per side, rigid, *glaucous,* arranged in clusters of 2–4, *spreading in different planes but all pointing upwards.* Inflorescences erect; *flowering branches 5–8; fruits almost globose but narrowed toward the base,* to 3 cm diameter.
Range and habitat. Brazil (Minas Gerais), known only from the Serra do Cipó; quartzitic rock outcrops and *campo rupestre,* at 1200–1300 m elevation.
Notes. Often associated with *Syagrus pleioclada,* which differs in its flaccid, drooping leaflets. *Syagrus glaucescens,* which also grows in the mountains of Minas Gerais also has glaucous leaves, but differs in its well-developed stem and 5-ranked leaves and its occurrence farther north in the Serra da Diamantina.

Syagrus flexuosa
(Map 294, Plate 30)
"Acumã," "côco de campo" (Bra)
Field characters. Stems small, clustered, or sometimes solitary, 1–5 m tall and 5–8(–10) cm diameter, often covered with persistent leaf bases. Leaves 7–15, *dark green;* rachis 0.5–1 m long; leaflets 38–80 per side, *narrow, linear,* rigid, in clusters of 2–5, *often whitish on lower surface.* Inflorescences with a woody, grooved peduncular bract; flowering branches 8–19; fruits ellipsoid, with a prominent beak, to 3.5 cm long and 1.5 cm diameter, yellowish.
Range and habitat. Eastern and central Brazil (Bahia, Goiás, Mato Grosso, Minas Gerais, São Paulo); *cerrado,* woodlands, and disturbed habitats, in fine sandy to rocky soils, to 1200 m elevation. Flowers and fruits are borne all year round.
Uses. It is often planted as an ornamental; the fruits are edible.

Syagrus glaucescens
(Map 295)
Field characters. Stems solitary, 0.5–5 m tall and 8–12 cm diameter. Leaves 5–10; *leaf bases persistent in 5 obvious rows;* rachis 0.6–1 m long; leaflets 59–79 per side, rigid, *glaucous,* in clusters of 3–5, arranged in different planes but all pointing upwards. Inflorescences with 8–17 flowering branches; *fruits almost conical,* 2.5–3 cm long and 1.6–2.5 cm diameter.
Range and habitat. Eastern Brazil (Minas Gerais, near Serra da Diamantina); common in *cerrado* and *campo rupestre* on rocky outcrops, at 700–1200 m elevation.
Notes. *Syagrus coronata* also has leaves in 5 vertical rows, but differs in its larger size and in the spinelike woody fibers of its leaf sheath and petiole.

Syagrus graminifolia
(Map 296)
"Acumão rasteiro" (Bra)
Field characters. Stems short and subterranean. Leaves to 1 m long; leaflets 23–25 per side, regularly arranged and spreading in the same plane. *Inflorescences with 2–7 flowering branches to 18 cm long;* fruits ellipsoid, to 2 cm long and 1.3 cm diameter, slightly beaked.
Range and habitat. Eastern Brazil (southern Goiás, Mato Grosso do Sul) and eastern Paraguay; in open areas or *cerrado.*
Notes. Very similar to the co-occurring *Syagrus petraea,* which usually has spicate inflorescences and clustered leaflets. *Syagrus lilliputiana,* a very small and poorly known palm

from the grasslands of Paraguay, with leaves about 40 cm long and 10 leaflets per side, is included here.

Syagrus harleyi
(Map 297)
"Côco de raposa" (Bra)

Field characters. Stems clustered, sometimes solitary, *short, and subterranean.* Leaves 3–8; rachis 0.6–1.8 m long, leaflets 14–57 per side, *bright green, regularly arranged, and spreading in the same plane.* Inflorescences with a woody, grooved, peduncular bract; flowering branches 5–31, to 15 cm long; fruits congested, ellipsoid to almost globose, 1.5–2.5 cm long and 1–2.5 cm diameter, *orange with scattered brown tomentum.*
Range and habitat. Eastern Brazil (Bahia); common in rock crevices of *campo rupestre* of the central sierras, at 400–1400 m elevation.
Uses. The waxy leaves are used to start domestic fires.
Notes. Palms from above 900 m elevation tend to have rigid leaflets, whereas those from lower elevations are softer and somewhat drooping. *Syagrus microphylla* and *S. werdermannii* differ from *S. harleyi* in their leaflets being glaucous on the upper surface and in their tendency to grow in less rocky areas. The leaflets of *S. microphylla* are clustered.

Syagrus inajai
(Map 298)
"Curua rana," "inaya-y" (Bra), "peh-peh" (Sur)

Field characters. Stems solitary, 3–15 m tall and 4–15 cm diameter. Leaves 15–18, to 3.5 m long; leaflets 51–110 per side, *rather flaccid,* irregularly arranged in clusters of 2–7 and spreading in different planes, *but the leaf not very plumose.* Inflorescences with a woody peduncular bract; flowering branches (6–)14–35; fruits ellipsoid, 3.2–4.5 cm long and 2–3 cm diameter, yellow, *the endocarp cavity triangular in cross section.*
Range and habitat. The Guianas and northern Brazil (Amapá, Amazonas, Maranhão, Pará); lowland rain forest and gallery forest on non-inundated soils, as well as in open areas on rocky soils, to 500 m elevation.
Uses. The leaves are used for thatching and are reported to be durable; the seeds are edible.
Notes. Very similar to *Syagrus orinocensis* from the northwestern Amazon region and adjacent *llanos* of Colombia and Venezuela. It differs in its endocarp cavity, which is triangular (not rounded) in cross section.

Syagrus leptospatha
(Map 299)

Field characters. Stems short and subterranean.

Leaf rachis to 50 cm long; leaflets to 9 per side, regularly arranged. *Inflorescences spicate, with papery peduncular bract;* fruits almost globose, 1–1.4 cm long and 0.8–1.2 cm diameter.
Range and habitat. Brazil (Mato Grosso); open, grassy areas.
Notes. Glassman (1987) reported that this species had a very narrow range and was probably extinct in the wild. Larry Noblick (personal communication) believes this species may actually belong in *Butia.*

Syagrus macrocarpa
(Map 300)
"Maria Rosa" (Bra)

Field characters. Stems solitary, 4–8 m tall and 10–20 cm diameter. Leaves 15–20, *dead leaves sometimes persisting on the palm for a long time;* rachis 1.2–2.2 m, *tomentose;* leaflets 110–153 per side, stiff, in clusters of 3–5. Inflorescences about 80 cm long; flowering branches 36–70; fruits ellipsoid, *6.5–7 cm long and 3–3.2 cm diameter,* green.
Range and habitat. Southeastern Brazil (southern Espírito Santo, southeastern Minas Gerais); rather uncommon on rocky, sandy soils in seasonal forest.

Syagrus microphylla
(Map 301)
"Ariri," "coquinho" (Bra)

Field characters. Stems very short and subterranean, solitary or sometimes clustered. Leaves 5–12; rachis 30–60 cm; leaflets 18–36 per side, *bluish green, arranged in clusters of 2–3.* Inflorescences as long as or shorter than the leaves, with a woody, grooved peduncular bract; *flowering branches 3–9, short;* fruits ovoid to globose, 1.5–2.5 cm long and 1–1.3 cm diameter, light green with brownish tomentum.
Range and habitat. Brazil (Bahia); *campo rupestre* or *caatinga* vegetation in the sierras, on white sandy to reddish clayey soils, at 800–1100 m elevation.
Uses. The liquid endosperm of young fruits has been used for the treatment of eye irritation (Noblick, 1991).

Syagrus oleracea
(Map 302)
"Catolé," "guariroba" (Bra)

Field characters. Stems solitary, 5–20 m tall and 25–30 cm diameter. Leaves 15–20, *spirally arranged, not in rows;* rachis 1.8–3.8 m long; leaflets 100–150 per side, rigid, glaucous green on upper surface, irregularly arranged in clusters of 2–5 and spreading in different planes. *Several old inflorescences and peduncular bracts typically hanging below leaves;* peduncular bract woody, deeply grooved; flowering branches 20–83; fruits ovoid, 4–5.5 cm long and 2.5–3 cm diameter, light greenish to yellow green, with a prominent beak.

Range and habitat. Eastern Brazil (Bahia, Ceará, Espírito Santo, Goiás, Minas Gerais, Paraíba, Paraná, Pernambuco, Rio de Janeiro) and eastern Paraguay; seasonal, semideciduous forests, in good soils, to 800 m elevation. The occurrence of this species in Paraguay has been questioned by Hahn (1990).

Uses. The edible fruits are sold in markets, both for the fleshy mesocarp and for the oily seeds. The bitter palm heart is used in cooking. It is commonly planted as an ornamental in western Bahia (Noblick, 1991).

Notes. Easily confused with *Syagrus coronata*, which differs in its 5-ranked leaves, the woody, spinelike petiole fibers, and the smaller fruits.

Syagrus orinocensis
(Map 303, Plate 31)
"Churrubay" (Col), "coquito" (Ven)

Field characters. Stems solitary or sometimes clustered, 1–12 m tall and 8–15 cm diameter. Leaves 8–10, to 3 m long; leaflets 70–107 per side, *rather flaccid,* irregularly arranged in clusters of 2–3, and spreading in different planes, *the leaf not markedly plumose.* Inflorescences with 19–37 flowering branches; fruits oblong-ellipsoid, 2.5–3.4 cm long and 2–3 cm diameter, yellow or brown.

Range and habitat. Colombia (Amazonas, Casanare, Guainía, Meta, Vaupés, Vichada) and Venezuela (Amazonas, Anzoátegui, Apure, Bolívar, Carabobo, Falcón, Miranda, Yaracuy); lowland rain forest or gallery forest, often on granitic outcrops, to 400 m elevation.

Notes. Very similar to *Syagrus inajai*, which differs in its triangular endocarp cavity and eastern distribution. Populations from northern Venezuela have been separated as a distinct species, *Syagrus stenopetala*, but were included by Glassman (1987) under *S. orinocensis.*

Syagrus petraea
(Map 304)
"Cocorito," "palma de las rocas" (Bol), "côco de vassoura," "ariri" (Bra), "guriri," (Par)

Field characters. Stems solitary or clustered, *short and subterranean.* Leaves 4–8; rachis 0.2–1.3 m long; leaflets 9–50 per side, regularly arranged and spreading in the same plane or clustered and spreading in slightly different planes. Inflorescences erect, to 60 cm long; peduncular bract woody, grooved; flowering branches sometimes to 9, *but commonly inflorescences spicate;* fruits ellipsoid, 2–3 cm long and 1–2 cm diameter, green with brown tomentum.

Range and habitat. Widespread throughout the *planalto* region of Brazil (Bahia, Mato Grosso do Sul, Minas Gerais, Pará, Piauí Rondônia, São Paulo), eastern Bolivia (Santa Cruz), and eastern Paraguay (Amambay, Caaguazú); *cerrado* vegetation, on sandy to red clayey soils, in both forested and open areas, often tolerating fire, at 600–900 m elevation (to 1800 m in Bolivia).

Uses. The leaves are tied together to make brooms and are used also for basketry; the mesocarp is occasionally eaten.

Notes. A widespread and variable species, ranging in size from small, grasslike plants, to larger palms with leaves to 1 m long. We include here *Syagrus loefgrenii,* a species kept separate by Glassman (1987).

Syagrus picrophylla
(Map 305)
"Côco de quaresma," "licuri" (Bra)

Field characters. Stems solitary, 3–7 m tall and 15–20 cm diameter. Leaves 7–12; rachis to 1.8 m long; leaflets 105–123 per side, rigid, irregularly arranged in clusters of 3–4. Inflorescences with a woody, grooved peduncular bract; flowering branches 29–64; fruits 3.5–4.5 cm long and 2–2.5 cm diameter, *cinnamon to orange-brown, the mesocarp sometimes splitting into 3 parts at apex.*

Range and habitat. Atlantic coast of Brazil (southern Bahia, Espírito Santo, Rio de Janeiro); coastal rain forest, steep slopes on granitic outcrops with shallow soils, at 300–350 m elevation.

Notes. Often regarded as conspecific with *Syagrus oleracea,* but separated by Noblick (1991) on the basis of its smaller, cinnamon to orange-brown fruits, smoother stem, and some floral characters, as well as its preference for wetter areas. In its splitting fruits it resembles *Lytocaryum.*

Syagrus pleioclada
(Map 306)
"Coqueirinho," "palmeirinha" (Bra)

Field characters. Stems solitary, *short and subterranean,* or up to 0.5 m tall and 13 cm diameter. Leaves 4–7, to 1.2 m long; rachis 35–97 cm long; leaflets 13–29 per side, flaccid, drooping, *in widely separated clusters of 2–4,* spreading in different planes. *Inflorescences with 6–21, 0.5–7(–18) cm long, gnarled flowering branches;* fruits ovoid, 2–3 cm long and 1.5–2.3 cm diameter, green.

Range and habitat. Brazil (Minas Gerais, Serra do Cipó, São Paulo); in open rocky areas, at 400–1300 m elevation.

Uses. The leaves are used for making brooms.

Notes. We include here *Syagrus menhandensis,* a species kept separate by Glassman (1987).

Syagrus pseudococos
(Map 307)
"Coco amargoso," "piririma" (Bra)
Field characters. Stems solitary, 10–15 m tall and to 25 cm diameter, *swollen at base.* Leaves 18–20, 2.1–2.2 m long; rachis 1.7–1.9 m long; leaflets 93–150 per side, in clusters of 2–4. Inflorescences with a very thick and woody peduncular bract; flowering branches 28–42; fruits ovoid, *with a prominent brown beak, 6–7 cm long and to 4 cm diameter, yellow, endocarp beaked; seed with deeply ruminate endosperm.*
Range and habitat. Brazil (Espírito Santo, Rio de Janeiro, São Paulo); forested areas and in pastures.
Notes. Previously treated as a genus of its own, *Barbosa,* based on the ruminate endosperm.

Syagrus romanzoffiana
(Map 308, Plate 31)
"Chirivá," pindó (Arg, Par), "jeribá," "guariroba" (Bra)
Field characters. Stems large, solitary, 10–15 m tall or more and 35–50 cm diameter. Leaves 7–15; *rachis 2.5–4.4 m long,* arching; leaflets 150–250 per side, irregularly arranged in clusters of 2–7 and spreading in different planes, *the tips bent and pendulous.* Inflorescences to 1.5 m long; flowering branches 80–280; fruits ovoid, 2–3 cm long and 1–2 cm diameter, yellow to orange, *the endocarp cavity very irregular in shape in cross section, with woody ridges that penetrate into the very irregular seed.*
Range and habitat. Central and southeast Brazil (Bahia, Espírito Santo, Goiás, Mato Grosso, Mato Grosso do Sul, Minas Gerais, Paraná, Rio Grande do Sul, Santa Catarina, São Paulo), eastern Paraguay (Amambay, Alto Paraná, Central, Guaira, Paraguarí), northern Argentina (Corrientes, Entre Ríos, Misiones), and eastern Uruguay (Rocha) and probably also Bolivia; in a variety of habitats, from seasonally dry forests, swampy areas, or *restinga.*
Uses. The fruits are edible; leaves and fruits are fed to cattle and broken seeds are fed to chickens; the palm heart is edible; and the durable stems are used for constructing saltwater piers. It is widely cultivated as an ornamental throughout tropical and subtropical areas of the world.
Notes. This species reaches one of the southernmost latitudes of any palm in the Americas, together with *Jubaea chilensis.* Previously treated as a separate, monotypic genus, *Arecastrum,* because of its irregular endocarp cavity. The fleshy mesocarp of ripe fruits is eaten by capuchin monkeys (*Cebus apella*) and brown howler monkeys (*Alouatta fusca*), whereas the endocarp of unripe fruits is broken by squir-

rels (*Sciurus* spp.), which thus act as predators (Azevedo Maia et al., 1987; Galetti et al., 1992). Similar relationships of mammals with other *Syagrus* species may exist, as many species in the genus have colorful, fleshy, fragrant fruits.

Syagrus ruschiana
(Map 309)
"Côco de pedra," "palmeirinho" (Bra)
Field characters. Stems *clustered,* 2–8 m tall and 4–12 cm diameter. Leaves 7–12, to 3 m long; rachis 1.2–2 m long; *leaflets 48–58 per side, regularly arranged and horizontally spreading in the same plane.* Inflorescences with 41–72 elongate, slender, flowering branches; fruits broadly ellipsoid, to 2.5 cm long and 2 cm diameter, bright orange with greenish apex, *the mesocarp often splitting into 3 parts at apex.*
Range and habitat. Southeastern Brazil (Espírito Santo and adjacent Minas Gerais); open areas on gneissic rocks, at 100–400 m elevation.
Uses. Recommended by Bondar (1964) as an attractive ornamental.
Notes. In its splitting fruits it resembles *Lytocaryum.*

Syagrus sancona
(Map 310, Plates 31 & 32)
"Sumuqué," "tiba" (Bol), "sarare" (Col, Ven)
Field characters. Stems solitary, 7–30 m tall and 20–30 cm diameter. Leaves 8–16, dark green, to 3.5 m long; rachis (1.5–)2.1–3 m; leaflets 122–188 per side, stiff, irregularly arranged in clusters of 2–5 and spreading in different planes. *Inflorescences with 78–200 flowering branches;* fruits ellipsoid, 2.8–3.2 cm long and 1.5–2 cm diameter, yellow or orangish, fleshy.
Range and habitat. Andes and adjacent lowlands from western Venezuela (Barinas, Bolívar) through Colombia (Antioquia, Caquetá, Cundinamarca, Meta, Norte de Santander, Putumayo, Risaralda, Tolima, Valle), Ecuador (El Oro), Peru (Loreto, Madre de Dios, San Martín, Ucayali), Brazil (Acre, Amazonas) and Bolivia (Beni, La Paz, Santa Cruz); lowland to premontane forest, gallery forest, and commonly left in disturbed areas, usually in drier, more seasonal regions, to 1200 m elevation.
Uses. The stems are used for fencing and for conducting water.
Notes. This is the tallest species in the genus and, with *Syagrus cardenasii,* the only species of *Syagrus* growing in the Andes.

Syagrus schizophylla
(Map 311, Plate 32)
"Aricuriroba," "licurioba" (Bra)
Field characters. Stems usually solitary but some-

times clustered, 1–4 m tall and 10–15 cm diameter (including the persistent leaf bases). Leaves 8–25, *in a rather flat-topped crown; leaf sheath with fibrous, spiny, serrated margins, typically persisting on the stem*; rachis 0.7–1.9 m long; leaflets 18–48 per side, rigid, regularly arranged, and spreading in the same plane. *Inflorescences with a long peduncle*; peduncular bract woody, grooved; flowering branches 14–32; fruits broadly ellipsoid to almost globose, 2–3 cm long and 1.5–2.5 cm diameter, *bright red-orange*, seed with ruminate endosperm.
Range and habitat. Atlantic coast of Brazil (Alagoas, Bahia, northern Espírito Santo, Pernambuco, Sergipe); along a narrow band of coastal *restinga* forest, in sandy soils, especially where fresh water is abundant, but also tolerant of salt spray.
Uses. The sweet-tasting mesocarp is edible.
Notes. Previously treated as a separate genus, *Arikuryroba*, based on the spiny petiole margins and ruminate endosperm.

Syagrus smithii
(Map 312)
"Catolé" (Bra)
Field characters. Stems solitary, 4–10 m tall and 5–8 cm diameter. Leaves 5–18, to 2.5–3 m long; rachis 1.9–2.4 m long; leaflets 83–94 per side, irregularly arranged and spreading in different planes, *the leaf rather flat or sometimes the leaf blade simple and narrowly elliptical*. Inflorescences with 9–20 flowering branches; fruits ellipsoid, 6–8 cm long and 3–4 cm diameter, yellow; endosperm ruminate.
Range and habitat. Northwestern Amazon region in Colombia (Amazonas), Peru (Amazonas, Loreto, Ucayali), and Brazil (Acre, western Amazonas); lowland rain forest on noninundated soils, to 400 m elevation.
Uses. The leaves are used for thatching temporary shelters; and the seeds are eaten and reported as delicious.
Notes. The large fruits are unmistakable; individuals with simple leaves are also very distinct. Sterile palms with pinnate leaves may prove difficult to separate from *Syagrus orinocensis* in the field, although the rather flat leaf may help.

Syagrus stratincola
(Map 313)
"Pali" (Guy)
Field characters. Stems clustered and forming clumps, 2–14 m tall and 5–10 cm diameter. Leaves 6–12, to 4 m long; rachis 1.5–2.5 m long; leaflets 57–82 per side, in clusters of 3–4. Inflorescences with 9–15 flowering branches; *fruits almost globose*, 4–4.5 cm diameter, yellowish green, *longitudinally grooved*.
Range and habitat. Suriname and French Guiana (and probably also Amapá, Brazil); lowland rain forest and open areas, especially on granite outcrops, at low elevations.
Notes. Syagrus inajai, the only other species in the area, differs in its typically solitary habit and ellipsoid fruits.

Syagrus vagans
(Map 314)
"Licurioba das caatingas," "pindoba" (Bra)
Field characters. Stems clustered, short, and subterranean. Leaves 10–30, *dark green, stiffly ascending*, up to 3 m long; *lower part of the leaf sheath with stiff, narrow, toothlike flattened fibers*; rachis 0.7–1.9 m long; leaflets 17–38 per side, *stiff*, both sides of the leaf forming an acute angle. Inflorescences erect, very long, often projected above leaves, with 15–45 long, flowering branches; *fruits narrowly ellipsoid*, 2.8–3.7 cm long and 1.5–1.8 cm diameter, yellowish green.
Range and habitat. Eastern Brazil (Bahia, northeastern Minas Gerais); arid *caatinga*, on sandy and gravelly soils but occasionally on lateritic soils, at 250–900 m elevation.
Uses. The leaves and inflorescences are used to feed livestock; the oily seeds are fed to pigs and chickens; and leaves are used for thatching and weaving hats.
Notes. The only short-stemmed palm of the *caatinga* in this area, but often associated with *Syagrus coronata*.

Syagrus werdermannii
(Map 315)
"Côco de vassoura," côco de peneira" (Bra)
Field characters. Stems solitary or clustered, *short and subterranean*. Leaves 4–8, to 1.5 m long; rachis 30–80 cm long; leaflets 10–20 per side, rigid, regularly arranged, or the lower ones sometimes in clusters of 2–3. *Inflorescences covered with a fine dense grayish-white tomentum*, erect, with a woody, grooved peduncular bract; flowering branches 6–18, fruits ovoid or obovoid, 2–2.5 cm long and 1.5 cm diameter, light green to yellow green.
Range and habitat. Brazil (southern Bahia, northern end of the Serra do Espinhaço); *cerrado* vegetation, at 800–1000 m elevation.
Uses. The leaves are used to make brooms and strainers.
Notes. Syagrus petraea, which also grows in the *cerrado*, has spicate inflorescences or up to 9 flowering branches and lacks the dense tomentum on the inflorescence.

46. LYTOCARYUM

This small and poorly known genus is closely related to *Syagrus*. Stems are small to medium sized and are often slightly leaning or curved. Leaves are pinnate, 7–22 in number, and gracefully spreading. Sheath, petiole, and rachis are often covered with elongate gray or brown hairs or scales. The leaflets are narrow, linear, and regularly arranged and spread in the same plane; they are gray on the lower surface. Inflorescences are branched to one order and are borne among the leaves. There are numerous flowering branches, covered with unisexual flowers that are arranged in threes of one central female and two lateral males. Fruits are one-seeded, ovoid to ellipsoid, and brownish. The fleshy outer layer (epicarp and mesocarp) splits regularly into three sections at maturity; this is one of the distinguishing features of the genus (although this also happens in a few species of *Syagrus*). The generic name refers to this and is derived from the Greek words "lyton," loosened, and "karyon," seed. The endocarp is thin and brittle compared to related genera (e.g., *Butia, Syagrus*) and there are three pores at the base. The endosperm is either homogeneous or ruminate, and the seedling leaf is simple or pinnate.

Lytocaryum contains two species which are narrowly distributed in southeastern Brazil in the Atlantic Coastal Forest. The genus is closely related to *Syagrus*, and the two species accepted here have at various times been included in that genus or in small segregate genera (e.g., *Microcoelum*). Glassman (1987) maintained the two species in separate genera, *Lytocaryum* and *Microcoelum*, but we have followed Uhl and Dransfield (1987) in placing them together. We accept only two species even though both Glassman and Uhl and Dransfield recognized three.

Lytocaryum hoehnei
(Map 316, Plate 32)

Field characters. Stems solitary, 1–5 m tall and to 10 cm diameter, often slightly leaning and covered with persistent leaf bases. Leaves 16–22; *leaflets 1.5–2 cm wide,* regularly arranged and spreading in the same plane, silvery gray on the lower surface. Inflorescences arching among the leaves; fruits ovoid, 3–3.3 cm long and 2–2.3 cm diameter, brown; *endosperm ruminate;* seedling leaf simple.

Range and habitat. Southern Brazil (São Paulo); forests on hillsides, at 800–1000 m elevation.

Notes. Glassman (1987) considered this species to be threatened with extinction because of habitat destruction. It is still abundant in some small parks in the city of São Paulo.

Lytocaryum weddellianum
(Map 317, Plate 32)

"Agué," "icá" (Bra)

Field characters. Stems solitary, 1–5 m tall and to 10 cm diameter. Leaves 7–20, the old ones persistent; petiole and rachis with *dense, gray or dark brown, elongate hairs or scales,* these soon falling; *leaflets 0.5–1.2 cm wide,* regularly arranged and spreading in the same plane, silvery gray on the lower surface. Inflorescences arching among the leaves; fruits ovoid to ellipsoid, 1.7–2.3 cm long and 1–1.7 cm diameter, brown; *endosperm homogeneous;* seedling leaf pinnate.

Range and habitat. Atlantic Coast of southern Brazil (Espírito Santo, Rio de Janeiro); lowland rain forest on steep slopes, usually below 1000 m elevation.

Notes. This species has been in cultivation as an indoor plant for several decades.

47. PARAJUBAEA

This genus takes its name from its resemblance to *Jubaea*. Although the two genera are similar they occupy quite different habitats. Stems are tall, stout, erect, solitary, and rough or smooth. Leaves are pinnate, 18–30 in number and form a large, graceful crown. Leaf sheaths and petioles are very fibrous on the margins. Leaflets are numerous, linear, deeply bifid at the tips, and regularly or slightly irregularly arranged, but usually spread in the same plane. Inflorescences are branched to one order (although the flowering branches of *Parajubaea cocoides* are sometimes branched again) and are borne among the leaves. The large, woody peduncular bract is grooved on the outer surface. Flowers are unisexual and are borne in threes of one central female and two lateral males on the lower part of the flowering branch and males only on the upper part. Male flowers have 13–18 stamens. Fruits are one- or two-seeded, oblong-ellipsoid or ovoid, and purple-green to brownish. The endocarp is thick and bony with three basal pores, and in one species it has prominent apical ridges. The endosperm is homogeneous and the seedling leaf is simple and linear.

Parajubaea contains two species (Moraes and Henderson, 1990) occurring in Andean regions of Bolivia and Ecuador and just reaching southern Colombia. The genus is very similar to other members of the Butiinae, particularly *Jubaea* and *Syagrus*, but can be distinguished by its unusual habitat.

Parajubaea cocoides
(Map 318)
"Coco," "coco cumbé" (Ecu)
Field characters. Stems usually smooth, to 16 m tall and 27–45 cm diameter. Leaves 20–30; leaflets regularly arranged and spreading in the same plane. Inflorescences borne among the leaves; fruits one-seeded, oblong-ellipsoid, greenish brown, 4–5.5 cm long and 2.8–4 cm diameter; *endocarp without prominent apical ridges.*
Range and habitat. Known only from cultivated plants in Andean towns in Ecuador (especially Quito) and southern Colombia (Pasto), at 2500–3000 m elevation.
Uses. It is cultivated as an ornamental tree for streets and parks.
Notes. The cultivated *Parajubaea cocoides* differs slightly from *P. torallyi*; it has an irregular staminodial ring (regular in *P. torallyi*), irregular branching of the flowering branches (unbranched in *P. torallyi*), and obscure endocarp

ridges (prominent in *P. torallyi*). Moraes and Henderson (1990) believed that since *P. cocoides* is only known from cultivated plants it probably originated from the wild *P. torallyi*.

Parajubaea torallyi
(Map 319, Plate 33)
"Janchicoco," "palmera zunca" (Bol)
Field characters. Stems solitary, rough, to 14 m tall and 25–35 cm diameter. Leaves 18–25; leaflets slightly irregularly arranged but spreading in more or less the same plane. Inflorescences borne among the leaves; fruits ovoid, one- to two-seeded, greenish brown, 3–7.5 cm long and 2–5 cm diameter; *endocarp with 3 prominent apical ridges.*
Range and habitat. Bolivia (Chuquisaca, Santa Cruz, and possibly Tarija); dry inter-Andean valleys, at 1500–2000 m elevation.
Uses. The fibers from the leaf sheaths and petioles are collected and locally woven into rope, twine, mattresses, and donkey panniers.

48. ALLAGOPTERA

This is a small but common genus in tropical areas of the eastern part of South America. Stems are short and subterranean or rarely aerial, solitary but sometimes appearing clustered, and often horizontal. There are two unusual features of the stem; it is occasionally forked and initially it is usually inverted so that the growing point is lower under the ground than the base. Leaves are pinnate, 4–10(–30) in number and are often somewhat glaucous. The sheaths are open, have fibrous margins, and are usually densely tomentose. The petiole is rather short. Leaflets are linear, gray-waxy on the lower and sometimes the upper surface, and often bifid at the tips. They are irregularly arranged in clusters and spread in different planes. It is the clustered nature of the leaflets that led to the generic name, from the Greek words "allage," meaning change, and "pteron," meaning feather. Inflorescences are spicate, erect, and borne among the leaves. Flowers are densely crowded on the short, stout flowering branch. They are borne in threes of one central female and two lateral males on the basal half of the branch, but on the top half there are male flowers only. Male flowers have 6–18 stamens. Female flowers (and fruits) are borne in distinct spirals. Fruits are one- to two-seeded, irregularly ovoid or obovoid, yellowish green, and often brown-tomentose. They are densely crowded and form a club-shaped infructescence. The endocarp is bony with three basal pores. The endosperm is homogeneous and the seedling leaf is simple and linear.

Allagoptera is a genus of four species (Noblick, 1991; Moraes, 1993), occurring in eastern and central South America, in Brazil, Bolivia, Paraguay, and Argentina. The species are all rather similar and are not easy to tell apart. Mostly, however, they have non-overlapping distributions.

Allagoptera arenaria
(Map 320, Plates 33 & 34)
"Caxandó," "côco da praia" (Bra)
Field characters. Stems horizontal, short, and subterranean (rarely upright and visible), sometimes forming dense colonies. Leaves 6–10(–15); leaflets irregularly arranged in clusters, each cluster 2–3 cm apart, spreading in different planes, *gray-waxy on the upper and lower surfaces, usually not bifid at the tips*; middle leaflets to 65 cm long. Inflorescences erect; fruits ovoid, yellowish green, smooth or with some tomentum, 1.2–2 cm long and 1–1.3 cm diameter, the persistent perianth enclosing about half the fruit.
Range and habitat. Atlantic coast of Brazil (Bahia, Espírito Santo, Rio de Janeiro, São Paulo); on dunes and adjacent *restinga* vegetation on sandy soils near the sea, often forming large stands, at 0–10 m elevation.
Uses. The fruits are edible.
Notes. Ormond and Leite (1987) reported inflorescences with all male flowers from near Rio de Janeiro.

Allagoptera brevicalyx
(Map 321)
"Buri da praia," "caxandó" (Bra)
Field characters. Stems short and subterranean. Leaves 4–8; leaflets irregularly arranged and spreading in different planes, *gray-waxy on the upper and lower surfaces, bifid at the tips*; middle leaflets to 25 cm long. Inflorescences erect; fruits ovoid, yellowish green, *smooth*, 1.5–2 cm long and 1–1.5 cm diameter, *the persistent perianth very short and only enclosing about one quarter of the fruit.*
Range and habitat. Atlantic coast of Brazil (Bahia, Sergipe); coastal dunes or dry woods near the sea, rarely occurring inland, at 0–20 m elevation.

Allagoptera campestris
(Map 322)
"Buri," "imburi" (Bra)
Field characters. Stems short and subterranean. Leaves 4–10; *leaflets irregularly arranged in clusters of 2–3, stiffly erect, and spreading in different planes, gray-waxy on the lower surface, usually bifid at the tips*; middle leaflets to 30 cm long. Inflorescences erect; fruits ovoid-ellipsoid, greenish yellow, *with loose, brown hairs*, 1.2–1.5 cm long and 0.5–0.7 cm diameter, the persistent perianth covering half the fruit.
Range and habitat. Brazil (Bahia, Goiás, Mato Grosso, Mato Grosso do Sul, Minas Gerais, Paraná, São Paulo), Paraguay (Amambay, Cordillera, San Pedro), and Argentina (Misiones); *cerrado* vegetation, at 600–1500 m elevation.
Uses. The immature fruits are edible.

Allagoptera leucocalyx
(Map 323)
"Motacuchí" (Bol), "côco da chapada," "guriri" (Bra)
Field characters. Stems creeping, short, and subterranean, rarely upright and then 1–2 m tall, occasionally forked. Leaves 6–30; leaflets irregularly arranged in clusters of 2–5, spreading in different planes, *waxy on the lower surface, bifid at the tips*; middle leaflets to 50 cm long. Inflorescences erect; fruits ovoid, orange-yellow, *densely covered with brown hairs*, 2.3–3 cm long and 1.5–2 cm diameter.
Range and habitat. Brazil (Bahia, Goiás, Mato Grosso, Mato Grosso do Sul, Minas Gerais, southern Pará, Paraná, São Paulo), Bolivia (Beni, Santa Cruz), Paraguay (Alto Paraguay, Amambay, Canendiyú, Concepción, Cordillera, Paraguarí), and Argentina (Misiones); open, dry, rocky places, often with sandy soils, at 200–700(–1000) m elevation.
Uses. The mesocarp and seeds are edible.

49. POLYANDROCOCOS

This genus is closely related to the preceding *Allagoptera* and can be regarded as a larger version. Stems are solitary, usually medium sized to tall but sometimes very short and subterranean (and then much resembling *Allagoptera*). Leaves are pinnate and 5–16 in number. Sheaths are open, fibrous on the margins, and slightly swollen but do not form a crownshaft. The petiole is rather short, and dead petioles often hang down below the crown of leaves. Leaflets are linear and usually irregularly arranged in indistinct clusters and spread in slightly different planes, but on short-stemmed plants the leaflets can be regularly arranged and spread in the same plane. Inflorescences are spicate and are borne among the leaves. The peduncle bears a prophyll and one, long, woody, persistent peduncular bract. The flowering branch is densely covered with unisexual flowers. The female flowers are borne on the basal part of the spike, with the male flowers on the apical part. Male flowers are unusual in having 60–120 stamens; the name of the genus alludes to this, literally meaning "the coconut with many stamens." Fruits are one-seeded, globose, but tend to be irregularly shaped because of dense crowding on the infructescence. In fact, the long, pendulous sausage-shaped infructescence densely covered with fruits is one of the most distinctive features of the genus. The thick endocarp has three basal pores. The seeds have slightly ruminate endosperm and the seedling leaf is simple.

Polyandrococos contains one species (Noblick, 1991), although Uhl and Dransfield (1987) reported two. It is distributed in southeastern Brazil, mostly in the Atlantic Coastal Forest.

Polyandrococos caudescens
(Map 324, Plate 34)
"Buri" (Bra)
Field characters. Stems solitary, rough, 4–8 m tall and 12–20 cm diameter, or occasionally short and subterranean. Leaves 5–16; leaflets linear, white-woolly on lower surface, irregularly arranged, and spreading in different planes but occasionally (on short-stemmed plants) regularly arranged and spreading in the same plane. Inflorescences borne among the leaves; infructescences pendulous, sausagelike with crowded fruits; fruits irregularly globose, 4–4.5 cm long and 3–3.5 cm diameter, greenish brown, one-seeded.
Range and habitat. Atlantic coast of Brazil (Alagoas, Bahia, Espírito Santo, Rio de Janeiro,

Sergipe); lowland rain forest or open areas, usually below 350 m elevation. It often persists in cleared areas.
Uses. The stems are used in construction, the leaves for thatching, and the fruits and seeds are occasionally eaten.
Notes. Noblick (1991) described the interesting variation in this species. In the northern part of its range, on infertile soils, some forms commonly have a short, subterranean stem, and in the southern part of the range other forms can have regularly arranged leaflets and sometimes these also have short stems. This variation on the edge of the range of a species is a very common phenomenon in American palms.

50. ATTALEA

This genus contains some of the largest and most abundant of American palms. It was named after an ancient Middle Eastern king, Attalus III Philometor, who was interested in medicinal plants. Stems are often very tall and stout, but there are also several species with short, subterranean stems. Leaves are pinnate and leaf number is very variable, ranging from three to thirty-five, but generally the taller species have more leaves and these are rather long. Individual leaflets are uniform throughout the genus; they are linear or linear-lanceolate and have a characteristic line of brown tomentum on one margin of the lower surface; this line widens at the leaflet apex. In some of the taller species the leaf rachis often gracefully arches so that some of the leaflets are arranged almost vertically. The large inflorescences are branched to one order and are always borne among the leaves, either on a short or long peduncle. They are surrounded by a very large, woody, grooved bract, and this is often persistent on the plant. Inflorescences are of two kinds, although both can occur on the same tree: either with all male flowers, or with mostly female flowers with a few male flowers. Male flowers are very variable, both in petal shape and stamen number, and these characters are important in species identification. Fruits are one- to several-seeded, but two- or three-seeded is the most common condition. They are ellipsoid, obovoid, oblong-ovoid, or rarely globose, generally very large and are either dull brown, yellow, orange-brown, or rarely dark purple. The endocarp is very thick and hard, with basal pores and variously arranged fibers. The endosperm is homogeneous and the seedling leaf is simple.

Attalea is a large and complex genus of twenty-nine species that is still incompletely understood. Although the species form a natural group, they have been divided, quite unnaturally, into at least six genera (*Attalea, Markleya, Maximiliana, Orbignya, Parascheelea, Scheelea*), distinguished from one another only by their male flowers (Henderson and Balick, 1991).

The four basic types of male flower are as follows (plate 36): petals flat, stamens 6–75, straight, shorter than the petals (*Attalea*); petals flat, stamens 6, straight, much longer than the petals (*Maximiliana*); petals cylindrical, stamens 6, straight, shorter than the petals (*Scheelea*); and petals flat in the middle but almost cylindrical below, stamens 12–24, coiled, shorter than the petals (*Orbignya*). There are many intermediate types, however, and separation of genera on this basis is unwarranted. The male flowers are indeed interesting; in *Attalea*, as in many groups of animals, it is the male sexual organs that vary, while the female ones are rather uniform. Inflorescences are also of great interest in their tendency to be unisexual. In some species, younger plants produce male inflorescences and older plants females. This phenomenon is poorly understood.

The understanding of the group is further complicated by the presence of hybridization between various species. Those that have been recorded are listed in table 5.

Another interesting feature of the genus is the ability of many species to persist and thrive in disturbed areas. A good example of this is the "babassu," *Attalea speciosa*. It now forms huge stands in areas where forest has been cleared, mostly on the southern fringes of the Amazon region. At least two short-stemmed species, *A. insignis* and *A. spectabilis*, also thrive in disturbed areas, the latter spreading by underground rhizomes. There are probably several reasons for this ability to grow in disturbed areas. The germination of these species is known as remote-tubular, which means that effectively the growing point of the seedling and juvenile plant is buried well under the ground and so is not destroyed by fire or agriculture. Also, the natural habitat of these species is open areas, such as river margins, clearings, or light gaps (Hogan, 1988), and thus they have the ability to grow in high-light areas, such as cleared pastures. It has also been suggested that when the natural seed predators (e.g., rodents such as agoutis and pacas) of these palms are removed by hunting, then the populations of palms are much larger (Terborgh, 1988). On the other hand, several studies have shown the importance of rodents to the dispersal of these palms; fruits that are not dispersed are predated by bruchid beetles (Janzen, 1971).

TABLE 5. HYBRIDS IN *ATTALEA*.

Parent 1	Hybrid	Parent 2
A. attaleoides	Unnamed hybrid	A. maripa
A. speciosa	x Attabignya minarum	A. oleifera
A. funifera	Unnamed hybrid	A. humilis
A. funifera	A. x piassabossu	A. oleifera
A. speciosa	Orbignya x teixeirana	A. eichleri

KEY TO THE SPECIES OF *ATTALEA*

1a. Mexico and Central America.
  2a. Stems short and subterranean.
    3a. Leaflets irregularly arranged in clusters and spreading in different
    planes .....*A. allenii.*
    3b. Leaflets regularly arranged and spreading in the same plane
    .....*A. iguadummat.*
  2b. Stems tall and aerial.
    4a. Male flowering branches short, to 15 cm long; sheath and petiole
    without stiff fibers on the margins .....*A. cohune.*
    4b. Male flowering branches elongate, 30–53 cm long; sheath and
    petiole margins with stout, stiff fibers .....*A. butyracea.*
1b. South America and the Caribbean.
  5a. Haiti .....*A. crassispatha.*
  5b. South America.
    6a. Pacific coast of Colombia and Ecuador, west of the Andes.
      7a. Stems short and subterranean; Colombia (Chocó, Nariño, Valle).
        8a. Leaflets regularly arranged and spreading in one plane; fruits
        11–14 cm long .....*A. cuatrecasana.*
        8b. Leaflets irregularly arranged and spreading in different
        planes; fruits 6–8 cm long .....*A. allenii.*
      7b. Stems tall and aerial; Colombia (Nariño) and Ecuador (El Oro,
      Esmeraldas, Guayas, Manabí) .....*A. colenda.*
    6b. Inter-Andean valleys of Colombia and South America east of the
    Andes.
    9a. Inter-Andean valleys of Colombia.
      10a. Stems tall and aerial.
        11a. Male flowering branches short, to 15 cm long; sheath and
        petiole without stiff fibers on the margins .....*A. cohune.*
        11b. Male flowering branches elongate, 30–53 cm long; sheath
        and petiole margins with stout, stiff fibers on the margins
        .....*A. butyracea.*
      10b. Stems short and subterranean.
        12a. Leaflets irregularly arranged and spreading in different
        planes .....*A. allenii.*
        12b. Leaflets regularly arranged and spreading in the same
        plane.
          13a. Río Cauca valley (Antioquia to Valle) .....*A. amygdalina.*

13b. Río Magdalena valley (Bolívar to Tolima and Cundinamarca) . . . . . *A. nucifera.*
9b. South America east of the Andes.
14a. Amazon region and adjacent areas, including Trinidad and Tobago.
15a. Stems tall and aerial.
16a. Leaflets irregularly arranged in clusters and spreading in different planes.
17a. Leaves conspicuously arranged in 5 vertical rows; petioles elongate, 2.4–3.3 m long . . . . . *A. maripa.*
17b. Leaves not arranged in distinctive rows; petioles not elongate.
18a. Fruits 12.5–13 cm long and 6.5–7 cm diameter; Peru (Loreto, Madre de Dios, Ucayali) and Brazil (Acre) . . . . . *A. tessmannii.*
18b. Fruits 6–11 cm long and 2.5–5 cm diameter; mostly southern and eastern Amazon region.
19a. Endocarp fibers in distinct clusters; widespread from Peru (Loreto) south to Bolivia (Santa Cruz) and Paraguay and east to Brazil (Goiás, Pará, Tocantins) . . . . . *A. phalerata.*
19b. Endocarp fibers not clustered; Suriname and Brazil (Pará) . . . . . *A. dahlgreniana.*
16b. Leaflets regularly arranged and spreading in the same plane (but note that *A. butyracea* with leaflets sometimes slightly irregular at base of rachis).
20a. Sheath and petiole with stout, stiff fibers on the margins . . . . . *A. butyracea.*
20b. Sheath and petiole without stiff fibers on the margins.
21a. Colombia (Amazonas) . . . . . *A. septuagenata.*
21b. Suriname, Brazil (Acre, Amazonas, Maranhão, Pará, Rondônia, Tocantins), Bolivia (Beni, Pando, Santa Cruz) . . . . . *A. speciosa.*
15b. Stems short and subterranean, rarely to 1.5 m tall.
22a. Leaflets irregularly arranged and spreading in different planes.
23a. Colombia (Amazonas, Caquetá, Casanare, Meta, Putumayo, Vaupés), Peru (Loreto) and Brazil (Acre, Amazonas) . . . . . *A. insignis.*
23b. Brazil (Maranhão, Mato Grosso, Pará, Tocantins) and Bolivia (Santa Cruz) . . . . . *A. eichleri.*
22b. Leaflets regularly arranged and spreading in the same plane.
24a. Male flowering branches 3–4 mm diameter, densely crowded with flowers; female flowering branches borne all around rachis.
25a. Open, white-sand areas west of junction of Río Vaupés and Río Negro in Colombia (Vaupés),

Venezuela (Amazonas), Brazil (Amazonas)

..... *A. luetzelburgii.*

25b. Rain forest or open areas, widespread north of
the Amazon in Colombia, the Guianas, Peru, and
Brazil.

26a. Fruits 3.5–4 cm long and 2–3 cm diameter;
Colombia (Amazonas, Guainía, Vaupés), Venezuela (Amazonas), the Guianas, Peru (Loreto),
and Brazil (Amapá, Amazonas, Pará) ..... *A. microcarpa.*

26b. Fruits 5–6 cm long and 3–4 cm diameter;
Brazil (Pará) ..... *A. spectabilis.*

24b. Male flowering branches 1–3 mm diameter, with
loosely spaced flowers; female flowering branches
borne all around rachis or absent from one
side.

27a. Female flowering branches borne all around
rachis; French Guiana, Suriname, and Brazil (Amazonas) ..... *A. attaleoides.*

27b. Female flowering branches borne on one side of
rachis; Colombia (Amazonas, Caquetá, Guainía,
Vaupés), Venezuela (Amazonas, Bolívar), Peru
(Loreto), and Brazil (Amazonas) ..... *A. racemosa.*

14b. Atlantic coastal forest and central Brazilian region including
Paraguay.

28a. Stems short and subterranean, rarely to 1 m tall.

29a. Leaflets irregularly arranged and spreading in different
planes.

30a. Massive palms; endocarp fibers in distinct clusters;
central Brazilian region ..... *A. phalerata.*

30b. Smaller palms; endocarp fibers scattered; Atlantic
coastal forest or central Brazilian region.

31a. Fruits 4–6 cm long and 3–5.5 cm diameter; *cerrado* vegetation inland in Brazil (Bahia, Goiás,
Minas Gerais, Piauí) ..... *A. exigua.*

31b. Fruits 10–15 cm long and 3–9 cm diameter; rain
forest vegetation near coast in Brazil (Alagoas,
Bahia, Sergipe) ..... *A. funifera.*

29b. Leaflets regularly arranged and spreading in the same
plane.

32a. Leaflets with conspicuous brown scales on the lower
surface; *cerrado* vegetation inland in Brazil (Bahia,
Goiás, Minas Gerais, Rio de Janeiro, São Paulo) and
Paraguay ..... *A. geraensis.*

32b. Leaflets without scales on lower surface; rain forest
vegetation near the coast in Brazil (Bahia, Espírito
Santo, Rio de Janeiro, São Paulo) ..... *A. humilis.*

28b. Stems tall and aerial.

33a. Leaflets regularly arranged and spreading in the same
plane.

34a. Open areas inland in Brazil (Bahia, Minas Gerais)
...... *A. speciosa.*
34b. Atlantic coastal forest of Brazil (Pernambuco to São Paulo).
   35a. North central Bahia   ...... *A. pindobassu.*
   35b. Coastal Pernambuco to São Paulo)   ...... *A. oleifera.*
33b. Leaflets irregularly arranged and spreading in different planes.
36a. Endocarp fibers in distinct clusters; central Brazilian region
...... *A. phalerata.*
36b. Endocarp fibers scattered or in indistinct clusters; Atlantic coastal forest.
  37a. Fruits 6–6.5 cm long and to 3 cm diameter; Brazil (Espírito Santo, Paraná, Rio de Janeiro, Santa Catarina, São Paulo)
...... *A. dubia.*
  37b. Fruits 10–15 cm long and 3–9 cm diameter; Brazil (Alagoas, Bahia, Sergipe)
...... *A. funifera.*

Attalea allenii
(Map 325)
"Taparín," "táparo" (Col), "igua," "mangué" (Pan)
Field characters. Stems short and subterranean. Leaves 8–15; *leaflets irregularly arranged in clusters and spreading in different planes,* several apical leaflets joined along their margins, leaving "windows" at the base. Inflorescences borne among the leaves on a short peduncle and often hidden among leaf litter; male flowers with flattened petals and 6 straight stamens; fruits 1–3-seeded, obovoid, 6–8 cm long and 3.5–5 cm diameter, light brown; endocarp fibers scattered.
Range and habitat. Atlantic slope of Panama (Bocas del Toro, Canal Area, Colón, Panamá, San Blas) and northwestern Colombia (Antioquia, Bolívar, Chocó, Cordoba, Valle); lowland rain forest on noninundated soils, below 500 m elevation.
Uses. Young leaves are used on Palm Sunday; the liquid endosperm is drunk and the seeds are eaten.

Attalea amygdalina
(Map 326)
"Táparo," "almendrón" (Col)
Field characters. Stems short and subterranean. Leaves 10–15, erect; *leaflets regularly arranged and spreading in the same plane.* Inflorescences borne among the leaves on a short peduncle; male flowers with flattened petals and 6–22 stamens; fruits ellipsoid to obovoid, 6–9 cm long and to 5 cm diameter, brown.
Range and habitat. Colombia, in the Río Cauca valley (Antioquia, Caldas, Quindio, Risaralda, Valle); dry to wet forested ravines, at 1000–1600 m elevation.

Uses. The seeds are edible. It was recommended by Ruiz (1984) as a promising economic species because of the high oil content of its seeds.
Notes. This species has had a confusing taxonomic history and has been known in the past by the name *Attalea victoriana.* Most of its former habitat is now converted into coffee plantations and the species is endangered (Bernal, 1989).

Attalea attaleoides
(Map 327, Plate 37)
"Palhera" (Bra), "macoupi blanc" (FrG)
Field characters. Stems short and subterranean. Leaves 8–11, forming a rosette which fills with leaf litter; petiole elongate; *leaflets regularly arranged and spreading in the same plane.* Inflorescences borne on a short peduncle, erect among the leaves; male flowers with linear petals and 6 stamens; fruits 2–3-seeded, oblong-ovoid, 4.5–5.5 cm long and 2–2.5 cm diameter, brownish; endocarp with few fibers.
Range and habitat. Central and eastern part of Amazon region in Suriname, French Guiana, and Brazil (Amapá, Amazonas, Pará); lowland forest on noninundated soils, at low elevations, rarely to 750 m.
Notes. Previously placed in *Scheelea,* but was probably nearer *Maximiliana.* Sometimes forms hybrids with *Attalea maripa.*

Attalea butyracea
(Map 328, Plates 34, 36, 37)
"Palla" (Bol), "jací" (Bra), "palma de vino," "palma real" (Col), "palma real" (CR), "corozo" (CR, Gua, Mex, Ven), "canambo" (Ecu), "coquito" (Gua), "coyol real" (Mex),

"palma real" (Pan), "shebon" (Per), "palma de agua," "yagua" (Ven)

Field characters. Stems tall and aerial, 3–20 m tall and 25–50 cm diameter, often covered with persistent leaf bases. Leaves 15–35, often curved, and then the leaflets held vertically; *sheath and petiole margins with stout, stiff fibers*; petiole short or absent; *leaflets regularly arranged and spreading in the same plane* (occasionally somewhat irregularly arranged, especially near the base of the leaf and on young plants). Inflorescences borne among the leaves; *male flowering branches elongate, 30–53 cm long*; male flowers with linear petals and 6 stamens; fruits 1–3-seeded, oblong-ovoid or ellipsoid-oblong, 4.5–8.5 cm long and 3–4.5 cm diameter, dull orange, yellow, or brown; endocarp fibers scattered.

Range and habitat. Widespread in Central America and northern South America in Mexico (Campeche, Chiapas, Oaxaca, Tabasco, Veracruz), Guatemala (Atlantic and Pacific coasts), Honduras (Gracias a Dios), Nicaragua (Pacific coast), Costa Rica (Pacific coast of Guanacaste, Puntarenas), Panama, Colombia (valleys of Ríos Cauca and Magdalena, Caribbean lowlands, eastern plains and Amazon region), Venezuela (widespread), Trinidad, Tobago, Ecuador (Napo), Peru (Huánuco, Loreto, Madre de Dios, Ucayali), Brazil (Acre, Amazonas), and Bolivia (Cochabamba, La Paz, Pando); seasonal and wet forest areas, common along river margins but also in open, savanna areas, usually below 300 m elevation but occasionally reaching 1000 m. It is very common in disturbed areas and it often persists in pastures.

Uses. The leaves are very widely used for thatching. Standley and Steyermark (1958) have described the importance of this species in Guatemala, where almost every part of the palm has some use. As in many other palms, different parts of the palm can have different local names. In Mexico the palm and the fruit are called "corozo," the leaves are called "manaca," the rachis is called "huilote," and the areas where the palm grows are called "manacales" (Hernández, 1945).

Notes. Previously placed in the genus *Scheelea*. This widespread species is very variable, especially since it spreads rapidly in disturbed, man-made habitats. In Central America (except for Costa Rica and Panama) and the Magdalena valley of Colombia, this species and *Attalea cohune* grow together in mixed stands. It differs from the latter by its male flowers with linear petals and six stamens. In northern South America the only other large *Attalea* with regularly arranged leaflets which grows with *A. butyracea* is *A. septuagenata*, which has male flowers with flattened petals and numerous stamens.

The patterns of flowering in this species and others in the genus are complex and poorly understood. Burret (1929b) described the sequence of inflorescences in this species (as *Scheelea preussii*). First 2–4 all-male inflorescences are produced followed by a female, and then the pattern is repeated.

A short-stemmed form occurs in the western Amazon region in Colombia (Amazonas) and Peru (Loreto), and this may deserve specific status.

Seed predation by bruchid beetles and rodents in Costa Rica and Panama has been studied by Janzen (1971), Wilson and Janzen (1972), Wright (1983), and Bradford and Smith (1977). Glanz et al. (1983) showed that in Panama the red-tailed squirrel, *Sciurus granatensis*, was the main arboreal seed predator of *Attalea butyracea*.

Attalea cohune

(Map 329)

"Cohune" (Bel, Gua, Hon, Mex), "corozo" (ElS, Gua, Hon), "manaca" (Hon)

Field characters. Stems tall and aerial, 6–20 m tall and 30–60 cm diameter. Leaves 15–30; sheath and petiole margins without stiff fibers; *leaflets regularly arranged and spreading in the same plane*. Inflorescences borne among the leaves on a long peduncle, pendulous in fruit; *male flowering branches to 15 cm long*; male flowers with flattened, incurved petals and up to 24 stamens, the anthers tightly coiled and twisted; fruits 1–3-seeded, ovoid or ellipsoid, 4–8 cm long and 3.3–4.5 cm diameter, brown or yellow-brown; endocarp fibers in inconspicuous or conspicuous clusters.

Range and habitat. Mexico (Campeche, Chiapas, Colima, Guerrero, Jalisco, Michoacan, Nayarit, Oaxaca, Quintana Roo, Tabasco), Belize, El Salvador, Guatemala (Alta Verapaz, Izabal, Petén), and Honduras (Atlántida, Islas de la Bahía) (and possibly reaching northwest Nicaragua); forest but now very abundant in disturbed areas, at low elevations. It possibly also occurs in the Magdalena valley of Colombia and may either have been introduced or have been overlooked in the intervening Costa Rica and Panama. Humans may have played a role in its distribution (Johannessen, 1957).

Uses. Oil is extracted from the seeds; and the leaves provide thatching material.

Notes. Previously placed in *Orbignya*. It is very abundant in parts of Central America. Furley (1975) has studied its role in soil formation.

Attalea colenda

(Map 330, Plate 35)

"Palma real" (Col, Ecu)

Field characters. Stems tall and aerial, to 30 m tall and 30–50 cm diameter. Leaves 15–25; petiole

long; *leaflets regularly arranged and spreading in the same plane.* Inflorescences borne among the leaves on a long peduncle; male flowers with flattened petals and 10–11 straight stamens; fruits 1–3-seeded, oblong, to 6 cm long and 3.5 cm diameter, orange-brown; endocarp fibers few or absent.
Range and habitat. Southwestern Colombia (Nariño) and western Ecuador (Azuay, El Oro, Esmeraldas, Guayas, Manabí); lowland rain forest or deciduous forest, but now mostly persisting in disturbed or cleared areas, below 900 m elevation.
Uses. The seeds from the huge inflorescences are gathered commercially and oil is extracted from them (Balslev and Henderson, 1987b). This is chemically similar to coconut and oil palm oil (Blicher-Mathiesen and Balslev, 1990).

Attalea crassispatha
(Map 331, Plate 35)
"Carossier" (Hai)
Field characters. Stems tall and aerial, to 20 m tall and 35 cm diameter. Leaves 15–19; *leaflets regularly arranged and spreading in the same plane.* Inflorescences borne among the leaves, on a short peduncle, and crowded among the leaf bases; male flowers with linear petals and 8–9 stamens, the anthers coiled and twisted; fruits one-seeded, ovoid, 3.5–4 cm long and 2 cm diameter, reddish; endocarp fibers few or absent.
Range and habitat. Southwestern peninsula of Haiti (Sud); in disturbed areas on slopes with limestone soil, at low elevations.
Uses. The seeds are eaten by children.
Notes. This is one of the rarest palms in the Americas (Henderson and Balick, 1991), with only about 25 individual trees known to still exist in Haiti. Its conservation status has been assessed by Timyan and Reep (1994). It is a very interesting species because of its unusual male flowers and disjunct distribution, being the only Caribbean *Attalea.*

Attalea cuatrecasana
(Map 332, Plate 35)
"Corozo," "táparo" (Col)
Field characters. Stems short and subterranean. Leaves 6–10; *leaflets regularly arranged and spreading in the same plane.* Inflorescences borne among the leaves; male flowers with flattened, incurved petals and 20–24 tightly coiled and twisted stamens; fruits 1–3-seeded, globose, *11–14 cm long and 7.5–9.5 cm diameter;* endocarp with inconspicuous fibers.
Range and habitat. Pacific coast of Colombia (Chocó, Nariño, Valle) and probably adjacent Ecudor; very wet lowland rain forest, at low elevations.

Notes. Previously placed in *Orbignya* and notable for its very large fruits.

Attalea dahlgreniana
(Map 333)
"Dois por dois," "perinão" (Bra), "maripa" (Sur)
Field characters. Stems tall and aerial, occasionally creeping along the ground but erect at the top, 2–15 m tall and 30–55 cm diameter. Leaves 12–20; *leaflets regularly to slightly irregularly arranged and spreading ± in the same plane.* Inflorescences borne among the leaves on a long peduncle; male flowers with flattened, incurved petals and 7–10 somewhat twisted stamens; fruits 1–3-seeded, ellipsoid-oblong, brownish, 6–9 cm long and 2.5–4 cm diameter; endocarp fibers scattered.
Range and habitat. Eastern Amazon region in Suriname and Brazil (Maranhão, Pará); lowland rain forest on noninundated soils, at low elevations.
Notes. Bondar (1957) described this species as *Markleya dahlgreniana* and speculated that it could be a hybrid between *Attalea speciosa* and *A. maripa.*

Attalea dubia
(Map 334)
"Babassu," "bacuaçu" (Bra)
Field characters. Stems tall and aerial, 5–7(–25) m tall and 20–35 cm diameter. Leaves about 35; *leaflets irregularly arranged in clusters and spreading in different planes.* Inflorescences borne among the leaves on a long peduncle; male flowers with flattened petals and 6–9 straight stamens; fruits 1–2-seeded, oblong, 6–6.5 cm long and to 3 cm diameter; endocarp fibers few, scattered near outer edge.
Range and habitat. Atlantic coast of Brazil (Espírito Santo, Paraná, Rio de Janeiro, Santa Catarina, São Paulo); lowland rain forest or persisting in disturbed areas.

Attalea eichleri
(Map 335)
"Indaya," "piassava" (Bra)
Field characters. Stems short and subterranean or rarely to 1.5 m tall. Leaves 4–8; *leaflets irregularly arranged in clusters and spreading in different planes.* Inflorescences borne among the leaves on short peduncles; male flowers with flattened, incurved petals and 17–20 coiled and twisted stamens; fruits 3–5-seeded, borne along one side of rachis only, ellipsoid-oblong, 7–8 cm long and 4–5.5 cm diameter, dark brown; endocarp fibers in inconspicuous or conspicuous clusters.
Range and habitat. Brazil (Bahia, Goiás, Maranhão, Mato Grosso, Pará, Piauí, Tocantins) and Bolivia (Santa Cruz); transition zone between

lowland forest and upland *cerrado,* on rocky slopes or seasonally dry forest, to 800 m elevation.
Notes. Previously placed in the genus *Orbignya.* Balick et al. (1987) have described a hybrid, *Orbignya* x *teixeirana,* between this species and *A. speciosa* (as *Orbignya phalerata*).

Attalea exigua
(Map 336)
"Catolé," "indaia rasteira" (Bra)
Field characters. Stems short and subterranean, sometimes appearing clustered. Leaves 4–8, strongly arched; *leaflets irregularly arranged in clusters and spreading in different planes.* Inflorescences borne among the leaves on short peduncles; male flowers with flattened petals and 6–9 straight stamens; fruits 1–2-seeded, obovoid, 4–6 cm long and 3–5.5 cm diameter, reddish orange to dark purple at maturity; endocarp fibers in rings.
Range and habitat. Brazil (Bahia, Goiás, Minas Gerais, and probably adjacent Piauí); *cerrado* vegetation, below 800 m elevation.
Uses. The endosperm is used to make candies and sweeten other foods.

Attalea funifera
(Map 337, Plate 35)
"Piaçava," "piassaba" (Bra)
Field characters. Stems usually tall and aerial, but small and subterranean at ends of range, (0–)1.5–15 m tall and 20–30 cm diameter. Leaves 5–15, with very long petioles, *sheaths and petioles with long fibers; leaflets irregularly arranged and spreading in different planes.* Inflorescences borne among the leaves on a long peduncle; male flowers with flattened petals and 6 straight stamens; fruits 1–3-seeded, obovoid to ellipsoid, 10–15 cm long and 3–9 cm diameter; endocarp fibers in indistinct clusters.
Range and habitat. Atlantic coast of Brazil (Alagoas, Bahia, Sergipe); lowland rain forest or *restinga,* especially near the sea on stabilized dunes, at low elevations.
Uses. The fibers from the leaf bases are an important item of commerce and are harvested in large amounts. Previously they were exported to Europe and used to make brooms; now they are commonly used as a source of thatching, especially of beach houses (Voeks, 1987). Most trees have had the fibers harvested (and the lower leaves removed).
Notes. Voeks (1988) has documented changing sexual expression in this species; younger plants generally produce inflorescences with male flowers, while older, taller plants produce inflorescences with female flowers. Voeks (1985) has shown that beetles, bees, and small flies are pollinators. At either end of the range

of this species, short, stemless plants occur (Noblick, 1991).

Attalea geraensis
(Map 338)
"Andaiá," "insiá" (Bra), "urucuri" (Par)
Field characters. Stems short and subterranean. Leaves 4–8, spreading; *leaflets regularly arranged and spreading in the same plane, with conspicuous, brown scales on the lower surface.* Inflorescences borne among the leaves on a short peduncle; male flowers with flattened petals and 6–10 straight stamens; fruits 1–6-seeded, obovoid or ovoid-ellipsoid, 5–7 cm long and 3–4.5 cm diameter, reddish brown; endocarp fibers few, scattered.
Range and habitat. Brazil (Bahia, Goiás, Minas Gerais, Rio de Janeiro, São Paulo) and Paraguay (Cordillera); *cerrado* vegetation or dry forest on sandy soils, especially in stream valleys.
Uses. The leaves are occasionally used for thatching; the seeds are sometimes eaten.

Attalea humilis
(Map 339)
"Pindoba," "catolé" (Bra)
Field characters. Stems short and subterranean or rarely to 1 m tall. Leaves 4–15, spreading; *leaflets regularly arranged and spreading in the same plane.* Inflorescences borne among the leaves on short peduncles; male flowers with flattened petals and 6 straight stamens; fruits 1–3-seeded, obovoid, 4–9 cm long and 2.5–8 cm diameter; brownish; endocarp fibers scattered.
Range and habitat. Atlantic Coastal Forest of Brazil (Bahia, Espírito Santo, Rio de Janeiro, São Paulo); low forest or *restinga* vegetation near the sea, often forming large colonies.

Attalea iguadummat
(Map 340)
"Igua dummat" (Pan: Kuna)
Field characters. Stems short and subterranean. Leaves 9–17; *leaflets regularly arranged and spreading in the same plane.* Inflorescences borne among the leaves on short peduncles; male flowers with linear petals and 8–10 straight stamens; fruits 1–3-seeded, obovoid, 7–10 cm long and 4.5–6.3 cm diameter.
Range and habitat. Atlantic slope in Panama (Colón, San Blas); lowland rain forest on non-inundated soils, below 500 m elevation.
Notes. It has the linear petals typical of *Scheelea* and the numerous stamens typical of *Attalea.*

Attalea insignis
(Map 341)
"Palha de flecha" (Bra), "yagua" (Col), "contillo" (Per)
Field characters. Stems short and subterranean. Leaves 9–11; petioles very long, 1.6–3.3 m;

leaflets irregularly arranged in clusters and spreading in different planes, the apical few leaflets joined at their tips only and leaving "windows" at the base. Inflorescences erect on long peduncles among the leaves, becoming pendulous in fruit; male flowers with linear petals and 6 stamens; fruits 2–3-seeded, ellipsoid-oblong, 7–7.5 cm long and 3.5–4 cm diameter; endocarp fibers scattered.
Range and habitat. Colombia (Amazonas, Caquetá, Casanare, Meta, Putumayo, Vaupés), Ecuador (Napo), Peru (Loreto), and western Brazil (Acre, Amazonas); understory of lowland rain forest and gallery forest, below 600 m elevation.
Notes. Previously placed in *Scheelea.* In some areas it has become a weed of cleared areas.

Attalea luetzelburgii
(Map 342)
"Curuaraua" (Bra), "curuá" (Col), "grua" (Ven)
Field characters. Stems short and subterranean. Leaves about 6; *leaflets regularly arranged and spreading in the same plane.* Inflorescences borne among the leaves on a short peduncle; male flowers with linear petals and 6 loosely coiled stamens; fruits one-seeded, ovoid, 5–5.5 cm long and 2–2.5 cm diameter; endocarp with inconspicuous fibers.
Range and habitat. Known from a small region west of the junction of the Río Vaupés and Río Negro, in northwestern Brazil (Amazonas), southeastern Colombia (Vaupés), and southwestern Venezuela (Amazonas); open, white-sand areas in the transition zone between forest and savanna.
Notes. First described as an *Orbignya* and then in its own genus, *Parascheelea.*

Attalea maripa
(Map 343, Plates 36 & 37)
"Cusi" (Bol), "anajá," "inajai" (Bra), "güichire" (Col), "inayo" (Ecu), "maripa" (FrG, Sur), "kukarit" (Guy), "inayuga" (Per), "cucurito" (Ven)
Field characters. Stems tall and aerial, 3.5–20 m tall and 20–33(–100) cm diameter. Leaves 10–22, *borne in 5 distinct vertical rows on long petioles; leaflets irregularly arranged in tight clusters and spreading in different planes.* Inflorescences persistent, borne among the leaves on a long peduncle; male flowers with 6 straight stamens, these much longer than the lanceolate petals; fruits 2–3-seeded, ellipsoid-oblong, brownish, 4–6 cm long and 2.5–3 cm diameter; endocarp fibers absent.
Range and habitat. Widespread in northern South America east of the Andes in Colombia (Amazonas, Caquetá, Guaviare, Guainía, Meta,

Putumayo, Vaupés, Vichada), Venezuela (Amazonas, Bolívar, Delta Amacuro, Monagas, Sucre), Trinidad, the Guianas, Ecuador (Napo), Peru (Loreto, Madre de Dios, Ucayali), Brazil (Acre, Amazonas, Maranhão, Mato Grosso, Mato Grosso do Sul, Pará, Rondônia), and Bolivia (Beni, Pando, Santa Cruz); lowland forest, secondary forest, open areas and especially abundant in disturbed areas, on noninundated soils, at low elevations.
Uses. The leaves are commonly used for thatching; and other parts of the palm provide many other minor uses.
Notes. This is one of the most distinct species of *Attalea* and in some respects resembles *Syagrus.* Previously placed in *Maximiliana* and may eventually be recognized at genus level.

Attalea microcarpa
(Map 344, Plate 37)
"Coco curuá" (Bra), "mavaco" (Col, Ven) "macoupi" (FrG), "catarina" (Per), "mountain maripa" (Sur)
Field characters. Stems short and subterranean. Leaves 6–16; *leaflets regularly arranged and spreading in the same plane.* Inflorescences erect, borne among the leaves; male flowers with flattened, incurved petals and 9–15 tightly coiled and twisted stamens; fruits 1–3-seeded, ovoid or obovoid, 3.5–4 cm long and 2–3 cm diameter, brownish; endocarp fibers inconspicuous.
Range and habitat. Northern Amazon region in Colombia (Amazonas, Guianía, Vaupés), Venezuela (Amazonas), the Guianas, Peru (Loreto), and Brazil (Amapá, Amazonas, Pará); lowland rain forest, semi-open areas, or forest margins in wet places on sandy soils, at low elevations.
Notes. Previously placed in the genus *Orbignya.* It forms hybrids with *Attalea speciosa* (Henderson, 1994). Pollination has been studied by Küchmeister et al. (1992) (as *Orbignya spectabilis*).

Attalea nucifera
(Map 345)
"Mangué" (Col)
Field characters. Stems short and subterranean. Leaves 7–13; *leaflets regularly arranged and spreading in the same plane.* Inflorescences borne among the leaves on a short peduncle; male flowers with flattened petals and 6–7 stamens; fruits 2–3-seeded, ellipsoid, 6.5–7 cm long and 4–5 cm diameter, brown; endocarp fibers scattered.
Range and habitat. Río Magdalena valley in Colombia (Bolívar, Norte de Santander, Santander, Tolima and Cundinamarca); dry to

wet areas, at 200–800 m elevation. Scarce in most of the area, but locally common in some places.

Attalea oleifera
(Map 346)
"Andaiá," "catolé" (Bra)
Field characters. Stems tall and aerial (1.5–)3–20 (–30) m tall and 30–40 cm diameter. Leaves 8–30, stiffly erect; *leaflets regularly arranged and spreading in the same plane.* Inflorescences borne among the leaves on a long peduncle; male flowers with flattened petals and 6–9 straight stamens; fruits 1–4-seeded, elongate or obovoid, 7–11 cm long and 4–6 cm diameter, rusty brown; endocarp fibers scattered or in small clusters.
Range and habitat. Atlantic coast of Brazil (Alagoas, Bahia, Espírito Santo, Pernambuco, Paraíba, Sergipe, and possibly São Paulo); transitional forest between coastal rain forest and *cerrado,* to 800 m elevation.
Uses. The leaves are commonly used for thatching.

Attalea phalerata
(Map 347)
"Motacú" (Bol), "urucuri" (Bra), "shapaja" (Per)
Field characters. Stems large and aerial, generally short, to 4(–10) m tall, 25–40(–60) cm diameter, often covered with persistent leaf bases. Leaves 11–30; *leaflets irregularly arranged and spreading in different planes, or regularly arranged and then only the tips spreading in different planes.* Inflorescences borne among the leaves on long peduncles; male flowers with linear petals and 6 stamens; fruits 1–4-seeded, ellipsoid-oblong, often angled by mutual pressure, 6–11 cm long and 3–5 cm diameter; *endocarp fibers in distinct clusters.*
Range and habitat. Widespread around the southern and western periphery of the Amazon region and in the *planalto* of Brazil, in Peru (Huánuco, Junín, Loreto, Madre de Dios, San Martin), Brazil (Acre, Goiás, Maranhão, Mato Grosso, Pará, Rondônia, Tocantins), Bolivia (Beni, La Paz, Pando), and Paraguay (Amambay, Concepción); open areas, gallery forest, disturbed forest, forest islands in savannas and lowland rain forest.
Uses. The leaves are an important source of thatching. In Amazonian Peru the ridges of roofs are thatched with the leaves of this palm, while the sloping part is made of *Geonoma deversa.* In Acre, Brazil, the endocarps are the preferred source of charcoal for the smoking of rubber.
Notes. Previously placed in *Scheelea.*

Attalea pindobassu
(Map 348)
"Côco palmeira," "pindobassú" (Bra)
Field characters. Stems tall and aerial, 5–15 m tall and 35–50 cm diameter. Leaves 15–25, stiffly erect; *leaflets regularly arranged and spreading in the same plane.* Inflorescences borne among the leaves on a long peduncle; male flowers with 8–12 straight stamens; fruits 1–5-seeded, obovoid, 7–9 cm long and 4.5–6 cm diameter; endocarp fibers scattered.
Range and habitat. Brazil (Bahia); seasonal forest on mountain slopes, at 350–1200 m elevation.
Notes. Very similar to *Attalea oleifera,* except for the number of stamens.

Attalea racemosa
(Map 349)
"Babassú" (Bra), "coco," "mavaco" (Col), "shebon enano" (Per)
Field characters. Stems solitary or rarely clustered, short, and subterranean. Leaves 8–35, with rusty-red tomentum on the petiole and rachis; *leaflets regularly arranged and spreading in the same plane, the basal leaflets widely spaced along rachis.* Inflorescences borne among the leaves on a long peduncle; male flowers with flattened petals and 19–42 straight stamens; fruits 1–2-seeded, globose, ellipsoid-oblong, or ovoid, 6–9 cm long and 4.5–5 cm diameter; endocarp fibers scattered or clustered.
Range and habitat. Northwestern Amazon region in Colombia (Amazonas, Caquetá, Guainía, Guaviare, Vaupés), southwestern Venezuela (Amazonas, Bolívar), Peru (Loreto), and Brazil (Amazonas); open areas, open forest or forest margins on sandy soils, at low elevations.

Attalea septuagenata
(Map 350)
"Kujita," "kuruá" (Col)
Field characters. Stems tall and aerial, 7–12 m tall and 25–30 cm diameter. Leaves 18–20; *leaflets regularly arranged and spreading in the same plane.* Inflorescences borne among the leaves on long peduncles; male flowers with flattened petals and 36–75 straight stamens; fruits 1–2-seeded, ellipsoid-oblong, 10–11.5 cm long and 5–6 cm diameter; endocarp fibers scattered.
Range and habitat. Colombia (Amazonas); known only from a small area of lowland rain forest, along the Río Miriti-Paraná, in low-lying, wet areas.

Attalea speciosa
(Map 351, Plate 36)
"Cusi" (Bol), "babaçu" (Bra)
Field characters. Stems tall and aerial, 3–15 m tall

and 25–41 cm diameter. Leaves 7–22; *leaflets regularly arranged* and spreading in the same plane. Inflorescences borne among the leaves on long peduncles, becoming pendulous in fruit; male flowers with flattened, incurved petals and 21–56 tightly coiled and twisted stamens; fruits 3–6-seeded, ellipsoid-oblong, 6.6–12.5 cm long and 3.7–9.9 cm diameter, dull brown; endocarp fibers scattered.

Range and habitat. Mostly south of the Amazon in Guyana, Suriname, Brazil (Acre, Amazonas, Bahia, Maranhão, Minas Gerais, Pará, Rondônia, Tocantins), and Bolivia (Beni, Pando); scattered in forest or open areas, but occurring in huge numbers in disturbed areas, e.g., in Maranhão, where the forest has been cut.

Uses. One of the most important of the oil-producing palms and extensively used in Brazil, especially in the state of Maranhão, as a source of oil and a host of other products. The natural and economic history of this palm has been summarized by Anderson et al. (1991).

Notes. Previously placed in *Orbignya.* Hybrids are known with a few other species. Munn et al. (1989–90) reported that hyacinth macaws relied heavily on fruits of *Attalea speciosa* (and *A. phalerata*) and with their incredibly powerful beaks could shear open the endocarp and eat the endosperm.

Attalea spectabilis
(Map 352)
"Curuá" (Bra)
Field characters. Stems short and subterranean, rarely to 1 m tall, spreading by rhizomes.

Leaves to 8; *leaflets regularly arranged and spreading in the same plane.* Inflorescences erect, borne among the leaves; male flowers with flattened, incurved petals and 8–15 tightly coiled and twisted stamens; fruits 1–2-seeded, ovoid or ellipsoid, 5–6 cm long and 3–4 cm diameter, brownish; endocarp fibers inconspicuous.

Range and habitat. Amazon region in Brazil (Pará); semi-open areas or forest margins in wet places on sandy soils, at low elevations.

Notes. Previously placed in *Orbignya.* This is a poorly known species that may be a hybrid between *Attalea microcarpa* and *A. speciosa.* In Pará it is an invasive weed of forestry plantations (Pires-O'Brien, 1993).

Attalea tessmannii
(Map 353, Plates 36 & 38)
"Cocão" (Bra), "conta" (Per)
Field characters. Stems tall and upright, 8–19 m tall and 30–40 cm diameter. Leaves about 12; *leaflets irregularly arranged and spreading in different planes.* Inflorescences borne among the leaves on long peduncles; male flowers with flattened petals and 10–14 straight stamens; fruits 2–3-seeded, ellipsoid-oblong, 12–13 cm long and 6–7 cm diameter; brownish; endocarp fibers scattered.

Range and habitat. Western Amazon region in Brazil (Acre) and Peru (Loreto, Madre de Dios, Ucayali); lowland rain forest on noninundated soils, at low elevations.

Uses. The endocarps of this and related species are used to smoke newly collected rubber.

51. BARCELLA

This genus of one species is very closely related to *Elaeis*, but is much smaller in all parts. The origin of the name is unknown, but may come from the town of Barcelos in Brazil, which is near to where the palm was first discovered by James Trail. Stems are short, subterranean, and solitary. Leaves are pinnate, about seven in number, arching, and arise directly from the ground. The petiole is nonspiny (unlike *Elaeis*) and decays into black fibers that persist around the base of the plant. The leaflets are linear, regularly arranged, and spread in the same plane. Inflorescences are borne among the leaves and are erect in flower and fruit. They have a woody, persistent peduncular bract (unlike the fibrous bract of *Elaeis*). Inflorescences are branched to one order and bear either all male flowers or male and female flowers; both types occur on the same plant. Inflorescences with both male and female flowers have female flowers at the base of basal flowering branches and male flowers on the upper part. Male flowers are sunken in small pits along the flowering branches. Fruits are one-seeded, irregularly ovoid, and orange. The endocarp is thick and bony with three lateral pores. The endosperm is homogeneous and the seedling leaf simple.

Barcella contains one species (Uhl and Dransfield, 1987), occurring only in the Amazon region north of the Rio Negro in Brazil. It grows in open vegetation on sandy soil. It is unlikely to be confused with any other genus.

Barcella odora
(Map 354, Plate 38)
"Piassaba braba," "piassabarana" (Bra)
Field characters. Stems solitary, short, and subterranean. Leaves about 7, arching, arising directly from the ground; leaflets linear, regularly arranged, and spreading in the same plane. Inflorescences borne among the leaves, erect; peduncular bract woody; fruits ovoid, 3.5 cm long and 2.5 cm diameter, orange.

Range and habitat. Amazon region of Brazil (Amazonas), north of the Rio Negro; low, shrubby vegetation on white-sand soil, called *campinarana* in Brazil (Henderson, 1986).
Uses. None recorded. The fibers from the petiole are persistent but are not strong enough to be of any use, hence the common name "piassabarana," which means "false piassaba"; the true piassaba in this region is *Leopoldinia piassaba.*

52. ELAEIS

A small genus of two species, unusual in that one occurs in Africa and the other in the Americas. Stems are solitary, moderate in size, and very thick. In the African oil palm they are tall and upright, and in the American oil palm they are somewhat creeping. In both cases they are rough with leaf scars. Leaves are pinnate, 20–40 in number, and are gracefully arching. The long petioles are covered with stout, recurved thorns. The numerous, linear leaflets are either regularly arranged and spreading in the same plane (in the American oil palm), or irregularly arranged in clusters and spreading in different planes (in the African oil palm), and this character easily distinguishes the two species. Inflorescences consist of massive heads tightly inserted among the leaf bases. They are branched to one order and have numerous, thick, flowering branches. These are closely packed together and covered, at least initially, with a fibrous peduncular bract. A characteristic of the branches is that they terminate in a sharp point. Flowers are borne in slight depressions along the branches and the males are densely crowded. Inflorescences are usually unisexual, but plants can bear both male and female inflorescences, but normally only one kind at a time; a series of all male inflorescences will eventually be followed by females. Fruits are densely packed in tight infructescences; individually they are one-seeded, irregularly ovoid or ellipsoid-oblong, and orange to red. The mesocarp is very oily, hence the common name, oil palm, and genus name, from the Greek word "elaia," meaning olive tree. The endocarp is thick and bony with three apical pores. The endosperm is homogeneous and the seedling leaf is narrow and simple.

Elaeis contains one species in the Old World, the African oil palm, and one in the Americas, the American oil palm (Bailey, 1933; Schultes, 1990). The African oil palm, *Elaeis guineensis,* is an extremely important oil crop and is now planted commercially in many parts of the world, including South and Central America. In some regions, such as Haiti and coastal Brazil, where there is a strong African tradition, it has become naturalized. It is commonly planted in many other places, especially as an ornamental in towns and cities. The American oil palm is less often cultivated but commonly grows in parts of Central America and northern Colombia and Venezuela and is scattered in other places.

Elaeis, together with *Raphia,* occurs in both Africa and the Americas. Because of this some have believed that the African oil palm was introduced to Africa from America (Cook, 1942), but there seems little evidence for this.

Elaeis oleifera

(Map 355, Plates 38 & 39)
"Caiaué" (Bra), "nolí" (Col), "ujun" (Hon: Mosquitia)
Field characters. Stems solitary, 1–6 m long and to 40 cm diameter, creeping at the base and becoming erect at the top. Leaves arching; leaflets 33–90 per side, regularly arranged and spreading in the same plane. Fruits ellipsoid-oblong, 2.5–3 cm long and 1.8–2 cm diameter, orange, orange-yellow or red.
Range and habitat. Central America in Honduras (Gracias a Dios), Nicaragua, Costa Rica, and Panama, and northern Colombia, and scattered localities in the Amazon region in Suriname, French Guiana, Peru, Ecuador, and Brazil; low-lying, wet areas along streams or rivers and often persisting in cleared areas. It may have been introduced into the Amazon region by Indians, given its sporadic distribution there and association with anthropogenic soils (Balée, 1989).
Uses. Oil is extracted from the mesocarp and used in cooking, but not to the same extent as that from the African oil palm. The oil is also used as a hair cream.

53. ACROCOMIA

This is a genus of two species, one very large and one very small, but both very spiny. Stems are either tall, spiny, and often swollen, or short and subterranean, and this easily distinguishes the two species. In the tall species the dead, spiny leaf bases sometimes persist on the stem. Leaves are pinnate, 2–6 in the smaller species and 10–30 in the taller species, where they form a dense crown. In fact, the derivation of the name comes from a combination of the Greek words "akros" and "kome," suggesting the crown of leaves. In the small species the leaves are small and resemble grass and are difficult to distinguish from surrounding vegetation. Leaflets are linear, irregularly arranged, and spreading in different planes and are glaucous on the lower surface. Inflorescences are always spiny, borne among the leaves, and are branched to one order. Flowers are unisexual, but males and females are borne on the same inflorescence. Female flowers are borne at the base of the flowering branches and male flowers are borne close together at the tops of the branches, where they are surrounded by distinctive "honeycomb" bracts. Fruits are one-seeded, globose, rather large, yellowish green to brown, and smooth or bristly. The epicarp is brittle and easily cracks. The endosperm is homogeneous and the seedling leaf is simple and linear.

Acrocomia contains two species (Henderson, 1994); one is widely distributed in drier regions throughout the American tropics, the other is restricted to *cerrado* vegetation of Brazil and Paraguay.

Acrocomia aculeata

(Map 356, Plate 39)
"Mbocayá" (Arg), "totaí" (Bol), "macaúba," "mucuja" (Bra), "corozo" (Col, Ven), "tamaco" (Col), "coyol" (CR, ElS, Hon, Mex), "corosse" (Hai)
Field characters. Stems spiny, large and aerial, 4–11 m tall and 10–35(–50) cm diameter, often swollen, sometimes covered with persistent, dead leaf bases. Leaves 10–30, grayish green; leaflets numerous, linear, whitish below, irregularly arranged and spreading in different planes, giving the leaf a plumose appearance. Inflorescences borne among the leaves; fruits globose, yellowish green, 2.5–5 cm diameter, smooth, the epicarp brittle and easily cracking at maturity.
Range and habitat. Throughout the American tropics from Mexico to Argentina, Bolivia, and Paraguay and also in the Antilles (but absent from Ecuador and Peru); open savannas, open woodlands, or often in disturbed areas and fields, in areas of seasonal rainfall, at low elevations but reaching 1200 m in the Colombian Andes. Its range has been greatly influenced by humans. Janzen (1983) considered it introduced to Costa Rica by pre-Columbian Indians, and Lentz (1990) reported that it was introduced into some sites in Mexico and Central America by the Maya.
Uses. This widespread palm has a host of uses. In many countries oil is extracted from the endosperm and the species is considered a promising oil-producing palm (Balick, 1979). In Honduras trees are felled and the sap is collected, fermented, and sold as palm wine (Balick, 1990, as *Acrocomia mexicana*).

Notes. A very widespread and variable species, which in the past has been overdescribed. Scariot et al. (1991) described phenology, floral biology, and pollination of this species near Brasília in Brazil. Plants flowered between August and December and fruited between June and March. Principal pollinators were curculionid, nitidulid, and scarab beetles.

Acrocomia hassleri
(Map 357, Plate 39)
"Coqueirinho do campo" (Bra)
Field characters. Stems short and subterranean.

Leaves 2–6, *grasslike*; leaflets linear, irregularly arranged, and loosely spreading. Inflorescences borne at ground level, among the leaves; flowering branches 5–15; fruits subglobose, 1.5–3 cm diameter, brown, minutely bristly.
Range and habitat. Southern Brazil (western Bahia, Goiás, Mato Grosso do Sul, Minas Gerais, Paraná, São Paulo) and Paraguay (Sierra de Amambay); widely scattered in *cerrado* vegetation.
Notes. Formerly placed in its own genus, *Acanthococos* (Hahn, 1991).

54. GASTROCOCOS

This genus of spiny palms is very closely related to *Acrocomia*, where it will probably be included after it has been more closely studied. The only difference between the two genera is the degree of joining of the sepals of male and female flowers and petals of female flowers. Stems are solitary, large, spiny, and very markedly swollen near the middle. The name of the genus comes from this swelling, and "gastro" comes from the Greek word meaning stomach or belly. Leaves are pinnate, spiny, and 10–15 in number. Leaflets are linear, gray-white on the lower surface, regularly to slightly irregularly arranged, and spread in one to a few planes. Inflorescences are branched to one order and are borne among the leaves. The peduncle bears a prophyll and large, spiny peduncular bract. Flowers are unisexual and arranged with female flowers near the base of the flowering branches, and the male flowers are crowded on the upper parts. Fruits are one-seeded, more or less globose, large, yellow or orange, and smooth. The endosperm is homogeneous and the seedling leaf is simple.

Gastrococos contains one species, in Cuba (Moore, 1967).

Gastrococos crispa
(Map 358, Plate 40)
"Corojo" (Cub)
Field characters. Stems solitary but usually several together in a clump, spiny (but becoming smooth with age), 8–18 m tall and 25–35 cm diameter, greatly swollen near the middle. Leaves 10–15, very spiny, cleanly falling when dead; leaflets linear, regularly to slightly irregularly arranged, and spreading in one to a few

planes, giving the leaves a somewhat plumose appearance. Inflorescences borne among the leaves, becoming pendulous in fruit; fruits more or less globose, 2.5–2.7 cm in diameter, yellow or orange, one-seeded.
Range and habitat. Cuba; widespread but uncommon in open, savanna areas on calcareous soils and persisting in fields and other disturbed areas, at low elevations.

55. AIPHANES

This large genus of small to medium-sized spiny palms is particularly diverse along the Andes. Stems are often slender, sometimes short and subterranean, solitary or clustered, and covered (often densely) with black spines. Leaves are pinnate (simple in *A. macroloba*), 3–15 in number, and spiny. The leaf sheath is open and the petiole is short or rarely elongate. Leaflets are few to numerous and are regularly or irregularly arranged along the rachis. Leaflets are wedge shaped or sometimes linear but always jagged at the tip. Due to their wedge-shaped, clustered, and rather short leaflets, species of *Aiphanes* are rather difficult to spot in the forest, unlike most other palms. Paradoxically, the name *Aiphanes* can be translated as "ever visible," probably referring to the large, red, infructescences of *Aiphanes aculeata*. Inflorescences are borne among the leaves and are spicate or branched to one order. The peduncle, peduncular bract, and rachis are usually elongate, with the peduncular bract persistent and pendulous. Flowers are borne in threes of one central female and two lateral males and are often brightly colored; male flowers have six stamens and female flowers have a staminodial ring. Fruits are one-seeded, usually rounded, smooth or sometimes spiny or covered in jelly, red to orange, or less often greenish white to purplish black. The endocarp is woody, with three germination pores near the middle, each surrounded by flattened fibers. The endosperm is homogeneous and the seedling leaf is spiny, slightly to deeply bifid with the outer margins jagged.

Aiphanes contains twenty-two species (Borchsenius and Bernal, in press), mostly distributed along the Andes in Colombia, Venezuela, Ecuador, Peru, and Bolivia, but a few species grow in the adjacent lowlands, reaching western Brazil (Acre, Amazonas) and western Panama and Costa Rica; one species grows in the Lesser Antilles. Many of the species are narrow endemics and most are concentrated in Colombia and Ecuador. They grow in the shade of rain forest, although a few prefer rather dry environments. They occur from sea level to 2800 m elevation, but most are found between 500 and 2000 m. Most species appear to be rather uncommon, and some have rather restricted ranges (Borchsenius and Bernal, in press). Bee and fly pollination have been recorded, but the pollination syndrome has been considered rather unspecialized; it has been suggested that this could account in part for the diversification of the genus in the Andean highlands (Borchsenius, 1993).

Aiphanes is the only American genus of spiny palms with leaflets jagged at the tips. *Bactris caryotifolia*, from eastern Brazil, also has spines and jagged leaflets, but it has an inflorescence with short peduncle, peduncular bract, and rachis, and its range does not overlap with that of *Aiphanes*.

Key to the Species of *Aiphanes*

1a. Stems solitary.
    2a. Hispaniola, Puerto Rico, and the Lesser Antilles; leaflets linear, regularly arranged, and spreading in the same plane   . . . . . *A. minima*.
    2b. Panama, Costa Rica, Trinidad, and South America.
        3a. Stems short and subterranean.
            4a. Leaflets linear.
                5a. Leaflets 5–13 per side; inflorescence with 5–34 flowering branches   . . . . . *A. weberbaueri*.
                5b. Leaflets 14–30 per side; inflorescence spicate.
                    6a. Leaflets 14–16 per side; high elevations in northeastern Peru   . . . . . *A. spicata*.
                    6b. Leaflets 18–30; lowlands of western Colombia   . . . . . *A. acaulis*.
            4b. Leaflets wedge shaped.
                7a. Eastern slopes of the Andes, and adjacent lowlands in Colombia, Ecuador, Peru, and Brazil.
                    8a. Leaflets pale grayish to silvery green on the lower surface   . . . . . *A. ulei*.
                    8b. Leaflets pale green on lower surface   . . . . . *A. weberbaueri*.

7b. Western slopes of the Andes in Ecuador ..... *A. chiribogensis.*
3b. Stems aerial.
  9a. Trinidad, Cordillera de la Costa of Venezuela and adjacent low-
    lands, and the eastern slopes of the Andes and adjacent lowlands
    from Colombia to Bolivia.
    10a. Stems more than 6 cm diameter; leaflets abruptly broadened
      at apex; in rather dry and seasonal habitats, often near human
      dwellings ..... *A. aculeata.*
    10b. Stems less than 6 cm diameter; leaflets linear to wedge
      shaped, but not abruptly broadened at apex; in rain forest.
      11a. Leaflets pale grayish to silvery green on the lower surface
        ..... *A. ulei.*
      11b. Leaflets pale green on lower surface.
        12a. Petiole to 50 cm long; male flowers purple ..... *A. weberbaueri.*
        12b. Petiole 90–105 cm long; male flowers orange ..... *A. deltoidea.*
  9b. Western slopes of the Andes and adjacent lowlands in Colombia
    and Ecuador, and valleys of Ríos Magdalena and Cauca in Co-
    lombia.
    13a. Leaflets abruptly broadened at apex; rather dry and seasonal
      habitats, often near human dwellings ..... *A. aculeata.*
    13b. Leaflets linear to wedge shaped, but not abruptly broadened
      at apex; rain forest.
      14a. Stems 10–21 m tall ..... *A. grandis.*
      14b. Stems to 9 m tall.
        15a. Leaflets broadly wedge shaped; under 800 m elevation
          ..... *A. tricuspidata.*
        15b. Leaflets narrowly wedge shaped or, if broadly wedge
        shaped, then above 800 m elevation.
          16a. Flowering branches of the upper half of the inflo-
            rescence less than 2 cm long, appressed to the rachis,
            the inflorescence superficially resembling a spike
            ..... *A. parvifolia.*
          16b. Flowering branches of the upper half of the inflo-
            rescence much longer than 2 cm.
            17a. Flowering branches thick and appressed to the
              rachis; ripe fruits brown or black, often enclosed
              in jelly ..... *A. gelatinosa.*
            17b. Flowering branches slender, not appressed to the
              rachis; ripe fruits red, not enclosed in jelly.
              18a. Leaflets 12–17 per side; western Ecuador,
                1500–2100 m elevation ..... *A. chiribogensis.*
              18b. Leaflets 23–35 per side; western Colombia,
                2000–2600 m elevation ..... *A. duquei.*
1b. Stems clustered.
  19a. Eastern Andean slopes and adjacent Amazon lowlands in Colombia,
    Ecuador, and Peru.
    20a. Leaves arranged in one plane.
      21a. Fruits greenish white, corky at top; Ecuador ..... *A. verrucosa.*
      21b. Fruits red, smooth; Colombia ..... *A. lindeniana.*

20b. Leaves spirally arranged.
   22a. Leaf sheath with yellow spines   . . . . . *A. erinacea.*
   22b. Leaf sheath with black spines.
      23a. Petiole to 50 cm long; male flowers purple   . . . . . *A. weberbaueri.*
      23b. Petiole 0.9–1 m long; male flowers orange   . . . . . *A. deltoidea.*
19b. Costa Rica, Panama, and western and central Andean slopes.
   24a. Leaves simple, or the apical leaflet very broad and with to 3 basal
      leaflets   . . . . . *A. macroloba.*
   24b. Leaves pinnate with more than 6 leaflets per side.
      25a. Inflorescences spicate; Colombia   . . . . . *A. simplex.*
      25b. Inflorescences branched.
         26a. Fruits densely covered with long, golden spines; leaves
            arranged in one plane; Cordillera Central and Occidental in
            Colombia   . . . . . *A. linearis.*
         26b. Fruits smooth or with short and scattered, black spines;
            leaves usually spirally arranged, occasionally arranged in one
            plane.
            27a. Flowering branches thickened and joined to rachis at
               base; western Andean slopes in southern Colombia and
               northern Ecuador   . . . . . *A. gelatinosa.*
            27b. Flowering branches not thickened and not joined to
               rachis at base.
               28a. Leaflets linear to lanceolate.
                  29a. Leaves arranged in one plane; fruits smooth
                               . . . . . *A. lindeniana.*
                  29b. Leaves spirally arranged; fruits minutely spinulose
                               . . . . . *A. hirsuta.*
               28b. Leaflets narrowly to broadly wedge shaped, widest at
                 apex; leaves spirally arranged.
                 30a. Leaflets abruptly widening at apex; western Ecuador
                   below 600 m elevation   . . . . . *A. eggersii.*
                 30b. Leaflets not abruptly widening near apex.
                   31a. Leaflets with shallowly incised tips.
                     32a. Leaf sheath with yellow spines   . . . . . *A. simplex.*
                     32b. Leaf sheath with black spines.
                         33a. Fruits minutely spinulose or smooth; Costa
                           Rica, Panama, and western slopes of the
                           Andes from Colombia to Ecuador   . . . . . *A. hirsuta.*
                     33b. Fruits smooth; Cordillera Central of
                         Colombia   . . . . . *A. lindeniana.*
                   31b. Leaflets with deeply incised tips; fruits smooth.
                     34a. Flowering branches densely covered in spi-
                       nules; leaflets spreading in different planes; leaf
                       sheath with yellow spines; western slopes of the
                       Andes from southern Colombia to southern
                       Ecuador   . . . . . *A. erinacea.*
                   34b. Flowering branches without spinules; leaflets
                       spreading in the same plane; leaf sheath with
                       black spines; Cordillera Central in Colombia
                                 . . . . . *A. leiostachys.*

Aiphanes acaulis
(Map 359)

Field characters. Stems short and subterranean. Leaves 8–10, arching, to 1.5 m long; *leaflets linear,* 18–30 per side, *regularly arranged and spreading in the same plane.* Inflorescences erect, *spicate;* flowers purple; fruits not known.

Range and habitat. Western Colombia (Chocó); deep shade of lowland rain forest, at 150–700 m elevation. Only two small populations are known.

Notes. Very similar to *Aiphanes spicata,* which differs in having 14–16 grouped leaflets per side, green-yellow flowers and in growing at higher elevations in northeastern Peru.

Aiphanes aculeata
(Map 360, Plate 40)
"Cocos rura" (Bol), "mararay" (Col), "corozo" (Col, Ecu), "macagüita," "marará" (Ven)

Field characters. Stems solitary, 3–10 m tall and 6–10 cm diameter, spiny. Leaves 10–15; leaflets 25–40 per side, irregularly arranged in clusters of 4–6, spreading in different planes, *abruptly widened at apex.* Inflorescences borne among the leaves, cream colored at anthesis; peduncular bract tough, usually spiny; flowering branches numerous; infructescences pendulous; fruits globose, (1–)1.6–2.3 cm diameter, bright red, rarely orange or white, with orange mesocarp.

Range and habitat. Trinidad, Cordillera de la Costa in Venezuela (Miranda, Sucre), and along the Andes in Venezuela (Barinas), Colombia (Antioquia, Casanare, Caldas, Cundinamarca, Meta, Quindío, Tolima, Valle), Peru (Cuzco, Huánuco, Madre de Dios), and Bolivia (Beni, La Paz, Pando, Santa Cruz), extending to adjacent areas of western Brazil (Acre), not found wild in Ecuador; dry forest, between sea level and 1700 m elevation, most common between 500 and 1500 m elevation. The gap in its range in Ecuador coincides with the wetter areas of the Amazon region there.

Uses. The fruits are sold in markets in Colombia, both for the epicarp and mesocarp, which is rich in carotene (Balick and Gerschoff, 1990) and for the seed, used in candies (Bernal, 1992). In the *llanos* of Colombia the endocarps are used to play games (Borchsenius and Bernal, in press). It is cultivated throughout the tropics, often under the name *Aiphanes caryotifolia.*

Notes. This is the most widely distributed and familiar species in the genus.

Aiphanes chiribogensis
(Map 361)

Field characters. Stems solitary, 0–3 m tall and 3–6 cm diameter, with black spines to 6 cm long. Leaves 5–9; leaflets 12–17 per side, in remote clusters of 1–3, wedge shaped. Inflorescences borne among the leaves; flowering branches to 30 (occasionally inflorescence spicate), pendulous, the lower ones often arising almost from the base of the peduncle, *all branches with a long basal flowerless part;* flowers pinkish to purple; fruit globose, 1–1.2 cm diameter, red.

Range and habitat. Western Ecuador (Azuay, Pichincha); montane rain forest, at 1500–2100 m elevation. Locally common in primary or slightly disturbed forest.

Aiphanes deltoidea
(Map 362)
"Shicashica" (Per)

Field characters. Stems solitary or in small clusters, 0.1–2 m tall and to 6 cm diameter, *with gray, flat spines to 6 cm long.* Leaves 10–12, to about 3 m long, including a petiole of about 1 m; leaflets 11–14 per side, in remote clusters of 2–3, wedge shaped. Inflorescences borne among the leaves; *flowering branches 49–60, spreading;* male flowers orange, female flowers greenish; fruits not known.

Range and habitat. Widespread throughout the western Amazon region in Colombia (Amazonas), Peru (Amazonas, Huánuco, Loreto), and Brazil (Amazonas); lowland rain forest in Amazon region at 300 m elevation and montane forests to 1650 m in the Andes of central Peru. Apparently very uncommon.

Notes. Very poorly known. It is closely related to *Aiphanes weberbaueri,* from which it can be distinguished by its longer petiole and orange male flowers.

Aiphanes duquei
(Map 363)

Field characters. Stems solitary, 4–5 m tall and 5 cm diameter, with black spines to 15 cm long. Leaves 8–9; leaflets 23–35 per side, arranged in remote clusters of 3–6, narrowly wedge shaped. Inflorescences borne among the leaves, fiercely armed, horizontally spreading; *flowering branches numerous, with 1–3 basal ones extremely long and hanging far from the rest of the inflorescence, with a basal flowerless part up to 90 cm long;* flowers purple; fruits globose, 0.9–1.2 cm long, with an apical beak 4–6 mm long, red.

Range and habitat. Cordillera Occidental of Colombia (Cauca, Valle); montane rain forest, at 2000–2600 m elevation.

Notes. It may now be restricted to two National Parks, Farallones de Cali and Munchique and the area between them, a total of less than 200 square kilometers.

Aiphanes eggersii
(Map 364)
"Corozo" (Ecu)

Field characters. Stems clustered, up to 10 in a clump, 1–6 m tall and 7–8 cm diameter, with gray or black spines to 10 cm long. Leaves 7–10; leaflets 50–65 per side, mostly in clusters of 4–10, narrowly wedge shaped, abruptly widening at apex. Inflorescences borne among the leaves, cream colored at anthesis; *flowering branches 35–75*; *peduncular bract woody*; fruits globose, 1.8–2 cm diameter, bright red.

Range and habitat. Coastal Ecuador (El Oro, Manabí); dry lowlands, below 600 m elevation. Locally common in semideciduous *Ceiba* forests, but often left over in pastures or planted near houses.

Uses. The mesocarp and seed are edible.

Notes. Very similar to *Aiphanes aculeata* (which is not wild in Ecuador), but is readily distinguished by its clustered habit and more numerous leaflets.

Aiphanes erinacea
(Map 365)

Field characters. Stems clustered, to 15 in a clump, 1.5–5 m tall and 2.5–5 cm diameter, with black spines to 10 cm long. Leaves 3–8, *the sheath and petiole normally with yellow spines*; leaflets 10–19 per side, in remote clusters of 2–3, strongly plicate, narrowly to broadly wedge shaped, *the apex fishtail shaped*. Inflorescences borne among the leaves, with a long peduncle armed with yellow spines; flowering branches few to many, *densely armed with minute hairlike spinules*; peduncular bract with small brown spines; male flowers rose to pale violet outside, white inside; fruits globose, 7–8 mm diameter, dark red, soon turning brown or black.

Range and habitat. Western slopes of the Andes from southern Colombia (Nariño) to southern Ecuador (Carchi, Cotopaxi, Esmeraldas, Los Ríos) and one isolated population from east of the Andes in Ecuador (Napo); primary to slightly disturbed premontane or montane rain forest, at 700–2100 m elevation.

Aiphanes gelatinosa
(Map 366)

Field characters. Stems solitary or clustered, 4–9 m tall and 5.5–10 cm diameter, with black spines to 20 cm long. Leaves 4–11, the lower ones borne horizontally; leaflets 16–30 per side, either linear and almost regularly arranged and spreading in the same plane, or narrowly wedge shaped and arranged in clusters and spreading in different planes. Inflorescences borne among the leaves, *one or three at each node; flowering branches 15–30, thick, closely appressed to the rachis; flowers densely arranged, the areas between them with flexuous spinules*; flowers white or cream; fruits rather closely packed, *often enclosed in jelly*, globose,

about 1.5 cm diameter, red with black apex, *becoming brown or shiny black at maturity*.

Range and habitat. Western slopes of the Andes in southern Colombia (Nariño, Valle) and northern Ecuador (Carchi); premontane to montane rain forest, at 800–1650 m elevation.

Notes. Two morphological variants of this species are known, which might deserve specific recognition. Plants in the northern and southern limits of the range have solitary stems, narrowly wedge-shaped leaflets arranged in clusters, and 3 inflorescences at each node, whereas plants from in between (southern Colombia) have clustered stems, linear leaflets that are almost regularly arranged, and a single inflorescence at each node.

Aiphanes grandis
(Map 367)

Field characters. Stems solitary, 10–21 m tall and to 17 cm diameter, with black spines. Leaves 7–10; *leaflets numerous*, arranged in clusters of 5–8, linear-lanceolate, the middle ones to 80 cm long and 8 cm wide. Inflorescences white at anthesis; peduncular bract long, woody, densely spiny; flowering branches about 200; infructescences pendulous; fruits globose, 2–2.3 cm diameter, dull green, *covered with soft, black, easily removed spinules about 1 mm long*.

Range and habitat. Southwestern Ecuador (El Oro, Loja); montane rain forest, at 1000–2000 m elevation and apparently most abundant around 1500 m. Locally common in a small area and sometimes left in cleared areas where it seems unable to regenerate.

Notes. This is the largest species of *Aiphanes*.

Aiphanes hirsuta
(Map 368, Plates 40 & 41)
"Cirquí" (Col)

Field characters. Stems clustered with up to 8 stems (rarely up to 20), 2–10 m tall and 2.5–10 cm diameter, with black spines. Leaves 4–8; leaflets 9–40 per side, in dense and remote clusters and spreading in different planes, or in loose clusters and appearing almost in the same plane, linear to broadly wedge shaped. Inflorescences borne among the leaves; flowering branches few to numerous, *densely covered with minute soft spinules*; fruits globose, 0.7–2 cm diameter, red or less often purple or white; *endocarp usually conspicuously pitted*.

Range and habitat. Costa Rica and western Panama, along the western slopes of the Andes in Colombia, to northwestern Ecuador, reaching the northern slopes of the Central Cordillera in Colombia (Antioquia); shade of premontane and montane rain forest, at 600–2000 m elevation, occasionally extending into the adjacent lowlands at 100 m. Sometimes left over in pastures, where it does not seem to regenerate.

Notes. One of the most complex species in the genus. Morphological variation forms a continuum, with a general tendency for an increase in size of all structures toward the south. It is divided into 4 subspecies (Borchsenius and Bernal, in press): subsp. *hirsuta*, with fewer than 30 flowering branches and leaf rachis less than 1.5 m, from Costa Rica (Puntarenas) and western Panama (Bocas del Toro, Coclé, Darién, Panamá) to western Colombia (Antioquia, Chocó); subsp. *kalbreyeri*, with linear leaflets arranged almost in the same plane, very thin flowering branches and fruits with minute, scattered, soft spinules, from western Colombia (Antioquia, Risaralda); subsp. *intermedia*, with long, narrowly wedge-shaped leaflets and numerous (60–90) flowering branches, from western Colombia (Chocó, Valle); and subsp. *fosteriorum*, with large stems and long, wedge-shaped leaflets and numerous flowering branches with few spinules, from southwestern Colombia (Valle, Nariño) to northwestern Ecuador (Esmeraldas).

Aiphanes leiostachys
(Map 369)
Field characters. Stems clustered, with up to 10 stems, 3.5–5 m tall and 3 cm diameter. Leaves about 11; leaflets 17–20 per side, in loose clusters of 2–4, appearing almost regularly arranged, *fishtail shaped.* Inflorescences borne among the leaves; flowering branches about 19, spineless; male flowers with purplish petals; fruits not known.
Range and habitat. Northern end of the Cordillera Central in Colombia (Antioquia); montane rain forest, at 1100 m elevation. Known only from a restricted area, this species is an element of the understory that does not survive deforestation and it is now endangered (Bernal, 1989).
Notes. Aiphanes erinacea is similar, but differs in its strongly grouped leaflets and densely spinulose flowering branches and also has a different range.

Aiphanes lindeniana
(Map 370, Plate 41)
"Mararay" (Col)
Field characters. Stems clustered, up to 10 per clump, rarely solitary, 1.5–7 m tall, 3–7(–10) cm diameter, with black spines to 10 cm. Leaves 4–10, *typically arranged in one plane,* rarely in different planes; leaflets 18–45 per side, in clusters of 2–7, *lanceolate to narrowly wedge shaped, normally rigid and strongly plicate, the margins lined with short spinules to 2 mm.* Inflorescences borne among the leaves; flowering branches to 68; flowers white to violet; fruits globose, 1.4–1.6 cm diameter, red to orange.
Range and habitat. Colombia, widespread along the Cordillera Central and Oriental (Antioquia, Boyacá, Caquetá, Cundinamarca, Huila, Norte de Santander, Quindío, Risaralda, Santander, Tolima); a conspicuous element in montane rain forest and often conserved in deforested areas but unable to regenerate there, at 1900–2700 m elevation.

Aiphanes linearis
(Map 371, Plates 41 & 42)
"Chirca," "corozo de agüita" (Col)
Field characters. Stems clustered, with 5–15 stems, 4–12 m tall and 12 cm diameter, *densely covered with black spines to 35 cm long.* Leaves 5–9 *arranged in one plane;* leaflets 35–48 per side, *linear to narrowly wedge shaped,* in clusters of 2–9, spreading in different planes. Inflorescences borne among the leaves; flowering branches 35–80, *conspicuously thickened in the basal part;* male flowers violet; fruits globose to conical, 2.2–4.5 cm long and 1.8–3.5 cm diameter, *densely packed, densely covered with golden spinules to 1 cm long.*
Range and habitat. Colombia, along the western slopes of the Cordillera Occidental and extending to the northern end of the Cordillera Central (Antioquia, Valle); montane rain forest and often conserved in pastures, at 1800–2500 m elevation.
Uses. The seeds are edible.

Aiphanes macroloba
(Map 372, Plate 42)
"Palmito" (Ecu)
Field characters. Stems clustered, 1–3 in a clump, to 2 m tall and 2–3 cm diameter, sparsely covered with black spines to 3 cm, often with suckers high on the stem. Leaves 5–8, *simple or with a large apical leaflet to 82 cm long, with jagged margins and 2–3 basal leaflets,* with soft spines to 1 cm long along the ribs. Inflorescences borne among the leaves, erect, *spicate; fruits ellipsoid,* to 1 cm long and 7 mm diameter, red or orange.
Range and habitat. Along the western slopes of the Andes from northwestern Colombia (Antioquia, Chocó) to northwestern Ecuador (Carchi, Esmeraldas); premontane or montane rain forest, at 600–1400 m elevation, rarely reaching as low as 100 m. It is typical of the shady and humid parts of the forests and does not survive deforestation.
Uses. The Coaiquer Indians in Ecuador eat the palm heart (Borchsenius and Bernal, in press).

Aiphanes minima
(Map 373)
"Macaw palm" (Bar), "grigri" (Mar, Vin, Dom, Luc); glouglou (Mar), "coyore" (PR)
Field characters. *Stems solitary,* (2–)5–18 m tall and 6–20 cm diameter, covered with black spines. Leaflets 18–34 per side, *linear.* Inflorescences borne among the leaves, to 2 m long, creamy white to yellow at anthesis; *flowering branches to 300*; fruits globose, 1.2–1.6 cm long and 1.4–1.7 cm diameter, red.
Range and habitat. Widespread throughout the Greater and Lesser Antilles in the Dominican Republic, Puerto Rico, Dominica, St. Vincent, St. Lucia, Martinique, Barbados and Grenada; limestone hills (Dominican Republic, Puerto Rico), and understory or the subcanopy of seasonal forest or rain forest, sometimes in deep shade.
Uses. The seed is edible. It is widely cultivated as an ornamental, often under the name *Aiphanes erosa.*

Aiphanes parvifolia
(Map 374, Plate 42)
Field characters. *Stems solitary,* (0.1–)1.5–2(–6) m tall and 2.5–3 cm diameter, nonspiny or with a few black spines. *Leaves 4–10, small, usually less than 1 m long*; leaflets 5–16 per side, *inserted in remote clusters of 2* (rarely 3) and spreading in different planes, narrowly to broadly wedge shaped, rarely linear, and then inserted almost regularly in the same plane. Inflorescences borne among the leaves and projected beyond them; *flowering branches numerous, slender, appressed to the rachis, those of the upper half of the inflorescence very short, less than 2 cm long*; fruits globose to ellipsoid, 0.7–1 cm long, orange to red.
Range and habitat. Colombia, in a small area at the northern end of the Cordillera Central (Antioquia) and found once on the western slopes of the Cordillera Occidental (Caldas); understory of primary or disturbed premontane or montane rain forest, at 800–1700 m elevation. Most of its range is subject to severe deforestation, and it does not grow in secondary forest nor in open areas and is thus endangered (Bernal, 1989).

Aiphanes simplex
(Map 375)
Field characters. *Stems clustered, to 20 per clump, very slender,* 2–4 m tall and 1–2 cm diameter, with scattered black spines to 4 cm long. Leaves 4–9; *sheath, petiole, and rachis with yellow flattened spines*; leaflets 9–16 per side, in remote clusters of 2–4, the margins lined with minute spinules. Inflorescences borne among the leaves, *spicate* or rarely with 4–12 flowering branches; male flowers purplish outside; fruits globose, 0.8–1 cm diameter, with a prominent beak, red at maturity.
Range and habitat. Colombia, throughout the Río Cauca basin and extending into adjacent areas in the upper Río Patía basin and into the western slopes of the Cordillera Occidental near Cali and near Frontino, where the passes are relatively low (Antioquia, Cauca, Quindío, Risaralda, Valle); common in patches of primary and secondary premontane or montane rain forest, sometimes near small streams, at 800–2200 m elevation, most abundant near 1600 m, where it may be locally a dominant component of the shrub layer.
Notes. All individuals known from the Río Cauca basin have spicate inflorescences; branched inflorescences are known only from the margins of the range of the species.

Aiphanes spicata
(Map 376)
Field characters. *Stems solitary, short and subterranean.* Leaves 9–12; leaflets 14–16 per side, arranged in clusters of 2–4, linear to narrowly wedge shaped. Inflorescences borne among the leaves, erect, *spicate*; male flowers green-yellow; fruits not known.
Range and habitat. Peru, known only from 2 neighboring localities in San Martín; montane rain forest dominated by *Dictyocaryum lamarckianum,* at 2000 m elevation.
Notes. Very similar to *Aiphanes acaulis,* from which it differs in its larger number of regularly arranged leaflets and purple male flowers; the range is also different.

Aiphanes tricuspidata
(Map 377)
Field characters. Stems solitary, sometimes creeping along the ground, to 4.5 m tall, 2.5–6 cm diameter. Leaves 8–10, *often with yellow spines on sheath and rachis*; leaflets 11–14 per side, *usually in remote clusters of 2, broadly wedge shaped, the apex trilobed, usually rather rough on the lower surface.* Inflorescences borne among the leaves; flowering branches to 52, minutely spinulose; flowers purple; fruits globose, 7–9 mm diameter, with a short beak, reddish brown at maturity.
Range and habitat. Pacific lowlands and adjacent foothills of Colombia (Cauca, Nariño, Valle) and Ecuador (Pichincha, El Oro); understory of lowland rain forest, often along streams, from sea level to 650 m elevation. It does not survive deforestation.

Aiphanes ulei
(Map 378)

"Chontaduro de nutria" (Col), "chontilla" (Ecu)

Field characters. *Stems solitary, short, and subterranean* or to 6 m tall and 2.5–5 cm diameter, with black spines to 7 cm. Leaves 6–15; leaflets 9–14 per side, *inserted in remote clusters of 2* (rarely of 3), broadly wedge shaped, *pale grayish to silvery-green on the lower surface*. Inflorescences borne among the leaves, erect, *normally exerted above the crown*; flowering branches 30–40, strongly appressed to rachis, *with flowers only on the lower surface*; fruits globose, to 7 mm diameter, with a beak 1–2 mm long.

Range and habitat. Western Amazon region and eastern Andean slopes in Colombia (Amazonas, Caquetá, Putumayo), Ecuador (Morona-Santiago, Napo, Pastaza), Peru (Loreto, San Martín), and Brazil (Acre, Amazonas); lowland rain forest, sometimes also in patches of disturbed or even secondary forest, to 1850 m elevation in Ecuador and to 1000 m in Peru.

Aiphanes verrucosa
(Map 379)

Field characters. *Stems clustered*, to 6 per clump, 2–5(–8) m tall and 4–5 cm diameter, densely covered with black spines to 8 cm. Leaves 3–5, *arranged in one plane; leaflets 58–70 per side*, arranged in clusters of 4–11, *narrow, lanceolate, the margins lined with short spinules*. Inflorescences borne among the leaves; flowering branches 50–65; fruits globose, to 3 cm diameter, *greenish white at maturity, first smooth, soon becoming corky at top*.

Range and habitat. Ecuador (Zamora-Chinchipe); primary or disturbed montane forest, at 2200–2800 m elevation.

Notes. Only one population of this species is known, in a small area subject to burning and firewood collecting. It is also likely to occur in the nearby Podocarpus National Park, but has not yet been recorded there.

Aiphanes weberbaueri
(Map 380)

"Chontilla" (Ecu)

Field characters. *Stems solitary*, or rarely with a few suckers at base, *short and subterranean* or to 1.5 m tall and 3.5–6 cm diameter. Leaves 5–13; leaflets 6–24 per side, linear to wedge shaped, in remote clusters of 2–3, or sometimes almost regularly arranged in the same plane (especially so in leaves with linear leaflets). Inflorescences with 5–34 flowering branches; male flowers purple; fruits globose, 0.7–1 cm diameter, red to purple.

Range and habitat. Eastern slopes of the Andes from southern Ecuador (Morona-Santiago, Pastaza) to southern Peru (Amazonas, Junín, Pasco, San Martín), extending into the adjacent Amazon lowlands in northern Peru (Loreto); montane rain forest, to 1950 m elevation. In the lowlands it grows both on lateritic soils and on white sands.

Notes. Variation of this species is not yet fully understood. It is closely related to *Aiphanes deltoidea*, from which it differs in its shorter petiole (to 46 cm vs. 0.9–1 m) and the purple (not orange) male flowers.

56. BACTRIS

This is one of the largest and spiniest American palm genera and it exhibits great morphological diversity. Stems range from short and subterranean to very large, from solitary to clustered, and from nonspiny to very spiny. The most common condition, however, is a medium-sized, spiny, clustered stem. In fact, the origin of the name *Bactris*, from the Greek word "bactron" meaning cane or staff, refers to the stems. Leaves are pinnate or simple and 4–20 in number. Leaflets are usually irregularly arranged in clusters and spread in different planes, but are occasionally regularly arranged. Most species have a short continuation of the leaf sheath above the point of insertion of the petiole, but this is absent in a few species, notably *Bactris gasipaes*. In one pinnate-leafed species, *B. caryotifolia*, the leaflets are wedge shaped and the tips are jagged. Almost all species have spines on the leaves, although in some the spines may be very small and obscure and confined to the tips of the leaflets. In some species the spines are flattened and are yellowish or grayish rather than the more usual black. Inflorescences are spicate or branched to one order and are usually borne among the leaves. The peduncular bract ranges from densely spiny to completely smooth. Flowering branches are usually thin, but they are very slender and filiform in one group of species. Flowers are unisexual, but both male and female flowers are borne on the same inflorescence. They are arranged in threes of one central female and two lateral males, although commonly males occur without the central female. Fruits are one-seeded, variously shaped from globose or ovoid to ellipsoid and they can be green, orange, red, or purple-black. They are usually smooth but several species have spinules or bristles. A group of species with purple-black fruits also has a staminodial ring, an obscure cuplike structure situated between the fruiting corolla and the fruit. The mesocarp is floury or juicy and this, together with the color, is a very good character for identifying the species. The thick, bony endocarp has three pores near the middle and is covered with various types of fibers.

Bactris contains sixty-four species, distributed throughout the tropical parts of the Americas, from southern Mexico to northern Paraguay and also in the Greater Antilles. They are most abundant in lowland rain forest, especially along river margins, but also occur in savannas and disturbed areas.

One of the largest American genera, it is also one of the most poorly known taxonomically. Although we recognize only sixty-four species here, over 250 have been proposed over the last two hundred years (Burret, 1933–34). However, many of these were described by botanists who had an extremely narrow species concept (e.g., Bailey, Barbosa Rodrigues, Burret) and who had limited material available for study. Now, with many more collections in herbaria and more realistic species concepts that take into account the great morphological variation within species, many of the older species are regarded as synonyms (Wessels Boer, 1965; Noblick, 1991; Sanders, 1991; Henderson, 1994; de Nevers et al., in press). There are, however, at least four large species complexes (*B. hirta, B. simplicifrons, B. maraja, B. major*) that are still very poorly understood and may eventually be split into several species, subspecies, or varieties.

KEY TO THE SPECIES OF *BACTRIS*

1a. Mexico, Central America, Pacific coast of Colombia and Ecuador, and lowlands of northern Colombia and Venezuela north and west of the Andes.
   2a. Stems 4–18 m tall and 6–25 cm diameter; leaflets 45–141 per side.
      3a. Sheath, petiole, and rachis with clustered spines; leaflets 45–60 per side   . . . . . *B. setulosa.*
      3b. Sheath, petiole, and rachis spines not clustered, in 3 rows; leaflets 92–141 per side.
         4a. Fruits ovoid, to 5 cm long and 3 cm diameter, widespread   . . . . . *B. gasipaes.*
         4b. Fruits subglobose to obovoid, 1–1.6 cm diameter; Colombia and Venezuela   . . . . . *B. macana.*
   2b. Stems usually less than 4 m tall and 6 cm diameter; leaflets usually fewer than 45 per side.
      5a. Leaf spines flattened, yellowish in the middle and darker at base and tip.
         6a. Leaflets sigmoid; fruits without staminodial ring; Costa Rica, Panama, and Colombia   . . . . . *B. maraja.*
         6b. Leaflets linear-lanceolate; fruits with staminodial ring; Colombia   . . . . . *B. brongniartii.*
      5b. Leaf spines not flattened, usually black.

7a. Flowering branches short, up to 5 cm long, 1–8 in number;
leaves simple and small, less than 70 cm long, or pinnate, and
then with a wide apical leaflet and a few basal leaflets.
  8a. Sheath, petiole, and rachis with a few black spines to 1 cm
long, interspersed with longer ones; Honduras to Panama and
the Pacific coast of Colombia and Ecuador   . . . . . *B. hondurensis.*
  8b. Sheath, petiole, and rachis without spines; Panama (San Blas)
and Colombia (Córdoba).
    9a. Inflorescences with 5–8 flowering branches; Panama (San
Blas)   . . . . . *B. charnleyae.*
    9b. Inflorescences spicate; Colombia (Córdoba)   . . . . . *B. simplicifrons.*
7b. Flowering branches more than 5 cm long, (3–) 5–90 in number;
leaves pinnate, usually with more than 4 leaflets or, if simple,
then more than 70 cm long.
  10a. Leaflets 59–68 per side, hairy on the lower surface; fruits
purple-black, covered in short bristles; eastern Panama, Colombia, and Venezuela   . . . . . *B. pilosa.*
  10b. Leaflets 48 or less per side, or the leaf simple, usually not
hairy on the lower surface; fruits not purple-black, or if purple-
black not covered in short bristles.
    11a. Flowering branches 40–90, very slender and filiform;
fruits spinulose or smooth.
      12a. Leaflets 31–45 per side, ± regularly arranged and
spreading in the same plane; fruits spinulose   . . . . . *B. barronis.*
      12b. Leaflets 16–29 per side, irregularly arranged and
spreading in different planes; fruits smooth   . . . . . *B. glandulosa.*
    11b. Flowering branches 51 or fewer, not filiform; fruits
smooth, rarely with bristles.
      13a. Flowering branches 14–25 cm long and to 3 mm diam-
eter; fruits covered with short, stiff bristles   . . . . . *B. coloniata.*
      13b. Flowering branches shorter and usually thinner (thick
in *B. major*); fruits smooth.
        14a. Fruits purple-black, with or without staminodial
ring; sheath, petiole, and rachis with spines 9–15 cm
long.
          15a. Leaflets not bifid at the tip; sheath, petiole, and
rachis with black spines; fruits ellipsoid to ovoid,
with a staminodial ring   . . . . . *B. major.*
          15b. Leaflets bifid at tip; sheath, petiole, and rachis
with yellowish (but black at base and tip) spines;
fruits depressed-globose   . . . . . *B. guineensis.*
        14b. Fruits orange or red, rarely purple-brown, without a
staminodial ring; sheath, petiole, and rachis with
spines less than 8.5 cm long.
          16a. Fruits purple-brown; leaflets often with spinules
to 2 cm long on the margins; eastern Costa Rica
(Alajuela, Heredia, Limón)   . . . . . *B. longiseta.*
          16b. Fruits orange-red; leaflets either without spinules
on the margins or with short spinules.

17a. Leaves strongly plicate, simple or partially pinnate, or with few (4–14) leaflets per side.
18a. Leaves simple; inflorescences erect ..... *B. militaris*
18b. Leaves pinnate or partially simple; inflorescences recurved.
19a. Nicaragua to Costa Rica; leaves simple
or with a few leaflets; fruits 1.1–1.2 cm
long ..... *B. grayumi.*
19b. Panama; leaves with 4–14 leaflets per
side; fruits 1.4–1.9 cm long ..... *B. kunorum.*
17b. Leaves not strongly plicate, pinnate with 8–
38(–80) leaflets per side.
20a. Peduncular bract covered with fine spines
to 1 cm long; leaflets elliptical to sigmoid;
Panama (Coclé, Panamá, San Blas)
..... *B. panamensis.*
20b. Peduncular bract spines coarse; leaflets not
elliptical to sigmoid.
21a. Sheath, petiole, and rachis with woolly
tomentum; leaflets 17–38(–80) per side;
Costa Rica, Panama, and Pacific coast of
Colombia and Ecuador ..... *B. coloradonis.*
21b. Sheath, petiole, and rachis without
woolly tomentum; leaflets 8–26 per side;
Mexico to Panama.
22a. Leaflets usually pubescent on lower
surface; Mexico to Nicaragua ..... *B. mexicana.*
22b. Leaflets not pubescent on lower surface; Nicaragua to Panama.
23a. Leaflets narrowly elliptical, with
spinules on the margins ..... *B. gracilior.*
23b. Leaflets linear or ovate to oblanceolate with 1–6 mm long spinules
on the margins.
24a. Fruiting calyx 3-lobed; sheath,
petiole and rachis densely spinulose ..... *B. dianeura.*
24b. Fruiting calyx simple; sheath,
petiole, and rachis not densely
spinulose ..... *B. caudata.*
1b. Rest of South America.
25a. Caribbean (Greater Antilles except Puerto Rico), excluding Trinidad
and Tobago ..... *B. plumeriana.*
25b. South America, including Trinidad and Tobago.
26a. Andes from Venezuela (including Coastal Cordillera and Peninsula
de Paria) and Colombia to Bolivia.
27a. Stems 2–4(–6) m tall and 1–3(–4) cm diameter; leaflets few or
leaf simple ..... *B. corossilla.*

27b. Stems 4–18 m tall and 6–25 cm diameter; leaflets 45–141 per side.

    28a. Sheath, petiole, and rachis with clustered spines; leaflets 45–60 per side   . . . . . *B. setulosa.*

    28b. Sheath, petiole, and rachis spines not clustered, in 3 rows; leaflets 92–141 per side.

        29a. Fruits ovoid, to 5 cm long and 3 cm diameter   . . . . . *B. gasipaes.*

        29b. Fruits subglobose to obovoid, 1–1.6 cm diameter   . . . . . *B. macana.*

26b. Rest of South America east of the Andes.

    30a. Amazon region and adjacent northern areas east and south of Andes (*llanos* in Colombia and Venezuela, Trinidad and Tobago), and adjacent southern areas south of the Amazon region (*llanos* of Bolivia, *pantanal, planalto* of Brazil, *chaco* of Paraguay).

        31a. Stems 4–18 m tall and 6–25 cm diameter; leaflets 45–141 per side.

            32a. Sheath, petiole, and rachis with clustered spines; leaflets 45–60 per side   . . . . . *B. setulosa.*

            32b. Sheath, petiole, and rachis spines not clustered, in 3 rows; leaflets 92–141 per side.

                33a. Fruits ovoid, to 5 cm long and 3 cm diameter   . . . . . *B. gasipaes.*

                33b. Fruits subglobose to obovoid, 1–1.6 cm diameter . . . . . *B. macana.*

        31b. Stems usually less than 4 m tall and 6 cm diameter; leaflets usually fewer than 45 per side.

            34a. Flowering branches densely covered with whitish, woolly hairs; leaf spines clustered and pointing in various directions.

                35a. Fruits oblong-ovoid, 1.5 cm long   . . . . *B. balanophora.*

                35b. Fruits widely obovoid, 0.7–1 cm long   . . . . *B. ptariana.*

            34b. Flowering branches not covered with woolly hairs; leaf spines not clustered.

                36a. Fruits globose, 0.5–0.8 cm diameter (rarely obovoid and to 1 cm diameter), red or orange; flowering branches few, 1–5(–13), short, 2.5–7 cm long, borne on a short rachis; stems slender, 0.1–2(–3) m long and 0.3–1(–2) cm diameter.

                    37a. Leaflets 30–35 per side, narrowly linear; flowering branches 7–13; Brazil (Pará)   . . . . . *B. syagroides.*

                    37b. Leaflets 2–30 per side, linear, linear-lanceolate or sigmoid, or commonly leaf simple; flowering branches 1–5(–8).

                        38a. Leaves usually spiny with rounded spines to 5 cm long; fruits spinulose or smooth; leaflets often hairy.

                          39a. Fruits spinulose; widespread   . . . . . *B. hirta.*

                          39b. Fruits smooth; French Guiana, Brazil (eastern Amazonas, Pará)   . . . . . *B. cuspidata.*

                        38b. Leaves usually lacking spines except for spinules at leaflet tip, or, if spiny then with short, flattened

spines to 1.5 cm long; fruits smooth; leaflets not
hairy.

40a. Peduncular bract densely spiny; blade with
prominent cross-veins; French Guiana and
Suriname   . . . . . *B. aubletiana.*

40b. Peduncular bract not spiny; leaflets without
cross-veins.

41a. Petiole densely reddish brown–tomentose;
inflorescence erect in flower and fruit . . . . . *B. killipii.*

41b. Petiole ± smooth; inflorescences curved
down in flower and fruit   . . . . . *B. simplicifrons.*

36b. Fruits various but more than 1 cm diameter; flowering
branches one to numerous, when few usually longer
than 2.5–7 cm, borne on a longer rachis; stems usually
stouter, or short and subterranean.

42a. Flowering branches 10–89, filiform, with the female
flowers regularly arranged along one side on basal
part of branch; fruits orange-red or yellowish, usually
spinulose.

43a. Leaves simple; stems short and subterranean,
rarely to 2 m tall   . . . . . *B. trailiana.*

43b. Leaves pinnate; stems either short and subterranean or tall and aerial.

44a. Fruits not spinulose; central Amazon region
in Brazil (Amazonas)   . . . . . *B. tefensis.*

44b. Fruits spinulose.

45a. Leaflets linear, regularly arranged, and
spreading in one plane; Suriname and
French Guiana   . . . . . *B. rhapidacantha.*

45b. Leaflets linear, linear-lanceolate, or sigmoid, irregularly arranged and spreading in
different planes.

46a. Stems short and subterranean, rarely to
1 m or more tall on older plants; flowering branches usually without spinules
                                        . . . . . *B. acanthocarpa.*

46b. Stems aerial, 1.5–6 m tall; flowering
branches usually with spinules.

47a. Leaflets linear, 61–70 cm long and
2.5–3 cm wide; fruits 1.2–2 cm diameter; the Guianas and eastern Brazil
(Amazonas, Pará)   . . . . . *B. acanthocarpoides.*

47b. Leaflets oblanceolate to sigmoid, 35–
60 cm long and 2.5–7 cm wide; fruits
to 2 cm diameter; the Guianas, Peru
to Brazil   . . . . . *B. pliniana.*

42b. Flowering branches fewer than 50, not slender and
filiform, not with the female flowers as above; fruits
variously colored, usually not spinulose.

48a. Fruits red, orange-red, dark rosy, rosy red, magenta-purple, yellowish brown, brownish, or green, smooth or with fleshy projections or bristles.

 49a. Sheath, petiole and rachis densely reddish brown–tomentose; fruits with either fleshy projections or bristles.

  50a. Flowering branches 14–25 cm long and to 3 mm diameter; leaf spines yellowish brown to black; fruits covered with short bristles; northeastern Peru (Amazonas)   . . . . . *B. coloniata.*

  50b. Flowering branches 6–12 cm long and 1 mm diameter; leaf spines black; fruits either with short bristles or fleshy projections.

   51a. Fruits dark rosy, rosy red, or magenta-purple, covered with fleshy projections
      . . . . . *B. constanciae.*

   51b. Fruits brownish, covered with short bristles   . . . . . *B. turbinocarpa.*

 49b. Sheath, petiole, and rachis not densely tomentose; fruits smooth.

  52a. Leaf spines flattened, gray or gray-black (darker at tip and base); fruits 5–8 mm long
     . . . . . *B. campestris.*

  52b. Leaf spines not flattened, black; fruits 0.7–1.5 cm long.

   53a. Fruits pear-shaped, markedly beaked, 2.5–3 cm long   . . . . . *B. fissifrons.*

   53b. Fruits depressed-globose, 1–2 cm long.

    54a. Leaflets 6–10 per side, lanceolate to almost sigmoid   . . . . . *B. oligoclada.*

    54b. Leaflets 33–58 per side, linear
      . . . . . *B. riparia.*

48b. Fruits purple-black, usually smooth.

 55a. Fruits without a staminodial ring.

  56a. Leaflets whitish brown on lower surface, briefly bifid apically.

   57a. Leaf spines to 4 cm long; Colombia (Amazonas), Venezuela (Amazonas), Peru (Loreto) and Brazil (Amazonas)   . . . . . *B. bidentula.*

   57b. Leaf spines to 10 cm long; Brazil (Mato Grosso, Rondônia), Bolivia (Beni, Santa Cruz) and Paraguay   . . . . . *B. glaucescens.*

  56b. Leaflets green on lower surface, bifid apically only in *B. elegans.*

   58a. Inflorescences spicate or forked.

    59a. Leaflets bifid at the tip, 1.5–2 cm wide   . . . . . *B. elegans.*

    59b. Leaflets not bifid at the tip, 3–4 cm wide, or leaf simple   . . . . . *B. tomentosa.*

58b. Inflorescences with 3–14 flowering
branches.
  60a. Leaf spines usually yellowish brown
  at middle and darker at tip and base;
  fruits widely depressed obovoid, 1–2
  cm diameter   . . . . . *B. maraja.*
  60b. Leaf spines not flattened, black; fruits
  depressed-globose to widely obovoid,
  markedly beaked, 2–2.5 cm diameter.
    61a. Sheath, petiole and rachis brown-
    tomentose; fruiting corolla spi-
    nulose   . . . . . *B. macroacantha.*
    61b. Sheath, petiole and rachis not to-
    mentose; fruiting corolla not spi-
    nulose   . . . . . *B. corossilla.*
55b. Fruits with a staminodial ring.
  62a. Leaf spines flattened, yellowish-brown at
  middle and darker at tip and base; flowering
  branches 15–33   . . . . . *B. brongniartii.*
  62b. Leaf spines not flattened, usually black;
  flowering branches 1–17.
    63a. Leaflets 16–52 per side or leaf simple;
    leaf rachis 0.4–2 m long.
      64a. Leaves simple or rarely partially pin-
      nate   . . . . . *B. bifida.*
      64b. Leaves pinnate with numerous leaf-
      lets.
        65a. Fruits very congested; flowering
        branches 1–3   . . . . . *B. concinna.*
        65b. Fruits loosely spaced; flowering
        branches (1–)2–17   . . . . . *B. major.*
    63b. Leaflets 2–11 per side; leaf rachis 8–55
    cm long.
      66a. Leaflets 8–11 per side; fruits 2.5–3
      cm long   . . . . . *B. gastoniana.*
      66b. Leaflets 1–3 per side; fruits 1.7–2 cm
      long   . . . . . *B. oligocarpa.*
30b. Atlantic coast of Brazil (Rio Grande do Norte to Rio Grande do
Sul).
67a. Leaflets wedge shaped with jagged apex   . . . . . *B. caryotifolia.*
67b. Leaflets not wedge shaped, with smooth apex, or leaf simple.
  68a. Fruits densely covered with short, bulbous-based spines;
  leaflets numerous, linear, gray on lower surface   . . . . . *B. hatschbachii.*
  68b. Fruits not densely covered with bulbous-based spines; leaflets not numerous, linear and gray on lower surface.
    69a. Flowering branches 10–46, slender, filiform, with the
    female flowers regularly arranged along one side on
    basal part of the flowering branches; fruits orange or
    red, spinulose   . . . . . *B. acanthocarpa.*

69b. Flowering branches fewer, not slender and filiform,
    not with the female flowers regularly arranged; fruits var-
    iously colored, usually not spinulose.
    70a. Flowering branches few, 1–6.
        71a. Leaf spines yellowish; leaflets regularly arranged
            and spreading in the same plane; fruits ellipsoid
                           . . . . . *B. horridispatha.*
        71b. Leaf spines black or brown; fruits globose.
            72a. Inflorescences spicate   . . . . . *B. bahiensis.*
            72b. Inflorescences with 2 or more flowering
                branches.
                73a. Sheath, petiole, and rachis densely covered
                    with white, woolly tomentum; flowering
                    branches 4–6   . . . . . *B. soeiroana.*
                73b. Sheath, petiole, and rachis not densely to-
                    mentose; flowering branches usually 4 or
                    fewer.
                    74a. Lower surface of leaves velvety; fruits
                        1.2–1.5 cm diameter, reddish purple
                             . . . . . *B. pickelii.*
                    74b. Lower surface of leaves not velvety;
                        fruits 0.5(–1) cm diameter, orange-red or
                        red, spinulose   . . . . . *B. hirta.*
    70b. Flowering branches numerous, usually more than 6.
        75a. Leaf spines black to reddish brown.
             76a. Sheath, petiole, and rachis with rounded,
                black spines; lower surface of leaflets gray
                             . . . . . *B. vulgaris.*
             76b. Sheath, petiole, and rachis with flattened,
                black or brown spines; lower surface of leaflets
                green   . . . . . *B. ferruginea.*
        75b. Leaf spines yellowish.
             77a. Stems less than 2 cm diameter; leaflets 25 or
                fewer per side; fruits yellow   . . . . . *B. glassmanii.*
             77b. Stems 4–10 cm diameter; leaflets 30 or more
                per side; fruits purple-black.
                78a. Inflorescences with 30 or more flowering
                    branches   . . . . . *B. ferruginea.*
                78b. Inflorescences with 12–27 flowering
                    branches   . . . . . *B. setosa.*

Bactris acanthocarpa
(Map 381, Plates 42 & 43)
"Marajá," "pupunha de mata" (Bra),
"chontaduro de los peces" (Col), "ñejilla"
(Per), "ceguera" (Ven)
Field characters. Stems solitary or clustered, *short
and subterranean* but occasionally reaching 1 m
tall and 3–6 cm diameter, then the internodes
very close together and nonspiny. Leaves 5–
15, pinnate; sheath, petiole, and rachis

scarcely to densely covered with black spines
to 8(–15) cm long; leaflets (3–)12–33 per
side, linear-lanceolate to almost sigmoid, irregularly arranged and spreading in different
planes. Inflorescences with 10–46 *slender, filiform flowering branches*; peduncular bract moderately to densely covered with black spines to
1 cm long; fruits very widely obovoid, 1–1.8 cm
diameter, orange or red, *covered with short spinules.*

Range and habitat. Amazon region of Colombia (Amazonas, Putumayo, Vaupés), Venezuela (Amazonas, Bolívar), the Guianas, Ecuador (Napo), Peru (Junín, Loreto, Madre de Dios, Pasco), Brazil (Acre, Amazonas, Maranhão, Pará, Rondônia), and Bolivia (Beni, Pando, Santa Cruz), and also in the Atlantic coastal forest of Brazil (Alagoas, Bahia, Espírito Santo, Paraíba, Pernambuco, Sergipe); lowland forest on noninundated soils at low elevations, occasionally to 1000 m.

Uses. The fruits are occasionally used, the mesocarp to make a medicine and the endocarps as beads.

Notes. Two leaf forms are recognized as varieties (Henderson, 1994); var. *acanthocarpa*, with more numerous (to 33), longer (45–60 cm), linear-lanceolate leaflets, widespread in the Amazon region and Atlantic coastal forest; and var. *intermedia*, with fewer (12–20), shorter (20–30 cm), sigmoid leaflets from French Guiana, Suriname, and Brazil (Amazonas).

A hybrid between this species and *Bactris oligoclada* is known from Venezuela (Wessels Boer, 1971).

Bactris acanthocarpoides
(Map 382)
"Marajá" (Bra), "ti-wara" (FrG), "jawi" (Guy), "hanaimaka" (Sur)
Field characters. Stems clustered, spiny, 2–4 m tall and 2–4 cm diameter. Leaves 8–15, pinnate; sheath, petiole, and rachis moderately to densely covered with somewhat flattened, black spines to 7 cm long; leaflets 20–37 per side, linear, irregularly arranged, and spreading in different planes. Inflorescences with *25–89 very slender and filiform flowering branches*; peduncular bract covered with somewhat soft, black, or brown spines, with longer, black spines interspersed; fruits very widely obovoid, 1.2–2 cm diameter, orange, yellowish, or red, *covered with short spinules.*
Range and habitat. Northeastern Amazon region of the Guianas and Brazil (Amazonas, Pará); lowland rain forest on noninundated soils or occasionally near streams, at low elevations.
Notes. Related to *Bactris acanthocarpa.*

Bactris aubletiana
(Map 383)
"Faux wi blanc" (FrG), "yuyba" (Sur)
Field characters. Stems clustered or solitary, 0.6–2 m tall and 0.3–0.5 cm diameter. Leaves 10–11, *simple, usually nonspiny (except for spinules at the tips); leaf blade bifid, with prominent cross-veins.* Inflorescences small with *1–3 flowering branches*; peduncular bract moderately to densely covered with soft, erect, black spines to 5 mm long; *fruits globose, 0.5–0.7 cm diameter, orange.*

Range and habitat. Suriname and French Guiana; lowland rain forest on noninundated soils, at low elevations.
Notes. Related to both *Bactris hirta* and *B. simplicifrons.*

Bactris bahiensis
(Map 384)
"Ouricana" (Bra)
Field characters. Stems clustered or occasionally solitary, nonspiny, 1–3 m tall and 0.5–1 cm diameter. Leaves 6–12, pinnate; sheath, petiole, and rachis nonspiny or with short, black spines to 8 mm long; leaflets 2–7 per side, linear, regularly or irregularly arranged and spreading in the same plane. *Inflorescences small, erect, spicate*; peduncular bract nonspiny, brown-tomentose; fruits globose, to 1.5 cm long and 1–1.2 cm diameter, yellow-green.
Range and habitat. Atlantic coast of Brazil (Bahia, Espírito Santo); lowland rain forest in noninundated areas, below 350 m elevation.
Notes. Related to *Bactris simplicifrons.*

Bactris balanophora
(Map 385)
"Marajá" (Bra), "chontaduro paso" (Col), "maswa" (Guy), "cubarro" (Ven)
Field characters. Stems clustered, 1.5–7 m tall and 2–3 cm diameter. Leaves 5–8, pinnate; sheath, petiole, and rachis with somewhat flattened, black spines to 3 cm long, *tending to be clustered and pointing in different directions*; leaflets 15–21 per side, linear-lanceolate, irregularly arranged, and spreading in different planes. Inflorescences with (5–)7–15 flowering branches, *densely covered with whitish, woolly hairs*; peduncular bract moderately to densely covered with stiff, black spines to 1 cm long; fruits oblong-ovoid, 1.5 cm long and 0.7–0.8 cm diameter, orange.
Range and habitat. Northern Amazon region in Colombia (Amazonas, Guainía, Vaupés), Venezuela (Amazonas) Guyana, and Brazil (Amazonas, Pará), usually north of the Amazon river; lowland rain forest in noninundated areas, below 600 m elevation.
Notes. One of the least specialized species in the genus (Sanders, 1991), because of its fruit fibers and shape. It is vegetatively similar to *Bactris ptariana*, but the fruits of this species are quite different.

Bactris barronis
(Map 386)
"Lata" (Col), "alar" (Pan: Kuna)
Field characters. Stems clustered, forming dense colonies, 2–8 m tall and 3.5–8 cm diameter. Leaves 4–9, pinnate; sheath, petiole, and rachis densely covered with black spines to 11

cm long; leaflets 31–45 per side, linear to linear-lanceolate, *more or less regularly arranged and spreading in the same plane, with prominent cross-veins. Inflorescences with 80–90 slender, filiform flowering branches*; peduncular bract densely covered with black spines to 1 cm long; fruits subglobose, 1–1.6 cm diameter, orange-red, *covered with short bristles.*

Range and habitat. Eastern Panama (Canal Area, Darién, Panamá, San Blas) and northwestern Colombia (Antioquia, Chocó, Valle); lowland rain forest in noninundated areas, to 700 m elevation.

Uses. In Panama the split stems are used to make floors.

Notes. A hybrid is known from Colombia between this species and *Bactris gasipaes* (Bernal and Henderson, in prep.).

Bactris bidentula
(Map 387)
"Chontilla" (Bol), "marajá de igapó" (Bra), "cubarro" (Ven)

Field characters. Stems clustered and forming dense clumps, spiny, 1.7–4 m tall and 3–4.5 cm diameter. Leaves 3–16, pinnate; sheath, petiole, and rachis densely whitish tomentose, moderately covered with *somewhat clustered,* black spines 3–4 cm long; leaflets 24–45 per side, linear to lanceolate, *briefly bifid apically, whitish brown on lower surface,* irregularly arranged and spreading in different planes. Inflorescences with 20–50 flowering branches; peduncular bract whitish brown with a few black spines to 2 cm long; fruits depressed-globose, 0.8–1.5 cm diameter, purple-black.

Range and habitat. Amazon region of Colombia (Amazonas), Venezuela (Amazonas), Peru (Loreto), Brazil (Amazonas, western Pará, Roraima); along margins of blackwater (occasionally white water) streams and rivers in areas liable to inundation.

Notes. Closely related to *Bactris glaucescens,* which occurs to the south, and to *B. guineensis,* which occurs to the north. The three species have a linear distribution.

Bactris bifida
(Map 388)
"Ubim de espinho" (Bra), "ñeja negra" (Per)

Field characters. Stems clustered, 1–4 m tall and 1–2 cm diameter, spiny. *Leaves simple,* rarely partly pinnate basally; sheath, petiole, and rachis moderately to densely covered with blackish brown, rounded to slightly flattened, spines to 7 cm long; *blade long and narrow, strongly plicate. Inflorescences with 1–2 flowering branches*; peduncular bract sparsely covered with black spines to 5 mm long; fruits narrowly ellipsoid or oblong-ellipsoid, 2.5 cm long and

1–1.5 cm diameter, *purple-black with juicy mesocarp; fruiting perianth with staminodial ring.*

Range and habitat. Western Amazon region in Colombia (Amazonas), Peru (Huánuco, Loreto, San Martin, Ucayali), and Brazil (Acre, Amazonas, Mato Grosso); lowland forest in wet places near streams and rivers, below 600 m elevation.

Bactris brongniartii
(Map 389, Plate 43)
"Marajá" (Bra), "chacarrá," "cubarro" (Col), "bango palm" (Guy), "ñejilla" (Per), "caña negra" (Ven)

Field characters. Stems clustered, *often forming large colonies by rhizomes,* spiny, 3–6(–9) m tall and 3.5–5(–8) cm diameter. Leaves 4–6, pinnate; sheath, petiole, and rachis moderately to densely covered with *flattened spines, yellowish brown in middle, black at base and tip;* leaflets (10–)23–34 per side, *linear-lanceolate, briefly bifid at the tip,* irregularly arranged and stiffly spreading in different planes. Inflorescences with 15–33 flowering branches; peduncular bract sparsely to densely covered with flattened, yellowish spines to 2 cm long; fruits depressed-globose, 1.5 cm diameter, *purple-black, juicy; fruiting perianth with staminodial ring.*

Range and habitat. Amazon region and adjacent areas in Colombia (Amazonas, Caquetá, Guainía, Guaviare, Meta, Putumayo, Vaupés, Vichada), Venezuela (Amazonas, Anzoátegui, Bolívar, Delta Amacuro), the Guianas, Peru (Loreto, Madre de Dios, Ucayali), Brazil (Acre, Amapá, Amazonas, Maranhão, Mato Grosso, Mato Grosso do Sul, Pará, Rondônia, Roraima), Bolivia (Beni, Pando, Santa Cruz), and reaching northern Colombia (Antioquia, Chocó, Santander); very common along river margins or seasonally inundated areas, at low elevations.

Uses. The fleshy fruits are commonly eaten.

Notes. Previously known under the incorrect name of *Bactris maraja.*

Bactris campestris
(Map 390, Plate 44)
"Mumbaca branca" (Bra), "cubarro" (Ven)

Field characters. Stems clustered and forming small clumps, spiny, 1–5 m tall and 3–4 cm diameter. Leaves 2–5, pinnate; *sheath, petiole, and rachis gray to ferruginous tomentose, with reddish brown or black scales, moderately covered with flattened, gray or gray-black (darker at base and tip) spines to 4 cm long;* leaflets 17–32 per side, linear or linear-lanceolate, irregularly arranged and spreading in different planes. Inflorescences with 8–39 *reddish brown tomentose flowering branches*; peduncular bract gray or brown-tomentose, with gray or brown spines to 1.5

cm long; fruits *globose, 5–8 mm diameter, red or orange-red.*

Range and habitat. Northeastern Amazon region in Colombia (Guainía, Vichada), Venezuela (Amazonas), the Guianas, Trinidad, and Brazil (Amapá, Amazonas, Pará, Roraima); often in poorly drained, wet areas in open white-sand savannas or adjacent forests on white sand, at low elevations or rarely to 800 m.

Bactris caryotifolia
(Map 391, Plate 44)
"Tucum branco" (Bra)
Field characters. Stems clustered, spiny, 1–1.5 m tall and 1–2 cm diameter. Leaves 10–12, pinnate; sheath, petiole, and rachis moderately covered with yellowish (darker at base and tip) spines to 5 cm long; leaflets 11–13 per side, *wedge shaped with broad, jagged apical margins, silvery gray on the lower surface,* irregularly arranged and spreading in different planes. Inflorescences with 4–6 flowering branches; peduncular bract moderately covered with black to yellow spines to 1.5 cm long; fruits globose or obovoid, 1–1.8 cm diameter, purple-black.
Range and habitat. Atlantic coast of Brazil (Bahia, Espírito Santo, Rio de Janeiro); primary and secondary lowland rain forest in noninundated areas, at low elevations.
Notes. This is a remarkable species, being the only *Bactris* with wedge-shaped leaflets with jagged apical margins. In this respect it resembles the other American genus with "fishtail" leaflets, *Aiphanes,* and also the Old World *Caryota* (hence the specific epithet).

Bactris caudata
(Map 392)
Field characters. Stems solitary or clustered, 1–5 m tall and 2–2.5 cm diameter. Leaves 5–8, pinnate; sheath, petiole, and rachis with few black spines to 7 cm long; leaflets 19–26 per side, linear to ovate, *with 1–3 mm long spinules on the margins,* irregularly arranged and spreading in different planes. Inflorescences with 18–31 flowering branches; peduncular bract sparsely to densely covered with short black spines; fruits obovoid, with prominent beak, 0.9–1.3 cm long and 1.1–1.2 cm diameter, orange-red.
Range and habitat. Southern Nicaragua (Río San Juan, Zelaya), Costa Rica (Alajuela, Cartago, Heredia), and Panama (Bocas del Toro); lowland rain forest, below 800 m elevation.

Bactris charnleyae
(Map 393)
Field characters. Stems clustered, 0.5–2 m tall

and 6–9 mm diameter. Leaves 3–6, *simple; sheath, petiole, and rachis without spines;* blade bifid, to 20 cm wide at middle, the lobes to 20 cm long. Inflorescences with *5–8 flowering branches; peduncular bract moderately covered with fine, straight spines to 2 cm long;* fruits globose, 5–8 mm diameter, orange or yellow.
Range and habitat. Central Panama (San Blas); lowland rain forest, to 300 m elevation.

Bactris coloniata
(Map 394)
"Uvito" (Pan)
Field characters. Stems clustered, spiny, forming open colonies, 3.5–7 m tall and 2–5 cm diameter. Leaves 5–7, pinnate; sheath, petiole, and rachis brown-tomentose, moderately to densely covered with yellowish brown to black, somewhat flattened, spines; leaflets (4–)14–23 per side, linear-lanceolate, elliptic or slightly sigmoid, irregularly arranged and spreading in different planes. *Inflorescences with 9–16, 14–25 cm long and to 3 mm thick flowering branches;* peduncular bract densely covered with appressed, brown, flattened spines; fruits depressed-globose, 1.5–2.5 cm diameter, yellowish brown, *covered with short, stiff, brown bristles (but becoming smooth at maturity).*
Range and habitat. Eastern Panama (Canal Area, Colón, Darién, Panamá, San Blas) and northwestern Colombia (Antioquia, Chocó), and a disjunct population east of the Andes in Peru (Amazonas); lowland rain forest in noninundated areas, to 700 m elevation.

Bactris coloradonis
(Map 395)
"Chacarrá" (Col), "coyolito" (Nic)
Field characters. Stems solitary or clustered, spiny, 1.5–10 m tall and 3–8 cm diameter. Leaves 2–6, pinnate or rarely simple; sheath, petiole, and rachis white-woolly tomentose, moderately to densely covered with black spines to 8.5 cm long; leaflets 17–38(–80) per side, linear-lanceolate, irregularly arranged and spreading in different planes, *usually with prominent cross veins.* Inflorescences with 20–51 flowering branches; peduncular bract sparsely to densely covered with spreading, black or brown spines to 1 cm long; fruits widely obovoid, to 1.5 cm long and 1.4–1.5 cm diameter, orange-red, *the fruiting corolla truncate.*
Range and habitat. Costa Rica (Heredia, Limón), Panama (Canal Area, Coclé, Colón, Darién, Panamá, San Blas, Veraguas), and the Pacific coast of Colombia (Antioquia, Chocó, Nariño, Valle) and Ecuador (Esmeraldas); lowland rain forest in noninundated areas, below 900 m elevation.

Bactris concinna
(Map 396, Plate 44)
"Marajaú" (Bol), "marajá" (Bra), "chontilla"
(Ecu), "ñejilla" (Per)
Field characters. Stems clustered, often forming
large colonies, (0.5–)2–8 m tall and 1.5–5 cm
diameter. Leaves 3–10, pinnate; sheath, petiole, and rachis densely covered with black
spines to 2 cm long, interspersed with fewer,
black or yellowish, spines to 10 cm long; leaflets 16–52 per side, *linear, linear-lanceolate, or
sigmoid, regularly arranged and spreading in the
same plane,* or less often irregularly arranged
and spreading in different planes. *Inflorescences
with 1–3(–6) flowering branches;* peduncular
bract moderately covered with black spines to
1.5 cm long; *fruits congested, irregularly and narrowly obovoid, 2–4.5 cm long and 1–2.5 cm diameter, purple-black; fruiting perianth with staminodial
ring.*
Range and habitat. Western Amazon region in
Colombia (Amazonas, Guainía, Putumayo),
Ecuador (Napo), Peru (Loreto, Madre de
Dios, San Martín, Ucayali), Brazil (Acre, Amazonas, northern Mato Grosso, Pará, Rondônia), and Bolivia (Beni, La Paz, Santa Cruz);
lowland rain forest along river margins and in
other wet places.
Uses. The fleshy fruits are edible and sold in local markets; they are also fed to domestic animals.
Notes. Depending on leaflet and fruit size, the
following three varieties are recognized (Henderson, 1994): var. *concinna*, with linear, regularly arranged, 45–70 cm long leaflets and
3.5–4.5 cm long fruits; var. *inundata*, with linear, regularly arranged, 15–52 cm long leaflets
and 2–2.5 cm long fruits; and var. *sigmoidea*,
with sigmoid, irregularly arranged leaflets. The
former two varieties can sometimes be found
together; the latter occurs more in the south
of the range of the species.

Bactris constanciae
(Map 397, Plate 45)
"Mumbaca" (Bra)
Field characters. Stems clustered, spiny, 1.5–5 m
tall and 2.5–5 cm diameter. Leaves 5–8, pinnate; *petiole elongate, to 1.4 m long, brown-tomentose;* sheath, petiole, and rachis lacking spines,
or with a few black spines to 7 cm long; leaflets
14–22 per side, *sigmoid, in widely spaced clusters*
and spreading in different planes. Inflorescences with 13–18 flowering branches; peduncular bract with a few, black spines to 1 cm
long; fruits globose, 1.5–2.5 cm diameter, *dark
red, rosy red, or magenta-purple, covered with fleshy,
spiny projections.*
Range and habitat. Northeastern Amazon region
in the Guianas and Brazil (Amazonas, Pará);

lowland rain forest in noninundated areas, to
350 m elevation.
Notes. This species has remarkable fruits, and is
generally uncommon throughout its range.

Bactris corossilla
(Map 398)
"Marajá" (Bra), "coquito" (Col), "ñejilla"
(Per), "macanillo" (Ven)
Field characters. Stems clustered, rarely solitary,
spiny, 2–4(–6) m tall and 1–3(–4) cm diameter. Leaves 6–8, simple or pinnate; sheath, petiole, and rachis with a moderate to dense covering of black spines to 5 cm long, *tending to be
grouped; blade simple or sometimes pinnate in the
lower half and then the leaflets linear,* clustered,
and spreading in different planes. Inflorescences with 4–14 flowering branches; peduncular bract densely covered with spreading,
soft, flexuous, brown spines; *fruits depressed-
globose with a prominent beak,* 2–2.5 cm long and
1.7–2 cm diameter, yellow, becoming purple-
black.
Range and habitat. Coastal Range and Andes of
Venezuela (Apure, Carabobo, Mérida, Táchira) and Colombia (Norte de Santander),
south to the western Amazon region of Colombia (Amazonas, Guainía, Meta, Vaupés),
Venezuela (Amazonas, Bolívar), Ecuador (Morona-Santiago, Napo, Pastaza), Peru (Amazonas, Loreto, San Martín, Ucayali), and Brazil
(Acre); lowland, premontane, or montane
rain forest on well-drained slopes, to 1400 m
elevation.
Notes. A rather heterogeneous and poorly
known species which may, on further study, be
split into two or more separate species.

Bactris cuspidata
(Map 399)
Field characters. Stems clustered, 1–1.5 m tall
and 6–8 mm diameter, usually without spines.
Leaves 4–5, pinnate; *sheath, petiole, and rachis
whitish tomentose,* moderately to densely covered with black spines to 2 cm long; leaflets 6–
13 per side, linear-lanceolate to sigmoid, irregularly arranged and spreading in different
planes, *scarcely to densely hairy on the lower surface. Inflorescences with 2–8 short (2.5–3.5 cm)
flowering branches; peduncular bract densely covered
with soft, straight, black spines to 1 cm long;* fruits
globose to obovoid, to 7 mm diameter, red.
Range and habitat. Central Amazon region in
French Guiana and Brazil (Amapá, Amazonas,
Pará); lowland rain forest on well-drained
soils, at low elevations or rarely to 800 m.
Notes. Related to both *Bactris hirta* and *B. simplicifrons;* some populations are of possible hybrid origin.

Bactris dianeura
(Map 400)

Field characters. Stems clustered, forming small colonies of 2–8 stems, 2–5(–10) m tall and 1–3 cm diameter, spiny. Leaves 5–7, pinnate; sheath, petiole, and rachis densely covered with black or reddish brown spines to 6.5 cm long; leaflets 14–20 per side, lanceolate to oblanceolate, *with spinules to 6 mm long on the margins,* usually with cross veins visible, irregularly arranged and spreading in different planes. Inflorescences with 7–17 flowering branches; peduncular bract densely covered with brown or black spines to 2 cm long; fruits subglobose or obovoid, 1.2–1.8 cm long and 1.2–1.6 cm diameter, bright orange.

Range and habitat. Nicaragua (Matagalpa), Costa Rica (Alajuela, Cartago, Guanacaste, Heredia, Limón, Puntarenas, San José) and Panama (Chiriquí); premontane or montane rain forest, at 600–1650 m elevation.

Bactris elegans
(Map 401, Plate 45)
"Marajá" (Bra), "moeroekoe" (Sur)

Field characters. Stems clustered, forming loose clumps, spiny, 1.5–3.5 m tall and 0.8–1.5 cm diameter. Leaves 6–13, pinnate; sheath, petiole, and rachis with a few black spines to 4 cm long; leaflets 17–32 per side, linear-lanceolate to almost sigmoid, *glossy green, unequally bifid at the tip, regularly arranged except for "gaps," spreading in the same plane. Inflorescences with (1–)2 flowering branches;* peduncular bract with few to many black spines to 1.5 cm long; fruits globose, 1.2–1.5 cm diameter, *purple-black.*

Range and habitat. Amazon region of Colombia (Amazonas), the Guianas, Brazil (Amazonas, Pará, Rondônia), and Bolivia (Pando); lowland rain forest in noninundated areas, below 350 m elevation.

Bactris ferruginea
(Map 402)
"Mané véio," "coquinho" (Bra)

Field characters. Stems clustered, spiny, 2.5–10 m tall and 4–10 cm diameter. Leaves 5–12, pinnate; *sheath, petiole, and rachis densely covered with black or yellow spines to 6 cm long;* leaflets 25–54 per side, sigmoid, irregularly arranged, and spreading in different planes. *Inflorescences with 17–49 flowering branches; peduncular bract very large, 30–75 cm long, with few, short, brown spines to 1.5 cm long, or spines absent;* fruits globose, 1.3–2 cm diameter, purple-black.

Range and habitat. Atlantic coast of Brazil (Alagoas, Bahia, Pernambuco, Sergipe); lowland rain forest, forest margins or secondary forest in noninundated areas, at low elevations.

Uses. The leaf fibers are extracted and woven into fishing lines.

Notes. In the northern part of the range of this species the leaf spines are black; in the southern part they are yellowish, and this form is recognized as var. *xanthacantha* (Noblick, 1991).

Bactris fissifrons
(Map 403)
"Ñejilla" (Per), "chontilla" (Col)

Field characters. Stems clustered, forming small clumps, 2–3 m tall and 1–3 cm diameter. Leaves 4–8, pinnate; sheath, petiole, and rachis scarcely to moderately covered with black spines to 4 cm long; leaflets 2–17 per side, linear-lanceolate with very long, thin tip, irregularly arranged and spreading in different planes. *Inflorescences with 2–5(–7), thick (to 5 mm) flowering branches;* peduncular bract moderately covered with black spines to 1 cm long; *fruits obovoid, markedly beaked,* 2.5–3 cm long and 1.5–2 cm diameter, yellowish, with a juicy mesocarp.

Range and habitat. Northwestern Amazon region in Colombia (Amazonas, Putumayo, Vaupés), Peru (Loreto), and Brazil (western Amazonas); lowland rain forest in noninundated areas, especially on river terraces, below 350 m elevation.

Bactris gasipaes
(Map 404, Plates 45 & 46)
"Chonta" (Bol, Ecu), "pupunha" (Bra), "chontaduro," "cachipay" (Col), "pejibaye" (CR, Gua, Nic), "parépou" (FrG), "paripie" (Guy), "pisbae" (Pan), "paripoe" (Sur), "peach palm" (Tri), "pijiguao" (Ven)

Field characters. Stems clustered or solitary, spiny or rarely without spines, *4–18 m tall and 10–25 cm diameter.* Leaves 9–20, pinnate; sheath, petiole, and rachis moderately to densely covered with black or brown spines to 1 cm long, those of petiole and rachis *in 3 distinct rows; sheath lacking an extension above the petiole; leaflets 92–123 per side,* linear, *with strongly unequal, bifid tips,* irregularly arranged and spreading in different planes, giving the leaf a plumose appearance. Inflorescences with 46–57 flowering branches; peduncular bract moderately to densely covered with black or brown spines to 1 cm long; *fruits ovoid, to 5 cm long and 3 cm diameter, yellow, orange, or red; mesocarp thick and edible; seed often absent.*

Range and habitat. Not known as a wild plant, but very widely cultivated throughout humid, tropical areas of Central and South America. It appears to be a selected form of *Bactris macana* (Bernal and Henderson, in prep.).

Uses. The fruits are an important part of the diet in many tropical areas. There are many local varieties, including one without spines and another without seeds in the fruits. In historical times they were probably much more important, not only as a food source but also in rituals and ceremonies (e.g., Reichel-Dolmatoff, 1989; Rival, 1993). Currently there are efforts to improve yields and also use the plants as a source of palm hearts (Clement and Mora Urpí, 1987; Mora Urpí et al. 1993).

Bactris gastoniana
(Map 405)
"Marajá" (Bra), "hanaimaka" (Sur)
Field characters. Stems solitary or clustered, *very short and subterranean or reaching 60 cm tall and 0.8–2 cm diameter.* Leaves 4–8, pinnate; sheath, petiole, and rachis with a few black spines to 4.5 cm long; *leaflets 8–11 per side, sigmoid,* irregularly arranged and spreading in different planes. *Inflorescences spicate;* peduncular bract densely covered with black or brown spines to 1.5 cm long; *fruits ellipsoid or widely ovoid, 2.5–3 cm long and 1.5–2 cm diameter, purple-black; fruiting perianth with staminodial ring.*
Range and habitat. Northeastern Amazon region in Suriname, French Guiana, and Brazil (Amapá, Amazonas, Pará); lowland rain forest on noninundated soils, below 500 m elevation.

Bactris glandulosa
(Map 406, Plate 46)
Field characters. Stems clustered or solitary, 1.5–5 m tall and 2–4.5 cm diameter, spiny. Leaves 4–6, pinnate; sheath, petiole, and rachis sparsely covered with black or yellowish spines to 5 cm long; leaflets 16–29 per side (or sometimes leaf simple), linear to narrowly elliptic, irregularly arranged and spreading in different planes, *with fine, golden pubescence on both or lower surface. Inflorescences with 40–50 slender, filiform flowering branches;* peduncular bract densely covered with fine, soft to stiff, black or yellowish spines; fruits globose, 0.5–1.6 cm diameter, red.
Range and habitat. Costa Rica (Cartago, Heredia, Limón, Puntarenas, San José), Panama (Bocas del Toro, Canal Area, Chiriquí, Coclé, San Blas, Veraguas), and northwestern Colombia (Antioquia, Chocó); lowland rain forest in noninundated areas, below 1000 m elevation.
Notes. It is divided into two varieties (de Nevers et al., in press): var. *glandulosa*, with sparsely spiny petiole and rachis and densely hairy leaflets; and var. *baileyana*, with spiny petiole and rachis and sparsely hairy leaflets. Both varieties often occur together.

Bactris glassmanii
(Map 407)
"Arirí" (Bra)
Field characters. Stems clustered or occasionally solitary, spiny, 1–3 m tall and 0.8–2 cm diameter. Leaves 3–8, pinnate; sheath, petiole, and rachis sparsely covered with *flattened, yellowish (with black base and tip) spines to 2 cm long;* leaflets 12–25 per side, linear to lanceolate, irregularly arranged and spreading in the same plane. Inflorescences with 4–24 flowering branches; peduncular bract curling downwards over the developing infructescence, sparsely covered with brown or yellow spines to 7 mm long; fruits globose, 0.6–2 cm diameter, yellow.
Range and habitat. Atlantic coast of Brazil (Alagoas, Bahia, Pernambuco, Sergipe); *restinga* or shrubby vegetation on sand dunes near the sea and in adjacent forest.
Notes. Fruits are larger in the southern part of its range in southern Bahia, and smaller to the north.

Bactris glaucescens
(Map 408)
"Chontilla" (Bol), "tucum" (Bra), "caranda" (Par)
Field characters. Stems clustered, 0.5–4 m tall and 2–4 cm diameter, spiny. Leaves 4–16, pinnate; *sheath, petiole, and rachis tomentose, with slightly clustered, black spines to 10 cm long;* leaflets 26–45 per side, oblanceolate, *briefly bifid at the tip, whitish brown on lower surface,* irregularly arranged, and stiffly spreading in different planes. Inflorescences with 32–42 flowering branches; peduncular bract whitish tomentose, moderately covered with straight, black spines to 1 cm long; fruits depressed-globose, 1.2–2 cm diameter, *purple-black,* with juicy mesocarp.
Range and habitat. Southwestern Amazon region and adjacent areas in Brazil (Goiás, Mato Grosso, Mato Grosso do Sul, Rondônia), Bolivia (Beni, Santa Cruz), and Paraguay (Amambay, Concepción, San Pedro); forest margins, gallery forest, or open places along stream margins or other wet places liable to seasonal inundation, at low elevations.
Notes. Very similar to *Bactris bidentula*, but occurs much farther to the south. Moraes and Sarmiento (1992) have discussed pollination of this species. It has a typical *Bactris* syndrome, with a short-lived, nocturnal pistillate anthesis followed by a very brief staminate anthesis and weevil pollinators.

Bactris gracilior
(Map 409)
"Biscoyol" (CR)

Field characters. Stems clustered, 2–4 m tall and to 2 cm diameter, spiny. Leaves 5–9, pinnate; sheath (petiole and rachis) moderately to densely covered with short, black spines; leaflets 10–24 per side, narrowly elliptical, irregularly arranged and spreading in different planes, *brownish-green on lower surface*. Inflorescences with 8–23 flowering branches; peduncular bract sparsely covered with black or brown spines, occasionally spines absent; fruits obovoid, 1–1.3 cm long, 0.9–1.1 cm diameter, orange.

Range and habitat. Atlantic slope in Central America in southern Nicaragua (Zelaya), Costa Rica (Alajuela, Heredia, Limón), and Panama (Bocas del Toro, Coclé, Colón, Darién, Panamá, San Blas); lowland rain forest, below 350 m elevation.

Bactris grayumi
(Map 410)

Field characters. Stems solitary, rarely clustered, 1.5–3.5 m tall and 2.2–3 cm diameter. Leaves 4–9, simple or pinnate, *strongly plicate*; sheath, petiole, and rachis sparsely covered with black spines to 6 cm long; simple leaves deeply bifid at the tip; pinnate leaves with a few, broad leaflets. Inflorescences with 18–25 flowering branches; peduncular bract almost without spines, or sparsely covered with black spines to 5 mm long; fruits obovoid with prominent beak, 1.1–1.2 cm long and 0.9–1.1 cm diameter, orange.

Range and habitat. Nicaragua (Chontales, Zelaya) and adjacent Costa Rica (Limón, San José); lowland rain forest, below 300 m elevation.

Bactris guineensis
(Map 411)
"Corozo," "lata" (Col), "biscoyol" (CR), "coyolito" (Nic), "uvita de monte" (Pan), "piritu," "uvita" (Ven)

Field characters. Stems clustered, often forming dense colonies, spiny, 0.8–3 m tall and 2.5–3 cm diameter. Leaves 5–6, pinnate; sheath, petiole, and rachis moderately to densely covered with *yellowish (but black at base and tip) spines to 9(–15) cm long*; leaflets 20–42 per side, linear, *bifid at the tip*, regularly to slightly irregularly arranged and spreading in different planes. Inflorescences with 20–30 flowering branches; peduncular bract moderately covered with yellowish, spreading spines to 1 cm long; fruits depressed-globose, 1.5–2 cm diameter, *purple-black*.

Range and habitat. Pacific slope of Nicaragua (Chontales, Granada), Costa Rica (Guanacaste, Puntarenas), Panama (Canal Area, Coclé, Los Santos, Panamá), and northern Col-

ombia (Antioquia, Atlántico, Bolívar, Córdoba, Guajira, Magdalena, Sucre), and northern Venezuela (Apure, Cojedes, Guárico, Monagas, Portuguesa); deciduous forest or open areas in seasonally dry regions, to 850 m elevation.

Uses. The stems were at one time used to make canes, and these were exported to Europe, where they were known as Tobago canes. This practice was known to Jacquin in 1763, and he used the Greek word "bactron," a cane or staff, for the genus. A refreshing drink is made with the fruits. Pollination has been studied in Costa Rica by Essig (1971).

Bactris hatschbachii
(Map 412)
"Brejaúva-mirim" (Bra)

Field characters. Stems clustered, forming large colonies, 3–5 m tall and to 2.5 cm diameter, spiny. Leaves pinnate; sheath, petiole, and rachis moderately covered with black spines to 3 cm long; leaflets numerous, *linear*, irregularly arranged and spreading ± in the same plane, *gray on the lower surface*. Inflorescences with 12–13 flowering branches; fruits depressed-globose, 2 cm diameter, *purple-black, densely covered with short, bulbous-based spines*.

Range and habitat. Southern Brazil (Paraná, São Paulo); lowland rain forest on noninundated soils, at low elevations.

Notes. A very rare species that is probably in danger of extinction. It is very interesting in its leaflets, which are gray on the lower surface, and fruits, which have spines. The fruits resemble those of *Bactris constanciae*, but the structure of the spines is different in the two species.

Bactris hirta
(Map 413, Plate 46)
"Marajá" (Bra), "chontaduro de rana" (Col), "kiskismaka" (Sur), "cubarro" (Ven)

Field characters. Stems clustered, 0.5–3 m tall and 1–2 cm diameter, without spines or covered with spiny leaf bases. Leaves 3–7; sheath and petiole with few to many black spines to 5 cm long; blade very variable, from simple or partially simple and then to 80 cm long and 20 cm wide, to regularly pinnate with leaflets linear or rarely sigmoid, 13–30 per side, regularly arranged and spreading in the same plane, *usually hairy on lower surface*. Inflorescences small, with *1–4(–5) erect, stiff, short (5–7 cm) flowering branches*; peduncular bract sparsely to densely covered with short, black spines; *fruits globose, 0.5(–1) cm diameter, orange-red or red, covered with spinules*.

Range and habitat. Amazon region of Colombia (Amazonas, Guainía, Putumayo, Vaupés, Vichada), Venezuela (Amazonas, Bolívar), the Guianas, Peru (Loreto, Madre de Dios), Brazil (Acre, Amapá, Amazonas, Pará, Rondônia), Bolivia (Pando), and Atlantic coast of Brazil (Bahia, Espírito Santo, Pernambuco); lowland rain forest on noninundated soils, to 800 m elevation.

Notes. Related to *Bactris simplicifrons* and extremely variable, especially in leaf form. The inflorescence, however, is usually consistent. It is divided into the following varieties (Henderson, 1994): var. *hirta*, the most widespread variety, with simple or pinnate leaves; var. *mollis*, from the western Amazon region in Colombia (Amazonas), Peru (Loreto), and Brazil (western Amazonas), with a dense covering of spinules to 3 cm long on the sheath, petiole, and rachis; and var. *pulchra*, from the central Amazon region, with smaller, simple leaves and the sheath and petiole usually lacking spines.

Bactris hondurensis
(Map 414)
"Biscoyol" (CR, Hon, Nic), "pacaya de danta" (Pan)
Field characters. Stems solitary or clustered, 1–2.5(–4) m tall and 0.5–1.5 cm diameter. Leaves 5–9; sheath, petiole, and rachis with few, black spines to 1 cm long, occasionally interspersed with yellowish or black spines to 2 cm long; *blade simple with a bifid tip, or occasionally the lower part of the blade irregularly pinnate with 1–8 sigmoid leaflets per side, usually softly hairy on the lower surface.* Inflorescences small with 3–7 flowering branches; peduncular bract moderately to densely covered with soft, spreading, yellowish, brown, or black spines to 1 cm long; fruits globose, 1.2–1.5 cm diameter, red to orange.
Range and habitat. Honduras (Atlántida), Nicaragua (Chontales, Jinotega, Zelaya), Costa Rica (Alajuela, Cartago, Guanacaste, Heredia, Limón, Puntarenas, San José), Panama (Bocas del Toro, Coclé, Colón, Darién, Panamá, San Blas, Veraguas), and the Pacific coast of Colombia (Antioquia, Chocó) and Ecuador (Esmeraldas); lowland rain forest in noninundated regions, to 1000 m elevation.

Bactris horridispatha
(Map 415)
"Tucum amarelo" (Bra)
Field characters. Stems clustered, spiny, 1–6 m tall and 1.5–3 cm diameter. Leaves 3–8, pinnate; sheath, petiole, and rachis densely covered with *yellowish (with black base and tip) spines to 5(–7) cm long;* leaflets 15–26 per side, linear, *regularly arranged and spreading in the same plane.* Inflorescences with 1–5 thick, flowering

branches; peduncular bract densely covered with yellowish to black, flattened spines to 2.5(–3) cm long; *fruits ellipsoid, (2.5–)3–3.5 cm long and 2.3–2.5 cm diameter, purple-black.*
Range and habitat. Atlantic coast of Brazil (Bahia); *restinga,* coastal forest, or secondary forest near the sea on sandy soil.

Bactris killipii
(Map 416, Plate 47)
"Marajá" (Bra), "ñejilla" (Per)
Field characters. Stems solitary or less often clustered, nonspiny, 10–60 cm tall and 1–1.5 cm diameter. Leaves 6–10, usually simple; sheath, petiole, and rachis without spines; *blade deeply bifid (rarely pinnate with 2–4 leaflets per side), the lobes lanceolate, stiff, and strongly plicate.* Inflorescences spicate, with an *erect flowering branch;* peduncular bract brown-tomentose, without spines; fruits ellipsoid, 1.4–1.5 cm long and 0.8–1 cm diameter, orange-red.
Range and habitat. Central Amazon region in Colombia (Amazonas, Vaupés), Peru (Loreto), and Brazil (Amazonas); lowland forest on noninundated soils, at low elevations.

Bactris kunorum
(Map 417)
Field characters. Stems clustered in tight clumps of 4–6 stems, 2–6 m tall and to 5 cm diameter, spiny. Leaves 4–9, pinnate; sheath, petiole, and rachis with moderate covering of black spines to 6 cm long; leaflets 4–14 per side, linear-lanceolate, *strongly plicate,* irregularly arranged, and spreading in different planes. Inflorescences with 24–30 flowering branches; peduncular bract sparsely covered with short, black spines to 5 mm long; fruits obovoid, beaked, 1.4–1.9 cm long and 1.3–2 cm long, orange or red.
Range and habitat. Central Panama (Panamá, San Blas) and Colombia (Valle); lowland or premontane rain forest, at 300–800 m elevation.

Bactris longiseta
(Map 418)
"Huiscoyol" (CR)
Field characters. Stems solitary or clustered, 3–4.5 m tall and 2–2.5 cm diameter, spiny. Leaves 6–7, pinnate; sheath, petiole, and rachis sparsely to densely covered with black spines to 7 cm long; leaflets 15–29 per side, linear to narrowly elliptic, regularly to slightly irregularly arranged, and spreading in the same or slightly different planes, *often with spinules to 2 cm long on the margins.* Inflorescences with 20–30 flowering branches; peduncular bract densely covered with erect, black or brown spines to 1 cm long; *fruits obovoid,*

beaked, 1.5–1.6 cm long and 1.5–1.6 cm diameter, purple-brown.
Range and habitat. Eastern Costa Rica (Alajuela, Heredia, Limón); lowland rain forest, below 750 m elevation.

Bactris macana
(Map 419, Plate 47)
"Chontilla" (Bol), "pupunha brava" (Bra), "chinamato" (Col), "pijuayo del monte" (Per), "macanilla" (Ven)
Field characters. Stems solitary or clustered, spiny, 9.5–12 m tall and 10–20 cm diameter. Leaves 8–17, pinnate; sheath, petiole, and rachis moderately to densely covered with black or brown spines to 1 cm long, those of petiole and rachis in 3 rows; sheath lacking an extension above the petiole; leaflets 92–141 per side, linear, with strongly unequal, bifid tips; irregularly arranged and spreading in different planes and giving the leaf a plumose appearance. Inflorescences with 40–70 flowering branches; peduncular bract moderately to densely covered with black or brown spines to 1 cm long; fruits subglobose to obovoid, 1–1.6 cm diameter, orange.
Range and habitat. Colombia (Antioquia, Guajira, Norte de Santander, Sucre, Valle) and Venezuela (Barinas, Cojedes, Zulia), and the southwestern Amazon region in Peru (Huánuco, Madre de Dios), Brazil (Acre, Rondônia), and Bolivia (Santa Cruz), absent from Ecuador; lowland rain forest in noninundated areas, below 600 m elevation.
Uses. The fruits are edible.
Notes. Apparently rare in the wild, especially in the southern part of its range, but of great interest in being the wild ancestor of the domesticated Bactris gasipaes (Bernal and Henderson, in prep.; see also Clement et al., 1989).

Bactris macroacantha
(Map 420)
"Marajá" (Bra)
Field characters. Stems clustered, often in dense clumps, 0.5–4 m tall and 2–4 cm diameter, spiny. Leaves 2–6, pinnate, spiny; sheath, petiole, and rachis densely brown-tomentose (often with a nontomentose strip on lower surface), with few to many black, rarely yellowish, spines to 8 cm long; leaflets 13–30 per side, oblanceolate to sigmoid, regularly or irregularly arranged, and spreading in one or different planes, with distinct, spinulose marginal veins. Inflorescences with 7–12 flowering branches; peduncular bract densely covered with brown or yellowish, strongly appressed, flattened spines; fruits widely obovoid, markedly beaked, 2.5–3.2 cm long and 2–2.3 cm diameter, purple-black, with juicy mesocarp.

Range and habitat. Western Amazon region in Colombia (Amazonas), Ecuador (Morona-Santiago), Peru (Amazonas, Cuzco, Huánuco, Loreto, Pasco, Ucayali), and Brazil (Amazonas, Pará); lowland rain forest on noninundated soils, at low elevations.

Bactris major
(Map 421, Plate 47)
"Hones" (Bel), "marayáu" (Bol), "marajá" (Bra), "lata" (Col), "zagrinette" (FrG), "huiscoyol" (ElS, Gua, Hon, Nic), "jahuacté" (Mex), "caña brava" (Pan), "cubarro" (Ven)
Field characters. Stems clustered, often forming large, dense clumps, spiny, 1–10 m tall and 2–6 cm diameter. Leaves 3–10, pinnate, spiny; sheath, petiole, and rachis with many short spines interspersed with longer, black spines to 11 cm long; leaflets 24–48 per side, linear, regularly arranged, and spreading in the same plane (rarely somewhat clustered). Inflorescences with (1–)5–17 thick (2–4 mm) flowering branches; peduncular bract sparsely to moderately covered with black, brown, or yellowish spines to 2 cm long; fruits irregularly ellipsoid to widely obovoid, 2.5–4.5 cm long and 1.3–3.5 cm diameter, purple-black; mesocarp juicy; fruiting perianth with staminodial ring.
Range and habitat. Southern Mexico (Chiapas, Oaxaca, Tabasco, Veracruz), Atlantic and Pacific slope of Central America, and all over northern South America, east and north of the Andes, as far south as Bolivia but not in Ecuador and Peru; drier, open areas or open forest, or gallery forest or forest patches, but always near groundwater.
Uses. The fruits, which have a juicy flesh, are widely eaten or used to flavor drinks.
Notes. It is divided into four varieties (Henderson, 1994), although in some cases the boundaries between them are not always clear: var. major, with inflorescences with (3–)5–10(–17) flowering branches and fruits 3.3–4.5 cm long and 2.3–3.5 cm diameter, from Mexico, Central America, northern Colombia (Atlántico, Antioquia, Bolívar, Córdoba, Meta, Sucre), Venezuela (Apure, Barinas, Cojedes, Monagas, Portuguesa, Yaracuy, Zulia), Trinidad, and the Guianas; var. megalocarpa, with inflorescences with 11–17 flowering branches and fruits 1.5–2 cm long and 2 cm diameter, from northeastern Venezuela (Bolívar, Monagas), Trinidad, the Guianas, and northeastern Brazil (Amapá, Pará); var. infesta, with inflorescences with (1–)2–5 flowering branches and fruits 2.5–3 cm long and 1.3–2 cm diameter, from Venezuela (Amazonas), the Guianas, Brazil (Acre, Amazonas, Maranhão, Mato Grosso, Pará, Rondônia), and Bolivia (Pando); and var. socialis, with inflorescences with 8–12 flow-

ering branches and fruits 3.5–4 cm long and
2–3 cm diameter, from Bolivia (Beni, Cochabamba, Pando, Santa Cruz).
Pollination of var. *major* has been studied in
Costa Rica by Essig (1971).

Bactris maraja
(Map 422, Plate 47)
"Chontilla" (Bol, Col, Per), "marajá" (Bra),
"chacarrá," "espina" (Col), "uvita" (Pan),
"ñeja" (Per), "piritu" (Sur, Ven), "uva de
montaña" (Ven)
Field characters. Stems clustered, usually forming open clumps, 2–7(–10) m tall and 1–4 cm
diameter, spiny. Leaves 3–10, pinnate, rarely
simple, spiny; *leaf spines flattened, usually yellowish brown at middle, darker at base and tip (occasionally dark throughout);* leaflets 6–22 per side,
sigmoid (rarely lanceolate), regularly or irregularly arranged, and spreading in the same or
different planes. Inflorescences with 3–17
flowering branches; fruits widely depressed,
obovoid, 1–2 cm diameter, *purple-black, occasionally minutely spinulose, with juicy mesocarp.*
Range and habitat. Widespread from Costa Rica
(Limón, Puntarenas) through Panama and
northern South America; various types of forest, usually on noninundated soils but occasionally in wet areas, at low elevations but occasionally reaching 1000 m.
Uses. The fruits are widely eaten.
Notes. It has long been known under the name
Bactris monticola, but this is incorrect. This is a
widespread and extremely variable species,
and the following 3 varieties are recognized
(Henderson, 1994): var. *chaetospatha,* with simple leaves and minutely spinulose fruits, from
Peru (Loreto) and Brazil (western Amazonas);
var. *juruensis,* with fewer (2–11) leaflets and
fewer (3–6) flowering branches, mostly from
the western Amazon region in Colombia
(Amazonas, Vaupés), French Guiana, Ecuador
(Napo), Peru (Loreto, Madre de Dios, Pasco),
Brazil (Acre, Amazonas, Pará), and Bolivia
(Beni, Cochabamba, La Paz); and var. *maraja,*
with more leaflets and more flowering
branches, the most widespread form.

Bactris mexicana
(Map 423)
"Huiscoyol" (Gua), "coyolillo" (Hon),
"chischi" (Mex), "biscoyol" (Nic)
Field characters. Stems clustered, 2–3 m tall and
2–3.5 cm diameter, spiny. Leaves 5–7, pinnate; sheath, petiole, and rachis moderately
to densely covered with black spines to 7 cm
long; leaflets 8–26 per side, linear to narrowly
elliptical, irregularly arranged and spreading
in different planes, *often minutely pubescent on
the lower surface.* Inflorescences with 12–36

flowering branches; peduncular bract densely
covered with black spines to 1 cm long; fruits
obovoid, to 1.2 cm long and 0.9–1.2 cm diameter, orange.
Range and habitat. Atlantic slope of Mexico
(Chiapas, Oaxaca, Tabasco, Veracruz), Guatemala (Alta Verapaz, Izabal, Petén), Belize,
Honduras (Atlántida Comayagua, Gracias a
Dios, Olancho), and Nicaragua (Zelaya); lowland rain forest, below 600 m elevation.

Bactris militaris
(Map 424)
Field characters. Stems clustered, 3–5 m tall and
2.5–4 cm diameter, spiny. Leaves 6–8; sheath,
petiole, and rachis sparsely covered with black
spines to 8.5 cm long; *blade simple, narrow,
strongly plicate, and stiffly erect, to 3 m long. Inflorescences erect in flower and fruit,* with 14–23
flowering branches; *peduncular bract densely tomentose, sparsely covered with brown spines to 4 mm
long;* fruits globose, 1.5–1.7 cm diameter, red.
Range and habitat. Atlantic coast of Costa Rica
(Limón) (and probably adjacent Nicaragua
and Panama) and less commonly Pacific coast
of Costa Rica (Puntarenas); low-lying swampy
areas near the sea, rarely to 400 m elevation.

Bactris oligocarpa
(Map 425, Plate 48)
Field characters. Stems solitary or occasionally
clustered, 0.2–1.5 m tall and 0.8–1 cm diameter. Leaves 4–10, pinnate or simple, spiny;
sheath, petiole, and rachis with scattered,
black spines to 3 cm long, occasionally spines
absent; *leaflets 1–3 per side, sigmoid,* regularly arranged and spreading in the same plane. *Inflorescences spicate;* peduncular bract with a few
spines; fruits widely ovoid, 1.7–2 cm long and
1–1.3 cm diameter, *purple-black, with juicy mesocarp; fruiting perianth with staminodial ring.*
Range and habitat. Central and northeastern
Amazon region in Suriname, French Guiana,
and Brazil (Amapá, Amazonas, Pará); lowland
rain forest on noninundated soils, at low elevations.

Bactris oligoclada
(Map 426)
"Yurua" (Guy), "corocillo" (Ven)
Field characters. Stems clustered, spiny or nonspiny, 1–3 m tall and 1–1.5 cm diameter.
Leaves 3–12, pinnate; sheath, petiole, and
rachis with few, long, black spines to 7 cm
long; leaflets 6–10 per side, *lanceolate to almost
sigmoid, lighter green on lower surface, in widely
spaced clusters,* spreading in different planes.
Inflorescences small, with 6–8 flowering
branches; peduncular bract densely covered
with short, black spines; fruits depressed-

globose, 1–1.5 cm diameter, orange-red (but maturing from green to white to yellow), with floury mesocarp.
Range and habitat. Venezuela (Bolívar) and Guyana; lowland rain forest, often on sandy soils in noninundated areas, at low elevations.

Bactris panamensis
(Map 427)
Field characters. Stems clustered, 1.5–3 m tall and 7–9 mm diameter. Leaves pinnate; sheath, petiole, and rachis densely to densely covered with black spines to 3 cm long; *leaflets 15–19 (–25) per side, narrowly elliptical to sigmoid,* irregularly arranged and spreading in different planes. Inflorescences with 8–12, *short (2–3.4 cm long)* flowering branches; *peduncular bract with fine black spines to 1 cm long;* fruits obovoid, 0.7–1 cm long and 7–8 mm diameter, orange.
Range and habitat. Panama (Coclé, Chiriquí, Panamá, San Blas); lowland to montane rain forest, at 350–1000 m elevation.

Bactris pickelii
(Map 428)
"Tucum mirim" (Bra)
Field characters. Stems clustered or solitary, 1–3 m tall and 1–1.5 cm diameter. Leaves 6–10; sheath, petiole, and rachis without spines or with scattered, brown or black spines to 2 cm long; blade pinnate or occasionally simple; *leaflets (1–)4–9 per side, sigmoid, lower surface velvety,* irregularly arranged and spreading in different planes. *Inflorescences small, erect, with 2–4 flowering branches;* peduncular bract densely covered with fine, short, black or brown spines; fruits globose, 1.2–1.5 cm diameter, reddish purple.
Range and habitat. Atlantic coast of Brazil (Alagoas, Bahia, Espírito Santo, Paraíba, Pernambuco, Sergipe); lowland rain forest in noninundated areas, at low elevations.

Bactris pilosa
(Map 429)
"Lata macho" (Col), "uvita" (Pan)
Field characters. Stems clustered and sometimes forming large clumps, or rarely solitary, 2–10 m tall and 2.5–4 cm diameter. Leaves 4–8, pinnate; sheath, petiole, and rachis moderately to densely covered with black or brown spines to 5 cm long; *leaflets 59–68 per side, linear, hairy on the lower surface,* regularly or irregularly arranged and spreading in the same or different planes. Inflorescences with 6–26 flowering branches; peduncular bract densely covered with soft, appressed brown spines interspersed with longer black spines; fruits de-

pressed obovoid, 2–2.5 cm long and 1.3–2 cm diameter, *purple-black, covered in short bristles.*
Range and habitat. Eastern Panama (Darién) to Colombia (Antioquia, Bolívar, Cesar, Chocó, Sucre, Tolima), Venezuela (Táchira, Zulia), and possibly Ecuador; lowland rain forest, below 600 m elevation.

Bactris pliniana
(Map 430)
"Marajá" (Bra), "zagrinette" (FrG), "hanaimaka" (Sur)
Field characters. Stems clustered, *1.5–3 m tall* and 2.5–5 cm diameter, spiny. Leaves 6–12, pinnate, spiny; sheath, petiole, and rachis with scattered, black spines to 7 cm long; leaflets 12–30 per side, *oblanceolate to sigmoid,* irregularly arranged in clusters and spreading in different planes. *Inflorescences with 20–60 filiform, flowering branches;* peduncular bract densely covered with soft, dark brown to yellowish spines to 1 cm long; fruits globose to widely obovoid, to 2 cm diameter, bright orange, *covered with short spinules,* with starchy mesocarp.
Range and habitat. Widespread in the Amazon region in the Guianas, Peru (Amazonas, Loreto), and Brazil (Acre, Amazonas); lowland rain forest in inundated areas, below 500 m elevation.
Notes. Closely related to *Bactris acanthocarpoides.*

Bactris plumeriana
(Map 431, Plate 48)
"Coco macaco" (Cub), "coco macaque" (Hai), "prickly pole" (Jam)
Field characters. Stems clustered, very spiny, *forming dense colonies, 4–10 m tall and 8–15 cm diameter.* Leaves 7–12, pinnate, densely black spiny; petiole spines in 3 longitudinal lines; leaflets 50–70 per side, linear, *spiny on margins,* irregularly arranged and spreading in different planes. Inflorescences with 40–60 flowering branches; *peduncular bract densely black spiny;* fruits globose or depressed-globose, 1–1.6 cm diameter, orange red.
Range and habitat. Cuba, Hispaniola (Dominican Republic, Haiti), Jamaica; forest (or open areas where forest has been cut) in hilly regions, below 500 m elevation.
Uses. The fruits are a source of food for domestic animals, especially pigs.
Notes. Specimens from Jamaica, which have been called *Bactris jamaicana,* are somewhat different and perhaps deserve specific status.

Bactris ptariana
(Map 432)
"Maswa" (Guy)
Field characters. Stems solitary or clustered, 2–3(–10) m tall and 3–4(–10) cm diameter, very

spiny. Leaves 5–9, pinnate, spiny; sheath, petiole, and rachis with *clusters of black spines to 3 cm long*; leaflets 15–18 per side, linear or linear-lanceolate, irregularly arranged in clusters and spreading in ± the same plane, sparsely spinulose on lower surface. Inflorescences with 12–18 flowering branches, *densely covered with very short, whitish hairs*; peduncular bract sparsely covered with black spines to 1 cm long; fruits widely obovoid, 0.7–1 cm long and 0.7–0.8 cm diameter, bright orange or red, with floury mesocarp.

Range and habitat. Venezuela (Bolívar) and Guyana; lowland to montane rain forest, usually on white-sand soils, at 50–2000 m elevation.

Notes. Populations from higher elevations (1000–2000 m) are larger, have more plicate leaflets with more spinules on the lower surface and larger inflorescences.

Bactris rhapidacantha
(Map 433)
"Ti-wara" (FrG)
Field characters. Stems solitary or clustered, *usually subterranean*, occasionally to 1.5 m long and 5–8 cm diameter. Leaves 8–15, pinnate; sheath, petiole, and rachis densely covered with black spines to 10 cm long; leaflets 25–40, linear, *regularly arranged and spreading in the same plane*. Inflorescences with *25–40 filiform, flowering branches*; fruits very widely obovoid, 1–1.5 cm diameter, orange-red, *covered with short spinules*, with starchy mesocarp.

Range and habitat. Suriname and French Guiana; lowland rain forest on noninundated soils, at low elevations.

Bactris riparia
(Map 434, Plates 48 & 49)
"Chontilla" (Bol, Col), "marajá" (Bra), "chontadurillo" (Col, Ecu), "ñejilla de canto de cocha" (Per)
Field characters. Stems clustered, *often forming large colonies, spiny, 3–10 m tall and 5–7.8 cm diameter*. Leaves 4–10, pinnate, spiny; sheath, petiole, and rachis densely covered with black spines to 7 cm long; *leaflets 33–58 per side, linear, usually with soft brown hairs on veins on lower surface*, irregularly arranged and spreading in different planes, giving the leaf a plumose appearance. Inflorescences with 24–36 flowering branches; peduncular bract moderately to densely covered with black spines; fruits depressed-globose, 1.5–2 cm diameter, orange-red or green, with floury mesocarp.

Range and habitat. Western Amazon region in Colombia (Amazonas, Putumayo), Ecuador (Napo), Peru (Loreto, Madre de Dios, Ucayali), Brazil (Acre, Amazonas, Mato Grosso,

Pará), and Bolivia (Beni, Pando, Santa Cruz); margins of blackwater (and occasionally whitewater) rivers and lakes, often where its roots are submerged by annual floods for part of the year.

Bactris setosa
(Map 435)
"Jucúm," "tucum" (Bra)
Field characters. Stems clustered, 2–6 m tall and 3–4 cm diameter, spiny. Leaves 2–5, pinnate; sheath, petiole, and rachis *sparsely covered with yellowish (black at base and tip) spines to 5.5 cm long*; leaflets 30–57 per side, linear, irregularly arranged and spreading in different planes. Inflorescences with 12–27 flowering branches; peduncular bract moderately covered with yellowish to black spines to 1 cm long; fruits depressed-globose, 1–1.5 cm long and 1.5–2 cm diameter, *purple-black*; mesocarp juicy.

Range and habitat. Atlantic coast of Brazil (Bahia, Espírito Santo, Paraná, Santa Catarina, São Paulo, Rio de Janeiro, Rio Grande do Sul) and possibly occurring farther inland; forest or open places, almost always in low-lying, wet areas.

Bactris setulosa
(Map 436, Plate 49)
"Jingapá" (Col), "chonta" (Ecu), "macana," "macanilla" (Ven)
Field characters. Stems clustered or less often solitary, densely spiny, *5–10 m tall and 6–10 cm diameter*. Leaves 4–9, pinnate; sheath, petiole, and rachis *very spiny with spines in clusters, to 4 cm long*; *leaflets 45–60 per side*, linear, irregularly arranged, and spreading in slightly different planes. *Inflorescences with 39–60 flowering branches*; peduncular bract densely covered in black spines to 1.5 cm long; fruits widely obovoid, 1.8–2 cm diameter, orange-red, with floury mesocarp, *with a cuplike corolla*.

Range and habitat. Andean region of Colombia (Antioquia, Chocó, Nariño, Valle), Venezuela (Anzoátegui, Barinas, Bolívar, Miranda, Monagas, Táchira, Zulia), Ecuador (El Oro, Esmeraldas, Los Ríos, Napo, Pichincha), and reaching Trinidad and possibly Suriname; lowland, premontane, or montane rain forest, sometimes in wet areas, between sea level and 1700 m elevation but most common in mountain areas between 500 and 1500 m.

Notes. One of the largest *Bactris* and the one that reaches the highest elevations. Bernal and Henderson (in prep.) consider it related to *Bactris gasipaes* and *B. macana*.

Bactris simplicifrons
(Map 437, Plate 50)
"Marajá" (Bra), "chontaduro de rana de

rastrojo" (Col), "chontaduro de tintín" (Ecu), "parapi-balli" (Guy), "ñejilla" (Per), "yuyba" (Sur), "cubarillo" (Ven)

Field characters. Stems clustered or solitary, usually nonspiny, *0.5–2 m tall and 0.3–1 cm diameter.* Leaves 5–9, pinnate or usually simple, very variable, often nonspiny except on extreme margins; sheath, petiole, and rachis occasionally spiny with flattened, black spines to 1.5 cm long; simple leaves with blade usually shaped like a whale's fin, rarely long and narrow; leaflets of pinnate leaves 2–5(–20) per side, linear to sigmoid. Inflorescences 5–10 cm long, *curved down, with 1(–5) flowering branches*; *fruits globose, 5(–8) mm diameter, red or orange*, with floury mesocarp.

Range and habitat. Throughout the Amazon region in Colombia, Venezuela, the Guianas, Ecuador, Peru, Brazil, and Bolivia, and just reaching Trinidad and northern Colombia (Córdoba); lowland forest on noninundated soils and also in semi-open, sandy areas, at both low and high (to 1800 m) elevations.

Notes. There is an extraordinary range in leaf shape and size in this species. Although some common forms repeatedly occur, there are many intermediates and division into varieties is not useful. Plants from higher elevations in the Guayana Highland region often have spiny leaves, and plants from open, white-sand areas often have very narrow, wedge-shaped leaves.

Bactris soeiroana
(Map 438)
"Jussa," "tucum" (Bra)
Field characters. Stems clustered, 0.7–1.5 m tall and 1–2 cm diameter. Leaves 4–10, pinnate; *sheath, petiole, and rachis densely covered with white, woolly tomentum,* sparsely covered with brown spines to 3 cm long; leaflets 8–17 per side, sigmoid, irregularly arranged and spreading in different planes. Inflorescences small with 4–6 flowering branches; peduncular bract reddish brown to gray-tomentose; fruits depressed-globose, to 1.5 cm diameter, yellow.
Range and habitat. Atlantic coast of Brazil (Bahia); *restinga* and shrubby vegetation on sand dunes near the sea.

Bactris syagroides
(Map 439)
Field characters. Stems clustered, *slender,* 0.6–1.5 m tall and 0.8–2 cm diameter, nonspiny. Leaves 5–8, pinnate; sheath, petiole, and rachis nonspiny or moderately covered with somewhat flattened, black spines to 1 cm long; *leaflets 30–35 per side, narrowly linear, regularly arranged, and spreading in the same plane. Inflorescences with 7–13 short (4–6 cm), flowering branches*; peduncular bract densely covered

with soft, black spines to 1 cm long; *fruits globose, to 7 mm diameter, orange-yellow,* with floury mesocarp.

Range and habitat. Eastern Amazon region in Brazil (Pará), where it is known only from the Rio Tapajós; lowland rain forest on noninundated soils, at low elevations.

Notes. This is an interesting species; although it is related to *Bactris simplicifrons,* it has many more flowering branches.

Bactris tefensis
(Map 440)
"Marajá" (Bra)
Field characters. Stems solitary or clustered, 0.8–1.5 m tall and 1.5–2 cm diameter. Leaves 4–10, pinnate; sheath, petiole, and rachis with a few, scattered black spines to 4 cm long; *leaflets 9–13 per side, sigmoid,* irregularly arranged, and spreading in different planes. Inflorescences with *numerous, filiform flowering branches*; fruits widely obovoid, 1 cm diameter, orange-red, with floury mesocarp; fruiting corolla densely spinulose.
Range and habitat. Central Amazon region in Brazil (Amazonas), known only from near Tefé; lowland rain forest on noninundated soils, at low elevations.
Notes. Related to both *Bactris acanthocarpa* and *B. acanthocarpoides,* but lacks spinules on the fruits.

Bactris tomentosa
(Map 441)
"Marajá" (Bra), "ñejilla" (Per)
Field characters. Stems clustered, 0.3–3 m tall and 0.8–1.6 cm diameter. Leaves 9–13, pinnate or simple; sheath, petiole, and rachis sparsely to moderately covered with flattened, yellowish or rounded, black spines to 3 cm long; simple leaves deeply bifid apically; leaflets of pinnate leaves 2–9 per side, sigmoid, irregularly arranged, and spreading in different planes, occasionally pilose on the lower surface. *Inflorescences spicate*; peduncular bract without spines or with a few black or yellowish spines to 1 cm long; fruits very widely obovoid, to 1.5 cm diameter, *purple-black, occasionally spinulose.*
Range and habitat. Amazon region of Colombia (Amazonas, Vaupés), French Guiana, Ecuador (Napo), Peru (Loreto, Madre de Dios, Pasco), Brazil (Acre, Amapá, Amazonas, Maranhão, Pará); lowland rain forest on noninundated soils, at low elevations.
Notes. This is a very variable species that is divided into two varieties (Henderson, 1994): var. *sphaerocarpa,* with sheath, petiole, and rachis with rounded, black spines, from the western half of the species range; and var.

tomentosa, with somewhat flattened, yellowish leaf spines, from the eastern half of the range.

Bactris trailiana
(Map 442, Plate 50)
"Ubussuhy" (Bra)

Field characters. Stems solitary, short, and subterranean, rarely to 2 m tall and 7 cm diameter. Leaves 7–10, *simple;* sheath, petiole, and rachis sparsely covered with black spines to 5 cm long, sometimes spines absent; *blade strongly plicate.* Inflorescences with about 23 *filiform* flowering branches; fruits very widely obovoid, 1.5 cm diameter, *orange-red, covered with black spinules*, with floury mesocarp.

Range and habitat. Amazon region of Colombia (Amazonas), Venezuela (Bolívar), the Guianas, Brazil (Amazonas, Pará), and Bolivia (Beni, Pando); lowland rain forest on noninundated soils, below 500 m elevation.

Notes. Closely related to *Bactris acanthocarpa*, but differs in its simple leaf.

Bactris turbinocarpa
(Map 443)

Field characters. Stems clustered, 1–1.7 m tall and 2–2.5 cm diameter, spiny. Leaves 6–13, pinnate; *sheath, petiole, and rachis densely reddish brown tomentose,* covered with few to numerous black spines to 9 cm long; leaflets 15–22 per side, linear-lanceolate, regularly arranged and spreading in the same plane. Inflorescences

with 8–12 flowering branches; peduncular bract densely covered with appressed black or brown spines to 1 cm long; fruits obovoid, *markedly beaked,* 2.5–3.5 cm long and 1.5–2 cm diameter, *brownish tomentose, covered with short, stiff bristles,* with floury mesocarp.

Range and habitat. Northeastern Amazon region in Suriname and Brazil (Pará); lowland rain forest on noninundated soils, at low elevations.

Notes. One specimen from Colombia (Chocó), incomplete and still unidentified, is remarkably similar to *Bactris turbinocarpa*.

Bactris vulgaris
(Map 444)
"Tucum," "tucum preto" (Bra)

Field characters. Stems clustered, spiny, 1–3 m tall and 2–3.5 cm diameter. Leaves 4–9, pinnate; sheath, petiole, and rachis sparsely to densely covered with black spines to 9 cm long; leaflets 21–46 per side, linear, *gray on the lower surface,* irregularly arranged and spreading in different planes. Inflorescences with 6–20 flowering branches; peduncular bract gray-tomentose, with a few black spines to 1 cm long; fruits depressed-globose, 1.8–2.4 cm diameter, purplish (yellowish when immature).

Range and habitat. Atlantic coast of Brazil (Bahia, Espírito Santo, Rio de Janeiro, São Paulo); lowland rain forest in noninundated areas, below 700 m elevation.

57. DESMONCUS

This widespread and common genus of spiny palms is easily recognizable by the climbing stems that characterize all but one species. Stems are long, thin, and flexible and often extend high into the surrounding vegetation. One species, *Desmoncus stans*, has short erect or leaning stems. Leaves are pinnate, 6–50 in number, and are usually widely spaced along the stem. Often they are alternately arranged on the upper part of the stem and then spread in one plane. The leaf sheath is usually spiny, cylindrical, closed, and it extends above the petiole into a long, tubelike structure. This completely encloses the stem up to the next petiole. The rachis is occasionally smooth, but usually has either short recurved spines or long straight spines on the lower surface, and this difference distinguishes the two commonest species. Leaflets are few to several per side of the rachis and are regularly arranged or less often in clusters. They are very variable in shape, even in the same species, and range from narrow and linear to broadly elliptical, and sometimes with a long filiform tail at the apex. Perhaps the most characteristic structure of *Desmoncus* is the tail-like extension of the rachis, known as the cirrus. The leaflets of the cirrus are much reduced to rigid, backward-pointing hooks, which act as grapnels and help the plant cling onto surrounding vegetation. The name of the genus is derived from these hooks, from the Greek words "desmos," meaning a band, and "ogkos," meaning a hook. Inflorescences are branched to one order (spicate in *D. stans*)

TABLE 6. HYBRIDS IN *DESMONCUS*.

Parent 1	Hybrid	Parent 2
D. phoenicocarpus	Unnamed hybrid	D. mitis
D. polyacanthos	Unnamed hybrid	D. mitis

and are borne among the leaves. They are usually solitary at each node, but in one species they are sometimes multiple. The peduncular bract is variously spiny with straight or recurved spines, but in one species it is tomentose and lacks spines. There are few to many short flowering branches, often on a long rachis. The unisexual flowers are borne in threes of a central female and two lateral males, but often only males occur. Fruits are one-seeded, ellipsoid to obovoid, rather small and red to orange-red at maturity. The mesocarp is fleshy and the thick endocarp has three lateral pores. The endosperm is homogeneous and the seedling leaf is bifid.

Desmoncus is a genus of perhaps no more than seven species (Henderson, 1994), distributed from southern Mexico to southern Brazil and Bolivia, mostly in forest borders, secondary forest, or other open areas, or sometimes in primary forest, from sea level to 1000 m elevation. This complex genus has never been revised in depth, and there is much confusion in separating species. Sixty-one species have been described so far, most of them based on poor collections and on an insufficient understanding of morphological variation. Wessels Boer (1965) first called attention to the great variation within a single species, depending on age and habitat, and he suggested that perhaps no more than ten species existed. Henderson (1994) recognized only seven species, a view followed in this guide. Taxonomy of the genus, however, is far from resolved, and the present treatment must be considered as provisional. Variation of some species, particularly *Desmoncus mitis*, is not yet well understood, and the reader should be aware that some plants are still hard to identify. Part of this confusion may be attributable to the frequent occurrence of hybrids in the genus. The hybrids in table 6 have been noted (Henderson, 1994).

Desmoncus represents the American equivalent of the Old World climbing palms, the rattans, although the two groups are unrelated. Nor are *Desmoncus* used to nearly the extent that rattans are, although they can be locally important on a small scale (Henderson and Chávez, 1993).

Seedlings of *Desmoncus* do not pass through a delayed, rosette-forming phase of establishment common to many palms. Instead, the stems begin to elongate after the second leaf opens. This fast stem elongation, together with its flexibility, enables plants to "move" toward light gaps (Putz, 1983).

Pollination of two Peruvian species has been shown to be effected by beetles, with a very similar syndrome to that in *Bactris*, with short-lived female flowers opening before the males and curculionid and nitidulid pollinators (Listabarth, 1992, 1994). Fruits are eaten by capuchin monkeys (*Cebus capucinus*) (Hladik and Hladik, 1969) and by different frugivorous birds, including the oil bird (*Steatornis caripensis*) (Snow, 1962).

Desmoncus cirrhiferus
(Map 445)
"Matamba" (Col), "bora negra" (Ecu)
Field characters. Stems clustered, to 5 m or more long and 1–2 cm diameter, green. Leaf sheaths tomentose, with short recurved spines to 5 mm long; rachis to 1.7 m long; *cirrus with*

short hooks; leaflets 5–11 per side, elliptical, to 20 cm long, *their tips ending in long, slender, and coiled tails to 11 cm long.* Inflorescences with 15–19 short flowering branches; fruits ellipsoid to almost globose, 1.5–2 long and 1–1.5 cm diameter, red.

Range and habitat. Coastal lowlands of Colombia

(Antioquia, Cauca, Chocó, Nariño, Valle) and around the north end of the western Andes into the Río Magdalena valley (Antioquia) and coastal Ecuador (Esmeraldas); lowland rain forest, to 800 m elevation.

Uses. The stems are used to weave baskets and for fish traps (Gentry, 1988); and the fruits are edible (Barfod and Balslev, 1988).

Notes. Unmistakable in the long tail at the apex of leaflets.

Desmoncus giganteus
(Map 446, Plate 50)
"Jacitara" (Bra), "vara casha" (Per)

Field characters. Stems solitary or clustered, 12–25 m long and 1.5–2 cm diameter. Leaves arranged in 2 rows along the upper part of the stem; leaf sheath very fibrous, densely armed with black spines to 3 cm long; petiole and rachis with black, straight spines; cirrus with stout hooks, but without spines; leaflets 5–7 per side, *very large,* 45–50 cm long and 7 cm wide, *glaucous on the lower surface.* Inflorescences with numerous flowering branches; *peduncular bract to 40 cm long, densely armed with black, straight spines to 2 cm long; fruits ellipsoid, 3–4 cm long and 1.5–2.5 cm diameter,* red, the thickened, persistent petals covering almost one-third of the fruit.

Range and habitat. Western Amazon region in Colombia (Vaupés), Ecuador (Napo), Peru (Loreto, Huánuco) and western Brazil (Acre); lowland rain forest in non-inundated areas, at low elevations.

Uses. The stems are used to weave various items (Henderson and Chávez, 1993).

Notes. This is the largest *Desmoncus,* but it is seldom collected and often difficult to see because the stems climb high into the canopy.

Desmoncus mitis
(Map 447, Plate 50)
"Jacitara" (Bra), "bejuco alcalde" (Col), "barahuasca" (Per)

Field characters. Stems clustered, 1–10 m long and 0.5–1 cm diameter, *mostly unarmed or sparsely armed with hooked spines.* Leaves 6–30; rachis and cirrus with short recurved spines; leaflets 3–24 per side, elliptical to almost linear. *Inflorescences with few (3–7), short, slender flowering branches along a rather long, slender rachis; peduncular bract usually unarmed, brown-tomentose;* fruits ellipsoid, 1–2.2 cm long and 0.5–1.5 cm diameter, red.

Range and habitat. Widespread in the western Amazon region from southeastern Colombia, western Venezuela, eastern Ecuador, eastern Peru, and western Brazil and northeastern Bolivia; lowland rain forest and forest margins, in inundated and noninundated areas, to 700 m elevation.

Uses. The stems are used for basketry and for tying beams in house construction (Galeano, 1991).

Notes. This is a highly variable species and still not well understood. Several morphological variants are found across its wide range; although at a particular place two or more forms can be readily separated, intermediate forms blur the margins. The following varieties were recognized by Henderson (1994): var. *leptoclonos,* with 2–3 elliptical leaflets per side and often the cirrus absent, from Brazil (Acre, Amazonas, Rondônia) and Bolivia (Beni, La Paz, Pando); var. *leptospadix,* with 5–7 elliptical to lanceolate leaflets per side, from Colombia (Amazonas) and Peru (Huánuco, Loreto, Madre de Dios); var. *mitis,* with 10–11 lanceolate leaflets per side, from Colombia (Amazonas), Venezuela (Amazonas), Ecuador (Napo), Peru (Loreto), and Brazil (Amazonas, Roraima); var. *rurrenabaquensis,* with a spiny leaf sheath and 22–24 linear leaflets per side, from Peru (Cusco, Madre de Dios) and Bolivia (Beni, La Paz); and var. *tenerrimus,* with large fruits 1.8–2.2 cm long and 1–1.5 cm diameter, from Colombia (Amazonas, Caquetá), Peru (Loreto) and Brazil (Acre, Amazonas).

Desmoncus orthacanthos
(Map 448, Plate 51)
"Basket tie-tie" (Bel) "bayal" (Bel, Gua, Hon, Mex), "urubamba" (Bol), "matamba" (Col, CR, Pan), "jacitara" (Bra), "karwari" (Guy), "balaire" (Hon), "ballí," "matambilla" (Mex), "bambamaka" (Sur), "grigri" (Tob), "camuari," "volador" (Ven)

Field characters. Stems clustered, 2–12 m long and 1.5–2 cm diameter. Leaves 10–50, arranged in two rows along the upper part of the stem; sheath sparsely to densely covered with short black spines; *petiole and rachis with straight (not recurved) spines to 6 cm long; cirrus without spines;* leaflets 7–25 per side, regularly or irregularly arranged, elliptical or linear, *often with black spines on the lower surface.* Inflorescences with 20–50 flowering branches; *peduncular bract covered with straight, black spines to 1 cm long;* fruits ellipsoid to obovoid or almost globose, 1.5–2 cm long and 1–1.5 cm diameter, red, orange, orange-yellow.

Range and habitat. Widespread from the Atlantic slope of southern Mexico through Central America to northern South America east of the Andes, to southern Brazil and Bolivia, also in Trinidad and Tobago; mostly in disturbed areas, secondary forest, river margins, and very common in coastal areas, usually at low elevations but rarely to 1000 m.

Uses. The stems are widely used for weaving baskets (Galeano and Bernal, 1987; Schultes, 1940).

Notes. The most widespread species in the genus, easily recognized by its straight rachis spines and cirrus without spines. It is, however, extremely variable, and it seems likely that on further study it will be found to be a species complex with many local varieties.

Desmoncus phoenicocarpus
(Map 449)
"Jacitara" (Bra), "kamuari" (Guy)

Field characters. Stems clustered, 2–3(–9) m long and 0.7–1 cm diameter. Leaves numerous; sheath unarmed or with scattered, short, straight spines; rachis to 70 cm, *with short, recurved spines*; leaflets 6–7 per side, elliptical, to 15 cm long and 4.5 cm wide. Inflorescences with 8–11 flowering branches, to 6 cm long; *peduncular bract armed with rather straight, short, dark spines with white, bulbous bases*; fruits globose to obovoid, 0.8–1 cm long and 0.8–1 cm diameter, orange to bright red.

Range and habitat. Northeastern Amazon region in Venezuela (Amazonas), the Guianas, and Brazil (Amapá, Amazonas, Maranhão, Pará, Roraima); forest margins or secondary forest, often on white-sand soils, to 700 m elevation.

Notes. Previously and erroneously known as *Desmoncus macroacanthos.*

Desmoncus polyacanthos
(Map 450, Plate 51)
"Jacitara," "espera-ai" (Bra), "bejuco alcalde" (Col), "kamawarri" (Guy), "vara casha" (Per), "bambakka," "bambamaka" (Sur), "voladora" (Ven)

Field characters. Stems clustered, 2–15 m long and 0.5–2 cm diameter. Leaves 15–25, in two rows either side of the upper part of the stem; sheath densely armed with black or brown spines to 2 cm long; *petiole, rachis, and cirrus with short, recurved spines*; leaflets 4–14 per side, regularly or irregularly arranged, lanceolate to elliptical. Inflorescences with 5–17 flowering branches; *peduncular bract covered with short, hooked, bulbous-based spines*; fruits ellipsoid to obovoid, 1–2.2 cm long and 0.8–1.8 cm diameter, red to orange.

Range and habitat. Widespread in northern South America east of the Andes, from eastern Colombia (Amazonas, Guianía, Meta, Putamayo, Vichada), southern Venezuela (Amazonas, Anzoátegui, Apure, Barinas, Bolívar, Carabobo, Delta Amacuro, Miranda), Trinidad, St. Vincent, the Guianas, eastern Ecuador (Napo), eastern Peru (Cusco, Loreto, Madre de Dios), Brazil (Acre, Alagoas, Amazonas, Amapá, Bahia, Espírito Santo, Goiás, Maranhão, Mato Grosso, Minas Gerais, Pernambuco, Rio de Janeiro, Roraima, Rondônia, Sergipe, Tocantins), and Bolivia (Pando, Santa Cruz); river banks, open areas, forest margins, understory of lowland forest, coastal areas, and gallery forest, to 1000 m elevation on eastern Andean slopes.

Uses. The stems are used for weaving baskets and sieves and for tying various items.

Notes. The great variation in leaf shape and spinyness of this species, depending on age and amount of light received, has been stressed by Wessels Boer (1965) and Galeano (1991). Two varieties were recognized by Henderson (1994), depending on fruit size: var. *polyacanthos*, with fruits 1–1.4 cm long and 0.8–1 cm diameter, the most widespread form; and var. *prunifer*, with fruits 1.5–2.2 cm long and 1.3–1.8 cm diameter, from Colombia (Amazonas), Ecuador (Napo), and Peru (Huánuco, Loreto, Pasco).

Desmoncus stans
(Map 451, Plate 51)

Field characters. Stems clustered, *erect or slightly creeping*, to 2.5 m tall and 1 cm diameter. Leaves 4–7; sheath with scattered, short spines; petiole and rachis with scattered, straight (not recurved) spines; *rachis not continued into a cirrus*; leaflets 3–7 per side, elliptical, *the tip narrowed into a long, slender tail. Inflorescences spicate*, to 20 cm long; fruits obovoid, to 2 cm long and 1.5 cm diameter, red.

Range and habitat. Costa Rica (Puntarenas, Osa Peninsula); locally common in primary forest on slopes and ridges, at 200–300 m elevation.

Notes. Unmistakable in its erect, nonclimbing habit, although easily overlooked in the forest. This species probably evolved as a neotenic (retaining juvenile characters) form of the climbing *Desmoncus cirrhiferus* of western Colombia, which shares the tail-like projection of the leaflet.

58. ASTROCARYUM

This genus contains some of the most spiny palms in the Americas, with sharp, black and flattened spines to 30 cm long covering the stems of some species. Stems are stout, moderate to large, sometimes short and subterranean, and solitary or clustered. They are either covered with persistent, spiny leaf bases, or clean and spiny. Spines on all parts of the plant are flattened and usually black. Leaves are pinnate, 3–30 in number, stiff and ascending in many species, and are always spiny. Leaflets are usually linear and are either regularly arranged and spread in the same plane, or irregularly arranged in clusters and spread in different planes. Occasionally the leaflets are incompletely split and the leaf appears almost simple. The lower surface of leaflets is whitish, and this usually serves to distinguish the genus from *Bactris*. Inflorescences are borne among the leaves and are branched to one order. The peduncle and peduncular bract are usually densely spiny. Flowering branches are numerous and the lower part bears unisexual flowers in threes of a central female and two lateral males, while the upper part bears only male flowers. The number of female flowers per flowering branch is important in identification. Male flowers have 3–12 stamens, although 6 is the most common number. Fruits are one-seeded, variously shaped but usually beaked, yellow, green orange, or brown, and smooth or spiny. In some species they are densely arranged and form a club-shaped infructescence. In a few species the epicarp splits open at maturity to reveal the brightly colored mesocarp. The endocarp is thick and bony, with three lateral pores, from which fibers radiate. The name of the genus is derived from the pattern of these fibers and comes from the Greek words "astron," meaning star, and "karyon," meaning nut. Endosperm is homogeneous and the seedling leaf is bifid.

Astrocaryum contains eighteen species distributed from Mexico to eastern Brazil; but most occur in the Amazon region, and this seems to be the center of distribution. They are almost exclusively lowland palms, seldom reaching 1200 m elevation. The last treatment of the genus as a whole was that of Burret (1934), but this work is imprecise and now out of date. Kahn and Millán (1992) have begun a modern revision of the genus (see also Henderson, 1994).

Some species are very important in food chains because of the abundance and edibility of their fruits. Many interesting associations have been described between the fruits of these palms and, for example, rodents (Smythe, 1989), monkeys (Terborgh, 1983), and fish (Piedade, 1985). Some species are of economic value, especially to aboriginal cultures.

KEY TO THE SPECIES OF *ASTROCARYUM*

1a. Central America to northwestern South America, west of the Andes, including inter-Andean valleys of Colombia.
  2a. Stems subterranean or very short; leaflets regularly arranged and spreading in the same plane; fruits purple, smooth; basins of Ríos Magdalena, Cauca and Sinú in Colombia . . . . . *A. malybo.*
  2a. Stems well developed; leaflets regularly or irregularly arranged; fruits not purple.
    3a. Leaflets irregularly arranged in clusters and spreading in different planes; fruits smooth or covered with minute spinules.
      4a. Infructescences erect among the leaves; peduncle 30–37 cm long; Atlantic slope of Costa Rica and Panama . . . . . *A. confertum.*
      4b. Infructescences pendulous below the leaves; peduncle to 1.7 m long; Atlantic coast of Panama and Pacific lowlands from Costa Rica to Ecuador . . . . . *A. standleyanum.*
    3b. Leaflets regularly arranged and spreading in the same plane; fruits smooth or covered with spinules.

5a. Leaflets narrow and equally wide; valley of Río Magdalena in Colombia   .....*A. triandrum.*

5b. Leaflets unequally wide; Central America.

  6a. Stems not covered with leaf bases; Mexico to Nicaragua   .....*A. mexicanum.*

  6b. Stems covered with persistent, spiny leaf bases; Nicaragua to Panama   .....*A. alatum.*

1b. Amazon region, Central Brazilian region, and Atlantic coast of Brazil.

  7a. Leaflets regularly arranged and spreading in the same plane; fruits densely crowded.

    8a. Atlantic coast of Brazil   .....*A. aculeatissimum.*

    8b. Amazon and central Brazilian region.

      9a. Stems clustered, slender, less than 10 cm diameter; leaves less than 3 m long; fruits bright orange, smooth   .....*A. gynacanthum.*

      9b. Stems solitary or, if clustered, more than 10 cm diameter; leaves usually more than 4 m long; fruits brown to orange, tomentose or spinulose.

        10a. Fruits orange-brown, with spinules on "shoulders" only; epicarp splitting regularly to expose the mesocarp; northeastern Amazon region   .....*A. paramacca.*

        10b. Fruits brown, completely tomentose or spinulose; epicarp usually not splitting.

          11a. Spines of petiole arranged in distinct, oblique rows; fruits covered with hard spinules; northeastern Amazon region   .....*A. sciophilum.*

          11b. Spines of petiole not in rows; fruits tomentose or covered with soft to hard spinules; widespread but mostly in the western Amazon region   .....*A. murumuru.*

  7b. Leaflets irregularly arranged and spreading in different planes; fruits usually loosely arranged.

    12a. Stem subterranean or short.

      13a. Leaflets 17–43 per side; central Brazil and eastern Bolivia   .....*A. campestre.*

      13b. Leaflets 55–103 per side; central and eastern Amazon region   .....*A. acaule.*

    12b. Stem tall and erect.

      14a. Stems clustered, usually forming clumps along river margins .....*A. jauari.*

      14b. Stems solitary or clustered, not forming clumps along river margins.

        15a. Stems solitary; forest, or often planted near dwellings.

          16a. Fruiting corolla with an entire margin; western Amazon region   .....*A. chambira.*

          16b. Fruiting corolla lobed; central and eastern Amazon region   .....*A. aculeatum.*

        15b. Stems usually clustered, rarely solitary; open areas, seldom planted.

          17a. Leaflets 50–72 per side; southwestern Amazon region   .....*A. huaimi.*

          17b. Leaflets 73–120 per side; northeastern Amazon region   .....*A. vulgare.*

Astrocaryum acaule
(Map 452)
"Tucumã-í" (Bra), "espina" (Col), "corozo" (Ven)

Field characters. Stems solitary, short and subterranean, rarely to 1 m tall. Leaves 5–9; leaflets 55–103 per side, *irregularly arranged in clusters and spreading in different planes.* Inflorescences erect; peduncular bract mottled brown-white, covered with black spines; *flowering branches with 2–3 female flowers at the base*, fruits obovoid, 2.5–3 cm long and 1.5–2 cm, yellow-green to orange when ripe, *smooth.*

Range and habitat. Amazon region in Colombia (Guainía, Meta, Vaupés, Vichada), Venezuela (Amazonas, Bolívar), Guyana and Brazil (Amazonas, Pará, Rondônia), especially common in upper Rio Negro region; lowland rain forest, streams banks, river islands, savanna margins, rocky outcrops, road margins or other disturbed areas, often on white-sand soils. In some places it is locally very abundant, but is generally uncommon in undisturbed forest.

Uses. The fruits are edible; and fibers are occasionally extracted from the leaves.

Astrocaryum aculeatissimum
(Map 453, Plate 51)
"Brejaúva" (Bra)

Field characters. Stems clustered or less often solitary, 4–8 m tall and 11–15 cm diameter, densely spiny. Leaves 10–20, spreading; leaflets 59–85 per side, *regularly arranged and spreading in the same plane.* Inflorescences pendulous; *flowering branches with one female flower at the base*, fruits obovoid, 3.5–4.5 cm long and 3–3.5 cm diameter, *scurfy brown with deciduous, black spinules.*

Range and habitat. Atlantic coast of Brazil (Bahia, Espírito Santo, Minas Gerais, Paraná, Rio de Janeiro, Santa Catarina, São Paulo); lowland rain forest on noninundated soils, or left in pastures, at low elevations.

Uses. The leaves are used for making brooms and hats; stems are used in house construction and bows and arrows; and the liquid endosperm is used medicinally (Noblick, 1991).

Astrocaryum aculeatum
(Map 454)
"Chonta," "panima" (Bol), "tucumã" "(Bra), "awara" (Guy), "cemau" (Sur), "tucuma" (Ven)

Field characters. Stems solitary, stout and erect, 8–20 m tall and 12–25(–40) cm diameter, covered with long black spines. Leaves 6–15, erect, to 6 m long; leaflets 73–130 per side, *irregularly arranged in clusters and spreading in different planes.* Inflorescences erect among the leaves; peduncular bract covered with black spines to 8 cm long; *flowering branches with 2–4*

female flowers at the base, fruits globose or obovoid, 4.5–6 cm long and 3.5–4.2 cm diameter, yellow-orange or yellow-green, *smooth; mesocarp fleshy; fruiting calyx and corolla lobed.*

Range and habitat. Central and eastern Amazon region of Colombia (Amazonas), Venezuela (Amazonas), Trinidad, the Guianas, Brazil (Acre, Amazonas, Pará, Rondônia), and Bolivia (Beni, Pando, Santa Cruz); most frequent in deforested areas and usually associated with present and past human settlements. It rarely occurs in lowland rain forest. It is probably introduced in some areas (Kahn and de Granville, 1992).

Uses. The orange, fleshy mesocarp is edible and the fruits are sold in markets in Leticia (Colombia), Tabatinga, and Manaus (Brazil).

Astrocaryum alatum
(Map 455, Plate 52)
"Coquito" (CR), "coquillo" (Pan)

Field characters. Stems solitary, 1.5–7 m tall and 10–17 cm diameter, covered with persistent, spiny leaf bases. Leaves 6–30, *strongly arching,* to 3 m long; leaflets numerous, unequally wide, regularly arranged and spreading in the same plane, *often closely inserted and leaf appearing almost simple and with serrate margins.* Inflorescences pendulous among the leaves; *flowering branches with one female flower at the base*, fruits obovoid to nearly globose, densely crowded, yellow-brown, loosely covered with straight black spinules; epicarp weakly splitting when mature.

Range and habitat. Atlantic slope in Nicaragua (Río San Juan, Zelaya), Costa Rica (Alajuela, Guanacaste, Heredia, Limón) and Panama (Bocas del Toro, Canal Area, Coclé, Colón, San Blas, Veraguas), and also Pacific slope in Costa Rica (Osa Peninsula, Puntarenas); lowland rain forest in well-drained or poorly drained soils, usually below 500 m elevation.

Notes. The Panama Canal marks the eastern end of its range. It is very similar to *Astrocaryum mexicanum,* and perhaps the two are conspecific.

Astrocaryum campestre
(Map 456)
"Jarivá," "tucum" (Bra)

Field characters. Stems solitary, short, and subterranean. Leaves 3–6, arching; leaflets 17–43 per side, *irregularly arranged in clusters (sometimes appearing almost regularly arranged) and spreading in different planes.* Inflorescences erect among the leaves, short and compact, and borne near ground level; peduncular bract brown-tomentose, with few, black spines; *flowering branches with 2–5 female flowers at the base*, fruits obovoid, 3–3.5 cm long and 2–2.5 cm diameter, orange or yellowish green, *smooth.*

Range and habitat. Central Brazil (Bahia, Goiás, Maranhão, Mato Grosso, Minas Gerais, southern Pará, Tocantins) and eastern Bolivia (Santa Cruz); open savannas or *cerrado*, in deep, sandy soils, to 1200 m elevation. It can be a persistent weed of fields.

Uses. Fibers from the young leaves are used to make fishing nets and similar items; and the fruits are edible.

Notes. The smallest species in the genus; plants from the extreme western part of the range in Bolivia are much larger than usual.

Astrocaryum chambira
(Map 457, Plate 52)
"Tucuma" (Bra), "chambira" (Col, Ecu, Per), "cumare" (Col, Ven), "coco" (Col, Ecu)

Field characters. Stems solitary, stout and erect, 3.5–30 m tall and 19–35 cm diameter, covered with black spines to 20 cm long. Leaves 9–16, erect, to 5 m or more long; *petiole in juvenile palms covered with yellowish, winged spines*; leaflets 120–175 per side, *irregularly arranged in clusters and spreading in different planes.* Inflorescences erect among the leaves; peduncular bract densely covered with short, black or brown spines; *flowering branches with (0–1)2–5 female flowers at the base*; fruits obovoid, 5–7 cm long and 4–5 cm diameter, yellow or yellowish green when ripe, *minutely spinulose*; *mesocarp fibrous, not fleshy; fruiting calyx frilled on the margin, corolla not lobed.*

Range and habitat. Western Amazon region in Colombia (Amazonas, Caquetá, Guaviare, Meta, Putumayo, Vaupés), Venezuela (Amazonas), Ecuador (Morona-Santiago, Napo), Peru (Amazonas, Loreto), and Brazil (Acre, Amazonas); lowland rain forest on noninundated soils and common in disturbed areas, at low elevations.

Uses. The fibers from the youngest, unexpanded leaves are commonly used to weave a variety of items, especially hammocks, fishing nets, and bags. It is often planted because of its usefulness.

Notes. Very similar to *Astrocaryum aculeatum*, but differs in its fruits.

Astrocaryum confertum
(Map 458)
"Coyolillo", "zurube" (CR), "pina-pina" (Pan)

Field characters. Stems solitary, stout and erect, 10–17 m tall and 14–20 cm diameter, densely covered with black spines to 17 cm long. Leaves 5–12, stiffly erect, to 4 m long; leaflets 114–123 per side, *irregularly arranged in clusters and spreading in different planes.* Inflorescences erect among the leaves; *flowering branches with several*

female flowers at the base; fruits obovoid, 3.3–3.7 cm long and 1.8–2 cm diameter, orange, minutely spinulose but appearing *smooth.*

Range and habitat. Atlantic slope of Costa Rica (Heredia, Limón) and Panama (San Blas); lowland rain forest on noninundated soils, to 250 m elevation.

Notes. Similar to and perhaps conspecific with *Astrocaryum standleyanum* (de Nevers et al., 1988).

Astrocaryum gynacanthum
(Map 459, Plates 52 & 53)
"Mumbaca" (Bra), "coco de puerco" (Col), "ti-warra" (FrG), "cubarro" (Ven)

Field characters. Stems clustered, 2–6(–12) m tall and 3–6(–10) cm diameter, covered with flattened spines to 15 cm long. Leaves 6–13, horizontally spreading, less than 3 m long; *leaflets 21–41 per side, regularly arranged and spreading in the same plane, the apical ones fused. Inflorescences pendulous; flowering branches with one female flower at the base*; fruits obovoid, 2.5–3 cm long and 1.2–1.5 cm diameter, smooth, *densely crowded, bright orange, and splitting regularly from the apex to show the orange, floury mesocarp*; fruiting calyx with flexuous, black spinules.

Range and habitat. Amazon region, most common in the eastern and central parts, in Colombia (Amazonas, Caquetá, Guainía, Putumayo, Vaupés, Vichada), Venezuela (Amazonas, Apure, Bolívar, Monagas), the Guianas, Brazil (Amapá, Amazonas, Maranhão, Pará, Rondônia), and Bolivia (Pando); common in the understory of lowland rain forest on noninundated soils, below 650(–850) m elevation.

Uses. The mesocarp is occasionally eaten; and Uitoto Indians in Colombia burn the palm heart to obtain vegetable salt (Galeano, 1991).

Astrocaryum huaimi
(Map 460)
"Chontilla" (Bol)

Field characters. Stems clustered or solitary, 3–7 m tall and 5–15 cm diameter, covered with long, flat, black spines. Leaves 6–12, erect, to 3.5 m long; leaflets 50–72 per side, *irregularly arranged in clusters and spreading in different planes.* Inflorescences erect among the leaves; *flowering branches with 2–3 female flowers at the base*; fruits ellipsoid, 3.5–4.5 cm long and 2–3 cm diameter, orange or orange-yellow, *smooth.*

Range and habitat. Southwestern periphery of the Amazon region in Peru (Madre de Dios), Brazil (Goiás, Mato Grosso), and Bolivia (Beni, La Paz, Santa Cruz); forest islands in savannas or deciduous forest, at low elevations.

Notes. Closely related to and perhaps not distinct from *Astrocaryum vulgare.*

Astrocaryum jauari
(Map 461, Plate 53)
"Jauari" (Bra), "güiridima," "alvarico" (Col, Ven), "yavarí" (Col), "chambirilla," "huiririma" (Ecu, Per), "sauarai" (Guy), "liba awara" (Sur)
Field characters. Stems clustered, forming large stands, rarely solitary, 5–13 m tall and 9–30 cm diameter. Leaves 6–15, stiffly erect, 4–5 m long; leaflets 56–148 per side, *irregularly arranged in clusters and spreading in different planes.* Inflorescences erect among the leaves; *flowering branches with 3–8 female flowers at the base*, fruits globose to obovoid, 2.5–3.5 cm long and 1.7–2.5 cm diameter, yellow to orange, smooth.
Range and habitat. Throughout the Amazon region in Colombia (Amazonas, Caquetá, Guainía, Guaviare, Putumayo, Vaupés, Vichada), Venezuela (Amazonas, Bolívar, Anzoátegui, Apure), the Guianas, Ecuador (Napo), Peru (Loreto), and Brazil (Acre, Amapá, Amazonas, Pará, Roraima); usually in large numbers along margins of large or small rivers, lakes, or frequently inundated areas.
Uses. The leaf rachis is used for weaving; the endocarps are used for necklaces (Borgtoft Pedersen and Balslev, 1990); and fruits are used as bait for fishing (Henderson, 1994). There is commercial palm heart canning business on the Rio Negro in Brazil, where this species is extremely abundant. Borgtoft Pedersen and Balslev (1990) consider that this species could be used in supplying food for fish farming in agroforestry systems.
Notes. The reproductive cycle seems to be associated with the annual fluctuation of river levels. Ripe fruits begin falling when rivers are at the highest levels and fruits are either predated or dispersed by fish (Piedade, 1985). The structure of some populations and reproductive biology can be found in Goulding (1989), Piedade (1985), and Borgtoft Pedersen and Balslev (1990). Schlüter et al. (1993) have studied the physiological and anatomical adaptations of seedlings to inundation. Young plants can be submerged for up to 300 days per year.

Astrocaryum malybo
(Map 462)
"Anchamba," "chingalé" (Col)
Field characters. Stems solitary, short and subterranean. Leaves 10–20, to 5 m long; leaflets 96–120 per side, *regularly arranged and horizontally spreading in the same plane.* Inflorescences erect; *flowering branches with 1–3 female flowers at the base*; fruits obovoid to ellipsoid, about 3.5 cm long and 2.6 cm diameter, purple to black, smooth.

Range and habitat. Colombia, middle and lower Magdalena valley, lower Cauca valley, and the Sinú valley (Antioquia, Bolívar, Córdoba, Sucre, Cundinamarca, Tolima, Santander); lowland rain forest, usually below 300 m elevation.
Uses. The veins of the leaflets from the very young leaves are used to make mats, baskets, and related handicrafts. In Colombia (Córdoba, Sucre) this is an important local industry. Populations have been severely reduced, both because of the destruction of its habitat and overexploitation of its leaves. It has been reported as a vulnerable species (Bernal, 1989).
Notes. An unusual species because it is the only one with both regularly arranged leaflets and 2–3 female flowers per flowering branch.

Astrocaryum mexicanum
(Map 463)
"Lancetilla" (Hon), "chocho," "chichón" (Mex)
Field characters. Stems solitary, 1.5–6(–8) m tall and 2.5–8 cm diameter, spiny, *without persistent leaf bases.* Leaves about 11, arching; leaflets 15–32 per side, unequally wide, the apical ones often not split and with toothed margins, *regularly arranged and spreading in the same plane.* Inflorescences erect; *flowering branches with one female flower at the base* (and infructescence appearing spicate); fruits ellipsoid to obovoid, 4–6 cm long and 4–6 cm diameter, *densely covered with short, black spinules*, brownish.
Range and habitat. Mexico (Chiapas, Oaxaca, Tabasco, Veracruz), Guatemala (Alta Verapaz, Izabal, Petén), Belize, El Salvador (San Miguel), Nicaragua (Zelaya), and Honduras (Atlántida, Gracias a Dios); locally very abundant in lowland rain forest on noninundated soils, at low elevations.
Uses. The young inflorescences and endosperm are eaten; the leaves are used for thatching; and the trunks are used as tool handles (Ibarra-Manriquez, 1988).
Notes. Various studies have been carried out in Mexico on the following ecological aspects of this species; pollen flow (Eguiarte et al., 1993), population structure and demography (Martinez-Ramos et al., 1988; Piñero et al., 1977, 1986), reproduction (Piñero et al., 1982; Piñero and Sarukhán, 1982), and pollination (Búrquez et al., 1987).

Astrocaryum murumuru
(Map 464, Plate 53)
"Chonta" (Bol), "murumuru" (Bra), "chuchana" (Col, Ecu), "huicungo" (Per)
Field characters. Stems solitary or clustered, short and subterranean or tall and aerial, (0–) 1.5–15 m tall and 10–30 cm diameter, spiny

but usually covered with persistent leaf bases. Leaves 6–15(–25), horizontally spreading, to 7 m long; leaflets 90–130 per side, *regularly arranged and spreading in the same plane*. Inflorescences erect among the leaves; *flowering branches with one female flower at the base*; fruits densely crowded, obovoid or elongate-obovoid, 3.5–9 cm long and 2.5–4.5 cm diameter, brown-tomentose or scarcely to densely covered with short, black spinules; mesocarp fleshy or fibrous.

Range and habitat. Widespread in the Amazon region in Colombia, Venezuela, the Guianas, Ecuador, Peru, Brazil, and Bolivia; lowland rain forest, usually along river margins or other periodically inundated areas, at low elevations but occasionally to 900 m on eastern Andean slopes.

Uses. The mesocarp of some varieties is occasionally eaten and leaves and stems are sometimes used in house construction.

Notes. The fruits are an important source of food for animals, particularly monkeys (Terborgh, 1983, 1986), squirrels (Emmons, 1984), and peccaries (Kiltie, 1981). Seed predation has been studied by Terborgh et al. (1993). Kahn and Millán (1992) divided this species into 13 separate species; here we follow Henderson (1994) and recognize these as fewer varieties. The first group, consisting of the following four varieties, has female flowers with a spinulose calyx as long or almost as long as the spinulose corolla: var. *ciliatum*, with corolla margins of fruits entire and spinulose, from Colombia (Amazonas); var. *ferrugineum*, with reddish brown hairs on the lower surface of the leaves, from near Manaus in Brazil (Amazonas); var. *huicungo*, with clustered stems and fruits 6.5–7.5 cm long with fleshy mesocarp, from Peru (Amazonas, western Loreto, San Martín); var. *javarense*, with solitary stems and fruits 3.5–6.5 cm long and fibrous mesocarp, from Peru (Loreto, Madre de Dios). The second group, consisting of the following four varieties, has the female flowers with a nonspiny calyx as long or shorter than the spinulose corolla: var. *murumuru*, with scurfy-tomentose fruits, widespread in the Amazon region; var. *perangustatum*, with spinulose fruits with a long, narrow basal part, from Peru (Pasco); var. *macrocalyx*, with solitary stems and spinulose fruits, from Colombia (Amazonas, Caquetá, Putumayo) and Peru (Loreto); and var. *urostachys*, with clustered stems and spinulose fruits, from Ecuador (Morona-Santiago, Napo) and Peru (Loreto).

Astrocaryum paramaca
(Map 465)
"Tucumã branco" (Bra), "counana" (FrG), "paramaka" (Sur)

Field characters. Stems solitary, short, and subterranean or less often to 8 m or more tall and 11 cm diameter. Leaves 10–15, erect; leaflets 55–100 per side, *regularly arranged and spreading in the same plane*. Inflorescences erect or pendulous, borne among the leaves; peduncular bract densely brown-velvety; *flowering branches with one female flower near the base, the lowermost part of the flowering branches with flexuous, black spinules*; fruits oblong, 3.5–4 cm long and 1.5–2 cm diameter, orange-brown, *with spinules on "shoulders" only*; epicarp splitting regularly at maturity to expose yellow mesocarp.

Range and habitat. Northeastern Amazon region in Suriname, French Guiana, and Brazil (Amapá, Amazonas, Pará); abundant in the understory of lowland rain forest, at low elevations.

Notes. Still somewhat problematic. Most plants have short and subterranean stems, but populations from either end of the range of the species have tall, upright stems. There may be two taxa here.

Astrocaryum sciophilum
(Map 466)
"Murumuru" (Bra), "mourou-mourou" (FrG), "counana" (Sur)

Field characters. Stems solitary, short and subterranean, or to 2 m tall. Leaves 7–12, stiffly erect, to 5 m long; petiole spines in oblique rows; leaflets 58–90 per side, *regularly arranged and spreading in the same plane.* Inflorescences erect among the leaves; *flowering branches with one female flower at the base*; fruits obovoid, clustered and borne in a club-shaped infructescence, 3–6 cm long and 2.5–4 cm diameter, brown, *moderately covered with short, black spinules.*

Range and habitat. Northeastern Amazon region in the Guianas and Brazil (Amapá, Amazonas, Pará); abundant in the understory of lowland rain forest on noninundated soils, at low elevations.

Notes. Demography has been studied by Sist (1989).

Astrocaryum standleyanum
(Map 467, Plate 54)
"Güérregue," "chunga" (Col), "mocora" (Ecu)

Field characters. Stems solitary, tall and stout, 6–15 m tall and 16–22 cm diameter, spiny. Leaves 11–18, horizontally spreading and somewhat curved, to 4 m long; leaflets 100–105 per side, *irregularly arranged and spreading in different planes.* Inflorescences erect among the leaves, becoming pendulous in fruit; *flowering branches with (1–)2–8 female flowers at the base*; fruits obovoid, 2.5–6 cm long and 2–3 cm diameter, orange, almost smooth or with minute spinules; mesocarp *orange,* fleshy.

Range and habitat. Pacific slope in Costa Rica (Puntarenas), Atlantic slope in Panama (Canal

Area, Panamá, San Blas), and Pacific lowlands of Colombia (Antioquia, Chocó, Cauca, Valle, Nariño) and Ecuador (Esmeraldas, Pichincha); most common in lowland rain forest on imperfectly drained soils, usually below 200 m elevation. It is commonly conserved in pastures.

Uses. Stems are used in house construction; the fruits are sometimes used to feed pigs; and fibers from the youngest leaves are used to weave various items.

Notes. The fruits are produced in very large numbers and are an important source of food for many animals. In Panama, Smythe (1989) studied seed survival and dispersal; and Glanz et al. (1983) showed that the red-tailed squirrel, *Sciurus granatensis*, was the main arboreal seed predator.

Astrocaryum triandrum
(Map 468)
"Cabecenegro" (Col)
Field characters. Stems solitary, up to 5 m tall and 12 cm diameter, usually with few spines. Leaves 6–8, erect, to 3 m long; leaflets 69–74 per side, *regularly arranged and horizontally spreading in the same plane.* Inflorescences erect among the leaves; *flowering branches with one female flower at the base*; male flowers with only 3 stamens; *fruits densely crowded*, obovoid, wedge-shaped at base, 4–6 cm long and 2.3 cm diameter, orange-brown, *densely covered, especially near the apex, with black spines.*

Range and habitat. A small area in the middle Magdalena valley of Colombia (Antioquia, Caldas); lowland rain forest on alluvial plains or gentle slopes, on acidic soils, below 500 m elevation. The habitat of this species has been drastically changed and it is considered vulnerable (Bernal, 1989; Galeano et al., 1988).

Uses. The trunks are used as posts for fences and for house construction.

Notes. The only species in the genus with 3 stamens. The fruits are eaten by peccaries (*Tayassu tajacu* and *T. pecari*).

Astrocaryum vulgare
(Map 469)
"Tucumã" (Bra), "awarra" (FrG, Sur)
Field characters. Stems clustered and forming small clumps or less often solitary, 4–10 m tall and 10–20 cm diameter, covered with black spines to 22 cm long. Leaves 8–16, stiffly erect; leaflets 73–120 per side, *irregularly arranged in clusters and spreading in different planes.* Inflorescences erect among the leaves; *flowering branches with 2–4 female flowers at the base of each branch*; fruits globose to ellipsoid, 4–5 cm long and 3–3.7 cm diameter, orange, *smooth.*

Range and habitat. Northeastern Amazon region in Suriname, French Guiana, and Brazil (Maranhão, Pará, Tocantins); lowland rain forest or forest patches in savannas, often in disturbed areas and common in old fields, on noninundated soils, at low elevations.

59. PHOLIDOSTACHYS

This is the first genus in the group of geonomoid palms (*Pholidostachys, Calyptrogyne, Calyptronoma, Asterogyne, Welfia, Geonoma*), and all are immediately recognizable by the numerous small pits in the flowering branches. Stems of *Pholidostachys* are moderate or rarely short, rather stout, usually solitary and erect or rarely creeping. Leaves are pinnate, 7–25 in number, and usually spread in a graceful crown. They are irregularly divided into several broad leaflets, and these always spread in the same plane, as in other geonomoid palms. Typically, sheaths and petioles (and inflorescences) are reddish brown tomentose. Inflorescences are spicate or branched to one order (and then rarely the basal branches bifurcate) and are borne among the leaves. Peduncular bracts are surprisingly variable for such a small genus and range from somewhat woody and deciduous to fibrous and persistent. The genus can usually be distinguished from other geonomoid palms by its thick flowering branches covered with closely spaced pits, and these pits are covered with overlapping, semicircular bracts. Flowers are arranged in threes of one central female and two lateral males, borne in pits along the flowering branches. Male and female flowers of all species are very similar to one another, and the species are distinguished mostly by inflorescence structure. Fruits are one-seeded, obovoid, or somewhat misshapen by mutual pressure, maroon-purple, brown, or black and have large fibers in the mesocarp. Seeds have homogeneous endosperm and the seedling leaf is bifid.

Pholidostachys is a small genus of four species (Wessels Boer, 1968; de Nevers, in press) distributed from Central America to northwestern South America in Colombia, Ecuador, Peru, and Brazil. Species usually grow in upland areas but can also be found in the lowlands. They always grow in forest and do not persist in disturbed areas. There is a fascinating progression from the enclosed inflorescences, covered by a fibrous peduncular bract, of *P. dactyloides* and *P. kalbreyeri*, to the completely open inflorescences with deciduous, woody bracts of *P. pulchra* and *P. synanthera*. Interestingly, in each pair of species, one has a spicate inflorescence while the other has a branched inflorescence. These two groups of species must have quite different pollination systems, but this has not been studied.

Wessels Boer (1968) included *Pholidostachys* in a more broadly conceived *Calyptrogyne*, in which he also placed *Calyptronoma*. This scheme has seldom been followed (Uhl and Dransfield, 1987; de Nevers and Henderson, 1988).

Pholidostachys dactyloides
(Map 470)
"Carmaná," "rabo de gallo" (Col)
Field characters. Stems solitary, 2–10 m tall and 6–9 cm diameter, erect. Leaves 7–20; leaflets 6–17 per side, to 10 cm wide. Inflorescences branched to one order; *peduncular bract fibrous, covering the flowering branches, decaying as the fruits develop; flowering branches 5–16,* (11–) 17–52 cm long and 0.5–1.3 cm wide; fruits obovoid, 1.3–1.5 cm long and 0.8–1.2 cm diameter, purple-black.
Range and habitat. Eastern Panama (Darién, Panamá) and Pacific slope in Colombia (Antioquia to Nariño) and Ecuador (Esmeraldas, Pichincha); lowland to montane rain forest, below 1500 m elevation.
Uses. The leaves are occasionally used for thatching and are said to be durable.

Pholidostachys kalbreyeri
(Map 471, Plate 54)
"Rabo de gallo" (Pan)
Field characters. Stems solitary, 0.3–3 m tall and 6–12 cm diameter, erect or creeping. Leaves 8–13; leaflets 5–7 per side, to 18 cm wide. *Inflorescences spicate or occasionally bifurcate; peduncular bract fibrous, covering the flowering branch(es), decaying as the fruits develop; flowering branch(es) 12–18 cm long and 1–2 cm wide;* fruits densely crowded and misshapen by mutual pressure, irregularly obovoid, 1.5–3.5 cm long, maroon.
Range and habitat. Panama (Coclé, San Blas, Veraguas) and Colombia (Antioquia, Chocó); wet areas near streams or in swamps, in lowland or premontane rain forest, at 60–750 m elevation.
Notes. A rare species, somewhat intermediate between *Pholidostachys pulchra* and *P. dactyloides.*

Pholidostachys pulchra
(Map 472)
Field characters. Stems solitary or occasionally clustered, 2–9 m tall and 3–6 cm diameter, erect. Leaves 10–23; leaflets 4–10 per side, to 7 cm wide. *Inflorescences spicate; peduncular bract fibrous, the inflorescence well exserted from the bract at flowering time; flowering branch (19–)40–50 cm long and 0.8–1.2 cm diameter;* fruits obovoid, to 2.8 cm long and 1.5 cm diameter, brown to purple-black.
Range and habitat. Atlantic slope of Nicaragua (Zelaya), Costa Rica (Heredia) through Panama (Bocas del Toro, Colón, San Blas, Veraguas) to Pacific slope of northwestern Colombia (Antioquia, Chocó, Valle) and possibly northwestern Ecuador; lowland or premontane rain forest, below 800 m elevation.

Pholidostachys synanthera
(Map 473, Plate 54)
"Ubim" (Bra), "chalar" (Col), "palmiche," "palmiche grande" (Per)
Field characters. Stems solitary, 1.8–5 m tall and 3–8 cm diameter, erect. Leaves 10–25; leaflets 5–17 per side, to 5 cm wide. *Inflorescences branched to one or two orders; peduncular bract somewhat woody, falling before flowering time; flowering branches 7–17, 40–64 cm long and 6–9 mm diameter, spreading;* fruits obovoid, 1.4–1.7 cm long and 0.8–1 cm diameter, black.
Range and habitat. Colombia (Amazonas, Antioquia, Chocó, Nariño, Santander), Ecuador (Carchi, Napo, Pastaza, Pichincha), Peru (Amazonas, Cusco, Junín, Loreto, Puno, San Martín), and Brazil (Amazonas); premontane or montane rain forest on steep slopes below 1500 m elevation, or in lowland rain forest on noninundated soils at low elevations in the western Amazon region.
Uses. The leaves are occasionally used for thatching.

60. WELFIA

This genus contains the tallest palms of the geonomoid group. Stems are large and solitary and reach the subcanopy of the forest. Leaves are pinnate, 10–30 in number, and are large and erect. Sheaths are open, brown tomentose, and have a few fibers on the margins. Petioles are usually very short or scarcely distinguishable from the sheath. Leaflets are numerous and are regularly arranged along the rachis and spread in the same plane. They are linear-lanceolate and are rather long and wide. The youngest leaves (and the seedling leaf), especially on young plants, are a very attractive reddish color when they first unfold. Inflorescences are borne below the leaves and are branched to one order, or the lowermost branches are bifurcate. Inflorescences have a short and recurved peduncle, a short rachis, and several long, very thick, angular, pendulous flowering branches. These are densely covered by large and deep flower pits. Remains of these characteristic branches are usually found on the ground at the base of the palms, and the genus can thus be recognized very easily in the field. Flowers are arranged in threes of one central female and two lateral males, borne in pits along the flowering branches. Male flowers are among the largest in the palm family and have to forty-two stamens. Fruits are one-seeded, almond-shaped, slightly compressed, keeled at the pointed apex, and reddish brown. Seeds have homogeneous endosperm and the seedling leaf is bifid.

Welfia contains just one species, occurring in the Central American region with an extension into the Andean region. In the last revision of the genus (Wessels Boer, 1968), two very closely related species, *Welfia regia* and *Welfia georgii*, were recognized. The differences between them are slight and are supported by supposedly different ecology and distribution; however, we recognize just one species. Plants from Andean slopes in Peru, (Huánuco, Pasco), discovered after Wessels Boer's 1968 work, are bigger than normal, with much bigger globose fruits (4–5 cm diameter), and these may represent a distinct species. More collections are needed to decide the matter.

Welfia regia
(Map 474, Plates 54 & 55)
"Amargo" (Col, Pan), "palma conga,"
"palmito" (CR), "camara" (Per)
Field characters. Stems solitary, 7–20 m tall and 10–15 cm diameter, grayish. Leaves 10–30, erect, and arching toward the apex, reddish when young; leaf sheath conspicuous; blade 3–6 m long; leaflets 40–90 per side, the middle ones to 1 m long and 5–10 cm wide. Inflorescences with a 10–15 cm long peduncle; flowering branches 5–12, pendulous, massive, up to 1 m long and 2.5–3.5 cm thick, with deep and large pits arranged in 8 vertical files; fruits almond shaped, 3.5–4.5 cm long and to 2 cm diameter, reddish brown.
Range and habitat. Central America in Honduras (Gracias a Dios), Nicaragua (Zelaya), throughout Costa Rica and Panama, western and central Colombia (Pacific lowlands from Chocó to Nariño, and Magdalena valley in Antioquia), and western Ecuador (Pichincha); lowland to montane rain forest on slopes and ridges, in areas of high rainfall, from sea level

to 1500 m elevation. Particularly common in the Pacific lowlands of Colombia and Ecuador, where it is an important element of the subcanopy.
Uses. The leaves are used for thatching and can last for several years; the trunks are used as house pillars in coastal areas because they are rot resistant when submerged in saltwater.
Notes. At first glance, the general appearance of *Welfia* is very similar to that of *Oenocarpus bataua*, with which it grows in some areas. *Welfia* is distinguished by its young reddish leaves, green lower leaf surface, and massive inflorescence branches. There are several ecological studies of this species in Costa Rica, which have been summarized by Vandermeer (1983). *Welfia* is widespread in the country but only common in areas of highest rainfall. There it grows well in small light gaps. Male flowers open first and are at anthesis during the day. The most probable pollinators are bees of the genus *Trigona*, but small beetles may also be important. Ripe fruits fall directly beneath the parent tree, but any seeds germinating there

are killed by falling leaves from the parent. Various animals feed on the edible mesocarp and nine different mammals and birds are dispersers. Seed predation was studied by Schupp and Frost (1989).

61. CALYPTRONOMA

This small genus is endemic to the Greater Antilles but closely related to the Central American *Calyptrogyne*. It is unusual among geonomoid palms in having a large, solitary stem and regularly pinnate leaves, and in this respect it differs from *Calyptrogyne* and resembles *Welfia*. Leaves are pinnate, 7–16 in number, and form a rather dense crown. Leaflets are lanceolate, regularly arranged, and spread in the same plane. Inflorescences are borne closely below the leaves and are branched to one or two orders. The peduncle is rather elongate and the flowering branches are numerous and form a close bunch. As in all other geonomoid palms, the flowers are borne in small pits along the flowering branches. Each pit contains three flowers—a central female and two lateral males. The flowers themselves are very small, but are unusual among palms in that female flowers have the tips of the petals joined into a cap (or "calyptra" in Latin, hence the generic name). This cap falls off (or is removed by pollinators) when the flowers open. In one species, *C. plumeriana*, the apex of the petals of the male flowers are also joined into a cap. Fruits are one-seeded, ovoid, and reddish brown. The endosperm is homogeneous and the seedling leaf is bifid.

Calyptronoma contains three species (Wessels Boer, 1968), distributed in the Greater Antilles. Our treatment differs slightly from that of Wessels Boer.

The pollination system of this genus should be interesting; the female flowers are similar to those of the bat-pollinated *Calyptrogyne* and the male flowers have both free and joined petals.

Calyptronoma occidentalis
(Map 475)
"Long thatch" (Jam)
Field characters. Stems solitary, 7–12 m tall and 17–20 cm diameter. Leaves 7–10; leaflets regularly arranged and spreading in the same plane. *Inflorescences with the basal few branches branched into 2–3 flowering branches, these 24–35 cm long and 7–8 mm diameter; fruits ovoid, 1–1.7 cm long and 0.7–1 cm diameter,* reddish brown, becoming black.
Range and habitat. Jamaica; waterlogged places near stream margins, to 800 m elevation.

Calyptronoma plumeriana
(Map 476)
"Confite," "manaca" (Cub)
Field characters. Stems solitary, 4–10 m tall and 10–20 cm diameter. Leaves 12–16; leaflets regularly arranged and spreading in the same plane. *Inflorescences with the few basal branches branched into 3–5 flowering branches, these 13–22 cm long and 4–5 mm diameter; fruits ovoid, 0.8–1.2 cm long and 0.5–0.7 cm diameter,* reddish brown, becoming black.
Range and habitat. Western and eastern Cuba

(Habana, Isla de Pinos, Oriente, Pinar del Río) and Hispaniola (Dominican Republic, Haiti); wet places near streams in lowland or mountainous areas.
Uses. The sweet-tasting petals of the staminate flowers are occasionally collected and eaten.

Calyptronoma rivalis
(Map 477, Plate 55)
"Coquito," "manaca" (DR), "palma" (Hai), "palma manaca" (PR)
Field characters. Stems solitary, 4–15 m tall and 15–30 cm diameter. Leaves 12–14; leaflets regularly arranged and spreading in the same plane. *Inflorescences with the few basal branches branched into 3–5 flowering branches, these 19–25 cm long and 4–5 mm diameter; fruits ovoid, 0.5–0.6 cm long and 0.4 cm diameter,* reddish brown, becoming black.
Range and habitat. Hispaniola (Dominican Republic, Haiti) and Puerto Rico; wet areas near streams. A very rare palm in both Haiti (Henderson et al., 1990) and Puerto Rico (Henderson, 1984b).
Uses. In Haiti the young leaves are cut before they open and the leaflets used for weaving; older leaves are used for thatching.

Notes. Unusual in that both male and female flowers have the petals joined into a cap. In Hispaniola, *Calyptronoma rivalis* occurs at low elevations, while *C. plumeriana* is found over 450 m elevation.

62. CALYPTROGYNE

This small genus of understory palms is confined to Central America and northwestern Colombia. Although closely related to *Calyptronoma*, species of *Calyptrogyne* resemble some species of *Geonoma* in their small habit, simple or unequally pinnate leaves, and spicate or branched inflorescences. Stems are short and subterranean, sometimes creeping along the ground, or aerial and erect. Leaves are pinnate and 6–21 in number. They are usually unequally divided or simple (regularly pinnate in *C. pubescens*) and closely resemble those of both *Geonoma* and *Asterogyne*. Inflorescences develop among the leaves and most species have an elongate, spicate inflorescence that is held well clear of the leaves; but in *C. anomala* the inflorescence is short and branched and not projecting. The genus can be distinguished from any other related palm by the peduncular bract, which is inserted at the top of the peduncle (except for *C. anomala*), just below the flowering branch. In most species it falls off just before flowering, leaving a circular scar around the peduncle; but in two species the bract is persistent. Flowers are small and arranged in threes of one central female and two lateral males sunken in pits along the flowering branch, as in other geonomoid palms. Female flowers of *Calyptrogyne* (and *Calyptronoma*) are unique among palms in that the tips of the petals of the female flowers are joined together like a cap over the flower, hence the name of the genus— "calyptra," from the Latin word meaning cap, and "gyne," meaning female flower. This cap falls from the flower, or is removed by pollinators, when the stigmas are receptive. Fruits are one-seeded, typically obovoid, black, and contrast with the flowering branches, which are an attractive bright red at fruiting time in most species. The mesocarp has a net of wide fibers. Endosperm is homogeneous and the seedling leaf is bifid.

Calyptrogyne contains eight species (Greg de Nevers, pers. comm.), distributed from Mexico through Central America and reaching northwestern Colombia. All species grow in the understory of lowland, premontane, or montane rain forest, rarely reaching over 1500 m elevation. They are small and rather delicate palms that do not persist in deforested areas.

Species of *Calyptrogyne* with a spicate inflorescence are unique among palms in being pollinated by bats (Beach, 1986). The elongate, erect or arching inflorescences of these species, which are held well clear of the leaves, allow bats to fly to the flowers, which open at dusk. The sweet-tasting "caps" of the female flowers are eaten by the bats and in the process they pollinate the flowers. The branched inflorescences of *C. anomala*, which are held near the ground, might be pollinated by nonflying mammals (de Nevers and Henderson, 1988).

Calyptrogyne differs from *Calyptronoma* mostly in its reduced size with associated leaf anatomy and its continental distribution, but both genera are very similar in flower and fruit structure. Both have been treated as a single genus (e.g., Burret, 1930; Wessels Boer, 1968).

Calyptrogyne allenii
(Map 478)
Field characters. Stems solitary, erect, 1–2.5 m tall and 1.5–2.5 cm diameter, canelike, with prominent leaf scars. Leaves irregularly pinnate. Inflores- cences spicate, projecting beyond the leaves, horizontal; peduncular bract falling before flowering and leaving a scar; fruits obovoid, 1– 1.5 cm long, brown, powdery on the surface.
Range and habitat. Atlantic slope of western Pan-

ama (Coclé, Panamá); lowland or premontane rain forest, at 200–800 m elevation.

Calyptrogyne anomala
(Map 479)
"Gwammu" (Pan)

Field characters. Stems solitary, *creeping, and partly subterranean.* Leaves 8–16, simple or with up to 4 irregular leaflets per side, these 3–9 cm wide. *Inflorescences short, with (1–)2–4 flowering branches, borne close to the ground; peduncular bract persistent, forming a "hood" over the inflorescences;* fruits ellipsoid, to 1.5 cm long and 1 cm diameter, black.

Range and habitat. Panama (Colón, San Blas); lowland rain forest on ridges or slopes, below 400 m elevation.

Uses. The leaves are occasionally used for thatching.

Notes. Unusual in its branched inflorescences and persistent peduncular bract; in this it approaches the Antillean *Calyptronoma.* In fact, this species could be used as an argument to combine the two genera.

Calyptrogyne condensata
(Map 480)

Field characters. Stems solitary, *short and subterranean, 4–8 cm diameter.* Leaves irregularly pinnate. Inflorescences spicate, erect; *peduncular bract woody and velvety,* falling before flowering time and leaving a scar; *flowering branch densely tomentose; flower pits crowded;* fruits obovoid, 1–1.5 cm long, brown.

Range and habitat. Atlantic slope of Costa Rica to western Panama (Bocas del Toro, Veraguas); lowland or premontane rain forest, to 900 m elevation.

Calyptrogyne costatifrons
(Map 481)

Field characters. Stems solitary, *erect, 1.2–4 m tall and 1.5–2.5 cm diameter, canelike with prominent leaf scars.* Leaves about 9, irregularly divided but most often with 3 broad leaflets, rarely simple. Inflorescences arching, pendulous; *peduncular bract striate,* falling before flowering; fruits obovoid, 1–1.5 cm long, black.

Range and habitat. Atlantic slope of eastern Panama (Colón, San Blas); lowland rain forest, to 600 m elevation.

Calyptrogyne ghiesbreghtiana
(Map 482, Plates 55 & 56)
"Coligallo" (CR), "capoca" (Gua)

Field characters. Stems solitary, *short and subterranean.* Leaves 9–21, irregularly divided, usually with 3–5 broad leaflets, sometimes simple. Inflorescences spicate, erect, or arching above the leaves; *peduncular bract striate,* falling before flowering time and leaving a scar; *flowering*

branch glabrous; fruits obovoid, 1.6–2 cm long, green to black.

Range and habitat. Atlantic slope from Mexico (Chiapas) through Belize, Guatemala, Honduras, Nicaragua, Costa Rica, and Panama and Pacific slope in Costa Rica (Puntarenas); lowland to montane rain forest, from sea level to 1500 m elevation.

Notes. Plants from higher elevations with narrower leaflets, which are constricted at the base have been called *Calyptrogyne brachystachys,* but we include this here. Plants from the Pacific coast of Colombia (northern Chocó) have a thicker, aerial stem, and seem to represent a distinct species (G. deNevers, pers. comm.).

Calyptrogyne kunaria
(Map 483)

Field characters. Stems solitary, *erect or partially creeping and then rooting, 1–2 m tall and 5–8 cm diameter.* Leaves 15–22, *simple and bifid;* leaf bases persistent and filling with leaf litter. Inflorescences spicate, arching, pendulous; peduncular bract falling before flowering time and leaving a scar; fruits oblong-obovoid, 1.6–2.8 cm long, 1.1–2.8 cm diameter, brown.

Range and habitat. Panama (San Blas; Cerro Brewster, Cerro Obu); premontane rain forest, at 500–900 m elevation.

Calyptrogyne pubescens
(Map 484)

Field characters. Stems solitary, *short, and subterranean.* Leaves 6–10, *divided into about 30 leaflets per side,* these regularly arranged. Inflorescences spicate, erect or arching, *densely tomentose; peduncular bract not falling before anthesis and not leaving a clean scar;* fruits oblong-obovoid, 1.1–1.4 cm long and 7–8 mm diameter, black.

Range and habitat. Atlantic slope of western Panama (Bocas del Toro); lowland rain forest, at 100–150 m elevation.

Notes. An unusual species in its regularly pinnate leaves and persistent peduncular bract.

Calyptrogyne trichostachys
(Map 485)

Field characters. Stems solitary, *short, and subterranean, 4–8 cm diameter.* Leaves 9–12, irregularly pinnate. Inflorescences spicate, erect or arching above the leaves; *peduncular bract densely brown-tomentose,* falling before flowering time and leaving a scar; *flower pits distantly spaced;* fruits obovoid, to 1 cm long and 6 mm diameter, purple-black.

Range and habitat. Atlantic slope in Costa Rica (Alajuela) and Panama (Bocas del Toro, Coclé, Veraguas); lowland to montane rain forest, to 1100 m elevation.

63. ASTEROGYNE

This small genus is of interest because of the isolated and restricted distributions of most species. Stems are rather stout, usually solitary and erect, but one species has clustered, partly creeping stems. Leaves are 8–25 in number, always simple and bifid, but commonly become split with age and then appear pinnate. Sheaths are open and petioles are short. Inflorescences are either spicate or branched to one order and then with few flowering branches. An unusual feature in some species is the presence of two peduncular bracts, rather than the usual one. The peduncle is elongate and the rachis very short, so that the flowering branches radiate from the top of the peduncle. The flowers are arranged in threes of one central female and two lateral males and like all other geonomoid palms, these are borne in pits along the flowering branches. Male flowers have 6–24 stamens. The derivation of the genus name is from the female flowers, which have spreading, star-shaped staminodes. Fruits are one-seeded, ellipsoid or ovoid, reddish brown but becoming purple-black at or after maturity. Endosperm is homogeneous and the seedling leaf is simple.

Asterogyne contains five species in Central America and northern South America (Wessels Boer, 1968; Henderson and Steyermark, 1986; de Granville and Henderson, 1988). Although one of them is relatively widespread, the other four have very small distributions and because of this must be considered threatened.

Asterogyne guianensis
(Map 486)
Field characters. Stems solitary, 1.5–2 m tall and 3.4–5 cm diameter, erect. Leaves 15–18, simple, bifid, the blade 1–1.1 m long and 35–40 cm wide. *Inflorescences spicate,* arching among the leaves; flowering branch 26–30 cm long and 1.5 cm diameter; fruits ellipsoid, to 2.5 cm long and 1.5 cm diameter, reddish.
Range and habitat. Southeastern French Guiana; known only from a small area of lowland rain forest in an inundated area, at 150 m elevation.
Notes. Notable for its isolated, very restricted distribution.

Asterogyne martiana
(Map 487, Plate 56)
"Cortadera," "rabihorcao" (Col), "pico" (Ecu), "capoca" (Gua), "pacuquilla" (Hon), "pata de gallo" (Nic)
Field characters. Stems solitary, 1–2 m or less tall and 3–5 cm diameter, erect or sometimes creeping and then rooting. Leaves 8–15, simple and bifid, the blade 0.7–1 m long and 15–25 cm wide. *Inflorescences usually branched,* arching among the leaves; *flowering branches (1–)5–8,* 15–25 cm long and 4–8 mm diameter, radiating from the apex of the long peduncle; fruits ellipsoid, 1.2 cm long and 6 mm diameter, reddish, becoming purple-black.
Range and habitat. Throughout Central America in Belize, Guatemala (Izabal), Honduras (Atlántida, Colón Cortés, Gracias a Dios, Santa

Bárbara), Nicaragua (Chontales, Zelaya), Costa Rica (Alajuela, Heredia, Limón, Puntarenas, San José), Panama (Bocas del Toro, Coclé, San Blas), northwestern Colombia (Antioquia, Cauca, Chocó, Nariño, Risaralda Valle), and the Magdalena valley, and just reaching northwestern Ecuador (Esmeraldas); lowland rain forest below 500 m elevation, but in Colombia also occurring in montane rain forest to 1100 m elevation.
Uses. The leaves are commonly used for thatching.
Notes. By far the most abundant and widespread species and a common component of the understory of the Central American region's rain forest. Pollination of this species was studied in Costa Rica by Schmid (1970a, 1970b), who found that the most important pollinators were syrphid flies. Various ecological aspects of this species have been studied in Costa Rica: leaf display and canopy structure (Chazdon, 1985), shade tolerance (Chazdon, 1986a), light variation and carbon gain (Chazdon, 1986b) and leaf support (Chazdon, 1986c).

Asterogyne ramosa
(Map 488)
Field characters. Stems solitary, to 3 m tall and 3–8 cm diameter. Leaves numerous, simple, bifid, the blade to 1 m long and 25 cm wide. *Inflorescences branched,* arching among the leaves; *flowering branches 4–6,* to 20 cm long and 5 mm diameter; fruits ellipsoid, 1.5–1.6 cm long and 5 mm diameter, reddish.

Range and habitat. Venezuela (Sucre, Peninsula de Paria); premontane rain forest on steep slopes, above 750 m elevation.

Asterogyne spicata
(Map 489, Plate 56)
"Palmito" (Ven)
Field characters. Stems solitary, 2–8 m tall and 4–5 cm diameter, erect. Leaves about 25, simple, bifid, the blade to 1 m long and 25 cm wide. *Inflorescences spicate*, arching among the leaves; flowering branch 25–40 cm long and 1–1.4 cm diameter; fruits ovoid, to 1.8 cm long and 7 mm diameter, reddish.
Range and habitat. Venezuela (Miranda, Parque Nacional de Guatopo); lowland to premontane rain forest on slopes, at 200–700 m elevation.
Uses. The leaves are used for thatching.

Notes. Quite abundant and protected in its restricted habitat.

Asterogyne yaracuyense
(Map 490)
Field characters. Stems clustered, 6–8 m tall and 5–8 cm diameter, erect or creeping at the base. Leaves 20–31, simple, bifid, the blade 1.2 m long and 30 cm wide. *Inflorescences branched*, arching among the leaves; *flowering branches 11–15*, to 32 cm long and 8 mm diameter; fruits unknown.
Range and habitat. Venezuela (Yaracuy, Cerro La Chapa); a small area of montane rain forest on slopes and ridges, at 1200–1400 m elevation.
Notes. This is another species having a very limited distribution and is possibly threatened with extinction (Henderson and Steyermark, 1986).

64. GEONOMA

This genus of small to medium-sized understory palms is one of the largest in the Americas. Species are abundant in the understory of all types of rain forest; the name of the genus reflects this, coming from the Greek words "geo," meaning earth or ground, and "nomos," meaning district or province. Together the two words come to mean a member of a colony or group. Stems are solitary or clustered, short to medium sized, often subterranean, usually canelike, brown (rarely green), and have conspicuous nodes. Leaves are pinnate or simple, 7–25 in number, and are often reddish when young. The sheath is open and the petiole is usually rather short; both are often brown-tomentose. Leaflets are few to many and almost always spread in one plane. They are of equal width, or commonly equal and unequal ones are mixed together. They range in shape from almost linear to sigmoid or sickle shaped. Inflorescences are borne among the leaves, rarely below the leaves and are spicate or branched from one to several orders. The prophyll is often very similar to the peduncular bract, and the length and shape of the peduncular bract, as well as its point of insertion, are important characters for separating some species. Flowers are arranged in threes of one central female and two lateral males, sunken in small and deep pits along the flowering branches. Each pit has two small bracts, or lips, which we refer to as lower lip and upper lip. The arrangement of the pits is quite variable; usually they are spirally arranged but sometimes they are whorled (i.e., with three pits at the same level around the flowering branch) or decussate (i.e., with opposite pairs of pits alternating along the flowering branch). Male flowers have six stamens (rarely 3 or 7–12), with unusual split anthers. Fruits are small, variable in form but usually globose or ellipsoid, one-seeded, black or purplish black, less commonly brown, green, reddish, or blue. The endosperm is homogeneous and the seedling leaf is bifid.

As treated here, *Geonoma* contains fifty-one species, widely distributed throughout the American tropics, from Mexico to Bolivia and southern Brazil, Paraguay, and just entering the Caribbean. They are typical of the forest understory in areas of high rainfall, where they usually are one of the commonest plants. The greatest concentration of species occurs in areas with an average annual rainfall of 2000 to 5000 mm, and no species are found in areas with less than 1000 mm annual rainfall (Wessels Boer, 1968). Elevational range is the widest for a palm genus, from sea level to 3150 m elevation. As a rule in the Andes, the largest species are found at the highest elevations, a situation mirrored in both *Prestoea* and *Chamaedorea* (Moraes et al., in press).

The last taxonomic treatment of the genus was that of Wessels Boer (1968), who recognized seventy-five species. Although this work was a great advance in our understanding of the genus, some confusion and overdescription remained. A modern revision, based on extensive fieldwork, is needed, and the treatment in this Guide is still somewhat tentative. *Geonoma* species show a great deal of morphological variation, especially in leaf shape and size. The identification of species, therefore, is somewhat difficult. Within the same species it is not uncommon for a complete range to exist between simple leaves and regularly pinnate leaves. The form of the inflorescences and the arrangement of the flowering pits are more conservative and are needed for identification.

Some species of *Geonoma* are perhaps the most variable of any palm in the Americas and at least eight can be considered as species complexes. Examples are *G. cuneata* in the Central American region; *G. jussieuana* and *G. undata* in the Andean region, and *G. interrupta* in the Central American and Andean regions; *G. macrostachys*, *G. maxima*, and *G. stricta* in the Amazon region; and *G. gamiova* and relatives in the Atlantic Coastal Forest region. One interesting and repeating pattern of variation is seen in the leaves, particularly in those of the smaller species. It is common to find a sequence of forms from simple, narrow, wedge-shaped leaves to simple, broad, wedge-shaped leaves, to pinnate leaves with straight leaflets, to pinnate leaves with sigmoid leaves. A better understanding of the factors underlying this variation would greatly simplify our understanding of the taxonomy of the genus. Chazdon (1991) has suggested that the changes in leaf size at reproductive maturity may have facilitated the adaptive radiation of *Geonoma* within the rain forest habitat.

The genus can be distinguished from other understory palms by the small pits in the flowering branches, something lacking in both *Chamaedorea* and *Hyospathe*, the most commonly confused genera. Furthermore, *Geonoma* species almost always have some kind of brown tomentum on the leaves or inflorescences, which is completely lacking in *Chamaedorea*. Differences between *Geonoma* and the other geonomoid genera are given in the generic key.

KEY TO THE SPECIES OF *GEONOMA*

1a. Lowlands of Central America and Pacific lowlands of western Colombia
    and Ecuador and inter-Andean valleys in Colombia; usually below 1000 m
    elevation.
    2a. Canelike palms; stems pencil-thin (less than 1 cm diameter).
        3a. Inflorescences spicate.
            4a. Leaves reddish on lower surface; inflorescences borne below the
                leaves; flowering branch to 20 cm long and 3 mm thick; Costa
                Rica and Panama   ..... *G. epetiolata*.
            4b. Leaves green on lower surface; inflorescences usually borne
                among the leaves; flowering branch usually more than 3 mm
                thick; South America
                5a. Peduncle shorter than flowering branch; Magdalena valley in
                    Colombia   ..... *G. stricta*.

    5b. Peduncle longer than flowering branch; western Ecuador
                                        ..... *G. cuneata.*
3b. Inflorescences branched.
    6a. Inflorescences branched to one order, usually with less than 10 flowering branches.
        7a. Flowering branches 2–5, very loosely pitted; stems usually less than 1 m tall; Magdalena valley, Chocó in Colombia, and western Ecuador   ..... *G. leptospadix.*
        7b. Flowering branches 3–25, densely pitted; stems usually 1–4 m tall.
            8a. Leaves erect, simple or divided into 3 sigmoid leaflets; flowering branches 3–7; pits spirally arranged; Panama and northwestern Colombia   ..... *G. divisa.*
            8b. Leaves spreading, usually divided into few (commonly 3 per side) to numerous leaflets; flowering branches 4–25; pits arranged in whorls of 3; widespread   ..... *G. deversa.*
    6b. Inflorescences branched to two or three orders, with more than 10 flowering branches.
        9a. Flowering branches threadlike (less than 1 mm thick), very loosely pitted.
            10a. Leaves simple, wedge-shaped; stems usually clustered; western Colombia and Ecuador   ..... *G. tenuissima.*
            10b. Leaves divided into 3 sigmoid leaflets; stems usually solitary; western Costa Rica   ..... *G. scoparia.*
        9b. Flowering branches thicker, 1–3 mm thick, more or less densely pitted.
            11a. Pits in whorls of 3   ..... *G. deversa.*
            11b. Pits spirally or decussately arranged, not in whorls of 3.
                12a. Leaves simple or pinnate with straight leaflets; fruits subglobose, 4–6 mm in diameter   ..... *G. concinna.*
                12b. Leaves simple or pinnate with sigmoid leaflets; fruits ovoid, 6–7 mm in diameter   ..... *G. triandra.*
2b. Larger palms; stems stouter or seldom short and subterranean.
    13a. Inflorescences spicate.
        14a. Leaves more than 1.2 m long, divided into a few broad leaflets; stems to 2.5 m tall and about 5 cm diameter; flowering branch 1 cm thick; fruits conspicuously rough, 1.8 cm long and 1.4 cm diameter; Panama and western Colombia   ..... *G. chococola.*
        14b. Leaves less than 1.2 m long, variously divided; stem less than 2.5 m tall and 5 cm diameter; flowering branch 1 cm thick or less; fruits not conspicuously rough, less than 1.8 cm long and 1.4 cm diameter.
            15a. Lower lip rounded and markedly projected over the flower pit and covering it; flowering branch orange in fruit; Colombia.
                16a. Leaves 45–60 cm long; flowering branch 15–32 cm long and 1 cm thick; fruits ovoid, 1–1.2 cm long and 6 mm diameter; Magdalena valley in Colombia   ..... *G. chlamydostachys.*
                16b. Leaves 30–50 cm long; flowering branch 7–10 cm long

and 2.5–6 mm thick; fruits 6 mm diameter; southwestern
Colombia ..... *G. paradoxa.*
15b. Lower lip not projected over the flower pit; flowering branch
purplish-red in fruit; Central America, Colombia and Ecuador.
17a. Stems forming large colonies along creek margins; leaflets
usually very narrow; mesocarp conspicuously fibrous ..... *G. linearis.*
17b. Stems solitary or clustered, not forming large colonies;
leaves simple or with several sigmoid to sickle-shaped leaflets; mesocarp not conspicuously fibrous ..... *G. cuneata.*
13b. Inflorescences branched.
18a. Inflorescences branched to one order (*G. ferruginea* sometimes
with basal branches forked).
19a. Leaves usually more than 1 m long, erect, simple or irregularly divided into several, wide, straight leaflets; inflorescences
erect, candelabrum-like; flowering branches 6–7 mm thick;
fruits 1–1.5 cm diameter, with minute warts ..... *G. congesta.*
19b. Leaves usually less than 1 m long, spreading; flowering
branches less than 6 mm thick; fruits smaller than 1 cm diameter, smooth.
20a. Flower pits in whorls of 3; widespread ..... *G. deversa.*
20b. Flower pits spirally arranged; Central America.
21a. Flowering branches less than 10 cm long, not pendulous; peduncle less than 12 cm long; usually above
700 m elevation ..... *G. ferruginea.*
21b. Flowering branches 20–35 cm long, pendulous; peduncle 20–50 cm long; below 350 m elevation ..... *G. longevaginata.*
18b. Inflorescences branched to several orders.
22a. Leaves usually less than 60 cm long; stems usually less than 3
cm diameter and 3 m tall; peduncle to 15 cm long; pits arranged in whorls of 3 ..... *G. deversa.*
22b. Leaves to 2 m long; stems usually larger; peduncle 20–50 cm
long; pits spirally arranged ..... *G. interrupta.*
1b. All other areas.
23a. Central American highlands, the Andes (including the Sierra Nevada
de Santa Marta), Cordillera de la Costa in Venezuela and other mountain areas, including the Guayana Highland (but excluding mountains
of coastal Brazil); usually above 1000 m elevation, rarely below.
24a. Inflorescences spicate or with 2–3 simple branches (to 4 branches
in *G. simplicifrons*)
25a. Peduncle with a thick tomentum ..... *G. orbignyana.*
25b. Peduncle without tomentum.
26a. Northwestern Venezuela and Guayana Highland; to 1400 m
elevation ..... *G. simplicifrons.*
26b. Widespread in Central America (Costa Rica, Panama) and
the Andes; to 3000 m elevation ..... *G. jussieauana.*
24b. Inflorescences branched 2–several orders, or if branched to one
order then with 4 or more flowering branches.
27a. Flowering branches less than 2 mm thick; usually below 1300 m
elevation.

28a. Flowering branches very loosely pitted; coastal Venezuela
..... *G. spinescens.*
28b. Flowering branches more or less densely pitted.
   29a. Stems less than 1 cm diameter; flowering branches less
     than 10 cm long; flower pits spirally arranged   ..... *G. concinna.*
   29b. Stems usually more than 1 cm diameter; flowering
     branches more than 10 cm long; flower pits whorled or in
     spirals.
     30a. Flower pits in whorls of 3; upper lip of pit present
..... *G. deversa.*
     30b. Flower pits spirally arranged, upper lip of pit absent
..... *G. interrupta.*
27b. Flowering branches more than 2 mm thick; at various elevations.
   31a. Below 1400 m elevation (seldom *G. undata* and *G. orbignyana*
     reaching this elevation).
     32a. Stems usually forming large clumps; flowering branches
       few, short, about 10 cm long; Central America   ..... *G. ferruginea.*
     32b. Stems solitary or clustered, not forming large clumps;
       flowering branches more numerous, usually more than 10
       cm long; Central America and the Andes.
       33a. Leaves divided into numerous narrow and stiff leaflets;
         northwestern coastal Venezuela   ..... *G. paraguanensis.*
       33b. Leaves simple or if divided the leaflets not stiff.
         34a. Flower pits in whorls of 3, upper lip present ..... *G. deversa.*
         34b. Flower pits spirally arranged, upper lip absent
..... *G. interrupta.*
   31b. Above 1400 m elevation, but in Guayana Highland rarely oc-
     curring below.
     35a. Leaves simple, less than 50 cm long, erect, strongly pli-
       cate, and leathery; Peru   ..... *G. trigona.*
     35b. Leaves pinnate or if simple, more than 50 cm long.
       36a. Flowering branches 5 mm thick or more.
         37a. Leaflets distantly spaced, usually more than 2.5 cm
           apart; stems rarely to 5 m tall and 6 cm diameter;
           peduncular bract persistent   ..... *G. orbignyana.*
         37b. Leaflets not distantly spaced or the leaf simple;
           stems larger, to 10 m tall and 10 cm diameter; pedun-
           cular bract deciduous.
           38a. Leaves simple or pinnate, leathery, plicate, usu-
             ally erect; fruits 1–1.5 cm long and 0.9–1.1 cm di-
             ameter   ..... *G. weberbaueri.*
           38b. Leaves pinnate with membranaceous leaflets, not
             leathery nor plicate, spreading; fruits 8–9 mm long
             and 6–7 mm diameter   ..... *G. undata.*
       36b. Flowering branches less than 5 mm thick.
         39a. Leaflets not leathery and rigid.
           40a. Peduncle elongate; peduncular bract inserted far
             from the base of the peduncle, persistent
..... *G. orbignyana.*

40b. Peduncle short; peduncular bract inserted at the
    base of the peduncle, deciduous   ..... *G. undata.*
39b. Leaflets leathery and rigid.
    41a. Leaves stiffly erect; Guayana Highland ..... *G. appuniana.*
    41b. Leaves spreading, rarely erect; the Andes   ..... *G. densa.*
23b. All other areas.
  42a. Amazon region and adjacent areas, including the Guianas and
  eastern slopes of the Andes below 1000 m elevation.
    43a. Inflorescences spicate (very rarely with 2–3 flowering branches).
      44a. Cane-like palms with stems pencil-thin, 1–2 cm diameter (sel-
      dom to 3 cm diameter in some forms of *G. stricta*).
        45a. Inflorescences covered with light brown tomentum; fruits
        pointed at apex, blue or black   ..... *G. stricta.*
        45b. Inflorescences without tomentum; fruits rounded at apex,
        black   ..... *G. arundinacea.*
      44b. Stouter palms with stems more than 2 cm diameter.
        46a. Leaves simple, 1–2 m long, forming an umbrella-like
        crown; stem 1.5–2 m tall; eastern Amazon region and
        French Guiana   ..... *G. oldemannii.*
        46b. Leaves pinnate or if simple, then smaller and spreading;
        western Amazon region.
          47a. Leaves pinnate; leaflets conspicuously thick and
          smooth, with two submarginal veins   ..... *G. camana.*
          47b. Leaves simple or, if pinnate, thin and without marginal
          veins.
            48a. Flowering branch about 1 cm thick, densely pitted.
              49a. Stems 0.5–1.5 m tall; fruits ovoid to ellipsoid,
              pointed at apex   ..... *G. polyandra.*
              49b. Stems subterranean or to 50 cm tall; fruits
              globose   ..... *G. macrostachys.*
            48b. Flowering branch less than 1 cm thick, not densely
            pitted.
              50a. Leaflets sickle-shaped; flowering branch purplish
              red in fruit   ..... *G. brongniartii.*
              50b. Leaflets straight or sigmoid; flowering branch
              orange in fruit   ..... *G. macrostachys.*
    43b. Inflorescences branched.
      51a. Canelike palms with pencil-thin stems.
        52a. Flowering branches less than 2 mm thick.
          53a. Clustered palms, forming large clumps in seasonally in-
          undated areas along river margins   ..... *G. laxiflora.*
          53b. Solitary palms, or if clustered, then not forming large
          clumps; noninundated areas.
            54a. Flowering branches densely pitted, the pits arranged
            in whorls of 3   ..... *G. deversa.*
            54b. Flowering branches loosely pitted, the pits not in
            whorls of 3.
              55a. Leaves simple or divided into a few broad leaf-
              lets, forming an umbrella-like crown; flowering
              branches bright red in fruit   ..... *G. leptospadix.*

55b. Leaves divided into several, usually narrow and
    sigmoid leaflets, not forming an umbrella-like
    crown; flowering branches orange in fruit   . . . . . *G. maxima.*
52b. Flowering branches more than 2 mm thick.
    56a. Stems forming large colonies in swampy areas along
        river margins; northeastern Amazon region   . . . . . *G. baculifera.*
    56b. Stems not forming large colonies, usually in non-inun-
        dated areas; mostly western Amazon region.
        57a. Flowering branches short (to 14 cm long), straight
            within the bud, with conspicuous purplish brown to-
            mentum   . . . . . *G. aspidiifolia.*
        57b. Flowering branches longer (usually more than 15
            cm long), folded and twisted within the bud, without
            conspicuous tomentum.
            58a. Leaves less than 30 cm long, usually simple
                                            . . . . . *G. arundinacea.*
            58b. Leaves 35–50 cm long, divided into 3 sigmoid
                leaflets per side, these contracted at base . . . . . *G. oligoclona.*
51b. Stouter palms with stems usually more than 1 cm diameter,
    or short and subterranean.
    59a. Stems forming large clumps in swampy areas, usually
        along river margins; eastern and southern Amazon
        region.
        60a. Leaves pinnate; inflorescences borne below the leaves;
            peduncle less than 20 cm long; flower pits decussate
                                                . . . . . *G. brevispatha.*
        60b. Leaves simple or pinnate; inflorescences borne among
            the leaves; peduncle more than 20 cm long; flower pits
            spirally arranged   . . . . . *G. baculifera.*
    59b. Stems not forming large clumps; usually in noninundated
        areas; mostly western Amazon region.
        61a. Flowering branches more than 5 mm thick.
            62a. Stems usually clustered; leaves plicate; peduncle less
                than 20 cm long   . . . . . *G. maxima.*
            62b. Stems solitary; leaves not plicate; peduncle 25–60
                cm long.
                63a. Stems less than 1 m tall; flowering branches to 6
                    mm thick, purplish brown in fruit   . . . . . *G. poeppigiana.*
                63b. Stems 1.5–4 m tall; flowering branches 8–13 mm
                    thick, orange-brown in fruit   . . . . . *G. triglochin.*
        61b. Flowering branches less than 5 mm thick
            64a. Flowering branches with pits in whorls of 3   . . . . . *G. deversa.*
            64b. Pits spirally arranged or at least not in whorls of 3.
                65a. Inflorescences branched to one order, with less
                    than 10 flowering branches.
                    66a. Stems clustered.
                        67a. Leaves divided into 3 sigmoid leaflets per
                            side, these contracted at the base   . . . . . *G. oligoclona.*
                        67b. Leaves simple or divided into few to sev-

eral leaflets per side, these not contracted at
the base.
68a. Peduncle short, to 6 cm long; flowering
branches straight within the bud; Brazil
(Acre) . . . . . *G. myriantha.*
68b. Peduncle 5–19 cm long; flowering
branches folded and twisted within the
bud . . . . . *G. maxima.*
66b. Stems solitary.
69a. Leaves simple or pinnate with a few leaflets, erect or forming an umbrella-like
crown.
70a. Stems less than 1 m tall . . . . . *G. poeppigiana.*
70b. Stems more than 1 m tall.
71a. Leaves strongly plicate, erect; peduncle less than 20 cm long . . . . . *G. maxima.*
71b. Leaves not plicate, horizontally
spreading, forming an umbrella-like
crown; peduncle more than 20 cm
long . . . . . *G. umbraculiformis.*
69b. Leaves simple or pinnate, spreading.
72a. Stems less than 1 m tall; leaf rachis covered with a brown tomentum
. . . . . *G. longepedunculata.*
72b. Stems more than 1 m tall; leaf rachis
without tomentum.
73a. Flowering branches densely pitted,
orange in fruit . . . . . *G. maxima.*
73b. Flowering branches loosely pitted,
red in fruit . . . . . *G. interrupta.*
65b. Inflorescences branched to 2–3 orders, with
more than 10 flowering branches.
74a. Upper lip of flower pits absent; flowering
branches red in fruit . . . . . *G. interrupta.*
74b. Upper lip of flower pits present; flowering
branches red or orange in fruit.
75a. Flowering branches tomentose, red in fruit
. . . . . *G. paniculigera.*
75b. Flowering branches not tomentose, orange
in fruit . . . . . *G. maxima.*
42b. Atlantic coast of eastern Brazil and adjacent inland areas, including Paraguay.
76a. Inflorescences spicate or with 2–7 flowering branches
77a. Stems 1.5–4 cm diameter, usually solitary, green to purplish;
inflorescences with 2–7 candelabrum-like flowering branches,
8–35 cm long and 3–6 mm thick, densely pitted, purplish red
. . . . . *G. rubescens.*
77b. Stems less than 1.5 cm diameter, usually clustered, brown; inflorescences spicate or with 2–6 flowering branches, 6–20 cm

long and 2–5 mm thick, rather loosely pitted, not purplish red
..... *G. pauciflora.*
76b. Inflorescences branched to 2–3 orders, usually with numerous flowering branches.
78a. Stems forming large clumps in swampy areas along stream margins; usually in inland areas, especially near streams in *cerrado* ..... *G. brevispatha.*
78b. Stems solitary or clustered, but not forming large clumps; mostly Atlantic coastal forest, occasionally inland in *cerrado*.
79a. Fruits ovoid, pointed at the apex ..... *G. gamiova.*
79b. Fruits globose to ovoid, usually rounded at apex.
80a. Leaflets narrow and numerous, each with 3 conspicuous principal veins on upper surface; flower pits decussate ..... *G. schottiana.*
80b. Leaflets few to numerous, narrow or broad, without 3 principal veins on upper surface; flower pits usually spirally arranged.
81a. Stems to 7 cm diameter; leaves to 1 m long; inflorescences branched to 2–3; peduncle to 30 cm long; flowering branches numerous, rather densely pitted; fruits to 1.6 cm diameter ..... *G. pohliana.*
81b. Stems about 1 cm diameter; leaves to 40 cm long; inflorescences branched to two orders; peduncle up to 10 cm long; rather few, loosely pitted flowering branches; fruits about 7 mm diameter ..... *G. gastoniana.*

Geonoma appuniana
(Map 491, Plate 57)
Field characters. Stems solitary, occasionally clustered, 1.5–10 m tall and (1.5–)5–8 cm diameter. Leaves 7–12, stiffly erect; *blade stiff and rather leathery,* to 1.5 m long and 70 cm wide, *divided into few to many unequal, plicate leaflets.* Inflorescences borne among the leaves in flower and below the leaves in fruit, branched to several orders; peduncle 10–25 cm long; rachis 8–50 cm long; flowering branches numerous, rather loosely pitted, 10–35 cm long and 2.5–4 mm thick, reddish in ripe fruit; pits spirally or rarely decussately arranged; fruits globose to ellipsoid, pointed at apex, about 1 cm diameter, black.
Range and habitat. Guayana Highland of Venezuela (Amazonas, Bolívar) and adjacent Guyana and Brazil (Amazonas) and just reaching Suriname and French Guiana; locally abundant on sandstone mountains, in exposed places or cloud forest, at (600–)1300–2300 m elevation.
Notes. A poorly known and extremely variable species. It is closely related to a group of high-elevation Andean species (*G. densa, G. undata,* and *G. weberbaueri*). The relationships among these are still not understood, and it is possible that *G. appuniana* represents an ecological variant of either *G. densa* or *G. undata* (see notes under *G. undata*). A recently described local form, *G. guianensis,* extends the range into the Guianas.

Geonoma arundinacea
(Map 492)
"Ubim" (Bra), "kamancha," "yunkip" (Per)
Field characters. Stems clustered, rarely solitary, *pencil thin,* erect or leaning, 0.5–2(–3) m tall and 0.5–1 cm diameter, brown to greenish. Leaves 4–10, erect; blade to 30 cm long, simple or irregularly divided into 2–3 unequal leaflets per side. Inflorescences borne among the leaves, below the leaves in fruit; *flowering branches 1–3, erect, to 25 cm long and 2–4 mm thick, folded and twisted in bud,* bright red in ripe fruit; pits spirally arranged; fruits ellipsoid, to 8 mm long and 6 mm diameter, black.
Range and habitat. Western Amazon region in Colombia (Amazonas, Putumayo), Ecuador (Napo, Pastaza), Peru (Amazonas, Huánuco, Loreto, Pasco), and Brazil (Amazonas); an uncommon species in the understory of lowland rain forest, on well-drained soils, usually below 500 m elevation (rarely to 1500 m on eastern Andean slopes in Ecuador).

Geonoma aspidiifolia
(Map 493, Plate 57)
Field characters. Stems clustered, pencil-thin, 1–3 m tall and 0.5–1 cm diameter. Leaves 7–12, loosely arranged on the upper part of the stem; blade 30–50 cm long, divided into 2–5, rarely more, broad and unequal to almost linear, sigmoid leaflets. Inflorescences small, developing below the leaves, branched to one order; *peduncle less than 10 cm long; rachis absent or very short; flowering branches 2–5, erect,* 5–14 cm long and 2–3 mm thick, reddish in fruit, with *conspicuous purplish brown tomentum;* pits spirally arranged; fruits globose or ellipsoid, pointed at apex, 0.8–1 cm long and 5–6 mm diameter, dark red or reddish purple, becoming black.
Range and habitat. Amazon region in Colombia (Amazonas), Guyana, and Brazil (Amazonas); a rather uncommon species in the understory of lowland rain forest on rather sandy soils, rarely in inundated areas, at low elevations but to 1350 m in the Guayana Highland.
Notes. Geonoma oligoclona is very similar but can be separated by its longer flowering branches and different range.

Geonoma baculifera
(Map 494)
"Ubim," "ubim grande" (Bra), "wai" (FrG), "meena" (Guy), "tas" (Sur), "palma cola de pescado," "palma San Pablo" (Ven)
Field characters. Stems clustered, usually forming large colonies, 1–4 m tall and 1–3 cm diameter, erect or partially creeping. Leaves 7–12; blade 70–90 cm long, *wedge shaped,* simple or irregularly divided into 2–several broad, or less commonly narrow, leaflets per side. Inflorescences borne among the leaves, erect, branched to one or rarely two orders; peduncle 20–44 cm long; *rachis almost absent or to 10 cm long; flowering branches 3–10,* 12–30 cm long and 3–4 mm thick, orange in fruit; pits spirally arranged; fruits ovoid to ellipsoid, 0.9–1.2 cm long and 5–8 mm diameter, black.
Range and habitat. Northeastern Amazon region in southern Venezuela (Amazonas, Bolívar), the Guianas, and Brazil (Amapá, Amazonas, Maranhão, Pará, Roraima); understory of lowland rain forest in swampy areas, sometimes forming large stands along river margins, below 650 m elevation.
Uses. The leaves are used for thatching.
Notes. Geonoma poeppigiana is similar, but grows in a different habitat and has a different range.

Geonoma brevispatha
(Map 495, Plate 57)
"Ouricana," "cana preta" (Bra), "guarika" (Par)

Field characters. Stems clustered, 1–4 m tall and 2.5–4 cm diameter, *usually forming large clumps.* Leaves 7–12; blade 40–60 cm long, divided into few to numerous narrow or broad leaflets. Inflorescences borne below or among the leaves, branched to 1–2 orders; peduncle 10–18 cm long; rachis 7–15 cm long; *flowering branches 3–9 (rarely more),* to 23 cm long and 1–3 mm thick; *pits usually decussately arranged;* fruits ellipsoid to globose, 0.8–1.1 cm long and 6–8 mm diameter, black.
Range and habitat. Central and southeastern Brazil, mostly in the *planalto* region, also Peru, Bolivia, and Paraguay; *cerrado* vegetation in swampy areas at stream edges, gallery forest, or lowland rain forest, at 400–1600 m elevation.
Notes. This widespread and variable species is divided into two varieties, although the boundary between them is not always clear (Henderson, 1994): var. *brevispatha,* with numerous linear leaflets and inflorescences borne below the leaves, from central and southeastern Brazil (Bahia, Distrito Federal, Goiás, Mato Grosso do Sul, Minas Gerais, Pará, Rondônia, Tocantins), Bolivia (Santa Cruz), and northern Paraguay (Alto Paraná, Amambay, Canandiyú); and var. *occidentale,* with few broad leaflets and inflorescences borne among the leaves, from Peru (Madre de Dios), Brazil (Rondônia), and Bolivia (La Paz, Pando).

Geonoma brongniartii
(Map 496)
"San Pablo" (Col), "ni-ní" (Ecu), "cululí" (Per)
Field characters. Stems solitary or rarely clustered, *subterranean or very short,* 0.3–1 m tall and 2–3.5 cm diameter. Leaves 5–13, blade to 1 m long, usually divided into 3–13 straight or sickle-shaped leaflets per side, these broad and narrow or all of them narrow and linear, rarely the blade simple. Inflorescences borne among the leaves, *spicate,* erect; peduncle to 60 cm long; flowering branch 14–43 cm long and 3–5 mm thick, *purplish red in fruit;* pits spirally and loosely to densely arranged; fruits globose, 5–8 mm diameter, black.
Range and habitat. Western Amazon region and adjacent eastern Andean slopes in Colombia (Amazonas, Caquetá, Meta, Putumayo), Ecuador (Napo), Peru (Ayacucho, Huánuco, Junín, Pasco, Loreto, Madre de Dios, Puno, San Martín, Ucayali), Brazil (Acre, Amazonas), and Bolivia (Beni, Cochabamba, La Paz, Santa Cruz); understory of lowland or premontane rain forest on well-drained soils on slopes or plains, but also in seasonally inundated areas, at 250–550 m elevation.

Uses. The leaves are occasionally used for thatching.

Notes. In general aspect it resembles some forms of *Geonoma macrostachys*, especially var. *acaulis* and var. *macrostachys*, with which it often grows. It can be separated by its slender and loosely pitted, purplish red flowering branch and sickle shaped (not sigmoid) leaflets. Pollination has been studied by Listabarth (1993, as *G. gracilis*).

Geonoma camana
(Map 497, Plate 57)
"Assai-rana," "juriti-ubim" (Bra), "hoja de guacamayo" (Ecu)
Field characters. Stems solitary, erect, rarely subterranean, 0.3–2 m tall and 2–4 cm diameter, rarely thicker. Leaves 5–14; blade to 2 m long, regularly or irregularly divided into 11–25, sigmoid or sickle-shaped leaflets per side, these broad or intermixed with narrow leaflets or all of them narrow, *each leaflet thick, markedly smooth, with conspicuous submarginal veins.* Inflorescences borne among the leaves, *spicate,* erect; peduncle to 1 m long, flowering branch 12–30 cm long and *about 1 cm thick,* reddish in fruit; pits spirally and *very densely arranged;* fruits ovoid to oblong, 1.1–1.3 cm long and 6–8 mm diameter, black.
Range and habitat. Western Amazon region in Colombia (Amazonas, Putumayo), Ecuador (Morona-Santiago, Napo), Peru (Loreto, Madre de Dios), and Brazil (Acre, Amazonas); understory of lowland rain forest, in well-drained or in swampy or imperfectly drained soils, sometimes forming large stands, below 700 m elevation.
Uses. The leaves are used for thatch. The whole palm is used by Miraña and Uitoto Indians in the Colombian Amazon to produce salt, which is obtained by burning the palm and then boiling and filtering the ashes. The salt is mixed with tobacco (Galeano, 1991).
Notes. Unmistakable because of its thick, smooth leaflets which have the appearance of a fern or cycad.

Geonoma chlamydostachys
(Map 498)
Field characters. Stems solitary, 1–2.5 m tall and about 2 cm diameter. Leaves 5–7; blade 45–60 cm long, usually divided into 3 leaflets, rarely more. Inflorescences borne among the leaves, *spicate,* peduncle to 43 cm long; flowering branch 15–32 cm long and *about 1 cm thick; pits spirally and very densely arranged, the lower lip of each projected over the pit;* fruits ovoid, acute at the apex, 1–1.2 cm long and to 6 mm diameter, black.
Range and habitat. Magdalena valley in Colombia (Antioquia); lowland to montane rain forest, at 300–1000 m elevation.
Notes. Closely related to *Geonoma paradoxa,* from the Pacific lowlands of Colombia and *G. macrostachys,* from the Amazon region.

Geonoma chococola
(Map 499)
Field characters. Stems solitary, to 2.5 m tall and 5 cm diameter. Leaves 9–12; blade 1.2–1.5 m long, irregularly divided into a few broad leaflets. Inflorescences borne among the leaves, *spicate;* peduncle to 1 m long; *flowering branch 20–25 cm long and 1 cm thick, orange-red in fruit; pits large, spirally and very densely arranged;* fruits globose, obovoid or ovoid, conspicuously rough, *to 1.8 cm long and 1.4 cm diameter,* black.
Range and habitat. Atlantic slope in Panama (Bocas del Toro) and Pacific lowlands of Colombia (Chocó to Valle); lowland rain forest on well-drained soils, below 500 m elevation.
Notes. Unusual in *Geonoma* in having to 12 stamens, instead of the usual 6, and large, rough fruits. A similar palm, recently collected in western Ecuador, has identical fruits but branched inflorescences and 6 stamens. It may represent an undescribed species or be a local form of *G. chococola.*

Geonoma concinna
(Map 500)
Field characters. Stems clustered, rarely solitary, *pencil-thin,* 1–3.5 m tall and 0.5–1 cm diameter, green, *forming colonies.* Leaves 8–11; blade 20–40 cm long, simple or divided into 2–3 broad leaflets per side. Inflorescences borne below the leaves, *branched to two or three orders;* peduncle about 10 cm long; flowering branches numerous, less than 10 cm long and 1–2 mm thick; pits spirally and densely arranged; fruits almost globose, pointed at apex, rough, 4–8 mm diameter, black.
Range and habitat. Panama (Coclé, Panamá, San Blas) and Colombia (Antioquia); well-drained places, at 100–1750 m elevation.
Notes. A poorly understood species that is known only from a few scattered localities, but rather common in Panama (San Blas).

Geonoma congesta
(Map 501)
"Cortadera," "cuchilleja" (Col), "caña de danta" (CR), "suita" (Hon)
Field characters. Stems clustered, *often in large clumps of 10–20 stems,* rarely solitary, to 7 m tall and 2–4 cm diameter, greenish to light brown. Leaves about 15, *usually erect,* less commonly spreading; *petiole with very sharp margins;* blade to 1.7 m long, irregularly divided into 3 or more leaflets per side, narrow and broad ones

intermixed, rarely the leaf simple. Inflorescences borne among or below the leaves, *branched to one order, erect; peduncle usually less than 10 cm long; rachis very short, to 10 cm long; flowering branches 3–13, stiff, spreading candelabrum-like, to 30 cm long and 6–7 mm thick, bright orange in fruit;* pits spirally and densely arranged; fruits globose or obovoid *rough,* 1–1.5 cm diameter, green or black.

Range and habitat. Central America in Honduras (Gracias a Dios), Nicaragua (Chantales, Río San Juan, Zelaya), Costa Rica (Alajuela, Guanacaste, Heredia, Limón, Puntarenas, San José), and Panama (Bocas del Toro, Darién, Panamá) and northwestern Colombia in the Pacific lowlands and Magdalena valley (Antioquia, Chocó); lowland or premontane rain forest on slopes or plains on well-drained soils, below 900 m elevation.

Uses. The leaves are used for thatching. The common name in Colombia, "cortadera" or "cuchilleja," refers to the sharp margins of the petioles, which sometimes cut the hands of people collecting the leaves.

Geonoma cuneata
(Map 502)
"Palmicha" (Col), "suita" (CR)
Field characters. Stems solitary or rarely clustered, subterranean or to 2 m tall and 1–5 cm diameter. Leaves 8–12; *blade to 1.2 m long* (rarely more), simple or irregularly to regularly divided in 2–15, straight to sigmoid or sickle shaped leaflets. Inflorescences borne among the leaves, erect, *spicate;* peduncle to about 1 m long; *flowering branch 5–36 cm long and 3–10 mm thick,* purplish in fruit; pits spirally and densely arranged; fruits ovoid to ellipsoid, to 8 mm long and 6 mm diameter, black.

Range and habitat. Widespread and common from Nicaragua (Chontales, Zelaya), Costa Rica (Alajuela, Cartago, Guanacaste, Heredia, Puntarenas, San José), Panama (Chiriquí, Coclé, Darién, Panamá, San Blas), western Colombia (Antioquia, Bolívar, Chocó, Cauca, Nariño, Valle), and Ecuador (Azuay, Carchi, Cotopaxi, Esmeraldas, Los Ríos, Pichincha); understory of lowland to montane rain forest, on well-drained soils, from sea level to 1200 m elevation but most common below 600 m.

Notes. An extremely variable species or species complex that is not yet fully understood. There are some consistencies in variation, which has allowed various forms, most of them occurring together, to be recognized as separate species (Wessels Boer, 1968) or varieties (Skov, 1989): var. *cuneata,* with leaves to 1.5 m long, simple or divided into several sickle-shaped leaflets; var. *gracilis,* with smaller

leaves, simple or divided into sickle-shaped leaflets; var. *procumbens,* with leaves less than 65 cm long, divided into several sigmoid leaflets; and var. *sodiroi,* with leaves less than 60 cm long, divided into sigmoid leaflets and with small inflorescences. Nevertheless, this separation has proved unsatisfactory since many intermediate forms occur throughout the whole range of the species. *G. cuneata* is rather similar to *G. jussieuana* for which it may be mistaken; however, the altitudinal ranges of the two species scarely overlap. Various ecological aspects of this species have been studied in Costa Rica (as *Geonoma cuneata*): leaf display and canopy structure (Chazdon, 1985), shade tolerance (Chazdon, 1986a), light variation and carbon gain (Chazdon, 1986b), leaf support (Chazdon, 1986c) and leaf predation by grasshoppers (Braker and Chazdon, 1993).

Geonoma densa
(Map 503)
Field characters. Stems solitary, to 8 m tall and 2.5–7 cm diameter, brown. Leaves 7–10; blade to 1.5 m long, divided into numerous (to 30 per side), *narrow, leathery, rigid, plicate leaflets.* Inflorescences borne below the leaves, branched to 2–3 orders; peduncle 10–25 cm long; rachis to 50 cm long; flowering branches numerous, 9–36 cm long and 2–3 mm thick; pits spirally and densely arranged; fruits ovoid, acute at the apex, about 5 mm long, black.

Range and habitat. Widely distributed throughout the Andes from Venezuela (Lara, Mérida, Monagas, Portuguesa, Yaracuy), Colombia (Antioquia, Boyacá, Chocó, Huila, Norte de Santander), possibly Ecuador, Peru (Cajamarca), and Bolivia (La Paz); montane or cloud forest, at 1800–2500 m elevation.

Notes. A very variable species with a patchy distribution. It is related to the group which includes *Geonoma undata, G. weberbaueri,* and *G. appuniana.* The relationships between these, however, are not fully understood, and they could represent one variable species. *Geonoma densa* is distinguished from the co-occurring *G. undata* and *G. weberbaueri* by its more slender flowering branches. Under severe conditions, such as on exposed ridges, the leaves become more plicate and leathery; this also occurs in *G. orbignyana.*

Geonoma deversa
(Map 504, Plate 58)
"Jatata" (Bol), "ubim" (Bra), "San Pablo" (Col), "chontillo" (Ecu), "palmiche" (Per), "palma de San Pablo" (Ven)
Field characters. Stems clustered, less commonly solitary, 1–4 m tall and 0.5–3 cm diameter, light brown or green. Leaves 7–18, *often loosely*

spaced along the upper part of the stem, the younger ones reddish; blade to 70 cm long, very variable, rarely simple, usually regularly divided into 3 almost sigmoid leaflets per side, or less often into many narrow and straight leaflets, or unequally wide leaflets, the apical ones broader, Inflorescences borne below the leaves, branched to 1–2 orders; peduncle less than 15 cm long; rachis 4–13 cm long; flowering branches 4–25, 11–32 cm long and 1–2.5 mm thick, dark orange to reddish in fruit; *pits arranged in whorls of 3*; fruits globose, 5–7 mm diameter, black.

Range and habit. Widespread and abundant in Central America in Belize, Honduras, Nicaragua, Costa Rica, and Panama and throughout northern South America in Colombia (Amazonas, Antioquia, Caquetá, Chocó, Meta, Nariño, Norte de Santander, Putumayo, Vaupés, Vichada), Venezuela (Amazonas, Apure, Barinas, Bolívar, Delta Amacuro, Mérida, Monagas, Táchira, Zulia), the Guianas, Ecuador (Esmeraldas, Morona-Santiago, Napo, Pastaza), Peru (Junín, Loreto, Madre de Dios, San Martín), Brazil (Acre, Amapá, Amazonas, Pará, Rondônia, Roraima), and Bolivia (Beni, Cochabamba, La Paz); understory of lowland or premontane rain forest, mostly on well-drained soils or rarely on seasonally inundated areas, below 600 m elevation or rarely to 1200 m. It commonly grows in disturbed areas, where it is often abundant.

Uses. The leaves are used for thatching and they are an important local resource in Peru and Bolivia (Rioja, 1992). It is used by the Uitoto Indians in Colombian Amazon to obtain salt by burning the whole plant and then boiling and filtering the ashes.

Notes. This is one of the most common and abundant palms in the understory of lowland rain forest in the American tropics. The arrangement of the pits, in whorls of three, is very characteristic, although leaves are very variable. It resembles *G. triandra* and some forms of *G. interrupta.*

Geonoma divisa
(Map 505)

Field characters. Stems clustered, *pencil-thin,* rarely solitary, to 3 m tall, green to light-brown. Leaves 5–10, erect, blade 30–70 cm long, simple and deeply bifid or divided into 3 broad sigmoid leaflets per side. Inflorescences borne below the leaves, branched to one order; peduncle to 6 cm long; *rachis very short; flowering branches 3–7, to 23 cm long and 2–3 mm thick*; pits spirally arranged; fruits globose, slightly pointed at apex, 5–7 mm diameter, black.

Range and habitat. Panama (Coclé) to northwestern Colombia (Antioquia, Chocó); a very

uncommon species in the understory of lowland rain forest, below 750 m elevation.

Geonoma epetiolata
(Map 506)

Field characters. Stems solitary, pencil-thin, to 2 m tall. Leaves 5–8, the new ones reddish; *petiole almost absent; blade simple, wedge shaped, obovoid, 20–60 cm long, reddish below.* Inflorescences borne among the leaves, but below the leaves in fruit, *spicate*; peduncle about 5 cm long; flowering branch to 20 cm long and 3 mm thick; pits spirally arranged; fruits ellipsoid, *longitudinally striate, strongly pointed at apex,* about 5 mm long, black.

Range and habitat. Costa Rica (Heredia) and Panama (Coclé, Colón, San Blas, Veraguas); understory of lowland or premontane rain forest, below 850 m elevation.

Geonoma ferruginea
(Map 507)

Field characters. Stems clustered, *sometimes forming large clumps,* 1–4 m tall and 2–2.5 cm diameter, light brown. Blade 50–60 cm long, usually regularly divided into 3 sickle-shaped leaflets per side, occasionally 10–15 per side, narrow leaflets present. Inflorescences borne below the leaves, branched to 1–2 orders; peduncle 5–9 cm long; rachis to 10 cm long; *flowering branches 4–13, short and thick, less than 10 cm long and 2–3.5 mm thick,* becoming reddish in fruit; pits densely and spirally arranged; fruits globose, slightly pointed at apex, 6–7 mm diameter, black.

Range and habitat. Central America in Guatemala (Izabal), Honduras (Yoro), Nicaragua (Boaco, Río San Juan, Zelaya), Costa Rica (Alajuela, Cartago, Guanacaste, Heredia, Puntarenas, San José), and Panama (Chiriquí); premontane to montane rain forest, at (100–) 700–1400 m elevation.

Notes. Very similar to *Geonoma longevaginata,* and perhaps both represent variation of one widespread species in Central America. More study throughout their range is needed. Meanwhile, *G. ferruginea* can be separated from *G. longevaginata* by its smaller leaves, shorter flowering branches, and its usually higher-elevation habitat.

Geonoma gamiova
(Map 508)
"Arecana," "gamiova" (Bra)

Field characters. Stems clustered, 2–4 m tall and to 3 cm diameter. Leaves 8–15; blade 50–80 cm long, divided into several unequal, narrow and broad sickle-shaped leaflets. Inflorescences branched to one or two orders; pedun-

cle to 30 cm long; rachis 10–15 cm long; flowering branches 8–13 or more, 20–30 cm long and *2–4 mm thick, often hairy*; pits loosely arranged; fruits ovoid, *markedly pointed at apex*, 1.1 cm long and 8 mm diameter, black.
Range and habitat. Southeastern Brazil (Paraná, Rio de Janeiro, Santa Catarina, São Paulo); forest in the coastal area, below 800 m elevation or rarely to 1300 m.
Notes. This species is part of a complex which includes *Geonoma schottiana, G. brevispatha, G. pohliana,* and *G. gastoniana. Geonoma gamiova* can be separated by its loosely pitted flowering branches and ovoid, pointed fruits.

Geonoma gastoniana
(Map 509)
Field characters. Stems solitary, 1–3 m tall and about 1 cm diameter. Leaves 5–8; blade about 40 cm long, divided into a few broad or many narrow leaflets. Inflorescences borne below the leaves, branched to 2 orders; peduncle about 10 cm long; rachis 10 cm long; flowering branches 20–25 cm long and *1–2 mm thick*; *pits loosely and spirally arranged*; fruits ovoid, about 7 mm diameter, black.
Range and habitat. Eastern Brazil (Goiás, Rio de Janeiro); mountain forest, to 1500 m elevation.
Notes. This is another poorly known species in the *Geonoma schottiana* complex, with which it is perhaps conspecific. Within this complex *G. gastoniana* can be distinguished by its small inflorescences with loosely pitted flowering branches.

Geonoma interrupta
(Map 510)
"Cortadera" (Col), "súrtuba" (CR), "chontilla," "caña brava" (Ecu), "palmiche" (Per), "coco macaque" (Hai, Mar), "chocho blanco" (Mex), "San Pablo" (Ven)
Field characters. Stems solitary or clustered with few(–10) stems, 0.1–7(–10) m tall and 2–12(–15) cm diameter, light brown. Leaves 6–23; blade to 2 m long, regularly or irregularly divided into 3–41 sickle-shaped leaflets per side, usually narrow leaflets intermixed with broad ones. Inflorescences borne below the leaves, less commonly among the leaves, branched to 1–3 orders; peduncle 5–50 cm long, rarely shorter; rachis 2–57 cm long; flowering branches 8–32, the basal ones again branched, *9–25 cm long and 1–3 mm thick*, reddish in fruit; *pits without an upper lip*; fruits globose, sometimes pointed at apex, 3–6 mm diameter, black.
Range and habitat. Widely distributed in Mexico (Veracruz, Oaxaca, Chiapas, Tabasco), Belize (Toledo), Guatemala (Alta Verapaz, Baja Vera

paz, Petén, San Marcos), Honduras (Atlántida, Colón, Cortez, Santa Bárbara, Yoro), Nicaragua (Zelaya), Costa Rica (Alajuela, Cartago, Guanacaste, Heredia, Limón, Puntarenas), Panama (Coclé, Panamá, San Blas), Trinidad, Haiti, Lesser Antilles (Dominica, Martinique), throughout Colombia (Antioquia, Caquetá, Chocó, Guajira, Magdalena, Meta, Nariño, Norte de Santander, Risaralda, Santander, Valle), northern Venezuela (Anzoátegui, Aragua, Barinas, Bolívar, Cojedes, Falcón, Lara, Mérida, Miranda, Monagas, Portuguesa, Sucre, Táchira, Yaracuy, Zulia), the Guianas, Ecuador (Esmeraldas, Morona-Santiago, Napo, Pastaza, Zamora-Chinchipe), Peru (Huánuco, Madre de Dios, San Martín), Brazil (Pará, Rondônia, Roraima), and Bolivia (Beni, La Paz); common in the understory of lowland to premontane rain forest, in well-drained soils on mountain slopes or in poorly drained soils, usually below 1000 m elevation but less commonly reaching 1400 m. It can also occur in disturbed or secondary forest. In Mexico it flowers from September to January and fruits from February to March (Ibarra-Manríquez, 1988).
Uses. In Mexico the trunks are used as handles for tools.
Notes. A widespread and variable species for which many names have been published and commonly used. The differences between these supposed species have been considered subtle and unsatisfactory (Moore, 1969b; Henderson, 1994). Commonly used names such as *G. oxycarpa, G. pinnatifrons,* and *G. euspatha* are here included in *G. interrupta. Geonoma rivalis,* a very localized form from river margins in a small area of the Magdalena valley in Colombia, seems to be a river-bank form. *G. membranacea,* described from Guatemala, is tentatively included here, but it could represent a distinct species because of its ovoid and larger fruits (8 mm long) (M. Grayum, pers. comm.). Two varieties are recognized (Henderson, 1994): var. *euspatha,* with the leaves usually irregularly divided into 3–10 leaflets, rarely the blade simple, in the Andean foothills and Amazon region in Colombia (Meta, Caquetá), Venezuela (Bolívar), the Guianas, Ecuador (Morona-Santiago, Napo), Brazil (Pará, Rondônia), and Bolivia (Beni, La Paz) and var. *interrupta,* with the leaves divided into more numerous leaflets, from throughout the range of the species. Pollination of the latter variety has been studied by Listabarth (1993b).

Geonoma jussieuana
(Map 511)
Field characters. Stems solitary, to 3 m tall and 1.5–2.5 cm diameter, rarely subterranean. Leaves 7–8; blade 30–80 cm long, simple or

regularly divided into 2–9 sickle-shaped to sigmoid leaflets per side, *more or less plicate and contracted at base, loosely spaced more than 2.5 cm apart along the rachis, the apical one broader.* Inflorescences borne among the leaves, *spicate,* rarely bifurcate or trifurcate; peduncle to 1 m long, with persistent, elongate, papery bracts; flowering branch 9–30 cm long and 3–6 mm thick, orange-red to purplish in fruit; pits usually large, loosely arranged; fruits globose to ellipsoid, pointed at apex, 0.6–1 cm long and 4–7 mm diameter, black.

Range and habitat. Mountain regions of Costa Rica (San José) and Panama (Chiriquí) and throughout the Andes in Colombia (Antioquia, Boyacá, Chocó, Cundinamarca, Huila, Putumayo, Tolima, Santander), Venezuela (Carabobo, Distrito Federal, Lara, Trujillo), Ecuador (Los Ríos, Morona-Santiago, Napo, Pastaza, Zamora-Chinchipe), Peru (Cajamarca, Huánuco, Junín, Pasco, San Martín), and Bolivia (Beni, La Paz, Santa Cruz); montane forest in well-drained soils, usually at 1800–3100 m elevation or rarely descending to 700 m. Sometimes it grows in very low forest at high elevations with *Espeletia* and *Polylepis.* The gap in its range in Panama seems to be due to the absence of suitable high-elevation forest in the eastern part of the country.

Uses. The leaves are occasionally used for thatching.

Notes. This is a typical high-elevation palm and is widespread and variable throughout its range. *Geonoma lehmannii,* a commonly used name for this species, is included here. *Geonoma dicranospadix,* which has spicate or branched inflorescences and flower pits lacking a distinct upper lip, is also tentatively included. Some individuals seem to be intermediate between *G. jussieauana* and the closely related and co-occurring *G. orbignyana,* also a widespread, variable, high-elevation species. This suggests that perhaps hybridization between these species occurs in the Andes.

Geonoma laxiflora
(Map 512, Plate 58)
"Ubim da varzea" (Bra), "ponilla" (Per)
Field characters. Stems clustered, *bamboolike, usually forming large colonies,* erect or leaning, 2–5 m tall, *pencil-thin,* green. Leaves 6–10; blade 25–60 cm long, *usually simple,* rarely with 2 wide leaflets per side. Inflorescences borne below the leaves, sometimes near the ground, branched to one, rarely two orders; *peduncle short (to 5 cm long); rachis short (4–8 cm long); flowering branches 4–9, long, slender, pendulous, to 35 cm long and 1–3 mm thick, orange in fruit; pits loosely and spirally arranged;* fruits globose, 0.7–1 cm diameter, black.

Range and habitat. Western Amazon region in Colombia (Amazonas), Ecuador (Napo), Peru (Loreto), Brazil (Acre, Amazonas), and Bolivia (Pando); understory of seasonally inundated lowland rain forest, along rivers and streams, at low elevations.

Geonoma leptospadix
(Map 513, Plate 58)
"Ubim," "ubim brava" (Bra), "sangapilla masha" (Per)
Field characters. Stems solitary or clustered, 0.5–2 m tall, *pencil-thin.* Leaves 6–17, *spreading umbrella-like,* blade less than 60 cm long, usually *oblong and simple or rarely divided into few sigmoid leaflets per side.* Inflorescences usually borne below the leaves, erect, branched to one, rarely two orders, several present at the same time; peduncle 6–20 cm long; rachis absent or to 7 cm long; flowering branches *2–5, stiff and erect, slender, thin,* to 20 cm long and 1–2 mm thick, red in fruit; pits loosely and spirally arranged; fruit globose, 5–8 mm diameter, black.

Range and habitat. Amazon region in Colombia (Amazonas), Venezuela (Bolívar), the Guianas, Ecuador (Pastaza), Peru (Huánuco, Junín, Loreto, Pasco, Ucayali), Brazil (Amapá, Amazonas, Maranhão, Rondônia, Roraima), and Bolivia (Beni); lowland rain forest on plains or slopes, on well-drained, noninundated soils, below 750 m elevation or rarely to 1200 m in the Guyana Highlands. Some specimens from northwestern Colombia (Chocó) and the Magdalena valley (Antioquia) and from Ecuador (Azuay, El Oro, Esmeraldas) also seem to belong to this species.

Uses. The leaves are occasionally used for thatching.

Notes. Unmistakable because of its small oblong leaves, with umbrella-like appearance and several contemporary inflorescences with erect, stiff, and slender flowering branches. Its distribution is very interesting; it is one of the few species that occurs mainly in the Amazon region and also in northwestern Colombia.

Geonoma linearis
(Map 514)
"Caló" (Col)
Field characters. Stems solitary or clustered, usually *forming large colonies,* 0.2–3 m tall and 1.5–4 cm diameter, often creeping and with numerous adventitious roots. Leaves 3–19, blade 30–70 cm long, divided into 4–18 narrow leaflets per side. Inflorescences borne among the leaves, erect, *spicate;* peduncle to 60 cm long; flowering branch 9.5–28 cm long and 4–7 mm thick, purplish green in fruit; pits densely arranged; fruits ovoid to subglobose, shortly

pointed at the apex, 6–8 mm long and 4–5 mm diameter, black, *the mesocarp very fibrous*.
Range and habitat. Pacific lowlands of Colombia (Chocó, Valle, Nariño) and northwestern Ecuador (Esmeraldas); forming large colonies confined to the banks of small, fast-flowing rivers, sometimes growing partially submerged.
Uses. In Ecuador it is reported to be a magic plant and used to cure stomach pains (Barfod and Balslev, 1988).
Notes. Closely related to *Geonoma cuneata*, of which it could represent a specialized form. It is one of the few palms in the world that grows in running water (Galeano and Skov, 1989).

Geonoma longepedunculata
(Map 515)
"Palmiche" (Per)
Field characters. Stems solitary, 0.1–1 m tall and 3–5 cm diameter, often creeping. Leaves 9–10; rachis 34–65 cm long, *covered with a distinct layer of brown tomentum*; blade rarely simple, usually divided into 3–11 unequal and sigmoid leaflets per side, the largest 30–40 cm long. Inflorescences borne among the leaves, erect, branched to one order; peduncle 28–40 cm long; rachis 5–11 cm long; flowering branches *4–7, straight and stiff, hairy*, 12–25 cm long and 2–3 mm thick; pits small, loosely and spirally arranged; fruits globose, 4–5 mm in diameter, black.
Range and habitat. Eastern Andean foothills and adjacent western Amazon basin in Colombia (Caquetá), Ecuador (Morona-Santiago, Napo, Pastaza), and Peru (Junín, Loreto, Pasco); lowland rain forest on noninundated, well-drained soils, at 200–700 m elevation.
Uses. The leaves are used for thatching.
Notes. Very similar to *Geonoma poeppigiana*, from which it can be separated by the tomentum on the leaf rachis and the absence of tomentum on the peduncle.

Geonoma longevaginata
(Map 516)
Field characters. Stems clustered, few, erect or leaning, 1–5 m tall and 2–3 cm in diameter, light brown. Leaves 6–7; blade about 1 m long, almost regularly divided into more than 10 (rarely only 3), almost equal, sickle-shaped or sigmoid leaflets per side. Inflorescences borne below the leaves, branched to one, rarely two orders; peduncle about 10 cm long; rachis 5–20 cm long; *flowering branches 5–11, pendulous*, 20–35 cm long and 2.5–3.5 cm thick, reddish in fruit; pits densely arranged; fruits globose, slightly pointed at apex, 5–7 mm diameter, black.
Range and habitat. Costa Rica (Heredia, Limón, Puntarenas) and Panama (San Blas); under-

story of lowland rain forest, on well-drained soils, below 350 m elevation.
Notes. See comments under *Geonoma ferruginea*.

Geonoma macrostachys
(Map 517, Plates 58 & 59)
"Ubim," "ubimzinho" (Bra), "calzón panga," "hoja de guacamayo" (Ecu), "wai" (FrG), "palmiche," "ponilla" (Per), "barubaru" (Ven)
Field characters. Stems solitary, rarely clustered, *short and subterranean* or rarely to 50 cm tall. Leaves 6–12, reddish when young; blade 0.3–1 m long and 30–50 cm wide, simple and strongly wedge shaped or regularly or irregularly divided into straight or sigmoid leaflets. Inflorescences borne among the leaves, erect, *spicate*; peduncle to 1.4 m long; flowering branch 6–28 cm long and 0.3–1 cm thick, orange in fruit; *pits densely and spirally arranged*; fruits globose, 0.5–1 cm diameter, black.
Range and habitat. Amazon region of Colombia (Amazonas, Caquetá, Putumayo, Vaupés, Vichada), Venezuela (Amazonas), the Guianas, Ecuador (Morona-Santiago, Napo), Peru (Loreto, Madre de Dios, Pasco, San Martin, Ucayali), Brazil (Acre, Amapá, Amazonas, Pará), and Bolivia (Beni, Pando); very common and widespread in lowland rain forest on well-drained soils or in seasonally inundated areas, below 600 m elevation.
Uses. The leaves are occasionally used for thatching.
Notes. This is a very variable species (Skov, 1989; Henderson, 1994) and even in the same place a large variation can be found in size and division of the leaves and size of the inflorescences. Although there are many intermediates, some distinctive forms can be easily recognized. These have been traditionally treated as separate species, but are here considered as varieties, following recent studies on the genus (Skov, 1989; Henderson, 1994): var. *macrostachys*, with strongly wedge-shaped, simple leaves, or the leaves divided with straight leaflets and the flowering branch about 1 cm thick with closely arranged pits, from the western Amazon region, usually in noninundated areas; var. *poiteauana*, with undivided and strongly wedge-shaped and plicate leaves or leaves divided with straight leaflets and the flowering branch less than 5 mm thick, with rather loosely arranged pits, from the eastern Amazon region, in inundated or noninundated forest; and var. *acaulis*, with nonwedge-shaped, divided leaves, with sigmoid leaflets and flowering branch less than 5 mm thick with closely or loosely arranged pits, from the western Amazon region, usually in seasonally inundated areas. Pollination of var. *macrostachys* has been studied in Ecuador (Olesen

and Balslev, 1990) and Peru (Listabarth, 1993b), and of var. *acaulis* in Peru by Listabarth (1993b).

Geonoma maxima
(Map 518, Plate 59)
"Ubim" (Bra), "pui paso" (Col), "baru-baru" (Col, Ven)
Field characters. Stems clustered, less commonly solitary, erect, 1–7 m tall and 0.5–5 cm in diameter, green to light brown. Leaves 4–20; the blade very variable, from less than 50 cm long to more than 1 m long, simple and strongly plicate, or regularly divided into several equal and narrow sickle-shaped or sigmoid leaflets, or irregularly divided into few unequal leaflets. Inflorescences borne among or below the leaves, branched to (one–)2 orders; peduncle to 20 cm long; rachis to 15 cm long; flowering branches to 13, erect, the basal ones often branched again, to 24 cm long and 1–6 mm thick, orange in fruit; pits spirally arranged; fruits ovoid or ellipsoid to globose, *to 1.6 cm long and 1.2 cm diameter,* black.
Range and habitat. Amazon region in Colombia, Venezuela, the Guianas, Ecuador, Peru, Brazil, and Bolivia, and Magdalena valley in Colombia; widespread in the understory of lowland rain forest, usually on noninundated soils or occasionally in inundated areas, below 500 m elevation but reaching 1300 m in the Guayana Highland.
Uses. The leaves are used for thatching; the young leaves are used to produce salt, after burning, cooking, and filtering. This salt is used to mix with tobacco paste.
Notes. A common and widespread species in the Amazon region. It is extremely variable and still poorly understood. Henderson (1994) recognized 4 more or less consistent forms which he treated as varieties. Nevertheless, many intermediates occur. The varieties are: var. *ambigua*, with leaves with wide apical and basal leaflets and narrower ones in between, from Venezuela (Bolívar, Delta Amacuro), the Guianas, and Brazil (Roraima); var. *chelidonura*, with plicate leaves, with 2 broad leaflets often interspersed with narrower leaflets, from Colombia (Amazonas, Putumayo, Vaupés and also in the Magdalena valley in Norte de Santander), Venezuela (Amazonas), Peru (Amazonas, Huánuco, Loreto, Madre de Dios, Pasco), Brazil (Acre, Amazonas, Pará, Rondônia), and Bolivia (Beni, La Paz, Pando); var. *maxima*, with regularly pinnate leaves with 9–31 equally wide, sigmoid leaflets, from Colombia (Amazonas, Caquetá, Guainía), Venezuela (Amazonas), French Guiana, Ecuador (Morona-Santiago, Napo, Pastaza), Peru (Amazonas, Loreto), Brazil (Amapá, Amazonas, Pará, Rondônia), and Bolivia (Beni,

Pando); and var. *spixiana,* with simple or partially pinnate, strongly plicate leaves, from Colombia (Amazonas) and Brazil (Amazonas).

Geonoma myriantha
(Map 519)
"Ubim" (Bra)
Field characters. Stems clustered, 2–5 m tall and 2.5–3 cm diameter. Leaves 9–14, pinnate; leaflets 3–19 per side, sigmoid. Inflorescences borne below the leaves, branched to 2–3 orders; *peduncle to 6 cm long;* flowering branches to 30, 28–30 cm long and 2.5 mm thick, straight within the bud; pits spirally arranged, *upper lip obscure or absent;* fruits globose to ellipsoid, 5–6 mm diameter, black.
Range and habitat. Brazil (Acre); lowland rain forest on noninundated soils, at low elevations.
Notes. A rare species with a restricted distribution.

Geonoma oldemannii
(Map 520, Plate 59)
"Ubimaçu" (Bra)
Field characters. Stems solitary or clustered, 1.5–2 m tall and 2–7 cm diameter, brown. Leaves 12–13, erect; blade 1–2 m long and 15–20 cm wide, *simple, wedge shaped.* Inflorescences borne among the leaves, erect, *spicate;* peduncle 35–45 cm long; *flowering branch 22–45 cm long and about 1 cm thick;* pits densely and spirally arranged; fruits globose, 1.2 cm long and 8 mm diameter, black.
Range and habitat. Eastern Amazon region in French Guiana and Brazil (Amapá, Pará); lowland rain forest on noninundated or inundated areas, at low elevations.
Uses. The leaves are used for thatching.

Geonoma oligoclona
(Map 521)
Field characters. Stems clustered, 1–2 m tall and 1–5 cm diameter. Leaves about 10; blade 35–50 cm long, *regularly divided into 3 sigmoid leaflets per side, these narrowed at the base. Inflorescences borne well below the leaves,* branched to one order; peduncle about 4 cm long; *rachis absent; flowering branches 3–10,* cylindrical, reddish in fruit, about 30 cm long and 4 mm thick; pits loosely and spirally arranged; fruits globose, 5 mm diameter, black.
Range and habitat. Western Amazon region in Colombia (Amazonas), Venezuela (Amazonas), and Brazil (Amazonas); very uncommon in lowland rain forest on well-drained soils, usually at low elevations but to 1000 m in the Guayana Highland.
Notes. Very similar to *Geonoma aspidiifolia;* see this for differences.

Geonoma orbignyana
(Map 522)
"Palmilla" (Col), "chile" (Ecu)

Field characters. Stems solitary or clustered, erect, rarely creeping, 1–5 m tall and 1.5–6 cm diameter, light brown. Leaves 6–15; blade 0.3–1.5 m long, rarely simple, irregularly or regularly divided into 2–20 broad and narrow, *mostly plicate and rigid leaflets per side, usually separated by more than 2.5 cm along the rachis.* Inflorescences borne among the leaves, branched to one order, or the lower branches bifurcate or trifurcate; with papery to leathery persistent bracts; peduncle 12–50 cm long, *covered initially (as the rachis and flowering branches) with a thick, woolly tomentum*; rachis to 16 cm long; *flowering branches 3–13, erect,* 5–23 cm long and 2.5–7 mm thick, purplish in fruit; pits loosely and spirally arranged; fruits ovoid, pointed at apex, 6–9 mm diameter, black.

Range and habitat. Nicaragua (Jinoteca), Costa Rica (Cartago, Heredia, Limón Puntarenas), Colombia (Antioquia, Boyacá, Cauca, Huila, Magdalena, Valle), Venezuela (Mérida, Táchira, Trujillo, Yaracuy), Ecuador (Azuay, Loja, Morona-Santiago, Napo, Zamora-Chinchipe), Peru (Amazonas, Cajamarca, Huánuco), Bolivia (Cochabamba, La Paz); understory of montane rain forest on slopes, at 1200–3150 m elevation. Its absence in Panama is probably due to the lower elevations in that country.

Uses. The leaves are locally traded for flower displays in Bogotá, Colombia (Bernal, 1992); and the stems are used for walking sticks.

Notes. One of the most common and widespread palms in Central American and Andean montane forest. It also reaches the highest elevations for any palm, and along with *Geonoma weberbaueri* and *Ceroxylon parvifrons* it can occur at over 3000 m elevation (Moraes et al., in press). It is also a very variable species and in consequence it has been overdescribed. It has been known most commonly by the names *G. lindeniana*, *G. marggraffia*, *G. hoffmanniana*, and *G. pachydicrana*. It is closely related to *G. jussieauana* and some intermediate individuals have been found, which could be hybrids. It is in need of detailed study. *Geonoma heinrichsiae*, described from the Andes in Ecuador, is tentatively included here.

Geonoma paradoxa
(Map 523)

Field characters. Stems solitary, very short, to 20 cm tall and 2 cm diameter. Leaves about 10; blade 30–50 cm long, *wedge shaped, simple or irregularly divided into 3–7 broad and sickle-shaped leaflets per side.* Inflorescences borne below the leaves, *spicate*; peduncle to 65 cm long; flower-

ing branch 7–10 cm long and 2.5–6 mm thick; pits conspicuous, densely and spirally arranged; fruits unknown.

Range and habitat. Pacific coast of southern Colombia (Cauca, Nariño, Valle); lowland rain forest on well-drained soils near sea level. There is a dubious record from eastern Ecuador (Morona-Santiago) at 1350–1650 m elevation (Skov, 1989), which seems to represent *G. jussieuana* (F. Borchsenius, pers. comm.).

Notes. A poorly known species, apparently restricted to a very small area. It may be related to *Geonoma macrostachys* from the Amazon and *G. chlamydostachys* from the Magdalena valley in Colombia.

Geonoma paraguanensis
(Map 524)

Field characters. Stems solitary, to 3 m tall and 2.5–6 cm in diameter, erect or creeping. Leaves with blade about 1 m long, divided into *numerous, narrow, leathery, stiff leaflets,* sometimes with some wider leaflets intermixed. Inflorescences borne among the leaves, branched 1–3 orders; peduncle 20–30 cm long; rachis about 12 cm long; flowering branches 12, to 10 cm long and 2.5–3.5 mm thick; pits spirally arranged; fruits globose, pointed at apex, about 6 mm diameter.

Range and habitat. Northwestern coastal area of Venezuela (Falcón); cloud forest on summits of isolated mountains, exposed to high winds, to 1400 m elevation.

Notes. A very poorly known species; it seems to be related to *Geonoma densa* and is perhaps merely a depauperate form.

Geonoma pauciflora
(Map 525)
"Ouricana" (Bra)

Field characters. Stems clustered, rarely solitary, erect, 1–3 m tall and 1–1.5 cm diameter, *pencil-thin*, light brown. Leaves 7–19; *blade oblong or lanceolate, wedge shaped,* 25–60 cm long, *simple or irregularly divided into a few broad leaflets,* sometimes with more narrow leaflets intermixed. Inflorescences borne among the leaves, *spicate or branched to one order*; peduncle 14–50 cm long; rachis to 25 cm long; flowering branches 6–20 cm long and 2–5 mm thick; pits rather loosely inserted in spirals or whorls; fruits globose or ovoid, slightly pointed at apex, 0.8–1.2 cm diameter, black.

Range and habitat. Atlantic coast of Brazil (Alagoas, Bahia, Espírito Santo, Paraná, Pernambuco, Rio de Janeiro, Santa Catarina, São Paulo); understory of lowland rain forest, on wet and well-drained lateritic clayey to sandy humus soils, on hillsides and mountain slopes, from sea level to 700 m elevation.

Notes. The smallest species of *Geonoma* in eastern Brazil. As noted by Noblick (1991), it has an interesting vegetative reproduction. The stems bend over until they make contact with the ground, then the stem at the base of the crown produces roots and begins a new clump of palms 3–4 m from the original parent cluster. It flowers from October to January and fruits are mature in May and June (Noblick, 1991). *Geonoma elegans* is included here, but perhaps deserves subspecific status.

Geonoma poeppigiana
(Map 526)
"Palmiche" (Per)
Field characters. *Stems solitary,* to 1 m tall, rarely more, and *2–5 cm diameter,* usually erect, brown, *with very close internodes.* Leaves 8–16, erect to horizontal; blade to 1.2 m long, *simple or divided into 2–5 unequal, broad leaflets per side.* Inflorescences borne among the leaves, erect, branched to one order; peduncle 30–60 cm long, *with whitish brown tomentum; rachis absent or to 15 cm long; flowering branches 2–9, erect and stiff,* to 50 cm long and 3–6 mm thick, purplish brown in fruit; pits small, spirally arranged; fruits globose to ovoid, 5–8 mm long and 5–6 mm diameter, dark brown to black.
Range and habitat. Western Amazon region in Colombia (Amazonas, Caquetá), Peru (Amazonas, Huánuco, Junín, Loreto, Madre de Dios, Pasco), and Brazil (Amazonas); understory of lowland rain forest on well-drained soils and also in places near white-sand formations, below 500 m elevation.
Uses. The leaves are used for thatching.
Notes. It resembles *Geonoma baculifera* and *G. longepedunculata.* The former has a different range and habitat and the latter lacks the distinctive whitish brown tomentum on the peduncle, which is conspicuous in *G. poeppigina.*

Geonoma pohliana
(Map 527, Plate 60)
"Ouricana," "ouricana-preta" (Bra)
Field characters. Stems clustered, rarely solitary, to 4 m tall and 7 cm in diameter. Leaves 6–15; blade to 1.2 m long, divided into few to many unequal sickle-shaped, narrow and broad leaflets, or sometimes all of them narrow. Inflorescences borne among leaves, branched to 2–3 orders; peduncle to 47 cm long; peduncular bract leathery, persistent or deciduous; rachis 10–50 cm long; *flowering branches numerous, 15–41 cm long and 1–5 mm thick; pits whorled or decussate, densely arranged;* fruit ovoid, pointed at apex, to 1.6 cm long, black.
Range and habitat. Atlantic coast of Brazil (Alagoas, Bahia, Ceará, Espírito Santo, Pernambuco, Rio de Janeiro); lowland to montane

rain forest on moist soils, also common in cocoa plantations, below 1800 m elevation.
Notes. This rather variable species is a member of the *Geonoma schottiana* complex. It can be distinguished from the latter by its densely pitted flowering branches. *Geonoma blanchettiana* and *G. fiscellaria* are included here, but both perhaps should be recognized as subspecific taxa.

Geonoma polyandra
(Map 528)
"Huasipanga" (Ecu)
Field characters. Stems solitary, 0.5–2.5 m tall and 1.5–5 cm in diameter, brown. Leaves 9–15; blade 0.8–2 m long, regularly divided into 8–22 straight to sigmoid, mostly narrow leaflets. Inflorescences borne among the leaves, *spicate, erect;* peduncle to 50 cm long; *flowering branch 21–30 cm long and about 1 cm thick,* orange in fruit; pits spirally and densely arranged; fruits ovoid or ellipsoid, pointed at apex, about 1 cm long and 6 mm diameter, black.
Range and habitat. Western Amazon region in Colombia (Caquetá) and Ecuador (Napo); lowland rain forest on noninundated soils, but near blackwater swamps, below 350 m elevation.
Uses. The leaves are used for thatching.
Notes. Similar to *Geonoma camana,* from which it can be separated by its less densely arranged pits and plicate leaflets without marginal veins. *Geonoma polyandra,* together with *G. chococola,* are the only species in the genus with more than 6 stamens (to 12).

Geonoma rubescens
(Map 529, Plate 60)
"Ouricana" (Bra)
Field characters. Stems solitary, erect, to 4 m tall and 1.5–4 cm diameter, *green to purplish.* Leaves 6–14, *purplish;* blade to 90 cm long, simple or divided into 2–8 rather broad, sickle-shaped leaflets per side, these sometimes contracted at the base. Inflorescences borne among the leaves, branched to one order; peduncle 7–20 cm long; *rachis less than 5 cm long; flowering branches 2–7, spreading candelabrum-like, 8–35 cm long and 3–6 mm thick, usually densely tomentose initially,* reddish in fruit; pits densely and spirally arranged; fruits globose, pointed at the apex, 0.7–1 cm diameter, black.
Range and habitat. Atlantic coast of Brazil (Bahia, Espírito Santo, Rio de Janeiro, São Paulo); understory of primary or disturbed lowland rain forest on lateritic clayey soils, at low elevations.
Notes. A rather variable species; *Geonoma rodeiensis* and *G. trinervis* are included here.

Geonoma schottiana
(Map 530)
"Ouricana" (Bra), "guarika" (Par: Guaraní)
Field characters. Stems clustered, forming clumps, occasionally solitary, 1–4 m tall and 2.5–4 cm diameter. Leaves 7–12; blade 0.4–1 m long, *usually regularly divided into numerous, very narrow sickle-shaped leaflets, each leaflet marked with 3 conspicuous veins on the upper surface.* Inflorescences borne among or below the leaves, branched to 2 orders; peduncle to 60 cm long; peduncular bract leathery, persistent; rachis to 20 cm long; flowering branches 7–17, 8–25 cm long and 1–3 mm thick, yellowish to dark orange in fruit; *pits loosely arranged, decussate;* fruits ovoid to globose, 0.8–1 cm diameter, black.
Range and habitat. Eastern Brazil (Espírito Santo, Goiás, Minas Gerais, Rio de Janeiro, Pará, Paraná, Tocantins); forest or gallery forest, at 400–1600 m elevation.
Notes. Part of a complex that includes *Geonoma brevispatha, G. pohliana, G. gamiova,* and *G. gastoniana.* An almost continuous gradient of variation is found, and the whole complex seems to be another example of a widespread, variable species, similar to the situation in *G. maxima.* It is in need of more detailed study. Traditionally *G. schottiana* has been distinguished from its relatives by its narrow leaflets with 3 conspicuous veins on the upper surface.

Geonoma scoparia
(Map 531, Plate 60)
Field characters. Stems solitary, 1.5–3 m tall, *pencil-thin,* greenish. Leaves 12–19; blade 40–60 cm long, divided into 3, rarely more, broad, sigmoid leaflets per side. Inflorescences borne below the leaves, branched to several orders; peduncle 2–4 cm long; flowering branches numerous, *threadlike,* 8.5–11 cm long; pits loosely and spirally arranged; fruits subglobose, 5–6 mm diameter, black.
Range and habitat. Costa Rica (Puntarenas); known only from a small area of lowland rain forest, at 100–300 m elevation.
Notes. This is a threatened species (Grayum and de Nevers, 1988). It is similar to both *Geonoma tenuissima* of Ecuador and *G. spinescens* from Venezuela, both of which differ in their clustered habit and simple leaves. Another species of *Geonoma* with threadlike flowering branches, probably undescribed, occurs on eastern Andean slopes in Ecuador and Peru at 1500–1600 m elevation.

Geonoma simplicifrons
(Map 532)
Field characters. Stems solitary or clustered, 1–3 m tall and 1–1.5 cm diameter. Leaves about 8;

blade 40–70 cm long, simple or divided into 2–4 somewhat sickle-shaped leaflets per side. Inflorescences borne among the leaves, *spicate or with 2–4 flowering branches;* peduncle 20–30 cm long; flowering branches 13–23 cm long and about 3 mm thick; *pits densely arranged, very small, without an upper lip;* fruits ovoid to globose, slightly pointed at apex, about 5 mm diameter, black.
Range and habitat. Cordillera de la Costa in northern Venezuela (Aragua, Carabobo, Distrito Federal, Miranda) and one record from the Guayana Highland in Venezuela (Amazonas); on mountain slopes in premontane or montane forest, at 400–1400 m elevation.
Notes. Resembles some forms of *G. jussieuana* and *G. orbignyana* and perhaps all three are conspecific.

Geonoma spinescens
(Map 533)
Field characters. Stems clustered, 1–2 m tall and 1–1.5 cm diameter. Leaves about 13; blade 60–80 cm long, simple and wedge shaped or divided into several leaflets. Inflorescences borne among the leaves, *branched to 3 orders;* peduncle about 10 cm long; rachis 10–15 cm long; flowering branches numerous, *threadlike,* to 10 cm long and 1–1.5 mm thick, reddish in fruit; pits loosely arranged; fruits ovoid, pointed at apex, 8 mm long and 6 mm diameter, black.
Range and habitat. Coastal area of Venezuela (Aragua, Carabobo, Yaracuy); understory of rain forest, at 750–1300 m elevation.
Notes. A poorly known species. By its threadlike flowering branches it resembles *Geonoma tenuissima* from Ecuador and *G. scoparia* from Costa Rica. The relationships among these three require more study.

Geonoma stricta
(Map 534, Plates 60 & 61)
"Ubim" (Bra), "palmicha" (Col), "chontilla" (Ecu), "palmiche" (Per)
Field characters. Stems solitary or clustered, 0.5–3 m tall, *pencil-thin,* green or brown. Leaves 5–12, sometimes arranged loosely along the apical part of the stem; *petiole often with thick reddish brown woolly tomentum;* blade simple, oblong or elliptic, very small to larger (14–75 cm long and 4–22 cm wide), or divided into 3 (or more) sigmoid leaflets per side. Inflorescences borne below the leaves, *spicate* (very rarely branched with 2–4 branches), erect; peduncle 1–13 cm long; flowering branches 3–25 cm long and 3–12 mm thick, *tomentose,* yellow-brown to dark red in fruit; pits spirally ar-

range; fruits ovoid to ellipsoid, 0.7–1.1 cm long and 5–7 mm diameter, blue or black at maturity.

Range and habitat. Amazon region in Colombia, Venezuela, the Guianas, Ecuador, Peru, Brazil, and Bolivia and also in the Chocó and the Magdalena valley in Colombia (Antioquia); understory of lowland rain forest, on well-drained soils, below 700 m elevation or rarely reaching 1000 m on eastern Andean slopes.

Uses. The leaves are used for thatching.

Notes. A rather wide and continuous variation in size of the whole plant and in division of the leaves can be seen throughout its geographical range. Some forms have been considered to represent different species (Wessels Boer, 1968) or varieties (Skov, 1989, as *G. pycnostachys*; Henderson, 1994). There are, however, many intermediates. Here we follow Henderson (1994) and recognize: var. *stricta*, with small, simple, parallel-sided, narrow leaves, from Colombia (Amazonas, Putumayo, the Magdalena valley, and the Pacific coast in Chocó), Venezuela (Amazonas), the Guianas, Ecuador (Morona-Santiago, Napo, Pastaza), Peru (Huánuco, Loreto, Pasco, Madre de Dios, San Martín), and Brazil (Acre, Amapá, Amazonas, Pará); var. *piscicauda*, with large, simple, oblanceolate, deeply bifid leaves, from Colombia (Amazonas, Caquetá, Putumayo), Ecuador (Napo, Pastaza, Santiago-Zamora), Peru (Loreto, Madre de Dios), Brazil (Acre, Amazonas); and var. *trailii*, with pinnate leaves and sigmoid leaflets, from Colombia (Amazonas, Vaupés), Ecuador (Morona-Santiago, Napo, Pastaza), Peru (Amazonas, Loreto, Madre de Dios, Pasco, Ucayali), Brazil (Acre, Amazonas), and Bolivia (Cochabamba, Pando), and with an outlying population in French Guiana and Brazil (Amapá).

Geonoma tenuissima
(Map 535)

Field characters. Stems clustered, to 3 m tall, *pencil-thin*, green to light brown. Leaves 6–8; blade 38–50 cm long and 11–13 cm wide, simple and wedge shaped. Inflorescences borne below the leaves, *branched to 3–4 orders*; peduncle 3–6 cm long, rachis 9–14 cm long; flowering branches numerous, *pendulous, threadlike*, 2–10 cm long and less than 1 mm thick, reddish in fruit; pits very loosely arranged; fruits globose, about 5 mm diameter, black or blue.

Range and habitat. Western Ecuador (Los Ríos, Pichincha) and probably Colombia (Valle); lowland rain forest, below 600 m elevation.

Notes. A very scarce and uncommon species, which has been considered threatened (Skov, 1989); see comments under *Geonoma scoparia.*

Geonoma triandra
(Map 536, Plate 61)
"Caña de loma" (Col)

Field characters. Stems clustered, forming clumps of about 15 stems, 1–3 m tall, *pencil-thin*, green or light brown. Leaves 4–8, arranged along the upper part of the stems, reddish when young; blade 25–50 cm long and 15–25 cm wide, simple or divided into 3–several sigmoid leaflets per side. Inflorescences borne among the leaves, branched to 2 orders; peduncle 10–20 cm long; rachis 5–10 cm long; *flowering branches numerous, 5–10 cm long and 1 mm thick*, reddish in fruit; pits loosely arranged; fruits ovoid, 6–7 mm diameter, black.

Range and habitat. Panama (Bocas del Toro, Darién, San Blas) and northwestern Colombia (Antioquia, Chocó); understory of lowland rain forest, sometimes on alluvial soils, from sea level to 1400 m elevation.

Notes. This is the only species of *Geonoma* with 3 stamens. In general aspect *G. triandra* resembles *G. deversa*, with which it grows. They can be separated by the threadlike flowering branches of *G. triandra.*

Geonoma triglochin
(Map 537)
"Daru" (Ecu: Siona)

Field characters. Stems solitary, erect or partially creeping, 1.5–4 m tall and 4–5 cm diameter, brown. Leaves 15–25, *spreading umbrella-like*; blade 0.7–1.9 m long and 25–50 cm wide, wedge shaped, simple or almost regularly divided into 3 broad leaflets per side. Inflorescences borne among the leaves, erect, branched to one order; peduncle 26–50 cm long; *rachis absent or to 14 cm long; flowering branches 2–8, erect, 10–30 cm long and 0.8–1.3 cm thick*, orange-brown in fruit; pits densely arranged; fruits globose to ellipsoid, not pointed at apex, *1–1.5 cm long*, black.

Range and habitat. Western Amazon region and adjacent Andean slopes in Colombia (Caquetá), Ecuador (Morona-Santiago, Napo), and Peru (Junín, Madre de Dios, Pasco); lowland to montane rain forest on slopes or plains in well-drained soils, below 100 m elevation but reaching 1150 m in Andean foothills.

Uses. The leaves are commonly used for thatching.

Notes. A rather uncommon species, but quite distinct with its stout trunk, large simple or almost simple leaves, inflorescences with few thick and densely pitted flowering branches and large fruits.

Geonoma trigona
(Map 538, Plate 61)

Field characters. Stems solitary, 2–3 m tall.

Leaves 5–7, erect; blade about 30 cm long, *simple, deeply bifid, strongly leathery, plicate, and wedge shaped.* Inflorescences borne among the leaves, erect, branched to one order; peduncle 30–40 cm long; *rachis almost absent; flowering branches 8–10, erect,* 0.8–1.1 cm long and 6–7 mm thick; pits densely arranged; fruits globose, about 1 cm long, black.

Range and habitat. Central Peruvian Andes (Huánuco, Pasco); shrubby xeromorphic vegetation locally called "pajonales" (Gentry, 1986), at 2650–2800 m elevation.

Notes. A very distinct species because of its strongly plicate, leathery leaves. In fact, it was originally described as a member of the Cyclanthaceae and mistakenly stayed in that family for almost two centuries (Gentry, 1986). It is similar in aspect to some forms of *Geonoma weberbaueri,* with which it grows. *Geonoma trigona* can be distinguished by its small and deeply bifid leaves and inflorescences branched to one order.

Geonoma umbraculiformis
(Map 539)
"Dhalebana" (Guy)

Field characters. Stems solitary, to 2 m tall and 2–2.5 cm diameter, brown. Leaves 12–27, erect to spreading, *umbrella-like*; blade 0.9–1.2 m long and 20–30 cm wide, wedge shaped, simple or irregularly divided into a few broad leaflets. Inflorescences borne among the leaves, branched to one order; peduncle 25–40 cm long; *rachis absent or to 5 cm long; flowering branches 2–5,* 15–20 cm long and 3–3.5 mm thick; pits loosely arranged; fruits globose, 0.9–1.3 cm diameter, black.

Range and habitat. Eastern Amazon region in the Guianas and Brazil (Amapá, Pará); lowland or premontane rain forest, on well-drained mountain slopes, in noninundated areas, at 300–750 m elevation.

Notes. Resembles *Geonoma triglochin* but this has much thicker and more densely pitted flowering branches and grows in the western Amazon region.

Geonoma undata
(Map 540, Plate 62)
"Palmiche" (Col), "macana," "colapato" (Ecu), "cum," "pamaca" (Gua), "capuca" (Hon)

Field characters. Stems solitary, erect, *to 10 m tall and 10 cm diameter,* light brown. Leaves 8–20; blade 1.4–2.5 m long, irregularly to almost regularly divided into 9–69 leaflets per side, broad and narrow, or all of them narrow, spreading in the same plane, rarely some of them positioned on a slightly different plane and pendulous at different lengths near the apex, giving the leaf a plumose appearance. Inflorescences borne below the leaves, *branched to 2–3 orders*; peduncle 15–32 cm long; rachis 54–69 cm long, with 11–24 primary branches, the basal ones branched again; flowering branches 12–47 cm long and 3–7 mm thick, green or reddish in fruit; pits densely arranged; fruits ovoid, pointed at apex, 8–9 mm long and 6–7 mm diameter, black.

Range and habitat. Lesser Antilles (Guadeloupe, Dominique, Martinique), Central America in Guatemala (Quezaltenango, Huehuetenango, Alta Verapaz, San Marcos, Zacapa), Belize (Toledo), Honduras (Francisco Morazán, Santa Bárbara), Nicaragua (Matagalpa), and Costa Rica (Guanacaste, Heredia, Limón, Puntarenas, San José), and throughout the Andes in South America from Colombia (Antioquia, Caquetá, Chocó, Huila, Risaralda) and Venezuela (Aragua, Barinas, Falcón, Portuguesa, Táchira, Trujillo), to Ecuador (Carchi, Cotopaxi, Morona-Santiago, Napo, Pastaza, Pichincha, Zamora-Chinchipe), Peru (Amazonas, Cusco, Huánuco, Pasco, San Martín), and Bolivia (La Paz, Santa Cruz); montane rain forest, at 1400–2400 m elevation. Not recorded in Panama, where appropriate elevations are scarce.

Uses. The leaves are occasionally used for thatching; the trunks are used for ax handles (Skov, 1989).

Notes. One of the largest and commonest *Geonoma* species, occurring in Central American mountains and throughout the Andes. It is rather variable, especially in the size and division of the leaves. *Geonoma seleri* and *G. helminthoclada* are included here. *Geonoma weberbaueri* is closely related and co-occurring in the Andes; it can be distinguished by its leathery, rigid, plicate leaves and thicker flowering branches. It also grows at higher elevations. Nevertheless, some plants seem to be intermediate between both species. Either there are hybrids, or the two should be considered as one variable species.

Geonoma weberbaueri
(Map 541, Plate 62)
"Palmiche" (Col)

Field characters. Stems solitary, *to 13 m tall and 5–14 cm diameter,* light brown. Leaves 8–12; blade 0.8–2.5 m long, regularly or irregularly divided into 8–42 mostly narrow leaflets per side, sometimes intermixed with broad leaflets, *these leathery and rigid, strongly plicate, sometimes erect, sometimes the blade simple and strongly wedge shaped and plicate.* Inflorescences borne below the leaves, *branched to 2–3 orders*; peduncle 15–63 cm long; rachis 30–70 cm long with 15–20 branches, lower ones branched again; *flowering branches numerous, to 20–30 cm long and 0.5–1.1 cm thick*; pits densely arranged; fruits ovoid, pointed at apex, 1–1.5 cm long and 0.9–1.1 cm diameter, black.

Range and habitat. Throughout the Andes in Colombia (Boyacá, Cauca, Cundinamarca, Magdalena, Nariño), Venezuela (Táchira), Ecuador (Napo, Pichincha, Zamora-Chinchipe), Peru (Huánuco, Pasco), and Bolivia (La Paz); montane rain forest, often near páramo, at 1800–3150 m elevation.

Uses. The trunks are used in house construction.

Notes. The tallest species of *Geonoma* and a common palm in montane forest. It also grows at the highest elevation for a palm, at 3150 m elevation, together with *Geonoma orbignyana* and *Ceroxylon parvifrons*. Here we include *G. solitaria* and *G. megalospatha*, formerly treated as separate species; see additional comments under *G. undata*.

65. PHYTELEPHAS

This and the following two genera make up the subfamily Phytelephantoideae, which contains the most unusual of all palms, especially in flower and fruit structure. Stems of *Phytelephas* are solitary or clustered, rather short and stout, erect or creeping, and are marked with prominent and very close leaf scars. In some species stems are short and subterranean, and then the palm appears as a large rosette of leaves arising directly from the ground. Leaves are pinnate, 8–35 in number, rather long, and lack tomentum. Leaflets are numerous, regularly arranged (often clustered in *P. aequatorialis*), and spread in the same plane. They are linear and narrow and in all species the leaflets are markedly smaller toward the apex, more so than in most other palms. Individual plants bear either male or female inflorescences, but not both. Male inflorescences consist of a long, pendulous, almost cylindrical rachis which bears many cream-colored, densely packed flowers. The sepals and petals are greatly reduced and the numerous stamens are the most conspicuous part of the inflorescences, making the whole thing reminiscent of a bottle brush. Individual male flowers have 150–700 stamens. Female inflorescences are much shorter than the males, and they are almost hidden among the leaf sheaths and often covered by litter. Each inflorescence has several very large flowers, densely arranged on a much-reduced rachis. Fruits are aggregated into large, rounded heads. Individual fruits are large, dark brown, and covered with many thick, woody, spiny projections. Each fruit contains several seeds. When the ripe fruits crack open they drop the seeds, which are covered with fleshy, orange or yellow mesocarp. Seeds are wedge shaped, with two flat sides and a rounded apex, and they are enclosed in a woody endocarp. Endosperm is homogeneous and the seedling leaf is large and pinnate.

Phytelephas contains six species, distributed from central Panama to southwestern Ecuador, in the basin of the Río Magdalena in Colombia and in the western Amazon region from southern Colombia to northwestern Bolivia. They grow mostly on alluvial soils, below 500 m elevation, but *P. aequatorialis* and *P. schottii* often reach 1000–1500 m. All species grow in rain forest, but *P. schottii* extends into rather dry areas.

Phytelephas, *Ammandra*, and *Aphandra* make up the subfamily Phytelephantoideae, an isolated group of uncertain relationships (Barfod, 1991). Inflorescence, flower, and fruit structure are so unusual for palms that nineteenth-century botanists placed *Phytelephas* in other plant families. The taxonomy of the subfamily has been studied recently (Barfod, 1991). The treatment in this Guide differs slightly from Barfod's, mostly in terms of ranking.

The name *Phytelephas* is derived from Greek words meaning vegetable ivory, in reference to the very hard, white to cream-colored endosperm, also known in commerce by its local name, "tagua." Vegetable ivory, or tagua, was an important trade item during the second half of the nineteenth century and early twentieth century (Acosta Solis, 1944), and it played a major role in the economy of Ecuador and Colombia (Bernal, 1992). Tagua was exported from South America and Panama into the United States and Europe, where it was used mainly for button manufacture. Defeated by plastics, tagua disappeared almost completely from trade in the 1930s (Barfod, 1989), but has begun to reappear recently (Ziffer, 1992; Calero Hidalgo, 1992).

On alluvial soils with periodic, short floods, *Phytelephas* palms often form large, rather homogeneous stands called "taguales" in Colombia and Ecuador. Taguales range in area from less than 1 hectare to 25 hectares or more. Although the extension of taguales was probably favored by man in the past, flood waters are perhaps the major disperses of the heavy seeds along the flood plains. Flooding must be responsible for the formation of taguales to a large extent. During an overnight flood of a small river in western Colombia, about thirty seeds were deposited in a 0.1-hectare plot of tagual (Rodrigo Bernal, pers. obs.). Rodents, such as pacas (*Agouti paca*) and agoutis (*Dasyprocta* spp.), carry the seeds away from the tagual and then eat the fleshy mesocarp, or bury the seeds for later retrieval (Zona and Henderson, 1989; Barfod, 1991; Bernal, pers. obs.). This behavior probably accounts also for dispersal of tagua, especially beyond river flood plains.

Inflorescences of *Phytelephas* are visited by different species of bees, flies, and beetles. The latter are by far the most numerous, and species of weevils in the genus *Phyllothrox* have been considered the most likely pollinators of *Phytelephas tenuicaulis* (Barfod et al., 1987, as *P. microcarpa*).

Phytelephas aequatorialis
(Map 542, Plate 62)
"Tagua" (Ecu)
Field characters. Stems solitary, 3–15 m tall and 25–30 cm diameter. Leaves 15–25, dead leaves hanging and persisting on the stem for some time; leaflets 100–140 per side, *irregularly arranged in groups of 2–7 and spreading in slightly different planes,* or almost regularly arranged and spreading in the same plane. *Male flowers borne on long stalks;* fruiting heads 15–20 per palm, about 30 cm diameter, with up to 12 fruits per head; seeds 5–6 per fruit.
Range and habitat. Ecuador, along the coastal plain from the Colombian to the Peruvian frontier; common in wet lowlands, ascending to 1500 m elevation on western Andean slopes. Abundant in Esmeraldas, where it forms large taguales along river banks, often as a component of agroforestry systems (Borgtoft Pedersen and Balslev, 1990). It is often left in pastures.
Uses. The source of all vegetable ivory exported from Ecuador, which is the major supplier of this commodity. Several factories produce button blanks made of vegetable ivory, most of them in the town of Manta (Barfod et al., 1990). There are several other minor uses. Liquid endosperm of unripe fruit is used as a drink or eaten after becoming harder and jel-

lylike; the orange fleshy mesocarp is a delicacy; and leaves are used for thatch. Koziol and Borgtoft Pedersen (1993) have discussed the use of this species in human and animal nutrition.
Notes. Palms in the lowlands tend to have the leaflets more uniformly arranged and spreading in one plane; palms on Andean slopes tend to be taller.

Phytelephas macrocarpa
(Map 543, Plate 63)
"Yarina" (Col, Ecu, Per)
Field characters. Stems solitary, rarely clustered, *short and subterranean* or sometimes creeping, then to 2 m long and 30 cm diameter. Leaves 12–20; leaflets 42–95 per side, *regularly arranged and spreading in the same plane. Male flowers sessile;* fruiting heads to 40 cm diameter, with 8–20 fruits; seeds 4–5 per fruit.
Range and habitat. Western Amazon region in Peru (Cusco, Huánuco, Junín, Loreto, Madre de Dios, Pasco, Ucayali), Brazil (Acre, western Amazonas), and Bolivia (Beni, La Paz, Pando); lowland rain forest on alluvial soils, at low elevations.
Notes. Barfod (1991) recognized two subspecies: subsp. *macrocarpa* and subsp. *tenuicaulis.* Here we give the latter specific status, following Henderson (1994). The two species have mostly nonoverlapping ranges.

Phytelephas schottii
(Map 544)
"Cabecinegro," "tagua" (Col)

Field characters. *Stems solitary, short and subterranean,* or if somewhat developed, then creeping. Leaves 10–15, to 7 m long, forming a rosette; leaflets about 100 per side, *regularly arranged and spreading in the same plane.* Inflorescences and infructescences borne at ground level and often hidden among leaf litter; *male flowers sessile;* fruiting heads to 30 cm diameter; seeds to 4 per fruit.

Range and habitat. Colombia, in the Río Magdalena valley (Boyacá, Cundinamarca, Huila, Santander, Tolima), an isolated population in the Río Cauca valley (Valle), and ascending onto the eastern slopes of the Cordillera Oriental in the upper basin of Río Catatumbo (Norte de Santander); dry to wet forest, at 500–1500 m elevation. Except for the middle Magdalena valley in Santander and Boyacá, where large populations still grow in forest remnants, the species has disappeared from most of its former range. It is also locally abundant in steep deforested areas in the upper Catatumbo river basin in Norte de Santander and along the Altamira-Florencia road (Huila) at 1000–1500 m elevation.

Uses. The seeds of this species were commercially exploited during the past tagua boom. Seeds from the middle Magdalena valley are the source of a locally renowned artisan industry centered in the highland town of Chiquinquirá (Barfod, 1989; Bernal, 1992).

Notes. Although this taxon was treated as a subspecies of *Phytelephas macrocarpa* by Barfod (1991), we recognize it as a distinct species. The solitary, subterranean stem is quite distinctive.

Phytelephas seemannii
(Map 545, Plate 63)
"Tagua," "antá" (Col, Pan)

Field characters. *Stems solitary, creeping, rooting at the lower surface and dying at the older parts,* to 4 m tall and 30 cm diameter, with many close leaf scars. Leaves 25–35, to 7 m long; leaflets about 90 per side, *regularly arranged and spreading in the same plane. Male flowers sessile;* fruiting heads to 30 cm diameter, with 5–9 fruits; seeds 5–7 per fruit.

Range and habitat. Central and eastern Panama (Bocas del Toro, Colón, San Blas, Veraguas), south along the Pacific coast of Colombia (Antioquia, Chocó, rare in Valle) and east to upper Río Sinú (Antioquia); lowland rain forest, forming large, dense, homogeneous stands on alluvial soils under forest shade, to 200 m elevation.

Uses. Seeds were extensively traded in the past and have recently begun to be reexploited. Leaves are used for thatching; liquid endosperm of unripe fruit is used as a drink or eaten when it becomes harder and jellylike; and the orange fleshy mesocarp is eaten as a delicacy.

Notes. Barfod (1991) recognized two subspecies on the basis of stem habit. This is a variable character, however, and subspecies separation seems unwarranted. In northwestern Colombia the unrelated *Elaeis oleifera* has the same growth habit and general appearance, but differs in the short, spiny leaf bases, the compact, branched male inflorescences, and the small, smooth, yellow to red oily fruits.

Phytelephas tenuicaulis
(Map 546, Plate 63)
"Tagua," "yarina" (Col, Ecu, Per)

Field characters. *Stems clustered, forming small clumps of 2–8 stems,* occasionally solitary, *1.5–7 m tall and 8–10 cm diameter,* rough with old leaf scars. Leaves 8–20; leaflets 35–73 per side, *regularly arranged and spreading in the same plane. Male flowers sessile;* fruits to 10 in a tight cluster, each fruit 6–9 cm long.

Range and habitat. Western Amazon region in Colombia (Putumayo), Ecuador (Napo, Pastaza), and Peru (Amazonas, Loreto); low-lying, inundated places near streams and rivers, occasionally on noninundated soils, at low elevations. Sometimes forming large stands (locally called "yarinales") in inundated forest.

Phytelephas tumacana
(Map 547)
"Tagua" (Col)

Field characters. *Stems solitary, to 5 m tall and 20 cm diameter.* Leaves 10–15, almost erect to erect, to 5 m long, old leaves hanging on the stem; leaflets 80–110 per side, *regularly arranged and spreading in the same plane. Male flowers borne on short stalks;* fruiting heads to 20 per palm, 20–25 cm diameter, with 5–8 fruits; seeds 5–6 per fruit.

Range and habitat. Pacific coast of Colombia (Tumaco area of Nariño); formerly in large stands on alluvial soils to 200 m elevation but now severely decimated and endangered (Bernal, 1989).

Uses. The seeds were formerly traded; leaves are used for thatching; and the fleshy mesocarp is edible.

Notes. Very similar to *Phytelephas aequatorialis,* which occurs just across the border in the adjacent lowlands in Ecuador, but differs in its male flowers with shorter stalks.

66. AMMANDRA

This genus of two species is restricted to northwestern South America, on either side of the Andes. Stems are solitary or clustered, short and subterranean, or sometimes aerial and then usually creeping. Leaves are pinnate, 12–20 in number, and the regularly arranged, linear leaflets spread in the same plane. Sheaths have a few fibers, but not nearly so many as *Aphandra*. Petioles are elongate and rounded in cross section. Individual plants bear either male or female inflorescences, but not both. Male inflorescences consist of a long rachis that is densely covered with very short flowering branches, each bearing flowers. There are 800–1200 stamens in each male flower. The genus gets its name from the small, numerous stamens and comes from the Greek words "ammos," meaning sand, and a modification of "aner," meaning man, alluding to the stamens. Female inflorescences are much more compact and consist of 6–10 flowers crowded on a greatly contracted rachis. Sepals and petals are very similar and are long and fleshy. The styles are even longer, and each has up to eight stigmas. Fruits are very similar to those of *Phytelephas* and *Aphandra* and are densely crowded into a large head, each with warty projections at the outermost part. Endosperm is very hard and homogeneous and the seedling leaf is pinnate.

Ammandra contains two species (Barfod, 1991). They differ from one another in the number of stamens. The genus differs from *Phytelephas* in its elongate, rounded petioles and in details of flower structure.

Ammandra dasyneura
(Map 548)
"Yarina," "yume" (Ecu)
Field characters. Stems short and subterranean, clustered with 2–7 stems. Leaves 6–8, erect; petiole very long, to 2 m, rounded; leaflets 35–60 per side, regularly arranged and spreading in the same plane. Inflorescences and infructescences borne at ground level and often covered by leaf litter; infructescences 20–25 cm diameter, with 4–10 fruits, the woody projections not markedly spiny, rather pyramidal or conical.
Range and habitat. A small area of the northwestern Amazon region in southern Colombia (Caquetá, Putumayo) and northern Ecuador (Napo), along the Río Putumayo; understory of lowland rain forest, usually not surviving in deforested areas, to 500 m elevation.

Ammandra decasperma
(Map 549 Plate 64)
"Cabecita" (Col)
Field characters. Stems short and subterranean or aerial and then usually creeping, solitary or in clusters of to 6. Leaves 6–10, erect; petiole to 3.5 m long, rounded; rachis as long as the petiole; leaflets 40–58 per side, regularly arranged and spreading in the same plane. Inflorescences and infructescences borne at ground level, often covered by litter; infructescences 20–25 cm diameter, with 3–10 fruits, the woody projections not markedly spiny, rather pyramidal or conical.
Range and habitat. Pacific coast of Colombia, west of the Andes (Antioquia, northern Cauca, Chocó, Valle); lowland rain forest, but seldom surviving deforestation, to 200 m elevation.
Uses. The very strong fibers of the petiole are used for weaving baskets and fans; and the soft, jelly-like immature endosperm is edible.

67. APHANDRA

This is the most recently described genus in the Americas. It is closely related to the preceding two genera, from which its name is derived. Stems are moderate to large and covered with closely spaced leaf scars. Leaves are pinnate, 10–20 in number, and form a dense crown. The elongate leaf sheaths disintegrate into a mass of persistent fibers that hang down and obscure the top of the stem. The long petiole is covered in conspicuous scales and these, together with the fibers, distinguish the genus from others. Leaflets are linear-lanceolate, regularly arranged, and spread in the same plane. Individual plants bear either male or female inflorescences, but not both. Inflorescences are borne among the leaves and are easy to see on plants from which the fibers have been harvested, otherwise they are obscured and difficult to see among the mass of fibers. Male inflorescences consist of a long rachis that is densely covered with very short flowering branches, each one bearing male flowers. There are 200–300 stamens in each flower. Female inflorescences are much more compact and consist of numerous flowers crowded onto a greatly contracted rachis. Sepals and petals are very similar and are long and fleshy. The styles are even longer, each with several stigmas. Fruits are very similar to those of *Phytelephas* and *Ammandra* and are densely crowded into a large head, each with woody projections on the outermost part. The mesocarp is fleshy and orange. Endosperm is very hard and homogeneous and the seedling leaf is pinnate.

Aphandra is a genus of one species distributed in the western Amazon region (Barfod, 1991). It differs from *Ammandra* and *Phytelephas* in its very fibrous leaf sheaths and scaly petioles and in details of flower structure.

Aphandra natalia
(Map 550, Plate 64)
"Piassaba" (Bra, Ecu), "tagua" (Ecu)
Field characters. Stems solitary, 3–11 m tall and 20–22 cm diameter. Leaves 10–20, to 8 m long; sheath and petiole 3–3.5 m long, the sheath very fibrous, the petiole scaly; leaflets 90–120 per side, regularly arranged and spreading in the same plane. Male inflorescences to 2 m long, the flowers in stalked clusters of 4. Infructescences to 5 per palm, 30–45 cm diameter, with 30–45 fruits per head; seeds to 6 per fruit.
Range and habitat. Eastern Andean foothills of Ecuador (Morona-Santiago, Napo) to the Amazon lowlands of Peru (Loreto, Ucayali) and Brazil (Acre, western Amazonas); lowland or premontane rain forest, on noninundated soils, to 800 m elevation, but found in cultiva-

tion to 1000 m in southern Ecuador (Borgtoft Pedersen and Balslev, 1990).
Uses. Leaf sheath fibers are used for making brooms, and these are an item of national trade in Ecuador and Peru. Local small-scale uses include edible mesocarp, immature fluid endosperm consumed as a beverage, leaves used for thatching, and male inflorescences used as cattle fodder. It was recommended as ideal for small-scale farming systems by Borgtoft Pedersen and Balslev (1990), and use and management were described by Borgtoft Pedersen (1992).
Notes. Pollination in Ecuador has been described by Ervik (1993). Two-day-old female inflorescences had a temperature at midnight of 19°C above ambient. The main pollinators were considered to be small curculionid beetles.

DISTRIBUTION MAPS

Venezuela
Guyana
Suriname
French Guiana
Colombia

Ecuador

Brazil

Peru

Bolivia

Tropic of Capricorn
Paraguay
Chile
Argentina
Uruguay

United States
Bahamas

Tropic of Cancer

Cuba

Mexico

Haiti
Dominican Republic

Belize
Jamaica
Hispaniola
Puerto Rico
Lesser Antilles

Guatemala
Guadeloupe
Dominica
Martinique

Honduras

El Salvador
Nicaragua

Tobago

Costa Rica
Trinidad

Panama

Venezuela

Colombia

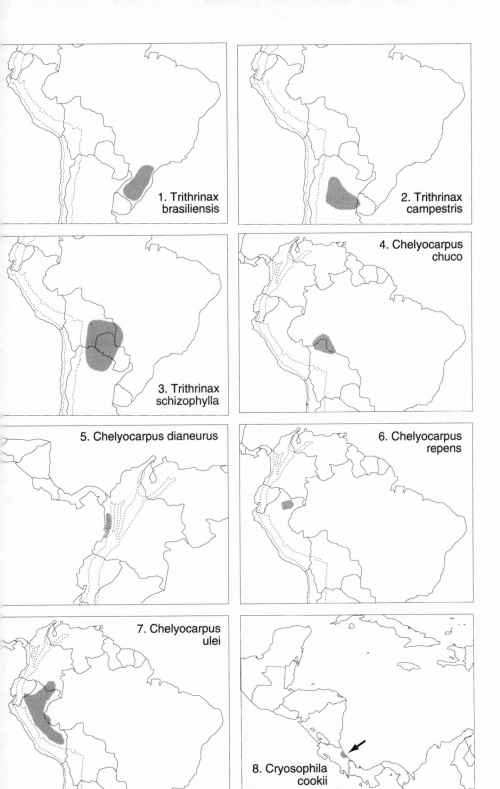

1. Trithrinax
brasiliensis

2. Trithrinax
campestris

3. Trithrinax
schizophylla

4. Chelyocarpus
chuco

5. Chelyocarpus dianeurus

6. Chelyocarpus
repens

7. Chelyocarpus
ulei

8. Cryosophila
cookii

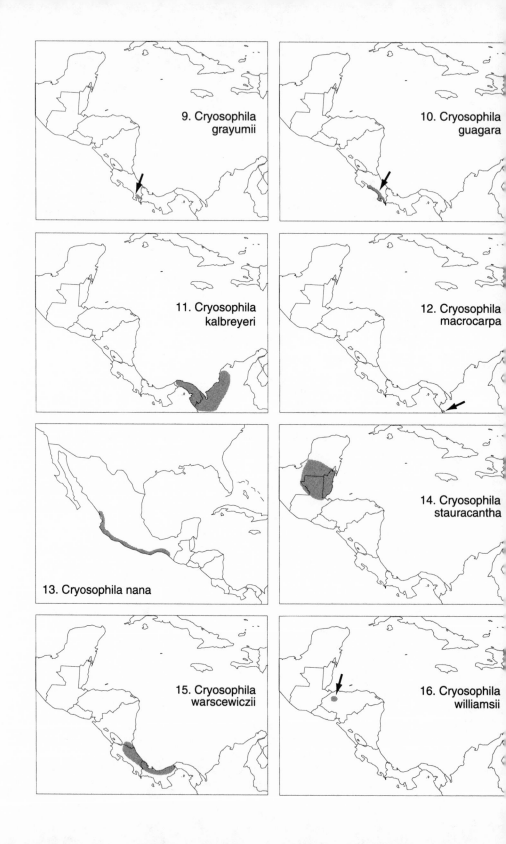

9. Cryosophila grayumii

10. Cryosophila guagara

11. Cryosophila kalbreyeri

12. Cryosophila macrocarpa

13. Cryosophila nana

14. Cryosophila stauracantha

15. Cryosophila warscewiczii

16. Cryosophila williamsii

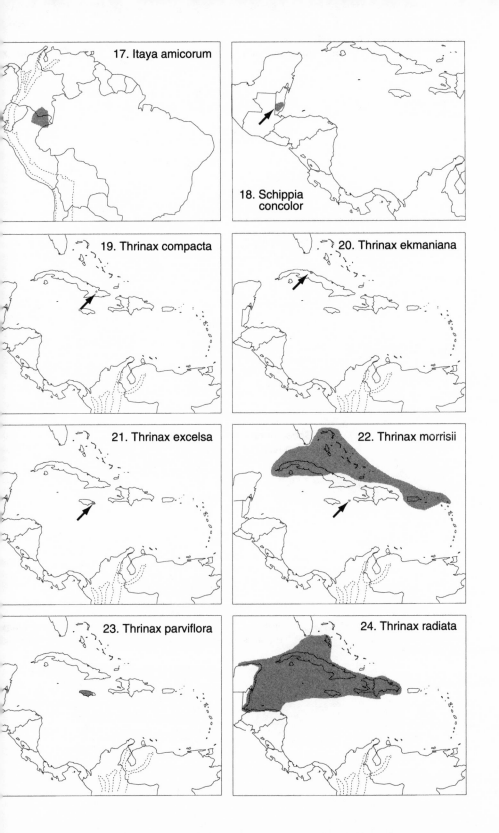

17. Itaya amicorum

18. Schippia concolor

19. Thrinax compacta

20. Thrinax ekmaniana

21. Thrinax excelsa

22. Thrinax morrisii

23. Thrinax parviflora

24. Thrinax radiata

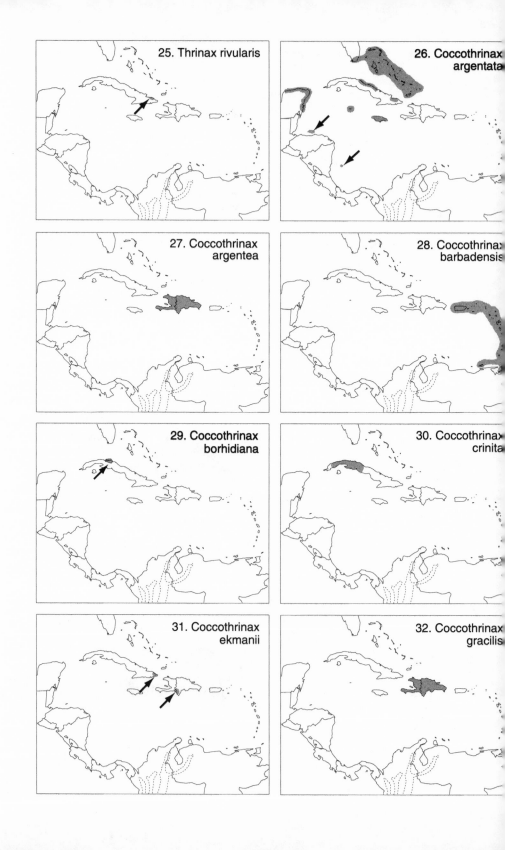

25. Thrinax rivularis

26. Coccothrinax
argentata

27. Coccothrinax
argentea

28. Coccothrinax
barbadensis

29. Coccothrinax
borhidiana

30. Coccothrinax
crinita

31. Coccothrinax
ekmanii

32. Coccothrinax
gracilis

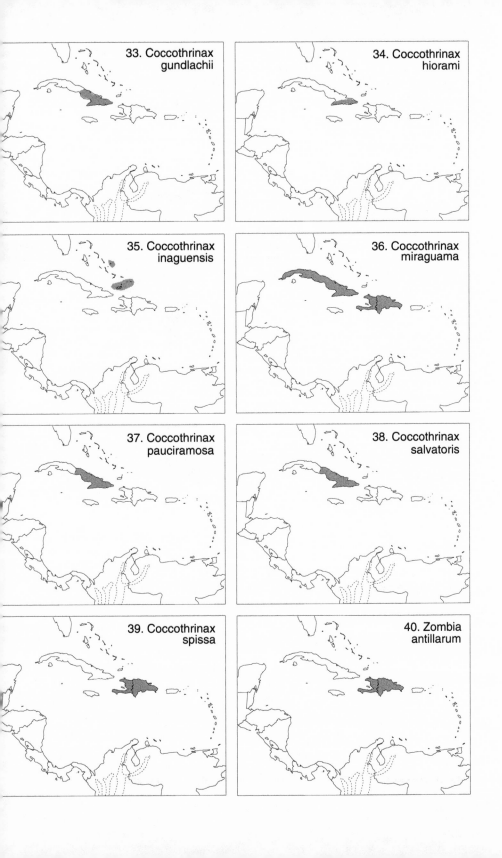

33. Coccothrinax gundlachii

34. Coccothrinax hiorami

35. Coccothrinax inaguensis

36. Coccothrinax miraguama

37. Coccothrinax pauciramosa

38. Coccothrinax salvatoris

39. Coccothrinax spissa

40. Zombia antillarum

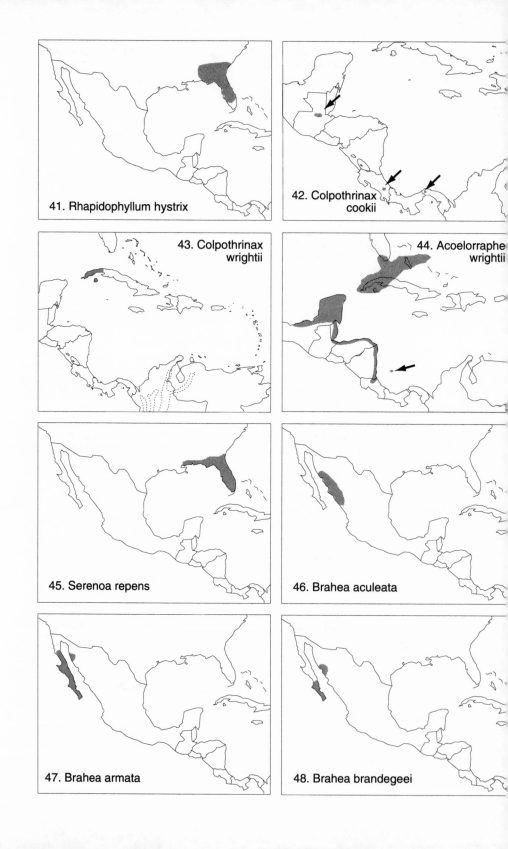

41. Rhapidophyllum hystrix

42. Colpothrinax
    cookii

43. Colpothrinax
    wrightii

44. Acoelorraphe
    wrightii

45. Serenoa repens

46. Brahea aculeata

47. Brahea armata

48. Brahea brandegeei

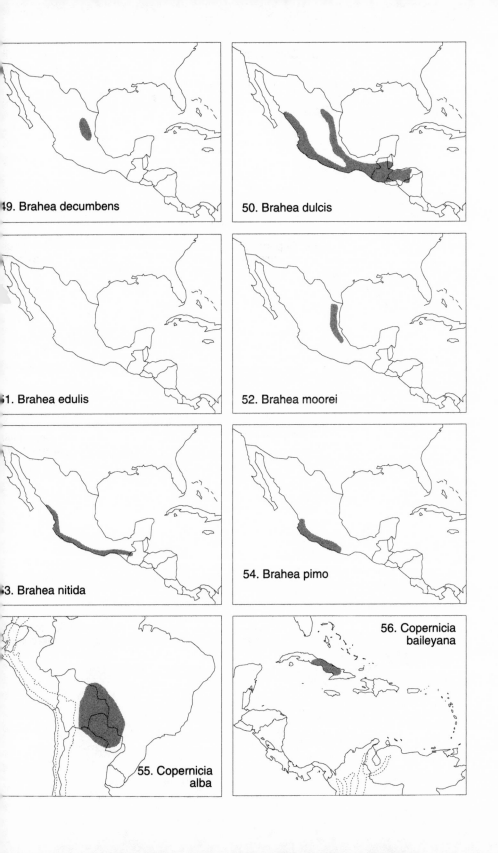

49. Brahea decumbens

50. Brahea dulcis

51. Brahea edulis

52. Brahea moorei

53. Brahea nitida

54. Brahea pimo

55. Copernicia alba

56. Copernicia baileyana

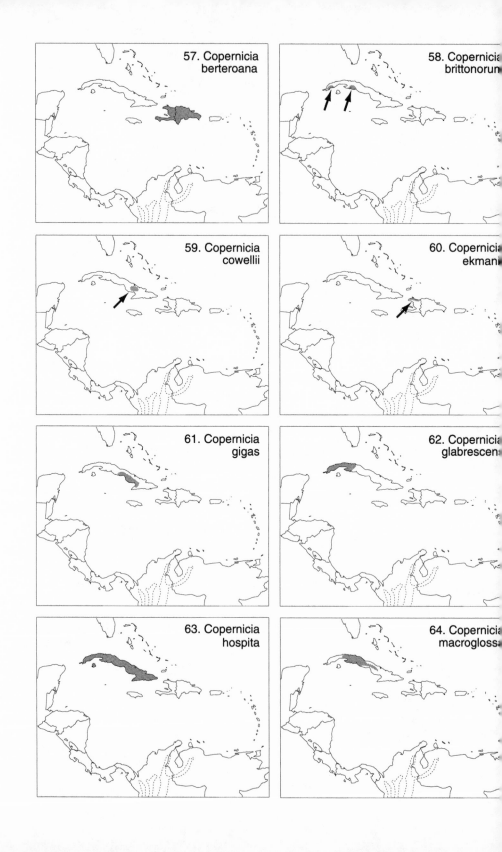

57. Copernicia
berteroana

58. Copernicia
brittonorum

59. Copernicia
cowellii

60. Copernicia
ekmani

61. Copernicia
gigas

62. Copernicia
glabrescens

63. Copernicia
hospita

64. Copernicia
macrglossa

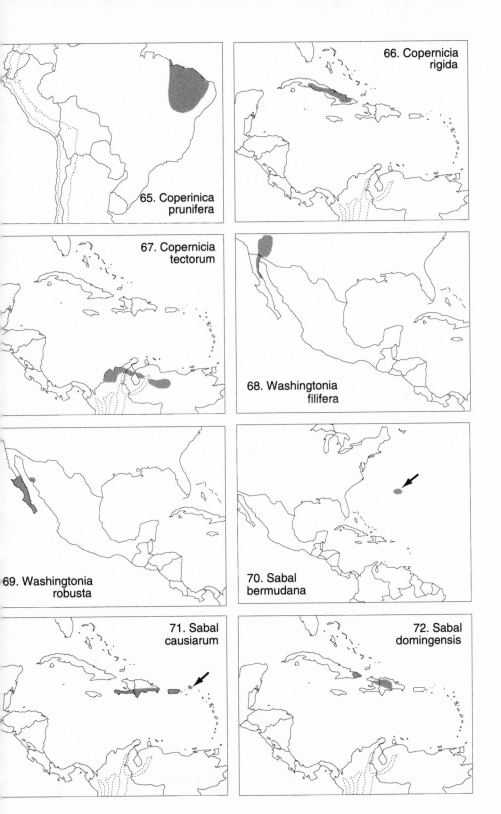

65. Coperinica prunifera

66. Copernicia rigida

67. Copernicia tectorum

68. Washingtonia filifera

69. Washingtonia robusta

70. Sabal bermudana

71. Sabal causiarum

72. Sabal domingensis

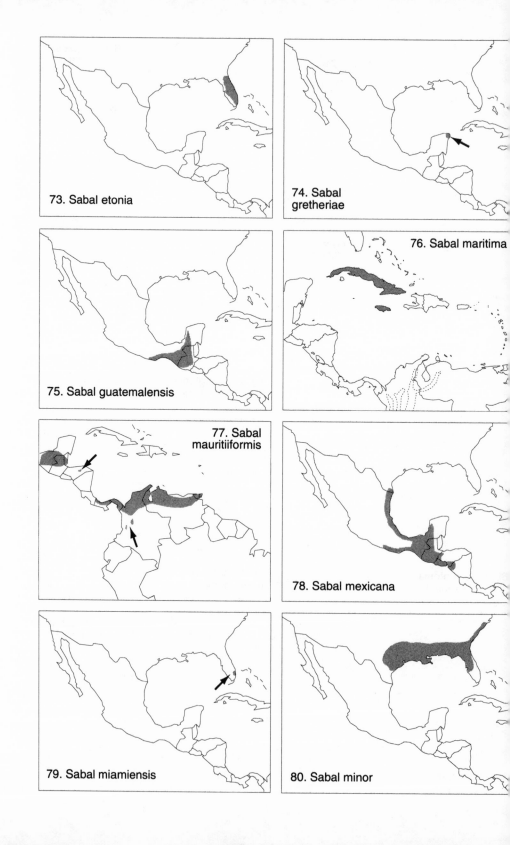

73. Sabal etonia

74. Sabal gretheriae

75. Sabal guatemalensis

76. Sabal maritima

77. Sabal mauritiiformis

78. Sabal mexicana

79. Sabal miamiensis

80. Sabal minor

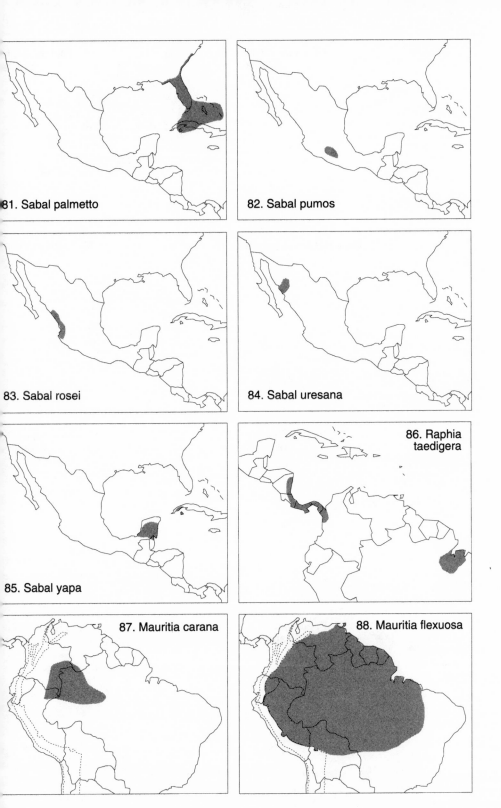

81. Sabal palmetto

82. Sabal pumos

83. Sabal rosei

84. Sabal uresana

85. Sabal yapa

86. Raphia taedigera

87. Mauritia carana

88. Mauritia flexuosa

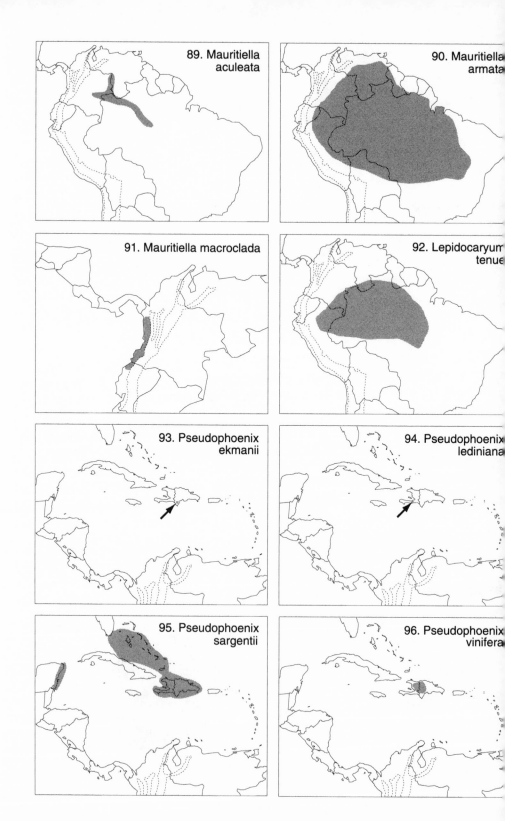

89. Mauritiella aculeata

90. Mauritiella armata

91. Mauritiella macroclada

92. Lepidocaryum tenue

93. Pseudophoenix ekmanii

94. Pseudophoenix lediniana

95. Pseudophoenix sargentii

96. Pseudophoenix vinifera

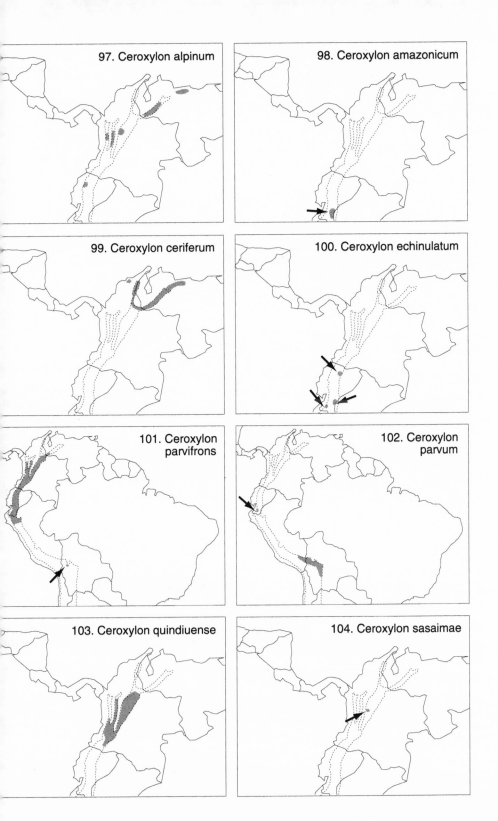

97. Ceroxylon alpinum

98. Ceroxylon amazonicum

99. Ceroxylon ceriferum

100. Ceroxylon echinulatum

101. Ceroxylon parvifrons

102. Ceroxylon parvum

103. Ceroxylon quindiuense

104. Ceroxylon sasaimae

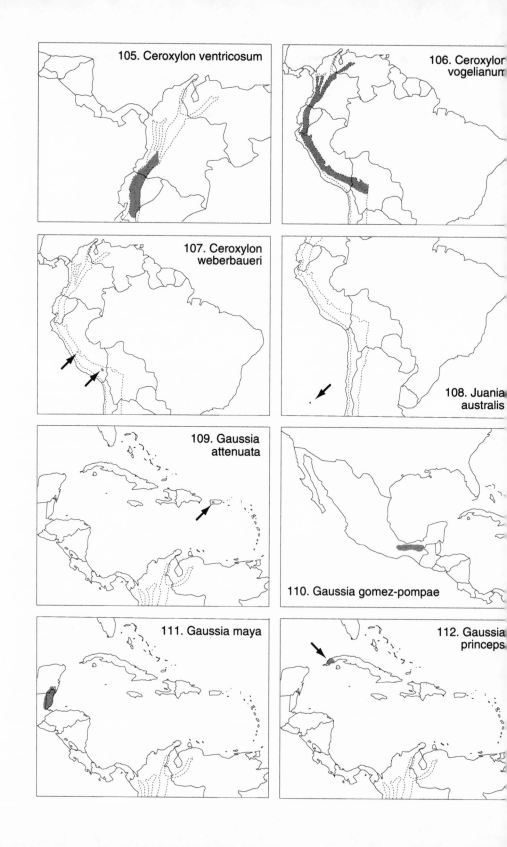

105. Ceroxylon ventricosum

106. Ceroxylon vogelianum

107. Ceroxylon weberbaueri

108. Juania australis

109. Gaussia attenuata

110. Gaussia gomez-pompae

111. Gaussia maya

112. Gaussia princeps

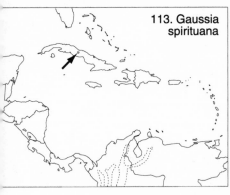

113. Gaussia
spirituana

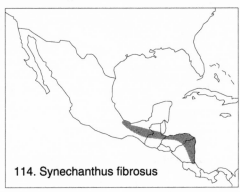

114. Synechanthus fibrosus

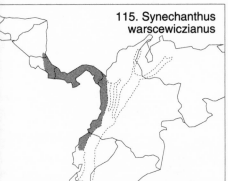

115. Synechanthus
warscewiczianus

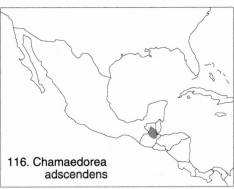

116. Chamaedorea
adscendens

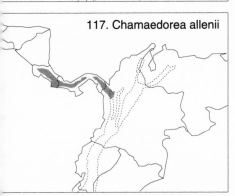

117. Chamaedorea allenii

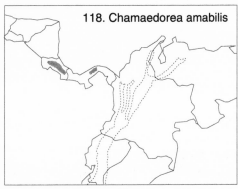

118. Chamaedorea amabilis

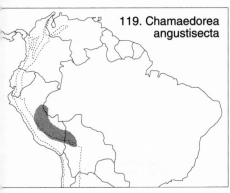

119. Chamaedorea
angustisecta

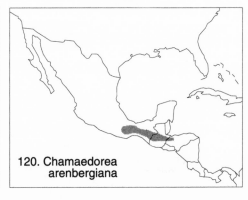

120. Chamaedorea
arenbergiana

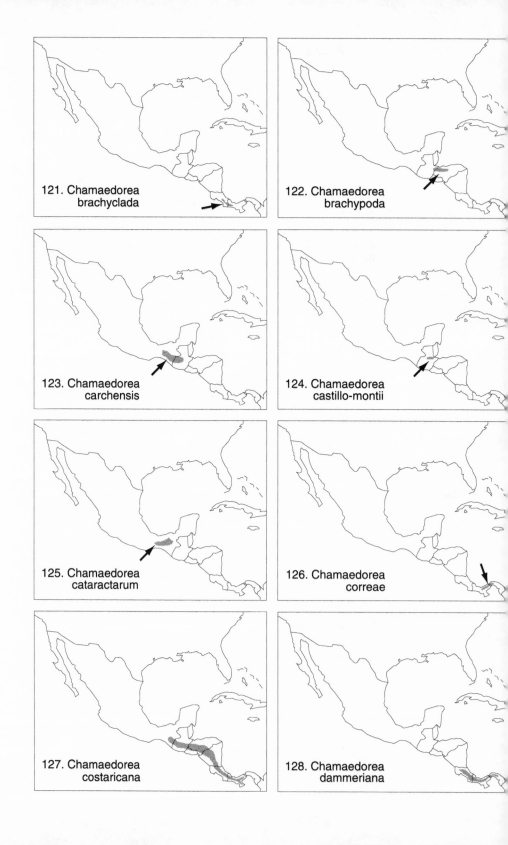

121. Chamaedorea
brachyclada

122. Chamaedorea
brachypoda

123. Chamaedorea
carchensis

124. Chamaedorea
castillo-montii

125. Chamaedorea
cataractarum

126. Chamaedorea
correae

127. Chamaedorea
costaricana

128. Chamaedorea
dammeriana

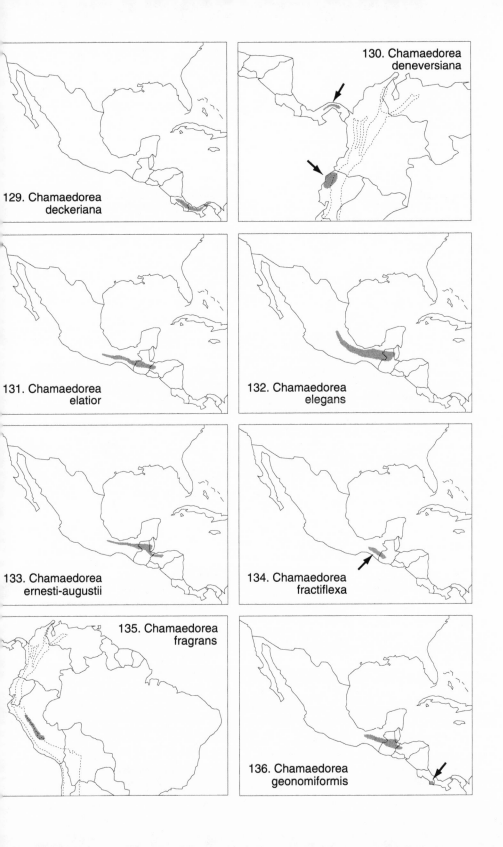

129. Chamaedorea
deckeriana

130. Chamaedorea
deneversiana

131. Chamaedorea
elatior

132. Chamaedorea
elegans

133. Chamaedorea
ernesti-augustii

134. Chamaedorea
fractiflexa

135. Chamaedorea
fragrans

136. Chamaedorea
geonomiformis

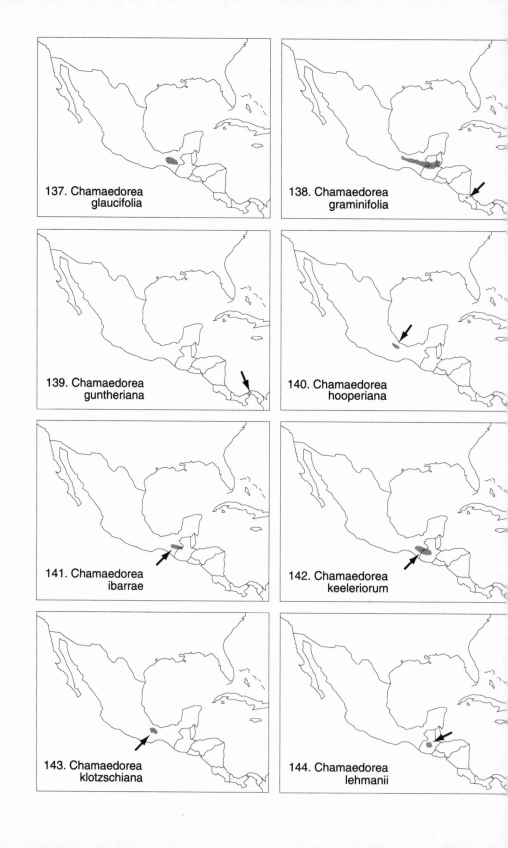

137. Chamaedorea
glaucifolia

138. Chamaedorea
graminifolia

139. Chamaedorea
guntheriana

140. Chamaedorea
hooperiana

141. Chamaedorea
ibarrae

142. Chamaedorea
keeleriorum

143. Chamaedorea
klotzschiana

144. Chamaedorea
lehmanii

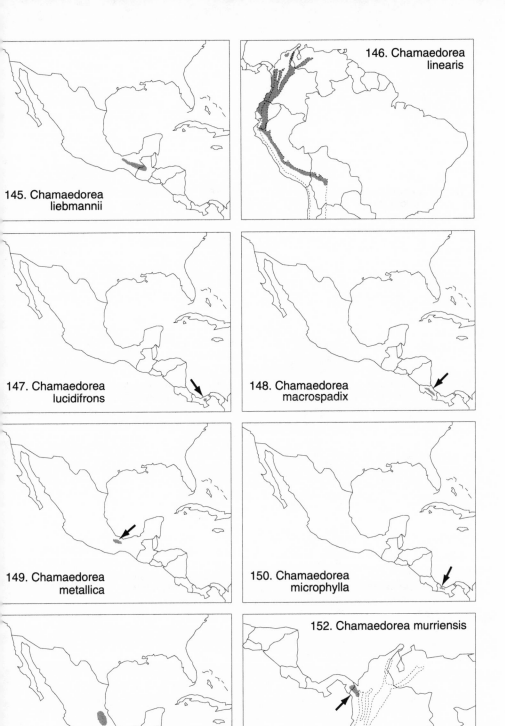

145. Chamaedorea liebmannii

146. Chamaedorea linearis

147. Chamaedorea lucidifrons

148. Chamaedorea macrospadix

149. Chamaedorea metallica

150. Chamaedorea microphylla

151. Chamaedorea microspadix

152. Chamaedorea murriensis

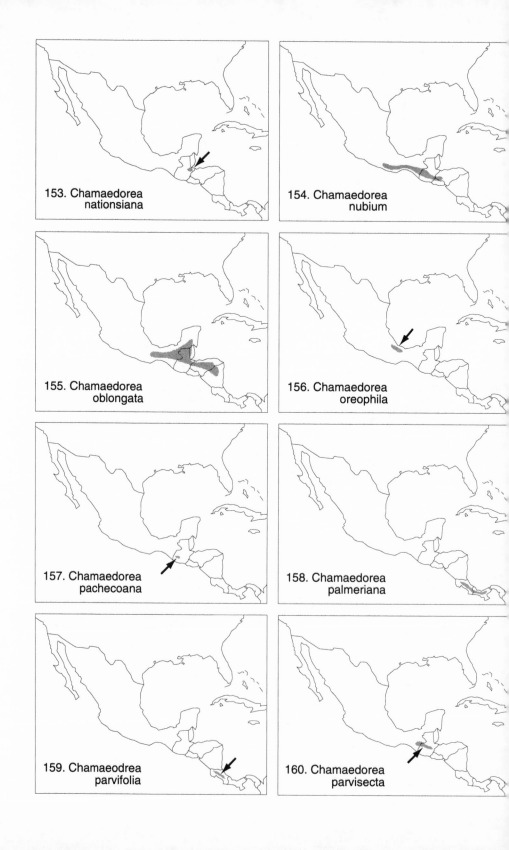

153. Chamaedorea
nationsiana

154. Chamaedorea
nubium

155. Chamaedorea
oblongata

156. Chamaedorea
oreophila

157. Chamaedorea
pachecoana

158. Chamaedorea
palmeriana

159. Chamaeodrea
parvifolia

160. Chamaedorea
parvisecta

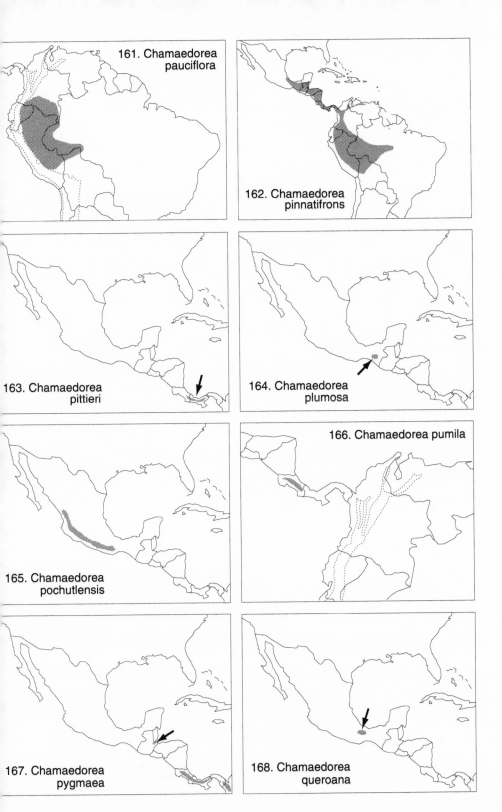

161. Chamaedorea
pauciflora

162. Chamaedorea
pinnatifrons

163. Chamaedorea
pittieri

164. Chamaedorea
plumosa

165. Chamaedorea
pochutlensis

166. Chamaedorea pumila

167. Chamaedorea
pygmaea

168. Chamaedorea
queroana

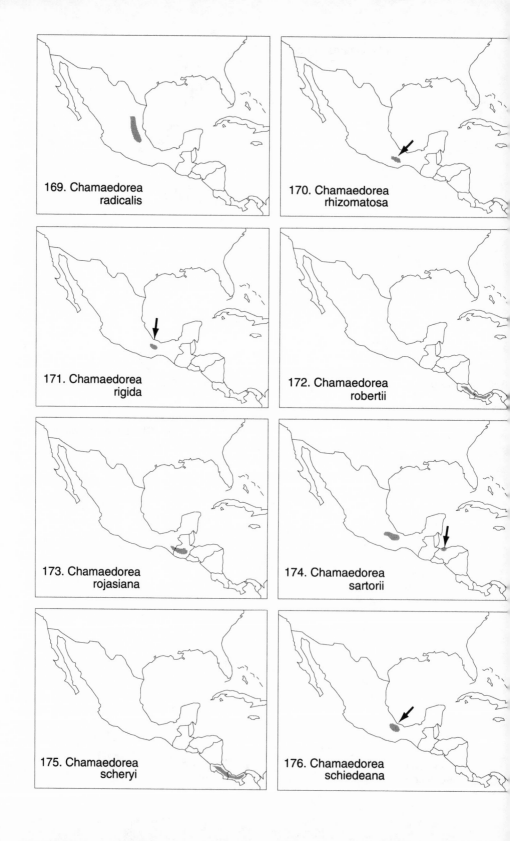

169. Chamaedorea
radicalis

170. Chamaedorea
rhizomatosa

171. Chamaedorea
rigida

172. Chamaedorea
robertii

173. Chamaedorea
rojasiana

174. Chamaedorea
sartorii

175. Chamaedorea
scheryi

176. Chamaedorea
schiedeana

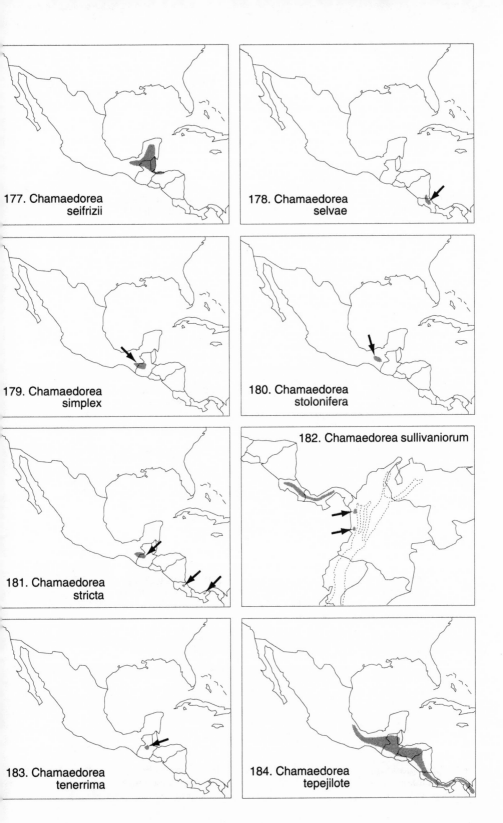

177. Chamaedorea
seifrizii

178. Chamaedorea
selvae

179. Chamaedorea
simplex

180. Chamaedorea
stolonifera

181. Chamaedorea
stricta

182. Chamaedorea sullivaniorum

183. Chamaedorea
tenerrima

184. Chamaedorea
tepejilote

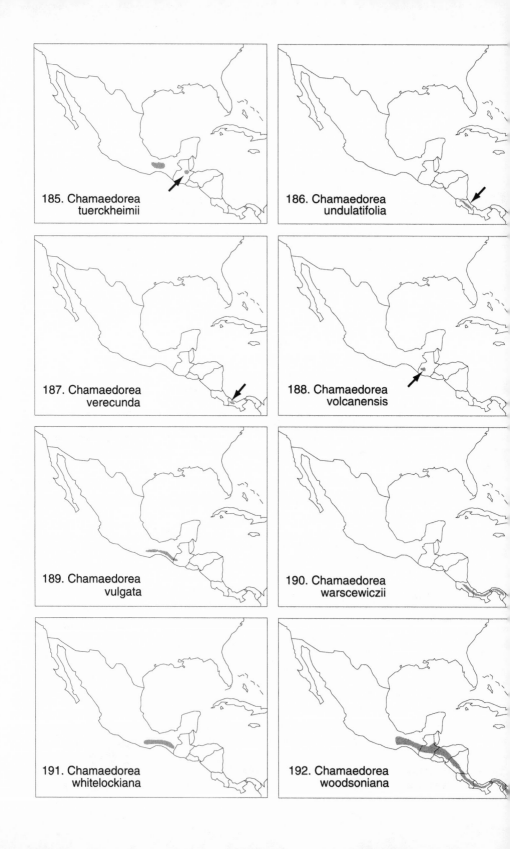

185. Chamaedorea
tuerckheimii

186. Chamaedorea
undulatifolia

187. Chamaedorea
verecunda

188. Chamaedorea
volcanensis

189. Chamaedorea
vulgata

190. Chamaedorea
warscewiczii

191. Chamaedorea
whitelockiana

192. Chamaedorea
woodsoniana

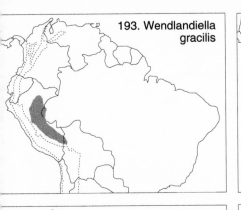

193. Wendlandiella
gracilis

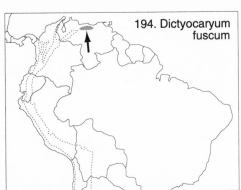

194. Dictyocaryum
fuscum

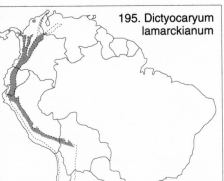

195. Dictyocaryum
lamarckianum

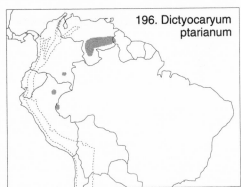

196. Dictyocaryum
ptarianum

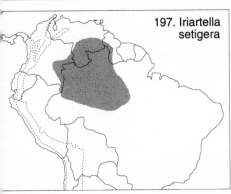

197. Iriartella
setigera

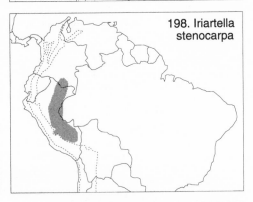

198. Iriartella
stenocarpa

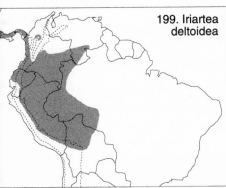

199. Iriartea
deltoidea

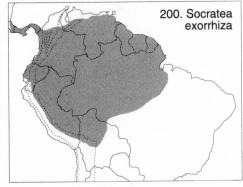

200. Socratea
exorrhiza

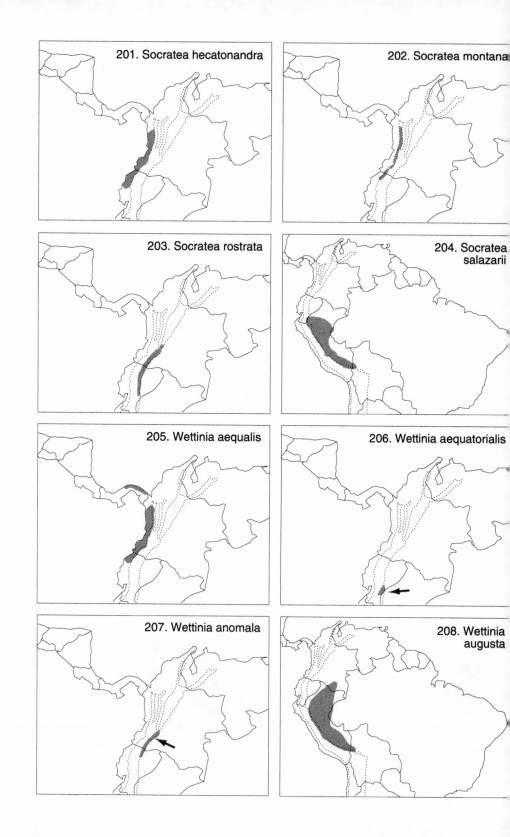

201. Socratea hecatonandra

202. Socratea montana

203. Socratea rostrata

204. Socratea salazarii

205. Wettinia aequalis

206. Wettinia aequatorialis

207. Wettinia anomala

208. Wettinia augusta

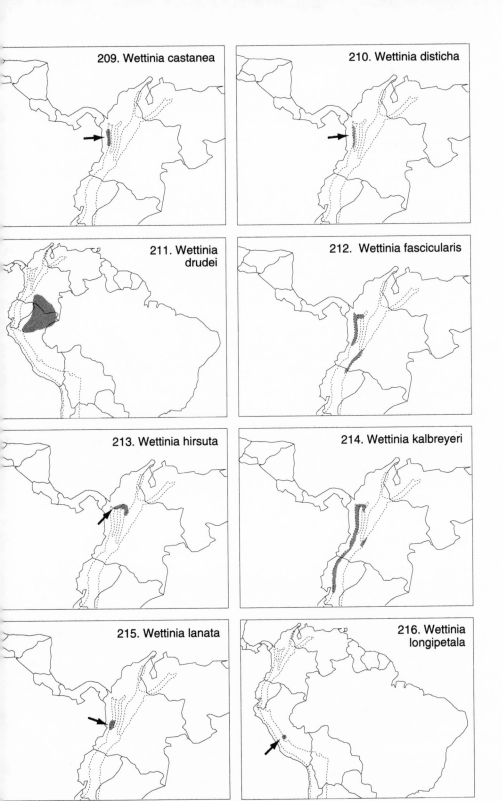

209. Wettinia castanea

210. Wettinia disticha

211. Wettinia drudei

212. Wettinia fascicularis

213. Wettinia hirsuta

214. Wettinia kalbreyeri

215. Wettinia lanata

216. Wettinia longipetala

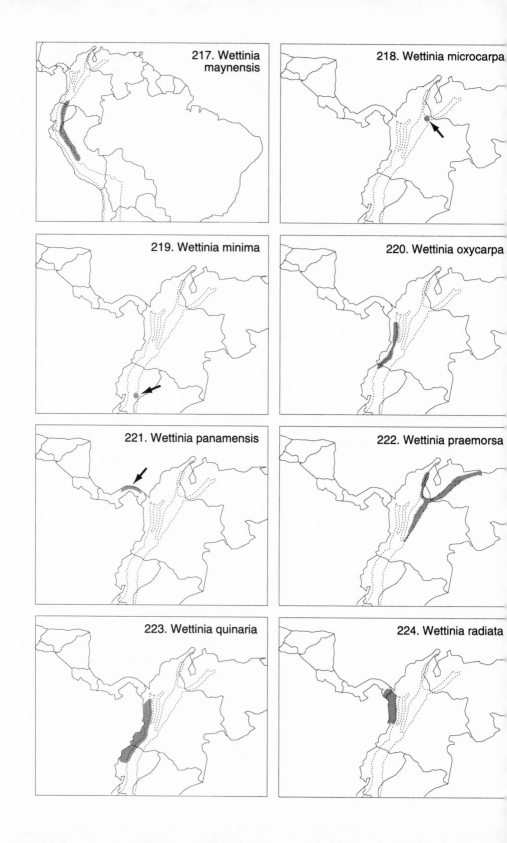

217. Wettinia maynensis

218. Wettinia microcarpa

219. Wettinia minima

220. Wettinia oxycarpa

221. Wettinia panamensis

222. Wettinia praemorsa

223. Wettinia quinaria

224. Wettinia radiata

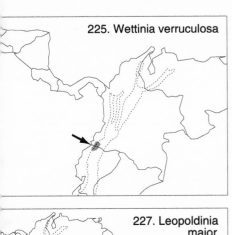

225. Wettinia verruculosa

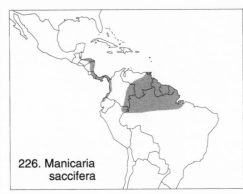

226. Manicaria saccifera

227. Leopoldinia major

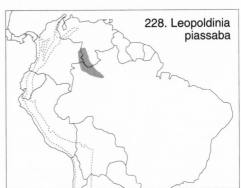

228. Leopoldinia piassaba

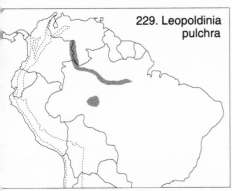

229. Leopoldinia pulchra

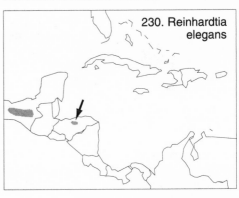

230. Reinhardtia elegans

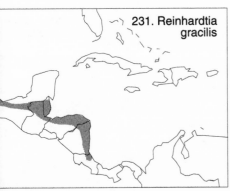

231. Reinhardtia gracilis

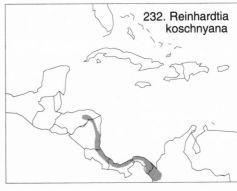

232. Reinhardtia koschnyana

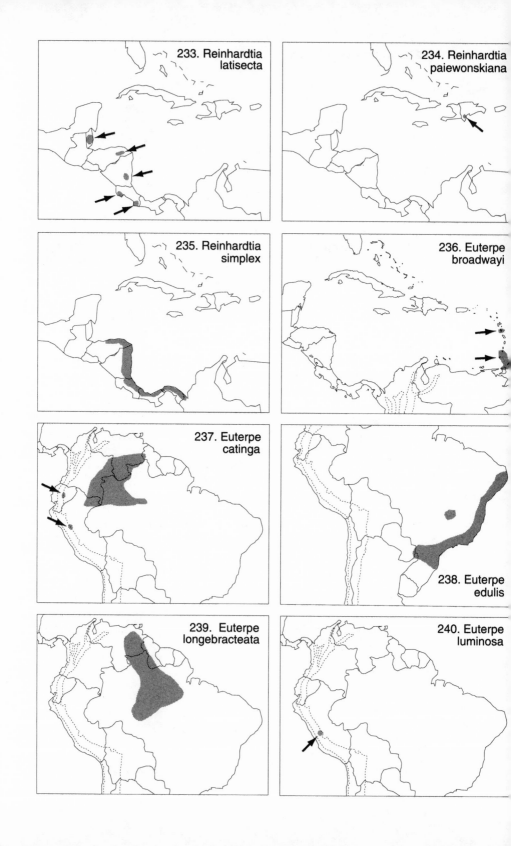

233. Reinhardtia latisecta

234. Reinhardtia paiewonskiana

235. Reinhardtia simplex

236. Euterpe broadwayi

237. Euterpe catinga

238. Euterpe edulis

239. Euterpe longebracteata

240. Euterpe luminosa

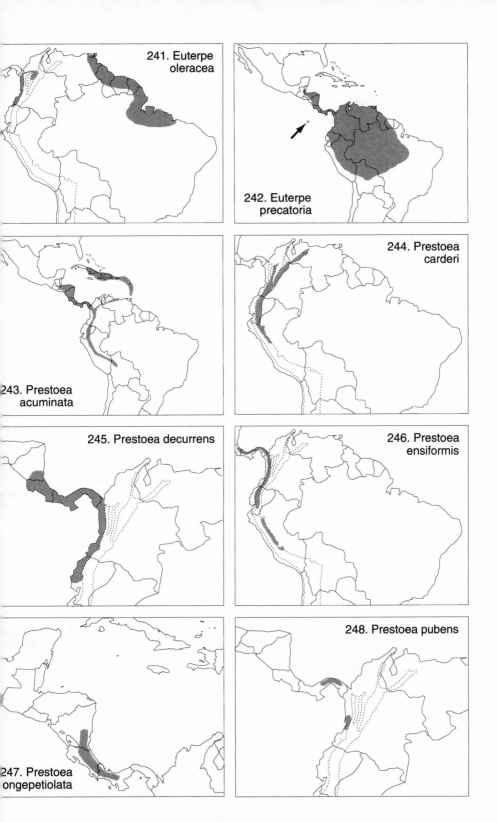

241. Euterpe oleracea

242. Euterpe precatoria

243. Prestoea acuminata

244. Prestoea carderi

245. Prestoea decurrens

246. Prestoea ensiformis

247. Prestoea longepetiolata

248. Prestoea pubens

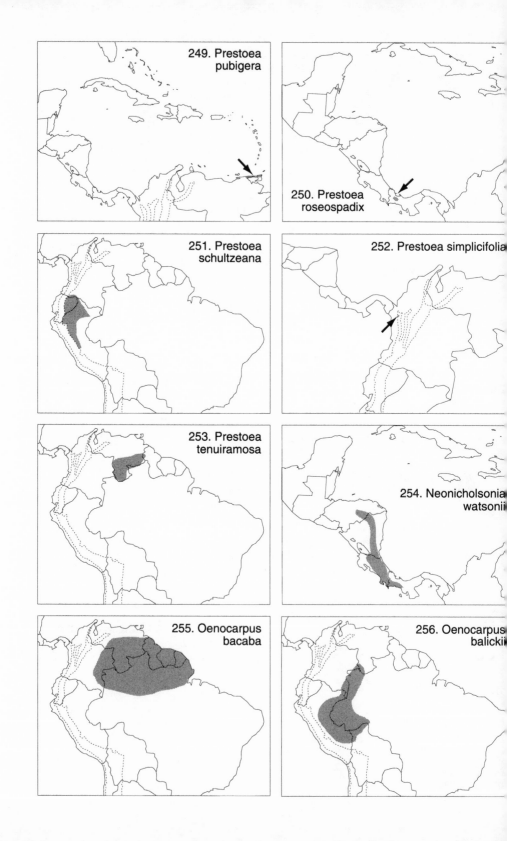

249. Prestoea pubigera

250. Prestoea roseospadix

251. Prestoea schultzeana

252. Prestoea simplicifolia

253. Prestoea tenuiramosa

254. Neonicholsonia watsonii

255. Oenocarpus bacaba

256. Oenocarpus balickii

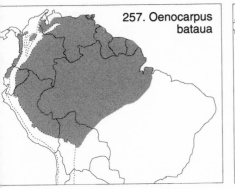

257. Oenocarpus
bataua

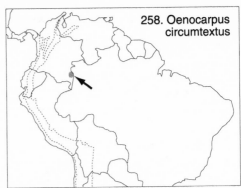

258. Oenocarpus
circumtextus

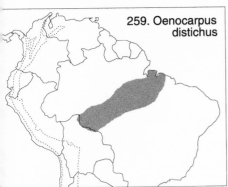

259. Oenocarpus
distichus

260. Oenocarpus
makeru

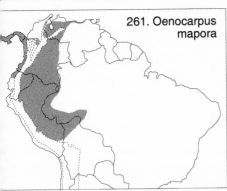

261. Oenocarpus
mapora

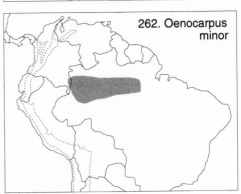

262. Oenocarpus
minor

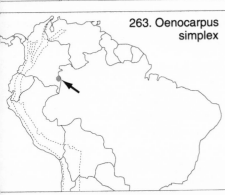

263. Oenocarpus
simplex

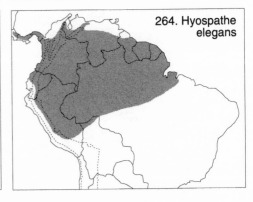

264. Hyospathe
elegans

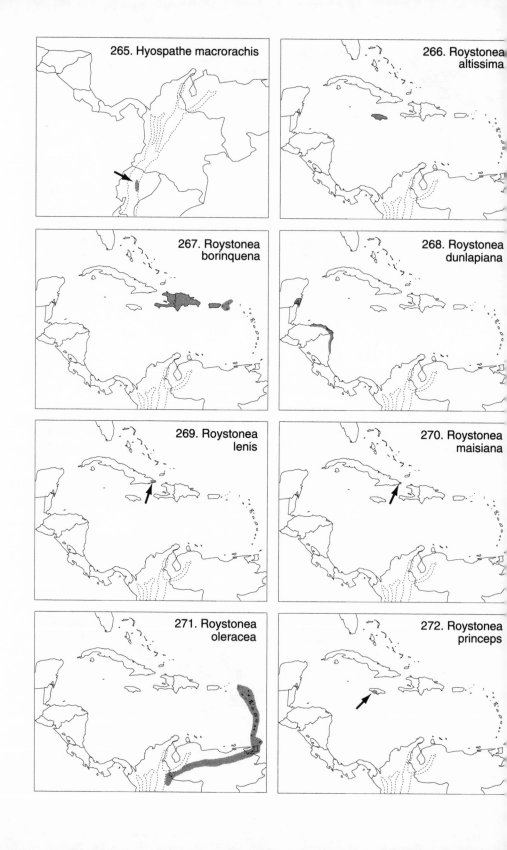

265. Hyospathe macrorachis

266. Roystonea altissima

267. Roystonea borinquena

268. Roystonea dunlapiana

269. Roystonea lenis

270. Roystonea maisiana

271. Roystonea oleracea

272. Roystonea princeps

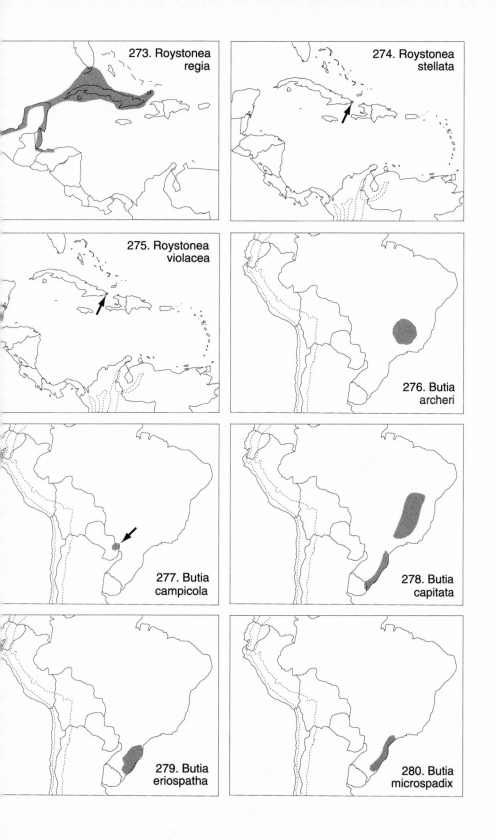

273. Roystonea regia

274. Roystonea stellata

275. Roystonea violacea

276. Butia archeri

277. Butia campicola

278. Butia capitata

279. Butia eriospatha

280. Butia microspadix

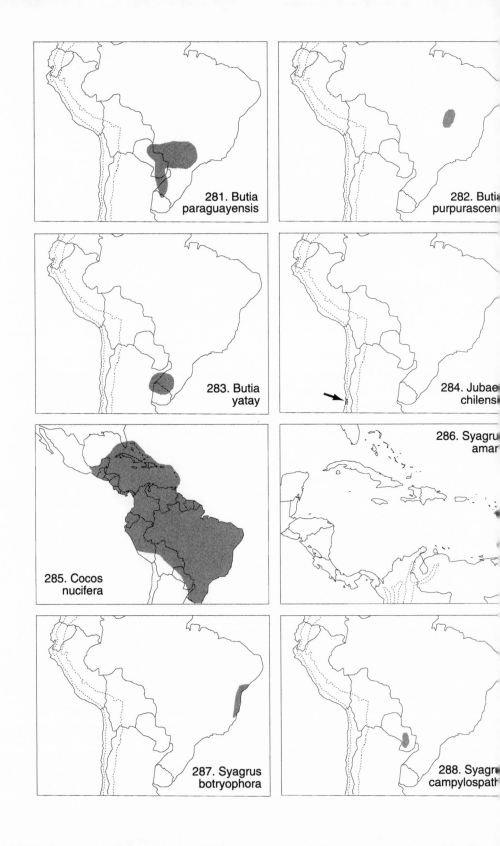

281. Butia
paraguayensis

282. Butia
purpurascen:

283. Butia
yatay

284. Jubae
chilens:

285. Cocos
nucifera

286. Syagru
amar

287. Syagrus
botryophora

288. Syagr
campylospath

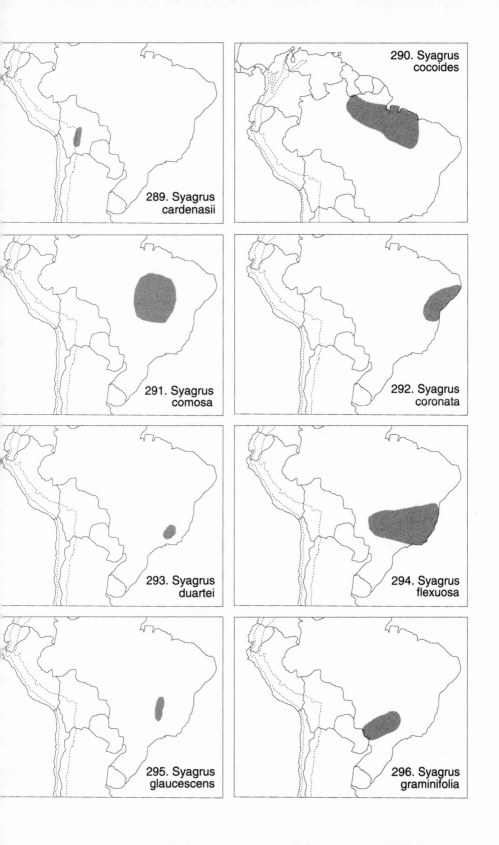

289. Syagrus
cardenasii

290. Syagrus
cocoides

291. Syagrus
comosa

292. Syagrus
coronata

293. Syagrus
duartei

294. Syagrus
flexuosa

295. Syagrus
glaucescens

296. Syagrus
graminifolia

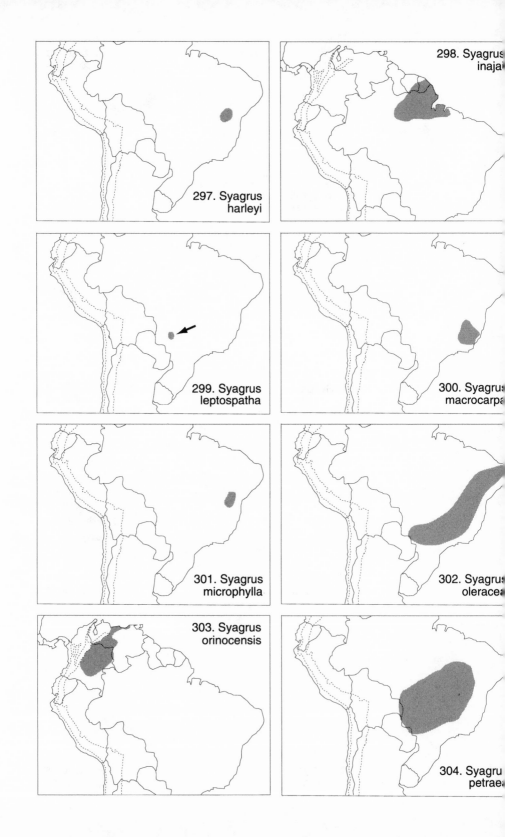

297. Syagrus harleyi

298. Syagrus inajai

299. Syagrus leptospatha

300. Syagrus macrocarpa

301. Syagrus microphylla

302. Syagrus oleracea

303. Syagrus orinocensis

304. Syagrus petraea

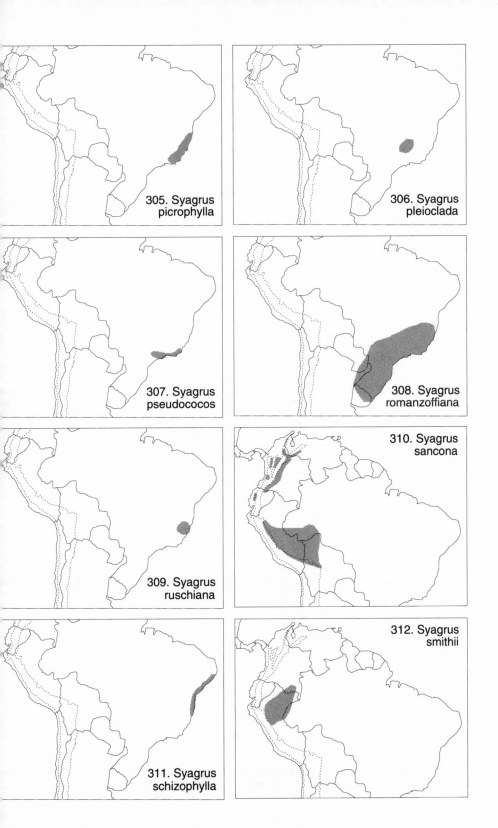

305. Syagrus
picrophylla

306. Syagrus
pleioclada

307. Syagrus
pseudococos

308. Syagrus
romanzoffiana

309. Syagrus
ruschiana

310. Syagrus
sancona

311. Syagrus
schizophylla

312. Syagrus
smithii

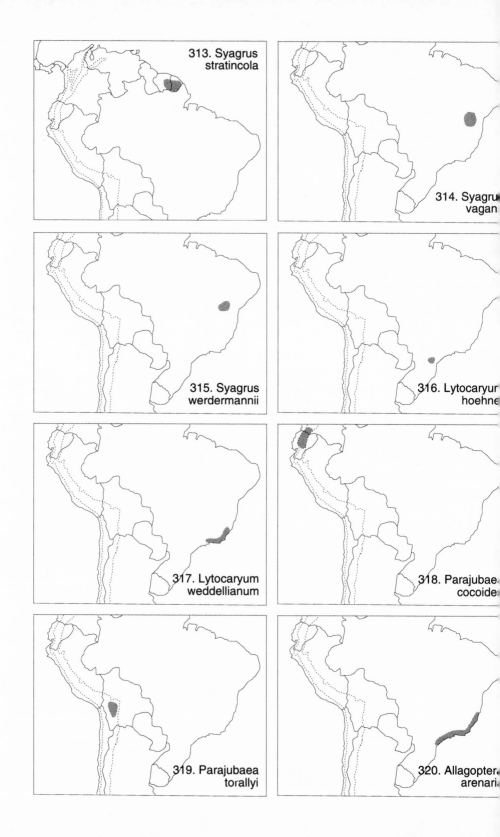

313. Syagrus stratincola

314. Syagru vagan

315. Syagrus werdermannii

316. Lytocaryur hoehne

317. Lytocaryum weddellianum

318. Parajubae cocoide:

319. Parajubaea torallyi

320. Allagopter arenari:

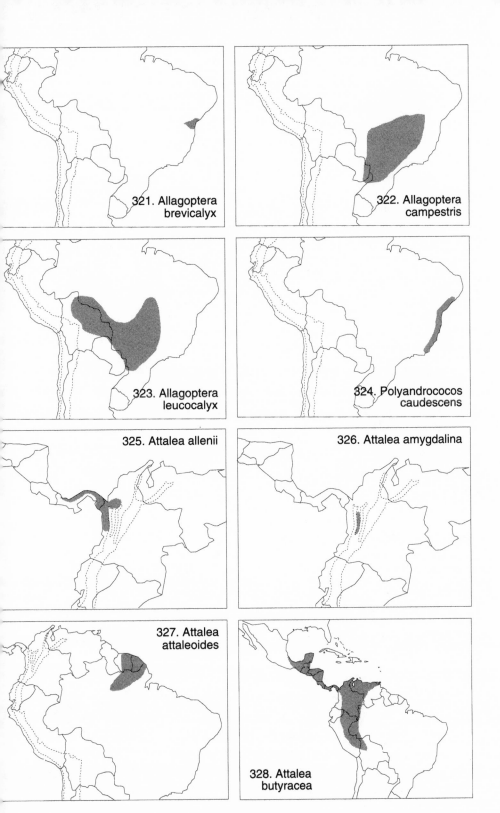

321. Allagoptera
brevicalyx

322. Allagoptera
campestris

323. Allagoptera
leucocalyx

324. Polyandrococos
caudescens

325. Attalea allenii

326. Attalea amygdalina

327. Attalea
attaleoides

328. Attalea
butyracea

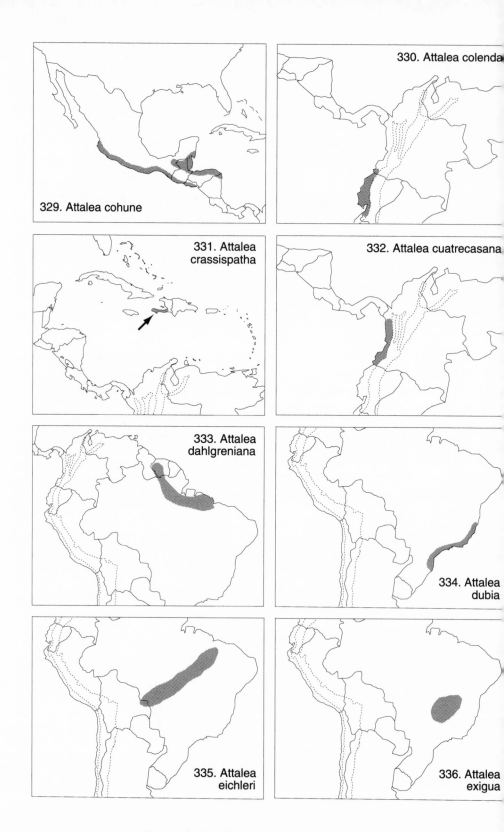

329. Attalea cohune

330. Attalea colenda

331. Attalea crassispatha

332. Attalea cuatrecasana

333. Attalea dahlgreniana

334. Attalea dubia

335. Attalea eichleri

336. Attalea exigua

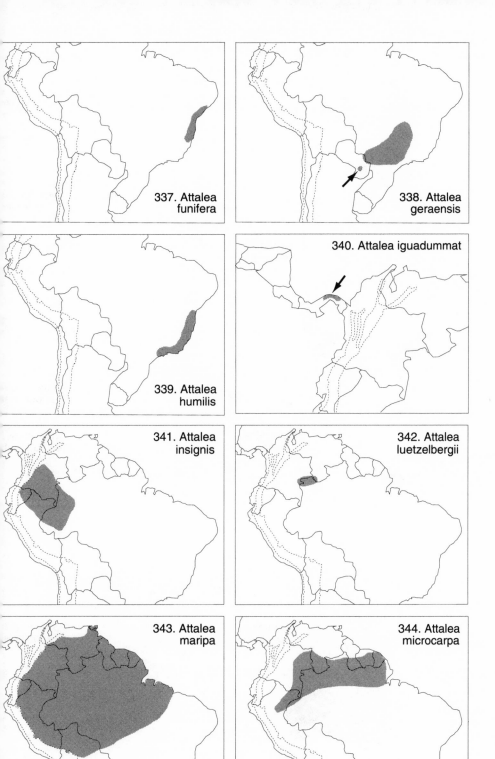

337. Attalea
funifera

338. Attalea
geraensis

339. Attalea
humilis

340. Attalea iguadummat

341. Attalea
insignis

342. Attalea
luetzelbergii

343. Attalea
maripa

344. Attalea
microcarpa

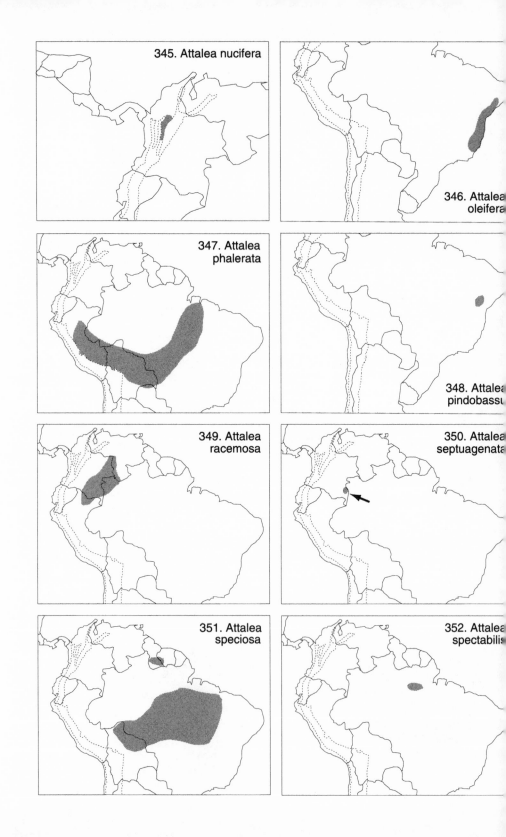

345. Attalea nucifera

346. Attalea oleifera

347. Attalea phalerata

348. Attalea pindobassu

349. Attalea racemosa

350. Attalea septuagenata

351. Attalea speciosa

352. Attalea spectabilis

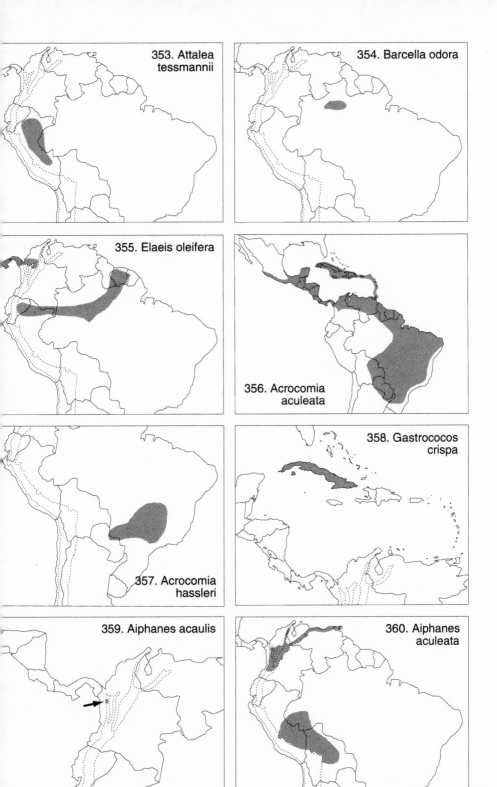

353. Attalea tessmannii

354. Barcella odora

355. Elaeis oleifera

356. Acrocomia aculeata

357. Acrocomia hassleri

358. Gastrococos crispa

359. Aiphanes acaulis

360. Aiphanes aculeata

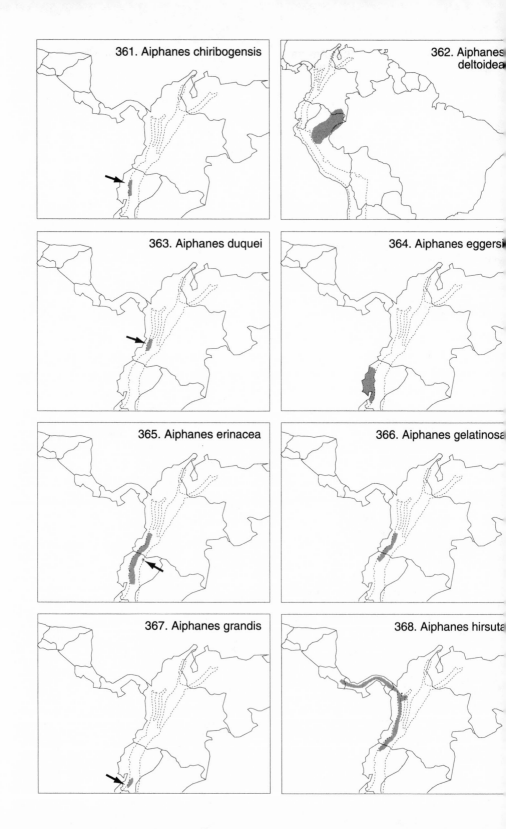

361. Aiphanes chiribogensis

362. Aiphanes deltoidea

363. Aiphanes duquei

364. Aiphanes eggersi

365. Aiphanes erinacea

366. Aiphanes gelatinosa

367. Aiphanes grandis

368. Aiphanes hirsuta

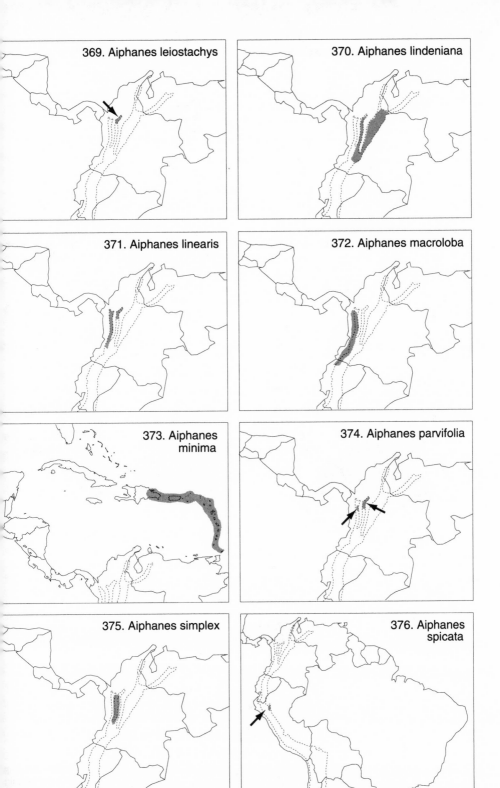

369. Aiphanes leiostachys

370. Aiphanes lindeniana

371. Aiphanes linearis

372. Aiphanes macroloba

373. Aiphanes minima

374. Aiphanes parvifolia

375. Aiphanes simplex

376. Aiphanes spicata

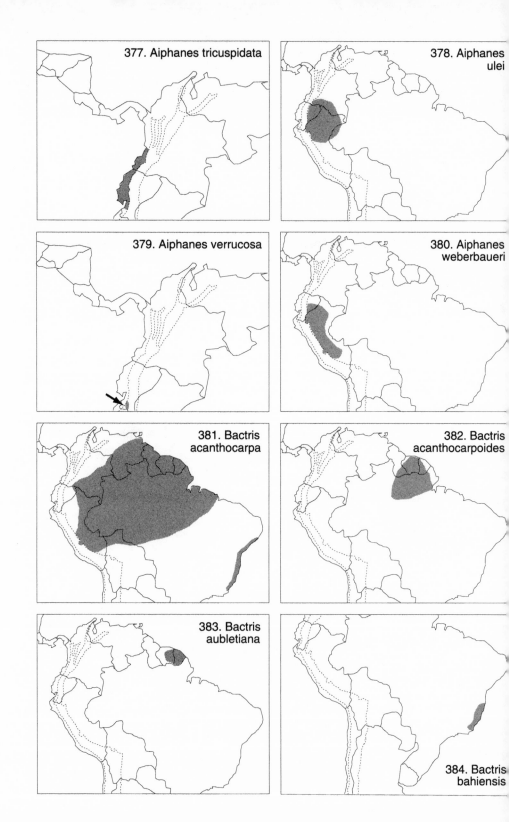

377. Aiphanes tricuspidata

378. Aiphanes ulei

379. Aiphanes verrucosa

380. Aiphanes weberbaueri

381. Bactris acanthocarpa

382. Bactris acanthocarpoides

383. Bactris aubletiana

384. Bactris bahiensis

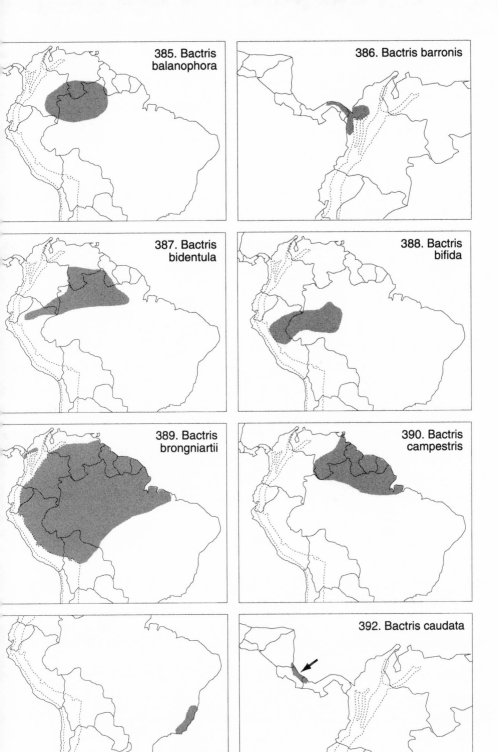

385. Bactris balanophora

386. Bactris barronis

387. Bactris bidentula

388. Bactris bifida

389. Bactris brongniartii

390. Bactris campestris

391. Bactris caryotifolia

392. Bactris caudata

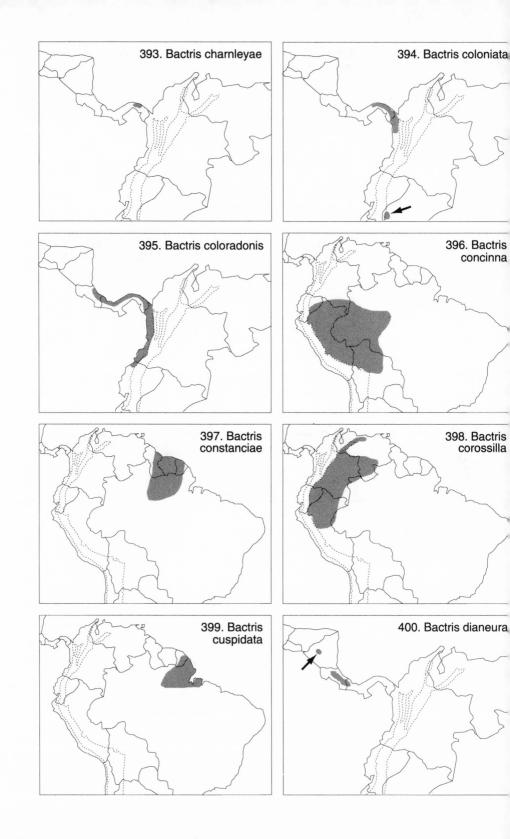

393. Bactris charnleyae

394. Bactris coloniata

395. Bactris coloradonis

396. Bactris concinna

397. Bactris constanciae

398. Bactris corossilla

399. Bactris cuspidata

400. Bactris dianeura

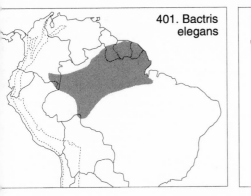

401. Bactris
elegans

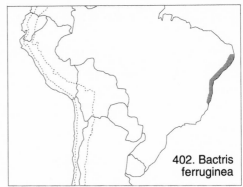

402. Bactris
ferruginea

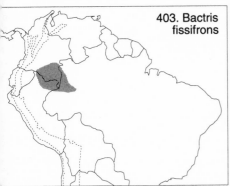

403. Bactris
fissifrons

404. Bactris
gasipaes

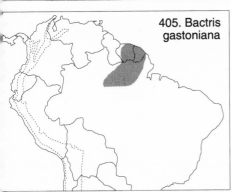

405. Bactris
gastoniana

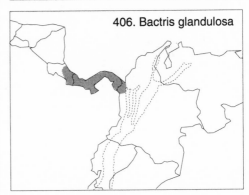

406. Bactris glandulosa

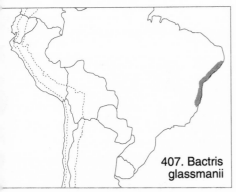

407. Bactris
glassmanii

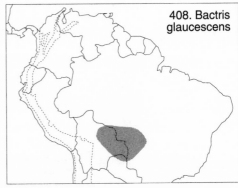

408. Bactris
glaucescens

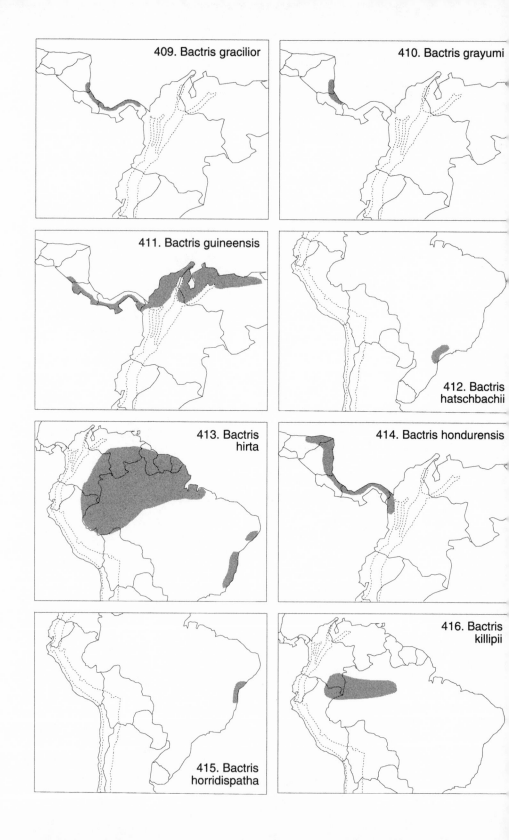

409. Bactris gracilior

410. Bactris grayumi

411. Bactris guineensis

412. Bactris hatschbachii

413. Bactris hirta

414. Bactris hondurensis

415. Bactris horridispatha

416. Bactris killipii

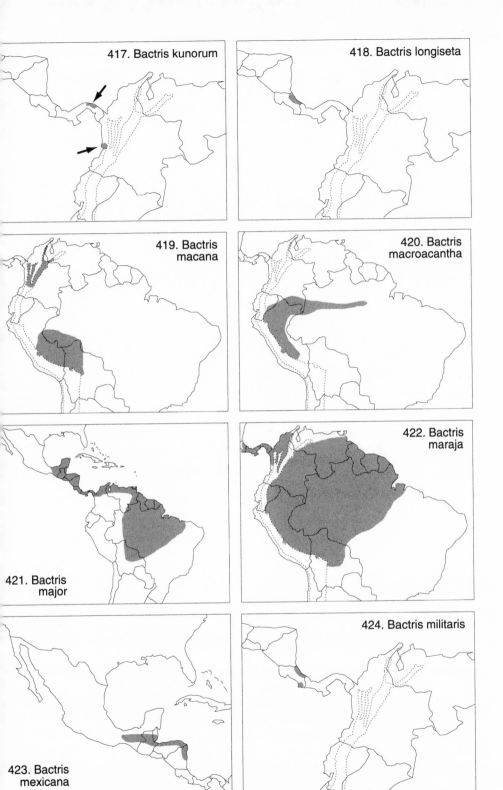

417. Bactris kunorum

418. Bactris longiseta

419. Bactris macana

420. Bactris macroacantha

421. Bactris major

422. Bactris maraja

423. Bactris mexicana

424. Bactris militaris

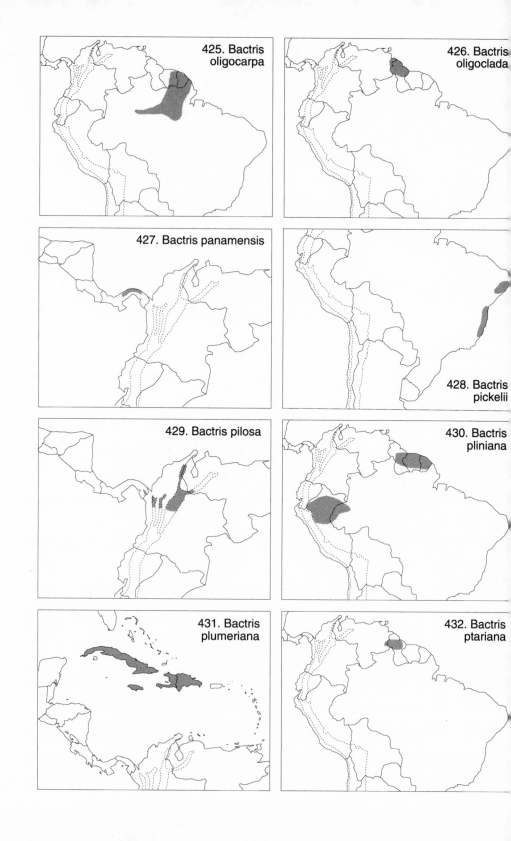

425. Bactris
oligocarpa

426. Bactris
oligoclada

427. Bactris panamensis

428. Bactris
pickelii

429. Bactris pilosa

430. Bactris
pliniana

431. Bactris
plumeriana

432. Bactris
ptariana

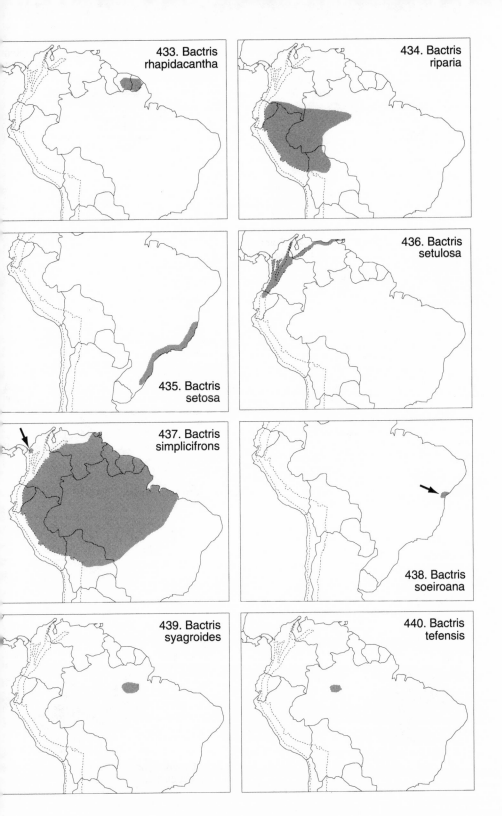

433. Bactris
rhapidacantha

434. Bactris
riparia

435. Bactris
setosa

436. Bactris
setulosa

437. Bactris
simplicifrons

438. Bactris
soeiroana

439. Bactris
syagroides

440. Bactris
tefensis

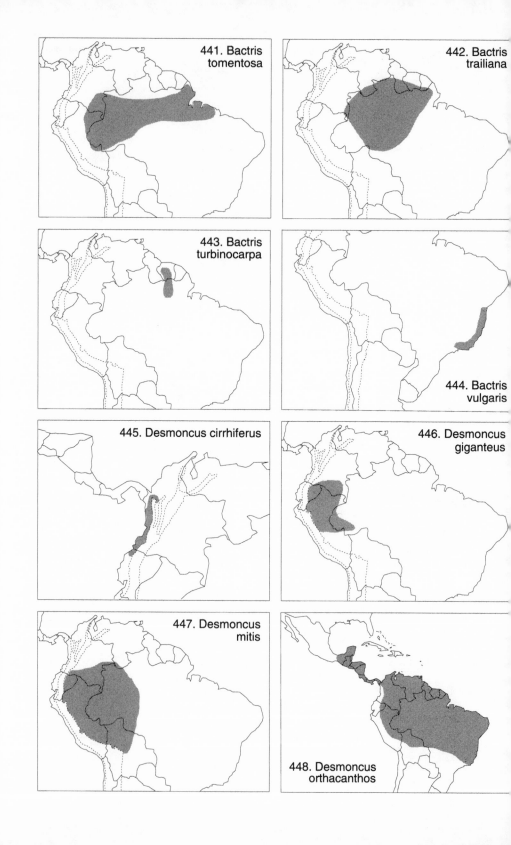

441. Bactris tomentosa

442. Bactris trailiana

443. Bactris turbinocarpa

444. Bactris vulgaris

445. Desmoncus cirrhiferus

446. Desmoncus giganteus

447. Desmoncus mitis

448. Desmoncus orthacanthos

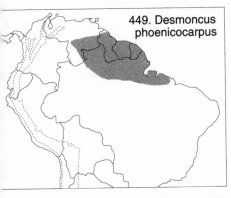

449. Desmoncus
phoenicocarpus

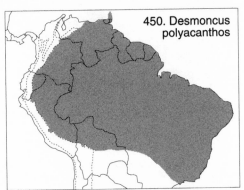

450. Desmoncus
polyacanthos

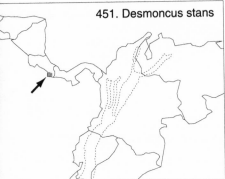

451. Desmoncus stans

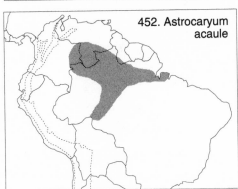

452. Astrocaryum
acaule

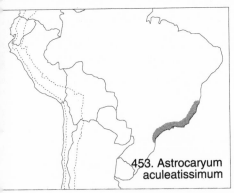

453. Astrocaryum
aculeatissimum

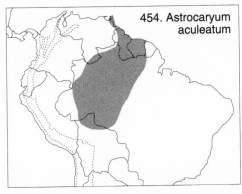

454. Astrocaryum
aculeatum

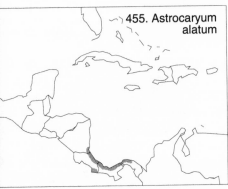

455. Astrocaryum
alatum

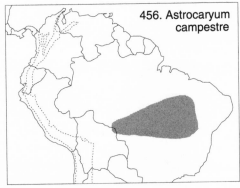

456. Astrocaryum
campestre

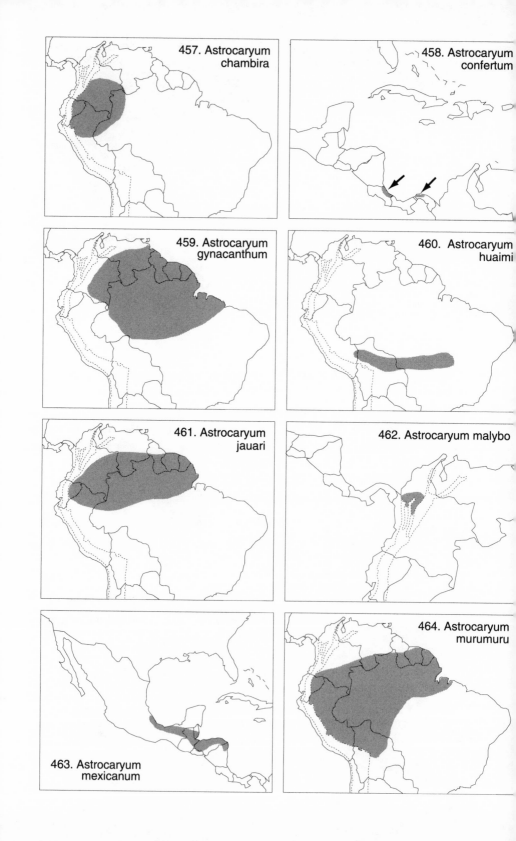

457. Astrocaryum chambira

458. Astrocaryum confertum

459. Astrocaryum gynacanthum

460. Astrocaryum huaimi

461. Astrocaryum jauari

462. Astrocaryum malybo

463. Astrocaryum mexicanum

464. Astrocaryum murumuru

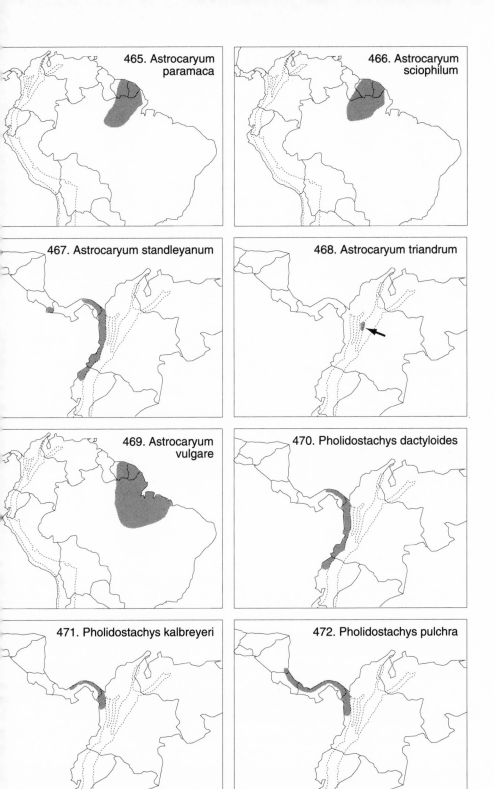

465. Astrocaryum paramaca

466. Astrocaryum sciophilum

467. Astrocaryum standleyanum

468. Astrocaryum triandrum

469. Astrocaryum vulgare

470. Pholidostachys dactyloides

471. Pholidostachys kalbreyeri

472. Pholidostachys pulchra

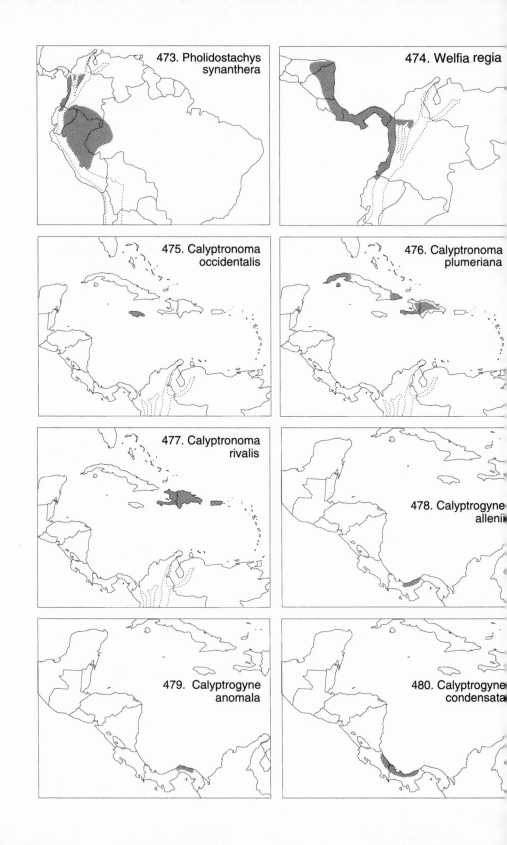

473. Pholidostachys
synanthera

474. Welfia regia

475. Calyptronoma
occidentalis

476. Calyptronoma
plumeriana

477. Calyptronoma
rivalis

478. Calyptrogyne
allenii

479. Calyptrogyne
anomala

480. Calyptrogyne
condensata

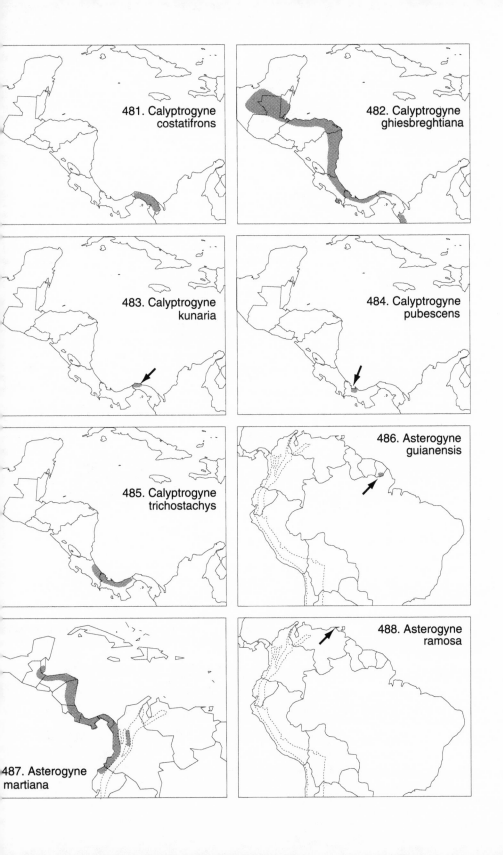

481. Calyptrogyne
costatifrons

482. Calyptrogyne
ghiesbreghtiana

483. Calyptrogyne
kunaria

484. Calyptrogyne
pubescens

485. Calyptrogyne
trichostachys

486. Asterogyne
guianensis

487. Asterogyne
martiana

488. Asterogyne
ramosa

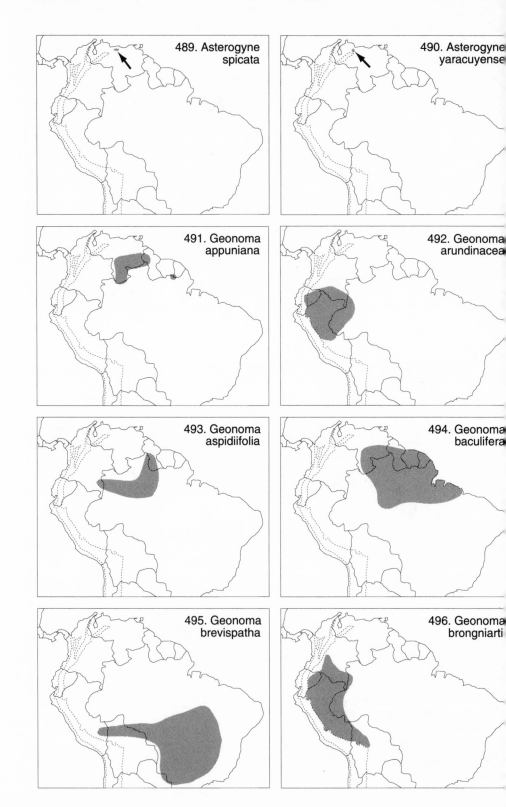

489. Asterogyne
spicata

490. Asterogyne
yaracuyense

491. Geonoma
appuniana

492. Geonoma
arundinacea

493. Geonoma
aspidiifolia

494. Geonoma
baculifera

495. Geonoma
brevispatha

496. Geonoma
brongniartii

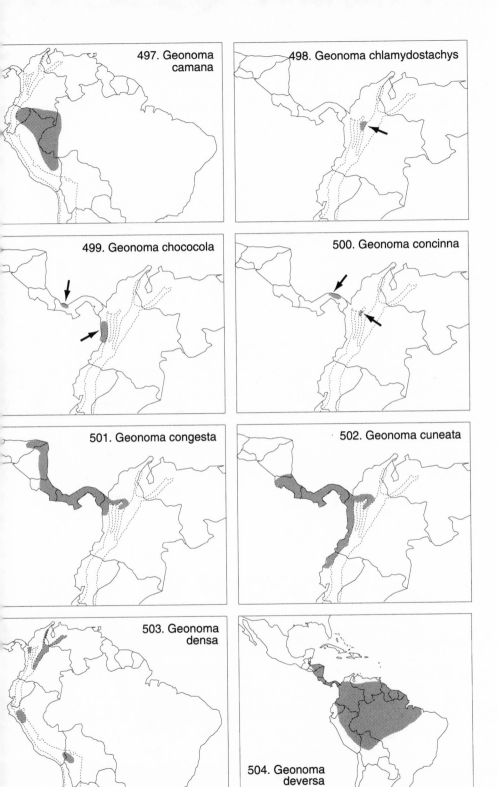

497. Geonoma camana

498. Geonoma chlamydostachys

499. Geonoma chococola

500. Geonoma concinna

501. Geonoma congesta

502. Geonoma cuneata

503. Geonoma densa

504. Geonoma deversa

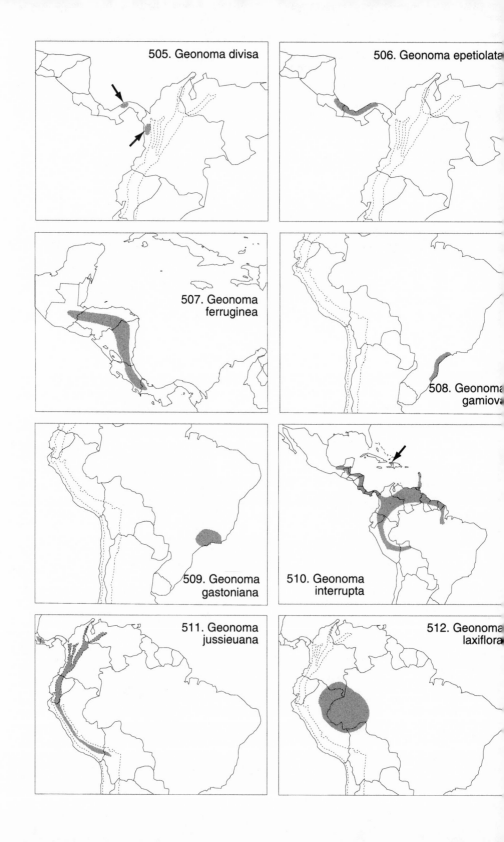

505. Geonoma divisa

506. Geonoma epetiolata

507. Geonoma ferruginea

508. Geonoma gamiova

509. Geonoma gastoniana

510. Geonoma interrupta

511. Geonoma jussieuana

512. Geonoma laxiflora

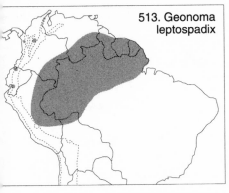

513. Geonoma leptospadix

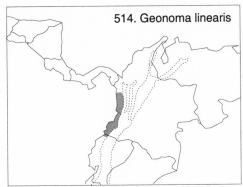

514. Geonoma linearis

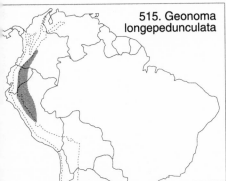

515. Geonoma longepedunculata

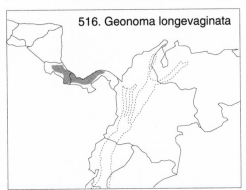

516. Geonoma longevaginata

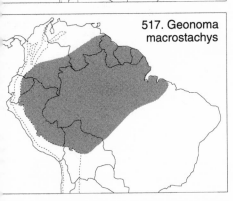

517. Geonoma macrostachys

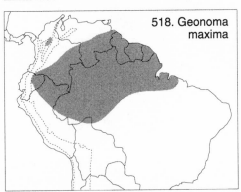

518. Geonoma maxima

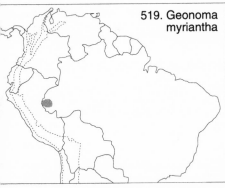

519. Geonoma myriantha

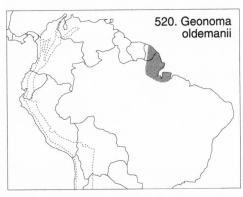

520. Geonoma oldemanii

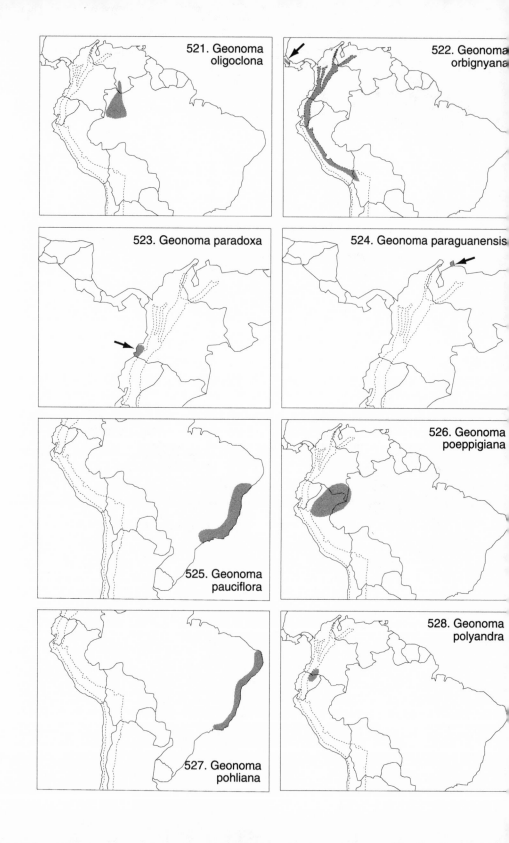

521. Geonoma oligoclona

522. Geonoma orbignyana

523. Geonoma paradoxa

524. Geonoma paraguanensis

525. Geonoma pauciflora

526. Geonoma poeppigiana

527. Geonoma pohliana

528. Geonoma polyandra

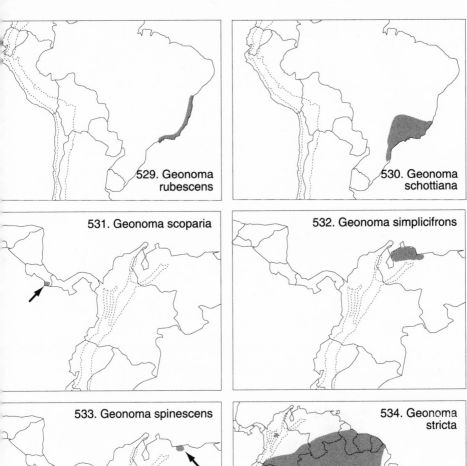

529. Geonoma
rubescens

530. Geonoma
schottiana

531. Geonoma scoparia

532. Geonoma simplicifrons

533. Geonoma spinescens

534. Geonoma
stricta

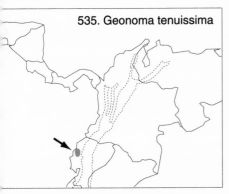

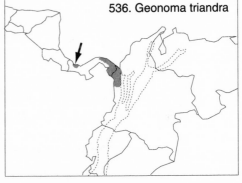

535. Geonoma tenuissima

536. Geonoma triandra

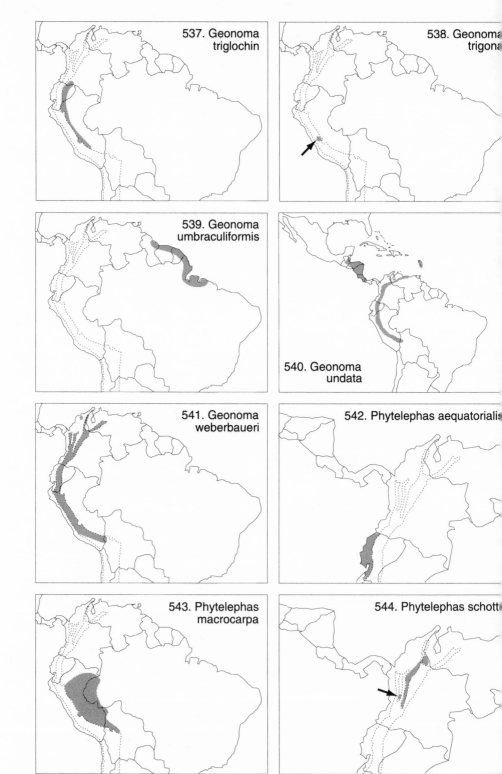

537. Geonoma triglochin

538. Geonoma trigona

539. Geonoma umbraculiformis

540. Geonoma undata

541. Geonoma weberbaueri

542. Phytelephas aequatorialis

543. Phytelephas macrocarpa

544. Phytelephas schotti

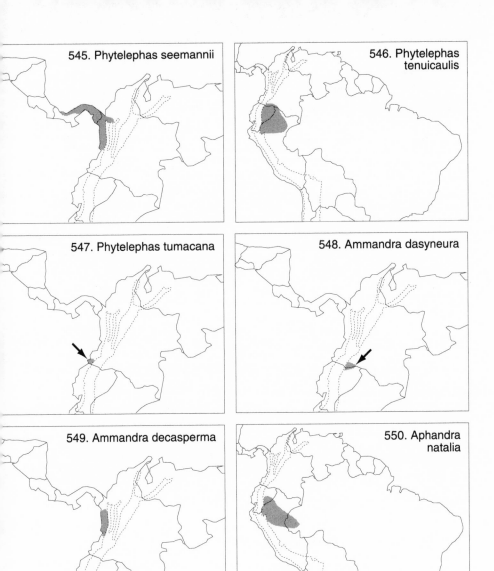

545. Phytelephas seemannii

546. Phytelephas tenuicaulis

547. Phytelephas tumacana

548. Ammandra dasyneura

549. Ammandra decasperma

550. Aphandra natalia

APPENDIXES

APPENDIX I

CHECKLISTS OF SPECIES BY COUNTRY

ARGENTINA

Acrocomia aculeata
Allagoptera campestris
Allagoptera leucocalyx
Butia paraguayensis
Butia yatay
Copernicia alba
Euterpe edulis
Syagrus romanzoffiana
Trithrinax campestris
Trithrinax schizophylla

BAHAMAS

Acoelorraphe wrightii
Coccothrinax argentata
Coccothrinax inaguensis
Cocos nucifera
Pseudophoenix sargentii subsp. *saonae* var.
  saonae
Roystonea regia
Sabal palmetto
Thrinax morrisii
Thrinax radiata

BELIZE

Acoelorraphe wrightii
Acrocomia aculeata
Asterogyne martiana
Astrocaryum mexicanum
Attalea cohune
Bactris major var. *major*
Bactris mexicana
Brahea dulcis
Calyptrogyne ghiesbreghtiana
Chamaedorea adscendens
Chamaedorea elegans
Chamaedorea ernesti-augustii
Chamaedorea geonomiformis
Chamaedorea graminifolia
Chamaedorea oblongata
Chamaedorea pinnatifrons
Chamaedorea seifrizii
Chamaedorea tepejilote
Chamaedorea woodsoniana
Cocos nucifera

Cryosophila stauracantha
Desmoncus orthacanthos
Euterpe precatoria var. *longevaginata*
Gaussia maya
Geonoma deversa
Geonoma interrupta var. *interrupta*
Geonoma undata
Manicaria saccifera
Pseudophoenix sargentii subsp. *sargentii*
Reinhardtia gracilis var. *gracilior*
Reinhardtia gracilis var. *gracilis*
Reinhardtia latisecta
Roystonea regia
Sabal mauritiiformis
Sabal yapa
Schippia concolor
Synechanthus fibrosus
Thrinax radiata

BERMUDA

Cocos nucifera
Sabal bermudana

BOLIVIA

Acrocomia aculeata
Aiphanes aculeata
Allagoptera leucocalyx
Astrocaryum aculeatum
Astrocaryum campestre
Astrocaryum gynacanthum
Astrocaryum huaimi
Astrocaryum murumuru var. *murumuru*
Attalea butyracea
Attalea eichleri
Attalea maripa
Attalea phalerata
Attalea speciosa
Bactris acanthocarpa var. *acanthocarpa*
Bactris brongniartii
Bactris concinna var. *inundata*
Bactris concinna var. *sigmoidea*
Bactris elegans
Bactris gasipaes
Bactris glaucescens
Bactris hirta var. *hirta*

Bactris macana
Bactris major var. infesta
Bactris major var. socialis
Bactris maraja var. juruensis
Bactris maraja var. maraja
Bactris riparia
Bactris simplicifrons
Bactris trailiana
Ceroxylon parvifrons
Ceroxylon parvum
Ceroxylon vogelianum
Chamaedorea angustisecta
Chamaedorea linearis
Chamaedorea pauciflora
Chamaedorea pinnatifrons
Chelyocarpus chuco
Copernicia alba
Desmoncus mitis var. leptoclonos
Desmoncus mitis var. rurrenabaquensis
Desmoncus orthacanthos
Desmoncus polyacanthos var. polyacanthos
Dictyocaryum lamarckianum
Euterpe precatoria var. longevaginata
Euterpe precatoria var. precatoria
Geonoma brevispatha var. brevispatha
Geonoma brevispatha var. occidentale
Geonoma brongniartii
Geonoma densa
Geonoma deversa
Geonoma interrupta var. interrupta
Geonoma interrupta var. euspatha
Geonoma jussieuana
Geonoma laxiflora
Geonoma leptospadix
Geonoma macrostachys var. acaulis
Geonoma macrostachys var. macrostachys
Geonoma maxima var. chelidonura
Geonoma maxima var. maxima
Geonoma orbignyana
Geonoma stricta var. piscicauda
Geonoma stricta var. stricta
Geonoma stricta var. trailii
Geonoma undata
Geonoma weberbaueri
Hyospathe elegans
Iriartea deltoidea
Mauritia flexuosa
Mauritiella martiana
Oenocarpus balickii
Oenocarpus bataua var. bataua
Oenocarpus distichus
Oenocarpus mapora
Parajubaea torallyi
Phytelephas macrocarpa

Prestoea acuminata
Socratea exorrhiza
Socratea salazarii
Syagrus cardenasii
Syagrus petraea
Syagrus romanzoffiana
Syagrus sancona
Trithrinax schizophylla
Wendlandiella gracilis var. simplicifrons
Wettinia augusta

BRAZIL

Acrocomia aculeata
Acrocomia hassleri
Aiphanes aculeata
Aiphanes deltoidea
Aiphanes ulei
Allagoptera arenaria
Allagoptera brevicalyx
Allagoptera campestris
Allagoptera leucocalyx
Aphandra natalia
Astrocaryum acaule
Astrocaryum aculeatissimum
Astrocaryum aculeatum
Astrocaryum campestre
Astrocaryum chambira
Astrocaryum gynacanthum
Astrocaryum huaimi
Astrocaryum jauari
Astrocaryum murumuru var. ferrugineum
Astrocaryum murumuru var. javarense
Astrocaryum murumuru var. murumuru
Astrocaryum paramaca
Astrocaryum sciophilum
Astrocaryum vulgare
Attalea attaleoides
Attalea butyracea
Attalea dahlgreniana
Attalea dubia
Attalea eichleri
Attalea exigua
Attalea funifera
Attalea geraensis
Attalea humilis
Attalea insignis
Attalea luetzelburgii
Attalea maripa
Attalea microcarpa
Attalea oleifera
Attalea phalerata
Attalea pindobassu
Attalea racemosa

Attalea speciosa
Attalea spectabilis
Attalea tessmannii
Bactris acanthocarpa var. acanthocarpa
Bactris acanthocarpa var. intermedia
Bactris acanthocarpoides
Bactris bahiensis
Bactris balanophora
Bactris bidentula
Bactris bifida
Bactris brongniartii
Bactris campestris
Bactris caryotifolia
Bactris concinna var. concinna
Bactris concinna var. inundata
Bactris concinna var. sigmoidea
Bactris constanciae
Bactris corossilla
Bactris cuspidata
Bactris elegans
Bactris ferruginea
Bactris fissifrons
Bactris gasipaes
Bactris gastoniana
Bactris glassmanii
Bactris glaucescens
Bactris hatschbachii
Bactris hirta var. hirta
Bactris hirta var. mollis
Bactris hirta var. pulchra
Bactris horridispatha
Bactris killipii
Bactris macana
Bactris macroacantha
Bactris major var. infesta
Bactris major var. megalocarpa
Bactris maraja var. chaetospatha
Bactris maraja var. juruensis
Bactris maraja var. maraja
Bactris oligocarpa
Bactris pickelli
Bactris pliniana
Bactris riparia
Bactris setosa
Bactris simplicifrons
Bactris soeiroana
Bactris syagroides
Bactris tefensis
Bactris tomentosa var. sphaerocarpa
Bactris tomentosa var. tomentosa
Bactris trailiana
Bactris turbinocarpa
Bactris vulgaris
Barcella odora

Butia archeri
Butia capitata
Butia eriospatha
Butia microspadix
Butia paraguayensis
Butia purpurascens
Butia yatay
Chamaedorea angustisecta
Chamaedorea pauciflora
Chamaedorea pinnatifrons
Chelyocarpus chuco
Chelyocarpus ulei
Cocos nucifera
Copernicia alba
Copernicia prunifera
Desmoncus giganteus
Desmoncus mitis var. leptoclonos
Desmoncus mitis var. mitis
Desmoncus mitis var. tenerrimus
Desmoncus orthacanthos
Desmoncus phoenicocarpus
Desmoncus polyacanthos var. polyacanthos
Dictyocaryum ptarianum
Elaeis oleifera
Euterpe catinga var. catinga
Euterpe catinga var. roraimae
Euterpe edulis
Euterpe longebracteata
Euterpe oleracea
Euterpe precatoria var. longevaginata
Euterpe precatoria var. precatoria
Geonoma appuniana
Geonoma arundinacea
Geonoma aspidiifolia
Geonoma baculifera
Geonoma brevispatha var. brevispatha
Geonoma brevispatha var. occidentale
Geonoma brongniartii
Geonoma camana
Geonoma deversa
Geonoma gamiova
Geonoma gastoniana
Geonoma interrupta var. interrupta
Geonoma interrupta var. euspatha
Geonoma laxiflora
Geonoma leptospadix
Geonoma macrostachys var. acaulis
Geonoma macrostachys var. macrostachys
Geonoma macrostachys var. poiteauana
Geonoma maxima var. ambigua
Geonoma maxima var. chelidonura
Geonoma maxima var. maxima
Geonoma maxima var. spixiana
Geonoma myriantha

Geonoma oldemannii
Geonoma oligoclona
Geonoma pauciflora
Geonoma poeppigiana
Geonoma pohliana
Geonoma rubescens
Geonoma schottiana
Geonoma stricta var. piscicauda
Geonoma stricta var. stricta
Geonoma stricta var. trailii
Geonoma umbraculiformis
Hyospathe elegans
Iriartea deltoidea
Iriartella setigera
Iriartella stenocarpa
Itaya amicorum
Leopoldinia major
Leopoldinia piassaba
Leopoldinia pulchra
Lepidocaryum tenue var. casquiarense
Lepidocaryum tenue var. gracile
Lepidocaryum tenue var. tenue
Lytocaryum hoehnei
Lytocaryum weddellianum
Manicaria saccifera
Mauritia carana
Mauritia flexuosa
Mauritiella aculeata
Mauritiella armata
Oenocarpus bacaba
Oenocarpus balickii
Oenocarpus bataua var. bataua
Oenocarpus distichus
Oenocarpus mapora
Oenocarpus minor
Pholidostachys synanthera
Phytelephas macrocarpa
Polyandrococos caudescens
Prestoea tenuiramosa
Raphia taedigera
Socratea exorrhiza
Socratea salazarii
Syagrus botryophora
Syagrus cocoides
Syagrus comosa
Syagrus coronata
Syagrus duartei
Syagrus flexuosa .
Syagrus glaucescens
Syagrus graminifolia
Syagrus harleyi
Syagrus inajai
Syagrus leptospatha
Syagrus macrocarpa

Syagrus microphylla
Syagrus oleracea
Syagrus petraea
Syagrus picrophylla
Syagrus pleioclada
Syagrus pseudococos
Syagrus romanzoffiana
Syagrus ruschiana
Syagrus sancona
Syagrus schizophylla
Syagrus smithii
Syagrus vagans
Syagrus werdermannii
Trithrinax brasiliensis
Trithrinax schizophylla
Wendlandiella gracilis var. gracilis
Wettinia augusta
Wettinia drudei

CHILE

Juania australis
Jubaea chilensis

COLOMBIA

Acoelorraphe wrightii
Acrocomia aculeata
Aiphanes acaulis
Aiphanes aculeata
Aiphanes deltoidea
Aiphanes duquei
Aiphanes erinacea
Aiphanes gelatinosa
Aiphanes hirsuta subsp. hirsuta
Aiphanes hirsuta subsp. kalbreyeri
Aiphanes hirsuta subsp. intermedia
Aiphanes leiostachys
Aiphanes lindeniana
Aiphanes linearis
Aiphanes macroloba
Aiphanes parvifolia
Aiphanes simplex
Aiphanes tricuspidata
Aiphanes ulei
Ammandra dasyneura
Ammandra decasperma
Asterogyne martiana
Astrocaryum acaule
Astrocaryum aculeatum
Astrocaryum chambira
Astrocaryum gynacanthum
Astrocaryum jauari
Astrocaryum malybo

Astrocaryum murumuru var. ciliatum
Astrocaryum murumuru var. macrocalyx
Astrocaryum standleyanum
Astrocaryum triandrum
Attalea allenii
Attalea amygdalina
Attalea butyracea
Attalea colenda
Attalea cuatrecasana
Attalea insignis
Attalea maripa
Attalea microcarpa
Attalea nucifera
Attalea racemosa
Attalea septuagenata
Bactris acanthocarpa var. acanthocarpa
Bactris balanophora
Bactris barronis
Bactris bidentula
Bactris bifida
Bactris brongniartii
Bactris campestris
Bactris coloniata
Bactris coloradonis
Bactris concinna var. concinna
Bactris concinna var. inundata
Bactris corossilla
Bactris elegans
Bactris fissifrons
Bactris gasipaes
Bactris glandulosa var. baileyana
Bactris glandulosa var. glandulosa
Bactris guineensis
Bactris hirta var. hirta
Bactris hirta var. mollis
Bactris hirta var. pulchra
Bactris hondurensis
Bactris killipii
Bactris kunorum
Bactris macana
Bactris macroacantha
Bactris major var. major
Bactris maraja var. juruensis
Bactris maraja var. maraja
Bactris pilosa
Bactris riparia
Bactris setulosa
Bactris simplicifrons
Bactris tomentosa var. sphaerocarpa
Bactris trailiana
Calyptrogyne ghiesbreghtiana
Ceroxylon alpinum subsp. alpinum
Ceroxylon ceriferum
Ceroxylon parvifrons

Ceroxylon quindiuense
Ceroxylon sasaimae
Ceroxylon ventricosum
Ceroxylon vogelianum
Chamaedorea allenii
Chamaedorea linearis
Chamaedorea murriensis
Chamaedorea pauciflora
Chamaedorea pinnatifrons
Chamaedorea pygmaea
Chamaedorea sullivaniorum
Chamaedorea tepejilote
Chelyocarpus dianeurus
Chelyocarpus ulei
Coccothrinax argentata
Cocos nucifera
Copernicia tectorum
Cryosophila kalbreyeri
Cryosophila macrocarpa
Desmoncus cirrhiferus
Desmoncus giganteus
Desmoncus mitis var. leptospadix
Desmoncus mitis var. mitis
Desmoncus mitis var. tenerrimus
Desmoncus orthacanthos
Desmoncus polyacanthos var. polyacanthos
Desmoncus polyacanthos var. prunifer
Dictyocaryum lamarckianum
Dictyocaryum ptarianum
Elaeis oleifera
Euterpe catinga var. catinga
Euterpe oleracea
Euterpe precatoria var. longevaginata
Euterpe precatoria var. precatoria
Geonoma arundinacea
Geonoma aspidiifolia
Geonoma brongniartii
Geonoma camana
Geonoma chlamydostachys
Geonoma chococola
Geonoma concinna
Geonoma congesta
Geonoma cuneata var. cuneata
Geonoma cuneata var. gracilis
Geonoma cuneata var. procumbens
Geonoma cuneata var. sodiroi
Geonoma densa
Geonoma deversa
Geonoma divisa
Geonoma interrupta var. interrupta
Geonoma interrupta var. euspatha
Geonoma jussieuana
Geonoma laxiflora
Geonoma leptospadix

Geonoma linearis
Geonoma longepedunculata
Geonoma macrostachys var. acaulis
Geonoma macrostachys var. macrostachys
Geonoma macrostachys var. poiteauana
Geonoma maxima var. chelidonura
Geonoma maxima var. maxima
Geonoma maxima var. spixiana
Geonoma oligoclona
Geonoma orbignyana
Geonoma paradoxa
Geonoma poeppigiana
Geonoma polyandra
Geonoma stricta var. piscicauda
Geonoma stricta var. stricta
Geonoma stricta var. trailii
Geonoma triandra
Geonoma triglochin
Geonoma undata
Geonoma weberbaueri
Hyospathe elegans
Iriartea deltoidea
Iriartella setigera
Iriartella stenocarpa
Itaya amicorum
Leopoldinia major
Leopoldinia piassaba
Leopoldinia pulchra
Lepidocaryum tenue var. casquiarense
Lepidocaryum tenue var. tenue
Manicaria saccifera
Mauritia carana
Mauritia flexuosa
Mauritiella aculeata
Mauritiella armata
Mauritiella macroclada
Oenocarpus bacaba
Oenocarpus balickii
Oenocarpus bataua var. bataua
Oenocarpus circumtextus
Oenocarpus makeru
Oenocarpus mapora
Oenocarpus minor
Oenocarpus simplex
Parajubaea cocoides
Pholidostachys dactyloides
Pholidostachys kalbreyeri
Pholidostachys pulchra
Pholidostachys synanthera
Phytelephas schottii
Phytelephas seemannii
Phytelephas tenuicaulis
Phytelephas tumacana
Prestoea acuminata

Prestoea carderi
Prestoea decurrens
Prestoea ensiformis
Prestoea pubens var. pubens
Prestoea schultzeana
Prestoea simplicifolia
Raphia taedigera
Reinhardtia koschnyana
Reinhardtia simplex
Roystonea oleracea
Sabal mauritiiformis
Socratea exorrhiza
Socratea hecatonandra
Socratea montana
Socratea rostrata
Syagrus orinocensis
Syagrus sancona
Syagrus smithii
Synechanthus warscewiczianus
Welfia regia
Wettinia aequalis
Wettinia anomala
Wettinia augusta
Wettinia castanea
Wettinia disticha
Wettinia drudei
Wettinia fascicularis
Wettinia hirsuta
Wettinia kalbreyeri
Wettinia lanata
Wettinia maynensis
Wettinia microcarpa
Wettinia oxycarpa
Wettinia praemorsa
Wettinia quinaria
Wettinia radiata
Wettinia verruculosa

COSTA RICA

Acoelorraphe wrightii
Acrocomia aculeata
Aiphanes hirsuta subsp. hirsuta
Asterogyne martiana
Astrocaryum alatum
Astrocaryum confertum
Astrocaryum standleyanum
Attalea butyracea
Bactris caudata
Bactris coloradonis
Bactris dianeura
Bactris gasipaes
Bactris glandulosa var. baileyana
Bactris glandulosa var. glandulosa

Bactris gracilior
Bactris grayumi
Bactris guineensis
Bactris hondurensis
Bactris longiseta
Bactris major var. major
Bactris maraja var. maraja
Bactris militaris
Calyptrogyne condensata
Calyptrogyne ghiesbreghtiana
Calyptrogyne trichostachys
Chamaedorea allenii
Chamaedorea amabilis
Chamaedorea brachyclada
Chamaedorea costaricana
Chamaedorea dammeriana
Chamaedorea deckeriana
Chamaedorea geonomiformis
Chamaedorea graminifolia
Chamaedorea macrospadix
Chamaedorea palmeriana
Chamaedorea parvifolia
Chamaedorea pinnatifrons
Chamaedorea pittieri
Chamaedorea pumila
Chamaedorea pygmaea
Chamaedorea robertii
Chamaedorea scheryi
Chamaedorea selvae
Chamaedorea stricta
Chamaedorea sullivaniorum
Chamaedorea tepejilote
Chamaedorea undulatifolia
Chamaedorea warscewiczii
Chamaedorea woodsoniana
Cocos nucifera
Colpothrinax cookii
Cryosophila cookii
Cryosphila grayumii
Cryosophila guagara
Cryosophila warscewiczii
Desmoncus orthacanthos
Desmoncus stans
Elaeis oleifera
Euterpe precatoria var. longevaginata
Geonoma congesta
Geonoma cuneata var. cuneata
Geonoma cuneata var. gracilis
Geonoma cuneata var. procumbens
Geonoma deversa
Geonoma ferruginea
Geonoma interrupta var. interrupta
Geonoma jussieuana
Geonoma longevaginata

Geonoma orbignyana
Geonoma scoparia
Geonoma undata
Iriartea deltoidea
Manicaria saccifera
Neonicholsonia watsonii
Oenocarpus mapora
Pholidostachys pulchra
Prestoea acuminata
Prestoea decurrens
Prestoea ensiformis
Prestoea longepetiolata
Raphia taedigera
Reinhardtia gracilis var. rostrata
Reinhardtia koschnyana
Reinhardtia latisecta
Reinhardtia simplex
Sabal mauritiiformis
Socratea exorrhiza
Synechanthus fibrosus
Synechanthus warscewiczianus
Welfia regia

CUBA

Acoelorraphe wrightii
Bactris plumeriana
Calyptronoma plumeriana
Coccothrinax argentata
Coccothrinax borhidiana
Coccothrinax crinita subsp. brevicrinis
Coccothrinax crinita subsp. crinita
Coccothrinax ekmanii
Coccothrinax gundlachii
Coccothrinax hiorami
Coccothrinax miraguama
Coccothrinax pauciramosa
Coccothrinax salvatoris
Cocos nucifera
Colpothrinax wrightii
Copernicia baileyana
Copernicia brittonorum
Copernicia cowellii
Copernicia gigas
Copernicia glabrescens
Copernicia hospita
Copernicia macroglossa
Copernicia rigida
Gastrococos crispa
Gaussia princeps
Gaussia spirituana
Prestoea acuminata
Pseuodphoenix sargentii subsp. saonae var.
    saonae

Roystonea lenis
Roystonea maisiana
Roystonea regia
Roystonea stellata
Roystonea violacea
Sabal domingensis
Sabal maritima
Sabal palmetto
Sabal yapa
Thrinax compacta
Thrinax ekmaniana
Thrinax morrisii
Thrinax radiata
Thrinax rivularis var. rivularis
Thrinax rivularis var. savannarum

DOMINICAN REPUBLIC

Acrocomia aculeata
Aiphanes minima
Bactris plumeriana
Calyptronoma plumeriana
Calyptronoma rivalis
Coccothrinax argentea
Coccothrinax ekmanii
Coccothrinax gracilis
Coccothrinax miraguama
Coccothrinax spissa
Cocos nucifera
Copernicia berteroana
Prestoea acuminata
Pseudophoenix ekmanii
Pseuodphoenix sargentii subsp. saonae var.
    saonae
Pseudophoenix vinifera
Reinhardtia paiewonskiana
Roystonea borinquena
Sabal causiarum
Sabal domingensis
Thrinax radiata
Zombia antillarum

ECUADOR

Aiphanes chiribogensis
Aiphanes eggersii
Aiphanes erinacea
Aiphanes gelatinosa
Aiphanes grandis
Aiphanes hirsuta subsp. fosteriorum
Aiphanes macroloba
Aiphanes tricuspidata
Aiphanes ulei
Aiphanes verrucosa

Aiphanes weberbaueri
Ammandra dasyneura
Aphandra natalia
Asterogyne martiana
Astrocaryum chambira
Astrocaryum jauari
Astrocaryum murumuru var. urostachys
Astrocaryum standleyanum
Attalea butyracea
Attalea colenda
Attalea insignis
Attalea maripa
Bactris acanthocarpa var. acanthocarpa
Bactris coloradonis
Bactris concinna var. concinna
Bactris concinna var. inundata
Bactris corossilla
Bactris gasipaes
Bactris hondurensis
Bactris macroacantha
Bactris maraja var. juruensis
Bactris maraja var. maraja
Bactris riparia
Bactris setulosa
Bactris simplicifrons
Bactris tomentosa var. sphaerocarpa
Ceroxylon alpinum subsp. ecuadorense
Ceroxylon amazonicum
Ceroxylon echinulatum
Ceroxylon parvifrons
Ceroxylon parvum
Ceroxylon ventricosum
Ceroxylon vogelianum
Chamaedorea deneversiana
Chamaedorea linearis
Chamaedorea pauciflora
Chamaedorea pinnatifrons
Chelyocarpus ulei
Cocos nucifera
Desmoncus cirrhiferus
Desmoncus giganteus
Desmoncus mitis var. mitis
Desmoncus orthacanthos
Desmoncus polyacanthos var. polyacanthos
Desmoncus polyacanthos var. prunifer
Dictyocaryum lamarckianum
Elaeis oleifera
Euterpe catinga var. roraimae
Euterpe oleracea
Euterpe precatoria var. longevaginata
Euterpe precatoria var. precatoria
Geonoma arundinacea
Geonoma brongniartii
Geonoma camana

Geonoma cuneata var. *cuneata*
Geonoma cuneata var. *gracilis*
Geonoma cuneata var. *procumbens*
Geonoma cuneata var. *sodiroi*
Geonoma deversa
Geonoma interrupta var. *interrupta*
Geonoma interrupta var. *euspatha*
Geonoma jussieuana
Geonoma laxiflora
Geonoma leptospadix
Geonoma linearis
Geonoma longepedunculata
Geonoma macrostachys var. *acaulis*
Geonoma macrostachys var. *macrostachys*
Geonoma maxima var. *chelidonura*
Geonoma maxima var. *maxima*
Geonoma orbignyana
Geonoma polyandra
Geonoma stricta var. *piscicauda*
Geonoma stricta var. *stricta*
Geonoma stricta var. *trailii*
Geonoma tenuissima
Geonoma triglochin
Geonoma undata
Geonoma weberbaueri
Hyospathe elegans
Hyospathe macrorachis
Iriartea deltoidea
Manicaria saccifera
Mauritia flexuosa
Mauritiella armata
Mauritiella macroclada
Oenocarpus bataua var. *bataua*
Oenocarpus mapora
Parajubaea cocoides
Pholidostachys dactyloides
Pholidostachys synanthera
Phytelephas aequatorialis
Phytelephas tenuicaulis
Prestoea acuminata
Prestoea carderi
Prestoea decurrens
Prestoea ensiformis
Prestoea schultzeana
Socratea exorrhiza
Socratea hecatonandra
Socratea montana
Socratea rostrata
Syagrus sancona
Synechanthus warscewiczianus
Welfia regia
Wettinia aequalis
Wettinia aequatorialis
Wettinia anomala

Wettinia drudei
Wettinia fascicularis
Wettinia kalbreyeri
Wettinia maynensis
Wettinia minima
Wettinia oxycarpa
Wettinia quinaria
Wettinia verruculosa

EL SALVADOR

Astrocaryum mexicanum
Attalea cohune
Bactris gasipaes
Bactris major var. *major*
Brahea dulcis
Chamaedorea costaricana
Chamaedorea nubium
Chamaedorea tepejilote
Cocos nucifera
Desmoncus orthacanthos
Sabal mexicana

FRENCH GUIANA

Acrocomia aculeata
Asterogyne guianensis
Astrocaryum aculeatum
Astrocaryum gynacanthum
Astrocaryum jauari
Astrocaryum murumuru var. *murumuru*
Astrocaryum paramaca
Astrocaryum sciophilum
Astrocaryum vulgare
Attalea attaleoides
Attalea maripa
Attalea microcarpa
Bactris acanthocarpa var. *acanthocarpa*
Bactris acanthocarpa var. *intermedia*
Bactris acanthocarpoides
Bactris aubletiana
Bactris brongniartii
Bactris campestris
Bactris constanciae
Bactris cuspidata
Bactris elegans
Bactris gasipaes
Bactris gastoniana
Bactris hirta var. *hirta*
Bactris major var. *major*
Bactris major var. *infesta*
Bactris maraja var. *juruensis*
Bactris maraja var. *maraja*
Bactris oligocarpa

Bactris pliniana
Bactris rhapidacantha
Bactris simplicifrons
Bactris tomentosa var. tomentosa
Cocos nucifera
Desmoncus orthacanthos
Desmoncus phoenicocarpus
Desmoncus polyacanthos var. polyacanthos
Elaeis oleifera
Euterpe oleracea
Euterpe precatoria var. precatoria
Geonoma appuniana
Geonoma baculifera
Geonoma deversa
Geonoma interrupta var. interrupta
Geonoma interrupta var. euspatha
Geonoma leptospadix
Geonoma macrostachys var. poiteauana
Geonoma maxima var. ambigua
Geonoma maxima var. maxima
Geonoma oldemannii
Geonoma stricta var. stricta
Geonoma umbraculiformis
Hyospathe elegans
Manicaria saccifera
Mauritia flexuosa
Oenocarpus bacaba
Oenocarpus bataua var. oligocarpa
Socratea exorrhiza
Syagrus inajai
Syagrus stratincola

GUATEMALA

Acoelorraphe wrightii
Acrocomia aculeata
Asterogyne martiana
Astrocaryum mexicanum
Attalea butyracea
Attalea cohune
Bactris gasipaes
Bactris major var. major
Bactris mexicana
Brahea dulcis
Brahea nitida
Calyptrogyne ghiesbreghtiana
Chamaedorea adscendens
Chamaedorea arenbergiana
Chamaedorea brachypoda
Chamaedorea carchensis
Chamaedorea castillo-montii
Chamaedorea costaricana
Chamaedorea elatior

Chamaedorea elegans
Chamaedorea ernesti-augustii
Chamaedorea fractiflexa
Chamaedorea geonomiformis
Chamaedorea graminifolia
Chamaedorea ibarrae
Chamaedorea keeleriorum
Chamaedorea lehmannii
Chamaedorea liebmannii
Chamaedorea nationsiana
Chamaedorea nubium
Chamaedorea oblongata
Chamaedorea pachecoana
Chamaedorea parvisecta
Chamaedorea pinnatifrons
Chamaedorea pygmaea
Chamaedorea rojasiana
Chamaedorea seifrizii
Chamaedorea simplex
Chamaedorea stricta
Chamaedorea tenerrima
Chamaedorea tepejilote
Chamaedorea tuerckheimii
Chamaedorea volcanensis
Chamaedorea vulgata
Chamaedorea woodsoniana
Cocos nucifera
Colpothrinax cookii
Cryosophila stauracantha
Desmoncus orthacanthos
Euterpe precatoria var. longevaginata
Gaussia maya
Geonoma ferruginea
Geonoma interrupta var. interrupta
Geonoma undata
Manicaria saccifera
Reinhardtia gracilis var. gracilior
Reinhardtia gracilis var. gracilis
Sabal guatemalensis
Sabal mauritiiformis
Synechanthus fibrosus

GUYANA

Acrocomia aculeata
Astrocaryum acaule
Astrocaryum aculeatum
Astrocaryum gynacanthum
Astrocaryum jauari
Astrocaryum murumuru var. murumuru
Astrocaryum sciophilum
Attalea maripa
Attalea microcarpa
Attalea speciosa

Bactris acanthocarpa var. *acanthocarpa*
Bactris acanthocarpoides
Bactris balanophora
Bactris brongniartii
Bactris campestris
Bactris constanciae
Bactris elegans
Bactris gasipaes
Bactris hirta var. *hirta*
Bactris major var. *infesta*
Bactris major var. *major*
Bactris maraja var. *maraja*
Bactris oligoclada
Bactris pliniana
Bactris ptariana
Bactris simplicifrons
Cocos nucifera
Desmoncus orthacanthos
Desmoncus phoenicocarpus
Desmoncus polyacanthos var. *polyacanthos*
Dictyocaryum ptarianum
Euterpe catinga var. *roraimae*
Euterpe longebracteata
Euterpe oleracea
Euterpe precatoria var. *precatoria*
Geonoma appuniana
Geonoma aspidiifolia
Geonoma baculifera
Geonoma deversa
Geonoma interrupta var. *euspatha*
Geonoma interrupta var. *interrupta*
Geonoma leptospadix
Geonoma macrostachys var. *poiteauana*
Geonoma maxima var. *ambigua*
Geonoma stricta var. *stricta*
Geonoma umbraculiformis
Hyospathe elegans
Iriartella setigera
Lepidocaryum tenue var. *gracile*
Manicaria saccifera
Mauritia flexuosa
Mauritiella armata
Oenocarpus bacaba
Oenocarpus bataua var. *oligocarpa*
Prestoea tenuiramosa
Socratea exorrhiza
Syagrus cocoides
Syagrus inajai

HAITI

Acrocomia aculeata
Attalea crassispatha
Bactris plumeriana

Calyptronoma plumeriana
Calyptronoma rivalis
Coccothrinax argentea
Coccothrinax ekmanii
Coccothrinax gracilis
Coccothrinax miraguama
Coccothrinax spissa
Cocos nucifera
Copernicia berteroana
Copernicia ekmanii
Geonoma interrupta var. *interrupta*
Prestoea acuminata
Pseudophoenix lediniana
Pseuodphoenix sargentii subsp. *saonae* var.
    navassana
Pseuodphoenix sargentii subsp. *saonae* var.
    saonae
Pseudophoenix vinifera
Roystonea borinquena
Sabal causiarum
Sabal domingensis
Thrinax morrisii
Thrinax radiata
Zombia antillarum

HONDURAS

Acoelorraphe wrightii
Acrocomia aculeata
Asterogyne martiana
Astrocaryum mexicanum
Attalea butyracea
Attalea cohune
Bactris gasipaes
Bactris hondurensis
Bactris major var. *major*
Bactris mexicana
Brahea dulcis
Calyptrogyne ghiesbreghtiana
Chamaedorea arenbergiana
Chamaedorea brachypoda
Chamaedorea costaricana
Chamaedorea elatior
Chamaedorea ernesti-augustii
Chamaedorea geonomiformis
Chamaedorea nubium
Chamaedorea oblongata
Chamaedorea pinnatifrons
Chamaedorea sartorii
Chamaedorea seifrizii
Chamaedorea tepejilote
Chamaedorea woodsoniana
Coccothrinax argentata
Cocos nucifera

Cryosophila williamsii
Desmoncus orthacanthos
Elaeis oleifera
Euterpe precatoria var. longevaginata
Geonoma congesta
Geonoma deversa
Geonoma ferruginea
Geonoma interrupta var. interrupta
Geonoma undata
Manicaria saccifera
Neonicholsonia watsonii
Reinhardtia elegans
Reinhardtia gracilis var. gracilior
Reinhardtia gracilis var. gracilis
Reinhardtia koschnyana
Reinhardtia latisecta
Reinhardtia simplex
Roystonea dunlapiana
Roystonea regia
Sabal mauritiiformis
Sabal mexicana
Synechanthus fibrosus
Thrinax radiata
Welfia regia

JAMAICA

Acrocomia aculeata
Bactris plumeriana
Calyptronoma occidentalis
Coccothrinax argentata
Cocos nucifera
Roystonea altissima
Roystonea princeps
Sabal maritima
Thrinax excelsa
Thrinax parviflora subsp. parviflora
Thrinax parviflora subsp. puberula
Thrinax radiata

LESSER ANTILLES

Acrocomia aculeata
Aiphanes minima
Coccothrinax barbadensis
Cocos nucifera
Desmoncus polyacanthos var. polyacanthos
Euterpe broadwayi
Geonoma interrupta var. interrupta
Geonoma undata
Prestoea acuminata
Pseudophoenix sargentii
Roystonea oleracea

Syagrus amara
Thrinax morrisii

MEXICO

Acoelorraphe wrightii
Acrocomia aculeata
Astrocaryum mexicanum
Attalea butyracea
Attalea cohune
Bactris gasipaes
Bactris major var. major
Bactris mexicana
Brahea aculeata
Brahea armata
Brahea brandegeei
Brahea decumbens
Brahea dulcis
Brahea edulis
Brahea moorei
Brahea nitida
Brahea pimo
Calyptrogyne ghiesbreghtiana
Chamaedorea arenbergiana
Chamaedorea carchensis
Chamaedorea cataractarum
Chamaedorea costaricana
Chamaedorea elatior
Chamaedorea elegans
Chamaedorea ernesti-augustii
Chamaedorea fractiflexa
Chamaedorea geonomiformis
Chamaedorea glaucifolia
Chamaedorea graminifolia
Chamaedorea hooperiana
Chamaedorea ibarrae
Chamaedorea keeleriorum
Chamaedorea klotzschiana
Chamaedorea liebmannii
Chamaedorea metallica
Chamaedorea microspadix
Chamaedorea nubium
Chamaedorea oblongata
Chamaedorea oreophila
Chamaedorea parvisecta
Chamaedorea pinnatifrons
Chamaedorea plumosa
Chamaedorea pochutlensis
Chamaedorea queroana
Chamaedorea radicalis
Chamaedorea rhizomatosa
Chamaedorea rigida
Chamaedorea rojasiana
Chamaedorea sartorii

Chamaedorea schiedeana
Chamaedorea seifrizii
Chamaedorea simplex
Chamaedorea stolonifera
Chamaedorea stricta
Chamaedorea tepejilote
Chamaedorea tuerckheimii
Chamaedorea vulgata
Chamaedorea whitelockiana
Chamaedorea woodsoniana
Coccothrinax argentata
Cocos nucifera
Cryosophila nana
Cryosophila stauracantha
Desmoncus orthacanthos
Gaussia gomez-pompae
Gaussia maya
Geonoma interrupta var. interrupta
Pseudophoenix sargentii subsp. sargentii
Reinhardtia elegans
Reinhardtia gracilis var. gracilior
Reinhardtia gracilis var. tenuissima
Roystonea dunlapiana
Roystonea regia
Sabal gretheriae
Sabal guatemalensis
Sabal mauritiiformis
Sabal mexicana
Sabal pumos
Sabal rosei
Sabal uresana
Sabal yapa
Synechanthus fibrosus
Thrinax radiata
Washingtonia filifera
Washingtonia robusta

NICARAGUA

Acoelorraphe wrightii
Acrocomia aculeata
Asterogyne martiana
Astrocaryum alatum
Astrocaryum mexicanum
Attalea butyracea
Bactris caudata
Bactris dianeura
Bactris gasipaes
Bactris gracilior
Bactris grayumi
Bactris guineensis
Bactris hondurensis
Bactris major var. major
Bactris mexicana

Brahea dulcis
Calyptrogyne ghiesbreghtiana
Chamaedorea costaricana
Chamaedorea oblongata
Chamaedorea pinnatifrons
Chamaedorea selvae
Chamaedorea tepejilote
Chamaedorea woodsoniana
Cocos nucifera
Cryosophila warscewiczii
Desmoncus orthacanthos
Elaeis oleifera
Euterpe precatoria var. longevaginata
Geonoma congesta
Geonoma cuneata var. cuneata
Geonoma deversa
Geonoma ferruginea
Geonoma interrupta var. interrupta
Geonoma jussieuana
Geonoma longevaginata
Geonoma orbignyana
Geonoma undata
Iriartea deltoidea
Manicaria saccifera
Neonicholsonia watsonii
Pholidostachys pulchra
Prestoea acuminata
Prestoea decurrens
Prestoea longepetiolata
Raphia taedigera
Reinhardtia gracilis var. gracilior
Reinhardtia gracilis var. gracilis
Reinhardtia gracilis var. rostrata
Reinhardtia koschyana
Reinhardtia latisecta
Reinhardtia simplex
Roystonea dunlapiana
Sabal mexicana
Socratea exorrhiza
Synechanthus fibrosus
Synechanthus warscewiczianus
Welfia regia

PANAMA

Acrocomia aculeata
Aiphanes hirsuta subsp. hirsuta
Asterogyne martiana
Astrocaryum alatum
Astrocaryum confertum
Astrocaryum standleyanum
Attalea allenii
Attalea butyracea
Attalea iguadummat

Bactris barronis
Bactris caudata
Bactris charnleyae
Bactris coloniata
Bactris coloradonis
Bactris dianeura
Bactris gasipaes
Bactris glandulosa var. baileyana
Bactris glandulosa var. glandulosa
Bactris gracilior
Bactris guineensis
Bactris hondurensis
Bactris kunorum
Bactris major var. major
Bactris maraja var. maraja
Bactris panamensis
Bactris pilosa
Calyptrogyne allenii
Calyptrogyne anomala
Calyptrogyne condensata
Calyptrogyne costatifrons
Calyptrogyne ghiesbreghtiana
Calyptrogyne kunaria
Calyptrogyne pubescens
Calyptrogyne trichostachys
Chamaedorea allenii
Chamaedorea amabilis
Chamaedorea brachyclada
Chamaedorea correae
Chamaedorea costaricana
Chamaedorea dammeriana
Chamaedorea deckeriana
Chamaedorea deneversiana
Chamaedorea guntheriana
Chamaedorea lucidifrons
Chamaedorea microphylla
Chamaedorea murriensis
Chamaedorea palmeriana
Chamaedorea pinnatifrons
Chamaedorea pittieri
Chamaedorea pygmaea
Chamaedorea robertii
Chamaedorea scheryi
Chamaedorea stricta
Chamaedorea sullivaniorum
Chamaedorea tepejilote
Chamaedorea verecunda
Chamaedorea warscewiczii
Chamaedorea woodsoniana
Cocos nucifera
Colpothrinax cookii
Cryosophila guagura
Cryosophila kalbreyeri
Cryosophila warscewiczii

Desmoncus orthacanthos
Dictyocaryum lamarckianum
Elaeis oleifera
Euterpe precatoria var. longevaginata
Geonoma chococola
Geonoma concinna
Geonoma congesta
Geonoma cuneata var. cuneata
Geonoma cuneata var. gracilis
Geonoma cuneata var. procumbens
Geonoma deversa
Geonoma divisa
Geonoma epetiolata
Geonoma ferruginea
Geonoma interrupta var. interrupta
Geonoma jussieuana
Geonoma longevaginata
Geonoma triandra
Hyospathe elegans
Iriartea deltoidea
Manicaria saccifera
Neonicholsonia watsonii
Oenocarpus bataua var. bataua
Oenocarpus mapora
Pholidostachys dactyloides
Pholidostachys kalbreyeri
Pholidostachys pulchra
Phytelephas seemannii
Prestoea acuminata
Prestoea decurrens
Prestoea ensiformis
Prestoea longepetiolata
Prestoea pubens var. semispicata
Prestoea roseospadix
Raphia taedigera
Reinhardtia koschnyana
Reinhardtia simplex
Sabal mauritiiformis
Socratea exorrhiza
Synechanthus warscewiczianus
Welfia regia
Wettinia aequalis
Wettinia panamensis
Wettinia radiata

PARAGUAY

Acrocomia aculeata
Acrocomia hassleri
Allagoptera campestris
Allagoptera leucocalyx
Attalea geraensis
Attalea phalerata
Bactris glaucescens

Butia campicola
Butia paraguayensis
Copernicia alba
Euterpe edulis
Geonoma brevispatha var. brevispatha
Syagrus campylospatha
Syagrus graminifolia
Syagrus oleracea
Syagrus petraea
Syagrus romanzoffiana
Trithrinax schizophylla

PERU

Aiphanes aculeata
Aiphanes deltoidea
Aiphanes spicata
Aiphanes ulei
Aiphanes weberbaueri
Aphandra natalia
Astrocaryum chambira
Astrocaryum huaimi
Astrocaryum jauari
Astrocaryum murumuru var. huincungo
Astrocaryum murumuru var. javarense
Astrocaryum murumuru var. macrocalyx
Astrocaryum murumuru var. murumuru
Astrocaryum murumuru var. perangustatum
Astrocaryum murumuru var. urostachys
Attalea butyracea
Attalea insignis
Attalea maripa
Attalea microcarpa
Attalea phalerata
Attalea racemosa
Attalea tessmannii
Bactris acanthocarpa var. acanthocarpa
Bactris bidentula
Bactris bifida
Bactris brongniartii
Bactris coloniata
Bactris concinna var. concinna
Bactris concinna var. inundata
Bactris concinna var. sigmoidea
Bactris corossilla
Bactris fissifrons
Bactris gasipaes
Bactris hirta var. hirta
Bactris hirta var. mollis
Bactris hirta var. pulchra
Bactris killipii
Bactris macana
Bactris macroacantha
Bactris maraja var. chaetospatha

Bactris maraja var. juruensis
Bactris maraja var. maraja
Bactris pliniana
Bactris riparia
Bactris simplicifrons
Bactris tomentosa var. sphaerocarpa
Ceroxylon parvifrons
Ceroxylon parvum
Ceroxylon vogelianum
Ceroxylon weberbaueri
Chamaedorea angustisecta
Chamaedorea fragrans
Chamaedorea linearis
Chamaedorea pauciflora
Chamaedorea pinnatifrons
Chelyocarpus repens
Chelyocarpus ulei
Desmoncus giganteus
Desmoncus mitis var. leptospadix
Desmoncus mitis var. mitis
Desmoncus mitis var. rurrenabaquensis
Desmoncus mitis var. tenerrimus
Desmoncus orthacanthos
Desmoncus polyacanthos var. polyacanthos
Desmoncus polyacanthos var. prunifer
Dictyocaryum lamarckianum
Dictyocaryum ptarianum
Elaeis oleifera
Euterpe catinga var. catinga
Euterpe catinga var. roraimae
Euterpe luminosa
Euterpe precatoria var. longevaginata
Euterpe precatoria var. precatoria
Geonoma arundinacea
Geonoma brevispatha var. occidentale
Geonoma brongniartii
Geonoma camana
Geonoma densa
Geonoma deversa
Geonoma interrupta var. interrupta
Geonoma jussieuana
Geonoma laxiflora
Geonoma leptospadix
Geonoma longepedunculata
Geonoma macrostachys var. acaulis
Geonoma macrostachys var. macrostachys
Geonoma maxima var. chelidonura
Geonoma maxima var. maxima
Geonoma orbignyana
Geonoma poeppigiana
Geonoma stricta var. piscicauda
Geonoma stricta var. stricta
Geonoma stricta var. trailii
Geonoma triglochin

Geonoma trigona
Geonoma undata
Geonoma weberbaueri
Hyospathe elegans
Iriartea deltoidea
Iriartella stenocarpa
Itaya amicorum
Lepidocaryum tenue var. *tenue*
Manicaria saccifera
Mauritia carana
Mauritia flexuosa
Mauritiella armata
Oenocarpus balickii
Oenocarpus bataua var. *bataua*
Oenocarpus mapora
Pholidostachys synanthera
Phytelephas macrocarpa
Phytelephas tenuicaulis
Prestoea acuminata
Prestoea carderi
Prestoea ensiformis
Prestoea schultzeana
Socratea exorrhiza
Socratea salazarii
Syagrus sancona
Syagrus smithii
Welfia sp.
Wendlandiella gracilis var. *gracilis*
Wendlandiella gracilis var. *polyclada*
Wendlandiella gracilis var. *simplicifrons*
Wettinia augusta
Wettinia drudei
Wettinia longipetala
Wettinia maynensis

PUERTO RICO

Aiphanes minima
Calyptronoma rivalis
Coccothrinax barbadensis
Cocos nucifera
Gaussia attenuata
Prestoea acuminata
Roystonea borinquena
Sabal causiarum
Thrinax morrisii

SURINAME

Acrocomia aculeata
Astrocaryum aculeatum
Astrocaryum gynacanthum
Astrocaryum jauari

Astrocaryum murumuru var. *murumuru*
Astrocaryum sciophilum
Astrocaryum paramaca
Astrocaryum vulgare
Attalea attaleoides
Attalea dahlgreniana
Attalea maripa
Attalea microcarpa
Attalea speciosa
Bactris acanthocarpa var. *intermedia*
Bactris acanthocarpoides
Bactris aubletiana
Bactris brongniartii
Bactris campestris
Bactris constanciae
Bactris elegans
Bactris gasipaes
Bactris gastoniana
Bactris hirta var. *hirta*
Bactris major var. *infesta*
Bactris major var. *major*
Bactris maraja var. *maraja*
Bactris oligocarpa
Bactris pliniana
Bactris rhapidacantha
Bactris simplicifrons
Bactris turbinocarpa
Cocos nucifera
Desmoncus orthacanthos
Desmoncus phoenicocarpus
Desmoncus polyacanthos var. *polyacanthos*
Elaeis oleifera
Euterpe oleracea
Euterpe precatoria var. *precatoria*
Geonoma appuniana
Geonoma baculifera
Geonoma deversa
Geonoma interrupta var. *euspatha*
Geonoma interrupta var. *interrupta*
Geonoma leptospadix
Geonoma macrostachys var. *poiteauana*
Geonoma maxima var. *ambigua*
Geonoma stricta var. *stricta*
Geonoma umbraculiformis
Hyospathe elegans
Manicaria saccifera
Mauritia flexuosa
Mauritiella armata
Oenocarpus bacaba
Oenocarpus bataua var. *oligocarpa*
Socratea exorrhiza
Syagrus inajai
Syagrus stratincola

TRINIDAD AND TOBAGO

Acrocomia aculeata
Aiphanes aculeata
Astrocaryum aculeatum
Attalea butyracea
Attalea maripa
Bactris campestris
Bactris gasipaes
Bactris major var. *infesta*
Bactris major var. *major*
Bactris major var. *megalocarpa*
Bactris setulosa
Bactris simplicifrons
Coccothrinax barbadensis
Cocos nucifera
Desmoncus orthacanthos
Desmoncus polyacanthos
Euterpe broadwayi
Euterpe oleracea
Euterpe precatoria var. *longevaginata*
Geonoma interrupta var. *interrupta*
Manicaria saccifera
Mauritia flexuosa
Oenocarpus bataua var. *oligocarpa*
Prestoea acuminata
Prestoea pubigera
Roystonea oleracea
Sabal mauritiiformis

UNITED STATES

Acoelorraphe wrightii
Coccothrinax argentata
Pseudophoenix sargentii subsp. *sargentii*
Rhapidophyllum hystrix
Roystonea regia
Sabal etonia
Sabal mexicana
Sabal miamiensis
Sabal minor
Sabal palmetto
Serenoa repens
Thrinax morrisii
Thrinax radiata
Washingtonia filifera

URUGUAY

Butia capitata
Butia paraguayensis
Butia yatay
Syagrus romanzoffiana
Trithrinax campestris

VENEZUELA

Acrocomia aculeata
Aiphanes aculeata
Asterogyne ramosa
Asterogyne spicata
Asterogyne yaracuyense
Astrocaryum acaule
Astrocaryum aculeatum
Astrocaryum chambira
Astrocaryum gynacanthum
Astrocaryum jauari
Astrocaryum murumuru var. *murumuru*
Attalea butyracea
Attalea luetzelburgii
Attalea maripa
Attalea microcarpa
Attalea racemosa
Bactris acanthocarpa var. *acanthocarpa*
Bactris balanophora
Bactris bidentula
Bactris brongniartii
Bactris campestris
Bactris corossilla
Bactris gasipaes
Bactris guineensis
Bactris hirta var. *hirta*
Bactris macana
Bactris major var. *infesta*
Bactris major var. *major*
Bactris major var. *megalocarpa*
Bactris maraja var. *maraja*
Bactris oligoclada
Bactris pilosa
Bactris ptariana
Bactris setulosa
Bactris simplicifrons
Bactris trailiana
Ceroxylon alpinum subsp. *alpinum*
Ceroxylon ceriferum
Ceroxylon parvifrons
Ceroxylon vogelianum
Chamaedorea linearis
Chamaedorea pinnatifrons
Coccothrinax barbadensis
Cocos nucifera
Copernicia tectorum
Desmoncus mitis var. *mitis*
Desmoncus orthacanthos
Desmoncus phoenicocarpus
Desmoncus polyacanthos var. *polyacanthos*
Dictyocaryum fuscum
Dictyocaryum lamarckianum
Dictyocaryum ptarianum

Euterpe catinga var. *catinga*
Euterpe catinga var. *roraimae*
Euterpe longebracteata
Euterpe oleracea
Euterpe precatoria var. *longevaginata*
Euterpe precatoria var. *precatoria*
Geonoma appuniana
Geonoma baculifera
Geonoma densa
Geonoma deversa
Geonoma interrupta var. *euspatha*
Geonoma interrupta var. *interrupta*
Geonoma jussieuana
Geonoma leptospadix
Geonoma macrostachys var. *acaulis*
Geonoma macrostachys var. *poiteauana*
Geonoma maxima var. *ambigua*
Geonoma maxima var. *chelidonura*
Geonoma maxima var. *maxima*
Geonoma oligoclona
Geonoma orbignyana
Geonoma paraguanensis
Geonoma simplicifrons
Geonoma spinescens
Geonoma stricta var. *stricta*
Geonoma undata
Geonoma weberbaueri

Hyospathe elegans
Iriartea deltoidea
Iriartella setigera
Leopoldinia major
Leopoldinia piassaba
Leopoldinia pulchra
Lepidocaryum tenue var. *casquiarense*
Manicaria saccifera
Mauritia carana
Mauritia flexuosa
Mauritiella aculeata
Mauritiella armata
Oenocarpus bacaba
Oenocarpus balickii
Oenocarpus bataua var. *bataua*
Oenocarpus bataua var. *oligocarpa*
Oenocarpus mapora
Prestoea acuminata
Prestoea carderi
Prestoea pubigera
Prestoea tenuiramosa
Roystonea oleracea
Sabal mauritiiformis
Socratea exorrhiza
Syagrus orinocensis
Syagrus sancona
Wettinia praemorsa

APPENDIX II

LIST OF ACCEPTED NAMES, SYNONYMS, HYBRIDS, AND UNCERTAIN NAMES

Accepted generic names are capitalized, bold face, and in alphabetical order, followed by generic synonyms. Accepted species are also in bold face and alphabetical order, and are followed by their synonyms. Each name is followed by its author, using abbreviations in Brummitt and Powell (1992). When "hort." precedes an author of a name it means that the name was first used in a horticultural publication (plant catalogs, etc.), and later validly published by that author. If a name is followed by "auct." it means that the name has been misapplied. When a synonym is preceded by a question mark it means that the name is doubtfully placed. Named hybrids, and their parents, are listed at the end of each genus, followed by uncertain names.

ACOELORRAPHE H. Wendl.
  Acanthosabal Prosch.
  Paurotis O. F. Cook
Acoelorraphe wrightii (Griseb. & H. Wendl.) H. Wendl. ex Becc.
  Acanthosabal caespitosa Prosch.
  Acoelorraphe arborescens (Sarg.) Becc.
  Acoelorraphe pinetorum Bartlett
  Acoelorraphe wrightii var. *geronensis* Becc.
  Brahea psilocalyx Burret
  Copernicia wrightii Griseb. & H. Wendl. ex Griseb.
  Paurotis androsana O. F. Cook
  Paurotis arborescens (Sarg.) O. F. Cook
  Paurotis psilocalyx (Burret) Lundell
  ?Paurotis schipii (Burret)
  Paurotis wrightii (Griseb. & H. Wendl.) Britton ex Britton & Schafer
  Serenoa arborescens Sarg.

ACROCOMIA Mart.
  Acanthococos Barb. Rodr.
Acrocomia aculeata (Jacq.) Lodd. ex Mart.
  Acrocomia antiguana L. H. Bailey
  Acrocomia antioquiensis Posada-Ar.
  Acrocomia belizensis L. H. Bailey
  Acrocomia christopherensis L. H. Bailey
  Acrocomia chunta Covas & Ragonese
  Acrocomia erioacantha Barb. Rodr.
  Acrocomia fusiformis (Sw.) Sweet
  Acrocomia glaucophylla Drude
  Acrocomia grenadana L. H. Bailey
  Acrocomia hospes L. H. Bailey
  Acrocomia ierensis L. H. Bailey

  Acrocomia intumescens Drude
  Acrocomia karukerana L. H. Bailey
  Acrocomia lasiospatha Mart.
  Acrocomia lasiospatha of Wallace
  Acrocomia media O. F. Cook
  Acrocomia mexicana Karw. ex Mart.
  Acrocomia microcarpa Barb. Rodr.
  Acrocomia mokayayba Barb. Rodr.
  Acrocomia odorata Barb. Rodr.
  Acrocomia panamensis L. H. Bailey
  Acrocomia pilosa León
  Acrocomia quisqueyana L. H. Bailey
  Acrocomia sclerocarpa Mart.
  Acrocomia sclerocarpa var. *wallaceana* Drude
  Acrocomia sclerocarpa of Bello y Espinosa
  Acrocomia spinosa (Mill.) H. E. Moore
  Acrocomia subinermis León ex L. H. Bailey
  Acrocomia totai Mart.
  Acrocomia ulei Dammer
  Acrocomia viegasii L. H. Bailey
  Acrocomia vinifera Oerst.
  Acrocomia wallaceana Becc.
  Bactris globosa Gaertn.
  Cocos aculeatus Jacq.
  Cocos fusiformis Sw.
  Palma spinosa Mill.
Acrocomia hassleri (Barb. Rodr.) Hahn
  Acanthococos emensis Toledo
  Acanthococos emensis var. *pubifolia* Toledo
  Acanthococos hassleri Barb. Rodr.
  Acanthococos sericea Burret

UNCERTAIN NAMES
  Acrocomia cubensis Lodd. ex H. Wendl.
  Acrocomia guianensis Lodd. ex G. Don

Acrocomia globosa Lodd. ex Mart.
Acrocomia horrida Lodd. ex Mart.
Acrocomia minor Lodd. ex G. Don
Acrocomia sphaerocarpa Desf.
Acrocomia tenuifrons Lodd. ex Mart.
Acrocomia zapotecis Karw. ex H. Wendl.

AIPHANES Willd.
  Curima O. F. Cook
  Marara H. Karst.
  Martinezia auct.
  Tilmia O. F. Cook
Aiphanes acaulis Galeano & R. Bernal
Aiphanes aculeata Willd.
  Aiphanes caryotifolia (Kunth) H. Wendl.
  Aiphanes elegans (Linden & H. Wendl.) H.
    Wendl.
  Aiphanes ernestii (Burret) Burret
  Aiphanes horrida (Jacq.) Burret
  Aiphanes killipii (Burret) Burret
  Aiphanes orinocensis Burret
  Aiphanes praemorsa (Poepp. ex Mart.)
    Burret
  Aiphanes truncata (Brongniart ex Mart.) H.
    Wendl.
  Bactris praemorsa Poepp. ex Mart.
  Caryota horrida Jacq.
  Euterpe aculeata (Willd.) Spreng.
  Marara aculeata (Willd.) H. Karst.
  Marara bicuspidata H. Karst.
  Marara caryotifolia (Kunth) H. Karst.
  Martinezia aculeata (Willd.) Klotzsch
  Martinezia aiphanes Mart.
  Martinezia caryotifolia Kunth
  Martinezia elegans Linden & H. Wendl.
  Martinezia ernestii Burret
  Martinezia killipii Burret
  Martinezia truncata Brongniart ex Mart.
  Tilmia caryotifolia (Kunth) O. F. Cook
Aiphanes chiribogensis Borchsenius &
  Balslev
Aiphanes deltoidea Burret
Aiphanes duquei Burret
Aiphanes eggersii Burret
Aiphanes erinacea (H. Karst.) H. Wendl.
  Marara erinacea H. Karst.
Aiphanes gelatinosa H. E. Moore
Aiphanes grandis Borchsenius & Balslev
Aiphanes hirsuta Burret
Aiphanes hirsuta subsp. **fosteriorum** (H. E.
  Moore) Borchsenius & R. Bernal
  Aiphanes fosteriorum H. E. Moore
Aiphanes hirsuta subsp. **hirsuta**
  Aiphanes fuscopubens L. H. Bailey

Aiphanes monostachys Burret
Aiphanes pachyclada Burret
Aiphanes hirsuta subsp. **intermedia**
  Borchsenius & R. Bernal
Aiphanes hirsuta subsp. **kalbreyeri** (Burret)
  Borchsenius & R. Bernal
  Aiphanes kalbreyeri Burret
Aiphanes leiostachys Burret
Aiphanes lindeniana (H. Wendl.) H. Wendl.
  Aiphanes concinna H. E. Moore
  Martinezia lindeniana H. Wendl.
Aiphanes linearis Burret
  Aiphanes echinocarpa Dugand
Aiphanes macroloba Burret
  Aiphanes chocoensis A. H. Gentry
  Aiphanes monostachys Burret
Aiphanes minima (Gaertn.) Burret
  Aiphanes acanthophylla (Mart.) Burret
  Aiphanes corallina (Mart.) H. Wendl.
  Aiphanes erosa (Linden) Burret
  Aiphanes luciana L. H. Bailey
  Aiphanes vincentiana L. H. Bailey
  Bactris acanthophylla Mart.
  Bactris erosa Mart.
  Bactris minima Gaertn.
  Curima colophylla O. F. Cook
  Curima corallina (Mart.) O. F. Cook
  Martinezia acanthophylla (Mart.) Burret
  Martinezia corallina Mart.
  Martinezia erosa Linden
Aiphanes parvifolia Burret
Aiphanes simplex Burret
Aiphanes spicata Borchsenius & R. Bernal
Aiphanes tricuspidata Borchsenius, R.
  Bernal & Ruiz
Aiphanes ulei (Dammer) Burret
  Aiphanes schultzeana Burret
  Martinezia ulei Dammer
Aiphanes verrucosa Borchsenius & Balslev
Aiphanes weberbaueri Burret
  Aiphanes tessmannii Burret

UNCERTAIN NAMES
  Aiphanes caryotides Blatter
  Aiphanes disticha (Linden) Burret
  Aiphanes gracilis Burret
  Aiphanes leiospatha Burret
  Martinezia abrupta Ruiz & Pav.
  Martinezia antiochensis Linden
  Martinezia disticha Linden
  Martinezia disticha Wallis ex Regel
  Martinezia granatensis H. Wendl.
  Martinezia leucophaeus hort.
  Martinezia minor Linden

Martinezia roezlii hort.
Martinezia ulei Dammer
Tilmia disticha (Linden) O. F. Cook

ALLAGOPTERA Nees
Diplothemium Mart.
Allagoptera arenaria (Gomes) Kuntze
Allagoptera littorale (Mart.) Kuntze
Allagoptera pumila Nees
Cocos arenaria Gomes
Diplothemium arenarium (Gomes) Vasc.
Diplothemium littorale Mart.
Diplothemium maritimum Mart.
Allagoptera brevicalyx Moraes
Allagoptera campestris (Mart.) Kuntze
Diplothemium campestre Mart.
Diplothemium campestre var. *genuinum* Drude
Diplothemium campestre var. *glaziovii* Dammer
Allagoptera leucocalyx (Mart.) Kuntze
Allagoptera anisitsii (Barb. Rodr.) H. E. Moore
Allagoptera campestris var. *orbignyi* (Drude) Kuntze
Allagoptera hassleriana (Barb. Rodr.) H. E. Moore
Diplothemium anisitsii Barb. Rodr.
Diplothemium campestre var. *orbignyi* Drude
Diplothemium hasslerianum Barb. Rodr.
Diplothemium jangadense S. Moore
Diplothemium leucocalyx Drude

UNCERTAIN NAMES
Diplothemium glaucescens W. Wats
Diplothemium henryanum Forest Brown

AMMANDRA O. F. Cook
Ammandra dasyneura (Burret) Barfod
Phytelephas dasyneura Burret
Ammandra decasperma O. F. Cook
Phytelephas decasperma (O. F. Cook) Dahlgren

APHANDRA Barfod
Aphandra natalia (Balslev & Henderson) Barfod
Ammandra natalia Balslev & Henderson

ASTEROGYNE H. Wendl. ex Hook. f.
Aristeyera H. E. Moore
Asterogyne guianensis Granv. & Henderson
Asterogyne martiana (H. Wendl.) H. Wendl. ex Hemsl.
Asterogyne minor Burret

Geonoma martiana H. Wendl.
Geonoma trifurcata Oerst.
Asterogyne ramosa (H. E. Moore) Wess. Boer
Aristeyera ramosa H. E. Moore
Asterogyne spicata (H. E. Moore) Wess. Boer
Aristeyera spicata H. E. Moore
Asterogyne yaracuyense Henderson & Steyerm.

ASTROCARYUM G. Mey.
Avoira Giseke
Hexopetion Burret
Toxophoenix Schott
Astrocaryum acaule Mart.
Astrocaryum giganteum Barb. Rodr.
Astrocaryum huebneri Burret
Astrocaryum luetzelburgii Burret
Astrocaryum aculeatissimum (Schott) Burret
Astrocaryum ayri Mart.
Toxophoenix aculeatissimum Schott
Astrocaryum aculeatum G. Mey.
Astrocaryum aureum Griseb.
Astrocaryum caudescens Barb. Rodr.
Astrocaryum macrocarpum Huber
Astrocaryum manoense Barb. Rodr.
Astrocaryum princeps Barb. Rodr.
Astrocaryum princeps var. *aurantiacum* Barb. Rodr.
Astrocaryum princeps var. *flavum* Barb. Rodr.
Astrocaryum princeps var. *sulphureum* Barb. Rodr.
Astrocaryum princeps var. *vitellinum* Barb. Rodr.
Astrocaryum tucuma Mart.
Astrocaryum alatum Loomis
Astrocaryum campestre Mart.
Astrocaryum chambira Burret
Astrocaryum vulgare of Wallace
Astrocaryum confertum H. Wendl. ex Burret
Astrocaryum polystachyum H. Wendl.
Astrocaryum gynacanthum Mart.
Astrocaryum gymopus Burret
Astrocaryum gynacanthum var. *dasychaetum* Burret
Astrocaryum gynacanthum var. *munbaca* Trail
Astrocaryum minus Trail
Astrocaryum minus var. *terrafirme* Drude
Astrocaryum munbaca Mart.
Astrocaryum rodriguesii var. *minus* (Trail) Barb. Rodr.
Astrocaryum vulgare of Warburg.

Astrocaryum huaimi Mart.
Astrocaryum huaimi var. *orbignyi* Drude
Astrocaryum leiospatha Barb. Rodr.
Astrocaryum leiospatha var. *sabulosum* Barb.
   Rodr.
Astrocaryum jauari Mart.
Astrocaryum guara Burret
Astrocaryum malybo H. Karst.
Astrocaryum mexicanum Liebm. ex Mart.
Astrocaryum ayri hort. ex Warburg
Astrocaryum cohune (Watson) Standl.
Astrocaryum rostratum Hook. f.
Astrocaryum warscwiczii Koch & Fint.
Bactris cohune Watson
Hexopetion mexicanum (Liebm. ex Mart.)
   Burret
Astrocaryum murumuru Mart.
Astrocaryum murumuru var. **ciliatum** (Kahn
   & Millán) Henderson
Astrocaryum ciliatum Kahn & Millán
Astrocaryum murumuru var. **ferrugineum**
   (Kahn & Millán) Henderson
Astrocaryum ferrugineum Kahn & Millán
Astrocaryum murumuru var. **huincungo**
   (Kahn & Millán) Henderson
Astrocaryum carnosum Kahn & Millán
Astrocaryum huicungo Dammer ex Burret
Astrocaryum scopatum Kahn & Millán
Astrocaryum murumuru var. **javarense**
   (Kahn & Millán) Henderson
Astrocaryum horridum Barb. Rodr.
Astrocaryum javarense (Trail) Drude
Astrocaryum paramaca var. *javarense* Trail
Astrocaryum murumuru var. **macrocalyx**
   (Kahn & Millán) Henderson
Astrocaryum cuatrecasanum Dugand
Astrocaryum macrocalyx Burret
Astrocaryum murumuru var. **murumuru**
Astrocaryum chonta Mart.
Astrocaryum gratum Kahn & Millán
Astrocaryum ulei Burret

Astrocaryum murumuru var. **perangustatum**
   (Kahn & Millán) Henderson
Astrocaryum perangustatum Kahn &
   Millán
Astrocaryum murumuru var. **urostachys**
   (Kahn & Millán) Henderson
Astrocaryum urostachys Burret
Astrocaryum paramaca Mart.
Astrocaryum acanthopodium Barb. Rodr.
Astrocaryum aculeatum of Barb. Rodr.
Astrocaryum paramaca var. *platyacantha*
   Drude

Astrocaryum rodriguesii Trail
Bactris paraensis Splitg. ex de Vriese
Astrocaryum sciophilum (Miq.) Pulle
Astrocaryum farinosum Barb. Rodr.
Astrocaryum plicatum Drude
Astrocaryum sociale Barb. Rodr.
Bactris sciophila Miq.
Astrocaryum standleyanum L. H. Bailey
Astrocaryum standleyanum var. *calimense*
   Dugand
Astrocaryum triandrum Galeano, R. Bernal
   & Kahn
Astrocaryum vulgare Mart.
Astrocaryum awarra de Vriese
Astrocaryum guianense Splitg. ex Mart.
Astrocaryum segregatum Drude
Astrocaryum tucuma of Wallace
Astrocaryum tucumoides Drude

UNCERTAIN NAMES
Astrocaryum argenteum hort.
Astrocaryum borsigianum Koch
Astrocaryum burity Barb. Rodr.
Astrocaryum chichon Linden
Astrocaryum echinatum Barb. Rodr.
Astrocaryum filare hort.
Astrocaryum flexuosum hort. ex H. Wendl.
Astrocaryum iriartoides Willis ex Regel
Astrocaryum jucuma Linden
Astrocaryum kewense Barb. Rodr.
Astrocaryum panamense Linden
Astrocaryum pictum hort.
Astrocaryum pumilum hort. ex H. Wendl.
Astrocaryum pygmaeum Drude
Astrocaryum sclerocarpum hort. ex H. Wendl.
Astrocaryum sclerophyllum Drude
Astrocaryum sechellarum hort. ex Baill.
Astrocaryum tenuifolium Linden
Astrocaryum trachycarpum Burret
Astrocaryum warszewiczii H. Karst.
Astrocaryum weddellii Drude
Avoira vulgaris Giseke

ATTALEA Kunth
Englerophoenix Kuntze
Lithocarpos O. Targ. Tozz.
Maximiliana Mart.
Orbignya Mart. ex Endl.
Parascheelea Dugand
Pindarea Barb. Rodr.
Sarinia O. F. Cook
Scheelea H. Karst.
Ynesa O. F. Cook

Attalea allenii H. E. Moore
Attalea amygdalina Kunth
  Attalea uberrima Dugand
  Attalea victoriana Dugand
Attalea attaleoides (Barb. Rodr.) Wess.
  Boer
  Attalea transitiva Barb. Rodr.
  Englerophoenix attaleoides (Barb. Rodr.)
    Barb. Rodr.
  Maximiliana attaleoides Barb. Rodr.
Attalea butyracea (Mutis ex L. f.) Wess.
  Boer
  Attalea cephalotes Poepp. ex Mart.
  ?Attalea gomphococca Mart.
  Attalea humboldtiana Spruce
  ?Attalea macrocarpa (Karst.) Burret
  Attalea macrolepis (Burret) Wess. Boer
  Attalea maracaibensis Mart.
  Attalea osmantha (Barb. Rodr.) Wess. Boer.
  Attalea pycnocarpa Wess. Boer
  Attalea rostrata Oersted
  Attalea wallisii Huber
  Cocos butyracea Mutis ex L. f.
  Cocos regia Liebm. ex Mart.
  Scheelea bassleriana Burret
  Scheelea brachyclada Burret
  Scheelea butyracea (Mutis ex L. f.) H. Karst.
    ex H. Wendl.
  Scheelea cephalotes (Poepp. ex Mart.) H.
    Karst.
  Scheelea costaricensis Burret
  Scheelea curvifrons L. H. Bailey
  Scheelea dryanderae Burret
  Scheelea excelsa H. Karst.
  ?Scheelea gomphococca (Mart.) Burret
  Scheelea huebneri Burret
  Scheelea humboldtiana (Spruce) Burret
  ?Scheelea kewensis Hook. f.
  Scheelea liebmannii Becc.
  Scheelea lundellii Bartlett
  ?Scheelea macrocarpa H. Karst.
  Scheelea macrolepis Burret
  Scheelea magdalenica Dugand
  Scheelea maracaibensis (Mart.) Burret
  Scheelea osmantha Barb. Rodr.
  Scheelea passargei Burret
  Scheelea preussii Burret
  Scheelea regia H. Karst.
  Scheelea rostrata (Oerst.) Burret
  Scheelea stenorhyncha Burret
  Scheelea tessmannii Burret

  Scheelea urbaniana Burret
  Scheelea wallisii (Huber) Burret
  Scheelea zonensis L. H. Bailey
Attalea cohune Mart.
  Cocos cocoyule Mart.
  Cocos guacuyule Liebm. ex Mart.
  Orbignya cohune (Mart.) Dahlgren ex
    Standl.
  Orbignya dammeriana Barb. Rodr.
  Orbignya guacuyule (Liebm. ex Mart.) E.
    Hern.
Attalea colenda (O. F. Cook) Balslev &
  Henderson
  Ynesa colenda O. F. Cook
Attalea crassispatha (Mart.) Burret
  Bornoa crassispatha O. F. Cook
  Cocos crassispatha Mart.
  Maximiliana crassispatha Mart.
Attalea cuatrecasana comb. nov.*
  Orbignya cuatrecasana Dugand
Attalea dahlgreniana (Bondar) Wess. Boer
  Markleya dahlgreniana Bondar
Attalea dubia (Mart.) Burret
  Attalea concinna (Barb. Rodr.) Burret
  Attalea indaya Drude
  Orbignya dubia Mart.
  Pindarea concinna Barb. Rodr.
  Pindarea dubia (Mart.) A. D. Hawkes
  Pindarea fastuosa Barb. Rodr.
Attalea eichleri (Drude) Henderson
  Orbignya campestris Barb. Rodr.
  Orbignya eichleri Drude
  Orbignya humilis Mart.
  Orbignya longibracteata Barb. Rodr.
  Orbignya macrocarpa Barb. Rodr.
  Orbignya teixeirana Bondar
  ?Orbignya urbaniana Dammer
Attalea exigua Drude
Attalea funifera Mart. ex Spreng.
  Attalea acaulis Burret
  Attalea funifera var. *acaulis* (Burret) Burret
  Lithocarpus cocciformis O. Targ. Tozz.
  Sarinia funifera (Mart. ex Spreng.) O. F.
    Cook
Attalea geraensis Barb. Rodr.
  Attalea guaranitica Barb. Rodr.
  Attalea monogyna Burret
Attalea humilis Mart. ex Spreng.
  Attalea borgesiana Bondar ex Dahlgren
  Attalea borgesiana of A. D. Hawkes
  Attalea compta var. *acaulis* Mart.

---

* *Attalea cuatrecasana* comb. nov. *Orbignya cuatrecasana* Dugand, Caldasia 2:285. 1943.
Type. Colombia. Valle: Río Naya, Feb 1943, *J. Cuatrecasas 13980* (holotype, COL).

Attalea iguadummat Nevers
Attalea insignis (Mart.) Drude
  Attalea goeldiana Huber
  Englerophoenix insignis (Mart.) Kuntze
  Maximiliana insignis Mart.
  Scheelea attaleoides H. Karst.
  Scheelea goeldiana (Huber) Burret
  Scheelea insignis (Mart.) H. Karst.
Attalea luetzelburgii (Burret) Wess. Boer
  Orbignya luetzelburgii Burret
  Parascheelea anchistropetala Dugand
  Parascheelea luetzelburgii (Burret) Duganc
Attalea maripa (Aubl.) Mart.
  Attalea cryptanthera Wess. Boer
  Attalea macropetala (Burret) Wess. Boer
  Attalea maripa (Corrêa) Mart.
  Attalea regia (Mart.) Wess. Boer
  Englerophoenix caribaea (Griseb. & H. Wendl. ex Griseb.) Kuntze
  Englerophoenix longirostrata (Barb. Rodr.) Barb. Rodr.
  Englerophoenix maripa (Corrêa) Kuntze
  Englerophoenix regia (Mart.) Kuntze
  Englerophoenix tetrasticha (Drude) Barb. Rodr.
  Maximiliana caribaea Griseb. & H. Wend ex Griseb.
  Maximiliana elegans H. Karst.
  Maximiliana longirostrata Barb. Rodr.
  Maximiliana macrogyne Burret
  Maximiliana macropetala (Burret) Wess. Boer
  Maximiliana maripa (Aubl.) Drude
  Maximiliana maripa (Corrêa) Drude
  Maximiliana martiana H. Karst.
  Maximiliana regia Mart.
  Maximiliana stenocarpa Burret
  Maximiliana tetrasticha Drude
  Palma maripa Aubl.
  Palma maripa Corrêa
  Scheelea tetrasticha (Drude) Burret
Attalea microcarpa Mart.
  Attalea agrestis Barb. Rodr.
  Attalea polysticha (Burret) Wess. Boer
  Attalea sagotii (Trail) Wess. Boer
  Orbignya agrestis (Barb. Rodr.) Burret
  Orbignya microcarpa (Mart.) Burret
  Orbignya polysticha Burret
  Orbignya sabulosa Barb. Rodr.
  Orbignya sagotii Trail ex Thurn
Attalea nucifera H. Karst.
Attalea oleifera Barb. Rodr.
  Attalea burretiana Bondar
  Attalea compta Mart.
  Attalea concentrista Bondar

Attalea phalerata Mart. ex Spreng.
  Attalea excelsa Mart. ex Spreng.
  Attalea parviflora Barb. Rodr.
  Attalea princeps Mart.
  Scheelea amylacea Barb. Rodr.
  Scheelea anisitsiana Barb. Rodr.
  Scheelea corumbaensis (Barb. Rodr.) Barb. Rodr.
  Scheelea lauromuelleriana Barb. Rodr.
  Scheelea leandroana Barb. Rodr.
  Scheelea martiana Burret
  Scheelea microspadix Burret
  Scheelea parviflora (Barb. Rodr.) Barb. Rodr.
  Scheelea phalerata (Mart. ex Spreng.) Burret
  Scheelea princeps (Mart.) H. Karst.
  Scheelea princeps var. *corumbaensis* Barb. Rodr.
  Scheelea quadrisperma Barb. Rodr.
  Scheelea quadrisulcata Barb. Rodr.
  Scheelea weberbaueri Burret
Attalea pindobassu Bondar
Attalea racemosa Spruce
  Attalea ferruginea Burret
  Orbignya racemosa (Spruce) Drude
Attalea septuagenata Dugand
Attalea speciosa Mart. ex Spreng.
  Attalea apoda Burret
  Attalea camposportoana Burret
  Attalea lydiae (Drude) Barb. Rodr.
  Attalea pixuna Barb. Rodr.
  Attalea spectabilis var. *polyandra* Drude
  Orbignya barbosiana Burret
  Orbignya huebneri Burret
  Orbignya lydiae Drude
  Orbignya macropetala Burret
  Orbignya martiana Barb. Rodr.
  Orbignya oleifera Burret
  Orbignya phalerata Mart.
  Orbignya pixuna (Barb. Rodr.) Barb. Rodr.
  Orbignya speciosa (Mart.) Barb. Rodr.
Attalea spectabilis Mart.
  Attalea monosperma Barb. Rodr.
  Attalea spectabilis var. *monosperma* (Barb. Rodr.) Drude
  Attalea spectabilis var. *typica* Drude
  Orbignya spectabilis (Mart.) Burret
Attalea tessmannii Burret

HYBRIDS
  x *Attabignya minarum* Balick, Anderson & Medeiros-Costa (*A. compta* x *A. oleifera*)
  Attalea piassabossu Bondar (*A. funifera* x *A. oleifera*)

Attalea x *voeksii* Noblick (*A. funifera* x *A. humilis*)

Orbignya x *teixeirana* (Bondar) Balick, Pinherio & Anderson (*A. eichleri* x *A. speciosa*)

UNCERTAIN NAMES
Attalea blepharopus Mart.
Attalea boehmei Drude
Attalea butyrosa Lodd. ex H. A. Wendl.
Attalea ceraensis Barb. Rodr.
Attalea coronata Lodd. ex H. Wendl.
Attalea grandis hort. ex H. A. Wendl.
Attalea hoehnei Burret
Attalea lapidea (Gaertn.) Burret
Attalea limbata Seem. ex H. Wendl.
Attalea macoupi Sagot ex Drude
Attalea magdalenae Linden
Attalea manaca Linden
Attalea purpurea Linden
Attalea puruensis Linden
Attalea rhynchocarpa Burret
Attalea rossii Lodd. ex Loud.
Attalea spinosa Meyen
Attalea tiasse Linden
Attalea venatorum Mart.
Cocos lapidea Gaertn.
Maximiliana argentinensis Speg.
Maximiliana jagua Seeman ex H. Wendl.
Maximiliana orenocensis Speg.
Maximiliana panamensis Linden
Maximiliana princeps Mart.
Maximiliana spiralis Linden
Maximiliana venatorum H. Wendl.
Orbignya cuci Kunth ex H. Wendl.
Orbignya macrostachya Drude ex Barb. Rodr.
Scheelea blepharopus (Mart.) Burret
Scheelea cubensis Burret
Scheelea dubia Burret
Scheelea imperialis hort.
Scheelea maripa hort. ex. H. Wendl.
Scheelea unguis Nichols.

BACTRIS Jacq. ex Scop.
Amylocarpus Barb. Rodr.
Augustinea H. Karst.
Guilielma Mart.
Pyrenoglyphis H. Karst.
Yuyba L. H. Bailey
Bactris acanthocarpa Mart.
Bactris acanthocarpa var. **acanthocarpa**
Astrocaryum humile Wallace
Bactris acanthocarpa Mart.
Bactris acanthocarpa var. *excapa* Barb. Rodr.

Bactris aculeifera Drude
Bactris bicuspidata Spruce
Bactris devia Burret
Bactris exscapa (Barb. Rodr.) Barb. Rodr.
Bactris humilis (Wallace) Burret
Bactris interruptepinnata Barb. Rodr.
Bactris leptochaete Burret
Bactris macrocalyx Burret
Bactris microcalyx Burret
Bactris mindellii Barb. Rodr.
Bactris pinnatisecta Burret
Bactris tarumanensis Barb. Rodr.
Pyrenoglyphis bicuspidata (Spruce) Burret
Bactris acanthocarpa var. **intermedia** Henderson
Bactris acanthocarpoides Barb. Rodr.
Bactris acanthocarpa var. *crispata* Drude
Bactris aubletiana Trail
Bactris bahiensis Noblick
Bactris balanophora Spruce
Astrocaryum aculeatum Wallace
Bactris barronis L. H. Bailey
Bactris bidentula Spruce
Bactris nigrispina Barb. Rodr.
Bactris palustris Barb. Rodr.
Bactris bifida Mart.
Bactris bifida var. *humaitensis* Trail
Bactris bifida var. *puruensis* Trail
Pyrenoglyphis bifida (Mart.) Burret
Pyrenoglyphis bifida var. *humaitensis* (Trail) Burret
Pyrenoglyphis bifida var. *puruensis* (Trail) Burret
Bactris brongniartii Mart.
Bactris burretii Glassman
Bactris marajaacu Barb. Rodr.
Bactris pallidispina Mart.
Bactris piscatorum Wedd. ex Drude
Bactris rivularis Barb. Rodr.
Bactris tenera (H. Karst.) H. Wendl.
Guilielma tenera H. Karst.
Pyrenoglyphis brongniartii (Mart.) Burret
Pyrenoglyphis microcarpa Burret
Pyrenoglyphis pallidispina (Mart.) Burret
Pyrenoglyphis piscatorum (Wedd. ex Drude) Burret
Pyrenoglyphis tenera (H. Karst.) Burret
Bactris campestris Poepp. ex Mart.
Bactris lanceolata Burret
Bactris leptocarpa Trail
Bactris savannarum Britton
Bactris caryotifolia Mart.
Bactris caudata H. Wendl. ex Burret
Bactris dasychaeta Burret
Bactris charnleyae Nevers & Grayum

Bactris coloniata L. H. Bailey
Bactris coloradonis L. H. Bailey
Bactris porschiana Burret
Bactris concinna Mart.
Bactris concinna var. **concinna**
Bactris concinna var. **inundata** Spruce
Bactris concinna subsp. *depauperata* Trail
Bactris concinna var. *depauperata* (Trail)
 Drude
Pyrenoglyphis concinna (Mart.) Burret
Pyrenoglyphis concinna var. *depauperata*
 (Trail) Burret
Pyrenoglyphis concinna var. *inundata*
 (Spruce) Burret
Bactris concinna var. **sigmoidea** Henderson
Bactris constanciae Barb. Rodr.
Bactris corossilla H. Karst.
Bactris cuesco Engel
Bactris duidae Steyerm.
Bactris duplex H. E. Moore
Bactris venezuelensis Steyerm.
Bactris cuspidata Mart.
Amylocarpus cuspidatus (Mart.) Barb. Rodr.
Amylocarpus floccosus (Spruce) Barb. Rodr.
Amylocarpus marajay (Barb. Rodr.) Barb.
 Rodr.
Amylocarpus mitis (Mart.) Barb. Rodr.
Bactris cuspidata var. *angustipinnata* Trail
Bactris cuspidata var. *coriacea* Trail
Bactris cuspidata var. *marajay* (Barb. Rodr.)
 Drude
Bactris cuspidata var. *mitis* (Mart.) Drude
Bactris floccosa Spruce
Bactris marajay Barb. Rodr.
Bactris mitis Mart.
Bactris mitis subsp. *mitis* Trail
Bactris dianeura Burret
Bactris elegans Barb. Rodr.
Bactris elegantissima Burret
Bactris ferruginea Burret
Bactris ferruginea var. **xanthacantha**
 Noblick
Bactris fissifrons Mart.
Bactris aristata Mart.
Bactris fissifrons var. *robusta* Trail
Pyrenoglyphis aristata (Mart.) Burret
Bactris gasipaes Kunth
Bactris ciliata (Ruiz & Pav.) Mart.
Bactris insignis (Mart.) Baillon
Bactris speciosa (Mart.) H. Karst.
Bactris speciosa var. *chichagui* (Mart.) H.
 Karst.
Bactris utilis (Oerst.) Benth. & Hook. f. ex
 Hemsl.

Guilielma chontaduro Triana
Guilielma ciliata (Ruiz & Pav.) H. Wendl.
Guilielma gasipaes (Kunth) L. H. Bailey
Guilielma gasipaes var. *chichagui* (H. Karst.)
 Dahlgren
Guilielma gasipaes var. *chontaduro* (Triana)
 Dugand
Guilielma gasipaes var *coccinea* (Barb. Rodr.)
 L. H. Bailey
Guilielma gasipaes var. *flava* (Barb. Rodr.)
 L. H. Bailey
Guilielma gasipaes var. *ochracea* (Barb.
 Rodr.) L. H. Bailey
Guilielma insignis Mart.
Guilielma speciosa Mart.
Guilielma speciosa var. *coccinea* Barb.
 Rodr.
Guilielma speciosa var. *flava* Barb. Rodr.
Guilielma speciosa var. *mitis* Drude
Guilielma speciosa var. *ochracea* Barb.
 Rodr.
Guilielma utilis Oerst.
Martinezia ciliata Ruiz & Pav.
Bactris gastoniana Barb. Rodr.
Pyrenoglyphis gastoniana (Barb. Rodr.)
 Burret
Bactris glandulosa Oerst.
Bactris glandulosa var. **baileyana** Nevers
Bactris baileyana H. E. Moore ex L. H.
 Bailey
Bactris glandulosa var. **glandulosa**
Bactris alleniana L. H. Bailey
Bactris bifida of Oerst.
Bactris fusca Oerst.
Bactris macrotricha Burret
Bactris oerstediana Trail
Bactris glassmanii Medeiros-Costa &
 Noblick
Bactris glaucescens Drude
Bactris gracilior Burret
Bactris aureodrupa L. H. Bailey
Bactris longipetiolata H. Wendl.
Bactris grayumii Nevers & Henderson
Bactris guineensis (L.) H. E. Moore
Aiphanes minima (Gaertn.) Burret
Bactris horrida Oerst.
Bactris minor Jacq.
Bactris oraria L. H. Bailey
Bactris piritu (H. Karst.) H. Wendl.
Bactris rotunda Stokes
Cocos guineensis L.
Guilielma piritu H. Karst.
Bactris hatschbachii Noblick
Bactris hirta Mart.

Bactris hirta var. **hirta**
Amylocarpus ericetinus (Barb. Rodr.) Barb.
Rodr.
Amylocarpus formosus (Barb. Rodr.) Barb.
Rodr.
Amylocarpus geonomoides (Drude) Barb.
Rodr.
Amylocarpus hirtus (Mart.) Barb. Rodr.
Amylocarpus hylophilus (Spruce) Barb.
Rodr.
Amylocarpus hylophilus var. *glabrescens*
(Drude) Barb. Rodr.
Amylocarpus linearifolius (Barb. Rodr.)
Barb. Rodr.
Amylocarpus pectinatus (Mart.) Barb.
Rodr.
Amylocarpus platispinus Barb. Rodr.
Amylocarpus setipinnatus (Barb. Rodr.)
Barb. Rodr.
Bactris atrox Burret
Bactris ericetina Barb. Rodr.
Bactris formosa Barb. Rodr.
Bactris geonomoides Drude
Bactris geonomoides var. *setosa* Drude
Bactris hoppii Burret
Bactris huebneri Burret
Bactris hylophila Spruce
Bactris hylophila var. *glabrescens* Drude
Bactris hylophila var. *macrocarpa* Drude
Bactris hylophila var. *nana* Trail ex Drude
Bactris integrifolia Wallace
Bactris linearifolia Barb. Rodr.
Bactris longipes Poepp. ex Mart.
Bactris longipes var. *exilis* Trail
Bactris microcarpa Spruce
Bactris pectinata Mart.
Bactris pectinata Wallace
Bactris pectinata subsp. *hylophila* (Spruce)
Trail
Bactris pectinata subsp. *hylophila* var.
setipinnata (Barb. Rodr.) Trail
Bactris pectinata subsp. *hylophila* var.
subintegrifolia Trail
Bactris pectinata subsp. *microcarpa* (Spruce)
Trail
Bactris pectinata subsp. *microcarpa* var. *nana*
Trail
Bactris pectinata subsp. *turbinata* (Spruce)
Trail
Bactris pectinata subsp. *turbinata* var.
spruceana Trail
Bactris platyspinus Barb. Rodr.
Bactris setipinnata Barb. Rodr.
Bactris simplicifrons of Spruce

Bactris turbinata Spruce
Bactris unaensis Barb. Rodr.
Bactris hirta var. **mollis** (Dammer)
Henderson
Bactris lakoi Burret
Bactris mollis Dammer
Bactris hirta var. **pulchra** (Trail) Henderson
Amylocarpus pulcher (Trail) Barb. Rodr.
Bactris hirta subsp. *pulchra* Trail
Bactris pulchra Trail
Bactris pulchra var. inermis Dammer
Bactris ulei Burret
Bactris hondurensis Standl.
Bactris paula L. H. Bailey
Bactris pubescens Burret
Bactris standleyana Burret
Bactris villosa H. Wendl. ex Hemsl.
Bactris wendlandiana Burret
Yuyba paula (L. H. Bailey) L. H. Bailey
Bactris horridispatha Noblick
Bactris killipii Burret
Bactris kunorum Nevers & Grayum
Bactris longiseta H. Wendl. ex Burret
Bactris polystachya H. Wendl.
Bactris macana (Mart.) Pittier
Bactris caribaea H. Karst.
Bactris dahlgreniana Glassman
Guilielma caribaea (H. Karst.) H. Wendl.
Guilielma microcarpa Huber
Guilielma macana Mart.
Bactris macroacantha Mart.
Bactris acanthospatha (Trail) Trail ex Drude
Bactris confluens var. *acanthospatha* Trail
Bactris platyacantha Burret
Bactris setiflora Burret
Bactris major Jacq.
Bactris major var. **infesta** (Mart.) Drude
Bactris chapadensis Barb. Rodr.
Bactris curuena (Trail) Trail ex Drude
Bactris exaltata Barb. Rodr.
Bactris gaviona (Trail) Trail ex Drude
Bactris infesta Mart.
Bactris major var. *mattogrossensis* Kuntze
Bactris mattogrossensis Barb. Rodr.
Bactris nemorosa Barb. Rodr.
Bactris pyrenoglyphoides A. D. Hawkes
Bactris socialis subsp. *curuena* Trail
Bactris socialis subsp. *gaviona* Trail
Pyrenoglyphis chapadensis (Barb. Rodr.)
Burret
Pyrenoglyphis curuena (Trail) Burret
Pyrenoglyphis exaltata (Barb. Rodr.) Burret
Pyrenoglyphis gaviona (Trail) Burret
Pyrenoglyphis hoppii Burret

Pyrenoglyphis infesta (Mart.) Burret
Pyrenoglyphis mattogrossensis (Barb. Rodr.) Burret
Pyrenoglyphis nemorosa (Barb. Rodr.) Burret
Bactris major var. **major**
Augustinea balanoidea Oerst.
Augustinea major (Jacq.) Oerst.
Augustinea ovata Oerst.
Bactris albonotata L. H. Bailey
Bactris augustinea L. H. Bailey
Bactris balanoidea (Oerst.) H. Wendl.
Bactris beata L. H. Bailey
Bactris broadwayi L. H. Bailey
Bactris cateri L. H. Bailey
Bactris chaetorachis Mart.
Bactris cruegeriana Griseb.
Bactris demerarana L. H. Bailey
Bactris ellipsoidalis L. H. Bailey
Bactris leucacantha Linden ex H. Wendl.
Bactris minax Miq.
Bactris obovoidea L. H. Bailey
Bactris ottostaffeana Barb. Rodr.
Bactris ovata (Oerst.) H. Wendl.
Bactris ovata Stokes
Bactris planifolia L. H. Bailey
Bactris subglobosa H. Wendl.
Bactris superior L. H. Bailey
Bactris swabeyi L. H. Bailey
Pyrenoglyphis balanoidea (Oerst.) H. Karst.
Pyrenoglyphis chaetorachis (Mart.) Burret
Pyrenoglyphis cruegeriana (Griseb.) Burret
Pyrenoglyphis leucacantha (Linden ex H. Wendl.) Burret
Pyrenoglyphis major (Jacq.) H. Karst.
Pyrenoglyphis ovata (Oerst.) H. Karst.
Pyrenoglyphis ottostapfeana (Barb. Rodr.) Burret
Pyrenoglyphis superior (L. H. Bailey) Burret
Bactris major var. **megalocarpa** (Trail) Henderson
Bactris megalocarpa Trail
Bactris major var. **socialis** Drude
Bactris socialis Mart.
Pyrenoglyphis socialis (Mart.) Burret
Bactris maraja Mart.
Bactris maraja var. **chaetospatha** (Mart.) Henderson
Bactris chaetospatha Mart.
Bactris maraja var. **juruensis** (Trail) Henderson
Bactris bella Burret
Bactris bijugata Burret
Bactris chlorocarpa Burret
Bactris incommoda Trail

Bactris juruensis Trail
Bactris juruensis var. *lissospatha* Trail
Bactris krichana Barb. Rodr.
Bactris microspadix Burret
Bactris penicillata Barb. Rodr.
Bactris piranga Trail
Bactris pulchella Burret
Bactris maraja var. **maraja**
Bactris actinoneura Drude & Trail
Bactris armata Barb. Rodr.
Bactris chaetochlamys Burret
Bactris chaetospatha var. *macrophylla* Drude
Bactris chloracantha Poepp. ex Mart.
Bactris divisicupula L. H. Bailey
Bactris elatior Wallace
Bactris erostrata Burret
Bactris fuscospina L. H. Bailey
Bactris granariuscarpa Barb. Rodr.
Bactris gymnospatha Burret
Bactris kamarupa Steyerm.
Bactris leptospadix Burret
Bactris leptotricha Burret
Bactris longicuspis Burret
Bactris longisecta Burret
Bactris macrocarpa Wallace
Bactris maraja subsp. *limnaia* Trail
Bactris maraja subsp. *maraja* Trail
Bactris maraja subsp. *sobralensis* Trail
Bactris maraja var. *limnaia* (Trail) Drude
Bactris maraja var. *sobralensis* (Trail) Drude
Bactris maraja var. *trailii* A. D. Hawkes
Bactris monticola Barb. Rodr.
Bactris paucijuga Barb. Rodr.
Bactris sigmoidea Burret
Bactris sobralensis (Trail) Barb. Rodr.
Bactris sobralensis var. *limnaia* (Trail) Barb. Rodr.
Bactris strictacantha Burret
Bactris sylvatica Barb. Rodr.
Bactris trichospatha Barb. Rodr.
Bactris trichospatha subsp. *jurutensis* Trail
Bactris trichospatha subsp. *trichospatha* Trail
Bactris trichospatha subsp. *trichospatha* var. *elata* Trail
Bactris trichospatha subsp. *trichospatha* var. *robusta* Trail
Bactris trichospatha var. *cararaucensis* A. D. Hawkes
Bactris trichospatha var. *jurutensis* (Trail) Drude
Bactris trichospatha var. *patens* Drude
Bactris trichospatha var. *robusta* (Trail) Drude
Bactris umbraticola Barb. Rodr.

Bactris umbrosa Barb. Rodr.
Pyrenoglyphis maraja (Mart.) Burret
Pyrenoglyphis rivularis (Barb. Rodr.) Burret
Bactris mexicana Mart.
Bactris acuminata Liebm. ex Mart.
Bactris baculifera Karw. ex Mart.
Bactris trichophylla Burret
Bactris militaris H. E. Moore
Bactris oligocarpa Barb. Rodr.
Bactris oligocarpa var. *brachycaulis* Trail
Pyrenoglyphis oligocarpa (Barb. Rodr.)
  Burret
Bactris oligoclada Burret
Bactris panamensis Nevers & Grayum
Bactris pickelli Burret
Bactris pilosa H. Karst.
Bactris granatensis (H. Karst.) H. Wendl.
Bactris hirsuta Burret
Guilielma granatensis H. Karst.
Bactris pliniana de Granv. & Henderson
Bactris plumeriana Mart.
Bactris chaetophylla Mart.
Bactris cubensis Burret
Bactris jamaicana L. H. Bailey
Bactris plumeriana of Becc.
Palma gracilis Mill.
Bactris ptariana Steyerm.
Bactris rhapidacantha Wess. Boer
Bactris riparia Mart.
Bactris coccinea Barb. Rodr.
Bactris inundata Mart.
Bactris littoralis Barb. Rodr.
Bactris longifrons Mart.
Guilielma mattogrossensis Barb. Rodr.
Bactris setosa Mart.
Bactris anisitsii Barb. Rodr.
Bactris cuyabensis Barb. Rodr.
Bactris escragnollei Glaz. ex Burret
Bactris fragrae Lindman
Bactris glaucescens var. *melanacantha* Drude
Bactris lindmanniana Drude ex Lindman
Bactris polyclada Burret
Bactris setosa var. *santensis* Barb. Rodr.
Bactris setulosa H. Karst.
Bactris bergantina Steyerm.
Bactris circularis L. H. Bailey
Bactris cuesa Crueg. ex Griseb.
Bactris cuvaro H. Karst.
Bactris falcata Johnston
Bactris kalbreyeri Burret
Bactris sworderiana Becc.
Bactris simplicifrons Mart.
Amylocarpus acanthocnemis (Mart.) Barb.
  Rodr.

Amylocarpus angustifolius Huber
Amylocarpus arenarius (Barb. Rodr.) Barb.
  Rodr.
Amylocarpus inermis (Trail ex Barb. Rodr.)
  Barb. Rodr.
Amylocarpus luetzelburgii (Burret) Burret
Amylocarpus microspathus (Barb. Rodr.)
  Barb. Rodr.
Amylocarpus simplicifrons (Mart.) Barb.
  Rodr.
Amylocarpus tenuissimus (Barb. Rodr.) Barb.
  Rodr.
Amylocarpus xanthocarpus (Barb. Rodr.)
  Barb. Rodr.
Bactris acanthocnemis Mart.
Bactris amoena Burret
Bactris arenaria Barb. Rodr.
Bactris brevifolia Spruce
Bactris carolensis Spruce
Bactris cuspidata var. *tenuis* (Wallace)
  Drude
Bactris dakamana (L. H. Bailey ex
  Maguire) Glassman
Bactris essequiboensis (L. H. Bailey ex
  Maguire) Glassman
Bactris gleasonii (L. H. Bailey) Glassman
Bactris gracilis Barb. Rodr.
Bactris huberiana Burret
Bactris inermis Trail ex Barb. Rodr.
Bactris inermis var. *tenuissimis* Barb. Rodr.
Bactris kuhlmanii Burret
Bactris kuhlmanii var. *aculeata* Burret
Bactris luetzelburgii Burret
Bactris luetzelburgii var. *anacantha* Burret
Bactris maguirei (L. H. Bailey ex Maguire)
  Steyerm.
Bactris microspatha Barb. Rodr.
Bactris mitis subsp. *inermis* Trail
Bactris mitis subsp. *tenuis* (Wallace) Trail
Bactris mitis subsp. *uaupensis* (Spruce)
  Trail
Bactris naevia Poepp. ex Burret
Bactris negrensis Spruce
Bactris negrensis var. *minor* Spruce
Bactris negrensis var. *carolensis* (Spruce)
  Burret
Bactris obovata Burret
Bactris paucisecta Burret
Bactris schultesii L. H. Bailey
Bactris simplex Burret
Bactris simplicifrons var. *acanthocnemis*
  (Mart.) Drude
Bactris simplicifrons var. *brevifolia* (Spruce)
  Trail

Bactris simplicifrons var. *carolensis* (Spruce) Trail
Bactris simplicifrons var. *negrensis* (Spruce) Trail
Bactris simplicifrons var. *subpinnata* Trail
Bactris soropanae Steyerm.
Bactris stahelii (L. H. Bailey) Glassman
Bactris tenuis Wallace
Bactris tenuis var. *inermis* (Trail) Burret
Bactris tenuissimis (Barb. Rodr.) Burret
Bactris trinitensis (L. H. Bailey) Glassman
Bactris uaupensis Spruce
Bactris xanthocarpa Barb. Rodr.
Yuyba dakamana L. H. Bailey ex Maguire
Yuyba essequiboensis L. H. Bailey ex Maguire
Yuyba gleasonii L. H. Bailey
Yuyba maguirei L. H. Bailey ex Maguire
Yuyba schultesii L. H. Bailey
Yuyba simplicifrons (Mart.) L. H. Bailey
Yuyba simplicifrons var. *acanthocnemis* (Mart.) A. D. Hawkes
Yuyba simplicifrons var. *subpinnata* (Trail) Hawkes
Yuyba stahelii L. H. Bailey ex Maguire
Yuyba trinitensis L. H. Bailey
Bactris soeiroana Noblick
Bactris syagroides Barb. Rodr. & Trial
Amylocarpus syagroides (Barb. Rodr. & Trail) Barb. Rodr.
Bactris multiramosa Burret
Bactris tefensis Henderson
Bactris tomentosa Mart.
Bactris tomentosa var. **sphaerocarpa** (Mart.) Henderson
Bactris angustifolia Dammer
Bactris sphaerocarpa Trail
Bactris sphaerocarpa subsp. *pinnatisecta* Trail
Bactris sphaerocarpa var. *ensifolia* Trail
Bactris sphaerocarpa var. *minor* Trail
Bactris sphaerocarpa var. *pinnatisecta* (Trail) A. D. Hawkes
Bactris sphaerocarpa var. *platyphylla* Trail
Bactris sphaerocarpa var. *schizophylla* Drude
Bactris tomentosa var. **tomentosa**
Bactris arundinacea (Trail) Drude
Bactris capillacea (Trail) Drude
Bactris capinensis Huber
Bactris eumorpha Trail
Bactris eumorpha subsp. *arundinacea* Trail
Bactris eumorpha subsp. *eumorpha*
Bactris tomentosa subsp. *capillacea* Trail
Bactris tomentosa var. *negrensis* A. D. Hawkes
Bactris tomentosa subsp. *tomentosa* Trail

Bactris trailiana Barb. Rodr.
Bactris acanthocarpa subsp. *trailiana* (Barb. Rodr.) Trail
Bactris turbinocarpa Barb. Rodr.
Pyrenoglyphis turbinocarpa (Barb. Rodr.) Burret
Bactris vulgaris Barb. Rodr.
Bactris glazioviana Drude

HYBRIDS
Bactris x *moorei* Wess. Boer

UNCERTAIN NAMES
Amylocarpus obovatus Burret
Bactris binoti hort. ex Hook. f.
Bactris bradei Burret
Bactris caracasana Lodd. ex Linden
Bactris caraja hort. ex Hook. f.
Bactris caravallana Linden
Bactris catel Linden
Bactris conferta H. Wendl. ex Burret
Bactris corazillo hort. ex H. Wendl.
Bactris cucullata H. Wendl.
Bactris dardanoi Medeiros-Costa
Bactris faucium Mart.
Bactris flavispina hort.
Bactris liboniana Linden
Bactris macanilla Linden
Bactris martineziaefolia hort. ex H. Wendl.
Bactris megistocarpa Burret
Bactris neromanni Voigt
Bactris pavoniana Mart.
Bactris puyamo Linden
Bactris sanctae-paulae Engel
Bactris spinosa Appun
Bactris tijucana Glaz.
Bactris tucum Burret
Bactris vexans Burret

BARCELLA Drude
Barcella odora (Trail) Drude
Elaeis odora Trail

BRAHEA Mart. ex Endl.
Erythea S. Watson
Glaucotheca O. F. Cook
Brahea aculeata (Brandegee) H. E. Moore
Erythea aculeata Brandegee
Glaucotheca aculeata (Brandegee) Johnston
Brahea armata S. Watson
Brahea armata var. *microcarpa* Becc.
Brahea clara (L. H. Bailey) Espejo & López-Ferrari
Brahea roezlii Linden

Erythea armata (S. Watson) Watson
Erythea clara L. H. Bailey
Erythea elegans Franceschi ex Becc.
Erythea roezlii (Linden) L. H. Bailey
Glaucotheca armata (S. Watson) O. F. Cook
Glaucotheca elegans (Franceschi ex Becc.)
 Johnston
Brahea brandegeei (Purpus) H. E. Moore
Erythea brandegeei Purpus
Erythea brandegeei var. *spiralis* Jones
?Erythea loretensis Jones
Glaucotheca brandegeei (Purpus) Johnston
Brahea decumbens Rzed.
Brahea dulcis (Kunth) Mart.
Acoelorraphe cookii Bartlett
?Acoelorraphe schippii (Burret) Dahlgren
Acoelorraphe salvadorensis (H. Wendl. ex
 Becc.) Bartlett
Brahea bella L. H. Bailey ·
Brahea berlandieri Bartlett
Brahea calcarea Liebm.
Brahea conzattii Bartlett
Brahea dulcis var. *montereyensis* Becc.
Brahea salvadorensis H. Wendl. ex Becc.
?Brahea schippii Burret
?Copernicia depressa Liebm.
Corypha dulcis Kunth
Corypha frigida Mohl ex Mart.
Erythea salvadorensis (H. Wendl. ex Becc.)
 H. E. Moore
Brahea edulis H. Wendl. ex Watson
Erythea edulis (H. Wendl.) Watson
Brahea moorei L. H. Bailey ex H. E. Moore
Brahea nitida André
Brahea prominens L. H. Bailey
Erythea brandegeei var. *spiralis* Jones
Brahea pimo Becc.
Acoelorraphe pimo (Becc.) Bartlett
Erythea pimo (Becc.) H. E. Moore

UNCERTAIN NAMES
Brahea calcarata Liebm. ex Linden
Brahea conduplicata Linden
Brahea frigida hort. ex Devansaye
Brahea glauca hort. ex Hook. f.
Brahea lucida hort. ex Hook. f.
Brahea nobilis hort. ex Hook. f.
Brahea robusta hort.

BUTIA (Becc.) Becc.
Butia archeri (Glassman) Glassman
Syagrus archeri Glassman

Butia campicola (Barb. Rodr.) Noblick
Cocos campicola Barb. Rodr.
Syagrus campicola (Barb. Rodr.) Becc.
Butia capitata (Mart.) Becc.
Butia capitata var. *elegantissima* (Chabaud)
 Becc.
Butia capitata var. *erythrospatha* (Chabaud)
 Becc.
Butia capitata var. *lilaceiflora* (Chabaud)
 Becc.
Butia capitata var. *nehrlingiana* (L. H.
 Bailey) L. H. Bailey
Butia capitata var. *odorata* (Barb. Rodr.)
 Becc.
Butia capitata var. *pulposa* (Barb. Rodr.)
 Becc.
Butia capitata var. *strictior* L. H. Bailey
Butia capitata var. *subglobosa* Becc.
Butia capitata var. *virescens* Becc.
Butia nehrlingiana L. H. Bailey
Cocos capitata Mart.
Cocos elegantissima Chabaud
Cocos erythrospatha Chabaud
Cocos lilaceifolia Chabaud
Cocos odorata Barb. Rodr.
Cocos pulposa Barb. Rodr.
Syagrus capitata (Mart.) Glassman
Butia eriospatha (Mart.) Becc.
Butia eriospatha subsp. *punctata* Bomhard
Cocos eriospatha Mart. ex Drude
Syagrus eriospatha (Mart.) Glassman
Butia microspadix Burret
Syagrus hatschbachii Glassman
Butia paraguayensis (Barb. Rodr.) L. H.
 Bailey
Butia arenicola (Barb. Rodr.) Burret
Butia yatay var. *paraguayensis* (Barb. Rodr.)
 Becc.
Cocos arenicola Barb. Rodr.
Cocos paraguayensis Barb. Rodr.
Syagrus arenicola (Barb. Rodr.) Frambach
 ex Dahlgren
Syagrus paraguayensis (Barb. Rodr.)
 Glassman
Butia purpurascens Glassman
Butia yatay (Mart.) Becc.
Cocos yatay Mart.
Syagrus yatay (Mart.) Glassman

HYBRIDS
x *Butiarecastrum nabonnandii* Robertson-
 Proschowsky

x *Butyagrus nabonnandii* (Robertson-Proschowsky) Vorster
(*Butia capitata* x *Syagrus romzanoffiana* = *Syagrus* x *fairchildensis* Glassman)

UNCERTAIN NAMES
Butia amadelpha (Barb. Rodr.) Burret
Butia bonneti Becc.
Butia dyerana (Barb. Rodr.) Burret
Butia leiospatha (Barb. Rodr.) Becc.
Butia poni (Hauman) Burret
Butia pungens Becc.
Butia stolonifera (Barb. Rodr.) Becc.
Butia wildemaniana (Barb. Rodr.) Burret
Cocos amadelpha Barb. Rodr.
Cocos barbosii Barb. Rodr.
Cocos capitata var *leiospatha* (Barb. Rodr.) Berger
Cocos dyerana Barb. Rodr.
Cocos leiospatha Barb. Rodr.
Cocos leiospatha var. *angustifolia* Drude
Cocos poni Hauman
Cocos stolonifera Barb. Rodr.
Cocos wildemaniana Barb. Rodr.
Syagrus amadelpha (Barb. Rodr.) Frambach ex Dahlgren
Syagrus dyerana (Barb. Rodr.) Becc.
Syagrus wildemaniana (Barb. Rodr.) Frambach ex Dahlgren

CALYPTROGYNE H. Wendl.
Calyptrogyne allenii (L. H. Bailey) Nevers
Geonoma allenii L. H. Bailey
Calyptrogyne anomala Nevers & Henderson
Calyptrogyne condensata (L. H. Bailey) Wess. Boer
Geonoma condensata L. H. Bailey
Calyptrogyne costatifrons (L. H. Bailey) Nevers
Geonoma costatifrons L. H. Bailey
Calyptrogyne ghiesbreghtiana (Linden & H. Wendl.) H. Wendl.
Calyptrogyne brachystachys H. Wendl.
Calyptrogyne donell-smithii (Dammer) Burret
Calyptrogyne glauca (Oerst.) H. Wendl.
Calyptrogyne sarapiquensis H. Wendl.
Calyptrogyne spicigera (Koch) Oerst.
Chamaedorea ghiesbreghtiana hort. in Kerch.
Geonoma donnell-smithii Dammer
Geonoma ghiesbreghtiana Linden & H. Wendl.
Geonoma glauca Oerst.
Geonoma spicigera Koch
Calyptrogyne kunaria Nevers

Calyptrogyne pubescens Nevers
Calyptrogyne trichostachys Burret

UNCERTAIN NAMES
Calyptrogyne elata H. Wendl.

CALYTRONOMA Griseb.
Cocops O. F. Cook
Calyptronoma occidentalis (Sw.) H. E. Moore
Calyptrogyne occidentalis (Sw.) M. Gómez
Calyptrogyne swartzii (Griseb. & H. Wendl.) Becc.
Calyptrogyne victorinii León
Calyptronoma swartzii (Griseb. & H. Wendl.) Griseb.
Geonoma swartzii Griseb. & H. Wendl.
Elaeis occidentalis Sw.
Calyptronoma plumeriana (Mart.) Lourteig
Calyptrogyne clementis León
Calyptrogyne dulcis (C. H. Wright ex Griseb.) M. Gómez
Calyptrogyne intermedia (Griseb. & H. Wendl.) M. Gómez
Calyptrogyne microcarpa León
Calyptronoma clementis (León) A. D. Hawkes
Calyptronoma clementis subsp. *orientensis* Muñiz & Borhidi
Calyptronoma clementis subsp. *clementis*
Calyptronoma dulcis (C. H. Wright ex Griseb.) L. H. Bailey
Calyptronoma intermedia (Griseb. & H. Wendl.) H. Wendl.
Calyptronoma microcarpa (León) A. D. Hawkes
Geonoma dulcis C. H. Wright ex Griseb.
Geonoma intermedia Griseb. & H. Wendl.
Geonoma plumeriana Mart.
Calyptronoma rivalis (O. F. Cook) L. H. Bailey)
Calyptrogyne quisqueyana (L. H. Bailey) León
Calyptrogyne rivalis (O. F. Cook) León
Calyptronoma quisqueyana L. H. Bailey
Cocops rivalis O. F. Cook

UNCERTAIN NAMES
Palma pinao Aubl.

CEROXYLON Bonpl. ex D. C.
Beethovenia Engel
Klopstockia H. Karst.
Ceroxylon alpinum Bonpl. ex D. C.

Ceroxylon alpinum subsp. **alpinum**
Ceroxylon andicola Humb. & Bonpl.
Ceroxylon ferrugineum André
Iriartea andicola (Humb. & Bonpl.) Spreng.
Ceroxylon alpinum subsp. **ecuadorense**
Galeano
Ceroxylon amazonicum Galeano
Ceroxylon ceriferum (H. Karst.) H. Wendl.
Beethovenia cerifera Engel
Ceroxylon andicola of H. Wendl.
Ceroxylon beethovenia Burret
Ceroxylon klopstockia Mart.
Ceroxylon schultzei Burret
Iriartea klopstockia hort. ex Watson
Klopstockia cerifera H. Karst.
Ceroxylon echinulatum Galeano
Ceroxylon parvifrons (Engel) H. Wendl.
Ceroxylon latisectum Burret
Ceroxylon mooreanum Galeano & R. Bernal
Ceroxylon sclerophyllum Dugand
Klopstockia parvifrons Engel
Ceroxylon parvum Galeano
Ceroxylon quindiuense (H. Karst.) H.
Wendl.
Ceroxylon floccosum Burret
Klopstockia quindiuensis H. Karst.
Ceroxylon sasaimae G. Galeano
Ceroxylon ventricosum Burret
Ceroxylon vogelianum (Engel) H. Wendl.
Ceroxylon coarctatum (Engel) H. Wendl.
Ceroxylon crispum Burret
Ceroxylon flexuosum Galeano & R. Bernal
Ceroxylon hexandrum Dugand
Ceroxylon verruculosum Burret
Klopstockia coarctata Engel
Klopstockia vogeliana Engel
Ceroxylon weberbaueri Burret

UNCERTAIN NAMES
Ceroxylon interruptum (H. Karst.) H. Wendl.
Ceroxylon niveum hort. ex H. Wendl.
Ceroxylon pityrophyllum (Mart.) H. Wendl.
Ceroxylon utile (H. Karst.) H. Wendl.
Cocos pityrophylla Mart.
Klopstockia interrupta H. Karst.
Klopstockia utilis H. Karst.

CHAMAEDOREA Willd.
Anothea O. F. Cook
Cladandra O. F. Cook
Collinia (Liebm.) Liebm. ex Oerst.
Dasystachys Oerst.
Discoma O. F. Cook

Docanthe O. F. Cook
Edanthe O. F. Cook
Eleutheropetalum (H. Wendl.) Oerst.
Encheila O. F. Cook
Kinetostigma Dammer
Kunthia Humb. & Bonpl.
Legnea O. F. Cook
Lobia O. F. Cook
Lophothele O. F. Cook
Mauranthe O. F. Cook
Meiota O. F. Cook
Migandra O. F. Cook
Morenia Ruiz & Pav.
Neanthe O. F. Cook
Nunnezharia Ruiz & Pav.
Nunnezia Willd.
Omanthe O. F. Cook
Paranthe O. F. Cook
Platythea O. F. Cook
Spathoscaphe Oerst.
Stachyophorbe (Liebm.) Liebm. ex Klotzsch
Stephanostachys (Klotzsch) Oerst.
Vadia O. F. Cook
Chamaedorea adscendens (Dammer)
Burret
Kinetostigma adscendens Dammer
Tuerckheimia adscendens Dammer
Chamaedorea allenii L. H. Bailey
Chamaedorea crucensis Hodel
Chamaedorea zamorae Hodel
Chamaedorea amabilis H. Wendl. ex
Dammer
Chamaedorea coclensis L. H. Bailey
Nunnezharia amabilis (H. Wendl. ex
Dammer) Kuntze
Chamaedorea angustisecta Burret
Chamaedorea leonis H. E. Moore
Chamaedorea arenbergiana H. Wendl.
Chamaedorea densiflora hort.
Chamaedorea gracilis hort. in H. Wendl.
Chamaedorea latifolia hort. in Nicholson
Chamaedorea latifrons hort. in H. Wendl.
Chamaedorea oblongata hort. in H. Wendl.
Nunnezharia arenbergiana (H. Wendl.)
Kuntze
Nunnezharia latifrons (hort. in H. Wendl.)
Kuntze
Spathoscaphe arenbergiana (H. Wendl.)
Oerst.
Chamaedorea brachyclada H. Wendl.
Nunnezharia brachyclada (H. Wendl.)
Kuntze
Chamaedorea brachypoda Standl. &
Steyerm.

Chamaedorea carchensis Standl. & Steyerm.
Chamaedorea benziei Hodel
Chamaedorea castillo-montii Hodel
Chamaedorea cataractarum Mart.
Chamaedorea atrovirens hort. in Kerchove
Chamaedorea flexuosa hort. in H. Wendl.
Chamaedorea lindeniana hort. in H. Wendl.
Chamaedorea martiana H. Wendl.
Encheila transversa O. F. Cook
Nunnezharia cataractarum (Mart.) Kuntze
Nunnezharia flexuosa (hort. in H. Wendl.)
    Kuntze
Nunnezharia martiana (H. Wendl.) Kuntze
Stachyophorbe cataractarum (Mart.) Klotzsch
Stephanostachys martiana (H. Wendl.)
    Oerst.
Vadia atrovirens (hort. in Kerchove) O. F.
    Cook
Vadia jotolana O. F. Cook
Chamaedorea correae Hodel & Uhl
Chamaedorea costaricana Oerst.
Chamaedorea biolleyi Guillaumin
Chamaedorea linearia L. H. Bailey
Chamaedorea quezalteca Standl. & Steyerm.
Chamaedorea seibertii L. H. Bailey
Legnea laciniata O. F. Cook
Nunnezharia costaricana (Oerst.) Kuntze
Omanthe costaricana O. F. Cook
Chamaedorea dammeriana Burret
Chamaedorea chazdoniae Hodel
Chamaedorea variabilis H. Wendl. ex Burret
Chamaedorea wedeliana L. H. Bailey
Chamaedorea deckeriana (Klotzsch) Hemsl.
Dasystachys deckeriana (Klotzsch) Oerst.
Morenia deckeriana hort. in Dammer
Nunnezharia deckeriana (Klotzsch) Kuntze
Stachyophorbe deckeriana Klotzsch
Chamaedorea deneversiana Grayum &
    Hodel
Chamaedorea elatior Mart.
Anothea scandens O. F. Cook
Chamaedorea affinis Liebm. in Mart.
Chamaedorea bambusoides Gerome
Chamaedorea bambusoides var. *graminifolia*
    Gerome
Chamaedorea bambusoides var. *juncea*
    Gerome
Chamaedorea desmoncoides H. Wendl.
Chamaedorea elatior var. *bambusoides* H.
    Wendl.
Chamaedorea elatior var. *desmoncoides* H.
    Wendl.
Chamaedorea montana Liebm. in Mart.
Chamaedorea regia hort. in H. Wendl.

Chamaedorea repens hort. in H. Wendl.
?*Chamaedorea resimpia* hort.
Chamaedorea resinifera H. Wendl.
Chamaedorea robusta hort. in H. Wendl.
Chamaedorea scandens Liebm. in Mart.
Chamaedorea scandens var. *bambusoides* H.
    Wendl. ex Dammer
Chamaedorea scandens var. *desmoncoides* H.
    Wendl. ex Dammer
Nunnezharia affinis (Liebm.) Kuntze
Nunnezharia desmoncoides (H. Wendl.)
    Kuntze
Nunnezharia elatior (Mart.) Kuntze
Nunnezharia oaxacensis Kuntze
Nunnezharia regia (hort. in H. Wendl.)
    Kuntze
Nunnezharia repens (hort. in H. Wendl.)
    Kuntze
Nunnezharia resinifera (H. Wendl.) Kuntze
Platythea graminea O. F. Cook
Chamaedorea elegans Mart.
Chamaedorea deppeana Klotzsch
Chamaedorea elegans ?var. *angustifolia* M.
    Martens & Galeotti
Chamaedorea elegantissima hort. in Kerch.
Chamaedorea helleriana Klotzsch
Chamaedorea humilis Liebm. ex Mart.
Chamaedorea lindeniana hort. in H. Wendl.
Chamaedorea martiana hort. in H. Wendl.
Chamaedorea pulchella Linden ex Hemsl.
Collinia deppeana (Klotzsch) Klotzsch
Collinia elegans (Mart.) Oerst.
Collinia elegans var. *angustifolia* (M. Martens
    & Galeotti) M. Martens & Galeotti
Collinia humilis (Liebm. ex Mart.) Oerst.
Kunthia deppii hort. in Zucc.
Neanthe bella O. F. Cook
Neanthe elegans (Mart.) O. F. Cook
Neanthe neesiana O. F. Cook
Nunnezharia elegans (Mart.) Kuntze
Nunnezharia humilis (Liebm. ex Mart.)
    Kuntze
Nunnezharia pulchella (Linden ex Hemsl.)
    Kuntze
Chamaedorea ernesti-augustii H. Wendl.
Chamaedorea glazioviana Drude ex
    Guillaumin
Chamaedorea latifrons hort. in H. Wendl.
Chamaedorea simplicifrons hort. in Heynh.
Eleutheropetalum ernesti-augustii (H. Wendl.)
    Oerst.
Geonoma coralliflora hort. in Chabaud
Geonoma latifrons hort. in H. Wendl.
Hyospathe elegans hort. in H. Wendl.

Morenia corallifera hort. in Ruffo
Morenia ernesti-augustii (H. Wendl.) H.
Wendl.
Nunnezharia ernesti-augustii (H. Wendl.)
Kuntze
Chamaedorea fractiflexa Hodel & Castillo
Chamaedorea fragrans (Ruiz & Pav.) Mart.
Chamaedorea cataractarum hort. in
Guillaumin
Chamaedorea gratissima hort. in Linden
Chamaedorea pavoniana H. Wendl. ex
Dammer
Chamaedorea ruizii H. Wendl. ex Dammer
Chamaedorea verschaffeltii hort. in Kerch.
Geonoma humilis hort. in Dammer
Nunnezharia fragrans Ruiz & Pav.
Chamaedorea geonomiformis H. Wendl.
Chamaedorea fenestra hort. in H. Wendl.
Chamaedorea humilis hort. in H. Wendl.
Chamaedorea tenella H. Wendl.
Geonoma fenestra hort. in Dammer
Nunnezharia geonomiformis (H. Wendl.)
Hook. f.
Nunnezharia tenella (H. Wendl.) Hook. f.
Chamaedorea glaucifolia H. Wendl.
Chamaedorea crucifolia hort. in Crouch
Chamaedorea elegantissima hort. in Kerch.
Chamaedorea glaucophylla hort. in Siebert &
Voss
Discoma glaucifolia O. F. Cook
Nunnezharia glaucifolia (H. Wendl.)
Kuntze
Chamaedorea graminifolia H. Wendl.
Chamaedorea schippii Burret
Nunnezharia graminifolia (H. Wendl.)
Kuntze
Chamaedorea guntheriana Hodel & Uhl
Chamaedorea hooperiana Hodel
Chamaedorea ibarrae Hodel
Chamaedorea keeleriorum Hodel & Castillo
Chamaedorea klotzschiana H. Wendl.
Nunnezharia klotzschiana (H. Wendl.)
Kuntze
Chamaedorea lehmannii Burret
Chamaedorea liebmannii Mart.
Chamaedorea aequalis Standl. & Steyerm.
?*Chamaedorea ferruginea* H. E. Moore
Chamaedorea liebmannii var. *lepidota* H.
Wendl. ex Dammer
Chamaedorea lepidota H. Wendl.
Chamaedorea velutina hort. in H. Wendl.
Collinia elatior Liebm.
Lophothele ramea O. F. Cook
Nunnezharia lepidota (H. Wendl.) Kuntze

Chamaedorea linearis (Ruiz & Pav.) Mart.
Chamaedorea formosa hort. in Bull
Chamaedorea latisecta (H. E. Moore) A. H.
Gentry
Chamaedorea megaphylla A. H. Gentry
Chamaedorea montana hort. in Siebert &
Voss
Chamaedorea poeppigiana (Mart.) A. H.
Gentry
Chamaedorea polyclada Burret
Chamaedorea smithii A. H. Gentry
Kunthia montana Humb. & Bonpl.
Martinezia linearis Ruiz & Pav.
Morenia caudata Burret
Morenia corallina H. Karst.
Morenia fragrans Ruiz & Pav.
Morenia latisecta H. E. Moore
Morenia lindeniana H. Wendl.
Morenia linearis (Ruiz & Pav.) Burret
Morenia macrocarpa Burret
Morenia microspadix Burret
Morenia montana (Ruiz & Pav.) Burret
Morenia poeppigiana Mart.
Morenia robusta Burret
Nunnezharia corallina (H. Karst.) Kuntze
Nunnezharia lindeniana (H. Wendl.)
Kuntze
Nunnezharia linearis (Ruiz & Pav.) Kuntze
Nunnezharia montana (Humb. & Bonpl.)
Kuntze
Nunnezharia morenia Kuntze
Nunnezharia poeppigiana (Mart.) Kuntze
Chamaedorea lucidifrons L. H. Bailey
Chamaedorea macrospadix Oerst.
Chamaedorea pedunculata Hodel & Uhl
Nunnezharia macrospadix (Oerst.) Kuntze
Chamaedorea metallica O. F. Cook ex
H. E. Moore
Chamaedorea microphylla H. Wendl.
Chamaedorea microspadix Burret
Chamaedorea murriensis Galeano
Chamaedorea macroloba Galeano
Chamaedorea nationsiana Hodel & Castillo
Chamaedorea nubium Standl. & Steyerm.
Chamaedorea skutchii Standl. & Steyerm.
Chamaedorea oblongata Mart.
Chamaedorea aurantiaca hort. in H. Wendl.
Chamaedorea biloba hort. in H. Wendl.
Chamaedorea corallina hort.
Chamaedorea corallocarpa hort. in Dammer
Chamaedorea fusca Standl. & Steyerm.
Chamaedorea lindeniana hort. in H. Wendl.
Chamaedorea lunata Liebm.
Chamaedorea paradoxa H. Wendl.

Chamaedorea scandens hort. in H. Wendl.
Chamaedorea schiedeana hort. in H. Wendl.
Mauranthe lunata (Liebm.) O. F. Cook
Morenia corallina hort. in Dammer
Morenia corallocarpa hort. in H. Wendl.
Nunnezharia biloba (hort. in H. Wendl.)
    Kuntze
Nunnezharia corallocarpa (hort. in
    Dammer) Kuntze
Nunnezharia lunata (Liebm.) Kuntze
Nunnezharia oblongata (Mart.) Kuntze
Nunnezharia paradoxa (H. Wendl.) Kuntze
Chamaedorea oreophila Mart.
Chamaedorea monostachys Burret
Nunnezharia oreophila (Mart.) Kuntze
Stachyophorbe filipes O. F. Cook
Stachyophorbe montana Liebm. ex Oerst.
Stachyophorbe oreophila (Mart.) O. F. Cook
Chamaedorea pachecoana Standl. &
    Steyerm.
Chamaedorea palmeriana Hodel & Uhl
Chamaedorea parvifolia Burret
Chamaedorea parvisecta Burret
Chamaedorea digitata Standl. & Steyerm.
Chamaedorea pulchra Burret
Paranthe violacea O. F. Cook
Chamaedorea pauciflora Mart.
Chamaedorea amazonica Dammer
Chamaedorea integrifolia (Trail) Dammer
Chamaedorea lechleriana H. Wendl. ex
    Dammer
Morenia integrifolia Trail
Morenia integrifolia var. *nigricans* Trail
Morenia pauciflora (Mart.) Drude
Nunnezharia integrifolia (Trail) Kuntze
Nunnezharia pauciflora (Mart.) Kuntze
Chamaedorea pinnatifrons (Jacq.) Oerst.
Borassus pinnatifrons Jacq.
Chamaedorea aguilariana Standl. & Steyerm.
Chamaedorea bartlingiana H. Wendl.
Chamaedorea bifurcata Oerst.
Chamaedorea boliviensis Dammer
Chamaedorea bracteata H. Wendl.
Chamaedorea brevifrons H. Wendl.
Chamaedorea concinna Burret
Chamaedorea concolor Mart.
Chamaedorea concolor hort. in H. Wendl.
Chamaedorea conocarpa Mart.
Chamaedorea depauperata Dammer
Chamaedorea dryanderae Burret
Chamaedorea falcifera H. E. Moore
Chamaedorea flavovirens H. Wendl.
Chamaedorea geonomoides (Spruce) Drude
Chamaedorea gracilis Willd.

Chamaedorea heilbornii Burret
Chamaedorea herrerae Burret
Chamaedorea holmgrenii Burret
Chamaedorea hoppii Burret
Chamaedorea kalbreyeriana H. Wendl. ex
    Burret
Chamaedorea lanceolata (Ruiz & Pav.) Kunth
Chamaedorea lanceolata var. *littoralis* Drude
Chamaedorea lindeniana H. Wendl.
Chamaedorea lindeniana hort. in H. Wendl.
Chamaedorea macroloba Burret
Chamaedorea membranacea Oerst.
Chamaedorea micrantha Burret
Chamaedorea minor Burret
Chamaedorea neurochlamys Burret
Chamaedorea oerstedii O. F. Cook & Doyle
Chamaedorea pacaya Oerst.
Chamaedorea rhombea Burret
Chamaedorea scandens hort. in H. Wendl.
Chamaedorea serpens Hodel
Chamaedorea verapazensis Hodel & Castillo
Chamaedorea weberbaueri Dammer ex Burret
Docanthe alba O. F. Cook
Hyospathe montana Mart.
Martinezia lanceolata Ruiz & Pav.
Nunnezharia bartlingiana (H. Wendl.)
    Kuntze
Nunnezharia bifurcata (Oerst.) Kuntze
Nunnezharia bracteata (H. Wendl.) Kuntze
Nunnezharia brevifrons (H. Wendl.) Kuntze
Nunnezharia concolor (Mart.) Kuntze
Nunnezharia conocarpa (Mart.) Kuntze
Nunnezharia flavovirens (H. Wendl.)
    Kuntze
Nunnezharia geonomoides Spruce
Nunnezharia lanceolata (Ruiz & Pav.)
    Kuntze
Nunnezharia membranacea (Oerst.) Kuntze
Nunnezharia pacaya (Oerst.) Kuntze
Nunnezharia pinnatifrons (Jacq.) Kuntze
Chamaedorea pittieri L. H. Bailey
Chamaedorea hageniorum L. H. Bailey
Chamaedorea plumosa Hodel
Chamaedorea pochutlensis Liebm.
Chamaedorea elatior hort. in H. Wendl.
Chamaedorea karwinskyana (H. Wendl.)
    Kuntze
?*Chamaedorea robusta* hort.
Nunnezharia karwinskyana (H. Wendl.)
    Kuntze
Nunnezharia pochutlensis (Liebm.) Kuntze
Chamaedorea pumila H. Wendl. ex
    Dammer
Chamaedorea minima Hodel

Chamaedorea nana N. E. Br.
Kinetostigma nana (N. E. Br.) Burret
Nunnezharia pumila (H. Wendl.) Kuntze
Chamaedorea pygmaea H. Wendl.
Chamaedorea stenocarpa Standl. & Steyerm.
Chamaedorea terryorum Standl.
Cladandra pygmaea (H. Wendl.) O. F. Cook
Nunnezharia pygmaea (H. Wendl.) Kuntze
Stachyophorbe pygmaea (H. Wendl.) Oerst.
Chamaedorea queroana Hodel
Chamaedorea radicalis Mart.
Chamaedorea pringlei S. Watson
Nunnezharia radicalis (Mart.) Kuntze
Chamaedorea rhizomatosa Hodel
Chamaedorea rigida H. Wendl. ex Dammer
Nunnezharia rigida (H. Wendl. ex
Dammer) Kuntze
Chamaedorea robertii Hodel & Uhl
Chamaedorea rojasiana Standl. & Steyerm.
Chamaedorea sartorii Liebm. in Mart.
Chamaedorea aurantiaca Brongn.
Chamaedorea hartwegii hort.
Chamaedorea mexicana hort. in Heynh.
Chamaedorea oblongata (H. Wendl.) H.
Wendl.
Chamaedorea oblongata var. *conferta* H.
Wendl.
Chamaedorea wobstiana hort. in Linden
Eleutheropetalum sartorii (Liebm.) Oerst.
Eleutheropetalum sartorii var. *conferta* H.
Wendl. in Burret
Morenia oblongata H. Wendl.
Morenia sartorii hort. in Ruffo
Nunnezharia aurantiaca (Brong.) Kuntze
Nunnezharia sartorii (Liebm.) Kuntze
Chamaedorea scheryi L. H. Bailey
Chamaedorea schiedeana Mart.
Chamaedorea gracilis hort. in H. Wendl.
Chamaedorea speciosa hort. in H. Wendl.
Kunthia xalapensis Otto & A. Dietr.
Nunnezharia schiedeana (Mart.) Kuntze
Chamaedorea seifrizii Burret
Chamaedorea erumpens H. E. Moore
Meiota campechana O. F. Cook
Chamaedorea selvae Hodel
Chamaedorea simplex Burret
Chamaedorea stolonifera H. Wendl. ex
Hook. f.
Chamaedorea stricta Standl. & Steyerm.
Chamaedorea sullivaniorum Hodel & Uhl
Chamaedorea tenerrima Burret
Lobia erosa O. F. Cook
Chamaedorea tepejilote Liebm.
Chamaedorea alternans H. Wendl.

Chamaedorea anomospadix Burret
Chamaedorea casperiana Klotzsch
Chamaedorea columbica Burret
Chamaedorea exorrhiza H. Wendl. ex
Guillaumin
Chamaedorea sphaerocarpa Burret
Chamaedorea wendlandiana (Oerst.) Hemsl.
Edanthe veraepacis O. F. Cook
Nunnezharia alternans (H. Wendl.) Kuntze
Nunnezharia casperiana (Klotzsch) Kuntze
Nunnezharia tepejilote (Liebm.) Kuntze
Nunnezharia wendlandiana (Oerst.) Kuntze
Stephanostachys casperiana (Klotzsch) Oerst.
Stephanostachys tepejilote (Klotzsch) Oerst.
Stephanostachys wendlandiana Oerst.
Chamaedorea tuerckheimii (Dammer)
Burret
Kinetostigma tuerckheimii (Dammer) Burret
Malortiea tuerckheimii Dammer
Chamaedorea undulatifolia Hodel & Uhl
Chamaedorea verecunda Grayum & Hodel
Chamaedorea volcanensis Hodel & Castillo
Chamaedorea vulgata Standl. & Steyerm.
Chamaedorea foveata Hodel
Chamaedorea warscewiczii H. Wendl.
Chamaedorea latipinna L. H. Bailey
Chamaedorea matae Hodel
Nunnezharia warscewiczii (H. Wendl.)
Kuntze
Chamaedorea whitelockiana Hodel & Uhl
Chamaedorea woodsoniana L. H. Bailey
Chamaedorea vistae Hodel & Uhl

UNCERTAIN NAMES
Chamaedorea atrovirens Mart.
Chamaedorea donnell-smithii Dammer
Chamaedorea ensifolia Liebm.
Nunnezharia atrovirens (Mart.) Kuntze

CHELYOCARPUS Dammer
Tessmanniodoxa Burret
Tessmanniophoenix Burret
Chelyocarpus chuco (Mart.) H. E. Moore
Acanthorrhiza chuco (Mart.) Drude
Tessmanniodoxa chuco (Mart.) Burret
Tessmanniophoenix chuco (Mart.) Burret
Thrinax chuco Mart.
Trithrinax chuco (Mart.) Walp.
Chelyocarpus dianeurus (Burret) H. E.
Moore
Tessmanniodoxa dianeura (Burret) Burret
Tessmanniophoenix dianeura Burret
Chelyocarpus repens Kahn & Mejía

Chelyocarpus ulei Dammer
Tessmanniophoenix longibracteata Burret

UNCERTAIN NAMES
Acanthorrhiza wallisii H. Wendl.
Chelyocarpus wallisii (H. Wendl.) Burret
Tessmanniophoenix wallisii (H. Wendl.) Burret

COCCOTHRINAX Sarg.
Haitiella L. H. Bailey
Thrincoma O. F. Cook
Thringis O. F. Cook
Coccothrinax argentata (Jacq.) L. H. Bailey
Coccothrinax fragrans Burret
Coccothrinax fragrans of L. H. Bailey
Coccothrinax garberi (Chapm.) Sarg.
Coccothrinax jamaicensis Read
Coccothrinax jucunda Sarg.
Coccothrinax jucunda var. *macrosperma* Becc.
Coccothrinax jucunda var. *marquesensis* Becc.
Coccothrinax litoralis León
Coccothrinax proctorii Read
Coccothrinax readii Quero
Palma argentata Jacq.
Thrinax argentea of Griseb. in part
Thrinax argentea var. *garberi* (Chapm.) Chapm.
Thrinax garberi Chapm.
Coccothrinax argentea (Lodd. ex Schult. & Schult. f.) Sarg. ex Becc.
Acanthorriza argentea (Lodd.) O. F. Cook
Coccothrinax argentea of Britton & Wilson
Thrinax argentea Lodd. ex Schult. & Schult. f.
Thrinax longistyla Becc.
Thrinax multiflora Mart. in part
Coccothrinax barbadensis (Lodd. ex Mart.) Becc.
Coccothrinax alta (O. F. Cook) Becc.
Coccothrinax australis L. H. Bailey
Coccothrinax boxii L. H. Bailey
Coccothrinax discreta L. H. Bailey
Coccothrinax dussiana L. H. Bailey
Coccothrinax eggersiana Becc.
Coccothrinax eggersiana var *sanctaecrucis* Becc.
Coccothrinax latifrons (O. F. Cook) Becc.
Coccothrinax laxa (O. F. Cook) Becc.
Coccothrinax martinicensis Becc.
Coccothrinax sabana L. H. Bailey

Coccothrinax sanctithomae Becc.
Thrinax barbadensis Lodd. ex Mart.
Thrincoma alta O. F. Cook
Thringis latifrons O. F. Cook
Thringis laxa O. F. Cook
Coccothrinax borhidiana Muñiz
Coccothrinax crinita (Griseb. & H. Wendl. ex C. H. Wright) Becc.
Coccothrinax crinita subsp. **brevicrinis** Borhidi & Muñiz
Coccothrinax crinita subsp. **crinita**
Thrinax crinita Griseb. & H. Wendl. ex C. H. Wright
Coccothrinax ekmanii Burret
Coccothrinax munizii Borhidi
Haitiella ekmanii (Burret) L. H. Bailey
Haitiella munizii (Borhidi) Borhidi
Coccothrinax gracilis Burret
Coccothrinax gundlachii León
Coccothrinax camagueyana Borhidi & Muñiz
Coccothrinax clarensis León
Coccothrinax clarensis subsp. *clarensis*
Coccothrinax hiorami León
Coccothrinax argentea subsp. *guantanamensis* (León) Borhidi & Muñiz
Coccothrinax argentea var. *guantanamensis* León
Coccothrinax guantanamensis (León) Muñiz & Borhidi
Coccothrinax inaguensis Read
? *Coccothrinax victorini* León
Coccothrinax miraguama (Kunth) León
Coccothrinax acuminata (Griseb. & H. Wendl. in Griseb.) Becc.
Coccothrinax acunana León
Coccothrinax alexandri León
Coccothrinax alexandri subsp. *alexandri*
Coccothrinax alexandri subsp. *nitida* (León) Borhidi & Muñiz
Coccothrinax alexandri var. *nitida* León
Coccothrinax baracoensis Borhidi & Muñiz
Coccothrinax bermudezii Muñiz
Coccothrinax concolor Burret
Coccothrinax cupularis (León) Muñiz & Borhidi
Coccothrinax elegans Muñiz & Borhidi
Coccothrinax fagildei Borhidi & Muñiz
Coccothrinax leonis Muñiz & Borhidi
Coccothrinax macroglossa (León) Muñiz & Borhidi
Coccothrinax miraguama subsp. *arenicola* (León) Borhidi & Muñiz
Coccothrinax miraguama subsp. *havanensis* (León) Borhidi & Muñiz

Coccothrinax miraguama subsp. *macroglossa* (León) Borhidi & Muñiz

Coccothrinax miraguama subsp. *roseocarpa* (León) Borhidi & Muñiz

Coccothrinax miraguama var. *arenicola* León

Coccothrinax miraguama var. *cupularis* León

Coccothrinax miraguama var. *havanensis* León

Coccothrinax miraguama var. *macroglossa* León

Coccothrinax miraguama var. *novogeronensis* Becc.

Coccothrinax miraguama var. *roseocarpa* León

Coccothrinax miraguano Becc.

Coccothrinax moaensis (Borhidi & Muñiz) Muñiz

Coccothrinax montana Burret

Coccothrinax orientalis (León) Muñiz & Borhidi

Coccothrinax rigida (Griseb. & H. Wendl.) Becc.

Coccothrinax saxicola León

Coccothrinax scoparia Becc.

Coccothrinax trinitensis Borhidi & Muñiz

Coccothrinax yuraguana (A. Rich.) León

Coccothrinax yuraguana supsp. *moaensis* Borhidi & Muñiz

Coccothrinax yuraguana subsp. *orientalis* (León) Borhidi

Coccothrinax yuraguana var. *orientalis* León

Copernicia miraguama (Kunth) Kunth

Corypha miraguama Kunth

Thrinax acuminata Griseb. & H. Wendl.

Thrinax miraguama (Kunth) Mart.

Thrinax stellata Lodd. ex Mart.

Thrinax yuraguana A. Rich.

Coccothrinax pauciramosa Burret

Coccothrinax clarensis subsp. *brevifolia* (León) Borhidi & Muñiz

Coccothrinax clarensis var. *brevifolia* León

Coccothrinax clarensis var. *perrigida* León

Coccothrinax garciana León

Coccothrinax microphylla Borhidi & Muñiz

Coccothrinax muricata León

Coccothrinax muricata var. *nipensis* Borhidi & Muñiz

Coccothrinax pseudorigida León

Coccothrinax pseudorigida var. *acaulis* León

Coccothrinax savannarum (León) Borhidi & Muñiz

Thrinax rigida Griseb. & H. Wendl.

Coccothrinax salvatoris León

Coccothrinax salvatoris subsp. *loricata* (León) Borhidi & Muñiz

Coccothrinax salvatoris subsp. *salvatoris*

Coccothrinax salvatoris var. *loricata* León

Coccothrinax yunquensis Borhidi & Muñiz

Coccothrinax spissa L. H. Bailey

COCOS L.
Cocos nucifera L.
Palma cocos Miller

COLPOTHRINAX Griseb. & H. Wendl.
Colpothrinax cookii Read
Colpothrinax wrightii Griseb. & H. Wendl. ex Siebert & Voss
Pritchardia wrightii (Griseb. & H. Wendl. ex Siebert & Voss) Becc.

COPERNICIA Mart. ex Endl.
Arrudaria Macedo
Coryphomia N. Rojas
Copernicia alba Morong ex Morong & Britton
Copernicia australis Becc.
Copernicia australis var. *alba* (Morong) Bertoni ex Hauman
Copernicia australis var. *nigra* (Morong) Bertoni ex Hauman
Copernicia cerifera of Mart.
Copernicia nigra Morong ex Becc.
Copernicia ramulosa Burret
Copernicia rubra Morong
Copernicia baileyana León
Copernicia baileyana f. *bifida* León
Copernicia baileyana var. *laciniosa* León
Copernicia fallaense León
Copernicia berteroana Becc.
Copernicia brittonorum León
Copernicia brittonorum var. *acuta* León
Copernicia brittonorum var. *sabaloense* León
Copernicia cowellii Britton & Wilson
Copernicia ekmanii Burret
Copernicia gigas E. Ekman ex Burret
Copernicia excelsa León
Copernicia vespertilionum (León) León
Copernicia glabrescens H. Wendl. ex Becc.
Copernicia glabrescens var. *glabrescens*
Copernicia glabrescens var. *havanensis* León
Copernicia glabrescens var. *ramosissima* (Burret) Muñiz & Borhidi
Copernicia ramosissima Burret
Copernicia hospita Mart.
Copernicia clarensis León
Copernicia curbeloi León
Copernicia curtisii Becc.
Copernicia x *escarzana* León

Copernicia holguinensis León
Copernicia hospita var. *clarensis* León
Copernicia humicola León
Copernicia molineti León
Copernicia molineti var. *cuneata* León
Copernicia occidentalis León
Copernicia pauciflora Burret
Copernicia roigii León
Copernicia sueroana (León) León
Copernicia sueroana var. *semiorbicularis* León
Copernicia textilis León
Copernicia yarey Burret
Copernicia yarey var. *robusta* León
Copernicia yarey var. *yarey*
Copernicia macroglossa H. Wendl. ex Becc.
Copernicia burretiana León
Copernicia leoniana Dahlgren & Glassman
Copernicia macroglossa of León
Copernicia torreana León
Copernicia prunifera (Mill.) H. E. Moore
Arrudaria cerifera (Arruda) Macedo
Copernicia cerifera (Arruda) Mart.
Corypha cerifera Arruda
Copernicia rigida Britton & Wilson
Copernicia clarkii León
Copernicia longiglossa León
Copernicia oxycalyx Burret
Copernicia rigida f. *fissilingua* León
Copernicia sueroana (León) León
Copernicia tectorum (Kunth) Mart.
Copernicia sanctae-martae Becc.
Corypha tectorum Kunth

HYBRIDS
Copernicia x *burretiana* (León) Muñiz & Borhidi (*C. macroglossa* x *C. hospita*)
Copernicia x *occidentalis* (León) Muñiz & Borhidi (*C. hospita* x *C. brittonorum*)
Copernicia schaferi Dahlgren & Glassman (*C. cowellii* x *C. hospita*)
Copernicia x *sueroana* León (*C. hospita* x *C. rigida*)
Copernicia x *textilis* (León) Dahlgren & Glassman (*C. hospita* x *C. baileyana*)
Copernicia x *vespertilionum* León (*C. gigas* x *C. rigida*)

UNCERTAIN NAMES
Copernicia barbadensis (Lodd. ex Mart.) H. Wendl.
Copernicia caranda Linden ex Becc.
Copernicia guibourtiana Pharm.
Copernicia macrophylla Roezl ex Gisard
Copernicia robusta hort. ex Linden

CRYOSOPHILA Blume
Acanthorrhiza H. Wendl.
Cryosophila cookii Bartlett
Cryosophila grayumii R. Evans
Cryosophila grayumii subsp. *gomezii* R. Evans
Cryosophila grayumii subsp. *grayumii*
Cryosophila guagara Allen
Cryosophila kalbreyeri (Dammer ex Burret) Dahlgren
Acanthorrhiza kalbreyeri Dammer ex Burret
Cryosophila kalbreyeri subsp. *bartlettii* R. Evans
Cryosophila kalbreyeri subsp. *cogolloi* R. Evans
Cryosophila kalbreyeri subsp. *kalbreyeri*
Cryosophila macrocarpa R. Evans
Cryosophila nana (Kunth) Blume ex Salomon
Acanthorrhiza aculeata (Liebm. ex Mart.) H. Wendl.
Acanthorrhiza mocini (Kunth) Hemsley
Chamaerops mocini Kunth
Copernicia nana (Kunth) Mart.
Corypha nana Kunth
Trithrinax aculeata Liebm. ex Mart.
Cryosophila stauracantha (Heynhold) R. Evans
Acanthorrhiza collinsii O. F. Cook
Acanthorrhiza stauracantha (Heynhold) Linden
Chamaerops stauracantha Heynhold
Cryosophila argentea Bartlett
Cryosophila bifurcata Lundell
Cryosophila warscewiczii (H. Wendl.) Bartlett
Acanthorrhiza warscewiczii H. Wendl.
Cryosophila albida Bartlett
Cryosophila williamsii Allen

DESMONCUS Mart.
Atitara Kuntze
Desmoncus cirrhiferus A. H. Gentry & Zardini
Desmoncus giganteus Henderson
Desmoncus mitis Mart.
Desmoncus mitis var. **leptoclonos** Henderson
Desmoncus leptoclonos of Dammer
Desmoncus mitis var. **leptospadix** (Mart.) Henderson
Atitara leptospadix (Mart.) Kuntze
Desmoncus leptospadix Mart.
Desmoncus mitis var. **mitis**
Atitara mitis (Mart.) Kuntze

Atitara pumila (Trail) Kuntze
Desmoncus mitis Mart.
Desmoncus pumilus Trail
Desmoncus setosus var. *mitescens* Drude
Desmoncus mitis var. **rurrenabaquensis**
Henderson
Desmoncus mitis var. **tenerrimus** (Mart.)
Henderson
Bactris tenerrima Mart.
Desmoncus tenerrimus (Mart.) Mart. ex
Burret
Desmoncus vacivus L. H. Bailey
Desmoncus orthacanthos Mart.
Atitara ataxacantha (Barb. Rodr.) Kuntze
Atitara chinantlensis (Liebm.) Kuntze
Atitara costaricensis Kuntze
Atitara cuyabensis (Barb. Rodr.) Barb.
Rodr.
Atitara drudeana Kuntze
Atitara horrida (Splitg. ex Mart.) Kuntze
Atitara lophacantha (Mart.) Barb. Rodr.
Atitara macrocarpa (Barb. Rodr.) Barb.
Rodr.
Atitara major (Crueg.) Kuntze
Atitara orthacantha (Mart.) Barb. Rodr.
Atitara palustris (Trail) Kuntze
Atitara prostrata (Lindm.) Barb. Rodr.
Atitara rudenta (Mart.) Barb. Rodr.
Desmoncus angustisectus Burret
Desmoncus anomalus Bartlett
Desmoncus apureanus L. H. Bailey
Desmoncus ataxacanthus Barb. Rodr.
Desmoncus brittonii L. H. Bailey
Desmoncus chinantlensis Liebm. ex Mart.
Desmoncus costaricensis (Kuntze) Burret
Desmoncus cuyabaensis Barb. Rodr.
Desmoncus demeraranus L. H. Bailey & H. E.
Moore
Desmoncus ferox Bartlett
Desmoncus hartii L. H. Bailey
Desmoncus horridus Splitg. ex Mart.
Desmoncus huebneri Burret
Desmoncus isthmius L. H. Bailey
Desmoncus kuhlmanii Burret
Desmoncus leiorhachis Burret
Desmoncus leptochaete Burret
Desmoncus longifolius Mart.
Desmoncus lophacanthos Mart.
Desmoncus luetzelburgii Burret
Desmoncus lundellii Bartlett
Desmoncus macrocarpus Barb. Rodr.
Desmoncus major Crueg. ex Griseb.
Desmoncus melanacanthos Drude

Desmoncus multijugus Steyerm.
Desmoncus myriacanthos Dugand
Desmoncus orthacanthos var. *mitis* Drude
Desmoncus orthacanthos var. *trailiana* Drude
Desmoncus palustris Trail
Desmoncus prostratus Lindman
Desmoncus quasillarius Bartlett
Desmoncus rudentum Mart.
Desmoncus schippii Burret
Desmoncus tobagonis L. H. Bailey
Desmoncus uaxactunensis Bartlett
Desmoncus velezii L. H. Bailey
Desmoncus werdermannii Burret
Desmoncus phoenicocarpus Barb. Rodr.
Atitara macrodon (Barb. Rodr.) Barb. Rodr.
Atitara nemorosa (Barb. Rodr.) Barb. Rodr.
Atitara phoenicocarpa (Barb. Rodr.) Kuntze
Desmoncus kaieteurensis L. H. Bailey
Desmoncus macrodon Barb. Rodr.
Desmoncus nemorosus Barb. Rodr.
Desmoncus parvulus L. H. Bailey
Desmoncus polyacanthos Mart.
Desmoncus polyacanthos var. **polyacanthos**
Atitara aerea (Drude) Barb. Rodr.
Atitara caespitosa (Barb. Rodr.) Barb. Rodr.
Atitara inermis (Barb. Rodr.) Barb. Rodr.
Atitara leptoclona (Drude) Barb. Rodr.
Atitara macroacantha (Mart.) Kuntze
Atitara oligacantha (Barb. Rodr.) Kuntze
Atitara oxyacantha (Mart.) Kuntze
Atitara paraensis Barb. Rodr.
Atitara phenogophylla (Drude) Kuntze
Atitara philippiana (Barb. Rodr.) Barb.
Rodr.
Atitara polyacantha (Mart.) Kuntze
Atitara pycnacantha (Mart.) Kuntze
Atitara riparia (Spruce) Kuntze
Atitara setosa (Mart.) Kuntze
Desmoncus aereus Drude
Desmoncus brevisectus Burret
Desmoncus caespitosus Barb. Rodr.
Desmoncus campylacanthus Burret
Desmoncus dasyacanthus Burret
Desmoncus duidensis Steyerm.
Desmoncus inermis Barb. Rodr.
Desmoncus latisectus Burret
Desmoncus leptoclonos Drude
Desmoncus longisectus Burret
Desmoncus macroacanthos Mart.
Desmoncus maguirei L. H. Bailey
Desmoncus mirandanus L. H. Bailey
Desmoncus oligacanthus Barb. Rodr.
Desmoncus oxyacanthos Mart.

Desmoncus paraensis (Barb. Rodr.) Barb. Rodr.
Desmoncus peraltus L. H. Bailey
Desmoncus phengophyllus Drude
Desmoncus philippianus Barb. Rodr.
Desmoncus polyacanthos var. *oxyacanthos* (Mart.) Drude
Desmoncus polyacanthos var. *angustifolia* Drude
Desmoncus prestoei L. H. Bailey
Desmoncus pycnacanthos Mart.
Desmoncus pycnacanthos var. *sarmentosus* Drude
Desmoncus riparius Spruce
Desmoncus setosus Mart.
Desmoncus ulei Dammer
Desmoncus polyacanthos var. **prunifer** (Mart.) Henderson
Atitara prunifera (Poepp. ex Mart.) Kuntze
Desmoncus prunifer Poepp. ex Mart.
Desmoncus stans Grayum & Nevers

UNCERTAIN NAMES
Atitara aculeata (H. Wendl.) Kuntze
Atitara americana (Lodd.) Kuntze
Atitara dubia (Lodd.) Kuntze
Atitara granatensis (hort.) Kuntze
Atitara latifrons (hort.) Kuntze
Atitara polyphylla (Poit. ex Desf.) Kuntze
Desmoncus aculeatus H. Wendl.
Desmoncus americanus Lodd. ex Loud.
Desmoncus andicola Pasq.
Desmoncus dubius Lodd. ex Loud.
Desmoncus glaber Mart. ex Burret
Desmoncus granatensis hort.
Desmoncus grandifolius Linden
Desmoncus intermedius Mart. ex H. Wendl.
Desmoncus latifrons hort.
Desmoncus panamensis Linden
Desmoncus peruvianus Dammer ex Burret
Desmoncus polyphyllus Poit. ex Desf.
Desmoncus wallisii Linden

DICTYOCARYUM H. Wendl.
Dahlgrenia Steyerm.
Dictyocaryum fuscum (H. Karst.) H. Wendl.
Iriartea altissima Appun
Iriartea altissima Klotzsch ex Al. Jahn
Iriartea altissima Klotzsch ex Linden
Iriartea fusca (H. Karst.) Drude
Socratea fusca H. Wendl.
Dictyocaryum lamarckianum (Mart.) H. Wendl.

Deckeria lamarckiana (Mart.) H. Karst.
Dictyocaryum globiferum Dugand
Dictyocaryum platysepalum Burret
Dictyocaryum schultzei Burret
Dictyocaryum superbum Burret
Iriartea lamarckianum Mart.
Dictyocaryum ptarianum (Steyerm.) H. E. Moore
Dahlgreniana ptariana Steyerm.

UNCERTAIN NAMES
Dictyocaryum glaucescens Linden
Dictyocaryum wallisii Bull
Dictyocaryum wallisii Linden

ELAEIS Jacq.
Alfonsia Kunth
Corozo Jacq. ex Giseke
Elaeis oleifera (Kunth) Cortés
Alfonsia oleifera Kunth
Corozo oleifera (Kunth) L. H. Bailey
Elaeis melanococca Mart.
Elaeis melanococca var. *semicircularis* Oersted

EUTERPE Mart.
Catis O. F. Cook
Plectis O. F. Cook
Rooseveltia O. F. Cook
Euterpe broadwayi Becc. ex Broadway
Euterpe broadwayana Becc.
Euterpe dominicana L. H. Bailey
Euterpe grenadana
Euterpe hagleyi
Euterpe catinga Wallace
Euterpe catinga var. **catinga**
Euterpe aurantiaca H. E. Moore
Euterpe caatinga Barb. Rodr.
Euterpe catinga var. *aurantiaca* Drude
Euterpe concinna Burret
Euterpe controversa Barb. Rodr.
Euterpe mollissima Spruce
Euterpe catinga var. **roraimae** (Dammer) Henderson & Galeano
Euterpe erubescens H. E. Moore
Euterpe montis-duida Burret
Euterpe ptariana Steyerm.
Euterpe roraimae Dammer
Euterpe edulis Mart.
Euterpe egusquizae Bertoni
Euterpe egusquizae Bertoni ex Hauman
Euterpe espiritosantensis Fernandes
Euterpe longebracteata Barb. Rodr.
Euterpe longespathacea Barb. Rodr. ex Huber

Euterpe luminosa Henderson, Galeano & Meza
Euterpe oleracea Mart.
Catis martiana O. F. Cook
Euterpe badiocarpa Barb. Rodr.
Euterpe beardii L. H. Bailey
Euterpe cuatrecasana Dugand
Euterpe precatoria Mart.
Euterpe precatoria var. **longevaginata**
(Mart.) Henderson
Euterpe kalbreyeri Burret
Euterpe karsteniana Engel
Euterpe leucospadix H. Wendl. ex Hemsl.
Euterpe longevaginata Mart.
Euterpe macrospadix Oerst.
Euterpe micorcarpa Burret
Euterpe panamensis Burret
Rooseveltia frankliniana O. F. Cook
Euterpe precatoria var. **precatoria**
Euterpe confertifolia L. H. Bailey
Euterpe jatapuensis Barb. Rodr.
Euterpe langloisii Burret
Euterpe oleracea of Engel
Euterpe petiolata Burret
Euterpe rhodoxyla Dugand
Euterpe stenophylla Trail
Euterpe subruminata Burret
Plectis oweniana O. F. Cook

UNCERTAIN NAMES
Euterpe antioquensis Linden
Euterpe brasiliana Oken
Euterpe elegans Linden
Euterpe filamentosa Blume
Euterpe gracilis Linden
Euterpe manihot Lodd. ex H. Wendl.
Euterpe menziesii Pritz.
Euterpe pisifera Gaertn.
Euterpe puruensis Linden
Euterpe speciosa hort.
Euterpe zamora hort.

GASTROCOCOS Morales
Gastrococos crispa (Kunth) H. E. Moore
Acrocomia armentalis (Morales) L. H. Bailey
Acrocomia crispa (Kunth) C. Baker ex Becc.
Acrocomia lasiospatha of Griseb.
Astrocaryum crispum (Kunth) Gomez Maca
Cocos crispa Kunth
Gastrococos armentalis Morales

GAUSSIA H. Wendl.
Aeria O. F. Cook
Opsiandra O. F. Cook

Gaussia attenuata (O. F. Cook) Becc.
Aeria attenuata O. F. Cook
Gaussia gomez-pompae (Quero) Quero
Opsiandra gomez-pompae Quero
Gaussia maya (O. F. Cook) Quero & Read
Opsiandra maya O. F. Cook
Gaussia princeps H. Wendl.
Gaussia spirituana Moya & Leiva

UNCERTAIN NAMES
Gaussia ghiesbreghti H. Wendl.
Gaussia portoricensis H. Wendl.

GEONOMA Willd.
Gynestum Poit.
Kalbreyera Burret
Roebelia Engel
Taenianthera Burret
Vouay Aubl.
Geonoma appuniana Spruce
Geonoma guianensis Read & Granv.
Geonoma roraimae Dammer
Geonoma arundinacea Mart.
Geonoma uleana Dammer
Geonoma aspidiifolia Spruce
Geonoma fusca Wess. Boer
Geonoma baculifera (Poit.) Kunth
Geonoma acutiflora Mart.
Geonoma baculifera var. *macrospatha*
(Spruce) Drude
Geonoma estevaniana Burret
Geonoma macrospatha Spruce
Gynestum baculiferum Poit.
Geonoma brevispatha Barb. Rodr.
Geonoma brevispatha var. **brevispatha**
Geonoma altissima Barb. Rodr.
Geonoma aricanga Barb. Rodr.
Geonoma calophyta Barb. Rodr.
Geonoma caudulata Loes.
Geonoma chapadensis Barb. Rodr.
Geonoma decussata Burret
Geonoma plurinervia Burret
Geonoma rupestris Barb. Rodr.
Geonoma schottiana var. *palustris* Warm. ex
Drude
Geonoma stenoschista Burret
Geonoma warmingii A. D. Hawkes
Geonoma weddelliana H. Wendl. ex Drude
Geonoma brevispatha var. **occidentale**
Henderson
Geonoma brongniartii Mart.
Geonoma cuneifolia Burret
Geonoma metensis Karst.
Geonoma werdermannii Burret

Geonoma camana Trail
Geonoma lagesiana Burret
Taenianthera camana (Trail) Burret
Taenianthera lagesiana (Dammer) Burret
Geonoma chlamydostachys Galeano
Geonoma chococola Wess. Boer
Geonoma concinna Burret
Geonoma congesta H. Wendl. ex Spruce
Geonoma calyptrogynoidea Burret
Geonoma cuneata H. Wendl. ex Spruce
Geonoma cuneata var. **cuneata**
Geonoma decurrens H. Wendl. ex Burret
Geonoma cuneata var. **gracilis** (H. Wendl.
ex Spruce) Skov
Geonoma gracilis H. Wendl ex Spruce
Geonoma obovata H. Wendl. ex Spruce
Geonoma cuneata var. **procumbens** (H.
Wendl. ex Spruce) Skov
Geonoma procumbens
Geonoma cuneata var. **sodiroi** (Dammer ex
Burret) Skov
Geonoma gibbosa Burret
Geonoma sodiroi Dammer ex Burret
Geonoma densa Linden & H. Wendl.
Geonoma barthia Engel
?*Geonoma pulchra* Engel
?*Geonoma uncibracteata* Burret
Geonoma deversa (Poit.) Kunth
Geonoma bartletii Dammer ex Burret
Geonoma desmarestii Mart.
Geonoma flacida H. Wendl. ex Spruce
Geonoma killipii Burret
Geonoma leptostachys Burret
Geonoma longepetiolata Oerst.
Geonoma macropoda Burret
Geonoma major Burret
Geonoma microspatha Spruce
Geonoma microspatha var. *pacimoensis* Spruce
Geonoma paniculigera Mart.
Geonoma paniculigera var. *cosmiophylla* Trail
Geonoma paniculigera subvar. *gramineifolia*
Trail
Geonoma paniculigera var. *microspatha*
(Spruce) Trail
Geonoma paniculigera var. *papyracea* Trail
Geonoma rectifolia Wallace
Geonoma tessmannii Burret
Geonoma trijugata Barb. Rodr.
Geonoma yauaperyensis Barb. Rodr.
Gynestum deversum Poit.
Geonoma divisa H. E. Moore
Geonoma epetiolata H. E. Moore
Geonoma ferruginea H. Wendl. ex Spruce
Geonoma microspadix H. Wendl.

Geonoma microstachys H. Wendl. ex Burret
Geonoma versiformis H. Wendl. ex Spruce
Geonoma gamiova Barb. Rodr.
Geonoma gastioniana Glaz. ex Drude
Geonoma wittigiana Glaz. ex Drude
Geonoma interrupta (Ruiz & Pav.) Mart.
Geonoma interrupta var. **euspatha** (Burret)
Henderson
Geonoma euspatha Burret
Geonoma karuaiana Steyerm.
Geonoma interrupta var. **interrupta**
Geonoma binervia Oerst.
Geonoma dominicana L. H. Bailey
Geonoma dryanderae Burret
Geonoma edulis H. Wendl. ex Spruce
Geonoma leptoclada Burret
Geonoma magnifica Linden & H. Wendl.
Geonoma martinicensis Mart.
Geonoma megaloptila Burret
?*Geonoma membranacea* H. Wendl. ex
Spruce
Geonoma mexicana Lieb. ex Mart.
Geonoma oxycarpa Mart.
Geonoma pinnatifrons Willd.
Geonoma pinnatifrons var. *vaga* (Griseb.)
Burret
Geonoma platybothros Burret
Geonoma pleeana Mart.
?*Geonoma polyclada* Burret
Geonoma preussii Burret
Geonoma purdieana Spruce
Geonoma ramossissima Burret
?*Geonoma rivalis* Kalbreyer ex Burret
Geonoma vaga Griseb.
Martinezia interrupta Ruiz & Pav.
Geonoma jussieuana Mart.
Geonoma acutangula Burret
?*Geonoma adscendens* Dammer ex Burret
Geonoma amoena Burret
?*Geonoma brachystachys* Burret
?*Geonoma campylostachys* Burret
?*Geonoma cernua* Burret
Geonoma cuneatoidea Burret
?*Geonoma dicranospadix* Burret
?*Geonoma frontinensis* Burret
Geonoma gracillima Burret
?*Geonoma grandifrons* Burret
?*Geonoma granditrijuga* Burret
Geonoma helminthostachys Burret
?*Geonoma kalbreyeri* Burret
Geonoma lehmanii Dammer ex Burret
?*Geonoma mucronata* Burret
Geonoma multisecta (Burret) Burret
Geonoma parvifrons Burret

?Geonoma pleioneura Burret
Taenianthera multisecta Burret
?Taenianthera weberbaueri Burret
Geonoma laxiflora Mart.
Geonoma beccariana Barb. Rodr.
Geonoma laxiflora var. *depauperata* Trail
Geonoma leptospadix Trail
Geonoma saramaccana L. H. Bailey
Geonoma linearis Burret
Geonoma longepedunculata Burret
Geonoma longevaginata H. Wendl. ex
  Spruce
Geonoma macrostachys Mart.
Geonoma macrostachys var. **acaulis** (Mart.)
  Skov
Geonoma acaulis Mart.
Geonoma acaulis subsp. *tapajotensis* Trail
Geonoma tapajotensis (Trail) Drude
Taenianthera acaulis (Mart.) Burret
Taenianthera gracilis Burret
Taenianthera minor Burret
Taenianthera oligosticha Burret
Taenianthera tapajotensis (Trail) Burret
Geonoma macrostachys var. **macrostachys**
Geonoma tamandua Trail
Geonoma woronowii Burret
Taenianthera macrostachys (Mart.) Burret
Taenianthera tamandua (Trail) Burret
Geonoma macrostachys var. **poiteauana**
  (Kunth) Henderson
Geonoma acaulis (Poit.) Burret
Geonoma chaunostachys Burret
Geonoma dammeri Huber
Geonoma poiteana Mart.
Geonoma poiteauana Kunth
Gynestum acaule Poit.
Taenianthera dammeri Burret
Taenianthera lakoi Burret
Geonoma maxima (Poit.) Kunth
Geonoma maxima var. **ambigua** (Spruce)
  Henderson
Geonoma ambigua Spruce
Geonoma robusta Burret
Geonoma schomburgkiana Spruce
Geonoma maxima var. **chelidonura**
  (Spruce) Henderson
Geonoma bijugata Barb. Rodr.
Geonoma brachyfoliata Barb. Rodr.
Geonoma chelidonura Spruce
Geonoma dasystachys Burret
Geonoma densiflora Spruce
Geonoma densiflora var. *monticola* Spruce
Geonoma falcata Barb. Rodr.
Geonoma furcifolia Barb. Rodr.

Geonoma huebneri Burret
Geonoma juruana Dammer
Geonoma lakoi Burret
Geonoma longisecta Burret
Geonoma palustris Barb. Rodr.
Geonoma parvisecta Burret
Geonoma personata Spruce
Geonoma speciosa Barb. Rodr.
Geonoma spruceana Trail
Geonoma spruceana subsp. *intermedia* var.
  major Trail
Geonoma spruceana subsp. *intermedia* var.
  tuberculata Trail
Geonoma spruceana subsp. *spruceana* var.
  heptasticha Trail
Geonoma spruceana subsp. *spruceana* var.
  micra Trail
Geonoma spruceana subsp. *spruceana* var.
  spruceana
Geonoma tuberculata Spruce
Geonoma maxima var. **maxima**
Geonoma camptoneura Burret
Geonoma capanemae Barb. Rodr.
Geonoma discolor Spruce
Geonoma hexasticha Spruce
Geonoma latisecta Burret
Geonoma multiflora Mart.
Geonoma negrensis Spruce
Geonoma paraensis Spruce
Geonoma spruceana subsp. *intermedia* var.
  compta Trail
Geonoma spruceana subsp. *intermedia* var.
  intermedia Trail
Geonoma uliginosa Barb. Rodr.
Gynestum maximum Poit.
Geonoma maxima var. **spixiana** (Mart.)
  Henderson
Geonoma grandisecta Burret
Geonoma spixiana Mart.
Geonoma myriantha Dammer
Geonoma oldemannii Granv.
Geonoma oligoclona Trail
Geonoma orbignyana Mart.
?Geonoma andina Burret
?Geonoma anomoclada Burret
Geonoma aulacophylla Burret
Geonoma campyloclada Burret
Geonoma euterpoidea Burret
?Geonoma floccosa Dammer ex Burret
Geonoma goniocarpa Burret
?Geonoma heinrichsiae Burret
Geonoma hoffmanniana H. Wendl. ex
  Spruce
Geonoma iodolepis Burret

Geonoma iodoneura Burret
Geonoma lepidota Burret
Geonoma leucotricha Burret
Geonoma lindeniana H. Wendl.
Geonoma linearifolia H. Karst.
?*Geonoma macroura* Burret
Geonoma marggraffia Engel
Geonoma microclada Burret
?*Geonoma molinillo* Burret
Geonoma pachydicrana Burret
Geonoma paleacea Burret
Geonoma plicata Burret
Geonoma pulcherrima Burret
Geonoma pumila Linden & H. Wendl.
Geonoma ramosa Engel
?*Geonoma rhytidocarpa* Burret
?*Geonoma tenuifolia* Burret
Geonoma wendlandiana Burret
Geonoma paradoxa Burret
Geonoma paraguanensis H. Karst.
Geonoma pauciflora Mart.
Geonoma bifurca Drude & H. Wendl.
Geonoma caespitosa H. Wendl. ex Drude
Geonoma elegans Mart.
Geonoma elegans var. *robusta* Drude
Geonoma olfersiana Klotzsch ex Drude
Geonoma porteana H. Wendl.
Geonoma poeppigiana Mart.
Geonoma oligoclada Burret
Geonoma pohliana Mart.
Geonoma barbigera Barb. Rodr.
Geonoma barbosiana Burret
Geonoma blanchetiana H. Wendl. ex Drude
Geonoma fiscellaria Mart. ex Drude
?*Geonoma kuhlmannii* Burret
Geonoma latifolia Burret
Geonoma luetzelburgii Burret
Geonoma macroclona Burret
Geonoma pilosa Barb. Rodr.
Geonoma tomentosa Barb. Rodr.
Geonoma trigonostyla Burret
Geonoma polyandra Burret
Geonoma rubescens H. Wendl. ex Drude
Geonoma platycaula Drude & Trail
Geonoma rodeiensis Barb. Rodr.
Geonoma trinervis Barb. Rodr.
Geonoma schottiana Mart.
Geonoma erythrospadice Barb. Rodr.
Geonoma hoehnei Burret
Geonoma schottiana var. *angustifolia* Drude
Geonoma schottiana var. *latifolia* Drude
Geonoma scoparia Grayum & Nevers
Geonoma simplicifrons Willd.
Geonoma fendleriana Spruce
Geonoma willdenowii Klotzsch

Geonoma spinescens H. Wendl.
Geonoma tenuis Burret
Geonoma stricta (Poit.) Kunth
Geonoma stricta var. **piscicauda** (Dammer)
    Henderson
Geonoma herthae Burret
Geonoma piscicauda Dammer
Geonoma wittiana Dammer
Geonoma stricta var. **stricta**
Geonoma lanceolata Burret
Geonoma maguirei L. H. Bailey
Geonoma pycnostachys Mart.
Gynestum strictum Poit.
Geonoma stricta var. **trailii** (Burret)
    Henderson
Geonoma bella Burret
Geonoma elegans var. *amazonica* Trail
Geonoma raimondii Burret
Geonoma trailii Burret
Geonoma trauniana Dammer
Geonoma tenuissima H. E. Moore
Geonoma triandra (Burret) Wess. Boer
Kalbreyera triandra Burret
Geonoma triglochin Burret
Geonoma trigona (Ruiz & Pav.) A. H.
    Gentry
Carludovica trigona Ruiz & Pav.
Ludovia trigona (Ruiz & Pav.) Pers.
Salmia trigona (Ruiz & Pav.) Willd.
Geonoma umbraculiformis Wess. Boer
Geonoma undata Klotzsch
Geonoma dussiana Becc.
Geonoma helminthoclada Burret
Geonoma hodgeorum L. H. Bailey
Geonoma macroclada Burret
Geonoma macrosiphon Burret
Geonoma margaritoides Engel
Geonoma molinae Glassman
Geonoma pachyclada Burret
Geonoma polyneura Burret
Geonoma seleri Burret
Geonoma weberbaueri Dammer ex Burret
?*Geonoma andicola* Burret
Geonoma megalospatha Burret
Geonoma solitaria (Engel) Al. Jahn
Geonoma stuebelii Burret
Roebelia solitaria Engel

UNCERTAIN NAMES
Geonoma amazonica hort. ex H. Wendl.
Geonoma antioquensis hort. ex H. Wendl.
Geonoma bluntii hort.
Geonoma brevibisecta Burret
Geonoma caudescens H. Wendl. ex Drude
Geonoma chiriquensis hort.

Geonoma compacta Linden
Geonoma congestissima Burret
Geonoma corallifera Hook. ex Morr.
Geonoma decora L. Lind. & Rodigas
Geonoma demarestei Pritz.
Geonoma frigida Linden
Geonoma furcifrons Drude
Geonoma gracilipes Dammer ex Burret
Geonoma herbstii hort.
Geonoma hoppii Burret
Geonoma imperialis Linden
Geonoma insignis Burret
Geonoma iraze Linden
Geonoma lacerata hort.
Geonoma latifrons hort. ex Burret
Geonoma longipes hort. ex H. Wendl.
Geonoma macrophylla Burret
Geonoma princeps Linden
Geonoma pulchella hort. ex Linden
Geonoma pynaertiana Sander
Geonoma riedeliana H. Wendl.
Geonoma saga Spruce
Geonoma seemannii hort.
Geonoma stenothyrsa Burret
Geonoma trichostachys Burret
Geonoma ventricosa Engel
Geonoma verdugo Linden
Geonoma verschaffelti hort.
Geonoma wallisii hort.
Geonoma zamorensis hort.

HYOSPATHE Mart.
Hyospathe elegans Mart.
Chamaedorea falcaria L. H. Bailey
Hyospathe brevipedunculata Dammer
Hyospathe concinna H. E. Moore
Hyospathe filiformis H. Wendl. ex Drude
Hyospathe gracilis H. Wendl. ex Drude
Hyospathe lehmannii Burret
Hyospathe maculata Steyerm.
Hyospathe micropetala Burret
Hyospathe pallida H. E. Moore
Hyospathe pittieri Burret
Hyospathe schultzeae Burret
Hyospathe simplex Burret
Hyospathe sodiroi Dammer
Hyospathe tessmannii Burret
Hyospathe ulei Dammer
Hyospathe weberbaueri Dammer ex Burret
Hyospathe wendlandiana Dammer
Hyospathe macrorachis Burret

UNCERTAIN NAMES
Hyospathe amaricaulis hort.
Hyospathe antioquensis hort.

Hyospathe chiriquensis hort.
Hyospathe elata hort. ex Hook. f.

IRIARTEA Ruiz & Pav.
Deckeria H. Karst.
Iriartea deltoidea Ruiz & Pav.
Deckeria corneto H. Karst.
Deckeria phaeocarpa (Mart.) H. Karst.
Deckeria ventricosa (Mart.) H. Karst.
Iriartea corneto (H. Karst.) H. Wendl.
Iriartea gigantea H. Wendl.
Iriartea megalocarpa Burret
Iriartea phaeocarpa Mart.
Iriartea ventricosa Mart.
Iriartea weberbaueri Burret

UNCERTAIN NAMES
Deckeria elegans Linden
Iriartea affinis H. Karst. ex Linden
Iriartea costata Linden
Iriartea glaucescens Linden
Iriartea leprosa Zippelius ex Macklot
Iriartea monogyna Zippelius ex Macklot
Iriartea nivea hort. ex Watson
Iriartea pygmaea Linden
Iriartea robusta hort. ex Kerch.
Iriartea sobolifera Linden
Iriartea xanthorhiza Klotzsch ex Linden
Iriartea zamorensis Kerch.
Iriartea zamorensis Linden

IRIARTELLA H. Wendl.
Cuatrecasea Dugand
Iriartella setigera (Mart.) H. Wendl.
Cuatrecasea spruceana (Barb. Rodr.)
  Dugand
Cuatrecasea vaupesana Dugand
Iriartea pruriens Spruce
Iriartea setigera Mart.
Iriartea spruceana Barb. Rodr.
Iriartella pruriens (Spruce) Barb. Rodr.
Iriartella spruceana (Barb. Rodr.) Barb.
  Rodr.
Iriartella setigera var *pruriens* Barb. Rodr.
Iriartella stenocarpa Burret
Iriartea stenocarpa (Burret) J. F. Macbr.
Iriartella ferreyrae H. E. Moore

ITAYA H. E. Moore
Itaya amicorum H. E. Moore

JUANIA Drude
Juania australis (Mart.) Drude ex Hook. f.
Ceroxylon australe Mart.
Morenia chonta Philippi
Nunnezharia chonta (Philippi) Kuntze

JUBAEA Kunth
  Micrococos Philippi
  Molinaea Bertero
Jubaea chilensis (Molina) Baillon
  Cocos chilensis (Molina) Kunth
  Jubaea spectabilis Kunth
  Micrococos chilensis (Molina) Philippi
  Molinaea micrococos Bertero
  Palma chilensis Molina

LEOPOLDINIA Mart.
Leopoldinia major Wallace
Leopoldinia piassaba Wallace
Leopoldinia pulchra Mart.
  Leopoldinia insignis Mart.

UNCERTAIN NAMES
  Leopoldinia laucheana hort.

LEPIDOCARYUM Mart.
Lepidocaryum tenue Mart.
Lepidocaryum tenue var. **casiquiarense**
  (Spruce) Henderson
  Lepidocaryum casiquiarense (Spruce) Drude
  Lepidocaryum guainiense (Spruce) Drude
  Mauritia casiquiarense Spruce
  Mauritia guainiensis Spruce
Lepidocaryum tenue var. **gracile** (Mart.)
  Henderson
  Lepidocaryum enneaphyllum Barb. Rodr.
  Lepidocaryum gracile Mart.
  Lepidocaryum gujanense Becc.
  Lepidocaryum macrocarpum (Drude) Becc.
  Lepidocaryum sexpartitum Trail & Barb.
    Rodr.
  Lepidocaryum tenue var. *sexpartitum* (Trail &
    Barb. Rodr.) Trail
  Lepidocaryum sexpartitum var. *macrocarpum*
    Drude
  Lepidocaryum sexpartitum var. *microcarpum*
    Drude
  Mauritia gracilis (Mart.) Spruce
Lepidocaryum tenue var. **tenue**
  Lepidocaryum allenii Dugand
  Lepidocaryum quadripartitum (Spruce)
    Drude
  Lepidocaryum tessmannii Burret
  Mauritia quadripartita Spruce
  Mauritia tenuis (Mart.) Spruce

LYTOCARYUM Tol.
  Microcoelum Burret & Potztal
Lytocaryum hoehnei (Burret) Tol.
  Syagrus hoehnei Burret

Lytocaryum weddellianum (H. Wendl.) Tol.
  Cocos insignis (hort. ex Drude) Mart. ex
    Hook. f.
  Cocos weddellianum H. Wendl.
  Glaziova insignis hort. ex Drude
  Glaziova martiana Glaz. ex Drude
  Lytocaryum insigne (hort. ex Drude) Tol.
  Lytocaryum weddellianum var. *cinereum*
    (Becc.) A. D. Hawkes
  Lytocaryum weddellianum var. *pinaertii* (hort.
    ex Nicholson) A. D. Hawkes
  Microcoelum insigne (hort. ex Drude)
    Burret & Potztal
  Microcoelum martianum (Glaz. ex Drude)
    Burret & Potztal
  Microcoelum weddellianum (H. Wendl.)
    H. E. Moore
  Syagrus insignis (hort. ex Drude) Becc.
  Syagrus weddelliana (H. Wendl.) Becc.
  Syagrus weddelliana var. *cinerea* Becc.
  Syagrus weddelliana var. *pinaertii* hort. ex
    Nicholson

MANICARIA Gaertn.
  Pilophora Jacq.
Manicaria saccifera Gaertn.
  Manicaria atricha Burret
  Manicaria saccifera var. *mediterranea* Trail
  Manicaria martiana Burret
  Manicaria plukenetii Griseb. & H. Wendl.
  Pilophora saccifera H. Wendl.
  Pilophora testicularis Jacq.

MAURITIA L. f.
Mauritia carana Wallace
  Orophoma carana (Wallace) Spruce
Mauritia flexuosa L. f.
  Mauritia flexuosa var. *venezuelana* Steyerm.
  Mauritia minor Burret
  Mauritia setigera Griseb. & H. Wendl.
  Mauritia sphaerocarpa Burret
  Mauritia vinifera Mart.

UNCERTAIN NAMES
  Mauritia piritu Linden
  Mauritia sagus Schult. f.

MAURITIELLA Burret
  Lepidococcus H. Wendl. & Drude
Mauritiella aculeata (Kunth) Burret
  Lepidococcus aculeatus (Kunth) H. Wendl. &
    Drude ex A. D. Hawkes
  Mauritia aculeata Kunth
  Mauritia aculeata of Mart.
  Mauritia amazonica Barb. Rodr.

Mauritia cataractarum (Dugand) Balick
Mauritia gracilis Wallace
Mauritia linnophilla Barb. Rodr.
Mauritiella cataractarum Dugand
Mauritiella armata (Mart.) Burret
  Lepidococcus armatus (Mart.) H. Wendl. &
    Drude ex H. Wendl.
  Lepidococcus duckei (Burret) H. Wendl. &
    Drude ex A. D. Hawkes
  Lepidococcus huebneri (Burret) H. Wendl. &
    Drude ex A. D. Hawkes
  Lepidococcus intermedius (Burret) H. Wendl.
    & Drude ex A. D. Hawkes
  Lepidococcus martianus (Spruce) H. Wendl.
    & Drude ex A. D. Hawkes
  Lepidococcus peruvianus (Becc.) H. Wendl.
    & Drude ex A. D. Hawkes
  Lepidococcus pumilus (Wallace) H. Wendl.
    & Drude ex A. D. Hawkes
  Lepidococcus subinermis (Spruce) A. D.
    Hawkes
  Mauritia armata Mart.
  Mauritia campylostachys (Burret) Balick
  Mauritia duckei (Burret) Balick
  Mauritia huebneri Burret
  Mauritia intermedia Burret
  Mauritia macrospadix (Burret) Balick
  Mauritia martiana Spruce
  Mauritia nannostachys (Burret) Balick
  Mauritia peruviana Becc.
  Mauritia pumila Wallace
  Mauritia subinermis (Spruce) Burret
  Mauritiella campylostachys Burret
  Mauritiella duckei Burret
  Mauritiella huebneri (Burret) Burret
  Mauritiella intermedia (Burret) Burret
  Mauritiella macrospadix Burret
  Mauritiella martiana (Spruce) Burret
  Mauritiella nannostachys Burret
  Mauritiella peruviana (Becc.) Burret
  Mauritiella pumila (Wallace) Burret
  Orophoma subinermis (Spruce) Drude
Mauritiella macroclada (Burret) Burret
  Lepidococcus macrocladus (Burret) A. D.
    Hawkes
  Mauritia macroclada Burret
  Mauritia pacifica (Dugand) Balick
  Mauritiella pacifica Dugand

NEONICHOLSONIA Dammer
  Bisnicholsonia Kuntze
  Woodsonia L. H. Bailey
Neonicholsonia watsonii Dammer
  Neonicholsonia georgei Dammer
  Woodsonia scheryi L. H. Bailey

OENOCARPUS Mart.
  Jessenia H. Karst.
Oenocarpus bacaba Mart.
  Oenocarpus bacaba var. *bacaba* Wess. Boer
  Oenocarpus bacaba var. *grandis* Wess. Boer
  Oenocarpus bacaba var. *xanthocarpa* Trail
  Oenocarpus baccata Cuervo Marquez
  Oenocarpus grandis Burret
  Oenocarpus hoppii Burret
Oenocarpus balickii Kahn
  Oenocarpus bacaba var. *parvus* Wess. Boer
Oenocarpus bataua Mart.
Oenocarpus bataua var. **bataua**
  Jessenia bataua (Mart.) Burret
  Jessenia polycarpa H. Karst.
  Jessenia repanda Engel
  Jessenia weberbaueri Burret
  Oenocarpus bataua subsp. *bataua* Balick
  Oenocarpus seje Cuervo Márquez
Oenocarpus bataua var. **oligocarpa** (Griseb.
    & H. Wendl.) Henderson
  Jessenia bataua subsp. *oligocarpa* (Griseb. &
    H. Wendl.) Balick
  Jessenia oligocarpa Griseb. & H. Wendl.
  Oenocarpus oligocarpa (Griseb. & H.
    Wendl.) Wess. Boer
Oenocarpus circumtextus Mart.
Oenocarpus distichus Mart.
  Oenocarpus discolor Barb. Rodr.
  Oenocarpus tarampabo Mart.
Oenocarpus makeru R. Bernal, Galeano &
    Henderson
Oenocarpus mapora H. Karst.
  Oenocarpus dryanderae Burret
  Oenocarpus macrocalyx Burret
  Oenocarpus mapora subsp. *dryanderae*
    (Burret) Balick
  Oenocarpus mapora subsp. *mapora* Balick
  Oenocarpus multicaulis Spruce
  Oenocarpus panamanus L. H. Bailey
Oenocarpus minor Mart.
  Oenocarpus huebneri Burret
  Oenocarpus intermedius Burret
  Oenocarpus microspadix Burret
  Oenocarpus minor subsp. *intermedius*
    (Burret) Balick
  Oenocarpus minor subsp. *minor* Balick
Oenocarpus simplex R. Bernal, Galeano &
    Henderson

HYBRIDS
  Oenocarpus x *andersonii* Balick

UNCERTAIN NAMES
  Jessenia amazonum Drude ex Mart.
  Jessenia glazioviana Dammer ex Engel

Oenocarpus altissimus Klotzsch ex H.
  Wendl.
Oenocarpus bolivianus hort. ex H. Wendl.
Oenocarpus calaber hort. ex H. Wendl.
Oenocarpus chiragua hort. ex H. Wendl.
Oenocarpus cubarro hort. ex H. Wendl.
Oenocarpus dealbatus hort. ex H. Wendl.
Oenocarpus edulis hort. ex Watson
Oenocarpus excelsus Mart.
Oenocarpus glaucus Mart.
Oenocarpus gracilis hort. ex H. Wendl.
Oenocarpus iriartoides Triana
Oenocarpus laguayra hort. ex H. Wendl.
Oenocarpus lutescens Mart.
Oenocarpus pulchellus Linden
Oenocarpus tenuis Mart.

PARAJUBAEA Burret
Parajubaea cocoides Burret
Parajubaea torallyi (Mart.) Burret
Diplothemium torallyi Mart.
Jubaea torallyi (Mart.) H. Wendl.
Polyandrococos torallyi (Mart.) Barb. Rodr.

PHOLIDOSTACHYS H. Wendl. & Hook. f.
Pholidostachys dactyloides H. E. Moore
Calyptrogyne dactyloides (H. E. Moore) Wess.
  Boer
Pholidostachys kalbreyeri H. Wendl. ex
  Burret
Pholidostachys pulchra H. Wendl. ex
  Burret
Calyptrogyne pulchra (H. Wendl. ex Burret)
  Burret
Geonoma amabilis H. Wendl. ex Dahlgren
Pholidostachys synanthera (Mart.) H. E.
  Moore
Calyptrogyne kalbreyeri Burret
Calyptrogyne robusta (Trail) Burret
Calyptrogyne synanthera (Mart.) Burret
? Calyptrogyne weberbaueri Burret
Calyptronoma kalbreyeri (Burret) L. H.
  Bailey
Calyptronoma robusta Trail
Calyptronoma synanthera (Mart.) L. H.
  Bailey
Calyptronoma weberbaueri (Burret) L. H.
  Bailey
Geonoma synanthera Mart.

PHYTELEPHAS Ruiz & Pav.
Elephantusia Willd.
Palandra O. F. Cook
Yarina O. F. Cook

Phytelephas aequatorialis Spruce
Palandra aequatorialis (Spruce) O. F. Cook
Phytelephas macrocarpa Ruiz & Pav.
Elephantusia macrocarpa (Ruiz & Pav.)
  Willd.
Elephantusia microcarpa (Ruiz & Pav.) Willd.
Phytelephas karstenii O. F. Cook
Phytelephas macrocarpa subsp. *macrocarpa*
Phytelephas microcarpa Ruiz & Pav.
Yarina microcarpa (Ruiz & Pav.) O. F. Cook
Phytelephas schottii H. Wendl.
Phytelephas macrocarpa subsp. *schottii* (H.
  Wendl.) Barfod
Phytelephas seemannii O. F. Cook
Phytelephas brachelus O. F. Cook
Phytelephas brachinus O. F. Cook
Phytelephas brevipes O. F. Cook
Phytelephas cornutus O. F. Cook
Phytelephas longiflora O. F. Cook
Phytelephas pittieri O. F. Cook
Phytelephas seemannii subsp. *brevipes* (O. F.
  Cook) Barfod
Phytelephas seemannii subsp. *seemannii*
Phytelephas tenuicaulis (Barfod)
  Henderson
Phytelephas macrocarpa subsp. *tenui-caulis*
  Barfod
Phytelephas tumacana O. F. Cook

UNCERTAIN NAMES
Phytelephas aureo-costata Linden
Phytelephas bonplandia Gaudich.
Phytelephas endlicheriana Gaudich.
Phytelephas humboldtiana Gaudich.
Phytelephas kunthiana Gaudich.
Phytelephas orbignyana Gaudich.
Phytelephas pavonii Gaudich.
Phytelephas persooniana Gaudich.
Phytelephas poeppigii Gaudich.
Phytelephas ruizii Gaudich.
Phytelephas willdenowiana Gaudich.

POLYANDROCOCOS Barb. Rodr.
Polyandrococos caudescens (Mart.) Barb.
  Rodr.
Allagoptera caudescens (Mart.) Kuntze
Diplothemium caudescens Mart.
Diplothemium pectinatum Barb. Rodr.
Polyandrococos pectinata (Barb. Rodr.) Barb.
  Rodr.

PRESTOEA Hook. f. ex Benth. & Hook. f.
Acrista O. F. Cook
Prestoea acuminata (Willd.) H. E. Moore
Acrista monticola O. F. Cook

Aiphanes pragra Kunth
Euterpe acuminata (Willd.) H. Wendl.
Euterpe andicola Brong. ex Mart.
Euterpe andina Burret
Euterpe aphanolepis Burret
Euterpe brevivaginata Mart.
Euterpe chaunostachys Burret
Euterpe dasystachys Burret
Euterpe frigida (Kunth) Burret
Euterpe globosa Gaertn.
Euterpe haenkeana Brong. ex Mart.
Euterpe manaele (Mart.) Griseb. & H.
    Wendl. ex Griseb.
Euterpe megalochlamys Burret
Euterpe microspadix Burret
Euterpe montana Graham
Euterpe oocarpa Burret
Euterpe pertenuis L. H. Bailey
Euterpe praga (Kunth) Spreng.
Euterpe purpurea Engel
Euterpe tobagonis L. H. Bailey
Euterpe trichoclada Burret
Euterpe zephyria Dugand
Oenocarpus caracasanus Mart.
Oenocarpus frigidus (Kunth) Spreng.
Oenocarpus utilis Klotzsch
Oreodoxa acuminata Willd.
Oreodoxa frigida Kunth
Oreodoxa manaele Mart.
Prestoea allenii H. E. Moore
Prestoea dasystachys (Burret) R. Bernal,
    Galeano & Henderson
Prestoea gregalis L. H. Bailey
Prestoea megalochlamys (Burret) H. E.
    Moore
Prestoea montana (Graham) Nicholson
Prestoea sabana L. H. Bailey
Prestoea trichoclada (Burret) Balslev &
    Henderson
Prestoea carderi Hook. f.
Euterpe brachyclada Burret
Euterpe brevicaulis Burret
Euterpe carderi (Hook. f.) Burret
Euterpe latisecta Burret
Euterpe parviflora Burret
Euterpe simplicifrons Burret
Geonoma carderi Bull
Prestoea brachyclada (Burret) R. Bernal,
    Galeano & Henderson
Prestoea cuatrecasasii H. E. Moore
Prestoea humilis Henderson & Steyerm.
Prestoea latisecta (Burret) R. Bernal,
    Galeano & Henderson
Prestoea simplicifrons (Burret) Henderson &
    Nevers

Prestoea decurrens (H. Wendl. ex Burret)
    H. E. Moore
Euterpe decurrens H. Wendl.
Prestoea ensiformis (Ruiz & Pav.) H. E.
    Moore
Martinezia ensiformis Ruiz & Pav.
Prestoea darienensis Henderson
Prestoea integrifolia Nevers & Henderson
Prestoea sejuncta L. H. Bailey
Prestoea longepetiolata (Oerst.) H. E.
    Moore
Euterpe brachyspatha Burret
Euterpe longepetiolata Oerst.
Euterpe simiarum (Standl. & Williams) H. E.
    Moore
Euterpe williamsii Glassman
Malortiea simiarum Standl. & Williams
Prestoea pubens H. E. Moore
Prestoea pubens var. **pubens**
Prestoea pubens var. **semispicata** (Nevers &
    Henderson) Henderson & Galeano
Prestoea semispicata Nevers & Henderson
Prestoea pubigera (Griseb. & H. Wendl.)
    Hook. f. ex Benth. & Hook. f.
Euterpe pubigera (Griseb. & H. Wendl.)
    Burret
Hyospathe pubigera Griseb. & H. Wendl.
Prestoea trinitensis Hook. f.
Prestoea roseospadix (L. H. Bailey) H. E.
    Moore
Euterpe roseospadix L. H. Bailey
Prestoea schultzeana (Burret) H. E. Moore
Euterpe schultzeana Burret
Prestoea asplundii H. E. Moore
Prestoea simplicifolia Galeano
Prestoea tenuiramosa (Dammer) H. E.
    Moore
Euterpe tenuiramosa Dammer
Prestoea steyermarkii H. E. Moore

PSEUDOPHOENIX H. Wendl. ex Sarg.
Chamaephoenix H. Wendl. ex Curtiss
Cyclospathe O. F. Cook
Sargentia H. Wendl. & Drude ex Salomon
Pseudophoenix ekmanii Burret
Pseudophoenix lediniana Read
Pseudophoenix elata O. F. Cook ex Burret
Pseudophoenix sargentii H. Wendl.
Pseudophoenix sargentii subsp. **saonae**
    (O. F. Cook) Read
Pseudophoenix sargentii subsp. **saonae** var.
    saonae
Cyclospathe northropii O. F. Cook
Pseudophoenix gracilis Ekman

Pseudophoenix linearis O. F. Cook
Pseudophoenix saonae O. F. Cook
Pseudophoenix sargentii subsp. **saonae** var.
navassana Read
Pseudophoenix navassana Ekman ex Burret
Pseudophoenix sargentii subsp. **sargentii**
Chamaephoenix sargentii (H. Wendl. ex
Sarg.) A. H. Curtis
Sargentia aricocca H. Wendl. & Drude
Pseudophoenix vinifera (Mart.) Becc.
Aeria vinifera (Mart.) O. F. Cook
Cocos vinifera (Mart.) Mart.
Euterpe vinifera Mart.
Gaussia vinifera (Mart.) H. Wendl.
Pseudophoenix insignis O. F. Cook
Raphia vinifera Descourt.

RAPHIA P. Beauv.
Sagus of Gaertn.
Raphia taedigera (Mart.) Mart.
Sagus taedigera Mart.
Metroxylon taedigerum (Mart.) Spreng.
Raphia vinifera var. *taedigera* Drude

REINHARDTIA Lieb.
Malortiea H. Wendl.
Reinhardtia elegans Liebm.
Reinhardtia gracilis (H. Wendl.) Drude ex
Dammer
Chamaedorea fenestrata hort. in H. Wendl.
Reinhardtia gracilis var. **gracilior** (Burret)
H. E. Moore
Reinhardtia gracilior Burret
Reinhardtia gracilis var. **gracilis**
Malortiea gracilis H. Wendl.
Reinhardtia gracilis var. **rostrata** (Burret)
H. E. Moore
Malortiea rostrata (Burret) L. H. Bailey
Reinhardtia rostrata Burret
Reinhardtia gracilis var. **tenuissima** H. E.
Moore
Reinhardtia koschnyana (H. Wendl. &
Dammer) Burret
Malortiea koschnyana H. Wendl. & Dammer
Malortiea pumila Dugand
Reinhardtia latisecta (H. Wendl.) Burret
Malortiea latisecta H. Wendl.
Reinhardtia paiewonskiana Read, Zanoni &
Mejía
Reinhardtia simplex (H. Wendl.) Drude ex
Dammer
Malortiea simplex H. Wendl.

UNCERTAIN NAMES
Malortiea intermedia H. Wendl.
Malortiea lacerata hort. ex H. Wendl.
Malortiea speciosa hort. ex H. Wendl.
Reinhardtia spinigera L. H. Bailey;

RHAPIDOPHYLLUM H. Wendl. & Drude
Rhapidophyllum hystrix (Pursh) H. Wendl.
& Drude
Chamaerops hystrix Pursh
Rhapis caroliniana hort. ex Kunth
Sabal hystrix (Pursh) Nutt.

ROYSTONEA O. F. Cook
Gorgasia O. F. Cook
Oreodoxa auct. not Willd.
Roystonea altissima (Mill.) H. E. Moore
Palma altissima Mill.
Roystonea jamaicana L. H. Bailey
Roystonea borinquena O. F. Cook
Oreodoxa borinquena (O. F. Cook) Reasoner
ex L. H. Bailey
Roystonea hispaniolana L. H. Bailey
Roystonea hispaniolana f. *altissima* Moscoso
Roystonea peregrina L. H. Bailey
Roystonea dunlapiana Allen
Roystonea lenis León
Roystonea regia var. *pinguis* L. H. Bailey
Roystonea maisiana (L. H. Bailey) Zona
Roystonea regia var. *maisiana* L. H. Bailey
Roystonea oleracea (Jacq.) O. F. Cook
Areca oleracea Jacq.
Euterpe caribaea Spreng.
Oreodoxa caribaea (Spreng.) Dammer
Oreodoxa charibaea Becc.
Oreodoxa oleracea (Jacq.) Mart.
Oreodoxa regia var. *jenmanii* Waby
Roystonea caribaea (Spreng.) Wilson
Roystonea oleracea var. *excelsior* L. H. Bailey
Roystonea venezuelana L. H. Bailey
Roystonea princeps (Becc.) Burret
Oreodoxa princeps Becc.
Roystonea regia (Kunth) O. F. Cook
Euterpe acuminata of Waby
Euterpe jenmanii C. H. Wright
Euterpe ventricosa C. H. Wright
Oenocarpus regius (Kunth) Spreng.
Oreodoxa oleracea of Griseb.
Oreodoxa regia Kunth
Palma elata Bartram
Roystonea elata (Bartram) Harper
Roystonea floridana O. F. Cook
Roystonea jenmanii (C. H. Wright) Burret
Roystonea regia var. *hondurensis* Allen

Roystonea ventricosa (C. H. Wright) L. H. Bailey
Roystonea stellata León
Roystonea violacea León

UNCERTAIN NAMES
Oreodoxa ghiesbreghtii hort.
Oreodoxa granatensis hort.
Oreodoxa ventricosa hort.
Roystonea aitia O. F. Cook

SABAL Adanson ex Guersent
Inodes O. F. Cook
Sabal bermudana L. H. Bailey
Inodes princeps (hort. ex Becc.) Ciferri & Giacom.
Sabal beccariana L. H. Bailey
Sabal princeps hort. ex Becc.
Sabal causiarum (O. F. Cook) Becc.
Inodes causiarum O. F. Cook
Inodes glauca Dammer
Sabal haitensis L. H. Bailey
Sabal questeliana L. H. Bailey
Sabal domingensis Becc.
Sabal neglecta Becc.
Sabal etonia Swingle ex Nash
Sabal adansonii var. *megacarpa* Chapm.
Sabal megacarpa (Chapm.) Small
Sabal gretheriae Quero
Sabal guatemalensis Becc.
Sabal maritima (Kunth) Burret
Corypha maritima Kunth
Copernicia maritima (Kunth) Mart.
Sabal florida Becc.
Sabal jamaicensis Becc.
Sabal mauritiiformis (H. Karst.) Griseb. ex H. Wendl.
Sabal allenii L. H. Bailey
Sabal glaucescens Lodd. ex H. E. Moore
Sabal morrisiana Bartlett ex L. H. Bailey
Sabal nematoclada Burret
Trithrinax mauritiaeformis H. Karst.
Sabal mexicana Mart.
Inodes exul O. F. Cook
Inodes mexicana (Mart.) Standl.
Inodes texana O. F. Cook
Sabal exul (O. F. Cook) L. H. Bailey
Sabal texana (O. F. Cook) Becc.
Sabal miamiensis Zona
Sabal minor (Jacq.) Persoon
Brahea minima (Nutt.) H. Wendl.
Chamaerops acaulis F. Michx.
Chamaerops lousiana Darby

Chamaerops sabaloides Baldwin ex W. Darlington
Corypha pumila Walt.
Sabal adansonii Guersent
Sabal adansonii var. *major* hort. ex Becc.
? *Sabal adiantinum* Rafinesque
Sabal deeringiana Small
Sabal lousiana (Darby) Bomhard
Sabal minima Nutt.
Sabal pumila (Walt.) Elliot
Rhapis acaulis Walter ex Willd.
Rhapis arundinacea Aiton
Sabal palmetto (Walt.) Lodd. ex Schult. & Schult. f.
Chamaerops palmetto (Walter) Michx.
Corypha palmetto Walter
Inodes palmetto (Walter) O. F. Cook
Inodes schwarzii O. F. Cook
Sabal bahamensis (Becc.) L. H. Bailey
Sabal jamesiana Small
Sabal palmetto var. *bahamensis* Becc.
Sabal parviflora Becc.
Sabal viatoris L. H. Bailey
Sabal pumos (Kunth) Burret
Copernicia pumos (Kunth) Mart.
Corypha pumos Kunth
Sabal dugesii S. Watson ex L. H. Bailey
Sabal rosei (O. F. Cook) Becc.
Erythea lorete O. F. Cook
Inodes rosei O. F. Cook
Sabal uresana var. *roseana* (O. F. Cook) I. M. Johnson
Sabal uresana Trelease
Inodes uresana (Trelease) O. F. Cook
Sabal yapa C. H. Wright ex Becc.
Inodes japa (Becc.) Standl.
Sabal mayarum Bartlett
Sabal peregrina L. H. Bailey
Sabal yucatanica L. H. Bailey

UNCERTAIN NAMES
Chamaerops glabra Mill.
Inodes blackburnia (Glazebrook) O. F. Cook
Inodes vestita O. F. Cook
Sabal acaulis J. Blanchard
Sabal australis hort. ex Pfister
Sabal blackburnia Glazebrook
Sabal blackburniana Glazebrook ex Schult. & Schult. f.
Sabal carat Lefroy
Sabal caroliniana hort. ex Poiret
Sabal chinensis hort. ex Becc.
Sabal coerulescens hort.
Sabal columnaris Lodd. ex Mart.

Sabal dealbata hort. ex Standl.
Sabal denisoni hort. ex Pfister
Sabal elata Lodd. ex Mart.
Sabal excelsa D. Morris
Sabal extonianum hort. ex Gentil
Sabal filamentosa H. Wendl. ex Pfister
Sabal floribunda Katzenstein
Sabal ghiesebrechtii hort. ex Pfister
Sabal giganteum Fulchiron ex Schult. & Schult. f.
Sabal glabra (Mill.) Sargent
Sabal glauca hort. ex L. H. Bailey
Sabal gluestrightii Eichhorn
Sabal graminifolia Lodd. ex Schult. & Schult. f.
Sabal havanensis Lodd. ex Mart.
Sabal henekenii Mart.
Sabal hoogendorpii hort. ex L. H. Bailey
Sabal japa Sauvalle
Sabal javanica hort. ex L. H. Bailey
Sabal longifolia hort. ex Pfister
Sabal longipedunculata hort. ex Gentil
Sabal magdalenae Linden
Sabal magdalenica Wallis ex Regel
Sabal megacarpa hort. ex Becc.
Sabal mexicana Sauvalle
Sabal mocini hort. ex Siebert & Voss
Sabal mocini hort. ex H. Wendl.
Sabal morrisiana Bartlett
Sabal nitida Dahlgren
Sabal oleracea Lodd. ex Mart.
Sabal palmetto Rein
Sabal picta hort. ex H. Wendl.
Sabal princeps hort. ex H. Wendl.
Sabal rubrum H. Cels. ex Schult. & Schult. f.
Sabal sanfordii Linden
Sabal schwarzii Becc.
Sabal speciosa hort. ex Ricasoli
Sabal spectabilis hort. ex Pfister
Sabal taurina Lodd. ex Mart.
Sabal tectorum hort. ex Ricasoli
Sabal umbraculifera Mart.
Sabal umbraculifera Reade
Sabal woodfordii Lodd. ex Mart.

SCHIPPIA Burret
Schippia concolor Burret

SERENOA Hook. f.
Diglossophyllum H. Wendl. ex Salomon
Serenoa repens (Bartram) Small
Brahea serrulata (F. Michx.) H. Wendl.
Chamaerops serrulata F. Michx.

Corypha obliqua Bartram
Corypha repens Bartram
Diglossophyllum serrulatum (F. Michx.) H. Wendl. ex Drude
Sabal serrulata (F. Michx.) Nutt. ex Schult. & Schult. f.
Sabal serrulata var. *minima* (Nutt.) Wood
Serenoa serrulata (F. Michx.) Nutt.

SOCRATEA H. Karst.
Metasocratea Dugand
Socratea exorrhiza (Mart.) H. Wendl.
Iriartea durissima Oerst.
Iriartea exorrhiza Mart.
Iriartea exorrhiza var *elegans* (H. Karst.) Drude
Iriartea exorrhiza var. *orbigniana* (Mart.) Drude
Iriartea orbignyana Mart.
Iriartea philonotia Barb. Rodr.
Socratea albolineata Steyerm.
Socratea durissima (Oerst.) H. Wendl.
Socratea elegans H. Karst.
Socratea gracilis Burret
Socratea hoppii Burret
Socratea macrochlamys Burret
Socratea microchlamys Burret
Socratea orbignyana (Mart.) H. Karst.
Socratea philonotia (Barb. Rodr.) Hook. f.
Socratea hecatonandra (Dugand) R. Bernal
Metasocratea hecatonandra Dugand
Socratea montana R. Bernal & Henderson
Socratea rostrata Burret
Socratea salazarii H. E. Moore

UNCERTAIN NAMES
Socratea forgetiana hort. ex L. H. Bailey

SYAGRUS Mart.
Arecastrum (Drude) Becc.
Arikury Becc.
Arikuryroba Barb. Rodr.
Barbosa Becc.
Chrysallidosperma H. E. Moore
Langsdorffia Raddi
Platenia H. Karst.
Rhyticocos Becc.
Syagrus amara (Jacq.) Mart.
Cocos amara Jacq.
Rhyticocos amara (Jacq.) Becc.
Syagrus botryophora (Mart.) Mart.
Arecastrum romanzoffianum var. *botryophora* (Mart.) Becc.
Cocos botryophora Mart.

Syagrus campylospatha (Barb. Rodr.) Becc.
  Cocos acaulis subsp. *glauca* Drude ex
    Lindman
  Cocos apaensis Barb. Rodr.
  Cocos campylospatha Barb. Rodr.
  Cocos hassleriana Barb. Rodr.
  Syagrus apaensis (Barb. Rodr.) Becc.
  Syagrus hassleriana (Barb. Rodr.) Becc.
Syagrus cardenasii Glassman
Syagrus cocoides Mart.
  Cocos drudei Becc.
  Cocos syagrus Drude
  Cocos weddellii Drude
  Syagrus brachyrhyncha Burret
  Syagrus cocoides var. *linearifolia* Barb. Rodr.
  Syagrus drudei (Becc.) Becc.
Syagrus comosa (Mart.) Mart.
  Cocos acaulis Drude
  Cocos comosa Mart.
  Syagrus acaulis (Drude) Becc.
Syagrus coronata (Mart.) Becc.
  Arecastrum romanzoffianum var. *ensifolium*
    (Drude) Becc.
  Cocos botryophora var. *ensifolia* Drude
  Cocos coronata Mart.
  Cocos coronata var. *todari* Becc.
  ?*Cocos quinquefaria* Barb. Rodr.
  Glaziovia treubiana Becc.
  Syagrus coronata var. *todari* (Becc.) Becc.
  Syagrus treubiana (Becc.) Becc.
Syagrus duartei Glassman
Syagrus flexuosa (Mart.) Becc.
  Cocos campestris Mart.
  Cocos flexuosa Mart.
  Cocos flexuosa var. *cataphracta* Mart.
  Cocos flexuosa var. *densiflora* Mart.
  Cocos urbaniana Dammer
  Syagrus campestris (Mart.) H. Wendl.
  Syagrus urbaniana (Dammer) Becc.
Syagrus glaucescens Glaz. ex Becc.
Syagrus graminifolia (Drude) Becc.
  Cocos graminifolia Drude
  Cocos graminifolia var. *glazioviana* Dammer
  Cocos graminifolia var. *nana* Drude
  Cocos lilliputiana Barb. Rodr.
  Syagrus graminifolia var. *glazioviana*
    (Dammer) Becc.
  Syagrus graminifolia var. *nana* (Drude)
    Becc.
  Syagrus lilliputiana (Barb. Rodr.) Becc.
Syagrus harleyi Glassman
Syagrus inajai (Spruce) Becc.
  Cocos aequatorialis Barb. Rodr.
  Cocos chavesiana Barb. Rodr. ex Becc.

Cocos inajai (Spruce) Trail
Cocos speciosa Barb. Rodr.
Maximiliana inajai Spruce
Syagrus aequatorialis (Barb. Rodr.) Barb.
  Rodr.
Syagrus chavesiana (Barb. Rodr.) Barb.
  Rodr.
Syagrus speciosa (Barb. Rodr.) Barb. Rodr.
Syagrus leptospatha Burret
Syagrus macrocarpa Barb. Rodr.
  Barbosa getuliana (Bondar) A. D. Hawkes
  Cocos getuliana Bondar
  Cocos macrocarpa (Barb. Rodr.) Barb. Rodr.
  Cocos procopiana Glaz. ex Drude
  Syagrus getuliana (Bondar) Glassman
Syagrus microphylla Burret
Syagrus oleracea (Mart.) Becc.
  Cocos oleracea Mart.
  Syagrus gomesii Glassman
Syagrus orinocensis (Spruce) Burret
  Cocos orinocensis Spruce
  Syagrus allenii Glassman
  Syagrus stenopetala Burret
Syagrus petraea (Mart.) Becc.
  Cocos glazioviana Dammer
  Cocos petraea Mart.
  Cocos petraea var. *alpina* (Drude) Glassman
  Cocos petraea var. *genuina* Drude
  Syagrus glazioviana (Dammer) Becc.
  Syagrus glazioviana var. *alpina* (Drude)
    Glassman
  Syagrus loefgrenii Glassman
  Syagrus petraea var. *alpina* Drude
  Syagrus rachidii Glassman
Syagrus picrophylla Barb. Rodr.
  Syagrus oleracea var. *platyphylla* (Drude)
    Becc.
  Cocos catechucarpa Barb. Rodr.
  Syagrus catechucarpa (Barb. Rodr.) Becc.
Syagrus pleioclada Burret
  Syagrus mendanhensis Glassman
Syagrus pseudococos (Raddi) Glassman
  Barbosa pseudococos (Raddi) Becc.
  Cocos mikaniana Mart.
  Langsdorffia pseudococos Raddi
  Syagrus mikaniana (Mart.) Mart.
Syagrus romanzoffiana (Cham.) Glassman
  Arecastrum romanzoffianum (Cham.) Becc.
  Arecastrum romanzoffianum var. *australe*
    (Mart.) Becc.
  Arecastrum romanzoffianum var. *genuinum*
    Becc.
  Arecastrum romanzoffianum var. *genuinum*
    minus Becc.

Arecastrum romanzoffianum var. *micropindo* Becc.
Cocos acrocomoides Drude
Cocos arechavaletana Barb. Rodr.
Cocos australis Mart.
Cocos datil Griseb. & Drude
Cocos geriba Barb. Rodr.
Cocos martiana Drude & Glaz.
Cocos plumosa Hook. f.
Cocos romanzoffiana Cham.
Syagrus ruschiana (Bondar) Glassman
Arikuryroba ruschiana (Bondar) Tol.
Cocos ruschiana Bondar
Syagrus sancona H. Karst.
Cocos argentea Engel
Cocos chiragua (H. Karst.) Becc.
Cocos sancona (H. Karst.) Hook. f.
Oenocarpus sancona (Kunth) Spreng.
Oreodoxa sancona Kunth
Platenia chiragua H. Karst.
Syagrus argentea (Engel) Becc.
Syagrus chiragua (H. Karst.) H. Wendl.
Syagrus ecuadorensis Becc.
Syagrus tessmannii Burret
Syagrus schizophylla (Mart.) Glassman
Arikury schizophylla (Mart.) Becc.
Arikuryroba capanemae Barb. Rodr.
Arikuryroba schizophylla (Mart.) L. H. Bailey
Cocos arikuryroba Barb. Rodr.
Cocos capanemae (Barb. Rodr.) Drude
Cocos schizophylla Mart.
Syagrus smithii H. E. Moore
Chrysallidosperma smithii H. E. Moore
Syagrus stratincola Wess. Boer
Syagrus vagans (Bondar) A. D. Hawkes
Cocos vagans Bondar
Syagrus werdermannii Burret

UNCERTAIN NAMES
Cocos chloroleuca Barb. Rodr.
Cocos cogniauxiana Barb. Rodr.
Cocos edulis Barb. Rodr.
Cocos petraea var. *platyphylla* Drude
Cocos purusana Huber
Cocos rupestris Barb. Rodr.
Cocos sapida (Barb. Rodr.) Becc.
Syagrus chloroleuca (Barb. Rodr.) Burret
Syagrus cogniauxiana (Barb. Rodr.) Becc.
Syagrus edulis Barb. Rodr.
Syagrus petraea var. *platyphylla* (Drude) Becc.
Syagrus purusana (Huber) Frambach ex Dahlgren
Syagrus sapida (Barb. Rodr.) Becc.

SYNECHANTHUS H. Wendl.
Rathea H. Karst.
Reineckea H. Karst.
Synechanthus fibrosus (H. Wendl.) H. Wendl.
Chamaedorea fibrosa H. Wendl.
Collinia fibrosa (H. Wendl.) Oerst.
Rathea fibrosa (H. Wendl.) H. Karst.
Synechanthus mexicanus L. H. Bailey ex H. E. Moore
Synechanthus warscewiczianus H. Wendl.
Reineckea triandra H. Karst.
Synechanthus angustifolius H. Wendl.
Synechanthus ecuadorensis Burret
Synechanthus panamensis H. E. Moore

THRINAX Sw.
Hemithrinax Hook. f.
Porothrinax H. Wendl. ex Griseb.
Simpsonia O. F. Cook
Thrinax compacta (Griseb. & H. Wendl.) Borhidi & Muñiz
Hemithrinax compacta (Griseb. & H. Wendl.) Hook. f.
Trithrinax compacta Griseb. & H. Wendl.
Thrinax ekmaniana (Burret) Borhidi & Muñiz
Hemithrinax ekmaniana Burret
Thrinax excelsa Lodd. ex Griseb.
Thrinax rex Britton & Harris
Thrinax morrisii H. Wendl.
Simpsonia microcarpa (Sarg.) O. F. Cook
Thrinax bahamensis O. F. Cook
Thrinax drudei Becc.
Thrinax ekmanii Burret
Thrinax keyensis Sarg.
Thrinax microcarpa Sarg.
Thrinax ponceana O. F. Cook
Thrinax praeceps O. F. Cook
Thrinax punctulata Becc.
Thrinax parviflora Sw.
Thrinax parviflora subsp. **parviflora**
Thrinax harrisiana Becc.
Thrinax tessellata Becc.
Thrinax parviflora subsp. **puberula** Read
Thrinax radiata Lodd. ex Schult. & Schult. f.
Coccothrinax martii (Griseb. & H. Wendl.) Becc.
Coccothrinax radiata (Lodd. ex Schult. & Schult. f.) Sarg.
Porothrinax pumilio H. Wendl. ex Griseb.
Thrinax floridana Sarg.

Thrinax martii Griseb. & H. Wendl. ex
  Griseb.
Thrinax wendlandiana Becc.
Thrinax rivularis (León) Borhidi & Muñ
Thrinax rivularis var. **rivularis**
Hemithrinax rivularis León
Thrinax rivularis var. **savannarum** Borhic
  & Muñiz
Hemithrinax savannarum León

UNCERTAIN NAMES
Thrinax altissima hort. ex N. Taylor
Thrinax arborea hort. ex Hook. f.
Thrinax aurantia Fulch. ex Kunth
Thrinax aurata hort. ex Kunth
Thrinax brasiliensis Mart.
Thrinax elegans hort. ex Schult. f.
Thrinax elegantissima hort. ex Hook f.
Thrinax ferruginea Lodd. ex Mart.
Thrinax gracilis hort. ex Schult. f.
Thrinax graminifolia hort. ex H. Wendl.
Thrinax grandis hort. ex Kerch.
Thrinax havanensis hort.
Thrinax maritima Lodd. ex Mart.
Thrinax mexicana Lodd. ex Mart.
Thrinax montana Lodd. ex Mart.
Thrinax parviflora Maycock
Thrinax pumila Fulch. ex Schult. f.
Thrinax robusta hort.
Thrinax tunica hort. ex Hook. f.
Thrinax tunicata Linden

TRITHRINAX Mart.
Chamaethrinax H. Wendl. & Pfister
Diodosperma H. Wendl.
Trithrinax brasiliensis Mart.
Trithrinax acanthocoma Drude
Trithrinax campestris (Burmeister) Druc
  & Griseb. ex Griseb.
Chamaethrinax hookeriana H. Wendl. &
  Pfister
Copernicia campestris Burmeister
Trithrinax schizophylla Drude
Diodosperma burity H. Wendl.
Trithrinax biflabellata Barb. Rodr.

WASHINGTONIA H. Wendl.
Neowashingtonia Sudw.
Washingtonia filifera (Linden) H. Wenc
Brahea filamentosa hort. ex S. Watson
Brahea filifera hort. ex S. Watson
Neowashingtonia filamentosa Sudw.
Neowashingtonia filifera (Linden) Sudw.
Pritchardia filifera Linden

Sabal filifera hort. ex André
Washingtonia filamentosa (H. Wendl. ex
  Franceschi) Kuntze
Washingtonia robusta H. Wendl.
Neowashingtonia robusta (H. Wendl.) A.
  Heller
Neowashingtonia sonorae (S. Watson) Rose
Washingtonia gracilis Parish
Washingtonia sonorae S. Watson

UNCERTAIN NAMES
Washingtonia gaudichaudii Kuntze
Washingtonia hildebrandtii Kuntze
Washingtonia lanigera Kuntze
Washingtonia martii Kuntze
Washingtonia pacifica Kuntze
Washingtonia pericularum Kuntze
Washingtonia remota Kuntze
Washingtonia thurstonii Kuntze
Washingtonia vuylstekeana Kuntze

WELFIA H. Wendl.
Welfia regia H. Wendl. ex André
Welfia georgii H. Wendl. ex Burret
Welfia microcarpa Burret

WENDLANDIELLA Dammer
Wendlandiella gracilis Dammer
Wendlandiella gracilis var. **gracilis**
Wendlandiella gracilis var. **polyclada**
  (Burret) Henderson
Wendlandiella polyclada Burret
Wendlandiella gracilis var. **simplicifrons**
  (Burret) Henderson
Wendlandiella simplicifrons Burret

WETTINIA Poepp. ex Endl.
Acrostigma O. F. Cook & Doyle
Catoblastus H. Wendl.
Catostigma O. F. Cook & Doyle
Wettinella O. F. Cook & Doyle
Wettiniicarpus Burret
Wettinia aequalis (O. F. Cook & Doyle) R.
  Bernal
Acrostigma equale O. F. Cook & Doyle
Catoblastus aequalis O. F. Cook & Doyle
?*Catoblastus velutinus* Burret
Catostigma aequale (O. F. Cook & Doyle)
  Burret
Wettinia aequatorialis R. Bernal
Wettinia anomala (Burret) R. Bernal
Catoblastus anomalus (Burret) Burret
Catostigma anomalum Burret

Wettinia augusta Poepp. ex Endl.
Wettinia poeppigii Kunth
Wettinia weberbaueri Burret
Wettinia castanea H. E. Moore & J. Dransf.
Wettinia disticha R. Bernal
Catoblastus distichus R. Bernal
Wettinia drudei (O. F. Cook & Doyle)
Henderson
Catoblastus drudei O. F. Cook & Doyle
Catoblastus pubescens var. *krinocarpa* (Trail)
Drude
Catostigma drudei (O. F. Cook & Doyle)
Burret
Iriartea pubescens var. *krinocarpa* Trail
Wettinia fascicularis (Burret) H. E. Moore
& J. Dransf.
Wettinia cladospadix (Dugand) H. E. Moore
& J. Dransf.
Wettiniicarpus cladospadix Dugand
Wettiniicarpus fascicularis Burret
Wettinia hirsuta Burret
Wettinia kalbreyeri (Burret) R. Bernal
Catoblastus inconstans (Dugand) Glassman
ex R. Bernal
Catoblastus kalbreyeri (Burret) Burret
Catoblastus megalocarpus (Burret) Burret
Catoblastus microcaryus (Burret) Burret
Catoblastus sphaerocarpus (Burret) Burret
Catostigma inconstans Dugand
Catostigma kalbreyeri Burret
Catostigma megalocarpum Burret
Catostigma microcaryum (Burret) Burret
Catostigma sphaerocarpum Burret
Catostigma sphaerocarpum var. *microcaryum*
Burret
Wettinia lanata R. Bernal
Wettinia longipetala A. H. Gentry
Wettinia maynensis Spruce
Catoblastus maynensis (Spruce) Drude
Wettinella maynensis (Spruce) O. F. Cook &
Doyle
Wettinia illaqueans Spruce

Wettinia microcarpa (Burret) R. Bernal
Catoblastus microcarpus Burret
Wettinia minima R. Bernal
Wettinia oxycarpa Galeano & R. Bernal
Wettinia panamensis R. Bernal
Wettinia praemorsa (Willd.) Wess. Boer
Catoblastus andinus Dugand
Catoblastus cuatrecasasii Dugand
Catoblastus engelii H. Wendl. ex Burret
Catoblastus mesocarpus Burret
Catoblastus praemorsus (Willd.) H. Wendl.
Catoblastus pubescens (H. Karst.) H.
Wendl.
Iriartea praemorsa (Willd.) Kl.
Iriartea pubescens H. Karst.
Oreodoxa praemorsa Willd.
Wettinia andina (Dugand) R. Bernal
Wettinia mesocarpa (Burret) Wess. Boer
Wettinia quinaria (O. F. Cook & Doyle)
Burret
Wettinella quinaria O. F. Cook & Doyle
Wettinia utilis Little
Wettinia radiata (O. F. Cook & Doyle) R.
Bernal
Catoblastus dryanderae (Burret) Burret
Catoblastus radiatus (O. F. Cook & Doyle)
Burret
Catostigma dryanderae Burret
Catostigma radiatum O. F. Cook & Doyle
Wettinia verruculosa H. E. Moore

ZOMBIA L. H. Bailey
Oothrinax (Becc.) L. H. Bailey
Zombia antillarum (Descourt. ex Jackson)
L. H. Bailey
Chamaerops antillarum Descourt. ex
Jackson
Coccothrinax anomala Becc.
Oothrinax anomala (Becc.) O. F. Cook
Zombia antillarum var. *gonzalezii* Jiménez

REFERENCES

Acosta Solis, M. 1944. *La Tagua.* Editorial Ecuador, Quito.

Aguilar, R. 1986. El género *Chamaedorea* Willd. (Palmae) en el estado de Veracruz. Lic. Tesis, Universidad Veracruzana.

Anderson, A. 1988. Use and management of native forests dominated by açaí palm (*Euterpe oleracea* Mart.) in the Amazon estuary. *Adv. Econ. Bot.* 6: 144–154.

Anderson, A., P. May, and M. Balick. 1991. *The Subsidy from Nature.* Columbia University Press, New York.

Anderson, R., and S. Mori. 1967. A preliminary investigation of *Raphia* palm swamps, Puerto Viejo, Costa Rica. *Turrialba* 17: 221–224.

Ayora, N., and R. Orellana. 1993. Physicochemical soil factors influencing the distribution of two coastal palms in Yucatan, Mexico. *Principes* 37: 82–91.

Azevedo Maia, A., F. Pompeu Serran, H. de Q. Boudet Fernandes, R. Ribeiro de Olivera, R. Fernandes de Oliveirta, A. Parucker, and T.M. Penna. 1987. Inferências faunísticas por vestígios vegetais. III: Interrelações do caxinguelê (*Sciurus aestuans ingramü*, Thomas 1901) com a palmeira baba-de-boi (*Syagrus romanzoffiana* (Chamisso) Glassman). *Atas Soc. Bot. Brasil* 3(11): 89–96.

Bailey, L. 1933. Certain palms of Panama. *Gentes Herb.* 3: 33–116.

———. 1936a. *Washingtonia. Gentes Herb.* 4: 53–82.

———. 1936b. 1. The Arecastrums. 2. The Butias. *Gentes Herb.* 4: 1–50.

———. 1937. *Erythea. Gentes Herb.* 4(3): 85–118.

———. 1940. *Acoelorraphe* vs. *Paurotis*—Silver-saw palm. *Gentes Herb.* 4: 361–365.

———. 1943. *Brahea* and an *Erythea. Gentes Herb.* 6(4): 177–197.

Balée, W. 1989. The culture of Amazonian forests. *Adv. Econ. Bot.* 7: 1–21.

Balick, M. 1979. Amazonian oil palms of promise: A survey. *Econ. Bot.* 33: 11–28.

———. 1986. Systematics and economic botany of the *Oenocarpus-Jessenia* (Palmae) complex. *Adv. Econ. Bot.* 3: 1–140.

———. 1990. Production of Coyol Wine from *Acrocomia mexicana* (Arecaceae) in Honduras. *Econ. Bot.* 44: 84–93.

Balick, M., and H. Beck. 1990. *Useful Palms of the World: A Synoptic Bibliography.* Columbia University Press, New York.

Balick, M., and S. Gershoff. 1990. A nutritional study of *Aiphanes caryotifolia* (Kunth) Wendl. (Palmae) fruit: An exceptional source of vitamin A and high quality protein from tropical America. *Adv. Econ. Bot.* 8: 35–40.

Balick, M., and D. Johnson. In press. An assessment of the conservation status of *Schippia concolor* Burret in Belize. *Principes.*

Balick, M., C. Pinheiro, and A. Anderson. 1987. Hybridization in the babassu palm complex: I. *Orbignya phalerata* x *O. eichleri. Amer. J. Bot.* 74: 1013–1032.

Balslev, H., and A. Henderson. 1987a. *Prestoea palmito. Principes* 31: 11.

———. 1987b. The identity of *Ynesa colenda* (Palmae). *Brittonia* 39: 1–6.

Balslev, H., and M. Moraes. 1989. Sinopsis de las palmeras de Bolivia. *AAU Report* 20: 1–107.

Barbosa Rodrigues, J. 1903. *Sertum Palmarum Brasiliensium.* 2 vols. Veuve Monnon, Brussels.

Barfod, A. 1989. The rise and fall of vegetable ivory. *Principes* 33: 181–190.

———. 1991. A monographic study of the subfamily Phytelephantoideae. *Opera Bot.* 105: 1–73.

Barfod, A., and H. Balslev. 1988. The use of palms by the Cayapas and Coaiqueres on the coastal plain of Ecuador. *Principes* 32(1): 29–42.

Barfod, A., A. Henderson, and H. Balslev. 1987. A note on the pollination of *Phytelephas microcarpa* (Palmae). *Biotropica* 19: 191–192.

Barfod, A., H. Borgtoft Pedersen, and B. Bergman. 1990. The vegetable ivory industry still exists and is doing fine in Ecuador. *Econ. Bot.* 44: 293–300.

Beach, J. 1986. Pollination biology of spadices and spicate inflorescences in Cyclanthaceae and Palmae. *Amer. J. Bot.* 73: 615–616.

Bentham, G., and J. Hooker. 1883. *Genera Plantarum.* Vol. 3(2). L. Reeve and Co., London.

Bernal, R. 1989. Endangerment of Colombian palms. *Principes* 33: 113–128.

———. 1992. Colombian palm products. In M. Plotkin and L. Famolare, eds., *The Sustainable Harvest and Marketing of Rainforest Products*. Island Press, Covelo, Calif.

———. In press. Nuevas especies y combinaciones en la subtribu Wettiniinae (Palmae). *Caldasia.*

Bernal, R., G. Galeano, and A. Henderson. 1991. Notes on *Oenocarpus* in the Colombian Amazon. *Brittonia* 43: 154–164.

Blicher-Mathiesen, U., and H. Balslev. 1990. *Attalea colenda* (Arecaceae), a potential lauric oil resource. *Econ. Bot.* 44: 360–368.

Blombery, A., and T. Rodd. 1982. *Palms.* Angus and Robertson, London.

Bondar, G. 1942. As ceras no Brasil e o licuri, *Cocos coronata* Mart. na Bahia. *Bol. Inst. Centr. Fomento Econ. Bahia* 11: 1–86.

———. 1957. Novo gênero e nova espécie de palmeiras da tribo Attaleinae. *Arq. Bot. Jard. Rio de Janeiro* 15: 49–55.

———. 1964. *Palmeiras do Brasil.* Instituto de Botânica, São Paulo.

Borchsenius, F. 1993. Flowering biology and insect visitors of three Ecuadorean *Aiphanes* species. *Principes* 37: 139–150.

Borchsenius, F., and R. Bernal. In press. *Aiphanes* (Palmae). *Flora Neotropica.*

Borgtoft Pedersen, H. 1992. Uses and management of *Aphandra natalia* (Palmae) in Ecuador. *Bull. Inst. fr. études andines* 21: 609–621.

Borgtoft Pederson, H., and H. Balslev. 1990. Ecuadorean palms for agroforestry. *AAU Report* 23: 1–122.

Borhidi, A., and O. Muñiz. 1983. *Catálogo de plantas Cubanas amenazadas o extinguidas*. Academia de Ciencias de Cuba.

———. 1985. Adiciones al catálogo de las palms de Cuba. *Acta Bot. Hung.* 31: 225–230.

Boyer, K. 1992. *Palms and Cycads beyond the Tropics.* Palm and Cycad Societies of Australia, Milton.

Bradford, D., and C. Smith. 1977. Seed predation and seed number in *Scheelea* palm fruits. *Ecology* 58: 667–673.

Braker, E., and R. Chazdon. 1993. Ecological, behavioural and nutritional factors influencing use of palms as host plants by a Neotropical forest grasshopper. *J. Trop. Ecol.* 9: 183–197.

Braun, A. 1976. Various observations on *Ceroxylon klopstockia*. *Principes* 20: 158–166.

Bristo, H. 1969. Autecology of saw palmetto (*Serenoa repens* (Bartr.) Small). Ph.D. diss., Duke University, Durham, N.C.

Brown, K. 1976a. Ecological studies of the cabbage palm, *Sabal palmetto*. I. Floral biology. *Principes* 20: 3–10.

————. 1976b. Ecological studies of the cabbage palm, *Sabal palmetto*. II. Dispersal, predation, and escape of seeds. *Principes* 20: 49–56.

Brummitt, R., and C. Powell. 1992. *Authors of Plant Names*. Royal Botanic Gardens, Kew, U.K.

Buckley, R., and H. Harries. 1984. Self-sown wild-type coconuts from Australia. *Biotropica* 16: 148–151.

Bullock, S. 1984. Biomass and nutrient allocation in a neotropical dioecious palm. *Oecologia* 63: 426–428.

Búrquez, A., J. Sarukhán, and A. Pedroza. 1987. Floral biology of a primary rain forest palm, *Astrocaryum mexicanum* Liebm. *Bot. J. Linn. Soc.* 94: 407–419.

Burret, M. 1929a. Die Gattung *Ceroxylon* Humb. et Bonpl. *Notizbl. Bot. Gart. Berlin-Dahlem* 10: 841–854.

————. 1929b. Die Palmengattungen *Orbignya, Attalea, Scheelea* und *Maximiliana*. *Notizbl. Bot. Gart. Berlin-Dahlem* 10: 651–701.

————. 1930. Geonomeae Americanae. *Bot. Jahrb. Syst.* 63: 123–270.

————. 1933–34. *Bactris* und verwandte Palmengattungen. *Repert. Spec. Nov. Regni Veg.* 34: 167–253.

————. 1934. Die Palmengattung *Astrocaryum* G.F.W. Meyer. *Repert. Spec. Nov. Regni Veg.* 35: 114–158.

Calero Hidalgo, R. 1992. The Tagua initiative in Ecuador: A community approach to tropical rain forest conservation. In M. Plotkin and L. Famolare, eds., *Sustainable Harvest and Marketing of Rain Forest Products*, pp. 263–273. Island Press, Covelo, Calif.

Calzavara, B. 1972. As possibilidades do açaizeiro no estuário amazônico. *Boletim, Faculdade de Ciências Agrárias do Pará* 5: 1–103.

Castillo Mont, J., N. Gallardo, and D. Johnson. 1994. The Pacaya palm (*Chamaedorea tepejilote:* Arecaceae) and its food use in Guatemala. *Econ. Bot.* 48: 68–75.

Chazdon, R. 1985. Leaf display, canopy structure, and light interception of two understory palm species. *Amer. J. Bot.* 72: 1493–1502.

————. 1986a. Physiological and morphological basis of shade tolerance in rain forest understory palms. *Principes* 30: 92–99.

————. 1986b. Light variation and carbon gain in rain forest understory palms. *J. Ecol.* 74: 995–1012.

————. 1986c. The costs of leaf support in understory palms: Economy versus safety. *Amer. Nat.* 127: 9–30.

————. 1991. Plant size and form in the understory palm genus *Geonoma*: Are species variations on a theme? *Amer. J. Bot.* 78: 680–694.

Clancy, K., and M. Sullivan. 1990. Distribution of the Needle Palm, *Rhapidophyllum hystrix*. *Castanea* 55: 31–39.

Clement, C., and J. Mora Urpí. 1987. Pejibaye palm (*Bactris gasipaes*, Arecaceae): Multi-use potential for the lowland humid tropics. *Econ. Bot.* 41: 302–311.

Clement, C., J. Aguiar, D. Arkcoll, J. Firmino, and R. Leandro. 1989. Pupunha brava (*Bactris dahlgreniana* Glassman): Progenitor da pupunha (*B. gasipaes* H.B.K.)? *Bol. Mus. Paraense Hist. Nat.* 5: 39–55.

Cook, O.F. 1942. The Brazilian origin for the commercial oil palm. *Sci. Monthly* 54: 577–590.

Cook, O., and C. Doyle. 1939. The edible pacaya palm of Alta Vera Paz. *Nat. Hort. Mag.* 18: 161–179.

Cornett, J. 1987a. Three palm species at Cataviña. *Principes* 31: 12–13.

———. 1987b. Cold tolerance in the desert fan palm, *Washingtonia filifera* (Arecaceae). *Madroño* 34: 57–62.

———. 1989. *Desert Palm Oasis.* Palm Springs Desert Museum, Palm Springs, Calif.

Crovetto, R., and B. Picinni. 1951. La vegetation de la Republica Argentina. I. Los Palmares de *Butia yatay. Revista Invest. Agric.* 4: 153–242.

Dahlgren, B., and S. Glassman. 1961. A revision of the genus *Copernicia. Gentes Herb.* 9: 1–40.

———. 1963. A revision of the genus *Copernicia.* 2. West Indian species. *Gentes Herb.* 9: 43–232.

Darwin, C. 1845. *Journal of the Researches into the Natural History and Geology of the Countries visited during the Voyage of H. M. S. Beagle round the World, under the Command of Captain FitzRoy, R. N.* 2d ed. John Murray, London.

de Granville, J.-J., and A. Henderson. 1988. A new species of *Asterogyne* (Palmae) from French Guiana. *Brittonia* 40: 76–80.

De los Heros, M., and J. Bueno Zárate. 1980–81. Posibilidades papeleras de pulpa al sulfato de peciolos de aguaje (*Mauritia flexuousa*). *Rev. Florestal del Perú* 10: 83–88.

de Nevers, G. In press. Certain palms of Panama. *Proc. Calif. Acad. Sci.*

de Nevers, G., and A. Henderson. 1988. A new *Calyptrogyne* (Palmae: Geonomeae) from Panama. *Syst. Bot.* 13: 428–431.

de Nevers, G., M. Grayum, and B. Hammel. 1988. *Astrocaryum confertum,* an enigmatic Costa Rican palm rediscovered. *Principes* 32: 91–95.

de Nevers, G., A. Henderson, and M. Grayum. In press. Mesoamerican *Bactris* (Palmae). *Proc. Calif. Acad. Sci.*

de Steven, D. 1986. Comparative demography of a clonal palm *Oenocarpus mapora* subsp. *mapora*) in Panama. *Principes* 30: 100–104.

Devall, M., and R. Kiester. 1987. Notes on *Raphia* at Corcovado. *Brenesia* 28: 89–96.

Di Silverio, F., G. D'Eramo, C. Lubrano, G. Flammia, A. Sciarra, E. Palma, M. Caponera, and F. Sciarra. 1992. Evidence that *Serenoa repens* extract displays an antiestrogenic activity in prostatic tissue of benign prostatic hypertrophy patients. *European Urology* 21: 309–314.

Dransfield, J. 1991. Arecaceae. In G. Zizka, *Flowering Plants of Easter Island,* pp. 64–65. Palmengarten, Frankfurt.

Dransfield, J., J. Flenley, S. King, D. Harkness, and S. Rapu. 1984. A recently extinct palm from Easter Island. *Nature* 312: 750–752.

Drude, O. 1887. Palmae. In A. Engler and K. Prantl, eds., *Die natürlichen Pflanzenfamilien,* vol. 2, part 3, pp. 1–93. Wilhelm Engelmann, Leipzig.

Durán, R., and M. Franco. 1992. Estudio demográfico de *Pseudophoenix sargentii. Bull. Inst. fr. études andines* 21: 609–621.

Eguiarte, L., A. Búrquez, J. Rodríguez, M. Martínez-Ramos, J. Sarukhán, and D. Piñero. 1993. Direct and indirect estimates of neighborhood and effective population size in a tropical palm, *Astrocaryum mexicanum. Evolution* 47: 75–87.

EMBRAPA (Empresa Brasileira de Pesquisa Agropecuária). 1987. *Palmito. 1° Encontro Nacional de Pesquisadores.* EMBRAPA, Curitiba, Brazil.

Emmons, L. 1984. Geographic variation in densities and diversities of non-flying mammals in Amazonia. *Biotropica* 16: 210–222.

Erikson, B. 1992. Some field observations of *Brahea* in Tamaulipas, Mexico. *Principes* 36(3): 128–132.

Ervik, F. 1993. Notes on the phenology and pollination of the dioecious palms *Mauritia flexuosa* (Calamoideae) and *Aphandra natalia* (Phytelephantoideae) in Ecuador. In W. Barthlott, C. Naumann, C. Schmidt-Loske, and K. Schuchmann, eds., *Animal-plant Interactions in Tropical Environments*, pp. 7–12. Zoologisches Forschungsinstitut und Museum Alexander Koenig, Bonn, Germany.

Essig, F. 1971. Observations in pollination in *Bactris. Principes* 15: 20–24.

Evans, R. 1992a. A monograph of *Cryosophila.* Ph.D. diss., University of Michigan, Ann Arbor.

———. 1992b. *Cryosophila macrocarpa* (Palmae), a new species from Chocó Department, Colombia. *Novon* 2: 58–61.

Fisher, J. 1974. Axillary and dichotomous branching in the palm *Chamaedorea. Amer. J. Bot.* 61: 1046–1056.

Fisher, J., and H. Moore. 1977. Multiple inflorescences in palms (Arecaceae): Their development and significance. *Bot. Jahrb. Syst.* 98: 573–611.

Fisher, J., and P. Tomlinson. 1973. Branch and inflorescence production in saw palmetto (Serenoa repens). *Principes* 17: 10–19.

Frangi, J., and A. Lugo. 1985. Ecosystem dynamics of a subtropical flood plain forest. *Ecol. Monogr.* 55: 351–369.

———. 1991. Hurricane damage to a flood plain forest in the Luquillo Mountains of Puerto Rico. *Biotropica* 23: 324–335.

Frangi, J., and M. Ponce. 1985. The root system of *Prestoea montana* and its ecological significance. *Principes* 29: 13–19.

Furley, P. 1975. The significance of the Cohune palm, *Orbignya cohune* (Mart.) Dahlgren, on the nature and in the development of the soil profile. *Biotropica* 7: 32–36.

Galeano, G. 1991. *Las palmas de la región de Araracuara.* Estudios en la Amazonia Colombiana. Vol 1. Tropenbos, Bogotá.

———. In press. Novedades en el género *Ceroxylon* (Palmae). *Caldasia.*

Galeano, G., and F. Skov. 1989. *Geonoma linearis*—a rheophytic palm from Colombia and Ecuador. *Principes* 33: 108–112.

Galeano, G., R. Bernal, and F. Kahn. 1988. Una nueva especie de *Astrocaryum* (Palmae) de Colombia. *Candollea* 43: 279–283.

Galeano, G., and R. Bernal. 1987. Palmas del Departamento de Antioquia. Región Occidental. Universidad Nacional de Colombia.

Galetti, M., M. Paschoal, and F. Pedroni. 1992. Predation on palm nuts (*Syagrus romanzoffiana*) by squirrels (*Sciurus ingrami*) in south-east Brazil. *J. Trop. Ecol.* 8: 121–123.

Gentry, A. 1986. Notes on Peruvian palms. *Ann. Missouri Bot. Gard.* 73: 158–165.

———. 1988. New species and a new combination for plants from trans-Andean South America. *Ann. Missouri Bot. Gard.* 75(4): 1429–1439.

Gibbons, M. 1993. *Palms.* Quintet Publishing, London.

Gillis, W. 1977. Unique setting of *Roystonea* in the Bahamas. *Principes* 21: 109–113.

Glanz, W., R. Thorington, J. Giacalone-Madden, and L. Heaney. 1983. Seasonal food use and demographic trends in *Sciurus.* In E. Leigh, A. Rand, and D. Windson, eds., *The Ecology of a Tropical Forest*, pp. 239–252. Smithsonian Institution Press, Washington, D.C.

Glassman, S. 1968. Studies in the palm genus *Syagrus* Mart. *Fieldiana Bot.* 31: 363–397.

——. 1970. A new hybrid in the palm genus *Syagrus* Mart. *Fieldiana Bot.* 32: 241–257.

——. 1972. *A Revision of B. E. Dahlgren's Index of American Palms.* Verlag von J. Cramer, Lehre.

——. 1979. A re-evaluation of the genus *Butia* with a description of a new species. *Principes* 23: 65–79.

——. 1987. Revision of the palm genus *Syagrus* Mart. and other selected genera in the *Cocos* alliance. *Illinois Biol. Monogr.* 56: 1–230.

Goulding, M. 1989. *Amazon: The Flooded Forest.* BBC Books, London.

Grayum, M., and G. de Nevers. 1988. New and rare understory palms from the Península de Osa, Costa Rica, and adjacent regions. *Principes* 32: 101–114.

Gruezo, W., and H. Harries. 1984. Self-sown, wild-type coconuts in the Philippines. *Biotropica* 16: 140–147.

Gubert, F. 1987. Descrição de duas áreas de ocorrência natural da palmácea *Trithrinax brasiliensis* no estado do Paraná. *Boletim FBCN* 22: 79–88.

Gunther, B., and Mahalick, P. 1988. *Brahea edulis* in the wild. *Principes* 32: 179–181.

Guzmán-Rivas, P. 1984. Coconut and other palm use in Mexico and the Philippines. *Principes* 28: 20–30.

Hahn, W. 1990. A synopsis of the Palmae of Paraguay. M.S. thesis, Cornell University, Ithaca, N.Y.

——. 1991. Notes on the genus *Acanthococos. Principes* 35: 167–171.

Harries, H. 1978. The evolution, dissemination and classification of *Cocos nucifera* L. *Bot. Rev.* 44: 265–319.

Henderson, A. 1984a. Observations on pollination of *Cryosophila albida. Principes* 28: 120–126.

——. 1984b. The native palms of Puerto Rico. *Principes* 28: 168–172.

——. 1985. Pollination of *Socratea exorrhiza* and *Iriartea ventricosa. Principes* 29: 64–71.

——. 1986. *Barcella odora. Principes* 30: 74–76.

——. 1990. Arecaceae. Part 1. Introduction and the Iriarteinae. *Flora Neotropica* 53: 1–100.

——. 1994. *The Palms of the Amazon.* Oxford University Press, New York.

Henderson, A., and M. Balick. 1991. *Attalea crassispatha,* a rare and endemic Haitian palm. *Brittonia* 43: 189–194.

Henderson, A., and F. Chávez. 1993. *Desmoncus* as a useful palm in the western Amazon basin. *Principes* 37: 184–186.

Henderson, A., and G. Galeano. In press. A revision of *Euterpe, Prestoea and Neonicholsonia* (Palmae). *Flora Neotropica.*

Henderson, A., and J. Steyermark. 1986. New palms from Venezuela. *Brittonia* 38: 309–313.

Henderson, A., M. Aubry, J. Timyan, and M. Balick. 1990. Conservation status of Haitian palms. *Principes* 34: 134–142.

Hernández, E. 1945. La distribución natural de la *Scheelea preussii* Burret, se extiende a Mexico. *Rev. Soc. Mexicana Hist. Nat.* 6: 145–152.

Hicks, B. 1989. Prehistoric development and dispersal of the desert fan palm. *Principes* 33: 33–39.

Hilty, S., and W. Brown. 1986. *A Guide of the Birds of Colombia.* Princeton University Press, Princeton, N.J.

Hladik A., and C.M. Hladik. 1969. Rapports trophiques entre vegetation et primates dans la forêt de Barro Colorado (Panama). *Terre et Vie* 116: 25–117.

Hodel, D. 1988. Letter. *Principes* 32: 95, 100.

——. 1992a. *The Chamaedorea Palms: The Species and Their Cultivation.* Allen Press, Lawrence, Kansas.

——. 1992b. Additions to *Chamaedorea* Palms: New species from Mexico and Guatemala and miscellaneous notes. *Principes* 36: 188–202.

Hogan, K. 1988. Photosynthesis in two neotropical palm species. *Functional Ecology* 2: 371–377.

Ibarra-Manríquez, G. 1988. The palms of a tropical rain forest in Veracruz, Mexico. *Principes* 32: 147–155.

Index Kewensis. 1993. *Index Kewensis on Compact Disc.* Oxford University Press, London.

Janzen, D. 1971. The fate of *Scheelea rostrata* fruits beneath the parent tree; predispersal attack by bruchids. *Principes* 15: 89–101.

——. 1983. *Acrocomia vinifera* (Coyol). In D. Janzen, ed., *Costa Rican Natural History*, pp. 184–185. University of Chicago Press, Chicago.

Johannessen, C. 1957. Man's role in the distribution of the Corozo palm. *Yearbook of the Association of Pacific Coast Geographers* 1957: 29–33.

Johnson, D. 1972. The carnauba wax palm (*Copernicia prunifera*). IV. Economic uses. *Principes* 16: 128–131.

Johnston, M. 1992. Soil-vegetation relationships in a tabonuco forest community in the Luquillo Mountains of Puerto Rico. *J. Trop. Ecol.* 8: 253–263.

Jones, J. 1983. An ecological study of the Florida Royal palm, *Roystonea elata* (Bartram) F. Harper. M.S. thesis, Florida Atlantic University, Boca Raton.

Kahn, F. 1988. A distichous *Mauritia flexuosa. Principes* 32: 88.

Kahn, F., and J.-J. de Granville. 1992. *Palms in Forest Ecosystems of Amazonia.* Springer-Verlag, Berlin.

Kahn, F., and K. Mejía. 1987. Notes on the biology, ecology, and use of a small Amazonian palm, *Lepidocaryum tessmannii. Principes* 31: 14–19.

——. 1988. A new species of *Chelyocarpus* (Palmae, Coryphoideae) from Peruvian Amazon. *Principes* 32: 69–72.

Kahn, F., and B. Millán. 1992. *Astrocaryum* (Palmae, Cocoeae, Bactridinae) in Amazonia. A preliminary treatment. *Bull. Inst. fr. et. andines* 21: 459–531.

Kiltie, R. 1981. Distribution of palm fruits on a rain forest floor: Why white-lipped peccaries forage near objects. *Biotropica* 13: 141–145.

Kowalska, M., R. Sanders, and C. Nauman. 1991. Phenolic constituents of *Coccothrinax* (Palmae). *Principes* 35: 142–146.

Koziol, M., and H. Borgtoft Pedersen. 1993. *Phytelephas aequatorialis* (Arecaceae) in human and animal nutrition. *Econ. Bot.* 47: 401–407.

Kubitzki, K. 1991. Dispersal and distribution in *Leopoldinia* (Palmae). *Nord. J. Bot.* 11: 429–432.

Küchmeister, H., G. Gottsberger, and I. Silberbauer-Gottsberger. 1992. Pollination biology of *Orbignya spectabilis*, a "monoecious" Amazonian palm. In W. Barthlott, C. Nauman, C. Schmidt-Loske and K. Schuchmann, eds., *Animal-Plant Interactions in Tropical Environments*, pp. 67–76. Zoologisches Forschungsinstitut und Museum Alexander Koenig, Bonn, Germany.

Lentz, D. 1990. *Acrocomia mexicana*: Palm of the ancient Mesoamericans. *J. Ethnobiol.* 10: 183–194.

León, H. 1939. Contribución al estudio de las palmas de Cuba. III. Género *Coccothrinax*. *Mem. Soc. Cubana Hist. Nat.* 13: 107–156.

Lescure, J.-P., L. Emperaire, and C. Franciscon. 1992. *Leopoldinia piassaba* Wallace (Arecaaceae): A few biological and economic data from the Rio Negro region (Brazil). *Forest Ecol. and Man.* 55: 83–86.

Listabarth, C. 1992. A survey of pollination strategies in the Bactridinae. *Bull. Inst. fr. ét. andines* 21: 699–714.

———. 1993a. Insect-induced pollination of the palm *Chamaedorea pinnatifrons* and pollination in the related *Wendlandiella* sp. *Biodiversity and Conservation* 2: 39–50.

———. 1993b. Pollination in *Geonoma macrostachys* and three congeners, *G. acaulis, g. gracilis* and *G. interrupta. Bot. Acta* 106: 455–514.

Lockett, L. 1991. Native Texas palms north of the lower Rio Grande valley: Recent discoveries. *Principes* 35: 64–71.

Lugo, A., and C. Batlle. 1987. Leaf production, growth rate, and age of the palm *Presotea montana* in the Luquillo Experimental Forest, Puerto Rico. *J. Trop. Ecol.* 3: 151–161.

Lugo, A., and Frangi, J. 1993. Fruit fall in the Luquillo Experimental Forest, Puerto Rico. *Biotropica* 25: 73–84.

McClenaghan, L., and A. Beauchamp. 1986. Low genetic differentiation among isolated populations of the California fan palm (*Washingtonia filifera*). *Evolution* 40: 315–322.

McCoy, R. 1983. *Lethal Yellowing of Palms*. University of Florida Press, Gainesville.

McVaugh, R. 1993. *Flora Novo-Galiciana*. Vol. 13. University of Michigan Press, Ann Arbor.

Magnano, S. de. 1973. *Trithrinax campestris* (Palmae): Inflorescencia y flor con especial referencia al gineceo. *Kurtziana* 7: 137–152.

Markley, K. 1955. Caranday—a source of palm wax. *Econ. Bot.* 9: 39–52.

Martinez-Ramos, M., J. Sarukhán, and D. Piñero. 1988. The demography of tropical trees in the context of forest gap dynamics: The case of *Astrocaryum mexicanum* at Los Tuxtlas tropical rain forest. In A. Davy, M. Hutchings, and A. Watkinson, eds., *Plant Population Ecology*, pp. 293–313. Blackwell Scientific Publications, Oxford.

Martius, C. 1823–37. *Historia Naturalis Palmarum*. Vol. 2, *Genera et species*. T. O. Weigel, Leipzig.

———. 1831–53. *Historia Naturalis Palmarum*. Vol. 1, *De Palmas Generatim*. T. O. Weigel, Leipzig.

———. 1837–53. *Historia Naturalis Palmarum*. Vol. 3, *Expositio systematica*. T. O. Weigel, Leipzig.

Medeiros-Costa, J., and S. Panizza. 1983. Palms of the Cerrado vegetation formation of São Paulo State, Brazil. *Principes* 27: 118–125.

Mendoza, A., and M. Franco. 1992. Integración clonal en una palma tropical. *Bull. Inst. fr. études andines* 21: 623–635.

Moore, H. 1951. Some American Corypheae. *Gentes Herb.* 8: 209–222.

———. 1956. The genus *Reinhardtia. Principes* 1: 127–145.

———. 1957. *Reinhardtia. Gentes Herb.* 8: 541–168.

———. 1967. The genus *Gastrococos* (Palmae-Cocoideae). *Principes* 11: 114–121.

————. 1969a. The genus *Juania* (Palmae-Arecoideae). *Gentes Herb.* 10: 385–393.

————. 1969b. The Geonomoid palms. *Taxon* 18: 230–232.

————. 1971. The genus *Synechanthus* (Palmae). *Principes* 15: 10–19.

————. 1972. *Chelyocarpus* and its allies *Cryosophila* and *Itaya* (Palmae). *Principes* 16: 67–88.

————. 1973. The major groups of palms and their distribution. *Gentes Herb.* 11: 27–140.

————. 1977. Endangerment at the specific and generic levels in palms. In G. Prance and T. Elias, eds., *Extinction Is Forever*, pp. 267–282. New York Botanical Garden, Bronx, N.Y.

————. 1982. Nomenclatural Notes. An overlooked name for the hybrid between *Arecastrum* and *Butia*. *Principes* 26: 50.

Moraes, M. 1991. Contribución al estudio del ciclo biológico de la palma *Copernicia alba* en un area ganadera (Espíritu, Beni, Bolivia). *Ecologia en Bolivia* 18: 1–20.

————. 1993. *Allagoptera brevicalyx* (Palmae), a new species from Bahia, Brazil. *Brittonia* 45: 21–24.

Moraes, M., and A. Henderson. 1990. The genus *Parajubaea* (Palmae). *Brittonia* 42: 92–99.

Moraes, M., and J. Sarmiento. 1992. Contribución al estudio de biología reproductiva de una especie de *Bactris* (Palmae) en el bosque de galería (Depto. Beni, Bolivia). *Bull. Inst. fr. ét. andines* 21: 685–698.

Moraes, M., G. Galeano, R. Bernal, H. Balslev, and A. Henderson. In press. Tropical Andean Palms (Arecaceae). In S. Churchill, H. Balslev, E. Forero, and J. Luteyn, eds., *Biodiversity and Conservation of Neotropical Montane Forests*. New York Botanical Garden, Bronx, N.Y.

Mora Urpí, J., L. Szott, M. Murillo, and V. Patío. 1993. *Cuarto Congreso Internacional sobre Biologá, Agronomá e Industrialización del Pijuayo*. Editorial de la Universidad de Costa Rica, San Jose, Costa Rica.

Moya, C., J. Martínez-Fortún, J. Ludgardo, J. García, and E. Rodríguez. 1989. Las Copernicias (Yareyes Y Jatas) en Sancti Spíritus. Palmas endémicas que necesitan protección. *Rev. Jardin Bot. Nacional* 10: 49–62.

Moya, C., A. Leiva, J. Valdés, J. Martínez-Fortún, and A. Hernandez. 1991. *Gaussia spirituana* Moya et Leiva, sp. nov.: Una nueva palma de Cuba Central. *Rev. Jardín Bot. Nacional* 12: 15–19.

Muñiz, O., and A. Borhidi. 1981. Palmas nuevas del género *Coccothrinax* Sarg. en Cuba. *Acta Bot. Acad. Sci. Hungaricae* 27: 439–454.

Munn, C., J. Thomsen, and C. Yamashita. 1989–90. The Hyacinth Macaw. *Audubon Wildlife Report* 1989–90: 405–419.

National Academy of Sciences. 1975. *Underexploited Tropical Plants with Promising Economic Value*. National Academy of Sciences, Washington, D.C.

Nauman, C. 1990. Intergeneric hybridization between *Coccothrinax* and *Thrinax* (Palmae: Coryphoideae). *Principes* 34: 191–198.

Nauman, C., and R. Sanders. 1991a. Preliminary classificatory studies in *Coccothrinax* (Palmae: Coryphoideae). *Selbyana* 12: 91–101.

————. 1991b. An annotated key to the cultivated species of *Coccothrinax*. *Principes* 35: 27–46.

Noblick, L. R. 1991. The indigenous palms of the state of Bahia, Brazil. Ph.D. diss., University of Illinois, Chicago.

Oldeman, R. 1969. Etude biologique des pinotières de la Guyane Française. *Cah. ORSTOM sér. Biol.* 10: 3–18.

Olesen, J., and H. Balslev. 1990. Flower biology and pollinators of the Amazonian monoecious palm, *Geonoma macrostachys*: A case of Bakerian mimicry. *Principes* 34: 181–190.

Orellana, R., and N. Ayora. 1993. Population structure of two palm species in a community of sand dune scrub in the Yucatán Peninsula, México. *Principes* 37: 26–34.

Ormond, W., and C. Leite. 1987. Ocorrência de inflorescência masculina em *Allagoptera arenaria* (Gomes) O. Kuntze—Palmae. *Bradea* 4: 358–361.

Otedoh, M. 1977. The African origin of *Raphia taedigera*—Palmae. *Nigerian Field* 42: 11–16.

———. 1982. A revision of the genus *Raphia* Beauv. (Palmae). *J. Nigerian Inst. Oil Palm Research* 6: 145–189.

Oyama, K. 1990. Variation in growth and reproduction in the neotropical dioecious palm *Chamaedorea tepejilote*. *J. Ecol.* 78: 648–663.

———. 1991. Seed predation by a curculionid beetle on the dioecious palm *Chamaedorea tepejilote*. *Principes* 35: 156–160.

———. 1993. Are age and height correlated in *Chamaedorea tepejilote* (Palmae)? *J. Trop. Ecol.* 9:381–385.

Oyama, K., and R. Dirzo. 1988. Biomass allocation in the dioecious tropical palm *Chamaedorea tepejilote* and its life history consequences. *Plant Species Biology* 3: 27–33.

———. 1991. Ecological aspects of the interaction between *Chamaedorea tepejilote*, a dioecious palm and *Calyptocephala marginipennis*, a herbivorous beetle, in a Mexican rain forest. *Principes* 35: 86–93.

Oyama, K., and A. Mendoza. 1990. Effects of defoliation on growth, reproduction, and survival of a neotropical dioecious palm, *Chamaedorea tepejilote*. *Biotropica* 22: 119–123.

Oyama, K., R. Dirzo, and G. Ibarra-Manriquez. 1992. Population structure of the dominant palm species in the understory of a Mexican lowland rain forest. *Tropics* 2: 23–28.

Padoch, C. 1988. Aguaje (*Mauritia flexuosa* L. f.) in the economy of Iquitos, Peru. *Adv. Econ. Bot.* 6: 214–224.

Palomino, G., and H. Quero. 1992. Karyotype analysis of three species of *Sabal*, (Palmae: Coryphoideae). *Cytologia* 57: 485–489.

Piedade, M. 1985. Ecologia e biologia reprodutiva de *Astrocaryum jauari* Mart. (Palmae) como exemplo de populacão adaptada às áreas inundáveis do Rio Negro (igapós). M.S. thesis, Universidade do Amazonas, Manaus, Brazil.

Pinard, M. 1993. Impacts of stem harvesting on populations of *Iriartea deltoidea* (Palmae) in an extractive reserve in Acre, Brazil. *Biotropica* 25: 2–14.

Piñero, D., and J. Sarukhán. 1982. Reproductive behavior and its individual variability in a tropical palm, *Astrocaryum mexicanum*. *J. Ecol.* 70: 461–472.

Piñero, D., J. Sarukhán, and E. González. 1977. Estudios demográficos en plantas. *Astrocaryum mexicanum* Liebm. 1. Estructura de las poblaciones. *Bol. Soc. Bot. Mexico* 37: 69–118.

Piñero, D., J. Sarukhán, and P. Alberdi. 1982. The costs of reproduction in a tropical palm, *Astrocaryum mexicanum*. *J. Ecol.* 70: 473–481.

Piñero, D., M. Martínez-Ramos, A. Mendoza, E. Alvarez-Bullya, and J. Sarukhán.

1986. Demographic studies in *Astrocaryum mexicanum* and their use in understanding community dynamics. *Principes* 30: 108–116.

Pingitore, E. 1978. Revision de las especies del género *Trithrinax. Revista Inst. Munic. Bot.* 4: 95–109.

Pires-O'Brien, M. 1993. Local distribution and ecology of "palha-preta"—a pioneer and invasive palm in Jari, Lower Amazon. *Principes* 37: 212–215.

Putz, F. 1979. Biology and human use of *Leopoldinia piassaba. Principes* 23: 149–156.

———. 1983. Developmental morphology of *Desmoncus isthmius,* a climbing colonial, cocosoid palm. *Principes* 27: 38–42.

Putz, F., and M. Holbrook. 1989. Strangler fig rooting habits and nutrient relations in the Llanos of Venezuela. *Amer. J. Bot.* 76: 781–788.

Quero, H. 1981. *Pseudophoenix sargentii* in the Yucatan Peninsula, Mexico. *Principes* 25: 63–72.

———. 1989. Flora genérica de arecáceas de México. Dr.Sc. thesis, Universidad Nacional Autónoma de México, Mexico.

———. 1991. *Sabal gretheriae,* a new species of palm from the Yucatan Peninsula, Mexico. *Principes* 35: 219–224.

Quero, H., and R. Read. 1986. A revision of the palm genus *Gaussia. Syst. Bot.* 11: 145–154.

Read, R. 1968. A study of *Pseudophoenix* (Palmae). *Gentes Herb.* 10: 169–213.

———. 1969. Some notes on *Pseudophoenix* and a key to the species. *Principes* 13: 77–79.

———. 1975. The genus *Thrinax* (Palmae: Coryphoideae). *Smithsonian Contr. Bot.* 19: 1–98.

———. 1979. *Palms of the Lesser Antilles.* Department of Botany, Smithsonian Institution, Washington, D.C.

———. 1988. Utilization of indigenous palms in the Caribbean (in relation to their abundance). *Adv. Econ. Bot.* 6: 137–143.

Read, R., T. Zanoni, and M. Mejía. 1987. *Reinhardtia paiewonskiana* (Palmae), a new species for the West Indies. *Brittonia* 39: 20–25.

Reichel-Dolmatoff, G. 1989. Biological and social aspects of the Yurupari complex of the Colombian Vaupés territory. *J. Lat. Amer. Lore* 15: 95–135.

Reitz, P. 1974. *Flora Ilustrada Catarinense: Palmeiras.* Santa Catarina, Brazil.

Rioja, G. 1992. The jatata project: the pilot experience of Chimane empowerment. In M. Plotkin and I. Famolare, eds., *Sustainable Harvest and Marketing of Rain Forest Products,* pp. 192–196. Island Press, Covelo, Calif.

Rival, L. 1993. The growth of family trees: Understanding Huaorani perceptions of the forest. *Man* 28: 635–652.

Roubik, D. 1989. *Ecology and Natural History of Tropical Bees.* Cambridge, University Press, Cambridge, U.K.

Ruiz, M. 1984. Contribución al conocimiento de la palma de almendrón. *Cespedesia* 13: 139–151.

Sanders, R. 1991. Cladistics of *Bactris* (Palmae): Survey of characters and refutation of Burret's classification. *Selbyana* 12: 105–133.

Scariot, A., E. Lleras, and J. Hay. 1991. Reproductive biology of the palm *Acrocomia aculeata* in Central Brazil. *Biotropica* 23: 12–22.

Schlüter, U., B. Furch, and C. Joly. 1993. Physiological and anatomical adaptations by young *Astrocaryum jauari* Mart. (Arecaceae) in periodically inundated biotopes of Central Amazonia. *Biotropica* 25: 384–396.

Schmid, R. 1970a. Notes on the reproductive biology of *Asterogyne martiana* (Palmae). I. Inflorescence and floral morphology; phenology. *Principes* 14: 3–9.

———. 1970b. Notes on the reproductive biology of *Asterogyne martiana* (Palmae). II. Pollination by syrphid flies. *Principes* 14: 39–49.

Schultes, R. 1940. Plantae Mexicanae V. *Desmoncus chinantlensis* and its utilization in native basketry. *Bot. Mus. Leafl.* 8: 134–140.

———. 1990. Taxonomic, nomenclatural and ethnobotanic notes on *Elaeis. Elaeis* 2: 172–187.

Schupp, W., and E. Frost 1989. Differential predation of *Welfia Georgei* seeds in treefall gaps and the forest understory. *Biotropica* 21: 200–203.

Shuey, A., and R. Wunderlin. 1977. The Needle Palm: *Rhapidophyllum hystrix. Principes* 21: 47–59.

Silberbauer-Gottsberger, I. 1973. Blüten- und Fruchtbiologie von *Butia leiospatha* (Arecaceae). *Oesterr. Bot. Z.* 121: 171–185.

Sist, P. 1989. Demography of *Astrocaryum sciophilum*, an understory palm of French Guiana. *Principes* 33: 142–151.

Sist, P., and H. Puig. 1987. Régénération, dynamique de populations et dissémination d'un palmier de Guyane française: *Jessenia bataua* (Mart.) Burret subsp. *oligocarpa* (Griseb. and H. Wendl.) Balick. *Adansonia* 3: 317–336.

Skov, F. 1989. HyperTaxonomy—a new tool for revisional work and a revision of *Geonoma* (Palmae) in Ecuador. Ph.D. thesis, Aarhus University, Denmark.

Skov, F., and H. Balslev. 1989. A revision of *Hyospathe* (Arecaceae). *Nord. J. Bot.* 9: 189–202.

Smythe, N. 1989. Seed survival in the palm *Astrocaryum standleyanum*: evidence for dependence upon its seed dispersers. *Biotropica* 21: 50–56.

Snow, D. 1962. The natural history of the oilbird, *Steatornis caripensis*, in Trinidad, W.I. Part 2. Population, breeding ecology, and food. *Zoologica* 47: 199–221.

Snow, D., and K. Snow. 1978. Palm fruits in the diet of the oilbird, *Steatornis caripensis. Principes* 22: 107–109.

Spruce, R. 1860. On *Leopoldinia piassaba*, Wallace. *J. Proc. Linn. Soc., Bot.* 4: 58–63.

Standley, P., and J. Steyermark. 1958. Palmae. Flora of Guatemala. *Fieldiana Bot.* 24: 196–299.

Strudwick, J., and G. Sobel. 1988. Uses of *Euterpe oleracea* Mart. in the Amazon estuary, Brazil. *Adv. Econ. Bot.* 6: 225–253.

Stuessy, T., R. Sanders, and O. Matthei. 1983. *Juania australis* revisited in the Juan Fernández Islands, Chile. *Principes* 27: 71–74.

Taboada, G. 1979. *Los murciélagos de Cuba.* Editorial Academica, Havana, Cuba.

Terborgh, J. 1983. *Five New World Primates.* Princeton University Press, Princeton, N.J..

———. 1986. Keystone plant resources in the tropical forest. In M. Soulé, ed., *Conserv. Biol.*, pp. 330–344. Sinauer, Sunderland, Mass.

———. 1988. The big things that run the world. *Conserv. Biol.* 2: 402–403.

Terborgh, J., E. Losos, M. Riley, and M. Riley. 1993. Predation by vertebrates and invertebrates on the seeds of five canopy tree species of an Amazonian forest. *Vegetatio* 107/108: 375–386.

Timyan, J., and S. Reep. 1994. Conservation status of *Attalea crassispatha* (Mart.) Burret, the rare and endemic oil palm of Haiti. *Biol. Conserv.* 68: 11–18.

Uhl, N., and J. Dransfield. 1987. *Genera Palmarum.* Allen Press, Lawrence, Kansas.

Uhl, N., and H. Moore. 1977. Correlations of inflorescence, flower structure, and floral anatomy with pollination in some palms. *Biotropica* 9: 170–190.

Urdaneta, H. 1981. *Planificación silvicultural de los bosques ricos en palma manaca (Euterpe oleracea), en el delta del Río Orinoco.* Universidad de los Andes, Mérida, Venezuela.

Urrego, L. 1987. Estudio preliminar de la fenología de la canangucha (*Mauritia flexuosa* L. f.). *Colombia Amazonica* 2: 57–81.

Vandermeer, J. 1983. *Welfia georgii* (Palmito, Palma Conga, Welfia Palm). In D. Janzen, ed., *Costa Rican Natural History,* pp. 346–349. University of Chicago Press, Chicago.

Van Valen, L. 1975. Life, death, and energy of a tree. *Biotropica* 7: 260–269.

Voeks, R. 1985. Preliminary observations on the reproductive ecology of the piassava palm (*Attalea funifera* Mart.). *An. Acad. Bras. Cienc.* 57: 524–525.

———. 1987. A biogeography of the piassava fiber palm (*Attalea funifera* Mart.) of Bahia, Brazil. Ph.D. diss., University of California, Berkeley.

———. 1988. Changing sexual expression of a Brazilian rain forest palm (*Attalea funifera* Mart.). *Biotropica* 20: 107–113.

Wallace, A. 1853. *Palm Trees of the Amazon and Their Uses.* Van Hoorst, London.

Weaver, P. 1992. An ecological comparison of canopy trees in the montane rain forest of Puerto Rico's Luquillo Mountains. *Caribbean J. Sci.* 28: 62–69.

Weissling, T., R. Giblin-Davis, and R. Scheffrahn. 1993. Laboratory and field evidence for male-produced aggregation pheromone in *Rhynchophorus cruentatus* (F.) (Coleoptera: Curculionidae). *J. Chem. Ecol.* 19: 1195–1203.

Wessels Boer, J. 1965. Palmae. *Flora of Suriname* 5(5): 1–172.

———. 1968. The geonomoid palms. *Verh. Kon. Ned. Akad. Wetensch, Afd. Natuurk., Tweede Sect. ser.* 2, 58: 1–202.

———. 1971. *Bactris* x *moorei,* a hybrid in palms. *Acta Bot. Neerl.* 20: 167–172.

Wilbert, J. 1976. *Manicaria saccifera* and its cultural significance among the Warao Indians of Venezuela. *Bot. Mus. Leafl.* 24: 275–335.

Wilson, D., and D. Janzen. 1972. Predation on *Scheelea* palm seeds by bruchid beetles: Seed density and distance from the parent palm. *Ecology* 53: 954–959.

Wright, S. 1983. The dispersion of eggs by a bruchid beetle among *Scheelea* palm seeds and the effect of distance to the parent palm. *Ecology* 64: 1016–1021.

Zanoni, T. 1991. The Royal palm on the island of Hispaniola. *Principes* 35: 49–54.

Ziffer, K. 1992. The Tagua initiative: Building the market for a rain forest product. In M. Plotkin and L. Famolare, eds., *Sustainable Harvest and Marketing of Rain Forest Products,* pp. 274–279. Island Press, Covelo, Calif.

Zizka, G. 1989. *Jubaea chilensis* (Molina) Baillon, die chilenische Honig- oder Coquitopalm. *Palmengarten* 1: 35–40.

Zona, S. 1990. A monograph of *Sabal* (Arecaceae: Coryphoideae). *Aliso* 12: 583–666.

———. 1991. Notes on *Roystonea* in Cuba. *Principes* 35: 225–233.

———. 1992. Distribution update: *Sabal domingensis* in Cuba. *Principes* 36: 34–35.

———. In press. A monograph of the genus *Roystonea. Flora Neotropica.*

Zona, S., and A. Henderson. 1989. A review of animal-mediated seed dispersal of palms. *Selbyana* 11: 6–21.

Zona, S., and W. Judd. 1986. *Sabal etonia* (Palmae): Systematics, distribution, ecology, and comparisons to other Florida scrub endemics. *Sida* 11: 417–427.

INDEX OF COMMON NAMES

coyore, 174
crespa, 110, 111
cubarillo, 196
cubarro, 185, 190, 192, 204
cuchilleja, 224
cucurito, 120, 162
cullulí, 223
cum, 235
cumare, 204
curuá, 162, 164
curua rana, 146
curuaraua, 162
cusi, 162, 163
cuyol, 127

daru, 234
desert palm, 62
dhalebana, 235
dois por dois, 160
don Pedrito, 132
dwarf palmetto, 66
dyaré, 59

escoba, 41
escobón, 40
escomfra, 119
espera-ai, 200
espina, 193, 203
everglades palm, 53

faux wi blanc, 184
fibra, 120

gamiova, 226
give-and-take, 41
glouglou, 174
grigri, 174, 199
grua, 162
guágara, 40, 119
guágara chica, 40
guáguara, 41
gualte, 110, 114, 115, 116, 117
guana cana, 65, 67
guanillo, 44
guanito, 51
guano, 47, 48, 50, 60
guano barbudo, 48
guano blanco, 60
guano cano, 60
guano de costa, 44
guano petate, 48
guano preto, 53
guarika, 223, 233
guariroba, 146, 148
guaya, 95
Guayaquil, 123
guayita, 95
guayita de los arroyos, 93
güérregue, 206
güichire, 162

güiridima, 205
guonay, 104
guriri, 147, 152
gwammu, 212
gwenn, 48

hairy Tom palmetto, 53
hanaimaka, 184, 189, 194
hoja de guacamayo, 224, 229
hoja redonda, 38
hones, 192
huacrapona, 109
huasi, 124
huasipanga, 232
huicungo, 205
huiririma, 205
huiscoyol, 191, 192, 193

icá, 150
igua, 158
igua dummat, 161
imburi, 152
inajai, 162
inaya-y, 146
inayo, 162
inayuga, 162
indaia rasteira, 161
indaya, 160
insiá, 161
irapai, 71
ite palm, 69

jací, 158
jacitara, 199, 200
jahuacté, 192
jamm de pay, 59
janchicoco, 151
jará, 119, 120
jarivá, 203
jata, 61
jatá, 144
jata de costa, 59
jata de Guanabacoa, 60
jata enana, 59
jata guatacuda, 61
jatata, 225
jatatilla, 100
jauari, 205
jawi, 184
jeribá, 148
jingapá, 195
jíquera, 119
jira, 110
juçara, 123
jucúm, 195
junco de bejuco, 94
jupatí, 68
juriti-ubim, 224
jussa, 196

INDEX OF SCIENTIFIC NAMES

Accepted names and their page numbers are in **boldface** and synonyms are in italics.

repens, **39,** 279
ulei, **39,** 280
wallisii, 280
Chrysallidosperma, 296
  smithii, 298
Cladandra, 275
  pygmaea, 279
Coccothrinax, 45, 280
  acuminata, 280
  acunana, 280
  alexandri, 280
  alexandri subsp. *alexandri,* 280
  alexandri subsp. *nitida,* 280
  alexandri var. *nitida,* 280
  alta, 280
  anomala, 300
  argentata, 47, 280
  argentea, 47, 280
  argentea, 280
  argentea subsp. *guantanamensis,* 280
  argentea var. *guantanamensis,* 280
  australis, 280
  baracoensis, 280
  barbadensis, 48, 280
  bermudezii, 280
  borhidiana, 48, 280
  boxii, 280
  camagueyana, 280
  clarensis, 280
  clarensis subsp. *brevifolia,* 281
  clarensis subsp. *clarensis,* 280
  clarensis var. *brevifolia,* 281
  clarensis var. *perrigida,* 281
  concolor, 280
  crinita, 48, 280
  crinita subsp. **brevicrinis, 48,** 280
  crinita subsp. **crinita, 48,** 280
  cupularis, 280
  discreta, 280
  dussiana, 280
  eggersiana, 280
  eggersiana var *sanctaecrucis,* 280
  ekmanii, 48, 280
  elegans, 280
  fagildei, 280
  fragrans, 280
  garberi, 280
  garciana, 281
  gracilis, 49, 280
  guantanamensis, 280
  gundlachii, 49, 280
  hiorami, 49, 280
  inaguensis, 49, 280
  jamaicensis, 280
  jucunda, 280
  jucunda var. *macrosperma,* 280
  jucunda var. *marquesensis,* 280
  latifrons, 280
  laxa, 280
  leonis, 280

litoralis, 280
macroglossa, 280
martii, 298
martinicensis, 280
microphylla, 281
miraguama, 49, 280
miraguama subsp. *arenicola,* 280
miraguama subsp. *havanensis,* 280
miraguama subsp. *macroglossa,* 281
miraguama subsp. *roseocarpa,* 281
miraguama var. *arenicola,* 281
miraguama var. *cupularis,* 281
miraguama var. *havanensis,* 281
miraguama var. *macroglossa,* 281
miraguama var. *novogeronensis,* 281
miraguama var. *roseocarpa,* 281
miraguano, 281
moaensis, 281
montana, 281
munizii, 280
muricata, 281
muricata var. *nipensis,* 281
orientalis, 281
pauciramosa, 50, 281
proctorii, 280
pseudorigida, 281
pseudorigida var. *acaulis,* 281
radiata, 298
readii, 280
rigida, 281
sabana, 280
salvatoris, 50, 281
salvatoris subsp. *loricata,* 281
salvatoris subsp. *salvatoris,* 281
salvatoris var. *loricata,* 281
sanctithomae, 280
savannarum, 281
saxicola, 281
scoparia, 281
spissa, 50, 281
trinitensis, 281
victorini, 280
yunquensis, 281
yuraguana, 281
yuraguana supsp. *moaensis,* 281
yuraguana subsp. *orientalis,* 281
yuraguana var. *orientalis,* 281
Cocops, 274
  rivalis, 274
Cocos, 139, 281
  acaulis, 297
  acaulis subsp. *glauca,* 297
  acrocomoides, 298
  aculeatus, 261
  aequatorialis, 297
  amadelpha, 274
  amara, 296
  apaensis, 297
  arechavaletana, 298
  arenaria, 263

precatoria, 124, 285
precatoria var. **longevaginata, 124,** 285
precatoria var. **precatoria, 124,** 285
ptariana, 284
pubigera, 293
purpurea, 293
puruensis, 285
rhodoxyla, 285
roraimae, 284
roseospadix, 293
schultzeana, 293
simiarum, 293
simplicifrons, 293
speciosa, 285
stenophylla, 285
subruminata, 285
tenuiramosa, 293
tobagonis, 293
trichoclada, 293
ventricosa, 294
vinifera, 294
williamsii, 293
zamora, 285
zephyria, 293

Gastrococos, 167, 285
armentalis, 285
crispa, 167, 285
Gaussia, 77, 285
attenuata, 77, 285
ghiesbreghti, 285
gomez-pompae, 78, 285
maya, 78, 285
portoricensis, 285
princeps, 78, 285
spirituana, 78, 285
vinifera, 294
Geonoma, 214, 285
acaulis, 287
acaulis subsp. *tapajotensis,* 287
acutangula, 286
acutiflora, 285
adscendens, 286
allenii, 274
altissima, 285
amabilis, 292
amazonica, 288
ambigua, 287
amoena, 286
andicola, 288
andina, 287
anomoclada, 287
antioquensis, 288
appuniana, 222, 285
aricanga, 285
arundinacea, 222, 285
aspidiifolia, 223, 285
aulacophylla, 287
baculifera, 223, 285
baculifera var. *macrospatha,* 285

barbigera, 288
barbosiana, 288
barthia, 286
bartletii, 286
beccariana, 287
bella, 288
bifurca, 288
bijugata, 287
binervia, 286
blanchetiana, 288
bluntii, 288
brachyfoliata, 287
brachystachys, 286
brevibisecta, 288
brevispatha, 223, 285
brevispatha var. **brevispatha, 223,** 285
brevispatha var. **occidentale, 223,** 285
brongniartii, 223, 285
caespitosa, 288
calophyta, 285
calyptrogynoidea, 286
camana, 224, 286
camptoneura, 287
campyloclada, 287
campylostachys, 286
capanemae, 287
carderi, 293
caudescens, 288
caudulata, 285
cernua, 286
chapadensis, 285
chaunostachys, 287
chelidonura, 287
chiriquensis, 288
chlamydostachys, 224, 286
chococola, 224, 286
compacta, 289
concinna, 224, 286
condensata, 274
congesta, 224, 286
congestissima, 289
corallifera, 289
coralliflora, 276
costatifrons, 274
cuneata, 225, 286
cuneata var. **cuneata, 225,** 286
cuneata var. **gracilis, 225,** 286
cuneata var. **procumbens, 225,** 286
cuneata var. **sodiroi, 225,** 286
cuneatoidea, 286
cuneifolia, 285
dammeri, 287
dasystachys, 287
decora, 289
decurrens, 286
decussata, 285
demarestei, 289
densa, 225, 286
densiflora, 287
densiflora var. *monticola,* 287

tenuifolia, 288
tenuis, 288
tenuissima, 234, 288
tessmannii, 286
tomentosa, 288
trailii, 288
trauniana, 288
triandra, 234, 288
trichostachys, 289
trifurcata, 263
triglochin, 234, 288
trigona, 234, 288
trigonostyla, 288
trijugata, 286
trinervis, 288
tuberculata, 287
uleana, 285
uliginosa, 287
umbraculiformis, 235, 288
uncibracteata, 286
undata, 235, 288
vaga, 286
ventricosa, 289
verdugo, 289
verschaffelti, 289
versiformis, 286
wallisii, 289
warmingii, 285
weberbaueri, 235, 288
weddelliana, 285
wendlandiana, 288
werdermannii, 285
willdenowii, 288
wittiana, 288
wittigiana, 286
woronowii, 287
yauaperyensis, 286
zamorensis, 289
Glaucotheca, 272
aculeata, 272
armata, 273
brandegeei, 273
elegans, 273
Glaziova insignis, 290
martiana, 290
treubiana, 297
Gorgasia, 294
Guilielma, 267
caribaea, 269
chontaduro, 268
ciliata, 268
gasipaes, 268
gasipaes var. *chichagui*, 268
gasipaes var. *chontaduro*, 268
gasipaes var. *coccinea*, 268
gasipaes var. *flava*, 268
gasipaes var. *ochracea*, 268
granatensis, 271
insignis, 268
macana, 269

mattogrossensis, 271
microcarpa, 269
piritu, 268
speciosa, 268
speciosa var. *coccinea*, 268
speciosa var. *flava*, 268
speciosa var. *mitis*, 268
speciosa var. *ochracea*, 268
tenera, 267
utilis, 268
Gynestum, 285
acaule, 287
baculiferum, 285
deversum, 286
maximum, 287
strictum, 288

Haitiella, 280
ekmanii, 280
munizii, 280
Hemithrinax, 298
compacta, 298
ekmaniana, 298
rivularis, 299
savannarum, 299
Hexopetion, 263
mexicanum, 264
Hyospathe, 132, 289
amaricaulis, 289
antioquensis, 289
brevipedunculata, 289
chiriquensis, 289
concinna, 289
elata, 289
elegans, 133, 289
elegans, 276
filiformis, 289
gracilis, 289
lehmannii, 289
macrorachis, 133, 289
maculata, 289
micropetala, 289
montana, 278
pallida, 289
pittieri, 289
pubigera, 293
schultzeae, 289
simplex, 289
sodiroi, 289
tessmannii, 289
ulei, 289
weberbaueri, 289
wendlandiana, 289

Inodes, 295
blackburnia, 295
causiarum, 295
exul, 295
glauca, 295
japa, 295

Andrew Henderson is Assistant Scientist at the New York Botanical Garden. Gloria Galeano and Rodrigo Bernal are Assistant Professors at the Instituto de Ciencias Naturales, Universidad Nacional de Colombia, Bogotá.

PLATES

PLATE 1. *Trithrinax brasiliensis*; habit; Brazil (top left). *Trithrinax schizophylla*; leaf sheath spines; Bolivia (top right). *Chelyocarpus dianeurus*; habit; Colombia (bottom left). *Chelyocarpus ulei*; flowers; Brazil (bottom right).

PLATE 2. *Cryosophila guagara*; habit; Costa Rica (top left). *Cryosophila guagara*; root spines; Costa Rica (top right). *Itaya amicorum*; leaf; Peru (bottom left). *Itaya amicorum*; flowers; Peru (bottom right).

PLATE 3. *Schippia concolor*; fruits; Belize (top left). *Thrinax ekmaniana*; habit; Cuba (top right). *Thrinax radiata*; habit; Cuba (bottom left). *Thrinax radiata*; fruits; Cuba (bottom right).

PLATE 4. *Thrinax radiata*; split leaf sheath; Cuba (top left). *Coccothrinax borhidiana*; habit; Cuba (top right). *Coccothrinax borhidiana*; fruits; Cuba (bottom left). *Coccothrinax crinita*; habit; Cuba (bottom right).

PLATE 5. *Coccothrinax miraguama*; habit; Cuba (top left). *Coccothrinax miraguama*; leaf sheath; Cuba (top right). *Zombia antillarum*; habit; Haiti (bottom left). *Rhapidophyllum hystrix*; leaf sheaths; Florida (bottom right).

PLATE 6. *Colpothrinax wrightii*; habit; Cuba (top left). *Acoelorraphe wrightii*; habit; Cuba (top right). *Serenoa repens*; habit; Florida (bottom left). *Brahea dulcis*; habit; Honduras (bottom right).

PLATE 7. *Copernicia alba*; habit; Bolivia (top left). *Copernicia berteroana*; habit; Haiti (top right). *Copernicia hospita*; habit; Cuba (bottom left). *Copernicia macro-glossa*; habit; Cuba (bottom right).

PLATE 8. *Copernicia prunifera*; habit; Brazil (top left). *Copernicia tectorum*; petioles; Colombia (top right). *Washingtonia filifera*; habit; cultivated (bottom left). *Sabal causiarum*; habit; Puerto Rico (bottom right).

PLATE 9. *Sabal mauritiiformis*; habit; Colombia (top left). *Sabal palmetto*; leaf
sheaths; Cuba (top right). *Sabal palmetto*; habit; Cuba (bottom left). *Raphia taedigera*; habit; Costa Rica (bottom right).

PLATE 10. *Raphia taedigera*; fruits; Brazil (top left). *Mauritia flexuosa*; habit; Brazil (top right). *Mauritia flexuosa*; fruits; Colombia (bottom left). *Mauritiella aculeata*; habit; Colombia (bottom right).

PLATE 11. *Mauritiella armata*; habit; Brazil (top left). *Lepidocaryum tenue*; habit; Peru (top right). *Lepidocaryum tenue*; fruits; Colombia (bottom left). *Pseudophoenix lediniana*; stem; Haiti (bottom right).

PLATE 12. *Pseudophoenix vinifera*; habit; Haiti (top left). *Ceroxylon parvifrons*; habit; Colombia (top right). *Ceroxylon quindiuense*; habit; Colombia (bottom left). *Ceroxylon quindiuense*; stem; Colombia (bottom right).

PLATE 13. *Ceroxylon ventricosum*; habit; habit; Ecuador (top left). *Ceroxylon vogelianum*; habit; Ecuador (top right). *Juania australis*; habit; Juan Fernández Islands (bottom left). *Gaussia attenuata*; roots; Puerto Rico (bottom right).

PLATE 14. *Gaussia princeps*; habit; Cuba (top left). *Synechanthus warscewiczianus*; habit; Costa Rica (top right). *Chamaedorea allenii*; habit; Costa Rica (bottom left). *Chamaedorea allenii*; fruits; Costa Rica (bottom right).

PLATE 15. *Chamaedorea linearis*; male flowers; Ecuador (top left). *Chamaedorea linearis*; female flowers and fruits; Ecuador (top right). *Chamaedorea pauciflora*; habit; Peru (bottom left). *Chamaedorea pinnatifrons*; habit; Brazil (bottom right).

PLATE 16. *Chamaedorea pinnatifrons*; fruits; Brazil (top left). *Chamaedorea tepejilote*; flowers; Costa Rica (top right). *Wendlandiella gracilis*; habit; Peru (bottom left). *Wendlandiella gracilis*; fruits; Bolivia (bottom right).

PLATE 17. *Dictyocaryum lamarckianum*; habit; Colombia (top left). *Iriartella setigera*; habit; Colombia (top right). *Iriartea deltoidea*; habit; Colombia (bottom left). *Iriartea deltoidea*; habit; Brazil (bottom right).

PLATE 18. *Socratea exorrhiza*; habit; Colombia (top left). *Socratea exorrhiza*; stilt root; Peru (top right). *Socratea salazarii*; flowers; Brazil (bottom left). *Wettinia castanea*; habit; Colombia (bottom right).

PLATE 19. *Wettinia disticha*; habit; Colombia (top left). *Wettinia fascicularis*; habit; Colombia (top right). *Wettinia fascicularis*; fruits; Colombia (bottom left). *Wettinia hirsuta*; flowers and fruits; Colombia (bottom right).

PLATE 20. *Wettinia kalbreyeri*; habit; Colombia (top left). *Wettinia quinaria*; flowers and fruits; Colombia (top right). *Manicaria saccifera*; habit; Brazil (bottom left). *Manicaria saccifera*; fruits; Colombia (bottom right).

PLATE 21. *Leopoldinia piassaba*; fibers; Colombia (top left). *Leopoldinia pulchra*; habit; Brazil (top right). *Reinhardtia koschnyana*; habit; Colombia (bottom left). *Reinhardtia latisecta*; habit; Costa Rica (bottom right).

PLATE 22. *Euterpe catinga*; leaf sheath; Brazil (top left). *Euterpe catinga*; habit; Venezuela (top right). *Euterpe oleracea*; habit; Brazil (bottom left). *Euterpe oleracea*; flowers; Brazil (bottom right).

PLATE 23. *Euterpe oleracea*; fruits; Brazil (top left). *Euterpe precatoria*; habit; Costa Rica (top right). *Prestoea acuminata*; habit; Colombia (bottom left). *Prestoea acuminata*; habit; Costa Rica (bottom right).

PLATE 24. *Prestoea carderi*; habit; Colombia (top left). *Prestoea decurrens*; habit; Colombia (top right). *Prestoea pubigera*; habit; Trinidad (bottom left). *Prestoea simplicifolia*; leaf; Colombia (bottom right).

PLATE 25. *Neonicholsonia watsonii*; habit; Costa Rica (top left). *Neonicholsonia wat-sonii*; fruits; Costa Rica (top right). *Oenocarpus balickii*; fruits; Brazil (bottom left). *Oenocarpus bataua*; habit; Colombia (bottom right).

PLATE 26. *Oenocarpus circumtextus*; habit; Colombia (top left). *Oenocarpus circum-textus*; fruits; Colombia (top right). *Oenocarpus distichus*; leaf sheaths; Brazil (bot-tom left). *Oenocarpus mapora*; habit; Brazil (bottom right).

PLATE 27. *Oenocarpus simplex*; habit; Colombia (top left). *Hyospathe elegans*; habit; Colombia (top right). *Hyospathe elegans*; flowers; Brazil (bottom left). *Roystonea oleracea*; habit; Trinidad (bottom right).

PLATE 28. *Roystonea regia*; habit; Cuba (top left). *Roystonea regia*; fruits; Cuba (top right). *Butia eriospatha*; habit; Brazil (bottom left). *Butia eriospatha*; peduncular bract; Brazil (bottom right).

PLATE 29. *Butia paraguayensis*; habit; Brazil (top left). *Jubaea chilensis*; habit; Chile (top right). *Jubaea chilensis*; stem; Chile (bottom left). *Cocos nucifera*; habit; Trinidad (bottom right).

PLATE 30. *Syagrus cardenasii*; flowers and fruits; Bolivia (top left). *Syagrus cocoides*; habit; Brazil (top right). *Syagrus cocoides*; fruits; Brazil (bottom left). *Syagrus flexuosa*; habit; Brazil (bottom right).

PLATE 31. *Syagrus orinocensis*; habit; Colombia (top left). *Syagrus romanzoffiana*; habit; Brazil (top right). *Syagrus romanzoffiana*; flowers; Brazil (bottom left). *Syagrus sancona*; habit; Colombia (bottom right).

PLATE 32. *Syagrus sancona*; flowers; Brazil (top left). *Syagrus schizophylla*; habit; Brazil (top right). *Lytocaryum hoehnei*; habit; Brazil (bottom left). *Lytocaryum weddellianum*; habit; Brazil (bottom right).

PLATE 33. *Parajubaea torallyi*; habit; Bolivia (top left). *Parajubaea torallyi*; flowers; Bolivia (top right). *Allagoptera arenaria*; habit; Brazil (bottom left). *Allagoptera arenaria*; female flowers; cultivated (bottom right).

PLATE 34. *Allagoptera arenaria*; fruits; Brazil (top left). *Polyandrococos caudescens*; habit; Brazil (top right). *Polyandrococos caudescens*; flowers; Brazil (bottom left). *Attalea butyracea*; habit; Costa Rica (bottom right).

PLATE 35. *Attalea colenda*; habit; Ecuador (top left). *Attalea crassispatha*; habit;
Haiti (top right). *Attalea cuatrecasana*; fruits; Colombia (bottom left). *Attalea
funifera*; habit; Brazil (bottom right).

PLATE 36. *Attalea butyracea*; male flowers; Colombia (top left). *Attalea maripa*; male flowers; Brazil (top right). *Attalea speciosa*; male flowers; Brazil (bottom left). *Attalea tessmannii*; male flowers; Brazil (bottom right).

PLATE 37. *Attalea maripa*; habit; Colombia (top left). *Attalea microcarpa*; fruits; Colombia (top right). *Attalea attaleoides*; fruits; Brazil (bottom left). *Attalea butyracea*; fruits; Colombia (bottom right).

PLATE 38. *Attalea tessmannii*; fruits; Brazil (top left). *Barcella odora*; flowers; Brazil (top right). *Barcella odora*; fruits; Brazil (bottom left). *Elaeis oleifera*; habit; Costa Rica (bottom right).

PLATE 39. *Elaeis oleifera*; fruits; Honduras (top left). *Acrocomia aculeata*; habit; Haiti (top right). *Acrocomia aculeata*; flowers; Brazil (bottom left). *Acrocomia hassleri*; habit; Brazil (bottom right).

PLATE 40. *Gastrococos crispa*; habit; Cuba (top left). *Aiphanes aculeata*; habit; Colombia (top right). *Aiphanes aculeata*; fruits; cultivated (bottom left). *Aiphanes hirsuta*; habit; Colombia (bottom right).

PLATE 41. *Aiphanes hirsuta*; leaf; Colombia (top left). *Aiphanes hirsuta*; fruits;
Colombia (top right). *Aiphanes lindeniana*; habit; Colombia (bottom left).
Aiphanes linearis; habit; Colombia (bottom right).

PLATE 42. *Aiphanes linearis*; fruits; Colombia (top left). *Aiphanes macroloba*; habit; Colombia (top right). *Aiphanes parvifolia*; leaf; Colombia (bottom left). *Bactris acanthocarpa*; habit; Brazil (bottom right).

PLATE 43. *Bactris acanthocarpa*; flowers; Brazil (top left). *Bactris acanthocarpa*; fruits; Brazil (top right). *Bactris brongniartii*; habit; Brazil (bottom left). *Bactris brongniartii*; spines; Brazil (bottom right).

PLATE 44. *Bactris campestris*; fruits; Brazil (top left). *Bactris caryotifolia*; habit; Brazil (top right). *Bactris concinna*; flowers; Peru (bottom left). *Bactris concinna*; fruits; Colombia (bottom right).

PLATE 45. *Bactris constanciae*; fruits; Brazil (top left). *Bactris elegans*; habit; Colombia (top right). *Bactris elegans*; fruits; Brazil (bottom left). *Bactris gasipaes*;
habit; Ecuador (bottom right).

PLATE 46. *Bactris gasipaes*; fruits; Ecuador (top left). *Bactris glandulosa*; flowers; Costa Rica (top right). *Bactris hirta*; habit; Colombia (bottom left). *Bactris hirta*; fruits; Brazil (bottom right).

PLATE 47. *Bactris killipii*; habit; Brazil (top left). *Bactris macana*; habit; Colombia (top right). *Bactris major*; habit; Trinidad (bottom left). *Bactris maraja*; fruits; Colombia (bottom right).

PLATE 48. *Bactris oligocarpa*; habit; Brazil (top left). *Bactris oligocarpa*; flowers and fruits; Brazil (top right). *Bactris plumeriana*; habit; Haiti (bottom left). *Bactris riparia*; habit; Colombia (bottom right).

PLATE 49. *Bactris riparia*; fruits; Brazil (top left). *Bactris setulosa*; habit; Colombia (top right). *Bactris setulosa*; stem; Colombia (bottom left). *Bactris setulosa*; fruits; Colombia (bottom right).

PLATE 50. *Bactris simplicifrons*; fruits; Colombia (top left). *Bactris trailiana*; habit; Brazil (top right). *Desmoncus giganteus*; habit; Brazil (bottom left). *Desmoncus mitis*; habit; Peru (bottom right).

PLATE 51. *Desmoncus orthacanthos*; leaf; Colombia (top left). *Desmoncus polya-canthos*; fruits; Colombia (top right). *Desmoncus stans*; leaflets; Costa Rica (bottom left). *Astrocaryum aculeatissimum*; habit; Brazil (bottom right).

PLATE 52. *Astrocaryum alatum*; habit; Costa Rica (top left). *Astrocaryum chambira*; habit; Colombia (top right). *Astrocaryum chambira*; spines; Peru (bottom left). *Astrocaryum gynacanthum*; habit; Colombia (bottom right).

PLATE 53. *Astrocaryum gynacanthum*; fruits; Colombia (top left). *Astrocaryum jauari*; fruits; Colombia (top right). *Astrocaryum murumuru*; habit; Brazil (bottom left). *Astrocaryum murumuru*; fruits; Colombia (bottom right).

PLATE 54. *Astrocaryum standleyanum*; fruits; Colombia (top left). *Pholidostachys kalbreyeri*; fruits; Panama (top right). *Pholidostachys synanthera*; habit; Ecuador (bottom left). *Welfia regia*; habit; Colombia (bottom right).

PLATE 55. *Welfia regia*; inflorescence; Colombia (top left). *Calyptronoma rivalis*;
habit; Haiti (top right). *Calyptronoma rivalis*; inflorescences; Haiti (bottom left).
Calyptrogyne ghiesbreghtiana; habit; Costa Rica (bottom right).

PLATE 56. *Calyptrogyne ghiesbreghtiana*; fruits; Costa Rica (top left). *Asterogyne martiana*; habit; Costa Rica (top right). *Asterogyne martiana*; fruits; Costa Rica (bottom left). *Asterogyne spicata*; flowers; Venezuela (bottom right).

PLATE 57. *Geonoma appuniana*; habit; Venezuela (top left). *Geonoma aspidiifolia*; fruits; Brazil (top right). *Geonoma brevispatha*; habit; Brazil (bottom left). *Geonoma camana*; habit; Brazil (bottom right).

PLATE 58. *Geonoma deversa*; habit; Peru (top left). *Geonoma laxiflora*; habit; Brazil (top right). *Geonoma leptospadix*; habit; Colombia (bottom left). *Geonoma macrostachys*; flowers; Brazil (bottom right).

PLATE 59. *Geonoma macrostachys*; fruits; Colombia (top left). *Geonoma maxima*; inflorescences; Brazil (top right). *Geonoma maxima*; fruits; Brazil (bottom left). *Geonoma oldemanii*; habit; French Guiana (bottom right).

PLATE 60. *Geonoma pohliana*; habit; Brazil (top left). *Geonoma rubescens*; inflorescences; Brazil (top right). *Geonoma scoparia*; inflorescence; Costa Rica (bottom left). *Geonoma stricta*; habit; Peru (bottom right).

PLATE 61. *Geonoma stricta*; inflorescences; Colombia (top left). *Geonoma stricta*; fruits; Colombia (top right). *Geonoma triandra*; habit; Colombia (bottom left). *Geonoma trigona*; habit; Peru (bottom right).

PLATE 62. *Geonoma undata*; habit; Colombia (top left). *Geonoma weberbaueri*; habit; Colombia (top right). *Geonoma weberbaueri*; habit; Colombia (bottom left). *Phytelephas aequatorialis*; male flowers; Ecuador (bottom right).

PLATE 63. *Phytelephas macrocarpa*; male flowers; Peru (top left). *Phytelephas seemannii*; habit; Colombia (top right). *Phytelephas tenuicaulis*; stem; Colombia (bottom left). *Phytelephas tenuicaulis*; fruits; Peru (bottom right).

PLATE 64. *Ammandra decasperma*; habit; Colombia (top left). *Aphandra natalia*; male flowers; Ecuador (top right). *Aphandra natalia*; female flowers; Ecuador (bottom left). *Aphandra natalia*; cross section of fruits; Brazil (bottom right).